CATECHISM
OF THE
CATHOLIC
CHURCH

CATECHISM OF THE CATHOLIC CHURCH

BURNS & OATES
A Continuum imprint
LONDON • NEW YORK

BURNS & OATES
A Continuum imprint
The Tower Building, 11 York Road, London SE1 7NX

First edition published May 1994
Reprinted 1994 (four times)
Revised edition first published 1999

Popular and definitive edition first published 2000

Reprinted 2002, 2003

British Library Cataloguing-in-Publication Data
A catalogue record for this book is available from the British Library

ISBN: 0-225-66867-X (hardback)
ISBN: 0-225-66868-8 (paperback)
ISBN: 0860123278 (Popular edition)

See p. xix for information on works frequently cited.

The design of the logo on the cover is taken from a Christian tombstone in the catacombs of Domitilla, in Rome, which dates from the end of the third century A.D. This pastoral image, of pagan origin, was used by Christians to symbolize the rest and the happiness of that the soul of the departed finds in eternal life.
This image also suggests certain characteristic aspects of the Catechism: Christ, the Good Shepherd who leads and protects his faithful (the lamb) by his authority (the staff), draws them by the melodious symphony of the truth (the panpipes) and makes them lie down in the shade of the 'tree of life', his redeeming Cross which opens paradise.

Typeset by August Filmsetting, Haydock St Helens
Printed and bound in Great Britain by Biddles Ltd, King's Lynn, Norfolk

CONTENTS

PART ONE
THE PROFESSION OF FAITH

SECTION ONE
'I BELIEVE' – 'WE BELIEVE'

v

SECTION TWO
THE PROFESSION OF THE CHRISTIAN FAITH
THE CREEDS

vi

PART TWO
THE CELEBRATION OF THE CHRISTIAN MYSTERY

SECTION ONE
THE SACRAMENTAL ECONOMY

CHAPTER ONE THE PASCHAL MYSTERY IN THE AGE OF THE CHURCH

ix

PART THREE
LIFE IN CHRIST

SECTION ONE
MAN'S VOCATION: LIFE IN THE SPIRIT

CHAPTER THREE   GOD'S SALVATION: LAW AND GRACE

SECTION TWO

THE TEN COMMANDMENTS

CHAPTER ONE   'YOU SHALL LOVE THE LORD YOUR GOD WITH ALL YOUR HEART, AND WITH ALL YOUR SOUL, AND WITH ALL YOUR MIND'

PART FOUR
CHRISTIAN PRAYER

SECTION ONE
PRAYER IN THE CHRISTIAN LIFE
WHAT IS PRAYER?

SECTION TWO
THE LORD'S PRAYER: 'OUR FATHER!'

ABBREVIATIONS

AA	Apostolicam actuositatem	IM	Inter mirifica
AAS	Acta Apostolicae Sedis	JB	Jerusalem Bible
AF	Lightfoot, Apostolic Fathers	LE	Laborem exercens
		LG	Lumen gentium
AG	Ad gentes	LH	Liturgy of the Hours
CA	Centesimus annus	LXX	Septuagint
CCEO	Corpus Canonum Ecclesiarum Orientalium	MC	Marialis cultus
		MD	Mulieris dignitatem
CChr	Corpus christianorum	MF	Mysterium fidei
CCL	Corpus christianorum, series latina	MM	Mater et magistra
		NA	Nostra aetate
CD	Christus Dominus	NCCB	National Conference of Catholic Bishops (USA)
CDF	Congregation for the Doctrine of the Faith		
		ND	Neuner–Dupuis, The Christian Faith in the Doctrinal Documents of the Catholic Church
CELAM	Latin American Episcopal Council		
CIC	Codex Iuris Canonici (1983)	OC	Rite of Confirmation
		OCF	Order of Christian Funerals
CL	Christifideles laici		
COD	Conciliorum oecumenicorum decreta	OCM	Ordo celebrandi matrimonium
		OCV	Ordo consecrationis virginum
CPG	Credo of the People of God	OE	Orientalium ecclesiarum
CSEL	Corpus scriptorum ecclesiasticorum latinorum	OP	Ordo poenitentiae
		OR	Office of Readings
CT	Catechesi tradendae	OT	Optatam totius
DeV	Dominum et Vivificantem	PC	Perfectae caritatis
DH	Dignitatis humanae	PG	Migne, Patrologia graeca
DM	Dives in misericordia	PL	Migne, Patrologia latina
DS	Denzinger–Schönmetzer, Enchiridion Symbolorum (1965)	PLS	Migne, Patrologia latina, Supplement
		PO	Presbyterorum ordinis
DV	Dei Verbum	PP	Populorum progressio
EN	Evangelii nuntiandi	PT	Pacem in terris
EP	Eucharistic Prayer	RBC	Rite of Baptism for Children
FC	Familiaris consortio	RCIA	Rite of Christian Initiation of Adults
GCD	General Catechetical Directory		
		RH	Redemptor hominis
GE	Gravissimum educationis	RMat	Redemptoris Mater
GILH	General Instruction on the Liturgy of the Hours	RMiss	Redemptoris missio
		RP	Reconciliatio et paenitentia
GIRM	General Instruction of the Roman Missal	SC	Sacrosanctum concilium
		SCG	Summa contra gentiles
GS	Gaudium et spes	SCh	Sources chrétiennes
HV	Humanae vitae	SRS	Sollicitudo rei socialis
ICEL	International Commission on English in the Liturgy	STh	Summa theologiae
		UR	Unitatis redintegratio

ACKNOWLEDGEMENTS

Biblical citations are mostly taken from the Revised Standard Version of the Bible, copyright 1973 by the Division of Christian Education of the National Council of the Churches of Christ in the United States of America; occasionally from the New Revised Standard Version of the Bible, Catholic Edition, copyright 1989 by the Division of Christian Education of the National Council of the Churches of Christ in the United States of America. Used by permission. All rights reserved.

Citations of documents of Vatican II are taken from *Vatican Council II: Conciliar and Postconciliar Documents*, ed. Austin Flannery OP (Dublin: Dominican Publications, 1975).

Citations of the Code of Canon Law are taken from *The Code of Canon Law: A Text and Commentary*, ed. James A. Coriden, Thomas J. Green and Donald E. Heintschel (New York/Mahwah NJ: Paulist Press, 1985).

Denzinger (DS) references are cited from *Christian Faith: Doctrinal Documents of the Catholic Church*, ed. J. Neuner and J. Dupuis (London: HarperCollins, 1992).

THE REVISED EDITION OF THE CATECHISM

The *Catechism of the Catholic* church was published in English in 1994. It proved an immediate success. However, no one could pretend that it was a particularly easy read. For many readers the waters were quite uncharted, and difficult to navigate.

Recently the definitive Latin version of the *Catechism* was published in Rome. This incorporated a considerable number of corrections and amendments – mostly fairly small – to the original text, as well as a much developed index. This present edition includes these changes to the original text. It also includes a guide for readers prepared for the French edition, to help chart the waters and to make reading the full text both easier and more profitable for the reader.

I warmly recommend this new edition of the *Catechism* for its corrected text, its developed index, and its thematic guide.

DAVID KONSTANT
Bishop of Leeds

APOSTOLIC CONSTITUTION
FIDEI DEPOSITUM

ON THE PUBLICATION OF THE

CATECHISM OF THE CATHOLIC CHURCH

PREPARED FOLLOWING

THE SECOND VATICAN ECUMENICAL COUNCIL

JOHN PAUL, BISHOP

SERVANT OF THE SERVANTS OF GOD

For Everlasting Memory

To my Venerable Brothers the Cardinals, Patriarchs, Archbishops, Bishops, Priests, Deacons and to all the People of God.

GUARDING THE DEPOSIT OF FAITH IS THE MISSION WHICH THE LORD ENTRUSTED TO HIS CHURCH, and which she fulfils in every age. The Second Vatican Ecumenical Council, which was opened 30 years ago by my predecessor Pope John XXIII, of happy memory, had as its intention and purpose to highlight the Church's apostolic and pastoral mission, and by making the truth of the Gospel shine forth to lead all people to seek and receive Christ's love which surpasses all knowledge (cf. *Eph* 3:19).

The principal task entrusted to the Council by Pope John XXIII was to guard and present better the precious deposit of Christian doctrine in order to make it more accessible to the Christian faithful and to all people of good will. For this reason the Council was not first of all to condemn the errors of the time, but above all to strive calmly to show the strength and beauty of the doctrine of the faith. 'Illumined by the light of this Council', the Pope said, 'the Church ... will become greater in spiritual riches and gaining the strength of new energies therefrom, she will look to the future without fear ... Our duty is to dedicate ourselves with an earnest will and without fear to that work which our era demands of us, thus pursuing the path which the Church has followed for 20 centuries.'[1]

With the help of God, the Council Fathers in four years of work were able to produce a considerable number of doctrinal statements and pastoral norms which were presented to the whole Church. There the Pastors and Christian faithful find directives for that 'renewal of thought, action, practices and moral virtue, of joy and hope, which was the very purpose of the Council'.[2]

After its conclusion, the Council did not cease to inspire the Church's life. In 1985 I was able to assert, 'For me, then – who had the special grace of participating in it and actively collaborating in its development – Vatican II has always been, and especially during these years of my Pontificate, the constant reference point of my every pastoral action, in the conscious commitment to implement its directives concretely and faithfully at the level of each Church and the whole Church.'[3]

In this spirit, on 25 January 1985, I convoked an extraordinary

---

[1] John XXIII, Discourse at the Opening of the Second Vatican Ecumenical Council, 11 October 1962: AAS 54 (1962), 788–91.

[2] Paul VI, Discourse at the Closing of the Second Vatican Ecumenical Council, 7 December 1965: AAS 58 (1966), 7–8.

[3] John Paul II, Discourse of 25 January 1985: *L'Osservatore Romano*, 27 January 1985.

assembly of the Synod of Bishops for the 20th anniversary of the close of the Council. The purpose of this assembly was to celebrate the graces and spiritual fruits of Vatican II, to study its teaching in greater depth in order that all the Christian faithful might better adhere to it, and to promote knowledge and application of it.

On that occasion the Synod Fathers stated: 'Very many have expressed the desire that a catechism or compendium of all Catholic doctrine regarding both faith and morals be composed, that it might be, as it were, a point of reference for the catechisms or compendiums that are prepared in various regions. The presentation of doctrine must be biblical and liturgical. It must be sound doctrine suited to the present life of Christians.'[4] After the Synod ended, I made this desire my own, considering it as 'fully responding to a real need of the universal Church and of the particular Churches'.[5]

For this reason we thank the Lord whole-heartedly on this day when we can offer the entire Church this 'reference text' entitled the *Catechism of the Catholic Church*, for a catechesis renewed at the living sources of the faith!

Following the renewal of the Liturgy and the new codification of the canon law of the Latin Church and that of the Oriental Catholic Churches, this catechism will make a very important contribution to that work of renewing the whole life of the Church, as desired and begun by the Second Vatican Council.

1. The Process and Spirit of Drafting the Text

The *Catechism of the Catholic Church* is the result of very extensive collaboration; it was prepared over six years of intense work done in a spirit of complete openness and fervent zeal.

In 1986, I entrusted a commission of twelve Cardinals and Bishops, chaired by Cardinal Joseph Ratzinger, with the task of preparing a draft of the catechism requested by the Synod Fathers. An editorial committee of seven diocesan Bishops, experts in theology and catechesis, assisted the commission in its work.

The commission, charged with giving directives and with overseeing the course of the work, attentively followed all the stages in editing the nine subsequent drafts. The editorial committee, for its part, assumed responsibility for writing the text, making the emendations requested by the commission and examining the

---

[4] *Final Report* of the Extraordinary Synod of Bishops, 7 December 1985: *Enchiridion Vaticanum*, vol. 9, II B a, n. 4: p. 1758, n. 1797.

[5] John Paul II, Discourse at the Closing of the Extraordinary Synod of Bishops, 7 December 1985, n. 6: AAS 78 (1986), 435.

observations of numerous theologians, exegetes and catechists, and, above all, of the Bishops of the whole world, in order to produce a better text. In the committee various opinions were compared with great profit, and thus a richer text has resulted whose unity and coherence are assured.

The project was the object of extensive consultation among all Catholic Bishops, their Episcopal Conferences or Synods, and theological and catechetical institutes. As a whole, it received a broadly favourable acceptance on the part of the Episcopate. It can be said that this *Catechism* is the result of the collaboration of the whole Episcopate of the Catholic Church, who generously accepted my invitation to share responsibility for an enterprise which directly concerns the life of the Church. This response elicits in me a deep feeling of joy, because the harmony of so many voices truly expresses what could be called the 'symphony' of the faith. The achievement of this *Catechism* thus reflects the collegial nature of the Episcopate; it testifies to the Church's catholicity.

2. Arrangement of the Material

A catechism should faithfully and systematically present the teaching of Sacred Scripture, the living Tradition in the Church and the authentic Magisterium, as well as the spiritual heritage of the Fathers, Doctors and saints of the Church, to allow for a better knowledge of the Christian mystery and for enlivening the faith of the People of God. It should take into account the doctrinal statements which down the centuries the Holy Spirit has intimated to his Church. It should also help to illumine with the light of faith the new situations and problems which had not yet emerged in the past.

This catechism will thus contain both the new and the old (cf. *Mt* 13:52), because the faith is always the same yet the source of ever new light.

To respond to this twofold demand, the *Catechism of the Catholic Church* on the one hand repeats the 'old', traditional order already followed by the Catechism of St Pius V, arranging the material in four parts: the *Creed*, the *Sacred Liturgy*, with pride of place given to the sacraments, the *Christian way of life*, explained beginning with the Ten Commandments, and finally, *Christian prayer*. At the same time, however, the contents are often presented in a 'new' way in order to respond to the questions of our age.

The four parts are related one to another: the Christian mystery is the object of faith (first part); it is celebrated and communicated in liturgical actions (second part); it is present to enlighten and sustain the children of God in their actions (third part); it is the basis for our prayer, the privileged expression of which is the *Our Father*, and it represents the object of our supplication, our praise and our intercession (fourth part).

The Liturgy itself is prayer; the confession of faith finds its proper place in the celebration of worship. Grace, the fruit of the sacraments, is the irreplaceable condition for Christian living, just as participation in the Church's Liturgy requires faith. If faith is not expressed in works, it is dead (cf. *Jas* 2:14–16) and cannot bear fruit unto eternal life.

In reading the *Catechism of the Catholic Church* we can perceive the wonderful unity of the mystery of God, his saving will, as well as the central place of Jesus Christ, the only-begotten Son of God, sent by the Father, made man in the womb of the Blessed Virgin Mary by the power of the Holy Spirit, to be our Saviour. Having died and risen, Christ is always present in his Church, especially in the sacraments; he is the source of our faith, the model of Christian conduct and the Teacher of our prayer.

3. The Doctrinal Value of the Text

The *Catechism of the Catholic Church*, which I approved 25 June last and the publication of which I today order by virtue of my Apostolic Authority, is a statement of the Church's faith and of catholic doctrine, attested to or illumined by Sacred Scripture, the Apostolic Tradition and the Church's Magisterium. I declare it to be a sure norm for teaching the faith and thus a valid and legitimate instrument for ecclesial communion. May it serve the renewal to which the Holy Spirit ceaselessly calls the Church of God, the Body of Christ, on her pilgrimage to the undiminished light of the Kingdom!

The approval and publication of the *Catechism of the Catholic Church* represent a service which the Successor of Peter wishes to offer to the Holy Catholic Church, to all the particular Churches in peace and communion with the Apostolic See: the service, that is, of supporting and confirming the faith of all the Lord Jesus' disciples (cf. *Lk* 22:32), as well as of strengthening the bonds of unity in the same apostolic faith.

Therefore, I ask all the Church's Pastors and the Christian faithful to receive this catechism in a spirit of communion and to use it assiduously in fulfilling their mission of proclaiming the faith and calling people to the Gospel life. This catechism is given to them that it may be a sure and authentic reference text for teaching catholic doctrine and particularly for preparing local catechisms. It is also offered to all the faithful who wish to deepen their knowledge of the unfathomable riches of salvation (cf. *Eph* 3:8). It is meant to support ecumenical efforts that are moved by the holy desire for the unity of all Christians, showing carefully the content and wondrous harmony of the catholic faith. The *Catechism of the Catholic Church*, lastly, is offered to every individual who asks us to give an account of the hope that is in us (cf. 1 *Pt* 3:15) and who wants to know what the Catholic Church believes.

This catechism is not intended to replace the local catechisms duly approved by the ecclesiastical authorities, the diocesan Bishops and the Episcopal Conferences, especially if they have been approved by the Apostolic See. It is meant to encourage and assist in the writing of new local catechisms, which take into account various situations and cultures, while carefully preserving the unity of faith and fidelity to catholic doctrine.

At the conclusion of this document presenting the *Catechism of the Catholic Church*, I beseech the Blessed Virgin Mary, Mother of the Incarnate Word and Mother of the Church, to support with her powerful intercession the catechetical work of the entire Church on every level, at this time when she is called to a new effort of evangelization. May the light of the true faith free humanity from the ignorance and slavery of sin in order to lead it to the only freedom worthy of the name (cf. *Jn* 8:32): that of life in Jesus Christ under the guidance of the Holy Spirit, here below and in the Kingdom of heaven, in the fullness of the blessed vision of God face to face (cf. 1 *Cor* 13:12; 2 *Cor* 5:6–8)!

Given 11 October 1992, the thirtieth anniversary of the opening of the Second Vatican Ecumenical Council, in the fourteenth year of my Pontificate.

Joannes Paulus PP. II

PROLOGUE

'FATHER,... this is eternal life, that they may know you, the only true God, and Jesus Christ whom you have sent.'[1] 'God our Saviour desires all men to be saved and to come to the knowledge of the truth.'[2] 'There is no other name under heaven given among men by which we must be saved'[3] – than the name of JESUS.

I. The Life of Man – to Know and Love God

1 God, infinitely perfect and blessed in himself, in a plan of sheer goodness freely created man to make him share in his own blessed life. For this reason, at every time and in every place, God draws close to man. He calls man to seek him, to know him, to love him with all his strength. He calls together all men, scattered and divided by sin, into the unity of his family, the Church. To accomplish this, when the fullness of time had come, God sent his Son as Redeemer and Saviour. In his Son and through him, he invites men to become, in the Holy Spirit, his adopted children and thus heirs of his blessed life.

2 So that this call should resound throughout the world, Christ sent forth the apostles he had chosen, commissioning them to proclaim the gospel: 'Go therefore and make disciples of all nations, baptizing them in the name of the Father and of the Son and of the Holy Spirit, teaching them to observe all that I have commanded you; and lo, I am with you always, to the close of the age.'[4] Strengthened by this mission, the apostles 'went forth and preached everywhere, while the Lord worked with them and confirmed the message by the signs that attended it.'[5]

3 Those who with God's help have welcomed Christ's call and freely responded to it are urged on by love of Christ to proclaim the Good News everywhere in the world. This treasure, received from the apostles, has been faithfully guarded by their successors. All Christ's faithful are called to hand it on from generation to generation, by professing the faith, by living it in fraternal sharing, and by celebrating it in liturgy and prayer.[6]

II. Handing on the Faith: Catechesis

4 Quite early on, the name *catechesis* was given to the totality of the Church's efforts to make disciples, to help men believe that

---

[1] Jn 17:3.
[2] 1 Tim 2:3–4.
[3] Acts 4:12.
[4] Mt 28:19–20.
[5] Mk 16:20.
[6] Cf. Acts 2:42.

Jesus is the Son of God so that believing they might have life in his name, and to educate and instruct them in this life, thus building up the body of Christ.[7]

5 'Catechesis is an *education in the faith* of children, young people and adults which includes especially the teaching of Christian doctrine imparted, generally speaking, in an organic and systematic way, with a view to initiating the hearers into the fullness of Christian life.'[8]

6 While not being formally identified with them, catechesis is built on a certain number of elements of the Church's pastoral mission which have a catechetical aspect, that prepare for catechesis, or spring from it. They are: the initial proclamation of the Gospel or missionary preaching to arouse faith; examination of the reasons for belief; experience of Christian living; celebration of the sacraments; integration into the ecclesial community; and apostolic and missionary witness.[9]

7 'Catechesis is intimately bound up with the whole of the Church's life. Not only her geographical extension and numerical increase, but even more her inner growth and correspondence with God's plan depend essentially on catechesis.'[10]

8 Periods of renewal in the Church are also intense moments of catechesis. In the great era of the Fathers of the Church, saintly bishops devoted an important part of their ministry to catechesis. St Cyril of Jerusalem and St John Chrysostom, St Ambrose and St Augustine, and many other Fathers wrote catechetical works that remain models for us.[11]

9 'The ministry of catechesis draws ever fresh energy from the councils. The Council of Trent is a noteworthy example of this. It gave catechesis priority in its constitutions and decrees. It lies at the origin of the *Roman Catechism*, which is also known by the name of that council and which is a work of the first rank as a summary of Christian teaching...'[12] The Council of Trent initiated a remarkable organization of the Church's catechesis. Thanks to the work of holy bishops and theologians such as St Peter Canisius, St Charles Borromeo, St Turibius of Mongrovejo or St Robert Bellarmine, it occasioned the publication of numerous catechisms.

10 It is therefore no surprise that catechesis in the Church has again attracted attention in the wake of the Second Vatican Council, which Pope Paul VI considered the great catechism of modern times. The *General Catechetical Directory* (1971), the sessions of the Synod of Bishops devoted to evangelization

---

[7] Cf. John Paul II, Apostolic Exhortation
   Catechesi tradendae 1; 2.
[8] *CT* 18.
[9] *CT* 18.

[10] *CT* 13.
[11] Cf. *CT* 12.
[12] *CT* 13.

(1974) and catechesis (1977), the apostolic exhortations *Evangelii nuntiandi* (1975) and *Catechesi tradendae* (1979), attest to this. The Extraordinary Synod of Bishops in 1985 asked 'that a catechism or compendium of all Catholic doctrine regarding both faith and morals be composed'.[13] The Holy Father, Pope John Paul II, made the Synod's wish his own, acknowledging that 'this desire wholly corresponds to a real need of the universal Church and of the particular Churches.'[14] He set in motion everything needed to carry out the Synod Fathers' wish.

III. The Aim and Intended Readership of the Catechism

11 This catechism aims at presenting an organic synthesis of the essential and fundamental contents of Catholic doctrine, as regards both faith and morals, in the light of the Second Vatican Council and the whole of the Church's Tradition. Its principal sources are the Sacred Scriptures, the Fathers of the Church, the liturgy, and the Church's Magisterium. It is intended to serve 'as a point of reference for the catechisms or compendia that are composed in the various countries'.[15]

12 This work is intended primarily for those responsible for catechesis: first of all the bishops, as teachers of the faith and pastors of the Church. It is offered to them as an instrument in fulfilling their responsibility of teaching the People of God. Through the bishops, it is addressed to redactors of catechisms, to priests, and to catechists. It will also be useful reading for all other Christian faithful.

IV. Structure of This Catechism

13 The plan of this catechism is inspired by the great tradition of catechisms which build catechesis on four pillars: the baptismal profession of faith (the *Creed*), the sacraments of faith, the life of faith (the *Commandments*), and the prayer of the believer (the *Lord's Prayer*).

Part One: *The Profession of Faith*

14 Those who belong to Christ through faith and Baptism must confess their baptismal faith before men.[16] First therefore the Catechism expounds revelation, by which God addresses and gives himself to man, and the faith by which man responds to God (*Section One*). The profession of faith summarizes the gifts that

---

[13] Extraordinary Synod of Bishops 1985, *Final Report* II B a, 4.

[14] John Paul II, Discourse at the Closing of the Extraordinary Synod of Bishops,

7 December 1985: AAS 78 (1986).

[15] Extraordinary Synod of Bishops 1985, *Final Report* II B a, 4.

[16] Cf. *Mt* 10:32; *Rom* 10:9.

God gives man: as the Author of all that is good; as Redeemer; and as Sanctifier. It develops these in the three chapters on our baptismal faith in the one God: the almighty *Father*, the Creator; his *Son* Jesus Christ, our Lord and Saviour; and the *Holy Spirit*, the Sanctifier, in the Holy Church (*Section Two*).

Part Two: *The Sacraments of Faith*

15 The second part of the Catechism explains how God's salvation, accomplished once for all through Christ Jesus and the Holy Spirit, is made present in the sacred actions of the Church's liturgy (*Section One*), especially in the seven sacraments (*Section Two*).

Part Three: *The Life of Faith*

16 The third part of the Catechism deals with the final end of man created in the image of God: beatitude, and the ways of reaching it – through right conduct freely chosen, with the help of God's law and grace (*Section One*), and through conduct that fulfils the twofold commandment of charity, specified in God's Ten Commandments (*Section Two*).

Part Four: *Prayer in the Life of Faith*

17 The last part of the Catechism deals with the meaning and importance of prayer in the life of believers (*Section One*). It concludes with a brief commentary on the seven petitions of the Lord's Prayer (*Section Two*), for indeed we find in these the sum of all the good things which we must hope for, and which our heavenly Father wants to grant us.

V. Practical Directions For Using This Catechism

18 This catechism is conceived as *an organic presentation* of the Catholic faith in its entirety. It should be seen therefore as a unified whole. Numerous cross-references in the margin of the text (italicized numbers referring to other paragraphs that deal with the same theme), as well as the analytical index at the end of the volume, allow the reader to view each theme in its relationship with the entirety of the faith.

19 The texts of Sacred Scripture are often not quoted word for word but are merely indicated by a reference ('**cf.**'). For a deeper understanding of such passages, the reader should refer to the Scriptural texts themselves. Such Biblical references are a valuable working-tool in catechesis.

20 The use of **small print** in certain passages indicates observations of an historical or apologetic nature, or supplementary doctrinal explanations.

21 The **quotations**, also in small print, from patristic, liturgical, magisterial or hagiographical sources, are intended to enrich the doctrinal presentations. These texts have often been chosen with a view to direct catechetical use.

22 *At the end of each thematic unit, a series of brief texts in small italics sums up the essentials of that unit's teaching in condensed formulae. These 'IN BRIEF' summaries may suggest to local catechists brief summary formulae that could be memorized.*

VI. Necessary Adaptations

23 The Catechism emphasizes the exposition of doctrine. It seeks to help deepen understanding of faith. In this way it is oriented towards the maturing of that faith, its putting down roots in personal life, and its shining forth in personal conduct.[17]

24 By design, this Catechism does not set out to provide the adaptation of doctrinal presentations and catechetical methods required by the differences of culture, age, spiritual maturity, and social and ecclesial condition among all those to whom it is addressed. Such indispensable adaptations are the responsibility of particular catechisms and, even more, of those who instruct the faithful:

> Whoever teaches must become 'all things to all men' (1 Cor 9:22), to win everyone to Christ... Above all, teachers must not imagine that a single kind of soul has been entrusted to them, and that consequently it is lawful to teach and form equally all the faithful in true piety with one and the same method! Let them realize that some are in Christ as newborn babes, others as adolescents, and still others as adults in full command of their powers.... Those who are called to the ministry of preaching must suit their words to the maturity and understanding of their hearers, as they hand on the teaching of the mysteries of faith and the rules of moral conduct.[18]

Above all – Charity

25 To conclude this Prologue, it is fitting to recall this pastoral principle stated by the *Roman Catechism*:

> The whole concern of doctrine and its teaching must be directed to the love that never ends. Whether something is proposed for belief, for hope or for action, the love of our Lord must always be made accessible, so that anyone can see that all the works of perfect Christian virtue spring from love and have no other objective than to arrive at love.[19]

---

[17] Cf. *CT* 20–22; 25.
[18] *Roman Catechism*, Preface 11; cf. 1 *Cor* 9:22; 1 *Pt* 2:2.

[19] *Roman Catechism*, Preface 10; cf. 1 *Cor* 13:8.

The central section of the sarcophagus of Junius Bassus, discovered underneath the 'Confessio' of the Basilica of St Peter in Rome and dating from the year 359.

Christ in glory, portrayed very young as a sign of his divinity, is seated on the throne of heaven, with Uranus, the pagan god of heaven, as his footstool. The apostles Peter and Paul stand on either side of Christ, towards whom they are turning and from whom they receive two scrolls: the new law.

As Moses had received the old law from God on Mount Sinai, now the apostles, represented by their two leaders, receive from Christ, the Son of God, the Lord of heaven and earth, the new law, no longer written on tablets of stone, but engraved by the Holy Spirit on the hearts of believers. Christ gives the strength to live according to the 'new life' (§ *1697*). He will fulfil in us what he has commanded for our benefit (cf. § *2074*).

Part One

THE PROFESSION OF FAITH

Section One

'I BELIEVE' – 'WE BELIEVE'

26 We begin our profession of faith by saying: 'I believe' or 'We believe'. Before expounding the Church's faith, as confessed in the Creed, celebrated in the liturgy and lived in observance of God's commandments and in prayer, we must first ask what 'to believe' means. Faith is man's response to God, who reveals himself and gives himself to man, at the same time bringing man a super-abundant light as he searches for the ultimate meaning of his life. Thus we shall consider first that search (*Chapter One*), then the divine Revelation by which God comes to meet man (*Chapter Two*), and finally the response of faith (*Chapter Three*).

Chapter One

MAN'S CAPACITY FOR GOD

I. The Desire For God

355, 1701

1718

27 The desire for God is written in the human heart, because man is created by God and for God; and God never ceases to draw man to himself. Only in God will he find the truth and happiness he never stops searching for:

> The dignity of man rests above all on the fact that he is called to commu-nion with God. This invitation to converse with God is addressed to man as soon as he comes into being. For if man exists it is because God has created him through love, and through love continues to hold him in existence. He cannot live fully according to truth unless he freely acknowledges that love and entrusts himself to his creator.[1]

843, 2566

2095–2109

28 In many ways, throughout history down to the present day, men have given expression to their quest for God in their religious beliefs and behaviour: in their prayers, sacrifices, rituals, medita-tions, and so forth. These forms of religious expression, despite the ambiguities they often bring with them, are so universal that one may well call man a *religious being*:

> From one ancestor [God] made all nations to inhabit the whole earth, and he allotted the times of their existence and the boundaries of the places where they would live, so that they would search for God and perhaps grope for him and find him – though indeed he is not far from each one of us. For 'in him we live and move and have our being.'[2]

---

[1] Vatican Council II, GS 19 § 1.   [2] *Acts* 17:26–28.

29   But this 'intimate and vital bond of man to God' (*GS* 19 § 1) can be forgotten, overlooked, or even explicitly rejected by man.[3]   2123–2128 Such attitudes can have different causes: revolt against evil in the world; religious ignorance or indifference; the cares and riches of this world; the scandal of bad example on the part of believers; currents of thought hostile to religion; finally, that attitude of sinful man which makes him hide from God out of fear and flee his   398 call.[4]

30   'Let the hearts of those who seek the LORD rejoice.'[5] Although man can forget God or reject him, He never ceases to call every   2567, 845 man to seek him, so as to find life and happiness. But this search for God demands of man every effort of intellect, a sound will, 'an upright heart', as well as the witness of others who teach him to   368 seek God.

> You are great, O Lord, and greatly to be praised: great is your power and your wisdom is without measure. And man, so small a part of your creation, wants to praise you: this man, though clothed with mortality and bearing the evidence of sin and the proof that you withstand the proud. Despite everything, man, though but a small a part of your creation, wants to praise you. You yourself encourage him to delight in your praise, for you have made us for yourself, and our heart is restless until it rests in you.[6]

II. Ways of Coming to Know God

31   Created in God's image and called to know and love him, the person who seeks God discovers certain ways of coming to know him. These are also called proofs for the existence of God, not in the sense of proofs in the natural sciences, but rather in the sense of 'converging and convincing arguments', which allow us to attain certainty about the truth.

These 'ways' of approaching God from creation have a twofold point of departure: the physical world, and the human person.

32   The *world*: starting from movement, becoming, contingency, and the world's order and beauty, one can come to a knowledge of   54, 337 God as the origin and the end of the universe.

> As St Paul says of the Gentiles: For what can be known about God is plain to them, because God has shown it to them. Ever since the creation of the

---

[3] *GS* 19 § 1.
[4] Cf. *GS* 19–21; *Mt* 13:22; *Gen* 3:8–10; *Jon* 1:3.
[5] *Ps* 105:3.
[6] St Augustine, *Conf.* 1, 1, 1: PL 32, 659–661.

world his invisible nature, namely, his eternal power and deity, has been clearly perceived in the things that have been made.[7]

And St Augustine issues this challenge: Question the beauty of the earth, question the beauty of the sea, question the beauty of the air distending and diffusing itself, question the beauty of the sky... question all these realities. All respond: 'See, we are beautiful.' Their beauty is a profession [confessio]. These beauties are subject to change. Who made them if not the Beautiful One [Pulcher] who is not subject to change?[8]

2500 **33** The *human person*: with his openness to truth and beauty, his
1730, 1776 sense of moral goodness, his freedom and the voice of his con-
1703 science, with his longings for the infinite and for happiness, man questions himself about God's existence. In all this he discerns signs
366 of his spiritual soul. The soul, the 'seed of eternity we bear in ourselves, irreducible to the merely material',[9] can have its origin only in God.

34 The world, and man, attest that they contain within themselves neither their first principle nor their final end, but rather that they participate in Being itself, which alone is without origin or end. Thus, in different ways, man can come to know that there exists a reality which is the first cause and final end of all things, a
199 reality 'that everyone calls "God"'.[10]

35 Man's faculties make him capable of coming to a knowledge of the existence of a personal God. But for man to be able to enter
50 into real intimacy with him, God willed both to reveal himself to man, and to give him the grace of being able to welcome this revelation in faith. The proofs of God's existence, however, can
159 predispose one to faith and help one to see that faith is not opposed to reason.

III. The Knowledge of God According to the Church

36 'Our holy mother, the Church, holds and teaches that God, the first principle and last end of all things, can be known with certainty from the created world by the natural light of human reason.'[11] Without this capacity, man would not be able to welcome God's revelation. Man has this capacity because he is created
355 'in the image of God'.[12]

37 In the historical conditions in which he finds himself, however,

---

[7] *Rom*. 1:19–20; cf. *Acts* 14:15, 17; 17:27–28; *Wis* 13:1–9.

[8] St Augustine, *Sermo* 241, 2: PL 38, 1134.

[9] *GS* 18 § 1; cf. 14 § 2.

[10] St Thomas Aquinas, *STh* I, 2, 3.

[11] Vatican Council I, *Dei Filius* 2: DS 3004; cf. 3026; Vatican Council II, *Dei Verbum* 6.

[12] Cf. *Gen* 1:27.

man experiences many difficulties in coming to know God by the 1960 light of reason alone:

> Though human reason is, strictly speaking, truly capable by its own natural power and light of attaining to a true and certain knowledge of the one personal God, who watches over and controls the world by his providence, and of the natural law written in our hearts by the Creator; yet there are many obstacles which prevent reason from the effective and fruitful use of this inborn faculty. For the truths that concern the relations between God and man wholly transcend the visible order of things, and, if they are translated into human action and influence it, they call for self-surrender and abnegation. The human mind, in its turn, is hampered in the attaining of such truths, not only by the impact of the senses and the imagination, but also by disordered appetites which are the consequences of original sin. So it happens that men in such matters easily persuade themselves that what they would not like to be true is false or at least doubtful.[13]

38 This is why man stands in need of being enlightened by God's revelation, not only about those things that exceed his understanding, but also 'about those religious and moral truths which of themselves are not beyond the grasp of human reason, so that even 2036 in the present condition of the human race, they can be known by all men with ease, with firm certainty and with no admixture of error'.[14]

IV. How Can We Speak About God?

39 In defending the ability of human reason to know God, the Church is expressing her confidence in the possibility of speaking 851 about him to all men and with all men, and therefore of dialogue with other religions, with philosophy and science, as well as with unbelievers and atheists.

40 Since our knowledge of God is limited, our language about him is equally so. We can name God only by taking creatures as our starting point, and in accordance with our limited human ways of knowing and thinking.

41 All creatures bear a certain resemblance to God, most especially man, created in the image and likeness of God. The manifold perfections of creatures – their truth, their goodness, their beauty – all reflect the infinite perfection of God. Consequently we can 213, 299 name God by taking his creatures' perfections as our starting

---

[13] Pius XII, *Humani generis* 561: DS 3875.
[14] Pius XII, *Humani generis* 561: DS 3876;

cf. *Dei Filius* 2: DS 3005; *DV* 6; St Thomas Aquinas, *STh* I, 1, 1.

point, 'for from the greatness and beauty of created things comes a corresponding perception of their Creator'.[15]

212, 300　42　God transcends all creatures. We must therefore continually purify our language of everything in it that is limited, image-bound or imperfect, if we are not to confuse our image of God –

370　'the inexpressible, the incomprehensible, the invisible, the ungraspable' – with our human representations.[16] Our human words always fall short of the mystery of God.

43　Admittedly, in speaking about God like this, our language is using human modes of expression; nevertheless it really does attain

206　to God himself, though unable to express him in his infinite simplicity. Likewise, we must recall that 'between Creator and creature no similitude can be expressed without implying an even greater dissimilitude';[17] and that 'concerning God, we cannot grasp what he is, but only what he is not, and how other beings stand in relation to him.'[18]

IN BRIEF

44　*Man is by nature and vocation a religious being. Coming from God, going toward God, man lives a fully human life only if he freely lives by his bond with God.*

45　*Man is made to live in communion with God in whom he finds happiness: 'When I am completely united to you, there will be no more sorrow or trials; entirely full of you, my life will be complete' (St Augustine, Conf. 10, 28, 39: PL 32, 795).*

46　*When he listens to the message of creation and to the voice of conscience, man can arrive at certainty about the existence of God, the cause and the end of everything.*

47　*The Church teaches that the one true God, our Creator and Lord, can be known with certainty from his works, by the natural light of human reason (cf. Vatican Council I, can. 2 §1: DS 3026).*

48　*We really can name God, starting from the manifold perfections of his creatures, which are likenesses of the infinitely perfect God, even if our limited language cannot exhaust the mystery.*

49　*'Without the Creator, the creature vanishes' (GS 36). This is the reason why believers know that the love of Christ urges them to bring the light of the living God to those who do not know him or who reject him.*

---

[15] *Wis* 13:5.
[16] Liturgy of St John Chrysostom, Anaphora.
[17] Lateran Council IV: DS 806.
[18] St Thomas Aquinas, *SCG* I, 30.

Chapter Two
GOD COMES TO MEET MAN

50 By natural reason man can know God with certainty, on the basis of his works. But there is another order of knowledge, which man cannot possibly arrive at by his own powers: the order of divine Revelation.[1] Through an utterly free decision, God has revealed himself and given himself to man. This he does by revealing the mystery, his plan of loving goodness, formed from all eternity in Christ, for the benefit of all men. God has fully revealed this plan by sending us his beloved Son, our Lord Jesus Christ, and the Holy Spirit.

36

1066

Article 1
THE REVELATION OF GOD

I. God Reveals His 'Plan of Loving Goodness'

51 'It pleased God, in his goodness and wisdom, to reveal himself and to make known the mystery of his will. His will was that men should have access to the Father, through Christ, the Word made flesh, in the Holy Spirit, and thus become sharers in the divine nature.'[2]

2823

1996

52 God, who 'dwells in unapproachable light', wants to communicate his own divine life to the men he freely created, in order to adopt them as his sons in his only-begotten Son.[3] By revealing himself God wishes to make them capable of responding to him, and of knowing him and of loving him far beyond their own natural capacity.

53 The divine plan of Revelation is realized simultaneously 'by deeds and words which are intrinsically bound up with each other'[4] and shed light on each another. It involves a specific divine pedagogy: God communicates himself to man gradually. He prepares him to welcome by stages the supernatural Revelation that is to culminate in the person and mission of the incarnate Word, Jesus Christ.

1953, 1950

> St Irenaeus of Lyons repeatedly speaks of this divine pedagogy using the image of God and man becoming accustomed to one another: The Word of God dwelt in man and became the Son of man in order to accustom

---

[1] Cf. *Dei Filius*: DS 3015.
[2] *DV* 2; cf. *Eph* 1:9; 2:18; 2 *Pt* 1:4.
[3] 1 *Tim* 6:16; cf. *Eph* 1:4–5.
[4] *DV* 2.

man to perceive God and to accustom God to dwell in man, according to the Father's pleasure.[5]

II. The Stages of Revelation

In the beginning God makes himself known

54 'God, who creates and conserves all things by his Word, provides men with constant evidence of himself in created realities. And furthermore, wishing to open up the way to heavenly salvation, he manifested himself to our first parents from the very beginning.'[6] He invited them to intimate communion with himself and clothed them with resplendent grace and justice.

55 This revelation was not broken off by our first parents' sin. 'After the fall, [God] buoyed them up with the hope of salvation, by promising redemption; and he has never ceased to show his solicitude for the human race. For he wishes to give eternal life to all those who seek salvation by patience in well-doing.'[7]

Even when he disobeyed you and lost your friendship
you did not abandon him to the power of death...
Again and again you offered a covenant to man.[8]

The covenant with Noah

56 After the unity of the human race was shattered by sin God at once sought to save humanity part by part. The covenant with Noah after the flood gives expression to the principle of the divine economy toward the 'nations', in other words, towards men grouped 'in their lands, each with [its] own language, by their families, in their nations'.[9]

57 This state of division into many nations is at once cosmic, social and religious. It is intended to limit the pride of fallen humanity,[10] united only in its perverse ambition to forge its own unity as at Babel.[11] But, because of sin, both polytheism and the idolatry of the nation and of its rulers constantly threaten this provisional economy with the perversion of paganism.[12]

58 The covenant with Noah remains in force during the times of the Gentiles, until the universal proclamation of the Gospel.[13] The

Margin references: 32, 374, 397, 410, 761, 401, 1219, 674

---

[5] St Irenaeus, *Adv. haeres.* 3, 20, 2: PG 7/1, 944; cf. 3, 17, 1; 4, 12, 4; 4, 21, 3.

[6] *DV* 3; cf. *Jn* 1:3; *Rom* 1:19–20.

[7] *DV* 3; cf. *Gen* 3:15; *Rom* 2:6–7.

[8] *Roman Missal*, Eucharistic Prayer IV, 118.

[9] *Gen* 10:5; cf. 9:9–10. 16; 10:20–31.

[10] Cf. *Acts* 17:26–27.

[11] Cf. *Wis* 10:5; *Gen* 11:4–6.

[12] Cf. *Rom* 1:18–25.

[13] Cf. *Gen* 9:16; *Lk* 21:24; *DV* 3.

Bible venerates several great figures among the Gentiles: Abel the just, the king-priest Melchisedek – a figure of Christ – and the upright 'Noah, Daniel, and Job'.[14] Scripture thus expresses the heights of sanctity that can be reached by those who live according to the covenant of Noah, waiting for Christ to 'gather into one the children of God who are scattered abroad'.[15]

2569

God chooses Abraham

59 In order to gather together scattered humanity God calls Abram from his country, his kindred and his father's house,[16] and makes him Abraham, that is, 'the father of a multitude of nations'. 'In you all the nations of the earth shall be blessed.'[17]

145, 2570

60 The people descended from Abraham would be the trustee of the promise made to the patriarchs, the chosen people, called to prepare for that day when God would gather all his children into the unity of the Church.[18] They would be the root on to which the Gentiles would be grafted, once they came to believe.[19]

760
762, 781

61 The patriarchs, prophets and certain other Old Testament figures have been and always will be honoured as saints in all the Church's liturgical traditions.

God forms his people Israel

62 After the patriarchs, God formed Israel as his people by freeing them from slavery in Egypt. He established with them the coven-ant of Mount Sinai and, through Moses, gave them his law so that they would recognize him and serve him as the one living and true God, the provident Father and just judge, and so that they would look for the promised Saviour.[20]

2060, 2574
1961

63 Israel is the priestly people of God, 'called by the name of the LORD', and 'the first to hear the word of God',[21] the people of 'elder brethren' in the faith of Abraham.

204, 2810
839

64 Through the prophets, God forms his people in the hope of salvation, in the expectation of a new and everlasting Covenant intended for all, to be written on their hearts.[22] The prophets proclaim a radical redemption of the People of God, purification from all their infidelities, a salvation which will include all the

711
1965

---

[14] Cf. Gen 14:18; Heb 7:3; Ezek 14:14.
[15] Jn 11:52.
[16] Gen 12:1.
[17] Gen 17:5; 12:3 (LXX); cf. Gal 3:8.
[18] Cf. Rom 11:28; Jn 11:52; 10:16.
[19] Cf. Rom 11:17–18, 24.

[20] Cf. DV 3
[21] Dt 28:10; Roman Missal, Good Friday, General Intercession VI; see also Ex 19:6.
[22] Cf. Is 2:2–4; Jer 31:31–34; Heb 10:16.

nations.[23] Above all, the poor and humble of the Lord will bear
489 this hope. Such holy women as Sarah, Rebecca, Rachel, Miriam,
Deborah, Hannah, Judith and Esther kept alive the hope of Israel's
salvation. The purest figure among them is Mary.[24]

III. Christ Jesus – 'Mediator and Fullness of All Revelation'[25]

God has said everything in his Word

65 'In many and various ways God spoke of old to our fathers by
the prophets, but in these last days he has spoken to us by a Son.'[26]
Christ, the Son of God made man, is the Father's one, perfect and
102 unsurpassable Word. In him he has said everything; there will be
no other word than this one. St John of the Cross, among others,
commented strikingly on *Hebrews* 1:1-2:

> In giving us his Son, his only Word (for he possesses no other), he spoke
> everything to us at once in this sole Word – and he has no more to say...
> because what he spoke before to the prophets in parts, he has now spoken
516 all at once by giving us the All Who is His Son. Any person questioning
> God or desiring some vision or revelation would be guilty not only of
> foolish behaviour but also of offending him, by not fixing his eyes
2717 entirely upon Christ and by living with the desire for some other
> novelty.[27]

There will be no further Revelation

66 'The Christian economy, therefore, since it is the new and
definitive Covenant, will never pass away; and no new public
revelation is to be expected before the glorious manifestation of
our Lord Jesus Christ.'[28] Yet even if Revelation is already complete, it has not been made completely explicit; it remains for
94 Christian faith gradually to grasp its full significance over the
course of the centuries.

67 Throughout the ages, there have been so-called 'private' revelations, some
of which have been recognized by the authority of the Church. They do not
84 belong, however, to the deposit of faith. It is not their role to improve or
93 complete Christ's definitive Revelation, but to help live more fully by it in a
certain period of history. Guided by the Magisterium of the Church, the *sensus*

---

[23] Cf. *Ezek* 36; *Is* 49:5–6; 53:11.
[24] Cf. *Zeph* 2:3; *Lk* 1:38.
[25] *DV* 2.
[26] *Heb* 1:1–2.
[27] St John of the Cross, *The Ascent of
Mount Carmel* 2, 22, 3–5 in *The
Collected Works of St John of the Cross*,
tr. K. Kavanaugh OCD and O.
Rodriguez OCD (Washington DC:
Institute of Carmelite Studies, 1979),
179–180: *LH*, Advent, week 2,
Monday, OR.
[28] *DV* 4; cf. 1 *Tim* 6:14; *Titus* 2:13.

fidelium knows how to discern and welcome in these revelations whatever constitutes an authentic call of Christ or his saints to the Church.

Christian faith cannot accept 'revelations' that claim to surpass or correct the Revelation of which Christ is the fulfilment, as is the case in certain non-Christian religions and also in certain recent sects which base themselves on such 'revelations'.

IN BRIEF

68 *By love, God has revealed himself and given himself to man. He has thus provided the definitive, superabundant answer to the questions that man asks himself about the meaning and purpose of his life.*

69 *God has revealed himself to man by gradually communicating his own mystery in deeds and in words.*

70 *Beyond the witness to himself that God gives in created things, he manifested himself to our first parents, spoke to them and, after the fall, promised them salvation (cf. Gen 3:15) and offered them his covenant.*

71 *God made an everlasting covenant with Noah and with all living beings (cf. Gen 9:16). It will remain in force as long as the world lasts.*

72 *God chose Abraham and made a covenant with him and his descendants. By the covenant God formed his people and revealed his law to them through Moses. Through the prophets, he prepared them to accept the salvation destined for all humanity.*

73 *God has revealed himself fully by sending his own Son, in whom he has established his covenant for ever. The Son is his Father's definitive Word; so there will be no further Revelation after him.*

Article 2
THE TRANSMISSION OF DIVINE REVELATION

74 God 'desires all men to be saved and to come to the knowledge of the truth':[29] that is, of Christ Jesus.[30] Christ must be proclaimed to all nations and individuals, so that this revelation may reach to the ends of the earth: *851*

> God graciously arranged that the things he had once revealed for the salvation of all peoples should remain in their entirety, throughout the ages, and be transmitted to all generations.[31]

I. The Apostolic Tradition

75 'Christ the Lord, in whom the entire Revelation of the most

---

[29] 1 *Tim* 2:4.
[30] Cf. *Jn* 14:6.

[31] *DV* 7; cf. 2 *Cor* 1:20; 3:16 – 4:6.

high God is summed up, commanded the apostles to preach the Gospel, which had been promised beforehand by the prophets, and which he fulfilled in his own person and promulgated with his own lips. In preaching the Gospel, they were to communicate the
171 gifts of God to all men. This Gospel was to be the source of all saving truth and moral discipline.'[32]

In the apostolic preaching...

76 In keeping with the Lord's command, the Gospel was handed on in two ways:

– *orally* 'by the apostles who handed on, by the spoken word of their preaching, by the example they gave, by the institutions they established, what they themselves had received – whether from the lips of Christ, from his way of life and his works, or whether they had learned it at the prompting of the Holy Spirit';[33]

– *in writing* 'by those apostles and other men associated with the apostles who, under the inspiration of the same Holy Spirit, committed the message of salvation to writing'.[34]

... continued in apostolic succession

77 'In order that the full and living Gospel might always be pre-
861 served in the Church the apostles left bishops as their successors. They gave them "their own position of teaching authority".'[35] Indeed, 'the apostolic preaching, which is expressed in a special way in the inspired books, was to be preserved in a continuous line of succession until the end of time.'[36]

78 This living transmission, accomplished in the Holy Spirit, is
174 called Tradition, since it is distinct from Sacred Scripture, though closely connected to it. Through Tradition, 'the Church, in her
1124, 2651 doctrine, life and worship, perpetuates and transmits to every generation all that she herself is, all that she believes.'[37] 'The sayings of the holy Fathers are a witness to the life-giving presence of this Tradition, showing how its riches are poured out in the practice and life of the Church, in her belief and her prayer.'[38]

79 The Father's self-communication made through his Word in the Holy Spirit, remains present and active in the Church: 'God, who spoke in the past, continues to converse with the Spouse of his beloved Son. And the Holy Spirit, through whom the living voice

---

[32] DV 7; cf. Mt 28:19–20; Mk 16:15.   1: PG 7/1, 848; Harvey, 2, 9.
[33] DV 7.   [36] DV 8 § 1.
[34] DV 7.   [37] DV 8 § 1.
[35] DV 7 § 2; St Irenaeus, *Adv. haeres.* 3, 3,   [38] DV 8 § 3.

of the Gospel rings out in the Church – and through her in the world – leads believers to the full truth, and makes the Word of Christ dwell in them in all its richness.'[39]

II. The Relationship between Tradition and Sacred Scripture

One common source...

80 'Sacred Tradition and Sacred Scripture, then, are bound closely together, and communicate one with the other. For both of them, flowing out from the same divine well-spring, come together in some fashion to form one thing, and move towards the same goal.'[40] Each of them makes present and fruitful in the Church the mystery of Christ, who promised to remain with his own 'always, to the close of the age'.[41]

... two distinct modes of transmission

81 '*Sacred Scripture* is the speech of God as it is put down in writing under the breath of the Holy Spirit.'[42]

'And [Holy] *Tradition* transmits in its entirety the Word of God which has been entrusted to the apostles by Christ the Lord and the Holy Spirit. It transmits it to the successors of the apostles so that, enlightened by the Spirit of truth, they may faithfully preserve, expound and spread it abroad by their preaching.'[43]   113

82 As a result the Church, to whom the transmission and interpretation of Revelation is entrusted, 'does not derive her certainty about all revealed truths from the holy Scriptures alone. Both Scripture and Tradition must be accepted and honoured with equal sentiments of devotion and reverence.'[44]

Apostolic Tradition and ecclesial traditions

83 The Tradition here in question comes from the apostles and hands on what they received from Jesus' teaching and example and what they learned from the Holy Spirit. The first generation of Christians did not yet have a written New Testament, and the New Testament itself demonstrates the process of living Tradition.

Tradition is to be distinguished from the various theological, disciplinary, liturgical or devotional traditions, born in the local churches over time. These are the particular forms, adapted to different places and times, in which the great Tradition is expressed. In the light of Tradition, these traditions can be retained, modified or even abandoned under the guidance of the Church's Magisterium.   *2041, 1202, 2684*

---

[39] *DV* 8 § 3; cf. *Col* 3:16.
[40] *DV* 9.
[41] *Mt* 28:20.

[42] *DV* 9.
[43] *DV* 9.
[44] *DV* 9.

III. The Interpretation of the Heritage of Faith

The heritage of faith entrusted to the whole of the Church

857, 871 84 The apostles entrusted the 'Sacred deposit' of the faith (the *depositum fidei*),[45] contained in Sacred Scripture and Tradition, to the whole of the Church. 'By adhering to [this heritage] the entire holy people, united to its pastors, remains always faithful to the teaching of the apostles, to the brotherhood, to the breaking of bread and the prayers. So, in maintaining, practising and pro- *2033* fessing the faith that has been handed on, there should be a remarkable harmony between the bishops and the faithful.'[46]

The Magisterium of the Church

85 'The task of giving an authentic interpretation of the Word of God, whether in its written form or in the form of Tradition, has *888–892* been entrusted to the living teaching office of the Church alone. Its *2032–2040* authority in this matter is exercised in the name of Jesus Christ.'[47] This means that the task of interpretation has been entrusted to the bishops in communion with the successor of Peter, the Bishop of Rome.

86 'Yet this Magisterium is not superior to the Word of God, but is its servant. It teaches only what has been handed on to it. At the *688* divine command and with the help of the Holy Spirit, it listens to this devotedly, guards it with dedication and expounds it faithfully. All that it proposes for belief as being divinely revealed is drawn from this single deposit of faith.'[48]

1548 87 Mindful of Christ's words to his apostles: 'He who hears you, *2037* hears me',[49] the faithful receive with docility the teachings and directives that their pastors give them in different forms.

The dogmas of the faith

888–892, 88 The Church's Magisterium exercises the authority it holds *032–2040* from Christ to the fullest extent when it defines dogmas, that is, when it proposes, in a form obliging the Christian people to an irrevocable adherence of faith, truths contained in divine Revelation or also when it proposes, in a definitive way, truths having a necessary connection with these.

[45] *DV* 10 § 1; cf. 1 *Tim* 6:20; 2 *Tim* 1:12–14 (Vulg.).

[46] *DV* 10 § 1; cf. *Acts* 2:42 (Greek); Pius XII, Apost. Const. *Munificentissimus Deus*, 1 November 1950: AAS 42 (1950), 756, taken along with the words of St Cyprian, *Epist.* 66, 8: CSEL 3/2, 733: 'The Church is the people united to its Priests, the flock adhering to its Shepherd.'

[47] *DV* 10 § 2.

[48] *DV* 10 § 2.

[49] *Lk* 10:16; cf. *LG* 20.

89 There is an organic connection between our spiritual life and 2625
the dogmas. Dogmas are lights along the path of faith; they illuminate it and make it secure. Conversely, if our life is upright, our
intellect and heart will be open to welcome the light shed by the
dogmas of faith.[50]

90 The mutual connections between dogmas, and their coherence, 114, 158
can be found in the whole of the Revelation of the mystery of
Christ.[51] 'In Catholic doctrine there exists an order or "hierarchy" 234
of truths, since they vary in their relation to the foundation of the
Christian faith.'[52]

The supernatural sense of faith

91 All the faithful share in understanding and handing on
revealed truth. They have received the anointing of the Holy
Spirit, who instructs them[53] and guides them into all truth.[54] 737

92 'The whole body of the faithful... cannot err in matters of 785
belief. This characteristic is shown in the supernatural appreciation
of faith (*sensus fidei*) on the part of the whole people, when, "from
the bishops to the last of the faithful", they manifest a universal
consent in matters of faith and morals.'[55]

93 'By this appreciation of the faith, aroused and sustained by the
Spirit of truth, the People of God, guided by the sacred teaching 889
authority (*Magisterium*),... receives... the faith, once for all delivered to the saints... The People unfailingly adheres to this faith,
penetrates it more deeply with right judgement, and applies it
more fully in daily life.'[56]

Growth in understanding the faith

94 Thanks to the assistance of the Holy Spirit, the understanding
of both the realities and the words of the heritage of faith is able to
grow in the life of the Church: 66
— 'through the contemplation and study of believers who ponder 2651
these things in their hearts';[57] it is in particular 'theological research
[which] deepens knowledge of revealed truth'.[58]
— 'from the intimate sense of spiritual realities which [believers] 2038, 2518

[50] Cf. *Jn* 8:31–32.
[51] Cf. Vatican Council I: DS 3016: *nexus mysteriorum*; *LG* 25.
[52] *UR* 11.
[53] Cf. 1 *Jn* 2:20, 27.
[54] Cf. *Jn* 16:13.
[55] *LG* 12; cf. St Augustine, *De praed. sanct.* 14, 27: PL 44, 980.
[56] *LG* 12; cf. *Jude* 3.
[57] *DV* 8 § 2; cf. *Lk* 2:19, 51.
[58] *GS* 62 § 7; cf. *GS* 44 § 2; *DV* 23; 24: *UR* 4.

experience',[59] the sacred Scriptures 'grow with the one who reads them.'[60]

– 'from the preaching of those who have received, along with their right of succession in the episcopate, the sure charism of truth'.[61]

95 'It is clear therefore that, in the supremely wise arrangement of God, sacred Tradition, Sacred Scripture and the Magisterium of the Church are so connected and associated that one of them cannot stand without the others. Working together, each in its own way, under the action of the one Holy Spirit, they all contribute effectively to the salvation of souls.'[62]

IN BRIEF

96 What Christ entrusted to the apostles, they in turn handed on by their preaching and writing, under the inspiration of the Holy Spirit, to all generations, until Christ returns in glory.

97 'Sacred Tradition and Sacred Scripture make up a single sacred deposit of the Word of God' (DV 10), in which, as in a mirror, the pilgrim Church contemplates God, the source of all her riches.

98 'The Church, in her doctrine, life and worship, perpetuates and transmits to every generation all that she herself is, all that she believes' (DV 8 § 1).

99 Thanks to its supernatural sense of faith, the People of God as a whole never ceases to welcome, to penetrate more deeply and to live more fully from the gift of divine Revelation.

100 The task of interpreting the Word of God authentically has been entrusted solely to the Magisterium of the Church, that is, to the Pope and to the bishops in communion with him.

Article 3
SACRED SCRIPTURE

I. Christ – The Unique Word of Sacred Scripture

101 In order to reveal himself to men, in the condescension of his goodness God speaks to them in human words: 'Indeed the words of God, expressed in the words of men, are in every way like human language, just as the Word of the eternal Father, when he took on himself the flesh of human weakness, became like men.'[63]

---

[59] DV 8 § 2.
[60] St Gregory the Great, Hom. in Ezek. 1, 7, 8: PL 76, 843D.
[61] DV 8 § 2.
[62] DV 10 § 3.
[63] DV 13.

102 Through all the words of Sacred Scripture, God speaks only *2763* one single Word, his one Utterance in whom he expresses himself *65* completely:[64]

> You recall that one and the same Word of God extends throughout Scripture, that it is one and the same Utterance that resounds in the mouths of all the sacred writers, since he who was in the beginning God with God has no need of separate syllables; for he is not subject to time.[65]

103 For this reason, the Church has always venerated the Scrip- *1100, 1184* tures as she venerates the Lord's Body. She never ceases to present *1378* to the faithful the bread of life, taken from the one table of God's Word and Christ's Body.[66]

104 In Sacred Scripture, the Church constantly finds her nourishment and her strength, for she welcomes it not as a human word, 'but as what it really is, the word of God'.[67] 'In the sacred books, the Father who is in heaven comes lovingly to meet his children, and talks with them.'[68]

II. Inspiration and Truth of Sacred Scripture

105 *God is the author of Sacred Scripture.* 'The divinely revealed realities, which are contained and presented in the text of Sacred Scripture, have been written down under the inspiration of the Holy Spirit.'[69]

'For Holy Mother Church, relying on the faith of the apostolic age, accepts as sacred and canonical the books of the Old and the New Testaments, whole and entire, with all their parts, on the grounds that, written under the inspiration of the Holy Spirit, they have God as their author, and have been handed on as such to the Church herself.'[70]

106 God inspired the human authors of the sacred books. 'To compose the sacred books, God chose certain men who, all the while he employed them in this task, made full use of their own faculties and powers so that, though he acted in them and by them, it was as true authors that they consigned to writing whatever he wanted written, and no more.'[71]

107 The inspired books teach the truth. 'Since therefore all that the inspired authors or sacred writers affirm should be regarded as

---

[64] Cf. *Heb* 1:1-3.
[65] St Augustine, *En. in Ps.* 103, 4, 1: PL 37, 1378; cf. *Ps* 104; *Jn* 1:1.
[66] Cf. *DV* 21.
[67] 1 *Th* 2:13; cf. *DV* 24.
[68] *DV* 21.
[69] *DV* 11.
[70] *DV* 11; cf. *Jn* 20:31; 2 *Tim* 3:16; 2 *Pt* 1:19-21; 3:15-16.
[71] *DV* 11.

702 affirmed by the Holy Spirit, we must acknowledge that the books of Scripture firmly, faithfully, and without error teach that truth which God, for the sake of our salvation, wished to see confided to the Sacred Scriptures.'[72]

108 Still, the Christian faith is not a 'religion of the book'. Christianity is the religion of the 'Word' of God, a word which is 'not a written and mute word, but the Word which is incarnate and living'.[73] If the Scriptures are not to remain a dead letter, Christ, the eternal Word of the living God, must, through the Holy Spirit, 'open [our] minds to understand the Scriptures.'[74]

III. The Holy Spirit, Interpreter of Scripture

109 In Sacred Scripture, God speaks to man in a human way. To interpret Scripture correctly, the reader must be attentive to what the human authors truly wanted to affirm, and to what God wanted to reveal to us by their words.[75]

110 In order to discover *the sacred authors' intention*, the reader must take into account the conditions of their time and culture, the literary genres in use at that time, and the modes of feeling, speaking and narrating then current. 'For the fact is that truth is differently presented and expressed in the various types of historical writing, in prophetical and poetical texts, and in other forms of literary expression.'[76]

111 But since Sacred Scripture is inspired, there is another and no less important principle of correct interpretation, without which Scripture would remain a dead letter. 'Sacred Scripture must be read and interpreted in the light of the same Spirit by whom it was written.'[77]

The Second Vatican Council indicates *three criteria* for interpreting Scripture in accordance with the Spirit who inspired it.[78]

112 1. *Be especially attentive 'to the content and unity of the whole Scripture'*. Different as the books which compose it may be, Scrip-
128 ture is a unity by reason of the unity of God's plan, of which Christ
368 Jesus is the centre and heart, open since his Passover.[79]

> The phrase 'heart of Christ' can refer to Sacred Scripture, which makes known his heart, closed before the Passion, as the Scripture was obscure.

---

[72] *DV* 11.
[73] St Bernard, *S. missus est hom.* 4, 11: PL 183, 86.
[74] Cf. *Lk* 24:45.
[75] Cf. *DV* 12 § 1.

[76] *DV* 12 § 2.
[77] *DV* 12 § 3.
[78] Cf. *DV* 12 § 4.
[79] Cf. *Lk* 24:25–27, 44–46.

But the Scripture has been opened since the Passion; since those who from then on have understood it, consider and discern in what way the prophecies must be interpreted.[80]

113 2. *Read the Scripture within 'the living Tradition of the whole Church'*. According to a saying of the Fathers, Sacred Scripture is *81* written principally in the Church's heart rather than in documents and records, for the Church carries in her Tradition the living memorial of God's Word, and it is the Holy Spirit who gives her the spiritual interpretation of the Scripture ('... according to the spiritual meaning which the Spirit grants to the Church'[81]).

114 3. *Be attentive to the analogy of faith.*[82] By 'analogy of faith' we mean the coherence of the truths of faith among themselves and *90* within the whole plan of Revelation.

The senses of Scripture

115 According to an ancient tradition, one can distinguish between two *senses* of Scripture: the literal and the spiritual, the latter being subdivided into the allegorical, moral and anagogical senses. The profound concordance of the four senses guarantees all its richness to the living reading of Scripture in the Church.

116 The *literal sense* is the meaning conveyed by the words of Scripture and discovered by exegesis, following the rules of sound interpretation: 'All other *110* senses of Sacred Scripture are based on the literal.'[83]

117 The *spiritual sense*. Thanks to the unity of God's plan, not only the text of *1101* Scripture but also the realities and events about which it speaks can be signs.

   1. The *allegorical sense*. We can acquire a more profound understanding of events by recognizing their significance in Christ; thus the crossing of the Red Sea is a sign or type of Christ's victory and also of Christian Baptism.[84]

   2. The *moral sense*. The events reported in Scripture ought to lead us to act justly. As St Paul says, they were written 'for our instruction'.[85]

   3. The *anagogical sense* (Greek: *anagōgē*, 'leading'). We can view realities and events in terms of their eternal significance, leading us toward our true home-land: thus the Church on earth is a sign of the heavenly Jerusalem.[86]

118 A medieval couplet summarizes the significance of the four senses:

The Letter speaks of deeds; Allegory to faith;
The Moral how to act; Anagogy our destiny.[87]

119 'It is the task of exegetes to work, according to these rules, towards a better understanding and explanation of the meaning of

---

[80] St Thomas Aquinas, *Expos. in Ps.* 21, 11; cf. *Ps* 22:14.

[81] Origen, *Hom. in Lev.* 5, 5: PG 12, 454D.

[82] Cf. *Rom* 12:6.

[83] St Thomas Aquinas, *STh* I, 1, 10, ad 1.

[84] Cf. 1 *Cor* 10:2.

[85] 1 *Cor* 10:11; cf. *Heb* 3:1 – 4:11.

[86] Cf. *Rev* 21:1 – 22:5.

[87] *Lettera gesta docet, quid credas allegoria, moralis quid agas, quo tendas anagogia.* Augustine of Dacia, *Rotulus pugillaris*, I: ed. A. Walz: *Angelicum* 6 (1929), 256.

Sacred Scripture in order that their research may help the Church to form a firmer judgement. For, of course, all that has been said about the manner of interpreting Scripture is ultimately subject to the judgement of the Church which exercises the divinely conferred commission and ministry of watching over and interpreting the Word of God.'[88]

113   But I would not believe in the Gospel, had not the authority of the Catholic Church already moved me.[89]

IV. The Canon of Scripture

1117   120 It was by the apostolic Tradition that the Church discerned which writings are to be included in the list of the sacred books.[90] This complete list is called the *canon* of Scripture. It includes 46 books for the Old Testament (45 if we count *Jeremiah* and *Lamentations* as one) and 27 for the New.[91]

The Old Testament: Genesis, Exodus, Leviticus, Numbers, Deuteronomy, Joshua, Judges, Ruth, 1 and 2 Samuel, 1 and 2 Kings, 1 and 2 Chronicles, Ezra and Nehemiah, Tobit, Judith, Esther, 1 and 2 Maccabees, Job, Psalms, Proverbs, Ecclesiastes, the Song of Songs, the Wisdom of Solomon, Sirach (Ecclesiasticus), Isaiah, Jeremiah, Lamentations, Baruch, Ezekiel, Daniel, Hosea, Joel, Amos, Obadiah, Jonah, Micah, Nahum, Habakkuk, Zephaniah, Haggai, Zachariah and Malachi.

The New Testament: the Gospels according to Matthew, Mark, Luke and John, the Acts of the Apostles, the Letters of St Paul to the Romans, 1 and 2 Corinthians, Galatians, Ephesians, Philippians, Colossians, 1 and 2 Thessalonians, 1 and 2 Timothy, Titus, Philemon, the Letter to the Hebrews, the Letters of James, 1 and 2 Peter, 1, 2 and 3 John, and Jude, and Revelation (the Apocalypse).

The Old Testament

121 The Old Testament is an indispensable part of Sacred Scrip-
1093   ture. Its books are divinely inspired and retain a permanent value,[92] for the Old Covenant has never been revoked.

122 Indeed, 'the economy of the Old Testament was deliberately
702   so oriented that it should prepare for and declare in prophecy the
763   coming of Christ, redeemer of all men.'[93] 'Even though they contain matters imperfect and provisional',[94] the books of the Old
708   Testament bear witness to the whole divine pedagogy of God's saving love: these writings 'are a storehouse of sublime teaching on God and of sound wisdom on human life, as well as a wonderful

---

[88] *DV* 12 § 3.

[89] St Augustine, *Contra epistolam Manichaei* 5, 6: PL 42, 176.

[90] Cf. *DV* 8 § 3.

[91] Cf. DS 179; 1334–1336; 1501–1504.

[92] Cf. *DV* 14.

[93] *DV* 15.

[94] *DV* 15.

treasury of prayers; in them, too, the mystery of our salvation is *2568*
present in a hidden way.'[95]

123 Christians venerate the Old Testament as true Word of God.
The Church has always vigorously opposed the idea of rejecting
the Old Testament under the pretext that the New has rendered it
void (Marcionism).

The New Testament

124 'The Word of God, which is the power of God for salvation
to everyone who has faith, is set forth and displays its power in a
most wonderful way in the writings of the New Testament'[96]
which hand on the ultimate truth of God's Revelation. Their central object is Jesus Christ, God's incarnate Son: his acts, teachings,
Passion and glorification, and his Church's beginnings under the
Spirit's guidance.[97]

125 The *Gospels* are the heart of all the Scriptures 'because they
are our principal source for the life and teaching of the Incarnate *515*
Word, our Saviour'.[98]

126 We can distinguish three stages in the formation of the Gospels:

1. *The life and teaching of Jesus.* The Church holds firmly that the four
Gospels, 'whose historicity she unhesitatingly affirms, faithfully hand on what
Jesus, the Son of God, while he lived among men, really did and taught for their
eternal salvation, until the day when he was taken up.'[99]

2. *The oral tradition.* 'For, after the ascension of the Lord, the apostles handed *76*
on to their hearers what he had said and done, but with that fuller understanding
which they, instructed by the glorious events of Christ and enlightened by the
Spirit of truth, now enjoyed.'[100]

3. *The written Gospels.* 'The sacred authors, in writing the four Gospels, *76*
selected certain of the many elements which had been handed on, either orally
or already in written form; others they synthesized or explained with an eye to
the situation of the churches, the while sustaining the form of preaching, but
always in such a fashion that they have told us the honest truth about Jesus.'[101]

127 The fourfold Gospel holds a unique place in the Church, as is
evident both in the veneration which the liturgy accords it and in *1154*
the surpassing attraction it has exercised on the saints at all times:

> There is no doctrine which could be better, more precious and more
> splendid than the text of the Gospel. Behold and retain what our Lord
> and Master, Christ, has taught by his words and accomplished by his
> deeds.[102]

---

[95] *DV* 15.
[96] *DV* 17; cf. *Rom* 1:16.
[97] Cf. *DV* 20.
[98] *DV* 18.
[99] *DV* 19; cf. *Acts* 1:1–2.

[100] *DV* 19.
[101] *DV* 19.
[102] St Caesaria the Younger to St
Richildis and St Radegunde: SCh 345,
480.

2705   But above all it's the gospels that occupy my mind when I'm at prayer;
my poor soul has so many needs, and yet this is the one thing needful. I'm
always finding fresh lights there; hidden meanings which had meant
nothing to me hitherto.[103]

The unity of the Old and New Testaments

128 The Church, as early as apostolic times,[104] and then constantly in her Tradition, has illuminated the unity of the divine
1094 plan in the two Testaments through *typology*, which discerns in
God's works of the Old Covenant prefigurations of what he
489 accomplished in the fullness of time in the person of his incarnate
Son.

129 Christians therefore read the Old Testament in the light of
651 Christ crucified and risen. Such typological reading discloses the
inexhaustible content of the Old Testament; but it must not make
us forget that the Old Testament retains its own intrinsic value as
2055 Revelation reaffirmed by our Lord himself.[105] Besides, the New
Testament has to be read in the light of the Old. Early Christian
catechesis made constant use of the Old Testament.[106] As an old
saying put it, the New Testament lies hidden in the Old and the
1968 Old Testament is unveiled in the New.[107]

130 Typology indicates the dynamic movement toward the fulfilment of the divine plan when 'God [will] be everything to
everyone.'[108] Nor do the calling of the patriarchs and the exodus
from Egypt, for example, lose their own value in God's plan, from
the mere fact that they were intermediate stages.

V. Sacred Scripture in the Life of the Church

131 'And such is the force and power of the Word of God that it
can serve the Church as her support and vigour, and the children
of the Church as strength for their faith, food for the soul, and a
pure and lasting fount of spiritual life.'[109] Hence 'access to Sacred
Scripture ought to be open wide to the Christian faithful.'[110]

132 'Therefore, the "study of the sacred page" should be the very
soul of sacred theology. The ministry of the Word, too – pastoral
94 preaching, catechetics and all forms of Christian instruction,
among which the liturgical homily should hold pride of place – is

---

[103] St Thérèse of Lisieux, *Autobiography of
a Saint*, tr. Ronald Knox (London:
Collins, 1960), 175.
[104] Cf. 1 *Cor* 10:6, 11; *Heb* 10:1; 1 *Pt* 3:21.
[105] Cf. *Mk* 12:29–31.
[106] Cf. 1 *Cor* 5:6–8; 10:1–11.

[107] Cf. St Augustine, *Quaest. in Hept.* 2,
73: PL 34, 623; cf. *DV* 16.
[108] 1 *Cor* 15:28.
[109] *DV* 21.
[110] *DV* 22.

healthily nourished and thrives in holiness through the Word of Scripture.'[111]

133 The Church 'forcefully and specifically exhorts all the Christian faithful... to learn "the surpassing knowledge of Jesus Christ", by frequent reading of the divine Scriptures. "Ignorance of the Scriptures is ignorance of Christ." '[112]   *2653* *1792*

IN BRIEF

134 *All Sacred Scripture is but one book, and this one book is Christ, 'because all divine Scripture speaks of Christ, and all divine Scripture is fulfilled in Christ' (Hugh of St Victor, De arca Noe 2, 8: PL 176, 642; cf. ibid. 2, 9: PL 176, 642–643).*

135 *'The Sacred Scriptures contain the Word of God and, because they are inspired, they are truly the Word of God' (DV 24).*

136 *God is the author of Sacred Scripture because he inspired its human authors; he acts in them and by means of them. He thus gives assurance that their writings teach without error his saving truth (cf. DV 11).*

137 *Interpretation of the inspired Scripture must be attentive above all to what God wants to reveal through the sacred authors for our salvation. What comes from the Spirit is not fully 'understood except by the Spirit's action' (cf. Origen, Hom. in Ex. 4, 5: PG 12, 320).*

138 *The Church accepts and venerates as inspired the 46 books of the Old Testament and the 27 books of the New.*

139 *The four Gospels occupy a central place because Christ Jesus is their centre.*

140 *The unity of the two Testaments proceeds from the unity of God's plan and his Revelation. The Old Testament prepares for the New and the New Testament fulfils the Old; the two shed light on each other; both are true Word of God.*

141 *'The Church has always venerated the divine Scriptures as she venerated the Body of the Lord' (DV 21): both nourish and govern the whole Christian life. 'Your word is a lamp to my feet and a light to my path' (Ps 119:105; cf. Is 50:4).*

---

[111] DV 24.
[112] DV 25; cf. Phil 3:8 and St Jerome, Commentariorum in Isaiam libri xviii prol.: PL 24, 17B.

Chapter Three
MAN'S RESPONSE TO GOD

142 *By his Revelation*, 'the invisible God, from the fullness of his love, addresses men as his friends, and moves among them, in order to invite and receive them into his own company.'¹ The 1102 adequate response to this invitation is faith.

143 *By faith*, man completely submits his intellect and his will to God.² With his whole being man gives his assent to God the revealer. Sacred Scripture calls this human response to God, the 2087 author of revelation, 'the obedience of faith'.³

Article 1
I BELIEVE

I. The Obedience of Faith

144 To obey (from the Latin *ob-audire,* to 'hear or listen to') in faith is to submit freely to the word that has been heard, because its truth is guaranteed by God, who is Truth itself. Abraham is the model of such obedience offered us by Sacred Scripture. The Virgin Mary is its most perfect embodiment.

Abraham – 'father of all who believe'

145 The *Letter to the Hebrews*, in its great eulogy of the faith of Israel's ancestors, lays special emphasis on Abraham's faith: 'By 59, 2570 faith, Abraham obeyed when he was called to go out to a place which he was to receive as an inheritance; and he went out, not knowing where he was to go.'⁴ By faith, he lived as a stranger and 489 pilgrim in the promised land.⁵ By faith, Sarah was given to conceive the son of the promise. And by faith Abraham offered his only son in sacrifice.⁶

1819 146 Abraham thus fulfils the definition of faith in *Hebrews* 11:1: 'Faith is the assurance of things hoped for, the conviction of things not seen':⁷ 'Abraham believed God, and it was reckoned to him as righteousness.'⁸ Because he was 'strong in his faith', Abraham became the 'father of all who believe'.⁹

147 The Old Testament is rich in witnesses to this faith. The *Letter to the Hebrews* proclaims its eulogy of the exemplary faith of the

---

¹ *DV* 2; cf. *Col* 1:15; 1 *Tim* 1:17; *Ex* 33:11; *Jn* 15:14–15; *Bar* 3:38 (Vulg.).
² Cf. *DV* 5.
³ Cf. *Rom* 1:5; 16:26.
⁴ *Heb* 11:8; cf. *Gen* 12:1–4.
⁵ Cf. *Gen* 23:4.
⁶ Cf. *Heb* 11:17.
⁷ *Heb* 11:1.
⁸ *Rom* 4:3; cf. *Gen* 15:6.
⁹ *Rom* 4:11, 18; 4:20; cf. *Gen* 15:5.

ancestors who 'received divine approval'.[10] Yet 'God had foreseen *839* something better for us': the grace of believing in his Son Jesus, 'the pioneer and perfecter of our faith'.[11]

Mary — 'Blessed is she who believed'

148 The Virgin Mary most perfectly embodies the obedience of faith. By faith Mary welcomes the tidings and promise brought by *494, 2617* the angel Gabriel, believing that 'with God nothing will be impossible' and so giving her assent: 'Behold I am the handmaid of the Lord; let it be [done] to me according to your word.'[12] Elizabeth greeted her: 'Blessed is she who believed that there would be a *506* fulfilment of what was spoken to her from the Lord.'[13] It is for this faith that all generations have called Mary blessed.[14]

149 Throughout her life and until her last ordeal[15] when Jesus her son died on the cross, Mary's faith never wavered. She never *969* ceased to believe in the fulfilment of God's word. And so the Church venerates in Mary the purest realization of faith. *507, 829*

II. 'I Know Whom I Have Believed'[16]

To believe in God alone

150 Faith is first of all a personal adherence of man to God. At the same time, and inseparably, it is a *free assent to the whole truth that God has revealed*. As personal adherence to God and assent to his truth, Christian faith differs from our faith in any human person. It is right and just to entrust oneself wholly to God and to believe *222* absolutely what he says. It would be futile and false to place such faith in a creature.[17]

To believe in Jesus Christ, the Son of God

151 For a Christian, believing in God cannot be separated from believing in the One he sent, his 'beloved Son', in whom the Father is 'well pleased'; God tells us to listen to him.[18] The Lord himself said to his disciples: 'Believe in God, believe also in me.'[19] We can believe in Jesus Christ because he is himself God, the Word made flesh: 'No one has ever seen God; the only Son, who is in the bosom of the Father, he has made him known.'[20] Because he 'has *424*

---

[10] *Heb* 11:2, 39.
[11] *Heb* 11:40; 12:2.
[12] *Lk* 1:37–38; cf. *Gen* 18:14.
[13] *Lk* 1:45.
[14] Cf. *Lk* 1:48.
[15] Cf. *Lk* 2:35.

[16] 2 *Tim* 1:12.
[17] Cf. *Jer* 17:5–6; *Pss* 40:5; 146:3–4.
[18] *Mk* 1:11; cf. 9:7.
[19] *Jn* 14:1.
[20] *Jn* 1:18.

seen the Father', Jesus Christ is the only one who knows him and can reveal him.[21]

To believe in the Holy Spirit

243, 683 152 One cannot believe in Jesus Christ without sharing in his Spirit. It is the Holy Spirit who reveals to men who Jesus is. For 'no one can say "Jesus is Lord", except by the Holy Spirit',[22] who 'searches everything, even the depths of God... No one comprehends the thoughts of God, except the Spirit of God.'[23] Only God knows God completely: we believe *in* the Holy Spirit because he is God.

232 *The Church never ceases to proclaim her faith in one only God: Father, Son and Holy Spirit.*

III. The Characteristics of Faith

Faith is a grace

552 153 When St Peter confessed that Jesus is the Christ, the Son of the living God, Jesus declared to him that this revelation did not come 'from flesh and blood', but from 'my Father who is in heaven'.[24] *Faith is a gift of God, a supernatural virtue infused by him.* 'Before this 1814 faith can be exercised, man must have the grace of God to move 1996 and assist him; he must have the interior helps of the Holy Spirit, who moves the heart and converts it to God, who opens the eyes 2606 of the mind and "makes it easy for all to accept and believe the truth".'[25]

Faith is a human act

154 Believing is possible only by grace and the interior helps of the Holy Spirit. But it is no less true that believing is an authen-1749 tically human act. Trusting in God and cleaving to the truths he has revealed is contrary neither to human freedom nor to human reason. Even in human relations it is not contrary to our dignity to believe what other persons tell us about themselves and their intentions, or to trust their promises (for example, when a man and a woman marry) to share a communion of life with one another. If this is so, still less is it contrary to our dignity to 'yield by faith the full submission of... intellect and will to God who reveals',[26] and to share in an interior communion with him.

---

[21] *Jn* 6:46; cf. *Mt* 11:27.
[22] 1 *Cor* 12:3.
[23] 1 *Cor* 2:10-11

[24] *Mt* 16:17; cf. *Gal* 1:15; *Mt* 11:25.
[25] *DV* 5; cf. DS 377; 3010.
[26] *Dei Filius* 3: DS 3008.

155 In faith, the human intellect and will co-operate with divine grace: 'Believing is an act of the intellect assenting to the divine truth by command of the will moved by God through grace.'[27] *2008*

Faith and understanding

156 What moves us to believe is not the fact that revealed truths appear as true and intelligible in the light of our natural reason: we believe 'because of the authority of God himself who reveals them, who can neither deceive nor be deceived'.[28] So 'that the submission of our faith might nevertheless be in accordance with reason, God willed that external proofs of his Revelation should be joined to the internal helps of the Holy Spirit.'[29] Thus the miracles of Christ and the saints, prophecies, the Church's growth and holiness, and her fruitfulness and stability 'are the most certain signs of divine Revelation, adapted to the intelligence of all'; they are 'motives of credibility' (*motiva credibilitatis*), which show that the assent of faith is 'by no means a blind impulse of the mind'.[30] *1063* *2465* *548* *812*

157 Faith is *certain*. It is more certain than all human knowledge because it is founded on the very word of God who cannot lie. To be sure, revealed truths can seem obscure to human reason and experience, but 'the certainty that the divine light gives is greater than that which the light of natural reason gives.'[31] 'Ten thousand difficulties do not make one doubt.'[32] *2088*

158 'Faith *seeks understanding*':[33] it is intrinsic to faith that a believer desires to know better the One in whom he has put his faith, and to understand better what He has revealed; a more penetrating knowledge will in turn call forth a greater faith, increasingly set afire by love. The grace of faith opens 'the eyes of your hearts'[34] to a lively understanding of the contents of Revelation: that is, of the totality of God's plan and the mysteries of faith, of their connection with each other and with Christ, the centre of the revealed mystery. 'The same Holy Spirit constantly perfects faith by his gifts, so that Revelation may be more and more profoundly understood.'[35] In the words of St Augustine, 'I *2705* *1827* *90*

---

[27] St Thomas Aquinas, *STh* II-II, 2, 9; cf. *Dei Filius* 3: DS 3010.
[28] *Dei Filius* 3: DS 3008.
[29] *Dei Filius* 3: DS 3009.
[30] *Dei Filius* 3: DS 3008–3010; cf. *Mk* 16:20; *Heb* 2:4.
[31] St Thomas Aquinas, *STh* II-II, 171, 5, obj. 3.
[32] John Henry Cardinal Newman, *Apologia pro vita sua* (London: Longman, 1878), 239.
[33] St Anselm, *Prosl.* prooem.: PL 153, 225A.
[34] *Eph* 1:18.
[35] *DV* 5.

2518 believe, in order to understand; and I understand, the better to believe.'[36]

159 *Faith and science*: 'Though faith is above reason, there can never be any real discrepancy between faith and reason. Since the same God who reveals mysteries and infuses faith has bestowed the 283 light of reason on the human mind, God cannot deny himself, nor can truth ever contradict truth.'[37] 'Consequently, methodical research in all branches of knowledge, provided it is carried out in a truly scientific manner and does not override moral laws, can 2293 never conflict with the faith, because the things of the world and the things of faith derive from the same God. The humble and persevering investigator of the secrets of nature is being led, as it were, by the hand of God in spite of himself, for it is God, the conserver of all things, who made them what they are.'[38]

The freedom of faith

160 To be human, 'man's response to God by faith must be free, and... therefore nobody is to be forced to embrace the faith 1738, 2106 against his will. The act of faith is of its very nature a free act.'[39] 'God calls men to serve him in spirit and in truth. Consequently they are bound to him in conscience, but not coerced... This fact received its fullest manifestation in Christ Jesus.'[40] Indeed, Christ invited people to faith and conversion, but never coerced them. 'For he bore witness to the truth but refused to use force to impose it on those who spoke against it. His kingdom... grows by the 616 love with which Christ, lifted up on the cross, draws men to himself.'[41]

The necessity of faith

161 Believing in Jesus Christ and in the One who sent him for our 432, 1257 salvation is necessary for obtaining that salvation.[42] 'Since "without faith it is impossible to please [God]" and to attain to the 846 fellowship of his sons, therefore without faith no one has ever attained justification, nor will anyone obtain eternal life "but he who endures to the end".'[43]

---

[36] St Augustine, *Sermo* 43, 7, 9: PL 38, 257–258.
[37] *Dei Filius* 4: DS 3017.
[38] GS 36 § 1.
[39] DH 10; cf. CIC, can. 748 § 2.
[40] DH 11.
[41] DH 11; cf. *Jn* 18:37; 12:32.
[42] Cf. *Mk* 16:16; *Jn* 3:36; 6:40 *et al.*
[43] *Dei Filius* 3: DS 3012; cf. *Mt* 10:22; 24:13 and *Heb* 11:6; Council of Trent: DS 1532.

Perseverance in faith

162 Faith is an entirely free gift that God makes to man. We can lose this priceless gift, as St Paul indicated to St Timothy: 'Wage the good warfare, holding faith and a good conscience. By rejecting conscience, certain persons have made shipwreck of their faith.'[44] To live, grow and persevere in the faith until the end we must nourish it with the word of God; we must beg the Lord to increase our faith;[45] it must be 'working through charity', abounding in hope, and rooted in the faith of the Church.[46]

2089

1037, 2016

2573, 2849

Faith – the beginning of eternal life

163 Faith makes us taste in advance the light of the beatific vision, the goal of our journey here below. Then we shall see God 'face to face', 'as he is'.[47] So faith is already the beginning of eternal life:

1088

> When we contemplate the blessings of faith even now, as if gazing at a reflection in a mirror, it is as if we already possessed the wonderful things which our faith assures us we shall one day enjoy.[48]

164 Now, however, 'we walk by faith, not by sight';[49] we perceive God as 'in a mirror, dimly' and only 'in part'.[50] Even though enlightened by him in whom it believes, faith is often lived in darkness and can be put to the test. The world we live in often seems very far from the one promised us by faith. Our experiences of evil and suffering, injustice and death, seem to contradict the Good News; they can shake our faith and become a temptation against it.

2846

309, 1502

1006

165 It is then we must turn to the *witnesses of faith*: to Abraham, who 'in hope... believed against hope';[51] to the Virgin Mary, who, in 'her pilgrimage of faith', walked into the 'night of faith'[52] in sharing the darkness of her son's suffering and death; and to so many others: 'Therefore, since we are surrounded by so great a cloud of witnesses, let us also lay aside every weight, and sin which clings so closely, and let us run with perseverance the race that is set before us, looking to Jesus the pioneer and perfecter of our faith.'[53]

2719

---

[44] 1 *Tim* 1:18–19.
[45] Cf. *Mk* 9:24; *Lk* 17:5; 22:32.
[46] *Gal* 5:6; *Rom* 15:13; cf. *Jas* 2:14–26.
[47] 1 *Cor* 13:12; 1 *Jn* 3:2.
[48] St Basil, *De Spiritu Sancto* 15, 36: PG 32, 132; cf. St Thomas Aquinas, *STh* II-II, 4, 1.

[49] 2 *Cor* 5:7.
[50] 1 *Cor* 13:12.
[51] *Rom* 4:18.
[52] *LG* 58; John Paul II, *RMat* 18.
[53] *Heb* 12:1–2.

Article 2
WE BELIEVE

166 Faith is a personal act – the free response of the human person to the initiative of God who reveals himself. But faith is not an isolated act. No one can believe alone, just as no one can live alone.
875 You have not given yourself faith as you have not given yourself life. The believer has received faith from others and should hand it on to others. Our love for Jesus and for our neighbour impels us to speak to others about our faith. Each believer is thus a link in the great chain of believers. I cannot believe without being carried by the faith of others, and by my faith I help support others in the faith.

1124 167 'I believe' (*Apostles' Creed*) is the faith of the Church professed personally by each believer, principally during Baptism. 'We believe' (*Niceno-Constantinopolitan Creed*) is the faith of the Church confessed by the bishops assembled in council or more generally by the liturgical assembly of believers. 'I believe' is also the
2040 Church, our mother, responding to God by faith as she teaches us to say both 'I believe' and 'We believe'.

I. 'Lord, Look upon the Faith of Your Church'

168 It is the Church that believes first, and so bears, nourishes and sustains my faith. Everywhere, it is the Church that first confesses the Lord: 'Throughout the world the holy Church acclaims you', as we sing in the hymn *Te Deum*; with her and in her, we are won over and brought to confess: 'I believe', 'We believe'. It is through the Church that we receive faith and new life in Christ by Baptism. In the *Rituale Romanum*, the minister of Baptism asks the
1253 catechumen: 'What do you ask of God's Church?' And the answer is: 'Faith.' 'What does faith offer you?' 'Eternal life.'[54]

169 Salvation comes from God alone; but because we receive the life of faith through the Church, she is our mother: 'We believe the Church as the mother of our new birth, and not *in* the Church as if
750 she were the author of our salvation.'[55] Because she is our mother,
2030 she is also our teacher in the faith.

II. The Language of Faith

170 We do not believe in formulae, but in those realities they

---

[54] *Roman Ritual*, Rite of Baptism of Adults.

[55] Faustus of Riez, *De Spiritu Sancto* 1, 2: PL 62, 11.

express, which faith allows us to touch. 'The believer's act [of faith] does not terminate in the propositions, but in the realities [which they express].'[56] All the same, we do approach these realities with the help of formulations of the faith which permit us to **186** express the faith and to hand it on, to celebrate it in community, to assimilate and live on it more and more.

171 The Church, 'the pillar and bulwark of the truth', faithfully **78** guards 'the faith which was once for all delivered to the saints'. She **857, 84** guards the memory of Christ's words; it is she who from generation to generation hands on the apostles' confession of faith.[57] As a mother who teaches her children to speak and so to understand and communicate, the Church our Mother teaches us the language **185** of faith in order to introduce us to the understanding and the life of faith.

III. Only One Faith

172 Through the centuries, in so many languages, cultures, peoples and nations, the Church has constantly confessed this one faith, received from the one Lord, transmitted by one Baptism, and grounded in the conviction that all people have only one God **813** and Father.[58] St Irenaeus of Lyons, a witness of this faith, declared:

173 'Indeed, the Church, though scattered throughout the whole world, even to the ends of the earth, having received the faith from the apostles and their disciples... guards [this preaching and **830** faith] with care, as dwelling in but a single house, and similarly believes as if having but one soul and a single heart, and preaches, teaches and hands on this faith with a unanimous voice, as if possessing only one mouth.'[59]

174 'For though languages differ throughout the world, the content of the Tradition is one and the same. The Churches established **78** in Germany have no other faith or Tradition, nor do those of the Iberians, nor those of the Celts, nor those of the East, of Egypt, of Libya, nor those established at the centre of the world...'[60] The Church's message 'is true and solid, in which one and the same way of salvation appears throughout the whole world.'[61]

---

[56] St Thomas Aquinas, STh II-II, 1, 2, ad 2.
[57] 1 Tim 3:15; Jude 3.
[58] Cf. Eph 4:4–6.
[59] St Irenaeus, Adv. haeres. 1, 10, 1–2: PG 7/1, 549–552.
[60] St Irenaeus, Adv. haeres. 1, 10, 1–2: PG 7/1, 552–553.
[61] St Irenaeus, Adv. haeres. 5, 20, 1: PG 7/2, 1177.

175 'We guard with care the faith that we have received from the Church, for without ceasing, under the action of God's Spirit, this deposit of great price, as if in an excellent vessel, is constantly being renewed and causes the very vessel that contains it to be renewed.'[62]

IN BRIEF

176 *Faith is a personal adherence of the whole man to God who reveals himself. It involves an assent of the intellect and will to the self-revelation God has made through his deeds and words.*

177 *'To believe' has thus a twofold reference: to the person, and to the truth: to the truth, by trust in the person who bears witness to it.*

178 *We must believe in no one but God: the Father, the Son and the Holy Spirit.*

179 *Faith is a supernatural gift from God. In order to believe, man needs the interior helps of the Holy Spirit.*

180 *'Believing' is a human act, conscious and free, corresponding to the dignity of the human person.*

181 *'Believing' is an ecclesial act. The Church's faith precedes, engenders, supports and nourishes our faith. The Church is the mother of all believers. 'No one can have God as Father who does not have the Church as Mother' (St Cyprian, De unit. 6: PL 4, 519).*

182 *We believe all 'that which is contained in the word of God, written or handed down, and which the Church proposes for belief as divinely revealed' (Paul VI, CPG § 20).*

183 *Faith is necessary for salvation. The Lord himself affirms: 'He who believes and is baptized will be saved; but he who does not believe will be condemned' (Mk 16:16).*

184 *'Faith is a foretaste of the knowledge that will make us blessed in the life to come' (St Thomas Aquinas, Comp. theol. 1, 2).*

---

[62] St Irenaeus, *Adv. haeres.* 3, 24, 1: PG 7/1, 966.

The Beatitudes by Evie Hone.

'The Beatitudes are at the heart of Jesus' preaching . . . [They] depict the countenance of Jesus Christ and portray his charity. They express the vocation of the faithful associated with the glory of his Passion and Resurrection; they shed light on the actions and attitudes characteristic of the Christian life; they are the paradoxical promises that sustain hope in the midst of tribulations' (§§ *1716, 1717*).

After she became a Catholic, Evie Hone's religious beliefs were a great inspiration for her artistic work. This stained glass window was made for the church in Tullabeg, Ireland in 1946 and is now situated with other stained glass windows by the artist in the Jesuit House at Manresa, Dublin.

Section Two

THE PROFESSION OF THE CHRISTIAN FAITH

THE CREEDS

185 Whoever says 'I believe' says 'I pledge myself to what *we* believe.' Communion in faith needs a common language of faith, *171, 949* normative for all and uniting all in the same confession of faith.

186 From the beginning, the apostolic Church expressed and handed on her faith in brief formulae normative for all.[1] But already very early on, the Church also wanted to gather the essential elements of her faith into organic and articulated summaries, intended especially for candidates for Baptism:

> This synthesis of faith was not made to accord with human opinions, but rather what was of the greatest importance was gathered from all the Scriptures, to present the one teaching of the faith in its entirety. And just as the mustard seed contains a great number of branches in a tiny grain, so too this summary of faith encompassed in a few words the whole knowledge of the true religion contained in the Old and the New Testaments.[2]

187 Such syntheses are called 'professions of faith' since they summarize the faith that Christians profess. They are called 'creeds' on account of what is usually their first word in Latin: *credo* ('I believe'). They are also called 'symbols of faith'.

188 The Greek word *symbolon* meant half of a broken object, for example, a seal presented as a token of recognition. The broken parts were placed together to verify the bearer's identity. The symbol of faith, then, is a sign of recognition and communion between believers. *Symbolon* also means a gathering, collection or summary. A symbol of faith is a summary of the principal truths of the faith and therefore serves as the first and fundamental point of reference for catechesis.

189 The first 'profession of faith' is made during Baptism. The symbol of faith is first and foremost the *baptismal* creed. Since Baptism is given 'in the name of the Father and of the Son and of *1237, 232* the Holy Spirit',[3] the truths of faith professed during Baptism are articulated in terms of their reference to the three persons of the Holy Trinity.

190 And so the Creed is divided into three parts: 'the first part speaks of the first divine Person and the wonderful work of

---

[1] Cf. *Rom* 10:9; 1 *Cor* 15:3-5, etc.   12: PG 33, 521-524.
[2] St Cyril of Jerusalem, *Catech. illum.* 5,   [3] *Mt* 28:19.

creation; the next speaks of the second divine Person and the mystery of his redemption of men; the final part speaks of the third divine Person, the origin and source of our sanctification.'[4] These are 'the three chapters of our [baptismal] seal'.[5]

191   'These three parts are distinct although connected with one another. According to a comparison often used by the Fathers, we call them *articles*. Indeed, just as in our bodily members there are certain articulations which distinguish and separate them, so too in this profession of faith, the name "articles" has justly and rightly been given to the truths we must believe particularly and distinctly."[6] In accordance with an ancient tradition, already attested to by St Ambrose, it is also customary to reckon the articles of the Creed as *twelve*, thus symbolizing the fullness of the apostolic faith by the number of the apostles.[7]

192   Through the centuries many professions or symbols of faith have been articulated in response to the needs of the different eras: the creeds of the different apostolic and ancient Churches,[8] e.g., the *Quicumque*, also called the Athanasian Creed;[9] the professions of faith of certain Councils, such as Toledo, Lateran, Lyons, Trent;[10] or the symbols of certain popes, e.g., the *Fides Damasi*[11] or the *Credo of the People of God* of Paul VI.[12]

193   None of the creeds from the different stages in the Church's life can be considered superseded or irrelevant. They help us today to attain and deepen the faith of all times by means of the different summaries made of it.

Among all the creeds, two occupy a special place in the Church's life:

194   *The Apostles' Creed* is so called because it is rightly considered to be a faithful summary of the apostles' faith. It is the ancient baptismal symbol of the Church of Rome. Its great authority arises from this fact: it is 'the Creed of the Roman Church, the See of Peter the first of the apostles, to which he brought the common faith'.[13]

195   *The Niceno-Constantinopolitan* or *Nicene Creed* draws its great authority from the fact that it stems from the first two ecumenical

---

[4] *Roman Catechism* I, 1, 3.
[5] St Irenaeus, *Dem. ap.* 100: SCh 62, 170.
[6] *Roman Catechism* I, 1, 4.
[7] Cf. St Ambrose, *Expl. symb.* 8: PL 17, 1196.
[8] Cf. DS 1–64.
[9] Cf. DS 75–76.
[10] Cf. DS 525–541; 800–802; 851–861; 1862–1870.
[11] Cf. DS 71–72.
[12] Paul VI, *CPG* (1968).
[13] St Ambrose, *Expl. symb.* 7: PL 17, 1196.

Councils (in 325 and 381). It remains common to all the great *242, 245,*
Churches of both East and West to this day.   *465*

196 Our presentation of the faith will follow the Apostles' Creed,
which constitutes, as it were, 'the oldest Roman catechism'. The
presentation will be completed however by constant references to
the Nicene Creed, which is often more explicit and more detailed.

197 As on the day of our Baptism, when our whole life was
entrusted to the 'standard of teaching',[14] let us embrace the Creed *1064*
of our life-giving faith. To say the Credo with faith is to enter into
communion with God, Father, Son and Holy Spirit, and also with
the whole Church which transmits the faith to us and in whose
midst we believe:

> This Creed is the spiritual seal, our heart's meditation and an ever-present *1274*
> guardian; it is, unquestionably, the treasure of our soul.[15]

THE CREED

THE APOSTLES' CREED

I believe in God
the Father almighty,
creator of heaven and earth.

I believe in Jesus Christ,
his only Son, our Lord.
He was conceived by the power
   of the Holy Spirit
and born of the Virgin Mary.
He suffered under Pontius Pilate,
was crucified, died, and was
   buried.
He descended to the dead.
On the third day he rose again.
He ascended into heaven
and is seated at the right hand
   of the Father.
He will come again
to judge the living and the dead.

THE NICENE CREED

We believe in one God,
the Father, the Almighty,
maker of heaven and earth,
of all that is, seen and unseen.

We believe in one Lord, Jesus
   Christ,
the only Son of God,
eternally begotten of the Father,
God from God, Light from Light,
true God from true God,
begotten, not made,
of one Being with the Father.
Through him all things were
   made.
For us men and for our salvation,
he came down from heaven:
by the power of the Holy Spirit
he became incarnate of the Virgin
   Mary,

---

[14] *Rom* 6:17.
[15] St Ambrose, *Expl. symb.* 1: PL 17,
   1193.

and became man.
For our sake he was crucified
    under Pontius Pilate;
he suffered death and was buried.
On the third day he rose again
in accordance with the Scriptures;
he ascended into heaven
and is seated at the right hand
    of the Father.
He will come again in glory
to judge the living and the dead,
and his kingdom will have no
    end.

I believe in the Holy Spirit,
the holy catholic Church,
the communion of saints,
the forgiveness of sins,
the resurrection of the body,
and the life everlasting.

Amen.

We believe in the Holy Spirit,
the Lord, the giver of life,
who proceeds from the Father
    and the Son.
With the Father and the Son he is
    worshipped and glorified.
He has spoken through the
    Prophets.
We believe in one holy
    catholic and apostolic Church.
We acknowledge one baptism
for the forgiveness of sins.
We look for the resurrection of
    the dead,
and the life of the world to come.

Amen.

Chapter One

I BELIEVE IN GOD THE FATHER

198 Our profession of faith begins with *God*, for God is the First
and the Last,[1] the beginning and the end of everything. The Credo
begins with God the *Father*, for the Father is the first divine person
of the Most Holy Trinity; our Creed begins with the creation of
heaven and earth, for creation is the beginning and the foundation
of all God's works.

---

[1] Cf. *Is* 44:6.

Article 1
'I BELIEVE IN GOD THE FATHER ALMIGHTY, CREATOR OF HEAVEN AND EARTH'

Paragraph 1. I Believe in God

199 'I believe in God': this first affirmation of the Apostles' Creed is also the most fundamental. The whole Creed speaks of God, and when it also speaks of man and of the world it does so in relation to God. The other articles of the Creed all depend on the first, just as the remaining Commandments make the first explicit. The other articles help us to know God better as he revealed himself progressively to men. 'The faithful first profess their belief in God.'[2]

2083

I. 'I Believe in One God'

200 These are the words with which the Niceno-Constantinopolitan Creed begins. The confession of God's oneness, which has its roots in the divine revelation of the Old Covenant, is inseparable from the profession of God's existence and is equally fundamental. God is unique; there is only one God: 'The Christian faith confesses that God is one in nature, substance and essence.'[3]

2085

201 To Israel, his chosen, God revealed himself as the only One: 'Hear, O Israel: The LORD our God is one LORD; and you shall love the LORD your God with all your heart, and with all your soul, and with all your might.'[4] Through the prophets, God calls Israel and all nations to turn to him, the one and only God: 'Turn to me and be saved, all the ends of the earth! For I am God, and there is no other... To me every knee shall bow, every tongue shall swear. "Only in the LORD, it shall be said of me, are righteousness and strength." '[5]

2083

202 Jesus himself affirms that God is 'the one Lord' whom you must love 'with all your heart, and with all your soul, and with all your mind, and with all your strength'.[6] At the same time Jesus gives us to understand that he himself is 'the Lord'.[7] To confess that Jesus is Lord is distinctive of Christian faith. This is not contrary to belief in the One God. Nor does believing in the Holy Spirit as 'Lord and giver of life' introduce any division into the One God:

446

152

> We firmly believe and confess without reservation that there is only one true God, eternal, infinite (*immensus*) and unchangeable, incomprehen-

42

---

[2] *Roman Catechism* I, 2, 2.
[3] *Roman Catechism* I, 2, 2.
[4] *Dt* 6:4-5.

[5] *Is* 45:22-24; cf. *Phil* 2:10-11.
[6] *Mk* 12:29-30.
[7] Cf. *Mk* 12:35-37.

sible, almighty and ineffable, the Father and the Son and the Holy Spirit;
three persons indeed, but one essence, substance or nature entirely
simple.[8]

II. God Reveals His Name

203 God revealed himself to his people Israel by making his name
known to them. A name expresses a person's essence and identity
2143 and the meaning of this person's life. God has a name; he is not an
anonymous force. To disclose one's name is to make oneself
known to others; in a way it is to hand oneself over by becoming
accessible, capable of being known more intimately and addressed
personally.

204 God revealed himself progressively and under different
names to his people, but the revelation that proved to be the
fundamental one for both the Old and the New Covenants was
63 the revelation of the divine name to Moses in the theophany of the
burning bush, on the threshold of the Exodus and of the covenant
on Sinai.

The living God

205 God calls Moses from the midst of a bush that burns without
being consumed: 'I am the God of your father, the God of Abra-
2575 ham, the God of Isaac, and the God of Jacob.'[9] God is the God of
the fathers, the One who had called and guided the patriarchs in
their wanderings. He is the faithful and compassionate God who
remembers them and his promises; he comes to free their descend-
268 ants from slavery. He is the God who, from beyond space and
time, can do this and wills to do it, the God who will put his
almighty power to work for this plan.

'I Am who I Am'

> Moses said to God, 'If I come to the people of Israel and say to them,
> "The God of your fathers has sent me to you", and they ask me, "What is
> his name?" what shall I say to them?' God said to Moses, 'I Am who I Am.'
> And he said, 'Say this to the people of Israel, "I Am has sent me to you".. .
> this is my name for ever, and thus I am to be remembered throughout all
> generations.'[10]

206 In revealing his mysterious name, YHWH ('I Am He who Is',
'I Am who Am' or 'I Am who I Am'), God says who he is and by

---

[8] Lateran Council IV: DS 800.   [10] *Ex* 3:13–15.
[9] *Ex* 3:6.

what name he is to be called. This divine name is mysterious just as God is mystery. It is at once a name revealed and something like the refusal of a name, and hence it better expresses God as what he is – infinitely above everything that we can understand or say: he is the 'hidden God', his name is ineffable, and he is the God who makes himself close to men.[11]

43

207 By revealing his name God at the same time reveals his faithfulness which is from everlasting to everlasting, valid for the past ('I am the God of your father'), as for the future ('I will be with you').[12] God, who reveals his name as 'I AM', reveals himself as the God who is always there, present to his people in order to save them.

208 Faced with God's fascinating and mysterious presence, man discovers his own insignificance. Before the burning bush, Moses takes off his sandals and veils his face in the presence of God's holiness.[13] Before the glory of the thrice-holy God, Isaiah cries out: 'Woe is me! I am lost; for I am a man of unclean lips.'[14] Before the divine signs wrought by Jesus, Peter exclaims: 'Depart from me, for I am a sinful man, O Lord.'[15] But because God is holy, he can forgive the man who realizes that he is a sinner before him: 'I will not execute my fierce anger. . . for I am God and not man, the Holy One in your midst.'[16] The apostle John says likewise: 'We shall. . . reassure our hearts before him whenever our hearts condemn us; for God is greater than our hearts, and he knows everything.'[17]

724

448

388

209 Out of respect for the holiness of God, the people of Israel do not pronounce his name. In the reading of Sacred Scripture, the revealed name (YHWH) is replaced by the divine title 'LORD' (in Hebrew *Adonai*, in Greek *Kyrios*). It is under this title that the divinity of Jesus will be acclaimed: 'Jesus is LORD.'

446

'A God merciful and gracious'

210 After Israel's sin, when the people had turned away from God to worship the golden calf, God hears Moses' prayer of intercession and agrees to walk in the midst of an unfaithful people, thus demonstrating his love.[18] When Moses asks to see his glory, God responds: 'I will make all my goodness pass before you, and will proclaim before you my name "the LORD" [YHWH].'[19] Then the

2116, 2577

---

[11] Cf. *Is* 45:15; *Judg* 13:18.
[12] *Ex* 3:6, 12.
[13] Cf. *Ex* 3:5–6.
[14] *Is* 6:5.
[15] *Lk* 5:8.
[16] *Hos* 11:9.
[17] 1 *Jn* 3:19–20.
[18] Cf. *Ex* 32; 33:12–17.
[19] *Ex* 33:18–19.

LORD passes before Moses and proclaims, 'YHWH, YHWH, a God merciful and gracious, slow to anger, and abounding in steadfast love and faithfulness'; Moses then confesses that the LORD is a forgiving God.[20]

211 The divine name, 'I AM' or 'HE IS', expresses God's faithfulness: despite the faithlessness of men's sin and the punishment it deserves, he keeps 'steadfast love for thousands'.[21] By going so far 604 as to give up his own Son for us, God reveals that he is 'rich in mercy'.[22] By giving his life to free us from sin, Jesus reveals that he himself bears the divine name: 'When you have lifted up the Son of man, then you will realize that "I AM".'[23]

God alone *IS*

212 Over the centuries, Israel's faith was able to manifest and deepen realization of the riches contained in the revelation of the divine name. God is unique; there are no other gods besides him.[24] 42 He transcends the world and history. He made heaven and earth: 'They will perish, but you endure; they will all wear out like a garment. . . .but you are the same, and your years have no end.'[25] 469 In God 'there is no variation or shadow due to change.'[26] God is 'HE WHO IS', from everlasting to everlasting, and as such remains 2086 ever faithful to himself and to his promises.

213 The revelation of the ineffable name 'I AM WHO AM' contains then the truth that God alone *IS*. The Greek Septuagint translation of the Hebrew Scriptures, and following it the Church's Tradition, understood the divine name in this sense: God is the fullness of Being and of every perfection, without origin and 41 without end. All creatures receive all that they are and have from him; but he alone *is* his very being, and he is of himself everything that he is.

III. God, 'HE WHO IS', Is Truth and Love

214 God, 'HE WHO IS', revealed himself to Israel as the one 'abounding in steadfast love and faithfulness'.[27] These two terms express summarily the riches of the divine name. In all his works 1062 God displays not only his kindness, goodness, grace and steadfast love, but also his trustworthiness, constancy, faithfulness and

---

[20] Ex 34:5–6; cf. 34:9.
[21] Ex 34:7.
[22] Eph 2:4.
[23] Jn 8:28 (Greek).

[24] Cf. Is 44:6.
[25] Ps 102:26–27.
[26] Jas 1:17.
[27] Ex 34:6.

truth. 'I give thanks to your name for your steadfast love and your faithfulness.'[28] He is the Truth, for 'God is light and in him there is no darkness'; 'God is love', as the apostle John teaches.[29]

God is Truth

215 'The sum of your word is truth; and every one of your righteous ordinances endures forever.'[30] 'And now, O LORD God, you are God, and your words are true';[31] this is why God's promises always come true.[32] God is Truth itself, whose words cannot deceive. This is why one can abandon oneself in full trust to the truth and faithfulness of his word in all things. The beginning of sin and of man's fall was due to a lie of the tempter who induced doubt of God's word, kindness and faithfulness.

2465

1063, 156

397

216 God's truth is his wisdom, which commands the whole created order and governs the world.[33] God, who alone made heaven and earth, can alone impart true knowledge of every created thing in relation to himself.[34]

295

32

217 God is also truthful when he reveals himself – the teaching that comes from God is 'true instruction'.[35] When he sends his Son into the world it will be 'to bear witness to the truth':[36] 'We know that the Son of God has come and has given us understanding, to know him who is true.'[37]

861

2466

God is Love

218 In the course of its history, Israel was able to discover that God had only one reason to reveal himself to them, a single motive for choosing them from among all peoples as his special possession: his sheer gratuitous love.[38] And thanks to the prophets Israel understood that it was again out of love that God never stopped saving them and pardoning their unfaithfulness and sins.[39]

295

219 God's love for Israel is compared to a father's love for his son. His love for his people is stronger than a mother's for her children. God loves his people more than a bridegroom his beloved; his love will be victorious over even the worst infidelities and will extend

239

796

---

[28] Ps 138:2; cf. Ps 85:11.
[29] 1 Jn 1:5; 4:8.
[30] Ps 119:160.
[31] 2 Sam 7:28.
[32] Cf. Dt 7:9.
[33] Cf. Wis 13:1–9.

[34] Cf. Ps 115:15; Wis 7:17–21.
[35] Mal 2:6.
[36] Jn 18:37.
[37] 1 Jn 5:20; cf. Jn 17:3.
[38] Cf. Dt 4:37; 7:8; 10:15.
[39] Cf. Is 43:1–7; Hos 2.

458   to his most precious gift: 'God so loved the world that he gave his only Son.'[40]

220   God's love is 'everlasting':[41] 'For the mountains may depart and the hills be removed, but my steadfast love shall not depart from you.'[42] Through Jeremiah, God declares to his people, 'I have loved you with an everlasting love; therefore I have continued my faithfulness to you.'[43]

221   But St John goes even further when he affirms that 'God is love':[44] God's very being is love. By sending his only Son and the
733, 851   Spirit of Love in the fullness of time, God has revealed his innermost secret:[45] God himself is an eternal exchange of love, Father,
257   Son and Holy Spirit, and he has destined us to share in that exchange.

IV. The Implications of Faith in One God

222   Believing in God, the only One, and loving him with all our being has enormous consequences for our whole life.

300   223   *It means coming to know God's greatness and majesty*: 'Behold, God is great, and we know him not.'[46] Therefore, we must 'serve God first'.[47]

224   *It means living in thanksgiving*: if God is the only One, everything we are and have comes from him: 'What have you that you
2637   did not receive?'[48] 'What shall I render to the LORD for all his bounty to me?'[49]

356, 360,   225   *It means knowing the unity and true dignity of all men*: everyone is
1700, 1934   made in the image and likeness of God.[50]

226   *It means making good use of created things*: faith in God, the only
339, 2402   One, leads us to use everything that is not God only insofar as it
2415   brings us closer to him, and to detach ourselves from it insofar as it turns us away from him:

My Lord and my God, take from me everything that distances me from you.
My Lord and my God, give me everything that brings me closer to you.
My Lord and my God, detach me from myself to give my all to you.[51]

---

[40] *Jn* 3:16; cf. *Hos* 11:1; *Is* 49:14–15; 62:4–5; *Ezek* 16; *Hos* 11.
[41] *Is* 54:8.
[42] *Is* 54:10; cf. 54:8.
[43] *Jer* 31:3.
[44] 1 *Jn* 4:8, 16.
[45] Cf. 1 *Cor* 2:7–16; *Eph* 3:9–12.

[46] *Job* 36:26.
[47] St Joan of Arc.
[48] 1 *Cor* 4:7.
[49] *Ps* 116:12.
[50] *Gen* 1:26.
[51] St Nicholas of Flüe; cf. *Mt* 5:29–30; 16:24–26.

227 *It means trusting God in every circumstance*, even in adversity. A 313, 2090
prayer of St Teresa of Jesus wonderfully expresses this trust:

> Let nothing trouble you / Let nothing frighten you
> Everything passes / God never changes
> Patience / Obtains all
> Whoever has God / Wants for nothing 2830
> God alone is enough.[52] 1723

IN BRIEF

228 'Hear, O Israel, the LORD our God is one LORD...' (*Dt 6:4; Mk 12:29*). 'The supreme being must be unique, without equal... If God is not one, he is not God' (*Tertullian, Adv. Marc., 1, 3, 5: PL 2, 274*).

229 Faith in God leads us to turn to him alone as our first origin and our ultimate goal, and neither to prefer anything to him nor to substitute anything for him.

230 Even when he reveals himself, God remains a mystery beyond words: 'If you understood him, it would not be God' (*St Augustine, Sermo 52, 6, 16: PL 38, 360 and Sermo 117, 3, 5: PL 38, 663*).

231 The God of our faith has revealed himself as HE WHO IS; and he has made himself known as 'abounding in steadfast love and faithfulness' (*Ex 34:6*). God's very being is Truth and Love.

Paragraph 2. The Father

I. 'In the name of the Father and of the Son and of the Holy Spirit'

232 Christians are baptized 'in the name of the Father and of the 1223
Son and of the Holy Spirit'.[53] Before receiving the sacrament, they
respond to a three-part question when asked to confess the Father,
the Son and the Spirit: 'I do.' 'The faith of all Christians rests on the 189
Trinity.'[54]

233 Christians are baptized in the *name* of the Father and of the
Son and of the Holy Spirit: not in their *names*,[55] for there is only
one God, the almighty Father, his only Son and the Holy Spirit:
the Most Holy Trinity.

---

[52] St Teresa of Jesus, *Poesías* 30 in *The Collected Works of St Teresa of Avila*, vol. III, tr. K. Kavanaugh OCD and O. Rodriguez OCD (Washington DC: Institute of Carmelite Studies, 1985), 386 no. 9, tr. John Wall.

[53] *Mt* 28:19.
[54] St Caesarius of Arles, *Sermo* 9, *Exp. symb.*: CCL 103, 47.
[55] Cf. Profession of faith of Pope Vigilius I (552): DS 415.

2157 234 The mystery of the Most Holy Trinity is the central mystery of Christian faith and life. It is the mystery of God in himself. It is therefore the source of all the other mysteries of faith, the light that enlightens them. It is the most fundamental and essential teaching 90 in the 'hierarchy of the truths of faith'.[56] The whole history of salvation is identical with the history of the way and the means by which the one true God, Father, Son and Holy Spirit, reveals 1449 himself to men 'and reconciles and unites with himself those who turn away from sin'.[57]

235 This paragraph expounds briefly (I) how the mystery of the Blessed Trinity was revealed, (II) how the Church has articulated the doctrine of the faith regarding this mystery, and (III) how, by the divine missions of the Son and the Holy Spirit, God the Father fulfils the 'plan of his loving goodness' of creation, redemption and sanctification.

236 The Fathers of the Church distinguish between theology (*theologia*) and 1066 economy (*oikonomia*). 'Theology' refers to the mystery of God's inmost life within the Blessed Trinity and 'economy' to all the works by which God reveals himself and communicates his life. Through the *oikonomia* the *theologia* is 259 revealed to us; but conversely, the *theologia* illuminates the whole *oikonomia*. God's works reveal who he is in himself; the mystery of his inmost being enlightens our understanding of all his works. So it is, analogously, among human persons. A person discloses himself in his actions, and the better we know a person, the better we understand his actions.

237 The Trinity is a mystery of faith in the strict sense, one of the "mysteries that are hidden in God, which can never be known 50 unless they are revealed by God'.[58] To be sure, God has left traces of his Trinitarian being in his work of creation and in his Revelation throughout the Old Testament. But his inmost Being as Holy Trinity is a mystery that is inaccessible to reason alone or even to Israel's faith before the Incarnation of God's Son and the sending of the Holy Spirit.

II. The Revelation of God as Trinity

The Father revealed by the Son

238 Many religions invoke God as 'Father'. The deity is often considered the 'father of gods and of men'. In Israel, God is called 'Father' inasmuch as he is Creator of the world.[59] Even more, God is Father because of the covenant and the gift of the law to Israel,

---

[56] GCD 43.
[57] GCD 47.

[58] *Dei Filius* 4: DS 3015.
[59] Cf. *Dt* 32:6; *Mal* 2:10.

'his first-born son'.[60] God is also called the Father of the king of Israel. Most especially he is 'the Father of the poor', of the *2443* orphaned and the widowed, who are under his loving protection.[61]

239 By calling God 'Father', the language of faith indicates two main things: that God is the first origin of everything and transcendent authority; and that he is at the same time goodness and loving care for all his children. God's parental tenderness can also be expressed by the image of motherhood,[62] which emphasizes God's immanence, the intimacy between Creator and creature. The language of faith thus draws on the human experience of parents, who are in a way the first representatives of God for man. But this experience also tells us that human parents are fallible and can disfigure the face of fatherhood and motherhood. We ought therefore to recall that God transcends the human *370* distinction between the sexes. He is neither man nor woman: he is God. He also transcends human fatherhood and motherhood, although he is their origin and *2779* standard:[63] no one is father as God is Father.

240 Jesus revealed that God is Father in an unheard-of sense: he is Father not only in being Creator; he is eternally Father in *2780* relation to his only Son who is eternally Son only in relation to his Father: 'No one knows the Son except the Father, and no *441–445* one knows the Father except the Son and any one to whom the Son chooses to reveal him.'[64]

241 For this reason the apostles confess Jesus to be the Word: 'In the beginning was the Word, and the Word was with God, and the Word was God'; as 'the image of the invisible God'; as the 'radiance of the glory of God and the very stamp of his nature'.[65]

242 Following this apostolic tradition, the Church confessed at the first ecumenical council at Nicaea (325) that the Son is 'con- *465* substantial' with the Father, that is, one only God with him.[66] The second ecumenical council, held at Constantinople in 381, kept this expression in its formulation of the Nicene Creed and confessed 'the only-begotten Son of God, eternally begotten of the Father, light from light, true God from true God, begotten not made, consubstantial with the Father'.[67]

The Father and the Son revealed by the Spirit

243 Before his Passover, Jesus announced the sending of 'another

---

[60] Ex 4:22.
[61] Cf. 2 Sam 7:14; Ps 68:6.
[62] Cf. Is 66:13; Ps 131:2.
[63] Cf. Ps 27:10; Eph 3:14; Is 49:15.
[64] Mt 11:27.
[65] Jn 1:1; Col 1:15; Heb 1:3.

[66] The English phrases 'of one being' and 'one in being' translate the Greek word *homoousios*, which was rendered in Latin by *consubstantialis*.
[67] Niceno-Constantinopolitan Creed; cf. DS 150.

683 Paraclete' (Advocate), the Holy Spirit. At work since creation,
2780 having previously 'spoken through the prophets', the Spirit will
now be with and in the disciples, to teach them and guide them
687 'into all the truth'.[68] The Holy Spirit is thus revealed as another
divine person with Jesus and the Father.

244 The eternal origin of the Holy Spirit is revealed in his mission
in time. The Spirit is sent to the apostles and to the Church both by
the Father in the name of the Son, and by the Son in person, once
he had returned to the Father.[69] The sending of the person of the
Spirit after Jesus' glorification[70] reveals in its fullness the mystery
732 of the Holy Trinity.

245 The apostolic faith concerning the Spirit was confessed by the
second ecumenical council at Constantinople (381): 'We believe in
152 the Holy Spirit, the Lord and giver of life, who proceeds from the
Father.'[71] By this confession, the Church recognizes the Father as
'the source and origin of the whole divinity'.[72] But the eternal
origin of the Spirit is not unconnected with the Son's origin: 'The
Holy Spirit, the third person of the Trinity, is God, one and equal
with the Father and the Son, of the same substance and also of the
same nature. . . Yet he is not called the Spirit of the Father alone,. . .
but the Spirit of both the Father and the Son.'[73] The Creed of the
Church from the Council of Constantinople confesses: 'With the
685 Father and the Son, he is worshipped and glorified.'[74]

246 The Latin tradition of the Creed confesses that the Spirit
'proceeds from the Father *and the Son* (*filioque*)'. The Council of
Florence in 1438 explains: 'The Holy Spirit is eternally from
Father and Son; He has his nature and subsistence at once (*simul*)
from the Father and the Son. He proceeds eternally from both as
from one principle and through one spiration. . . And, since the
Father has through generation given to the only-begotten Son
everything that belongs to the Father, except being Father, the
Son has also eternally from the Father, from whom he is eternally
born, that the Holy Spirit proceeds from the Son.'[75]

247 The affirmation of the *filioque* does not appear in the Creed confessed in 381
at Constantinople. But Pope St Leo I, following an ancient Latin and Alexandrian tradition, had already confessed it dogmatically in 447,[76] even before

---

[68] Cf. *Gen* 1:2; Nicene Creed (DS 150);
Jn 14:17, 26; 16:13.
[69] Cf. *Jn* 14:26; 15:26; 16:14.
[70] Cf. *Jn* 7:39.
[71] Nicene Creed; cf. DS 150.
[72] Council of Toledo VI (638): DS 490.

[73] Council of Toledo XI (675): DS 527.
[74] Nicene Creed; cf. DS 150.
[75] Council of Florence (1439): DS 1300–
1301.
[76] Cf. Leo I, *Quam laudabiliter* (447): DS
284.

Rome, in 451 at the Council of Chalcedon, came to recognize and receive the Symbol of 381. The use of this formula in the Creed was gradually admitted into the Latin liturgy (between the eighth and eleventh centuries). The introduction of the *filioque* into the Niceno-Constantinopolitan Creed by the Latin liturgy constitutes moreover, even today, a point of disagreement with the Orthodox Churches.

248 At the outset the Eastern tradition expresses the Father's character as first origin of the Spirit. By confessing the Spirit as he 'who proceeds from the Father', it affirms that he *comes from* the Father *through* the Son.[77] The Western tradition expresses first the consubstantial communion between Father and Son, by saying that the Spirit proceeds from the Father and the Son (*filioque*). It says this, 'legitimately and with good reason',[78] for the eternal order of the divine persons in their consubstantial communion implies that the Father, as 'the principle without principle',[79] is the first origin of the Spirit, but also that as Father of the only Son, he is, with the Son, the single principle from which the Holy Spirit proceeds.[80] This legitimate complementarity, provided it does not become rigid, does not affect the identity of faith in the reality of the same mystery confessed.

III. The Holy Trinity in the Teaching of the Faith

The formation of the Trinitarian dogma

249 From the beginning, the revealed truth of the Holy Trinity has been at the very root of the Church's living faith, principally by means of Baptism. It finds its expression in the rule of baptismal faith, formulated in the preaching, catechesis and prayer of the Church. Such formulations are already found in the apostolic writings, such as this salutation taken up in the Eucharistic liturgy: 'The grace of the Lord Jesus Christ and the love of God and the fellowship of the Holy Spirit be with you all.'[81] *683 189*

250 During the first centuries the Church sought to clarify her Trinitarian faith, both to deepen her own understanding of the faith and to defend it against the errors that were deforming it. This clarification was the work of the early councils, aided by the theological work of the Church Fathers and sustained by the Christian people's sense of the faith. *94*

251 In order to articulate the dogma of the Trinity, the Church had to develop her own terminology with the help of certain notions of philosophical origin: 'substance', 'person' or 'hypostasis', 'relation' and so on. In doing this, she did not submit the faith to human wisdom, but gave a new and unprecedented

---

[77] *Jn* 15:26; cf. *AG* 2.
[78] Council of Florence (1439): DS 1302.
[79] Council of Florence (1442): DS 1331.
[80] Cf. Council of Lyons II (1274): DS

850.
[81] *2 Cor* 13:14; cf. *1 Cor* 12:4–6; *Eph* 4:4–6.

meaning to these terms, which from then on would be used to signify an
170 ineffable mystery, 'infinitely beyond all that we can humanly understand'.[82]

252 The Church uses (I) the term 'substance' (rendered also at
times by 'essence' or 'nature') to designate the divine being in its
unity, (II) the term 'person' or 'hypostasis' to designate the Father,
Son and Holy Spirit in the real distinction among them, and (III)
the term 'relation' to designate the fact that their distinction lies in
the relationship of each to the others.

The dogma of the Holy Trinity

253 *The Trinity is One*. We do not confess three Gods, but one
God in three persons, the 'consubstantial Trinity'.[83] The divine
persons do not share the one divinity among themselves but each
2789 of them is God whole and entire: 'The Father is that which the Son
is, the Son that which the Father is, the Father and the Son that
590 which the Holy Spirit is, i.e. by nature one God.'[84] In the words of
the Fourth Lateran Council (1215), 'Each of the persons is that
supreme reality, viz., the divine substance, essence or nature.'[85]

254 *The divine persons are really distinct from one another*. 'God is one
but not solitary.'[86] 'Father', 'Son', 'Holy Spirit' are not simply
468 names designating modalities of the divine being, for they are
689 really distinct from one another: 'He is not the Father who is the
Son, nor is the Son he who is the Father, nor is the Holy Spirit he
who is the Father or the Son.'[87] They are distinct from one another
in their relations of origin: 'It is the Father who generates, the Son
who is begotten, and the Holy Spirit who proceeds.'[88] *The divine
Unity is Triune*.

255 *The divine persons are relative to one another*. Because it does not
divide the divine unity, the real distinction of the persons from one
another resides solely in the relationships which relate them to one
another: 'In the relational names of the persons the Father is related
240 to the Son, the Son to the Father, and the Holy Spirit to both.
While they are called three persons in view of their relations, we
believe in one nature or substance.'[89] Indeed 'everything (in them)
is one where there is no opposition of relationship.'[90] 'Because of
that unity the Father is wholly in the Son and wholly in the Holy

---

[82] Paul VI, *CPG* § 2.

[83] Council of Constantinople II (553): DS 421.

[84] Council of Toledo XI (675): DS 530:26.

[85] Lateran Council IV (1215): DS 804 .

[86] *Fides Damasi*: DS 71.

[87] Council of Toledo XI (675): DS 530:25.

[88] Lateran Council IV (1215): DS 804.

[89] Council of Toledo XI (675): DS 528.

[90] Council of Florence (1442): DS 1330.

Spirit; the Son is wholly in the Father and wholly in the Holy Spirit; the Holy Spirit is wholly in the Father and wholly in the Son.'[91]

256 St Gregory of Nazianzus, also called 'the Theologian', entrusts this summary of Trinitarian faith to the catechumens of Constantinople:

236, 684

> Above all guard for me this great deposit of faith for which I live and fight, which I want to take with me as a companion, and which makes me bear all evils and despise all pleasures: I mean the profession of faith in the Father and the Son and the Holy Spirit. I entrust it to you today. By it I am soon going to plunge you into water and raise you up from it. I give it to you as the companion and patron of your whole life. I give you but one divinity and power, existing one in three, and containing the three in a distinct way. Divinity without disparity of substance or nature, without superior degree that raises up or inferior degree that casts down... the infinite co-naturality of three infinites. Each person considered in himself is entirely God... the three considered together... I have not even begun to think of unity when the Trinity bathes me in its splendour. I have not even begun to think of the Trinity when unity grasps me...[92]

84

IV. The Divine Works and the Trinitarian Missions

257 'O blessed light, O Trinity and first Unity!'[93] God is eternal blessedness, undying life, unfading light. God is love: Father, Son and Holy Spirit. God freely wills to communicate the glory of his blessed life. Such is the 'plan of his loving kindness', conceived by the Father before the foundation of the world, in his beloved Son: 'He destined us in love to be his sons' and 'to be conformed to the image of his Son', through 'the spirit of sonship'.[94] This plan is a 'grace [which] was given to us in Christ Jesus before the ages began', stemming immediately from Trinitarian love.[95] It unfolds in the work of creation, the whole history of salvation after the fall, and the missions of the Son and the Spirit, which are continued in the mission of the Church.[96]

221
758

292

850

258 The whole divine economy is the common work of the three divine persons. For as the Trinity has only one and the same nature, so too does it have only one and the same operation: 'The Father, the Son and the Holy Spirit are not three principles of creation but one principle.'[97] However, each divine person

686

---

[91] Council of Florence (1442): DS 1331.
[92] St Gregory of Nazianzus, *Oratio* 40, 41: PG 36, 417.
[93] *LH*, Hymn for Evening Prayer.
[94] *Eph* 1:4–5, 9; *Rom* 8:15, 29.
[95] *2 Tim* 1:9–10.
[96] Cf. *AG* 2–9.
[97] Council of Florence (1442): DS 1331; cf. Council of Constantinople II (553): DS 421.

performs the common work according to his unique personal property. Thus the Church confesses, following the New Testament, 'one God and Father from whom all things are, and one Lord Jesus Christ, through whom all things are, and one Holy Spirit in whom all things are'.[98] It is above all the divine missions of the Son's Incarnation and the gift of the Holy Spirit that show forth the properties of the divine persons.

259 Being a work at once common and personal, the whole divine economy makes known both what is proper to the divine persons, and their one divine nature. Hence the whole Christian life is a communion with each of the divine persons, without in any way separating them. Everyone who glorifies the Father does so through the Son in the Holy Spirit; everyone who follows Christ does so because the Father draws him and the Spirit moves him.[99]

236

260 The ultimate end of the whole divine economy is the entry of God's creatures into the perfect unity of the Blessed Trinity.[100] But even now we are called to be a dwelling for the Most Holy Trinity: 'If a man loves me', says the Lord, 'he will keep my word, and my Father will love him, and we will come to him, and make our home with him':[101]

1050, 1721

1997

> O my God, Trinity whom I adore, help me forget myself entirely so to establish myself in you, unmovable and peaceful as if my soul were already in eternity. May nothing be able to trouble my peace or make me leave you, O my unchanging God, but may each minute bring me more deeply into your mystery! Grant my soul peace. Make it your heaven, your beloved dwelling and the place of your rest. May I never abandon you there, but may I be there, whole and entire, completely vigilant in my faith, entirely adoring, and wholly given over to your creative action.[102]

2565

IN BRIEF

261 *The mystery of the Most Holy Trinity is the central mystery of the Christian faith and of Christian life. God alone can make it known to us by revealing himself as Father, Son and Holy Spirit.*

262 *The Incarnation of God's Son reveals that God is the eternal Father and that the Son is consubstantial with the Father, which means that, in the Father and with the Father, the Son is one and the same God.*

---

[98] Council of Constantinople II: DS 421.
[99] Cf. Jn 6:44; Rom 8:14.
[100] Cf. Jn 17:21–23.
[101] Jn 14:23.
[102] Prayer of Blessed Elizabeth of the Trinity.

263 *The mission of the Holy Spirit, sent by the Father in the name of the Son (Jn 14:26) and by the Son 'from the Father' (Jn 15:26), reveals that, with them, the Spirit is one and the same God. 'With the Father and the Son he is worshipped and glorified' (Nicene Creed).*

264 *'The Holy Spirit proceeds from the Father as the first principle and, by the eternal gift of this to the Son, from the communion of both the Father and the Son' (St Augustine, De Trin. 15, 26, 47: PL 42, 1095).*

265 *By the grace of Baptism 'in the name of the Father and of the Son and of the Holy Spirit', we are called to share in the life of the Blessed Trinity, here on earth in the obscurity of faith, and after death in eternal light (cf. Paul VI, CPG § 9).*

266 *'Now this is the Catholic faith: We worship one God in the Trinity and the Trinity in unity, without either confusing the persons or dividing the substance; for the person of the Father is one, the Son's is another, the Holy Spirit's another; but the Godhead of the Father, Son and Holy Spirit is one, their glory equal, their majesty coeternal' (Athanasian Creed: DS 75; ND 16).*

267 *Inseparable in what they are, the divine persons are also inseparable in what they do. But within the single divine operation each shows forth what is proper to him in the Trinity, especially in the divine missions of the Son's Incarnation and the gift of the Holy Spirit.*

Paragraph 3. The Almighty

268 Of all the divine attributes, only God's omnipotence is named in the Creed: to confess this power has great bearing on our lives. 222 We believe that his might is *universal*, for God who created everything also rules everything and can do everything. God's power is *loving*, for he is our Father, and *mysterious*, for only faith can discern it when it 'is made perfect in weakness'.[103]

'He does whatever he pleases'[104]

269 The Holy Scriptures repeatedly confess the *universal* power of God. He is called the 'Mighty One of Jacob', the 'LORD of hosts', the 'strong and mighty' one. If God is almighty 'in heaven and on earth', it is because he made them.[105] Nothing is impossible with God, who disposes his works according to his will.[106] He is the Lord of the universe, whose order he established and which remains wholly subject to him and at his disposal. He is master of 303

---

[103] Cf. *Gen* 1:1; *Jn* 1:3; *Mt* 6:9; 2 *Cor* 12:9; cf. 1 *Cor* 1:18.
[104] *Ps* 115:3.

[105] *Gen* 49:24; *Is* 1:24 etc.; *Pss* 24:8–10; 135:6.
[106] Cf. *Jer* 27:5; 32:17; *Lk* 1:37.

history, governing hearts and events in keeping with his will: 'It is always in your power to show great strength, and who can withstand the strength of your arm?'[107]

'You are merciful to all, for you can do all things'[108]

270 God is the *Father* Almighty, whose fatherhood and power shed light on one another: God reveals his fatherly omnipotence by the way he takes care of our needs; by the filial adoption that he gives us ('I will be a father to you, and you shall be my sons and daughters, says the Lord Almighty'):[109] finally by his infinite mercy, for he displays his power at its height by freely forgiving sins.

271 God's almighty power is in no way arbitrary: 'In God, power, essence, will, intellect, wisdom, and justice are all identical. Nothing therefore can be in God's power which could not be in his just will or his wise intellect.'[110]

The mystery of God's apparent powerlessness

272 Faith in God the Father Almighty can be put to the test by the experience of evil and suffering. God can sometimes seem to be absent and incapable of stopping evil. But in the most *mysterious* way God the Father has revealed his almighty power in the voluntary humiliation and Resurrection of his Son, by which he conquered evil. Christ crucified is thus 'the power of God and the wisdom of God. For the foolishness of God is wiser than men, and the weakness of God is stronger than men.'[111] It is in Christ's Resurrection and exaltation that the Father has shown forth 'the immeasurable greatness of his power in us who believe'.[112]

273 Only faith can embrace the mysterious ways of God's almighty power. This faith glories in its weaknesses in order to draw to itself Christ's power.[113] The Virgin Mary is the supreme model of this faith, for she believed that 'nothing will be impossible with God', and was able to magnify the Lord: 'For he who is mighty has done great things for me, and holy is his name.'[114]

274 'Nothing is more apt to confirm our faith and hope than holding it fixed in our minds that nothing is impossible with God. Once our reason has grasped the idea of God's almighty power, it

---

[107] *Wis* 11:21; cf. *Esth* 4:17b; *Prov* 21:1; *Tob* 13:2.
[108] *Wis* 11:23.
[109] 2 *Cor* 6:18; cf. *Mt* 6:32.
[110] St Thomas Aquinas, *STh* I, 25, 5, ad 1.
[111] 1 *Cor* 1:24-25.
[112] *Eph* 1:19-22.
[113] Cf. 2 *Cor* 12:9; *Phil* 4:13.
[114] *Lk* 1:37, 49.

will easily and without any hesitation admit everything that [the Creed] will afterwards propose for us to believe – even if they be great and marvellous things, far above the ordinary laws of nature.'[115]

IN BRIEF

275 With Job, the just man, we confess: 'I know that you can do all things, and that no purpose of yours can be thwarted' (Job 42:2).

276 Faithful to the witness of Scripture, the Church often addresses her prayer to the 'almighty and eternal God' ('omnipotens sempiterne Deus...'), believing firmly that 'nothing will be impossible with God' (Gen 18:14; Lk 1:37; Mt 19:26).

277 God shows forth his almighty power by converting us from our sins and restoring us to his friendship by grace. 'God, you show your almighty power above all in your mercy and forgiveness...' (Roman Missal, 26th Sunday, Opening Prayer).

278 If we do not believe that God's love is almighty, how can we believe that the Father could create us, the Son redeem us and the Holy Spirit sanctify us?

Paragraph 4. The Creator

279 'In the beginning God created the heavens and the earth.'[116] Holy Scripture begins with these solemn words. The profession of faith takes them up when it confesses that God the Father almighty is 'Creator of heaven and earth' (Apostles' Creed), 'of all that is, seen and unseen' (Nicene Creed). We shall speak first of the Creator, then of creation and finally of the fall into sin from which Jesus Christ, the Son of God, came to raise us up again.

280 Creation is the foundation of 'all God's saving plans', the *288* 'beginning of the history of salvation'[117] that culminates in Christ. Conversely, the mystery of Christ casts conclusive light on the mystery of creation and reveals the end for which 'in the beginning God created the heavens and the earth': from the beginning, *1043* God envisaged the glory of the new creation in Christ.[118]

281 And so the readings of the Easter Vigil, the celebration of the new creation in Christ, begin with the creation account; likewise in the Byzantine liturgy, the account of creation always constitutes the first reading at the vigils of the great *1095*

---

[115] Roman Catechism I, 2, 13.
[116] Gen 1:1.
[117] GCD 51.
[118] Gen 1:1; cf. Rom 8:18–23.

feasts of the Lord. According to ancient witnesses the instruction of catechumens for Baptism followed the same itinerary.[119]

I. Catechesis on Creation

282 Catechesis on creation is of major importance. It concerns the very foundations of human and Christian life: for it makes explicit the response of the Christian faith to the basic question that men of all times have asked themselves:[120] 'Where do we come from?' 'Where are we going?' 'What is our origin?' 'What is our end?' 'Where does everything that exists come from and where is it going?' The two questions, the first about the origin and the second about the end, are inseparable. They are decisive for the meaning and orientation of our life and actions.

1730

283 The question about the origins of the world and of man has been the object of many scientific studies which have splendidly enriched our knowledge of the age and dimensions of the cosmos, the development of life-forms and the appearance of man. These discoveries invite us to even greater admiration for the greatness of the Creator, prompting us to give him thanks for all his works and for the understanding and wisdom he gives to scholars and researchers. With Solomon they can say: 'It is he who gave me unerring knowledge of what exists, to know the structure of the world and the activity of the elements... for wisdom, the fashioner of all things, taught me.'[121]

159

341

284 The great interest accorded to these studies is strongly stimulated by a question of another order, which goes beyond the proper domain of the natural sciences. It is not only a question of knowing when and how the universe arose physically, or when man appeared, but rather of discovering the meaning of such an origin: is the universe governed by chance, blind fate, anonymous necessity, or by a transcendent, intelligent and good Being called 'God'? And if the world does come from God's wisdom and goodness, why is there evil? Where does it come from? Who is responsible for it? Is there any liberation from it?

285 Since the beginning the Christian faith has been challenged by responses to the question of origins that differ from its own. Ancient religions and cultures produced many myths concerning origins. Some philosophers have said that everything is God, that the world is God, or that the development of the world is the development of God (Pantheism). Others have said that the world is a necessary emanation arising from God and returning to him. Still others have affirmed the existence of two eternal principles, Good and Evil, Light and Darkness, locked in permanent conflict (Dualism, Manichaeism). According to some of these conceptions, the world (at least the physical world) is evil, the product of a fall, and is thus to be rejected or left behind (Gnosticism). Some admit that the world was made by God, but as by a watch-maker who, once he

296

---

[119] Cf. Egeria, *Peregrinatio ad loca sancta* 46: PLS I, 1047; St Augustine, *De catechizandis rudibus* 3, 5: PL 40, 256.

[120] Cf. *NA* 2.
[121] *Wis* 7:17–22.

has made a watch, abandons it to itself (Deism). Finally, others reject any transcendent origin for the world, but see it as merely the interplay of matter that has always existed (Materialism). All these attempts bear witness to the permanence and universality of the question of origins. This inquiry is distinctively human. *28*

286 Human intelligence is surely already capable of finding a response to the question of origins. The existence of God the Creator can be known with certainty through his works, by the light of *32* human reason,[122] even if this knowledge is often obscured and disfigured by error. This is why faith comes to confirm and enlighten reason in the correct understanding of this truth: 'By *37* faith we understand that the world was created by the word of God, so that what is seen was made out of things which do not appear.'[123]

287 The truth about creation is so important for all of human life that God in his tenderness wanted to reveal to his People every- *107* thing that is salutary to know on the subject. Beyond the natural knowledge that every man can have of the Creator,[124] God progressively revealed to Israel the mystery of creation. He who chose the patriarchs, who brought Israel out of Egypt, and who by choosing Israel created and formed it, this same God reveals himself as the One to whom belong all the peoples of the earth, and the whole earth itself; he is the One who alone 'made heaven and earth'.[125]

288 Thus the revelation of creation is inseparable from the revelation and forging of the covenant of the one God with his People. Creation is revealed as the first step towards this covenant, the first *280, 2569* and universal witness to God's all-powerful love.[126] And so, the truth of creation is also expressed with growing vigour in the message of the prophets, the prayer of the psalms and the liturgy, and in the wisdom sayings of the Chosen People.[127]

289 Among all the Scriptural texts about creation, the first three chapters of *Genesis* occupy a unique place. From a literary stand- *390* point these texts may have had diverse sources. The inspired authors have placed them at the beginning of Scripture to express in their solemn language the truths of creation – its origin and its end in God, its order and goodness, the vocation of man, and finally the drama of sin and the hope of salvation. Read in the light

---

[122] Cf. Vatican Council I, can. 2 § 1: DS 3026.
[123] *Heb* 11:3.
[124] Cf. *Acts* 17:24–29; *Rom* 1:19–20.

[125] Cf. *Is* 43:1; *Pss* 115:15; 124:8; 134:3.
[126] Cf. *Gen* 15:5; *Jer* 33:19–26.
[127] Cf. *Is* 44:24; *Ps* 104; *Prov* 8:22–31.

111 of Christ, within the unity of Sacred Scripture and in the living Tradition of the Church, these texts remain the principal source for catechesis on the mysteries of the 'beginning': creation, fall, and promise of salvation.

II. Creation – Work of the Holy Trinity

290 'In the beginning God created the heavens and the earth':[128] three things are affirmed in these first words of Scripture: the eternal God gave a beginning to all that exists outside of himself; he alone is Creator (the verb 'create' – Hebrew *bara* – always has God for its subject). The totality of what exists (expressed by the *326* formula 'the heavens and the earth') depends on the One who gives it being.

241 291 'In the beginning was the Word. . . and the Word was God. . . all things were made through him, and without him was not anything made that was made.'[129] The New Testament reveals that God created everything by the eternal Word, his beloved Son. *331* In him 'all things were created, in heaven and on earth. . . all things were created through him and for him. He is before all things, and in him all things hold together.'[130] The Church's faith likewise *703* confesses the creative action of the Holy Spirit, the 'giver of life', 'the Creator Spirit' (*Veni, Creator Spiritus*), the 'source of every good'.[131]

292 The Old Testament suggests and the New Covenant reveals the creative action of the Son and the Spirit,[132] inseparably one with that of the Father. This creative co-operation is clearly affirmed in the Church's rule of faith: 'There exists but one God. . . he is the Father, God, the Creator, the author, the giver of order. He made all things *by himself*, that is, by his Word and by his Wisdom', 'by the Son and the Spirit' who, so to speak, are 'his *699, 257* hands'.[133] Creation is the common work of the Holy Trinity.

III. 'The World Was Created for the Glory of God'

293 Scripture and Tradition never cease to teach and celebrate this *337, 344* fundamental truth: 'The world was made for the glory of God.'[134] St Bonaventure explains that God created all things 'not to

---

[128] *Gen* 1:1.
[129] *Jn* 1:1–3.
[130] *Col* 1:16–17.
[131] Cf. Nicene Creed: DS 150; Hymn *Veni, Creator Spiritus*; Byzantine Troparion of Pentecost Vespers, 'O

heavenly King, Consoler'.
[132] Cf. *Pss* 33:6; 104:30; *Gen* 1:2–3.
[133] St Irenaeus, *Adv. haeres.* 2, 30, 9; 4, 20, 1: PG 7/1, 822, 1032.
[134] *Dei Filius*, can. § 5: DS 3025.

increase his glory, but to show it forth and to communicate it',[135] 1361
for God has no other reason for creating than his love and goodness: 'Creatures came into existence when the key of love opened
his hand.'[136] The First Vatican Council explains:

> This one, true God, of his own goodness and 'almighty power', not for 759
> increasing his own beatitude, nor for attaining his perfection, but in
> order to manifest this perfection through the benefits which he bestows
> on creatures, with absolute freedom of counsel 'and from the beginning
> of time, made out of nothing both orders of creatures, the spiritual and
> the corporeal...'[137]

294 The glory of God consists in the realization of this manifestation and communication of his goodness, for which the world
was created. God made us 'to be his sons through Jesus Christ,
according to the purpose of his will, *to the praise of his glorious* 2809
grace',[138] for 'the glory of God is man fully alive; moreover man's
life is the vision of God: if God's revelation through creation has 1722
already obtained life for all the beings that dwell on earth, how
much more will the Word's manifestation of the Father obtain life
for those who see God.'[139] The ultimate purpose of creation is that
God 'who is the creator of all things may at last become "all in all"', 1992
thus simultaneously assuring his own glory and our beatitude.'[140]

IV. The Mystery of Creation

God creates by wisdom and love

295 We believe that God created the world according to his
wisdom.[141] It is not the product of any necessity whatever, nor of
blind fate or chance. We believe that it proceeds from God's free
will; he wanted to make his creatures share in his being, wisdom
and goodness: 'For you created all things, and by your will they 216, 1951
existed and were created.'[142] Therefore the Psalmist exclaims: 'O
LORD, how manifold are your works! In wisdom you have made
them all'; and 'The LORD is good to all, and his compassion is over
all that he has made.'[143]

God creates 'out of nothing'

296 We believe that God needs no pre-existent thing or any help
in order to create, nor is creation any sort of necessary emanation 285

---

[135] St Bonaventure, *In II Sent.* I, 2, 2, 1.
[136] St Thomas Aquinas, *Sent.* II, prol.
[137] *Dei Filius* 1: DS 3002; cf. Lateran
   Council IV (1215): DS 800.
[138] *Eph* 1:5–6.
[139] St Irenaeus, *Adv. haeres.* 4, 20, 7: PG

7/1, 1037.
[140] *AG* 2; cf. 1 *Cor* 15:28.
[141] Cf. *Wis* 9:9.
[142] *Rev* 4:11.
[143] *Pss* 104:24; 145:9.

from the divine substance.[144] God creates freely 'out of nothing':[145]

> If God had drawn the world from pre-existent matter, what would be so extraordinary in that? A human artisan makes from a given material whatever he wants, while God shows his power by starting from nothing to make all he wants.[146]

338 297 Scripture bears witness to faith in creation 'out of nothing' as a truth full of promise and hope. Thus the mother of seven sons encourages them for martyrdom:

> I do not know how you came into being in my womb. It was not I who gave you life and breath, nor I who set in order the elements within each of you. Therefore the Creator of the world, who shaped the beginning of man and devised the origin of all things, will in his mercy give life and breath back to you again, since you now forget yourselves for the sake of his laws... Look at the heaven and the earth and see everything that is in them, and recognize that God did not make them out of things that existed. Thus also mankind comes into being.[147]

1375 298 Since God could create everything out of nothing, he can also, through the Holy Spirit, give spiritual life to sinners by creat-
992 ing a pure heart in them,[148] and bodily life to the dead through the Resurrection. God 'gives life to the dead and calls into existence the things that do not exist.'[149] And since God was able to make light shine in darkness by his Word, he can also give the light of faith to those who do not yet know him.[150]

God creates an ordered and good world

299 Because God creates through wisdom, his creation is ordered:
339 'You have arranged all things by measure and number and weight.'[151] The universe, created in and by the eternal Word, the 'image of the invisible God', is destined for and addressed to man, himself created in the 'image of God' and called to a personal relationship with God.[152] Our human understanding, which
41, 1147 shares in the light of the divine intellect, can understand what God tells us by means of his creation, though not without great effort and only in a spirit of humility and respect before the Creator and his work.[153] Because creation comes forth from God's goodness, it

---

[144] Cf. *Dei Filius*, cann. 2–4: DS 3022–3024.

[145] Lateran Council IV (1215): DS 800; cf. DS 3025.

[146] St Theophilus of Antioch, *Ad Autolycum* II, 4: PG 6, 1052.

[147] 2 *Macc* 7:22–23, 28.

[148] Cf. *Ps* 51:12.

[149] *Rom* 4:17.

[150] Cf. *Gen* 1:3; 2 *Cor* 4:6.

[151] *Wis* 11:20.

[152] *Col* 1:15; *Gen* 1:26.

[153] Cf. *Ps* 19:2–5; *Job* 42:3.

shares in that goodness – 'And God saw that it was good... very good'[154] – for God willed creation as a gift addressed to man, an inheritance destined for and entrusted to him. On many occasions the Church has had to defend the goodness of creation, including that of the physical world.[155]

358

2415

God transcends creation and is present to it

300 God is infinitely greater than all his works: 'You have set your glory above the heavens.'[156] Indeed, God's 'greatness is unsearchable'.[157] But because he is the free and sovereign Creator, the first cause of all that exists, God is present to his creatures' inmost being: 'In him we live and move and have our being.'[158] In the words of St Augustine, God is 'higher than my highest and more inward than my innermost self'.[159]

42, 223

God upholds and sustains creation

301 With creation, God does not abandon his creatures to themselves. He not only gives them being and existence, but also, and at every moment, upholds and sustains them in being, enables them to act and brings them to their final end. Recognizing this utter dependence with respect to the Creator is a source of wisdom and freedom, of joy and confidence:

1951, 396

> For you love all things that exist, and detest none of the things that you have made; for you would not have made anything if you had hated it. How would anything have endured, if you had not willed it? Or how would anything not called forth by you have been preserved? You spare all things, for they are yours, O Lord, you who love the living.[160]

V. God Carries Out His Plan: Divine Providence

302 Creation has its own goodness and proper perfection, but it did not spring forth complete from the hands of the Creator. The universe was created 'in a state of journeying' (*in statu viae*) toward an ultimate perfection yet to be attained, to which God has destined it. We call 'divine providence' the dispositions by which God guides his creation toward this perfection:

> By his providence God protects and governs all things which he has made, 'reaching mightily from one end of the earth to the other, and ordering all things well'. For 'all are open and laid bare to his eyes', even

---

[154] *Gen* 1:4, 10, 12, 18, 21, 31.
[155] Cf. DS 286; 455–463; 800; 1333; 3002.
[156] *Ps* 8:1; cf. *Sir* 43:28.
[157] *Ps* 145:3.
[158] *Acts* 17:28.
[159] St Augustine, *Conf.* 3, 6, 11: PL 32, 688.
[160] *Wis* 11:24–26.

those things which are yet to come into existence through the free action of creatures.[161]

303 The witness of Scripture is unanimous that the solicitude of divine providence is *concrete* and *immediate*; God cares for all, from the least things to the great events of the world and its history. The sacred books powerfully affirm God's absolute sovereignty over the course of events: 'Our God is in the heavens; he does whatever he pleases.'[162] And so it is with Christ, 'who opens and no one shall shut, who shuts and no one opens'.[163] As the book of Proverbs states: 'Many are the plans in the mind of a man, but it is the purpose of the LORD that will be established.'[164]

304 And so we see the Holy Spirit, the principal author of Sacred Scripture, often attributing actions to God without mentioning any secondary causes. This is not a 'primitive mode of speech', but a profound way of recalling God's primacy and absolute Lordship over history and the world,[165] and so of educating his people to trust in him. The prayer of the Psalms is the great school of this trust.[166]

305 Jesus asks for childlike abandonment to the providence of our heavenly Father who takes care of his children's smallest needs: 'Therefore do not be anxious, saying, "What shall we eat?" or "What shall we drink?"... Your heavenly Father knows that you need them all. But seek first his kingdom and his righteousness, and all these things shall be yours as well.'[167]

Providence and secondary causes

306 God is the sovereign master of his plan. But to carry it out he also makes use of his creatures' co-operation. This use is not a sign of weakness, but rather a token of almighty God's greatness and goodness. For God grants his creatures not only their existence, but also the dignity of acting on their own, of being causes and principles for each other, and thus of co-operating in the accomplishment of his plan.

307 To human beings God even gives the power of freely sharing in his providence by entrusting them with the responsibility of 'subduing' the earth and having dominion over it.[168] God thus enables men to be intelligent and free causes in order to complete the work of creation, to perfect its harmony for their own good and that of their neighbours. Though often unconscious collabor-

---

[161] Vatican Council I, *Dei Filius* 1: DS 3003; cf. *Wis* 8:1; *Heb* 4:13.
[162] *Ps* 115:3.
[163] *Rev* 3:7.
[164] *Prov* 19:21.

[165] Cf. *Is* 10:5–15; 45:5–7; *Dt* 32:39; *Sir* 11:14.
[166] Cf. *Pss* 22; 32; 35; 103; 138; *et al.*
[167] *Mt* 6:31–33; cf. 10:29–31.
[168] Cf. *Gen* 1:26–28.

ators with God's will, they can also enter deliberately into the divine plan by their actions, their prayers and their sufferings.[169] They then fully become 'God's fellow workers' and co-workers for his kingdom.[170]

2738

618, 1505

308 The truth that God is at work in all the actions of his creatures is inseparable from faith in God the Creator. God is the first cause who operates in and through secondary causes: 'For God is at work in you, both to will and to work for his good pleasure.'[171] Far from diminishing the creature's dignity, this truth enhances it. Drawn from nothingness by God's power, wisdom and goodness, it can do nothing if it is cut off from its origin, for 'without a Creator the creature vanishes.'[172] Still less can a creature attain its ultimate end without the help of God's grace.[173]

970

Providence and the scandal of evil

309 If God the Father almighty, the Creator of the ordered and good world, cares for all his creatures, why does evil exist? To this question, as pressing as it is unavoidable and as painful as it is mysterious, no quick answer will suffice. Only Christian faith as a whole constitutes the answer to this question: the goodness of creation, the drama of sin and the patient love of God who comes to meet man by his covenants, the redemptive Incarnation of his Son, his gift of the Spirit, his gathering of the Church, the power of the sacraments and his call to a blessed life to which free creatures are invited to consent in advance, but from which, by a terrible mystery, they can also turn away in advance. *There is not a single aspect of the Christian message that is not in part an answer to the question of evil.*

164, 385

2850

310 But why did God not create a world so perfect that no evil could exist in it? With infinite power God could always create something better.[174] But with infinite wisdom and goodness God freely willed to create a world 'in a state of journeying' towards its ultimate perfection. In God's plan this process of becoming involves the appearance of certain beings and the disappearance of others, the existence of the more perfect alongside the less perfect, both constructive and destructive forces of nature. With physical good there exists also *physical evil* as long as creation has not reached perfection.[175]

412

1042–1050

---

[169] Cf. Col 1:24.
[170] 1 Cor 3:9; 1 Th 3:2; Col 4:11.
[171] Phil 2:13; cf. 1 Cor 12:6.
[172] GS 36 § 3.

[173] Cf. Mt 19:26; Jn 15:5; 14:13.
[174] Cf. St Thomas Aquinas, STh I, 25, 6.
[175] Cf. St Thomas Aquinas, SCG III, 71.

311 Angels and men, as intelligent and free creatures, have to
396 journey toward their ultimate destinies by their free choice and
preferential love. They can therefore go astray. Indeed, they have
1849 sinned. Thus has *moral evil*, incommensurably more harmful than
physical evil, entered the world. God is in no way, directly or
indirectly, the cause of moral evil.[176] He permits it, however,
because he respects the freedom of his creatures and, mysteriously,
knows how to derive good from it:

> For almighty God..., because he is supremely good, would never allow
> any evil whatsoever to exist in his works if he were not so all-powerful
> and good as to cause good to emerge from evil itself.[177]

312 In time we can discover that God in his almighty providence
can bring a good from the consequences of an evil, even a moral
evil, caused by his creatures: 'It was not you', said Joseph to his
brothers, 'who sent me here, but God... You meant evil against
me; but God meant it for good, to bring it about that many people
should be kept alive.'[178] From the greatest moral evil ever com-
598–600 mitted – the rejection and murder of God's only Son, caused by
the sins of all men – God, by his grace that 'abounded all the
1994 more',[179] brought the greatest of goods: the glorification of Christ
and our redemption. But for all that, evil never becomes a good.

227 313 'We know that in everything God works for good for those
who love him.'[180] The constant witness of the saints confirms this
truth:

> St Catherine of Siena said to 'those who are scandalized and rebel against
> what happens to them': 'Everything comes from love, all is ordained for
> the salvation of man, God does nothing without this goal in mind.'[181]

> St Thomas More, shortly before his martyrdom, consoled his daughter:
> 'Nothing can come but that that God wills. And I make me very sure that
> whatsoever that be, seem it never so bad in sight, it shall indeed be the
> best.'[182]

> Dame Julian of Norwich: 'Here I was taught by the grace of God that I
> should steadfastly keep me in the faith... and that at the same time I
> should take my stand on and earnestly believe in what our Lord shewed
> in this time – that "all manner [of] thing shall be well." '[183]

---

[176] Cf. St Augustine, *De libero arbitrio* 1,
1, 2: PL 32, 1221–1223; St Thomas
Aquinas, *STh* I-II, 79, 1.

[177] St Augustine, *Enchiridion* 11, 3: PL 40,
236.

[178] *Gen* 45:8; 50:20; cf. *Tob* 2:12–18
(Vulgate).

[179] Cf. *Rom* 5:20.

[180] *Rom* 8:28.

[181] St Catherine of Siena, *Dialogue* IV,
138 'On Divine Providence'.

[182] *The Correspondence of Sir Thomas More*,
ed. Elizabeth F. Rogers (Princeton:
Princeton University Press, 1947),
letter 206, lines 661–663.

[183] Julian of Norwich, *The Revelations of
Divine Love*, tr. James Walshe SJ
(London: 1961), ch. 32, 99–100.

314 We firmly believe that God is master of the world and of its history. But the ways of his providence are often unknown to us. Only at the end, when our partial knowledge ceases, when we see God 'face to face',[184] will we fully know the ways by which – even through the dramas of evil and sin – God has guided his creation to that definitive *sabbath* rest[185] for which he created heaven and earth.

1040
2550

IN BRIEF

315 *In the creation of the world and of man, God gave the first and universal witness to his almighty love and his wisdom, the first proclamation of the 'plan of his loving goodness', which finds its goal in the new creation in Christ.*

316 *Though the work of creation is attributed to the Father in particular, it is equally a truth of faith that the Father, Son and Holy Spirit together are the one, indivisible principle of creation.*

317 *God alone created the universe, freely, directly and without any help.*

318 *No creature has the infinite power necessary to 'create' in the proper sense of the word, that is, to produce and give being to that which had in no way possessed it (to call into existence 'out of nothing') (cf. DS 3624)..*

319 *God created the world to show forth and communicate his glory. That his creatures should share in his truth, goodness and beauty – this is the glory for which God created them.*

320 *God created the universe and keeps it in existence by his Word, the Son 'upholding the universe by his word of power' (Heb 1:3), and by his Creator Spirit, the giver of life.*

321 *Divine providence consists of the dispositions by which God guides all his creatures with wisdom and love to their ultimate end.*

322 *Christ invites us to filial trust in the providence of our heavenly Father (cf. Mt 6:26–34), and St Peter the apostle repeats: 'Cast all your anxieties on him, for he cares about you' (1 Pt 5:7; cf. Ps 55:23).*

323 *Divine providence works also through the actions of creatures. To human beings God grants the ability to co-operate freely with his plans.*

324 *The fact that God permits physical and even moral evil is a mystery that God illuminates by his Son Jesus Christ who died and rose to vanquish evil. Faith gives us the certainty that God would not permit an evil if he did not cause a good to come from that very evil, by ways that we shall fully know only in eternal life.*

---

[184] 1 Cor 13:12. [185] Cf. Gen 2:2.

Paragraph 5. Heaven and Earth

325 The Apostles' Creed professes that God is 'creator of heaven and earth'. The Nicene Creed makes it explicit that this profession includes 'all that is, seen and unseen'.

290   326 The Scriptural expression 'heaven and earth' means all that exists, creation in its entirety. It also indicates the bond, deep within creation, that both unites heaven and earth and distinguishes the one from the other: 'the earth' is the world of men, while 'heaven' or 'the heavens' can designate both the firmament *1023, 2794* and God's own 'place' – 'our Father in heaven' and consequently the 'heaven' too which is eschatological glory. Finally, 'heaven' refers to the saints and the 'place' of the spiritual creatures, the angels, who surround God.[186]

327 The profession of faith of the Fourth Lateran Council (1215) affirms that God 'from the beginning of time made at once (*simul*) *296* out of nothing both orders of creatures, the spiritual and the corporeal, that is, the angelic and the earthly, and then (*deinde*) the human creature, who as it were shares in both orders, being composed of spirit and body.'[187]

I. The Angels

The existence of angels – a truth of faith

328 The existence of the spiritual, non-corporeal beings that *150* Sacred Scripture usually calls 'angels' is a truth of faith. The witness of Scripture is as clear as the unanimity of Tradition.

Who are they?

329 St Augustine says: ' "Angel" is the name of their office, not of their nature. If you seek the name of their nature, it is "spirit"; if you seek the name of their office, it is "angel": from what they are, "spirit", from what they do, "angel".'[188] With their whole beings the angels are *servants* and messengers of God. Because they 'always behold the face of my Father who is in heaven' they are the 'mighty ones who do his word, hearkening to the voice of his word'.[189]

330 As purely *spiritual* creatures angels have intelligence and will: they are personal and immortal creatures, surpassing in perfection

---

[186] *Pss* 115:16; 19:2; *Mt* 5:16.
[187] Lateran Council IV (1215): DS 800; cf. DS 3002 and Paul VI, *CPG* § 8.

[188] St Augustine, *En. in Ps.* 103, 1, 15: PL 37, 1348.
[189] *Mt* 18:10; Ps 103:20.

all visible creatures, as the splendour of their glory bears witness.[190]

Christ 'with all his angels'

331 Christ is the centre of the angelic world. They are *his* angels: 'When the Son of man comes in his glory, and all the angels with him. . .'[191] They belong to him because they were created *through* and *for* him: 'for in him all things were created in heaven and on earth, visible and invisible, whether thrones or dominions or principalities or authorities – all things were created through him and for him.'[192] They belong to him still more because he has made them messengers of his saving plan: 'Are they not all ministering spirits sent forth to serve, for the sake of those who are to obtain salvation?'[193] 291

332 Angels have been present since creation and throughout the history of salvation, announcing this salvation from afar or near and serving the accomplishment of the divine plan: they closed the earthly paradise; protected Lot; saved Hagar and her child; stayed Abraham's hand; communicated the law by their ministry; led the People of God; announced births and callings; and assisted the prophets, just to cite a few examples.[194] Finally, the angel Gabriel announced the birth of the Precursor and that of Jesus himself.[195]

333 From the Incarnation to the Ascension, the life of the Word incarnate is surrounded by the adoration and service of angels. When God 'brings the firstborn into the world, he says: "Let all God's angels worship him." '[196] Their song of praise at the birth of Christ has not ceased resounding in the Church's praise: 'Glory to God in the highest!'[197] They protect Jesus in his infancy, serve him in the desert, strengthen him in his agony in the garden, when he could have been saved by them from the hands of his enemies as Israel had been.[198] Again, it is the angels who 'evangelize' by proclaiming the Good News of Christ's Incarnation and Resurrection.[199] They will be present at Christ's return, which they will announce, to serve at his judgement.[200] 559

---

[190] Cf. Pius XII, *Humani generis*: DS 3891; *Lk* 20:36; *Dan* 10:9–12.
[191] *Mt* 25:31.
[192] *Col* 1:16.
[193] *Heb* 1:14.
[194] Cf. *Job* 38:7 (where angels are called 'sons of God'); *Gen* 3:24; 19; 21:17; 22:11; *Acts* 7:53; *Ex* 23:20–23; *Judg* 13; 6:11–24; *Is* 6:6; 1 *Kings* 19:5.

[195] Cf. *Lk* 1:11, 26.
[196] *Heb* 1:6.
[197] *Lk* 2:14.
[198] Cf. *Mt* 1:20; 2:13, 19; 4:11; 26:53; *Mk* 1:13; *Lk* 22:43; 2 *Macc* 10:29–30; 11:8.
[199] Cf. *Lk* 2:8–14; *Mk* 16:5–7.
[200] Cf. *Acts* 1:10–11; *Mt* 13:41; 24:31; *Lk* 12:8–9.

The angels in the life of the Church

334 In the meantime, the whole life of the Church benefits from the mysterious and powerful help of angels.[201]

1138 335 In her liturgy, the Church joins with the angels to adore the thrice-holy God. She invokes their assistance (in the funeral liturgy's *In Paradisum deducant te angeli...*['May the angels lead you into Paradise...']). Moreover, in the 'Cherubic Hymn' of the Byzantine Liturgy, she celebrates the memory of certain angels more particularly (St Michael, St Gabriel, St Raphael, and the guardian angels).

1020 336 From its beginning until death, human life is surrounded by their watchful care and intercession.[202] 'Beside each believer stands an angel as protector and shepherd leading him to life.'[203] Already here on earth the Christian life shares by faith in the blessed company of angels and men united in God.

II. The Visible World

290 337 God himself created the visible world in all its richness, diversity and order. Scripture presents the work of the Creator symbolically as a succession of six days of divine 'work', concluded by the 'rest' of the seventh day.[204] On the subject of creation, the sacred text teaches the truths revealed by God for our salvation,[205] permitting us to 'recognize the inner nature, the value and the
293 ordering of the whole of creation to the praise of God.'[206]

338 *Nothing exists that does not owe its existence to God the Creator.*
297 The world began when God's word drew it out of nothingness; all existent beings, all of nature, and all human history are rooted in this primordial event, the very genesis by which the world was constituted and time begun.[207]

339 *Each creature possesses its own particular goodness and perfection.*
2501 For each one of the works of the 'six days' it is said: 'And God saw that it was good.' 'By the very nature of creation, material being is endowed with its own stability, truth and excellence, its own
299 order and laws.'[208] Each of the various creatures, willed in its own

---

[201] Cf. *Acts* 5:18–20; 8:26–29; 10:3–8; 12:6–11; 27:23–25.
[202] Cf. *Mt* 18:10; *Lk* 16:22; *Pss* 34:7; 91:10–13; Job 33:23–24; *Zech* 1:12; *Tob* 12:12.
[203] St Basil. *Adv. Eunomium* III, 1: PG 29. 656B.

[204] *Gen* 1:1 – 2:4.
[205] Cf. *DV* 11.
[206] *LG* 36 § 2.
[207] Cf. St Augustine, *De Genesi adv. Man.* 1, 2, 4: PL 34, 175.
[208] *GS* 36 § 1.

being, reflects in its own way a ray of God's infinite wisdom and goodness. Man must therefore respect the particular goodness of *226* every creature, to avoid any disordered use of things which would be in contempt of the Creator and would bring disastrous consequences for human beings and their environment.

340 God wills the *interdependence of creatures*. The sun and the *1937* moon, the cedar and the little flower, the eagle and the sparrow: the spectacle of their countless diversities and inequalities tells us that no creature is self-sufficient. Creatures exist only in dependence on each other, to complete each other, in the service of each other.

341 The *beauty of the universe*: The order and harmony of the created world results from the diversity of beings and from the relationships which exist among them. Man discovers them progressively as the laws of nature. They call forth the admiration of *283* scholars. The beauty of creation reflects the infinite beauty of the *2500* Creator and ought to inspire the respect and submission of man's intellect and will.

342 The *hierarchy of creatures* is expressed by the order of the 'six days', from the less perfect to the more perfect. God loves all his *310* creatures[209] and takes care of each one, even the sparrow. Nevertheless, Jesus said: 'You are of more value than many sparrows', or again: 'Of how much more value is a man than a sheep!'[210]

343 *Man is the summit* of the Creator's work, as the inspired *355* account expresses by clearly distinguishing the creation of man from that of the other creatures.[211]

344 There is a *solidarity among all creatures* arising from the fact that *293, 1939,* all have the same Creator and are all ordered to his glory: *2416*

> May you be praised, O Lord, in all your creatures, especially brother sun, by whom you give us light for the day; he is beautiful, radiating great splendour, and offering us a symbol of you, the Most High...
> May you be praised, my Lord, for sister water, who is very useful and *1218* humble, precious and chaste...
> May you be praised, my Lord, for sister earth, our mother, who bears and feeds us, and produces the variety of fruits and dappled flowers and grasses...
> Praise and bless my Lord, give thanks and serve him in all humility.[212]

---

[209] Cf. *Ps* 145:9.
[210] *Lk* 12:6–7; *Mt* 12:12.
[211] Cf. *Gen* 1:26.

[212] St Francis of Assisi, *Canticle of the Creatures*.

345 *The sabbath – the end of the work of the six days.* The sacred text says that 'on the seventh day God finished his work which he had done', that the 'heavens and the earth were finished', and that God 'rested' on this day and sanctified and blessed it.[213] These inspired words are rich in profitable instruction:

346 In creation God laid a foundation and established laws that remain firm, on which the believer can rely with confidence, for they are the sign and pledge of the unshakeable faithfulness of God's covenant.[214] For his part man must remain faithful to this foundation, and respect the laws which the Creator has written into it.

347 Creation was fashioned with a view to the sabbath and therefore for the worship and adoration of God. Worship is inscribed in the order of creation.[215] As the rule of St Benedict says, nothing should take precedence over 'the work of God', that is, solemn worship.[216] This indicates the right order of human concerns.

348 The sabbath is at the heart of Israel's law. To keep the commandments is to correspond to the wisdom and the will of God as expressed in his work of creation.

349 The *eighth day.* But for us a new day has dawned: the day of Christ's Resurrection. The seventh day completes the first creation. The eighth day begins the new creation. Thus, the work of creation culminates in the greater work of redemption. The first creation finds its meaning and its summit in the new creation in Christ, the splendour of which surpasses that of the first creation.[217]

IN BRIEF

350 *Angels are spiritual creatures who glorify God without ceasing and who serve his saving plans for other creatures: 'The angels work together for the benefit of us all' (St Thomas Aquinas, STh I, 114, 3, ad 3).*

351 *The angels surround Christ their Lord. They serve him especially in the accomplishment of his saving mission to men.*

352 *The Church venerates the angels who help her on her earthly pilgrimage and protect every human being.*

---

[213] *Gen* 2:1–3.
[214] Cf. *Heb* 4:3–4; *Jer* 31:35–37; 33:19–26.
[215] Cf. *Gen* 1:14.
[216] St Benedict, *Regula* 43, 3: PL 66, 675–676.

[217] Cf. *Roman Missal*, Easter Vigil 24, prayer after the first reading.

353 *God willed the diversity of his creatures and their own particular good-ness, their interdependence and their order. He destined all material creatures for the good of the human race. Man, and through him all creation, is destined for the glory of God.*

354 *Respect for laws inscribed in creation and the relations which derive from the nature of things is a principle of wisdom and a foundation for morality.*

Paragraph 6. Man

355 'God created man in his own image, in the image of God he created him, male and female he created them.'[218] Man occupies a unique place in creation: (I) he is 'in the image of God'; (II) in his own nature he unites the spiritual and material worlds; (III) he is created 'male and female'; (IV) God established him in his friendship.   *1700*   *343*

I. 'In the Image of God'

356 Of all visible creatures only man is 'able to know and love his creator'.[219] He is 'the only creature on earth that God has willed for its own sake',[220] and he alone is called to share, by knowledge and love, in God's own life. It was for this end that he was created, and this is the fundamental reason for his dignity: *1703, 2258*   *225*

> What made you establish man in so great a dignity? Certainly the incalculable love by which you have looked on your creature in yourself! You are taken with love for her; for by love indeed you created her, by love you have given her a being capable of tasting your eternal Good.[221]   *295*

357 Being in the image of God the human individual possesses the dignity of a *person*, who is not just something, but someone. He is capable of self-knowledge, of self-possession and of freely giving himself and entering into communion with other persons. And he is called by grace to a covenant with his Creator, to offer him a response of faith and love that no other creature can give in his stead.   *1935*   *1877*

358 God created everything for man,[222] but man in turn was created to serve and love God and to offer all creation back to him: *299, 901*

> What is it that is about to be created, that enjoys such honour? It is man — that great and wonderful living creature, more precious in the eyes of

---

[218] *Gen* 1:27.
[219] *GS* 12 § 3.
[220] *GS* 24 § 3.
[221] St Catherine of Siena, *Dialogue* IV, 13

'On Divine Providence': *LH*, Sunday, week 19, OR.
[222] Cf. *GS* 12 § 1; 24 § 3; 39 § 1.

God than all other creatures! For him the heavens and the earth, the sea and all the rest of creation exist. God attached so much importance to his salvation that he did not spare his own Son for the sake of man. Nor does he ever cease to work, trying every possible means, until he has raised man up to himself and made him sit at his right hand.[223]

359 'In reality it is only in the mystery of the Word made flesh that *1701* the mystery of man truly becomes clear.'[224]

388, 411 St Paul tells us that the human race takes its origin from two men: Adam and Christ... The first man, Adam, he says, became a living soul, the last Adam a life-giving spirit. The first Adam was made by the last Adam, from whom he also received his soul, to give him life... The second Adam stamped his image on the first Adam when he created him. That is why he took on himself the role and the name of the first Adam, in order that he might not lose what he had made in his own image. The first Adam, the last Adam: the first had a beginning, the last knows no end. The last Adam is indeed the first; as he himself says: 'I am the first and the last.'[225]

225, 404, 360 Because of its common origin *the human race forms a unity*, for *775, 831,* 'from one ancestor [God] made all nations to inhabit the whole *842* earth':[226]

O wondrous vision, which makes us contemplate the human race in the unity of its origin in God... in the unity of its nature, composed equally in all men of a material body and a spiritual soul; in the unity of its immediate end and its mission in the world; in the unity of its dwelling, the earth, whose benefits all men, by right of nature, may use to sustain and develop life; in the unity of its supernatural end: God himself, to whom all ought to tend; in the unity of the means for attaining this end;... in the unity of the redemption wrought by Christ for all.[227]

361 'This law of human solidarity and charity',[228] without excluding the rich variety of persons, cultures and peoples, assures *1939* us that all men are truly brethren.

II. 'Body and Soul but Truly One'

362 The human person, created in the image of God, is a being at *1146, 2332* once corporeal and spiritual. The biblical account expresses this reality in symbolic language when it affirms that 'then the LORD God formed man of dust from the ground, and breathed into his nostrils the breath of life; and man became a living being.'[229] Man, whole and entire, is therefore *willed* by God.

---

[223] St John Chrysostom, *In Gen. sermo* 2, 1: PG 54, 587D–588A.

[224] GS 22 § 1.

[225] St Peter Chrysologus, *Sermo* 117: PL 52, 520–521.

[226] *Acts* 17:26; cf. *Tob* 8:6.

[227] Pius XII, Enc. *Summi pontificatus* 3; cf. NA 1.

[228] Pius XII, *Summi pontificatus* 3.

[229] *Gen* 2:7.

363 In Sacred Scripture the term 'soul' often refers to human *life* or the entire human *person*.[230] But 'soul' also refers to the inner-most aspect of man, that which is of greatest value in him,[231] that by which he is most especially in God's image: 'soul' signifies the *spiritual principle* in man. *1703*

364 The human *body* shares in the dignity of 'the image of God': it is a human body precisely because it is animated by a spiritual soul, and it is the whole human person that is intended to become, in the body of Christ, a temple of the Spirit:[232] *1004*

> Man, though made of body and soul, is a unity. Through his very bodily condition he sums up in himself the elements of the material world. Through him they are thus brought to their highest perfection and can raise their voice in praise freely given to the Creator. For this reason man may not despise his bodily life. Rather he is obliged to regard his body as good and to hold it in honour since God has created it and will raise it up on the last day.[233] *2289*

365 The unity of soul and body is so profound that one has to consider the soul to be the 'form' of the body:[234] i.e., it is because of its spiritual soul that the body made of matter becomes a living, human body; spirit and matter, in man, are not two natures united, but rather their union forms a single nature.

366 The Church teaches that every spiritual soul is created imme-diately by God – it is not 'produced' by the parents – and also that it is immortal: it does not perish when it separates from the body at death, and it will be reunited with the body at the final Resurrec-tion.[235] *1005* *997*

367 Sometimes the soul is distinguished from the spirit: St Paul for instance prays that God may sanctify his people 'wholly', with 'spirit and soul and body' kept sound and blameless at the Lord's coming.[236] The Church teaches that this distinction does not introduce a duality into the soul.[237] 'Spirit' signifies that from creation man is ordered to a supernatural end and that his soul can gratuitously be raised beyond all it deserves to communion with God.[238] *2083*

---

[230] Cf. *Mt* 16:25–26; *Jn* 15:13; *Acts* 2:41.
[231] Cf. *Mt* 10:28; 26:38; *Jn* 12:27; 2 *Macc* 6:30.
[232] Cf. 1 *Cor* 6:19–20; 15:44–45.
[233] *GS* 14 § 1; cf. *Dan* 3:57–80.
[234] Cf. Council of Vienne (1312): DS 902.
[235] Cf. Pius XII, *Humani generis*: DS 3896; Paul VI, *CPG* § 8; Lateran Council V

(1513): DS 1440.
[236] 1 *Th* 5:23.
[237] Cf. Council of Constantinople IV (870): DS 657.
[238] Cf. Vatican Council I, *Dei Filius*: DS 3005; *GS* 22 § 5; *Humani generis*: DS 3891.

478, 582,
1431,
764, 2517,
2562, 2843

368 The spiritual tradition of the Church also emphasizes the *heart*, in the biblical sense of the depths of one's being, where the person decides for or against God.[239]

2331-2336 ## III. 'Male and Female He Created Them'

Equality and difference willed by God

369 Man and woman have been *created*, which is to say, *willed* by God: on the one hand, in perfect equality as human persons; on the other, in their respective beings as man and woman. 'Being man' or 'being woman' is a reality which is good and willed by God: man and woman possess an inalienable dignity which comes to them immediately from God their Creator.[240] Man and woman are both with one and the same dignity 'in the image of God'. In their 'being-man' and 'being-woman', they reflect the Creator's wisdom and goodness.

239, 42 **370** In no way is God in man's image. He is neither man nor woman. God is pure spirit in which there is no place for the difference between the sexes. But the respective 'perfections' of man and woman reflect something of the infinite perfection of God: those of a mother and those of a father and husband.[241]

'Each for the other' – 'A unity in two'

1605 **371** God created man and woman *together* and willed each *for* the other. The Word of God gives us to understand this through various features of the sacred text. 'It is not good that the man should be alone. I will make him a helper fit for him.'[242] None of the animals can be man's partner.[243] The woman God 'fashions' from the man's rib and brings to him elicits on the man's part a cry of wonder, an exclamation of love and communion: 'This at last is bone of my bones and flesh of my flesh.'[244] Man discovers woman as another 'I', sharing the same humanity.

372 Man and woman were made 'for each other' – not that God left them half-made and incomplete: he created them to be a communion of persons, in which each can be 'helpmate' to the other, for they are equal as persons ('bone of my bones. . .') and complementary as masculine and feminine. In marriage God unites them in such a way that, by forming 'one flesh',[245] they can transmit
1652, 2366 human life: 'Be fruitful and multiply, and fill the earth.'[246] By

---

[239] Cf. *Jer* 31:33; *Dt* 6:5; 29:3; *Is* 29:13;
  Ezek 36:26; *Mt* 6:21; *Lk* 8:15; *Rom* 5:5.
[240] Cf. *Gen* 2:7, 22.
[241] Cf. *Is* 49:14-15; 66:13; *Ps* 131:2-3;
  Hos 11:1-4; *Jer* 3:4-19.
[242] *Gen* 2:18.
[243] *Gen* 2:19-20.
[244] *Gen* 2:23.
[245] *Gen* 2:24.
[246] *Gen* 1:28.

transmitting human life to their descendants, man and woman as spouses and parents co-operate in a unique way in the Creator's work.[247]

373 In God's plan man and woman have the vocation of 'subduing' the earth[248] as stewards of God. This sovereignty is not to be an arbitrary and destructive domination. God calls man and *307* woman, made in the image of the Creator 'who loves everything that exists',[249] to share in his providence toward other creatures; hence their responsibility for the world God has entrusted to them. *2415*

IV. Man in Paradise

374 The first man was not only created good, but was also established in friendship with his Creator and in harmony with himself *54* and with the creation around him, in a state that would be surpassed only by the glory of the new creation in Christ.

375 The Church, interpreting the symbolism of biblical language in an authentic way, in the light of the New Testament and Tradition, teaches that our first parents, Adam and Eve, were constituted in an original 'state of holiness and justice'.[250] This grace of original holiness was 'to share in. . .divine life'.[251]   *1997*

376 By the radiance of this grace all dimensions of man's life were confirmed. As long as he remained in the divine intimacy, man would not have to suffer or die.[252] The inner harmony of the *1008, 1502* human person, the harmony between man and woman,[253] and finally the harmony between the first couple and all creation, comprised the state called 'original justice'.

377 The 'mastery' over the world that God offered man from the beginning was realized above all within man himself: *mastery of self*. The first man was unimpaired and ordered in his whole being because he was free from the triple concupiscence[254] that subju- *2514* gates him to the pleasures of the senses, covetousness for earthly goods, and self-assertion, contrary to the dictates of reason.

378 The sign of man's familiarity with God is that God places him in the garden.[255] There he lives 'to till it and keep it'. Work is not *2427* yet a burden,[256] but rather the collaboration of man and woman with God in perfecting the visible creation.   *2415*

---

[247] Cf. GS 50 § 1.
[248] Gen 1:28.
[249] Wis 11:24.
[250] Cf. Council of Trent (1546): DS 1511.
[251] Cf. LG 2.
[252] Cf. Gen 2:17; 3:16, 19.
[253] Cf. Gen 2:25.
[254] Cf. 1 Jn 2:16.
[255] Cf. Gen 2:8.
[256] Gen 2:15; cf. 3:17–19.

379 This entire harmony of original justice, foreseen for man in God's plan, will be lost by the sin of our first parents.

IN BRIEF

380 '*Father,... you formed man in your own likeness and set him over the whole world to serve you, his creator, and to rule over all creatures' (Roman Missal, EP IV, 118).*

381 *Man is predestined to reproduce the image of God's Son made man, the 'image of the invisible God' (Col 1:15), so that Christ shall be the first-born of a multitude of brothers and sisters (cf. Eph 1:3–6; Rom 8:29).*

382 *'Man, though made of body and soul, is a unity' (GS 14 § 1). The doctrine of the faith affirms that the spiritual and immortal soul is created immediately by God.*

383 *'God did not create man a solitary being. From the beginning, "male and female he created them" (Gen 1:27). This partnership of man and woman constitutes the first form of communion between persons' (GS 12 § 4).*

384 *Revelation makes known to us the state of original holiness and justice of man and woman before sin: from their friendship with God flowed the happiness of their existence in paradise.*

Paragraph 7. The Fall

385 God is infinitely good and all his works are good. Yet no one can escape the experience of suffering or the evils in nature which seem to be linked to the limitations proper to creatures: and above all to the question of moral evil. Where does evil come from? 'I *309* sought whence evil comes and there was no solution', said St Augustine,[257] and his own painful quest would only be resolved by his conversion to the living God. For 'the mystery of lawlessness' is clarified only in the light of the 'mystery of our religion'.[258] The revelation of divine love in Christ manifested at the *457, 1848* same time the extent of evil and the superabundance of grace.[259] We must therefore approach the question of the origin of evil by *539* fixing the eyes of our faith on him who alone is its conqueror.[260]

I. Where Sin Abounded, Grace Abounded All the More

The reality of sin

386 Sin is present in human history; any attempt to ignore it or to

---

[257] St Augustine. *Conf.* 7, 7, 11: PL 32, 739.
[258] 2 *Th* 2:7; 1 *Tim* 3:16.
[259] Cf. *Rom* 5:20.
[260] Cf. *Lk* 11:21–22; *Jn* 16:11; 1 *Jn* 3:8.

give this dark reality other names would be futile. To try to understand what sin is, one must first recognize *the profound relation of man to God*, for only in this relationship is the evil of sin unmasked *1847* in its true identity as humanity's rejection of God and opposition to him, even as it continues to weigh heavy on human life and history.

387 Only the light of divine Revelation clarifies the reality of sin and particularly of the sin committed at mankind's origins. Without the knowledge Revelation gives of God we cannot recognize *1848* sin clearly and are tempted to explain it as merely a developmental flaw, a psychological weakness, a mistake, or the necessary consequence of an inadequate social structure, etc. Only in the knowledge of God's plan for man can we grasp that sin is an abuse of the *1739* freedom that God gives to created persons so that they are capable of loving him and loving one another.

Original sin – an essential truth of the faith

388 With the progress of Revelation, the reality of sin is also illuminated. Although to some extent the People of God in the Old Testament had tried to understand the pathos of the human *431* condition in the light of the history of the fall narrated in *Genesis*, *208* they could not grasp this story's ultimate meaning, which is revealed only in the light of the death and Resurrection of Jesus Christ.[261] We must know Christ as the source of grace in order to know Adam as the source of sin. The Spirit-Paraclete, sent by the *359* risen Christ, came to 'convict the world concerning sin',[262] by *729* revealing him who is its Redeemer.

389 The doctrine of original sin is, so to speak, the 'reverse side' of the Good News that Jesus is the Saviour of all men, that all need salvation and that salvation is offered to all through Christ. The *422* Church, which has the mind of Christ,[263] knows very well that we cannot tamper with the revelation of original sin without undermining the mystery of Christ.

How to read the account of the fall

390 The account of the fall in *Genesis* 3 uses figurative language, *289* but affirms a primeval event, a deed that took place *at the beginning of the history of man*.[264] Revelation gives us the certainty of faith that

---

[261] Cf. *Rom* 5:12–21.   [263] Cf. 1 *Cor* 2:16.
[262] *Jn* 16:8.   [264] Cf. *GS* 13 § 1.

the whole of human history is marked by the original fault freely committed by our first parents.[265]

II. The Fall of the Angels

391 Behind the disobedient choice of our first parents lurks a seductive voice, opposed to God, which makes them fall into death out of envy.[266] Scripture and the Church's Tradition see in this being a fallen angel, called 'Satan' or the 'devil'.[267] The Church teaches that Satan was at first a good angel, made by God: 'The devil and the other demons were indeed created naturally good by God, but they became evil by their own doing.'[268]

2538

392 Scripture speaks of a *sin* of these angels.[269] This 'fall' consists in the free choice of these created spirits, who radically and irrevocably *rejected* God and his reign. We find a reflection of that rebellion in the tempter's words to our first parents: 'You will be like God.'[270] The devil 'has sinned from the beginning'; he is 'a liar and the father of lies'.[271]

1850

393 It is the *irrevocable* character of their choice, and not a defect in the infinite divine mercy, that makes the angels' sin unforgivable. 'There is no repentance for the angels after their fall, just as there is no repentance for men after death.'[272]

1033–1037
1022

394 Scripture witnesses to the disastrous influence of the one Jesus calls 'a murderer from the beginning', who would even try to divert Jesus from the mission received from his Father.[273] 'The reason the Son of God appeared was to destroy the works of the devil.'[274] In its consequences the gravest of these works was the mendacious seduction that led man to disobey God.

538–540
550

2846–2849

395 The power of Satan is, nonetheless, not infinite. He is only a creature, powerful from the fact that he is pure spirit, but still a creature. He cannot prevent the building up of God's reign. Although Satan may act in the world out of hatred for God and his kingdom in Christ Jesus, and although his action may cause grave injuries – of a spiritual nature and, indirectly, even of a physical nature – to each man and to society, the action is permitted by divine providence which with strength and gentleness guides

309

1673

412

---

265 Cf. Council of Trent: DS 1513; Pius XII: DS 3897; Paul VI: AAS 58 (1966), 654.
266 Cf. Gen 3:1–5; Wis 2:24.
267 Cf. Jn 8:44; Rev 12:9.
268 Lateran Council IV (1215): DS 800.
269 Cf. 2 Pt 2:4.

270 Gen 3:5.
271 1 Jn 3:8; Jn 8:44.
272 St John Damascene, De fide orth. 2, 4: PG 94, 877.
273 Jn 8:44; cf. Mt 4:1–11.
274 1 Jn 3:8.

human and cosmic history. It is a great mystery that providence should permit diabolical activity, but 'we know that in everything *2850–2854* God works for good with those who love him.'[275]

III. Original Sin

Freedom put to the test

396 God created man in his image and established him in his friendship. A spiritual creature, man can live this friendship only in free submission to God. The prohibition against eating 'of the tree *1730, 311* of the knowledge of good and evil' spells this out: 'for in the day that you eat of it, you shall die.'[276] The 'tree of the knowledge of good and evil'[277] symbolically evokes the insurmountable limits that man, being a creature, must freely recognize and respect with trust. Man is dependent on his Creator, and subject to the laws of creation and to the moral norms that govern the use of freedom. *301*

Man's first sin

397 Man, tempted by the devil, let his trust in his Creator die in *1707, 2541* his heart and, abusing his freedom, *disobeyed* God's command. This is what man's first sin consisted of.[278] All subsequent sin would be disobedience toward God and lack of trust in his *1850, 215* goodness.

398 In that sin man *preferred* himself to God and by that very act scorned him. He chose himself over and against God, against the *2084* requirements of his creaturely status and therefore against his own good. Constituted in a state of holiness, man was destined to be fully 'divinized' by God in glory. Seduced by the devil, he wanted to 'be like God', but 'without God, before God, and not in accord- *2113* ance with God'.[279]

399 Scripture portrays the tragic consequences of this first dis-obedience. Adam and Eve immediately lose the grace of original holiness.[280] They become afraid of the God of whom they have conceived a distorted image – that of a God jealous of his preroga-tives.[281]

400 The harmony in which they had found themselves, thanks to original justice, is now destroyed: the control of the soul's spiritual faculties over the body is shattered; the union of man and woman *1607*

---

[275] *Rom* 8:28.
[276] *Gen* 2:17.
[277] *Gen* 2:17.
[278] Cf. *Gen* 3:1–11; *Rom* 5:19.

[279] St Maximus the Confessor, *Ambigua*: PG 91, 1156C; cf. *Gen* 3:5.
[280] Cf. *Rom* 3:23.
[281] Cf. *Gen* 3:5–10.

2514 becomes subject to tensions, their relations henceforth marked by lust and domination.[282] Harmony with creation is broken: visible creation has become alien and hostile to man.[283] Because of man, creation is now subject 'to its bondage to decay'.[284] Finally, the consequence explicitly foretold for this disobedience will come true: man will 'return to the ground',[285] for out of it he was taken.
602, 1008 *Death makes its entrance into human history.*[286]

1865 401 After that first sin, the world is virtually inundated by sin.
2259 There is Cain's murder of his brother Abel and the universal corruption which follows in the wake of sin. Likewise, sin frequently manifests itself in the history of Israel, especially as infidelity to the God of the Covenant and as transgression of the Law of Moses. And even after Christ's atonement, sin raises its head in countless ways among Christians.[287] Scripture and the Church's Tradition
1739 continually recall the presence and *universality of sin in man's history*:

> What Revelation makes known to us is confirmed by our own experience. For when man looks into his own heart he finds that he is drawn towards what is wrong and sunk in many evils which cannot come from his good creator. Often refusing to acknowledge God as his source, man has also upset the relationship which should link him to his last end; and at the same time he has broken the right order that should reign within himself as well as between himself and other men and all creatures.[288]

The consequences of Adam's sin for humanity

402 All men are implicated in Adam's sin, as St Paul affirms: 'By one man's disobedience many (that is, all men) were made sinners': 'sin came into the world through one man and death through sin, and so death spread to all men because all men sinned...'[289] The
430, 605 Apostle contrasts the universality of sin and death with the universality of salvation in Christ. 'Then as one man's trespass led to condemnation for all men, so one man's act of righteousness leads to acquittal and life for all men.'[290]

403 Following St Paul, the Church has always taught that the
2606 overwhelming misery which oppresses men and their inclination towards evil and death cannot be understood apart from their connection with Adam's sin and the fact that he has transmitted to us a sin with which we are all born afflicted, a sin which is the

---

[282] Cf. *Gen* 3:7–16.
[283] Cf. *Gen* 3:17, 19.
[284] *Rom* 8:21.
[285] *Gen* 3:19; cf. 2:17.
[286] Cf. *Rom* 5:12.

[287] Cf. *Gen* 4:3–15; 6:5, 12; *Rom* 1:18–32; 1 *Cor* 1 – 6; *Rev* 2 – 3.
[288] *GS* 13 § 1.
[289] *Rom* 5:12, 19.
[290] *Rom* 5:18.

'death of the soul'.[291] Because of this certainty of faith, the Church baptizes for the remission of sins even tiny infants who have not *1250* committed personal sin.[292]

404 How did the sin of Adam become the sin of all his descendants? The whole human race is in Adam 'as one body of one man'.[293] By this 'unity of the human race' all men are implicated in *360* Adam's sin, as all are implicated in Christ's justice. Still, the transmission of original sin is a mystery that we cannot fully understand. But we do know by Revelation that Adam had received *50* original holiness and justice not for himself alone, but for all human nature. By yielding to the tempter, Adam and Eve committed a *personal sin*, but this sin affected *the human nature* that they would then transmit *in a fallen state*.[294] It is a sin which will be transmitted by propagation to all mankind, that is, by the transmission of a human nature deprived of original holiness and justice. And that is why original sin is called 'sin' only in an analogical sense: it is a sin 'contracted' and not 'committed' – a state and not an act.

405 Although it is proper to each individual,[295] original sin does not have the character of a personal fault in any of Adam's descendants. It is a deprivation of original holiness and justice, but human nature has not been totally corrupted: it is wounded in the natural powers proper to it, subject to ignorance, suffering and the dominion of death, and inclined to sin – an inclination to evil that is called 'concupiscence'. Baptism, by imparting the life of Christ's *2515* grace, erases original sin and turns a man back towards God, but *1264* the consequences for nature, weakened and inclined to evil, persist in man and summon him to spiritual battle.

406 The Church's teaching on the transmission of original sin was articulated more precisely in the fifth century, especially under the impulse of St Augustine's reflections against Pelagianism, and in the sixteenth century, in opposition to the Protestant Reformation. Pelagius held that man could, by the natural power of free will and without the necessary help of God's grace, lead a morally good life; he thus reduced the influence of Adam's fault to bad example. The first Protestant reformers, on the contrary, taught that original sin has radically perverted man and destroyed his freedom; they identified the sin inherited by each man with the tendency to evil (*concupiscentia*), which would be insurmountable. The Church pronounced on the meaning of the data of Revelation on original sin especially at the second Council of Orange (529)[296] and at the Council of Trent (1546).[297]

---

[291] Cf. Council of Trent: DS 1512.
[292] Cf. Council of Trent: DS 1514.
[293] St Thomas Aquinas, *De malo* 4, 1.
[294] Cf. Council of Trent: DS 1511–1512.

[295] Cf. Council of Trent: DS 1513.
[296] DS 371–372.
[297] Cf. DS 1510–1516.

A hard battle. . .

407 The doctrine of original sin, closely connected with that of
2015 redemption by Christ, provides lucid discernment of man's situation and activity in the world. By our first parents' sin, the devil
2852 has acquired a certain domination over man, even though man
remains free. Original sin entails 'captivity under the power of
him who thenceforth had the power of death, that is, the devil'.[298]
Ignorance of the fact that man has a wounded nature inclined to
evil gives rise to serious errors in the areas of education, politics,
1888 social action[299] and morals.

408 The consequences of original sin and of all men's personal sins
put the world as a whole in the sinful condition aptly described in
St John's expression, 'the sin of the world'.[300] This expression can
also refer to the negative influence exerted on people by commu-
1865 nal situations and social structures that are the fruit of men's sins.[301]

409 This dramatic situation of 'the whole world [which] is in the
2516 power of the evil one'[302] makes man's life a battle:

> The whole of man's history has been the story of dour combat with the
> powers of evil, stretching, so our Lord tells us, from the very dawn of
> history until the last day. Finding himself in the midst of the battlefield
> man has to struggle to do what is right, and it is at great cost to himself,
> and aided by God's grace, that he succeeds in achieving his own inner
> integrity.[303]

IV. 'You Did Not Abandon Him to the Power of Death'

410 After his fall, man was not abandoned by God. On the contrary, God calls him and in a mysterious way heralds the coming
55, 705 victory over evil and his restoration from his fall.[304] This passage
1609, 2568 in *Genesis* is called the *Protoevangelium* ('first gospel'): the first
675 announcement of the Messiah and Redeemer, of a battle between
the serpent and the Woman, and of the final victory of a descend-
ant of hers.

411 The Christian tradition sees in this passage an announcement
359, 615 of the 'New Adam' who, because he 'became obedient unto death,
even death on a cross', makes amends superabundantly for the
disobedience of Adam.[305] Furthermore many Fathers and Doctors

---

[298] Council of Trent (1546): DS 1511; cf.
    Heb 2:14.
[299] Cf. John Paul II, *CA* 25.
[300] *Jn* 1:29.
[301] Cf. John Paul II, *RP* 16.

[302] 1 *Jn* 5:19; cf. 1 *Pt* 5:8.
[303] *GS* 37 § 2.
[304] Cf. *Gen* 3:9, 15.
[305] Cf. 1 *Cor* 15:21–22, 45; Phil 2:8; *Rom*
    5:19–20.

of the Church have seen the woman announced in the 'Proto-evangelium' as Mary, the mother of Christ, the 'new Eve'. Mary benefited first of all and uniquely from Christ's victory over sin: she was preserved from all stain of original sin and by a special *491* grace of God committed no sin of any kind during her whole earthly life.[306]

412 But *why did God not prevent the first man from sinning?* St Leo *310* the Great responds, 'Christ's inexpressible grace gave us blessings better than those the demon's envy had taken away.'[307] And St *395* Thomas Aquinas wrote, 'There is nothing to prevent human nature's being raised up to something greater, even after sin; God permits evil in order to draw forth some greater good. Thus St *272* Paul says, "Where sin increased, grace abounded all the more"; and the *Exsultet* sings, "O happy fault,... which gained for us so great a Redeemer!" '[308]   *1994*

IN BRIEF

413 'God did not make death, and he does not delight in the death of the living... It was through the devil's envy that death entered the world' (Wis 1:13; 2:24).

414 Satan or the devil and the other demons are fallen angels who have freely refused to serve God and his plan. Their choice against God is definitive. They try to associate man in their revolt against God.

415 'Although set by God in a state of rectitude man, enticed by the evil one, abused his freedom at the very start of history. He lifted himself up against God, and sought to attain his goal apart from him' (GS 13 § 1).

416 By his sin Adam, as the first man, lost the original holiness and justice he had received from God, not only for himself but for all human beings.

417 Adam and Eve transmitted to their descendants human nature wounded by their own first sin and hence deprived of original holiness and justice; this deprivation is called 'original sin'.

418 As a result of original sin, human nature is weakened in its powers, subject to ignorance, suffering and the domination of death, and inclined to sin (this inclination is called 'concupiscence').

---

[306] Cf. Pius IX, *Ineffabilis Deus*: DS 2803; Council of Trent: DS 1573.
[307] St Leo the Great, *Sermo* 73, 4: PL 54, 396.

[308] St Thomas Aquinas, *STh* III, 1, 3, ad 3; cf. *Rom* 5:20.

419 *'We therefore hold, with the Council of Trent, that original sin is transmitted with human nature, "by propagation, not by imitation" and that it is... "proper to each"'* (Paul VI, CPG § 16).

420 *The victory that Christ won over sin has given us greater blessings than those which sin had taken from us: 'where sin increased, grace abounded all the more'* (Rom 5:20).

421 *Christians believe that 'the world has been established and kept in being by the Creator's love; has fallen into slavery to sin but has been set free by Christ, crucified and risen to break the power of the evil one...'* (GS 2 § 2).

Chapter Two

I BELIEVE IN JESUS CHRIST, THE ONLY SON OF GOD

The Good News: God has sent his Son

422 'But when the time had fully come, God sent forth his Son, born of a woman, born under the law, to redeem those who were under the law, so that we might receive adoption as sons.'[1] This is 'the gospel of Jesus Christ, the Son of God':[2] God has visited his people. He has fulfilled the promise he made to Abraham and his descendants. He acted far beyond all expectation – he has sent his own 'beloved Son'.[3]

423 We believe and confess that Jesus of Nazareth, born a Jew of a daughter of Israel at Bethlehem at the time of King Herod the Great and the emperor Caesar Augustus, a carpenter by trade, who died crucified in Jerusalem under the procurator Pontius Pilate during the reign of the emperor Tiberius, is the eternal Son of God made man. He 'came from God',[4] 'descended from heaven',[5] and 'came in the flesh'.[6] For 'the Word became flesh and dwelt among us, full of grace and truth; we have beheld his glory, glory as of the only Son from the Father... And from his fullness have we all received, grace upon grace.'[7]

424 Moved by the grace of the Holy Spirit and drawn by the Father, we believe in Jesus and confess: 'You are the Christ, the Son

*Marginal references: 389 (at 422); 2763 (at 422); 683 (at 424).*

---

[1] *Gal* 4:4–5.
[2] *Mk* 1:1.
[3] *Mk* 1:11; cf. *Lk* 1:55, 68.
[4] *Jn* 13:3.
[5] *Jn* 3:13; 6:33.
[6] 1 *Jn* 4:2.
[7] *Jn* 1:14, 16.

of the living God.'[8] On the rock of this faith confessed by St Peter, *552*
Christ built his Church.[9]

'To preach. . . the unsearchable riches of Christ'[10]

425 The transmission of the Christian faith consists primarily in
proclaiming Jesus Christ in order to lead others to faith in him.
From the beginning, the first disciples burned with the desire to
proclaim Christ: 'We cannot but speak of what we have seen and
heard.'[11] And they invite people of every era to enter into the joy *850, 858*
of their communion with Christ:

> That which was from the beginning, which we have heard, which we
> have seen with our eyes, which we have looked upon and touched with
> our hands, concerning the word of life – the life was made manifest, and
> we saw it, and testify to it, and proclaim to you the eternal life which was
> with the Father and was made manifest to us – that which we have seen
> and heard we proclaim also to you, so that you may have fellowship with
> us; and our fellowship is with the Father and with his Son Jesus Christ.
> And we are writing this that our joy may be complete.[12]

At the heart of catechesis: Christ

426 'At the heart of catechesis we find, in essence, a Person, the *1698*
Person of Jesus of Nazareth, the only Son from the Father. . .who
suffered and died for us and who now, after rising, is living with us
forever.'[13] To catechize is 'to reveal in the Person of Christ the
whole of God's eternal design reaching fulfilment in that Person. It
is to seek to understand the meaning of Christ's actions and words *513*
and of the signs worked by him.'[14] Catechesis aims at putting
'people . . . in communion . . . with Jesus Christ: only he can lead us
to the love of the Father in the Spirit and make us share in the life of *260*
the Holy Trinity.'[15]

427 In catechesis 'Christ, the Incarnate Word and Son of God,. . .
is taught – everything else is taught with reference to him – and it *2145*
is Christ alone who teaches – anyone else teaches to the extent that
he is Christ's spokesman, enabling Christ to teach with his lips. . .
Every catechist should be able to apply to himself the mysterious
words of Jesus: "My teaching is not mine, but his who sent *876*
me." '[16]

---

[8] Mt 16:16.
[9] Cf. Mt 16:18; St Leo the Great, Sermo 4,
3: PL 54, 150–152; 51, 1: PL 54,
309B; 62, 2: PL 54, 350–351; 83, 3: PL
54, 431–432.
[10] Eph 3:8.

[11] Acts 4:20.
[12] 1 Jn 1:1–4.
[13] CT 5.
[14] CT 5.
[15] CT 5.
[16] CT 6; cf. Jn 7:16.

428 Whoever is called 'to teach Christ' must first seek 'the surpassing worth of knowing Christ Jesus'; he must suffer 'the loss of all things. . .' in order to 'gain Christ and be found in him', and 'to know him and the power of his resurrection, and [to] share his sufferings, becoming like him in his death, that if possible [he] may attain the resurrection from the dead'.[17]

429 From this loving knowledge of Christ springs the desire to proclaim him, to 'evangelize', and to lead others to the 'yes' of faith in Jesus Christ. But at the same time the need to know this faith better makes itself felt. To this end, following the order of the Creed, Jesus' principal titles – 'Christ', 'Son of God', and 'Lord' (*article 2*) – will be presented. The Creed next confesses the chief mysteries of his life – those of his Incarnation (*article 3*), Paschal mystery (*articles 4 and 5*) and glorification (*articles 6 and 7*).

851

Article 2

'AND IN JESUS CHRIST, HIS ONLY SON, OUR LORD'

I. Jesus

430 Jesus means in Hebrew: 'God saves.' At the annunciation, the angel Gabriel gave him the name Jesus as his proper name, which expresses both his identity and his mission.[18] Since God alone can forgive sins, it is God who, in Jesus his eternal Son made man, 'will save his people from their sins'.[19] In Jesus, God recapitulates all of his history of salvation on behalf of men.

210

402

431 In the history of salvation God was not content to deliver Israel 'out of the house of bondage'[20] by bringing them out of Egypt. He also saves them from their sin. Because sin is always an offence against God, only he can forgive it.[21] For this reason Israel, becoming more and more aware of the universality of sin, will no longer be able to seek salvation except by invoking the name of the Redeemer God.[22]

1850, 1441

388

432 The name 'Jesus' signifies that the very name of God is present in the person of his Son, made man for the universal and definitive redemption from sins. It is the divine name that alone brings salvation, and henceforth all can invoke his name, for Jesus united himself to all men through his Incarnation,[23] so that 'there is no

2666

589

389

---

[17] *Phil* 3:8–11.
[18] Cf. *Lk* 1:31.
[19] *Mt* 1:21; cf. 2:7.
[20] *Dt* 5:6.

[21] Cf. *Ps* 51:4, 12.
[22] Cf. *Ps* 79:9.
[23] Cf. *Jn* 3:18; *Acts* 2:21; 5:41; 3 *Jn* 7; *Rom* 10:6–13.

other name under heaven given among men by which we must be 161 saved.'[24]

433 The name of the Saviour God was invoked only once in the year by the high priest in atonement for the sins of Israel, after he had sprinkled the mercy seat in the Holy of Holies with the sacri- 615 ficial blood. The mercy seat was the place of God's presence.[25] When St Paul speaks of Jesus whom 'God put forward as an expiation by his blood', he means that in Christ's humanity 'God was in Christ reconciling the world to himself.'[26]

434 Jesus' Resurrection glorifies the name of the Saviour God, for from that time on it is the name of Jesus that fully manifests the 2812 supreme power of the 'name which is above every name'.[27] The evil spirits fear his name; in his name his disciples perform miracles, for the Father grants all they ask in this name.[28] 2614

435 The name of Jesus is at the heart of Christian prayer. All liturgical prayers conclude with the words 'through our Lord Jesus Christ'. The *Hail Mary* reaches its high point in the words 2676 'blessed is the fruit of thy womb, Jesus.' The Eastern prayer of the 2667–2668 heart, the *Jesus Prayer*, says: 'Lord Jesus Christ, Son of God, have mercy on me, a sinner.' Many Christians, such as St Joan of Arc, have died with the one word 'Jesus' on their lips.

II. Christ

436 The word '*Christ*' comes from the Greek translation of the Hebrew *Messiah*, which means 'anointed'. It became the name 690, 695 proper to Jesus only because he accomplished perfectly the divine mission that 'Christ' signifies. In effect, in Israel those consecrated to God for a mission that he gave were anointed in his name. This was the case for kings, for priests and, in rare instances, for prophets.[29] This had to be the case all the more so for the Messiah whom God would send to inaugurate his kingdom definitively.[30] It was necessary that the Messiah be anointed by the Spirit of the Lord at once as king and priest, and also as prophet.[31] Jesus fulfilled the messianic hope of Israel in his threefold office of priest, prophet 711–716, and king. 783

---

[24] *Acts* 4:12; cf. 9:14; *Jas* 2:7.
[25] Cf. *Ex* 25:22; *Lev* 16:2, 15–16; *Num* 7:89; *Sir* 50:20; *Heb* 9:5, 7.
[26] *Rom* 3:25; 2 *Cor* 5:19.
[27] *Phil* 2:9–10; cf. *Jn* 12:28.
[28] Cf. *Acts* 16:16–18; 19:13–16; *Mk* 16:17; *Jn* 15:16.

[29] Cf. *Ex* 29:7; *Lev* 8:12; 1 *Sam* 9:16; 10:1; 16:1, 12–13; 1 *Kings* 1:39; 19:16.
[30] Cf. *Ps* 2:2; *Acts* 4:26–27.
[31] Cf. *Is* 11:2; 61:1; *Zech* 4:14; 6:13; *Lk* 4:16–21.

525   437 To the shepherds, the angel announced the birth of Jesus as the
Messiah promised to Israel: 'To you is born this day in the city of
486   David a Saviour, who is Christ the Lord.'[32] From the beginning he
was 'the one whom the Father consecrated and sent into the
world', conceived as 'holy' in Mary's virginal womb.[33] God called
Joseph to 'take Mary as your wife, for that which is conceived in
her is of the Holy Spirit', so that Jesus, 'who is called Christ',
should be born of Joseph's spouse into the messianic lineage of
David.[34]

438 Jesus' messianic consecration reveals his divine mission, 'for
727   the name "Christ" implies "he who anointed", "he who was
anointed" and "the very anointing with which he was anointed".
The one who anointed is the Father, the one who was anointed is
the Son, and he was anointed with the Spirit who is the anointing.'[35] His eternal messianic consecration was revealed during the
535   time of his earthly life at the moment of his baptism by John, when
'God anointed Jesus of Nazareth with the Holy Spirit and with
power', 'that he might be revealed to Israel'[36] as its Messiah. His
works and words will manifest him as 'the Holy One of God'.[37]

439 Many Jews and even certain Gentiles who shared their hope
528–529   recognized in Jesus the fundamental attributes of the messianic
547   'Son of David', promised by God to Israel.[38] Jesus accepted his
rightful title of Messiah, though with some reserve because it was
understood by some of his contemporaries in too human a sense, as
essentially political.[39]

440 Jesus accepted Peter's profession of faith, which acknowledged him to be the Messiah, by announcing the imminent Pas-
552   sion of the Son of Man.[40] He unveiled the authentic content of his
messianic kingship both in the transcendent identity of the Son of
Man 'who came down from heaven', and in his redemptive mission as the suffering Servant: 'The Son of Man came not to be
served but to serve, and to give his life as a ransom for many.'[41]
550, 445   Hence the true meaning of his kingship is revealed only when he is
raised high on the cross.[42] Only after his Resurrection will Peter be
able to proclaim Jesus' messianic kingship to the People of God:

[32] Lk 2:11.
[33] Jn 10:36; cf. Lk 1:35.
[34] Mt 1:20; cf. 1:16; Rom 1:1; 2 Tim 2:8;
    Rev 22:16.
[35] St Irenaeus, Adv. haeres. 3, 18, 3: PG
    7/1, 934.
[36] Acts 10:38; Jn 1:31.
[37] Mk 1:24; Jn 6:69; Acts 3:14.

[38] Cf. Mt 2:2; 9:27; 12:23; 15:22; 20:30;
    21:9, 15.
[39] Cf. Jn 4:25–26; 6:15; 11:27; Mt
    22:41–46; Lk 24:21.
[40] Cf. Mt 16:16–23.
[41] Jn 3:13; Mt 20:28; cf. Jn 6:62; Dan 7:13;
    Is 53:10–12.
[42] Cf. Jn 19:19–22; Lk 23:39–43.

'Let all the house of Israel therefore know assuredly that God has made him both Lord and Christ, this Jesus whom you crucified.'[43]

III. The Only Son of God

441 In the Old Testament, 'son of God' is a title given to the angels, the Chosen People, the children of Israel, and their kings.[44] It signifies an adoptive sonship that establishes a relationship of particular intimacy between God and his creature. When the promised Messiah-King is called 'son of God', it does not necessarily imply that he was more than human, according to the literal meaning of these texts. Those who called Jesus 'son of God', as the Messiah of Israel, perhaps meant nothing more than this.[45]

442 Such is not the case for Simon Peter when he confesses Jesus as 'the Christ, the Son of the living God', for Jesus responds solemnly: 'Flesh and blood has not *revealed* this to you, but *my Father* who is in heaven.'[46] Similarly Paul will write, regarding his conversion on the road to Damascus, 'When he who had set me apart before I was born, and had called me through his grace, was pleased to reveal his Son to me, in order that I might preach him among the Gentiles...'[47] 'And in the synagogues immediately [Paul] proclaimed Jesus, saying, "He is the Son of God." '[48] From the beginning this acknowledgment of Christ's divine sonship will be the centre of the apostolic faith, first professed by Peter as the Church's foundation.[49] **552** **424**

443 Peter could recognize the transcendent character of the Messiah's divine sonship because Jesus had clearly allowed it to be so understood. To his accusers' question before the Sanhedrin, 'Are you the Son of God, then?' Jesus answered, 'You say that I am.'[50] Well before this, Jesus referred to himself as 'the Son' who knows the Father, as distinct from the 'servants' God had earlier sent to his people; he is superior even to the angels.[51] He distinguished his sonship from that of his disciples by never saying 'our Father', except to command them: 'You, then, pray like this: "Our Father" ', and he emphasized this distinction, saying 'my Father and your Father'.[52] **2786**

---

[43] *Acts* 2:36.
[44] Cf. *Dt* 14:1; (LXX) 32:8; *Job* 1:6; *Ex* 4:22; *Hos* 2:1; 11:1; *Jer* 3:19; *Sir* 36:11; *Wis* 18:13; 2 *Sam* 7:14; *Ps* 82:6.
[45] Cf. 1 *Chr* 17:13; *Ps* 2:7; *Mt* 27:54; *Lk* 23:47.
[46] *Mt* 16:16–17.

[47] *Gal* 1:15–16.
[48] *Acts* 9:20.
[49] Cf. 1 *Th* 1:10; *Jn* 20:31; *Mt* 16:18.
[50] *Lk* 22:70; cf. *Mt* 26:64; *Mk* 14:61–62.
[51] Cf. *Mt* 11:27; 21:34–38; 24:36.
[52] *Mt* 5:48; 6:8–9; 7:21; *Lk* 11:13; *Jn* 20:17.

444 The Gospels report that at two solemn moments, the Baptism and the Transfiguration of Christ, the voice of the Father designates Jesus his 'beloved Son'.[53] Jesus calls himself the 'only Son of God', and by this title affirms his eternal pre-existence.[54] He asks for faith in 'the name of the only Son of God'.[55] In the centurion's exclamation before the crucified Christ, 'Truly this man was the Son of God',[56] that Christian confession is already heard. Only in the Paschal mystery can the believer give the title 'Son of God' its full meaning.

536, 554

445 After his Resurrection, Jesus' divine sonship becomes manifest in the power of his glorified humanity. He was 'designated Son of God in power according to the Spirit of holiness by his Resurrection from the dead'.[57] The apostles can confess: 'We have beheld his glory, glory as of the only Son from the Father, full of grace and truth.'[58]

653

IV. LORD

446 In the Greek translation of the Old Testament, the ineffable Hebrew name YHWH, by which God revealed himself to Moses,[59] is rendered as *Kyrios*, 'Lord'. From then on, '*Lord*' becomes the more usual name by which to indicate the divinity of Israel's God. The New Testament uses this full sense of the title 'Lord' both for the Father and – what is new – for Jesus, who is thereby recognized as God Himself.[60]

209

447 Jesus ascribes this title to himself in a veiled way when he disputes with the Pharisees about the meaning of *Psalm* 110, but also in an explicit way when he addresses his apostles.[61] Throughout his public life, he demonstrated his divine sovereignty by works of power over nature, illnesses, demons, death and sin.

548

448 Very often in the Gospels people address Jesus as 'Lord'. This title testifies to the respect and trust of those who approach him for help and healing.[62] At the prompting of the Holy Spirit, 'Lord' expresses the recognition of the divine mystery of Jesus.[63] In the encounter with the risen Jesus, this title becomes adoration: 'My Lord and my God!' It thus takes on a connotation of love and

208, 683

---

[53] Cf. *Mt* 3:17; cf. 17:5.
[54] *Jn* 3:16; cf. 10:36.
[55] *Jn* 3:18.
[56] *Mk* 15:39.
[57] *Rom* 1:3; cf. *Acts* 13:33.
[58] *Jn* 1:14.

[59] Cf. *Ex* 3:14.
[60] Cf. 1 *Cor* 2:8.
[61] Cf. *Mt* 22:41–46; cf. *Acts* 2:34–36; *Heb* 1:13; *Jn* 13:13.
[62] Cf. *Mt* 8:2; 14:30; 15:22; *et al.*
[63] Cf. *Lk* 1:43; 2:11.

affection that remains proper to the Christian tradition: 'It is the *641* Lord!'[64]

449 By attributing to Jesus the divine title 'Lord', the first confessions of the Church's faith affirm from the beginning that the power, honour and glory due to God the Father are due also to Jesus, because 'he was in the form of God',[65] and the Father mani- *461* fested the sovereignty of Jesus by raising him from the dead and *653* exalting him into his glory.[66]

450 From the beginning of Christian history, the assertion of Christ's lordship over the world and over history has implicitly *668–672* recognized that man should not submit his personal freedom in an absolute manner to any earthly power, but only to God the Father and the Lord Jesus Christ: Caesar is not 'the Lord'.[67] 'The *2242* Church. . . believes that the key, the centre and the purpose of the whole of man's history is to be found in its Lord and Master.'[68]

451 Christian prayer is characterized by the title 'Lord', whether in the invitation to prayer ('The Lord be with you'), its conclusion ('through Christ our Lord') or the exclamation full of trust and *2664–2665* hope: *Maran atha* ('Our Lord, come!') or *Marana tha* ('Come, *2817* Lord!') – 'Amen. Come, Lord Jesus!'[69]

IN BRIEF

452 *The name Jesus means 'God saves'. The child born of the Virgin Mary is called Jesus, 'for he will save his people from their sins' (Mt 1:21): 'there is no other name under heaven given among men by which we must be saved' (Acts 4:12).*

453 *The title 'Christ' means 'Anointed One' (Messiah). Jesus is the Christ, for 'God anointed Jesus of Nazareth with the Holy Spirit and with power' (Acts 10:38). He was the one 'who is to come' (Lk 7:19), the object of 'the hope of Israel' (Acts 28:20).*

454 *The title 'Son of God' signifies the unique and eternal relationship of Jesus Christ to God his Father: he is the only Son of the Father (cf. Jn 1:14, 18; 3:16, 18); he is God himself (cf. Jn 1:1). To be a Christian, one must believe that Jesus Christ is the Son of God (cf. Acts 8:37; 1 Jn 2:23).*

455 *The title 'Lord' indicates divine sovereignty. To confess or invoke Jesus as Lord is to believe in his divinity. 'No one can say "Jesus is Lord" except by the Holy Spirit' (1 Cor 12:3).*

---

[64] Jn 20:28; 21:7.
[65] Cf. Acts 2:34–36; Rom 9:5; Titus 2:13; Rev 5:13; Phil 2:6.
[66] Cf. Rom 10:9; 1 Cor 12:3; Phil 2:9–11.
[67] Cf. Rev 11:15; Mk 12:17; Acts 5:29.
[68] GS 10 § 3; cf. 45 § 2.
[69] 1 Cor 16:22; Rev 22:20.

Article 3

'HE WAS CONCEIVED BY THE POWER OF THE HOLY SPIRIT, AND WAS BORN OF THE VIRGIN MARY'

Paragraph 1. The Son of God Became Man

I. Why Did the Word Become Flesh?

456 With the Nicene Creed, we answer by confessing: '*For us men and for our salvation* he came down from heaven; by the power of the Holy Spirit, he became incarnate of the Virgin Mary, and was made man.'

457 The Word became flesh for us *in order to save us by reconciling us with God*, who 'loved us and sent his Son to be the expiation for our sins': 'the Father has sent his Son as the Saviour of the world', and 'he was revealed to take away sins':[70]

607

Sick, our nature demanded to be healed; fallen, to be raised up; dead, to rise again. We had lost the possession of the good; it was necessary for it to be given back to us. Closed in the darkness, it was necessary to bring us the light; captives, we awaited a Saviour; prisoners, help; slaves, a liberator. Are these things minor or insignificant? Did they not move God to descend to human nature and visit it, since humanity was in so miserable and unhappy a state?[71]

385

458 The Word became flesh *so that thus we might know God's love*: 'In this the love of God was made manifest among us, that God sent his only Son into the world, so that we might live through him.'[72] 'For God so loved the world that he gave his only Son, that whoever believes in him should not perish but have eternal life.'[73]

219

459 The Word became flesh *to be our model of holiness*: 'Take my yoke upon you, and learn from me.' 'I am the way, and the truth, and the life; no one comes to the Father, but by me.'[74] On the mountain of the Transfiguration, the Father commands: 'Listen to him!'[75] Jesus is the model for the Beatitudes and the norm of the new law: 'Love one another as I have loved you.'[76] This love implies an effective offering of oneself, after his example.[77]

520, 823

2012

717, 1965

460 The Word became flesh *to make us 'partakers of the divine nature'*:[78] 'For this is why the Word became man, and the Son of God became the Son of man: so that man, by entering into communion

1391

---

[70] 1 Jn 4:10; 4:14; 3:5.
[71] St Gregory of Nyssa, *Orat. catech.* 15: PG 45, 48B.
[72] 1 Jn 4:9.
[73] Jn 3:16.
[74] Mt 11:29; Jn 14:6.
[75] Mk 9:7; cf. Dt 6:4–5.
[76] Jn 15:12.
[77] Cf. Mk 8:34.
[78] 2 Pt 1:4.

with the Word and thus receiving divine sonship, might become a son of God.'[79] 'For the Son of God became man so that we might become God.'[80] 'The only-begotten Son of God, wanting to make us sharers in his divinity, assumed our nature, so that he, made man, might make men gods.'[81]

1265

1988

II. The Incarnation

461 Taking up St John's expression, 'The Word became flesh',[82] the Church calls 'Incarnation' the fact that the Son of God assumed a human nature in order to accomplish our salvation in it. In a hymn cited by St Paul, the Church sings the mystery of the Incarnation:

653, 661

449

> Have this mind among yourselves, which is yours in Christ Jesus, who, though he was in the form of God, did not count equality with God a thing to be grasped, but emptied himself, taking the form of a servant, being born in the likeness of men. And being found in human form he humbled himself and became obedient unto death, even death on a cross.[83]

462 The *Letter to the Hebrews* refers to the same mystery:

> Consequently, when Christ came into the world, he said, 'Sacrifices and offerings you have not desired, but a body have you prepared for me; in burnt offerings and sin offerings you have taken no pleasure. Then I said, Lo, I have come to do your will, O God.'[84]

463 Belief in the true Incarnation of the Son of God is the distinctive sign of Christian faith: 'By this you know the Spirit of God: every spirit which confesses that Jesus Christ has come in the flesh is of God.'[85] Such is the joyous conviction of the Church from her beginning whenever she sings 'the mystery of our religion': 'He was manifested in the flesh.'[86]

90

III. True God and True Man

464 The unique and altogether singular event of the Incarnation of the Son of God does not mean that Jesus Christ is part God and part man, nor does it imply that he is the result of a confused mixture of the divine and the human. He became truly man while remaining truly God. Jesus Christ is true God and true man.

---

[79] St Irenaeus, *Adv. haeres.* 3, 19, 1: PG 7/1, 939.
[80] St Athanasius, *De inc.* 54, 3: PG 25, 192B.
[81] St Thomas Aquinas, *Opusc.* 57, 1–4.
[82] *Jn* 1:14.

[83] *Phil* 2:5–8; cf. *LH*, Saturday, Canticle at Evening Prayer.
[84] *Heb* 10:5–7, citing *Ps* 40:6–8 ([7–9] LXX).
[85] 1 *Jn* 4:2.
[86] 1 *Tim* 3:16.

88 During the first centuries, the Church had to defend and clarify this truth of faith against the heresies that falsified it.

465 The first heresies denied not so much Christ's divinity as his true humanity (Gnostic Docetism). From apostolic times the Christian faith has insisted on the true incarnation of God's Son 'come in the flesh'.[87] But already in the third century, the Church in a council at Antioch had to affirm against Paul of Samosata that Jesus Christ is Son of God by nature and not by adoption. The first

242 ecumenical council of Nicaea in 325 confessed in its Creed that the Son of God is 'begotten, not made, of the same substance (*homoousios*) as the Father', and condemned Arius, who had affirmed that the Son of God 'came to be from things that were not' and that he was 'from another substance' than that of the Father.[88]

466 The Nestorian heresy regarded Christ as a human person joined to the divine person of God's Son. Opposing this heresy, St Cyril of Alexandria and the third ecumenical council, at Ephesus in 431, confessed 'that the Word, uniting to himself in his person the flesh animated by a rational soul, became man.'[89] Christ's humanity has no other subject than the divine person of the Son of God, who assumed it and made it his own, from his conception. For this reason the Council of Ephesus proclaimed in 431 that Mary truly

495 became the Mother of God by the human conception of the Son of God in her womb: 'Mother of God, not that the nature of the Word or his divinity received the beginning of its existence from the holy Virgin, but that, since the holy body, animated by a rational soul, which the Word of God united to himself according to the hypostasis, was born from her, the Word is said to be born according to the flesh.'[90]

467 The Monophysites affirmed that the human nature had ceased to exist as such in Christ when the divine person of God's Son assumed it. Faced with this heresy, the fourth ecumenical council, at Chalcedon in 451, confessed:

> Following the holy Fathers, we unanimously teach and confess one and the same Son, our Lord Jesus Christ: the same perfect in divinity and perfect in humanity, the same truly God and truly man, composed of rational soul and body; consubstantial with the Father as to his divinity and consubstantial with us as to his humanity; 'like us in all things but sin'. He was begotten from the Father before all ages as to his divinity and

---

[87] Cf. 1 *Jn* 4:2–3; 2 *Jn* 7.
[88] Council of Nicaea I (325): DS 130, 126.
[89] Council of Ephesus (431): DS 250.
[90] Council of Ephesus: DS 251.

in these last days, for us and for our salvation, was born as to his humanity of the virgin Mary, the Mother of God.[91]

We confess that one and the same Christ, Lord, and only-begotten Son, is to be acknowledged in two natures without confusion, change, division or separation. The distinction between the natures was never abolished by their union, but rather the character proper to each of the two natures was preserved as they came together in one person (*prosopon*) and one hypostasis.[92]

468 After the Council of Chalcedon, some made of Christ's human nature a kind of personal subject. Against them, the fifth ecumenical council, at Constantinople in 553, confessed that 'there is but one *hypostasis* [or person], which is our Lord Jesus Christ, *one of the Trinity*.'[93] Thus everything in Christ's human nature is to be *254* attributed to his divine person as its proper subject, not only his miracles but also his sufferings and even his death: 'He who was crucified in the flesh, our Lord Jesus Christ, is true God, Lord of *616* glory, and one of the Holy Trinity.'[94]

469 The Church thus confesses that Jesus is inseparably true God and true man. He is truly the Son of God who, without ceasing to *212* be God and Lord, became a man and our brother:

'What he was, he remained and what he was not, he assumed', sings the Roman Liturgy.[95] And the liturgy of St John Chrysostom proclaims and sings: 'O only-begotten Son and Word of God, immortal being, you who deigned for our salvation to become incarnate of the holy Mother of God and ever-virgin Mary, you who without change became man and were crucified, O Christ our God, you who by your death have crushed death, you who are one of the Holy Trinity, glorified with the Father and the Holy Spirit, save us!'[96]

IV. How Is the Son of God Man?

470 Because 'human nature was assumed, not absorbed',[97] in the mysterious union of the Incarnation, the Church was led over the course of centuries to confess the full reality of Christ's human soul, with its operations of intellect and will, and of his human body. In parallel fashion, she had to recall on each occasion that Christ's human nature belongs, as his own, to the divine person of

---

[91] Council of Chalcedon (451): DS 301; cf. *Heb* 4:15.
[92] Council of Chalcedon: DS 302.
[93] Council of Constantinople II (553): DS 424.
[94] Council of Constantinople II (553): DS 432; cf. DS 424; Council of Ephesus, DS 255.

[95] *LH*, 1 January, Antiphon for Morning Prayer; cf. St Leo the Great, *Sermo in nat. Dom.* 1, 2; PL 54, 191–192.
[96] Liturgy of St John Chrysostom, Troparion *O monogenēs*.
[97] *GS* 22 § 2.

the Son of God, who assumed it. Everything that Christ is and
516 does in this nature derives from 'one of the Trinity'. The Son of
God therefore communicates to his humanity his own personal
626 mode of existence in the Trinity. In his soul as in his body, Christ
thus expresses humanly the divine ways of the Trinity:[98]

> The Son of God... worked with human hands; he thought with a human
2599   mind. He acted with a human will, and with a human heart he loved.
> Born of the Virgin Mary, he has truly been made one of us, like to us in
> all things except sin.[99]

Christ's soul and his human knowledge

471 Apollinarius of Laodicaea asserted that in Christ the divine
Word had replaced the soul or spirit. Against this error the Church
confessed that the eternal Son also assumed a rational, human
363 soul.[100]

472 This human soul that the Son of God assumed is endowed
with a true human knowledge. As such, this knowledge could not
in itself be unlimited: it was exercised in the historical conditions of
his existence in space and time. This is why the Son of God could,
when he became man, 'increase in wisdom and in stature, and in
favour with God and man',[101] and would even have to inquire for
himself about what one in the human condition can learn only
from experience.[102] This corresponded to the reality of his voluntary emptying of himself, taking 'the form of a slave'.[103]

473 But at the same time, this truly human knowledge of God's
Son expressed the divine life of his person.[104] 'The human nature
of God's Son, *not by itself but by its union with the Word*, knew and
showed forth in itself everything that pertains to God.'[105] Such is
first of all the case with the intimate and immediate knowledge
240 that the Son of God made man has of his Father.[106] The Son in his
human knowledge also showed the divine penetration he had into
the secret thoughts of human hearts.[107]

474 By its union to the divine wisdom in the person of the Word
incarnate, Christ enjoyed in his human knowledge the fullness of
understanding of the eternal plans he had come to reveal.[108] What

---

[98] Cf. Jn 14:9–10.
[99] GS 22 § 2.
[100] Cf. Damasus I: DS 149.
[101] Lk 2:52.
[102] Cf. Mk 6:38; 8:27; Jn 11:34; etc.
[103] Phil 2:7.
[104] Cf. St Gregory the Great, 'Sicut aqua'
   ad Eulogium, Epist. Lib. 10, 39: PL 77,

1097Aff.; DS 475.
[105] St Maximus the Confessor, Qu. et dub.
   66: PG 90, 840A.
[106] Cf. Mk 14:36; Mt 11:27; Jn 1:18; 8:55;
   etc.
[107] Cf. Mk 2:8; Jn 2:25; 6:61; etc.
[108] Cf. Mk 8:31; 9:31; 10:33–34;
   14:18–20, 26–30.

he admitted to not knowing in this area, he elsewhere declared himself not sent to reveal.[109]

Christ's human will

475 Similarly, at the sixth ecumenical council, Constantinople III in 681, the Church confessed that Christ possesses two wills and two natural operations, divine and human. They are not opposed to each other, but co-operate in such a way that the Word made flesh willed humanly in obedience to his Father all that he had decided divinely with the Father and the Holy Spirit for our salvation.[110] Christ's human will 'does not resist or oppose but rather submits to his divine and almighty will.'[111]

2008
2824

Christ's true body

476 Since the Word became flesh in assuming a true humanity, Christ's body was finite.[112] Therefore the human face of Jesus can be portrayed; at the seventh ecumenical council (Nicaea II in 787) the Church recognized its representation in holy images to be legitimate.[113]

1159–1162
2129–2132

477 At the same time the Church has always acknowledged that in the body of Jesus 'we see our God made visible and so are caught up in love of the God we cannot see.'[114] The individual characteristics of Christ's body express the divine person of God's Son. He has made the features of his human body his own, to the point that they can be venerated when portrayed in a holy image, for the believer 'who venerates the icon is venerating in it the person of the one depicted'.[115]

The heart of the Incarnate Word

478 Jesus knew and loved us each and all during his life, his agony and his Passion, and gave himself up for each one of us: 'The Son of God... loved me and gave himself for me.'[116] He has loved us all with a human heart. For this reason, the Sacred Heart of Jesus, pierced by our sins and for our salvation,[117] 'is quite rightly considered the chief sign and symbol of that... love with which the divine Redeemer continually loves the eternal Father and all human beings' without exception.[118]

487
368
2669
766

---

[109] Cf. *Mk* 13:32; *Acts* 1:7.
[110] Cf. Council of Constantinople III (681): DS 556–559.
[111] Council of Constantinople III: DS 556.
[112] Cf. Council of the Lateran (649): DS 504.
[113] Cf. *Gal* 3:1; cf. Council of Nicaea II

(787): DS 600–603.
[114] *Roman Missal*, Preface of Christmas I.
[115] Council of Nicaea II: DS 601.
[116] *Gal* 2:20.
[117] Cf. *Jn* 19:34.
[118] Pius XII, Enc. *Haurietis aquas* (1956): DS 3924; cf. DS 3812.

IN BRIEF

479 At the time appointed by God, the only Son of the Father, the eternal Word, that is, the Word and substantial Image of the Father, became incarnate; without losing his divine nature he has assumed human nature.

480 Jesus Christ is true God and true man, in the unity of his divine person; for this reason he is the one and only mediator between God and men.

481 Jesus Christ possesses two natures, one divine and the other human, not confused, but united in the one person of God's Son.

482 Christ, being true God and true man, has a human intellect and will, perfectly attuned and subject to his divine intellect and divine will, which he has in common with the Father and the Holy Spirit.

483 The Incarnation is therefore the mystery of the wonderful union of the divine and human natures in the one person of the Word.

Paragraph 2. 'Conceived by the Power of the Holy Spirit and Born of the Virgin Mary'

I. Conceived by the Power of the Holy Spirit. . .

484 The Annunciation to Mary inaugurates 'the fullness of time',[119] the time of the fulfilment of God's promises and preparations. Mary was invited to conceive him in whom the 'whole *461* fullness of deity' would dwell 'bodily'.[120] The divine response to her question, 'How can this be, since I know not man?', was given *721* by the power of the Spirit: 'The Holy Spirit will come upon you.'[121]

689 485 The mission of the Holy Spirit is always conjoined and *723* ordered to that of the Son.[122] The Holy Spirit, 'the Lord, the giver of Life', is sent to sanctify the womb of the Virgin Mary and divinely fecundate it, causing her to conceive the eternal Son of the Father in a humanity drawn from her own.

486 The Father's only Son, conceived as man in the womb of the Virgin Mary, is 'Christ', that is to say, anointed by the Holy Spirit, *437* from the beginning of his human existence, though the manifestation of this fact takes place only progressively: to the shepherds, to the magi, to John the Baptist, to the disciples.[123] Thus the

---

[119] Gal 4:4.
[120] Col 2:9.
[121] Lk 1:34–35 (Greek).

[122] Cf. Jn 16:14–15.
[123] Cf. Mt 1:20; 2:1–12; Lk 1:35; 2:8–20; Jn 1:31–34; 2:11.

whole life of Jesus Christ will make manifest 'how God anointed Jesus of Nazareth with the Holy Spirit and with power.'[124]

II. ...Born of the Virgin Mary

487 What the Catholic faith believes about Mary is based on what it believes about Christ, and what it teaches about Mary illumines in turn its faith in Christ. 963

Mary's predestination

488 'God sent forth his Son', but to prepare a body for him,[125] he wanted the free co-operation of a creature. For this, from all eternity God chose for the mother of his Son a daughter of Israel, a young Jewish woman of Nazareth in Galilee, 'a virgin betrothed to a man whose name was Joseph, of the house of David; and the virgin's name was Mary':[126]

> The Father of mercies willed that the Incarnation should be preceded by assent on the part of the predestined mother, so that just as a woman had a share in the coming of death, so also should a woman contribute to the coming of life.[127]

489 Throughout the Old Covenant the mission of many holy women *prepared* for that of Mary. At the very beginning there was Eve; despite her disobedience, she receives the promise of a posterity that will be victorious over the evil one, as well as the promise that she will be the mother of all the living.[128] By virtue of this promise, Sarah conceives a son in spite of her old age.[129] Against all human expectation God chooses those who were considered powerless and weak to show forth his faithfulness to his promises: Hannah, the mother of Samuel; Deborah; Ruth; Judith and Esther; and many other women.[130] Mary 'stands out among the poor and humble of the Lord, who confidently hope for and receive salvation from him. After a long period of waiting the times are fulfilled in her, the exalted Daughter of Sion, and the new plan of salvation is established.'[131] 722 410 145 64

The Immaculate Conception

490 To become the mother of the Saviour, Mary 'was enriched by God with gifts appropriate to such a role.'[132] The angel Gabriel

---

[124] *Acts* 10:38.
[125] *Gal* 4:4; *Heb* 10:5.
[126] *Lk* 1:26–27.
[127] *LG* 56; cf. *LG* 61.
[128] Cf. *Gen* 3:15, 20.

[129] Cf. *Gen* 18:10–14; 21:1–2.
[130] Cf. 1 *Cor* 1:17; 1 *Sam* 1.
[131] *LG* 55.
[132] *LG* 56.

2676, 2853 at the moment of the annunciation salutes her as 'full of grace'.[133] In fact, in order for Mary to be able to give the free assent of her faith to the announcement of her vocation, it was necessary that *2001* she be wholly borne by God's grace.

491 Through the centuries the Church has become ever more *411* aware that Mary, 'full of grace' through God,[134] was redeemed from the moment of her conception. That is what the dogma of the Immaculate Conception confesses, as Pope Pius IX proclaimed in 1854:

> The most Blessed Virgin Mary was, from the first moment of her conception, by a singular grace and privilege of almighty God and by virtue of the merits of Jesus Christ, Saviour of the human race, preserved immune from all stain of original sin.[135]

492 The 'splendour of an entirely unique holiness' by which Mary is 'enriched from the first instant of her conception' comes wholly from Christ: she is 'redeemed, in a more exalted fashion, *2011* by reason of the merits of her Son'.[136] The Father blessed Mary *1077* more than any other created person 'in Christ with every spiritual blessing in the heavenly places' and chose her 'in Christ before the foundation of the world, to be holy and blameless before him in love'.[137]

493 The Fathers of the Eastern tradition call the Mother of God 'the All-Holy' (*Panagia*), and celebrate her as 'free from any stain of sin, as though fashioned by the Holy Spirit and formed as a new creature'.[138] By the grace of God Mary remained free of every personal sin her whole life long.

'Let it be done to me according to your word. . .'

494 At the announcement that she would give birth to 'the Son of the Most High' without knowing man, by the power of the Holy *148, 2617* Spirit, Mary responded with the obedience of faith, certain that 'with God nothing will be impossible': 'Behold, I am the handmaid of the Lord; let it be [done] to me according to your word.'[139] Thus, giving her consent to God's word, Mary becomes the mother of Jesus. Espousing the divine will for salvation wholeheartedly, without a single sin to restrain her, she gave her- *968* self entirely to the person and to the work of her Son; she did so in

---

[133] *Lk* 1:28.
[134] *Lk* 1:28.
[135] Pius IX, *Ineffabilis Deus* (1854): DS 2803.

[136] *LG* 53, 56.
[137] Cf. *Eph* 1:3-4.
[138] *LG* 56.
[139] *Lk* 1:28-38; cf. *Rom* 1:5.

order to serve the mystery of redemption with him and dependent on him, by God's grace:[140]

> As St Irenaeus says, 'Being obedient she became the cause of salvation for herself and for the whole human race.'[141] Hence not a few of the early Fathers gladly assert...: 'The knot of Eve's disobedience was untied by Mary's obedience: what the virgin Eve bound through her disbelief, Mary loosened by her faith.'[142] Comparing her with Eve, they call Mary 'the Mother of the living' and frequently claim: 'Death through Eve, life through Mary.'[143]   *726*

Mary's divine motherhood

495 Called in the Gospels 'the mother of Jesus', Mary is acclaimed by Elizabeth, at the prompting of the Spirit and even before the birth of her son, as 'the mother of my Lord'.[144] In fact, the One whom she conceived as man by the Holy Spirit, who truly became her Son according to the flesh, was none other than the Father's eternal Son, the second person of the Holy Trinity. Hence the Church confesses that Mary is truly *'Mother of God'* (*Theotokos*).[145]   *466, 2677*

Mary's virginity

496 From the first formulations of her faith, the Church has confessed that Jesus was conceived solely by the power of the Holy Spirit in the womb of the Virgin Mary, affirming also the corporeal aspect of this event: Jesus was conceived 'by the Holy Spirit without human seed'.[146] The Fathers see in the virginal conception the sign that it truly was the Son of God who came in a humanity like our own. Thus St Ignatius of Antioch at the beginning of the second century says:

> You are firmly convinced about our Lord, who is truly of the race of David according to the flesh, Son of God according to the will and power of God, truly born of a virgin,... he was truly nailed to a tree for us in his flesh under Pontius Pilate... he truly suffered, as he is also truly risen.[147]

497 The Gospel accounts understand the virginal conception of Jesus as a divine work that surpasses all human understanding and

---

[140] Cf. LG 56.

[141] St Irenaeus, *Adv. haeres.* 3, 22, 4: PG 7/1, 959A.

[142] St Irenaeus, *Adv. haeres.* 3, 22, 4: PG 7/1, 959A.

[143] LG 56; St Epiphanius, *Panarion* 2, 78, 18: PG 42, 728CD–729AB; St Jerome, *Ep.* 22, 21: PL 22, 408.

[144] Lk 1:43; Jn 2:1; 19:25; cf. Mt 13:55; et al.

[145] Council of Ephesus (431): DS 251.

[146] Council of the Lateran (649): DS 503; cf. DS 10–64.

[147] St Ignatius of Antioch, *Ad Smyrn.* 1–2: *Apostolic Fathers*, ed. J. B. Lightfoot (London: Macmillan, 1889), II/2, 289–293; SCh 10. 154–156; cf. *Rom* 1:3; Jn 1:13.

possibility:[148] 'That which is conceived in her is of the Holy Spirit', said the angel to Joseph about Mary his fiancée.[149] The Church sees here the fulfilment of the divine promise given through the prophet Isaiah: 'Behold, a virgin shall conceive and bear a son.'[150]

498 People are sometimes troubled by the silence of St Mark's Gospel and the New Testament Epistles about Jesus' virginal conception. Some might wonder if we were merely dealing with legends or theological constructs not claiming to be history. To this we must respond: Faith in the virginal conception of Jesus met with the lively opposition, mockery or incomprehension of non-believers, Jews and pagans alike;[151] so it could hardly have been motivated by pagan mythology or by some adaptation to the ideas of the age. The meaning of this event is accessible only to faith, which understands in it the 'connection of these mysteries with one another'[152] in the totality of Christ's mysteries, from his Incarnation to his Passover. St Ignatius of Antioch already bears witness to this connection: 'Mary's virginity and giving birth, and even the Lord's death escaped the notice of the prince of this world: these three mysteries worthy of proclamation were accomplished in God's silence.'[153]

Mary – 'ever-virgin'

499 The deepening of faith in the virginal motherhood led the Church to confess Mary's real and perpetual virginity even in the act of giving birth to the Son of God made man.[154] In fact, Christ's birth 'did not diminish his mother's virginal integrity but sanctified it.'[155] And so the liturgy of the Church celebrates Mary as *Aeiparthenos*, the 'Ever-virgin'.[156]

500 Against this doctrine the objection is sometimes raised that the Bible mentions brothers and sisters of Jesus.[157] The Church has always understood these passages as not referring to other children of the Virgin Mary. In fact James and Joseph, 'brothers of Jesus', are the sons of another Mary, a disciple of Christ, whom St Matthew significantly calls 'the other Mary'.[158] They are close relations of Jesus, according to an Old Testament expression.[159]

501 Jesus is Mary's only son, but her spiritual motherhood extends to all men whom indeed he came to save: 'The Son whom she brought forth is he whom God placed as the first-born among

[148] Cf. *Mt* 1:18–25; *Lk* 1:26–38.
[149] *Mt* 1:20.
[150] *Is* 7:14 (LXX), quoted in *Mt* 1:23 (Greek).
[151] Cf. St Justin, *Dial.* 99, 7: PG 6, 708–709; Origen, *Contra Celsum* 1, 32, 69: PG 11, 720–721; *et al.*
[152] *Dei Filius* 4: DS 3016.
[153] St Ignatius of Antioch, *Ad Eph.* 19, 1: AF II/2, 76–80; cf. 1 *Cor* 2:8.

[154] Cf. DS 291; 294; 427; 442; 503; 571; 1880.
[155] *LG* 57.
[156] Cf. *LG* 52.
[157] Cf. *Mk* 3:31–35; 6:3; 1 *Cor* 9:5; *Gal* 1:19.
[158] *Mt* 13:55; 28:1; cf. *Mt* 27:56.
[159] Cf. *Gen* 13:8; 14:16; 29:15; etc.

many brethren, that is, the faithful in whose generation and formation she co-operates with a mother's love.'[160]

970

Mary's virginal motherhood in God's plan

502 The eyes of faith can discover in the context of the whole of Revelation the mysterious reasons why God in his saving plan 90 wanted his Son to be born of a virgin. These reasons touch both on the person of Christ and his redemptive mission, and on the welcome Mary gave that mission on behalf of all men.

503 Mary's virginity manifests God's absolute initiative in the Incarnation. Jesus has only God as Father. 'He was never estranged from the Father because of the human nature which he assumed... He is naturally Son of the Father as to 422 his divinity and naturally son of his mother as to his humanity, but properly Son of the Father in both natures.'[161]

504 Jesus is conceived by the Holy Spirit in the Virgin Mary's womb because he is *the New Adam*, who inaugurates the new creation: 'The first man was from 359 the earth, a man of dust; the second man is from heaven.'[162] From his conception, Christ's humanity is filled with the Holy Spirit, for God 'gives him the Spirit without measure.'[163] From 'his fullness' as the head of redeemed humanity 'we have all received, grace upon grace.'[164]

505 By his virginal conception, Jesus, the New Adam, ushers in *the new birth* of children adopted in the Holy Spirit through faith. 'How can this be?'[165] Partici- 1265 pation in the divine life arises 'not of blood nor of the will of the flesh nor of the will of man, but of God'.[166] The acceptance of this life is virginal because it is entirely the Spirit's gift to man. The spousal character of the human vocation in relation to God[167] is fulfilled perfectly in Mary's virginal motherhood.

506 Mary is a virgin because her virginity is *the sign of her faith* 'unadulterated by any doubt', and of her undivided gift of herself to God's will.[168] It is her faith 1814 that enables her to become the mother of the Saviour: 'Mary is more blessed 148 because she embraces faith in Christ than because she conceives the flesh of Christ.'[169]

507 At once virgin and mother, Mary is the symbol and the most perfect 967 realization of the Church: 'the Church indeed... by receiving the word of God in faith becomes herself a mother. By preaching and Baptism she brings forth sons, who are conceived by the Holy Spirit and born of God, to a new and immortal life. She herself is a virgin, who keeps in its entirety and purity the faith she pledged to her spouse.'[170]

149

---

[160] LG 63; cf. Jn 19:26–27; Rom 8:29; Rev 12:17.
[161] Council of Friuli (796): DS 619; cf. Lk 2:48–49.
[162] I Cor 15:45, 47.
[163] Jn 3:34.
[164] Jn 1:16; cf. Col 1:18.

[165] Lk 1:34; cf. Jn 3:9.
[166] Jn 1:13.
[167] Cf. 2 Cor 11:2.
[168] LG 63; cf. I Cor 7:34–35.
[169] St Augustine, De virg. 3: PL 40, 398.
[170] LG 64; cf. 63.

> ## IN BRIEF
>
> 508 From among the descendants of Eve, God chose the Virgin Mary to be
> the mother of his Son. 'Full of grace', Mary is 'the most excellent fruit of
> redemption' (SC 103): from the first instant of her conception, she was totally
> preserved from the stain of original sin and she remained pure from all per-
> sonal sin throughout her life.
>
> 509 Mary is truly 'Mother of God' since she is the mother of the eternal Son
> of God made man, who is God himself.
>
> 510 Mary 'remained a virgin in conceiving her Son, a virgin in giving birth
> to him, a virgin in carrying him, a virgin in nursing him at her breast, always
> a virgin' (St Augustine, Serm. 186, 1: PL 38, 999): with her whole being she
> is 'the handmaid of the Lord' (Lk 1:38).
>
> 511 The Virgin Mary 'co-operated through free faith and obedience in
> human salvation' (LG 56). She uttered her yes 'in the name of all human
> nature' (St Thomas Aquinas, STh III, 30, 1). By her obedience she became
> the new Eve, mother of the living.

Paragraph 3. The Mysteries of Christ's Life

512 Concerning Christ's life the Creed speaks only about the
mysteries of the Incarnation (conception and birth) and Paschal
mystery (passion, crucifixion, death, burial, descent into hell,
resurrection and ascension). It says nothing explicitly about the
1163 mysteries of Jesus' hidden or public life, but the articles of faith
concerning his Incarnation and Passover do shed light on the *whole*
of his earthly life. 'All that Jesus did and taught, from the beginning until the day when he was taken up to heaven',[171] is to be seen
in the light of the mysteries of Christmas and Easter.

513 According to circumstances catechesis will make use of all the
561, 426 richness of the mysteries of Jesus. Here it is enough merely to
indicate some elements common to all the mysteries of Christ's life
(I), in order then to sketch the principal mysteries of Jesus' hidden
(II) and public (III) life.

I. Christ's Whole Life Is Mystery

514 Many things about Jesus of interest to human curiosity do not
figure in the Gospels. Almost nothing is said about his hidden life
at Nazareth, and even a great part of his public life is not recounted.[172] What is written in the Gospels was set down there 'so that

---

[171] *Acts* 1:1–2.   [172] Cf. *Jn* 20:30.

you may believe that Jesus is the Christ, the Son of God, and that believing you may have life in his name.'[173]

515 The Gospels were written by men who were among the first to have the faith[174] and wanted to share it with others. Having known in faith who Jesus is, they could see and make others see the traces of his mystery in all his earthly life. From the swaddling clothes of his birth to the vinegar of his Passion and the shroud of his Resurrection, everything in Jesus' life was a sign of his mystery.[175] His deeds, miracles and words all revealed that 'in him the whole fullness of deity dwells bodily.'[176] His humanity appeared as 'sacrament', that is, the sign and instrument, of his divinity and of the salvation he brings: what was visible in his earthly life leads to the invisible mystery of his divine sonship and redemptive mission. *126* *609, 774* *477*

Characteristics common to Jesus' mysteries

516 Christ's whole earthly life – his words and deeds, his silences and sufferings, indeed his manner of being and speaking – is *Revelation* of the Father. Jesus can say: 'Whoever has seen me has seen the Father', and the Father can say: 'This is my Son, my Chosen; listen to him!'[177] Because our Lord became man in order to do his Father's will, even the least characteristics of his mysteries manifest 'God's love... among us'.[178] *65* *2708*

517 Christ's whole life is a mystery of *redemption*. Redemption comes to us above all through the blood of his cross,[179] but this mystery is at work throughout Christ's entire life: *606* *1115*
—already in his Incarnation through which by becoming poor he enriches us with his poverty;[180]
– in his hidden life which by his submission atones for our disobedience;[181]
– in his word which purifies its hearers;[182]
– in his healings and exorcisms by which 'he took our infirmities and bore our diseases';[183]
– and in his Resurrection by which he justifies us.[184]

518 Christ's whole life is a mystery of *recapitulation*. All Jesus did, *2748*

---

[173] Jn 20:31.
[174] Cf. Mk 1:1; Jn 21:24.
[175] Cf. Lk 2:7; Mt 27:48; Jn 20:7.
[176] Col 2:9.
[177] Jn 14:9; Lk 9:35; cf. Mt 17:5; Mk 9:7, 'my beloved Son'.
[178] 1 Jn 4:9.

[179] Cf. Eph 1:7; Col 1:13–14; 1 Pt 1:18–19.
[180] Cf. 2 Cor 8:9.
[181] Cf. Lk 2:51.
[182] Cf. Jn 15:3.
[183] Mt 8:17; cf. Is 53:4.
[184] Cf. Rom 4:25.

said and suffered had for its aim restoring fallen man to his original
vocation:

> When Christ became incarnate and was made man, he recapitulated in
> himself the long history of mankind and procured for us a 'short cut' to
> salvation, so that what we had lost in Adam, that is, being in the image
> and likeness of God, we might recover in Christ Jesus.[185] For this reason
> Christ experienced all the stages of life, thereby giving communion with
> God to all men.[186]

668

Our communion in the mysteries of Jesus

793
602
519 All Christ's riches 'are for every individual and are every-
body's property.'[187] Christ did not live his life for himself but *for
us*, from his Incarnation 'for us men and for our salvation' to his
death 'for our sins' and Resurrection 'for our justification'.[188] He is
still 'our advocate with the Father', who 'always lives to make
intercession' for us.[189] He remains ever 'in the presence of God on
1085 our behalf, bringing before him all that he lived and suffered for
us'.[190]

520 In all of his life Jesus presents himself as *our model*. He is 'the
459 perfect man',[191] who invites us to become his disciples and follow
359 him. In humbling himself, he has given us an example to imitate,
2607 through his prayer he draws us to pray, and by his poverty he calls
us to accept freely the privation and persecutions that may come
our way.[192]

2715 521 Christ enables us *to live in him* all that he himself lived, and *he
lives it in us*. 'By his Incarnation, he, the Son of God, has in a certain
way united himself with each man.'[193] We are called only to
1391 become one with him, for he enables us as the members of his
Body to share in what he lived for us in his flesh as our model:

> We must continue to accomplish in ourselves the stages of Jesus' life and
> his mysteries and often to beg him to perfect and realize them in us and in
> his whole Church. . . For it is the plan of the Son of God to make us and
> the whole Church partake in his mysteries and to extend them to and
> continue them in us and in his whole Church. This is his plan for fulfilling
> his mysteries in us.[194]

---

[185] St Irenaeus, *Adv. haeres.* 3, 18, 1: PG
7/1, 932.
[186] St Irenaeus, *Adv. haeres.* 3, 18, 7: PG
7/1, 937; cf. 2, 22, 4.
[187] John Paul II, *RH* 11.
[188] 1 *Cor* 15:3; *Rom* 4:25.
[189] 1 *Jn* 2:1; *Heb* 7:25.

[190] *Heb* 9:24.
[191] *GS* 38; cf. *Rom* 15:5; *Phil* 2:5.
[192] Cf. *Jn* 13:15; *Lk* 11:1; *Mt* 5:11–12.
[193] *GS* 22 § 2.
[194] St John Eudes: *LH*, week 33, Friday,
OR.

II. The Mysteries of Jesus' Infancy and Hidden Life

The preparations

522 The coming of God's Son to earth is an event of such immen- *711*
sity that God willed to prepare for it over centuries. He makes *762*
everything converge on Christ: all the rituals and sacrifices, figures
and symbols of the 'First Covenant'.[195] He announces him
through the mouths of the prophets who succeeded one another in
Israel. Moreover, he awakens in the hearts of the pagans a dim
expectation of this coming.

523 *St John the Baptist* is the Lord's immediate precursor or fore- *717–720*
runner, sent to prepare his way.[196] 'Prophet of the Most High',
John surpasses all the prophets, of whom he is the last.[197] He inaugurates the Gospel, already from his mother's womb welcomes
the coming of Christ, and rejoices in being 'the friend of the bridegroom', whom he points out as 'the Lamb of God, who takes
away the sin of the world'.[198] Going before Jesus 'in the spirit and
power of Elijah', John bears witness to Christ in his preaching, by
his Baptism of conversion, and through his martyrdom.[199]

524 When the Church celebrates *the liturgy of Advent* each year,
she makes present this ancient expectancy of the Messiah, for by
sharing in the long preparation for the Saviour's first coming, the *1171*
faithful renew their ardent desire for his second coming.[200] By
celebrating the precursor's birth and martyrdom, the Church
unites herself to his desire: 'He must increase, but I must
decrease.'[201]

The Christmas mystery

525 Jesus was born in a humble stable, into a poor family.[202]
Simple shepherds were the first witnesses to this event. In this
poverty heaven's glory was made manifest.[203] The Church never *437, 2443*
tires of singing the glory of this night:

> The Virgin today brings into the world the Eternal
> And the earth offers a cave to the Inaccessible.
> The angels and shepherds praise him
> And the magi advance with the star,
> For you are born for us,
> Little Child, God eternal![204]

---

[195] *Heb* 9:15.
[196] Cf. *Acts* 13:24; *Mt* 3:3.
[197] *Lk* 1:76; cf. 7:26; *Mt* 11:13.
[198] *Jn* 1:29; cf. *Acts* 1:22; *Lk* 1:41; 16:16; *Jn* 3:29.
[199] *Lk* 1:17; cf. *Mk* 6:17–29.
[200] Cf. *Rev* 22:17.
[201] *Jn* 3:30.
[202] Cf. *Lk* 2:6–7.
[203] Cf. *Lk* 2:8–20.
[204] Kontakion of Romanos the Melodist.

526 To become a child in relation to God is the condition for
entering the kingdom.[205] For this, we must humble ourselves and
become little. Even more: to become 'children of God' we must be
'born from above' or 'born of God'.[206] Only when Christ is
formed in us will the mystery of Christmas be fulfilled in us.[207]
Christmas is the mystery of this 'marvellous exchange':

460

> O marvellous exchange! Man's Creator has become man, born of the
> Virgin. We have been made sharers in the divinity of Christ who hum-
> bled himself to share our humanity.[208]

536

The mysteries of Jesus' infancy

527 Jesus' *circumcision*, on the eighth day after his birth,[209] is the
sign of his incorporation into Abraham's descendants, into the
580 people of the covenant. It is the sign of his submission to the
Law[210] and his deputation to Israel's worship, in which he will
participate throughout his life. This sign prefigures that 'circum-
1214 cision of Christ' which is Baptism.[211]

439 528 The *Epiphany* is the manifestation of Jesus as Messiah of Israel,
Son of God and Saviour of the world. The great feast of Epiphany
celebrates the adoration of Jesus by the wise men (*magi*) from the
East, together with his baptism in the Jordan and the wedding feast
at Cana in Galilee.[212] In the magi, representatives of the neighbouring pagan religions, the Gospel sees the first-fruits of the
nations, who welcome the good news of salvation through the
Incarnation. The magi's coming to Jerusalem in order to pay
homage to the king of the Jews shows that they seek in Israel, in the
messianic light of the star of David, the one who will be king of the
nations.[213] Their coming means that pagans can discover Jesus and
worship him as Son of God and Saviour of the world only by
711–716, turning towards the Jews and receiving from them the messianic
122 promise as contained in the Old Testament.[214] The Epiphany
shows that 'the full number of the nations' now takes its 'place in
the family of the patriarchs', and acquires *Israelitica dignitas*[215] (is
made 'worthy of the heritage of Israel').

---

[205] Cf. *Mt* 18:3–4.
[206] *Jn* 3:7; 1:13; 1:12; cf. *Mt* 23:12.
[207] Cf. *Gal* 4:19.
[208] *LH*, 1 January, Antiphon I of Evening
Prayer.
[209] Cf. *Lk* 2:21.
[210] Cf. *Gal* 4:4.
[211] Cf. *Col* 2:11–13.
[212] *Mt* 2:1; cf. *LH*, Epiphany, Evening

Prayer II, Antiphon at the *Canticle of
Mary.*
[213] Cf. *Mt* 2:2; *Num* 24:17–19; *Rev* 22:16.
[214] Cf. *Jn* 4:22; *Mt* 2:4–6.
[215] St Leo the Great, *Sermo* 3 *in epiphania
Domini* 1–3, 5: PL 54. 242; *LH*,
Epiphany, OR; *Roman Missal*, Easter
Vigil 26. Prayer after the third
reading.

529 The *presentation of Jesus in the temple* shows him to be the *583* firstborn Son who belongs to the Lord.[216] With Simeon and Anna, all Israel awaits its *encounter* with the Saviour – the name given to this event in the Byzantine tradition. Jesus is recognized as the long-expected Messiah, the 'light to the nations' and the 'glory *439* of Israel', but also 'a sign that is spoken against'. The sword of sorrow predicted for Mary announces Christ's perfect and unique *614* oblation on the cross that will impart the salvation God had 'prepared in the presence of all peoples'.

530 The *flight into Egypt* and the massacre of the innocents[217] make manifest the opposition of darkness to the light: 'He came to his own home, and his own people received him not.'[218] Christ's whole life was lived under the sign of persecution. His own share it *574* with him.[219] Jesus' departure from Egypt recalls the exodus and presents him as the definitive liberator of God's people.[220]

The mysteries of Jesus' hidden life

531 During the greater part of his life Jesus shared the condition of the vast majority of human beings: a daily life spent without evident greatness, a life of manual labour. His religious life was *2427* that of a Jew obedient to the law of God,[221] a life in the community. From this whole period it is revealed to us that Jesus was 'obedient' to his parents and that he 'increased in wisdom and in stature, and in favour with God and man.'[222]

532 Jesus' obedience to his mother and legal father fulfils the *2214–2220* fourth commandment perfectly and was the temporal image of his filial obedience to his Father in heaven. The everyday obedience of Jesus to Joseph and Mary both announced and anticipated the obedience of Holy Thursday: 'Not my will. . .'[223] The obedience *612* of Christ in the daily routine of his hidden life was already inaugurating his work of restoring what the disobedience of Adam had destroyed.[224]

533 The hidden life at Nazareth allows everyone to enter into fellowship with Jesus by the most ordinary events of daily life:

> The home of Nazareth is the school where we begin to understand the life of Jesus – the school of the Gospel. First, then, a lesson of *silence*. May *2712* esteem for silence, that admirable and indispensable condition of mind,

---

[216] Cf. *Lk* 2:22–39; *Ex* 13:2, 12–13.
[217] Cf. *Mt* 2:13–18.
[218] *Jn* 1:11.
[219] Cf. *Jn* 15:20.
[220] Cf. *Mt* 2:15; *Hos* 11:1.
[221] Cf. *Gal* 4:4.
[222] *Lk* 2:51–52.
[223] *Lk* 22:42.
[224] Cf. *Rom* 5:19.

2204 revive in us... A lesson on *family life*. May Nazareth teach us what family life is, its communion of love, its austere and simple beauty, and its sacred and inviolable character... A lesson of *work*. Nazareth, home of the 'Carpenter's Son', in you I would choose to understand and proclaim the severe and redeeming law of human work... To conclude, I want to greet all the workers of the world, holding up to them their great pattern,
2427 their brother who is God.[225]

583 534 The *finding of Jesus in the temple* is the only event that breaks the silence of the Gospels about the hidden years of Jesus.[226] Here Jesus lets us catch a glimpse of the mystery of his total consecration
259 to a mission that flows from his divine sonship: 'Did you not know that I must be about my Father's work?'[227] Mary and Joseph did
964 not understand these words, but they accepted them in faith. Mary 'kept all these things in her heart' during the years Jesus remained hidden in the silence of an ordinary life.

III. The Mysteries of Jesus' Public Life

The baptism of Jesus

535 Jesus' public life begins with his baptism by John in the Jor-
719–720 dan.[228] John preaches 'a baptism of repentance for the forgiveness of sins'.[229] A crowd of sinners[230] – tax collectors and soldiers, Pharisees and Sadducees, and prostitutes – come to be baptized by him. 'Then Jesus appears.' The Baptist hesitates, but Jesus insists
701 and receives baptism. Then the Holy Spirit, in the form of a dove,
438 comes upon Jesus and a voice from heaven proclaims, 'This is my beloved Son.'[231] This is the manifestation ('Epiphany') of Jesus as Messiah of Israel and Son of God.

606 536 The baptism of Jesus is on his part the acceptance and inauguration of his mission as God's suffering Servant. He allows himself to be numbered among sinners; he is already 'the Lamb of God, who takes away the sin of the world'.[232] Already he is anticipating the 'baptism' of his bloody death.[233] Already he is coming
1224 to 'fulfil all righteousness', that is, he is submitting himself entirely to his Father's will: out of love he consents to this baptism of death for the remission of our sins.[234] The Father's voice responds to the
444 Son's acceptance, proclaiming his entire delight in his Son.[235] The

---

[225] Paul VI at Nazareth, 5 January 1964: *LH*, Feast of the Holy Family, OR.
[226] Cf. *Lk* 2:41–52.
[227] *Lk* 2:49 alt.
[228] Cf. *Lk* 3:23; *Acts* 1:22.
[229] *Lk* 3:3.
[230] Cf. *Lk* 3:10–14; *Mt* 3:7; 21:32.
[231] *Mt* 3:13–17.
[232] *Jn* 1:29; cf. *Is* 53:12.
[233] Cf. *Mk* 10:38; *Lk* 12:50.
[234] *Mt* 3:15; cf. 26:39.
[235] Cf. *Lk* 3:22; *Is* 42:1.

Spirit whom Jesus possessed in fullness from his conception comes
to 'rest on him'.[236] Jesus will be the source of the Spirit for all   727
mankind. At his baptism 'the heavens were opened'[237] – the
heavens that Adam's sin had closed – and the waters were sanctified by the descent of Jesus and the Spirit, a prelude to the new   739
creation.

537 Through Baptism the Christian is sacramentally assimilated
to Jesus, who in his own baptism anticipates his death and resurrec-   1262
tion. The Christian must enter into this mystery of humble self-
abasement and repentance, go down into the water with Jesus in
order to rise with him, be reborn of water and the Spirit so as to
become the Father's beloved son in the Son and 'walk in newness
of life':[238]

> Let us be buried with Christ by Baptism to rise with him; let us go down   628
> with him to be raised with him; and let us rise with him to be glorified
> with him.[239]

> Everything that happened to Christ lets us know that, after the bath of
> water, the Holy Spirit swoops down upon us from high heaven and that,
> adopted by the Father's voice, we become sons of God.[240]

Jesus' temptations

538 The Gospels speak of a time of solitude for Jesus in the desert
immediately after his baptism by John. Driven by the Spirit into
the desert, Jesus remains there for forty days without eating; he
lives among wild beasts, and angels minister to him.[241] At the end
of this time Satan tempts him three times, seeking to compromise   394
his filial attitude toward God. Jesus rebuffs these attacks, which
recapitulate the temptations of Adam in Paradise and of Israel in   518
the desert, and the devil leaves him 'until an opportune time'.[242]

539 The evangelists indicate the salvific meaning of this mysterious event: Jesus is the new Adam who remained faithful just where
the first Adam had given in to temptation. Jesus fulfils Israel's   397
vocation perfectly: in contrast to those who had once provoked
God during forty years in the desert, Christ reveals himself as
God's Servant, totally obedient to the divine will. In this, Jesus is
the devil's conqueror: he 'binds the strong man' to take back his   385
plunder.[243] Jesus' victory over the tempter in the desert anticipates

---

[236] Jn 1:32–33; cf. Is 11:2.
[237] Mt 3:16.
[238] Rom 6:4.
[239] St Gregory of Nazianzus, Oratio 40, 9:
    PG 36, 369.
[240] St Hilary of Poitiers, In Matth. 2, 5:
    PL 9, 927.
[241] Cf. Mk 1:12–13.
[242] Lk 4:13.
[243] Cf. Ps 95:10; Mk 3:27.

609   victory at the Passion, the supreme act of obedience of his filial love for the Father.

2119   540 Jesus' temptation reveals the way in which the Son of God is Messiah, contrary to the way Satan proposes to him and the way
2849   men wish to attribute to him.[244] This is why Christ vanquished the
519   Tempter *for us*: 'For we have not a high priest who is unable to sympathize with our weaknesses, but one who in every respect has been tested as we are, yet without sinning.'[245] By the solemn forty
1438   days of *Lent* the Church unites herself each year to the mystery of Jesus in the desert.

'The kingdom of God is at hand'

541   'Now after John was arrested, Jesus came into Galilee, preaching the gospel of God, and saying: "The time is fulfilled,
2816   and the kingdom of God is at hand: repent, and believe in the
763   gospel." '[246] 'To carry out the will of the Father Christ inaugurated the kingdom of heaven on earth.'[247] Now the Father's will is 'to raise up men to share in his own divine life'.[248] He does
768   this by gathering men around his Son Jesus Christ. This gathering
669, 865   is the Church, 'on earth the seed and beginning of that kingdom'.[249]

542   Christ stands at the heart of this gathering of men into the
2233   'family of God'. By his word, through signs that manifest the reign of God, and by sending out his disciples, Jesus calls all people to come together around him. But above all in the great Paschal mystery – his death on the cross and his Resurrection – he would accomplish the coming of his kingdom. 'And I, when I am lifted
789   up from the earth, will draw all men to myself.' Into this union with Christ all men are called.[250]

The proclamation of the kingdom of God

543   *Everyone* is called to enter the kingdom. First announced to the children of Israel, this messianic kingdom is intended to accept
764   men of all nations.[251] To enter it, one must first accept Jesus' word:

> The word of the Lord is compared to a seed which is sown in a field; those who hear it with faith and are numbered among the little flock of Christ have truly received the kingdom. Then, by its own power, the seed sprouts and grows until the harvest.[252]

---

[244] Cf. *Mt* 16:21–23.
[245] *Heb* 4:15.
[246] *Mk* 1:14–15.
[247] *LG* 3.
[248] *LG* 2.

[249] *LG* 5.
[250] *Jn* 12:32; cf. *LG* 3.
[251] Cf. *Mt* 8:11; 10:5–7; 28:19.
[252] *LG* 5; cf. *Mk* 4:14, 26–29; *Lk* 12:32.

544 The kingdom belongs *to the poor and lowly*, which means 709
those who have accepted it with humble hearts. Jesus is sent to
'preach good news to the poor';[253] he declares them blessed, for 2443
'theirs is the kingdom of heaven.'[254] To them – the 'little ones' – 2546
the Father is pleased to reveal what remains hidden from the wise
and the learned.[255] Jesus shares the life of the poor, from the cradle
to the cross; he experiences hunger, thirst and privation.[256] Jesus
identifies himself with the poor of every kind and makes active
love toward them the condition for entering his kingdom.[257]

545 Jesus invites *sinners* to the table of the kingdom: 'I came not to 1443, 588
call the righteous, but sinners.'[258] He invites them to that conversion without which one cannot enter the kingdom, but shows
them in word and deed his Father's boundless mercy for them and 1846, 1439
the vast 'joy in heaven over one sinner who repents'.[259] The
supreme proof of his love will be the sacrifice of his own life 'for
the forgiveness of sins'.[260]

546 Jesus' invitation to enter his kingdom comes in the form of
parables, a characteristic feature of his teaching.[261] Through his 2613
parables he invites people to the feast of the kingdom, but he also
asks for a radical choice: to gain the kingdom, one must give
everything.[262] Words are not enough, deeds are required.[263] The
parables are like mirrors for man: will he be hard soil or good earth
for the word?[264] What use has he made of the talents he has received?[265] Jesus and the presence of the kingdom in this world are
secretly at the heart of the parables. One must enter the kingdom, 542
that is, become a disciple of Christ, in order to 'know the secrets of
the kingdom of heaven'.[266] For those who stay 'outside', everything remains enigmatic.[267]

The signs of the kingdom of God

547 Jesus accompanies his words with many 'mighty works and
wonders and signs', which manifest that the kingdom is present in 670
him and attest that he was the promised Messiah.[268]   439

---

[253] *Lk* 4:18; cf. 7:22.
[254] *Mt* 5:3.
[255] Cf. *Mt* 11:25.
[256] Cf. *Mt* 21:18; Mk 2:23–26; *Jn* 4:6–7;
19:28; *Lk* 9:58.
[257] Cf. *Mt* 25:31–46.
[258] *Mk* 2:17; cf. 1 *Tim* 1:15.
[259] *Lk* 15:7; cf. 7:11–32.
[260] *Mt* 26:28.

[261] Cf. *Mk* 4:33–34.
[262] Cf. *Mt* 13:44–45; 22:1–14.
[263] Cf. *Mt* 21:28–32.
[264] Cf. *Mt* 13:3–9.
[265] Cf. *Mt* 25:14–30.
[266] *Mt* 13:11.
[267] *Mk* 4:11; cf. *Mt* 13:10–15.
[268] *Acts* 2:22; cf. *Lk* 7:18–23.

2616, 156   548 The signs worked by Jesus attest that the Father has sent him. They invite belief in him.[269] To those who turn to him in faith, he grants what they ask.[270] So miracles strengthen faith in the One who does his Father's works; they bear witness that he is the Son of God.[271] But his miracles can also be occasions for 'offence';[272] they are not intended to satisfy people's curiosity or desire for magic.
447   Despite his evident miracles some people reject Jesus; he is even
574   accused of acting by the power of demons.[273]

1503   549 By freeing some individuals from the earthly evils of hunger, injustice, illness and death,[274] Jesus performed messianic signs. Nevertheless he did not come to abolish all evils here below,[275] but
440   to free men from the gravest slavery, sin, which thwarts them in their vocation as God's sons and causes all forms of human bondage.[276]

550 The coming of God's kingdom means the defeat of Satan's:
394   'If it is by the Spirit of God that I cast out demons, then the
1673   kingdom of God has come upon you.'[277] Jesus' *exorcisms* free some individuals from the domination of demons. They anticipate
440, 2816   Jesus' great victory over 'the ruler of this world'.[278] The kingdom of God will be definitively established through Christ's cross: 'God reigned from the wood.'[279]

'The keys of the kingdom'

551 From the beginning of his public life Jesus chose certain men,
858   twelve in number, to be with him and to participate in his mission.[280] He gives the Twelve a share in his authority and 'sent them out to preach the kingdom of God and to heal.'[281] They remain
765   associated for ever with Christ's kingdom, for through them he directs the Church:

> As my Father appointed a kingdom for me, so do I appoint for you that you may eat and drink at my table in my kingdom, and sit on thrones judging the twelve tribes of Israel.[282]

153, 880   552 Simon Peter holds the first place in the college of the Twelve;[283] Jesus entrusted a unique mission to him. Through a

[269] Cf. Jn 5:36; 10:25, 38.
[270] Cf. Mk 5:25–34; 10:52; etc.
[271] Cf. Jn 10:31–38.
[272] Mt 11:6.
[273] Cf. Jn 11:47–48; Mk 3:22.
[274] Cf. Jn 6:5–15; Lk 19:8; Mt 11:5.
[275] Cf. Lk 12:13–14; Jn 18:36.
[276] Cf. Jn 8:34–36.
[277] Mt 12:26, 28.

[278] Jn 12:31; cf. Lk 8:26–39.
[279] LH, Lent, Holy Week, Evening Prayer, Hymn Vexilla Regis: Regnavit a ligno Deus.
[280] Cf. Mk 3:13–19.
[281] Lk 9:2.
[282] Lk 22:29–30.
[283] Cf. Mk 3:16; 9:2; Lk 24:34; 1 Cor 15:5.

revelation from the Father, Peter had confessed: 'You are the
Christ, the Son of the living God.' Our Lord then declared to him: *442*
'You are Peter, and on this rock I will build my Church, and the
gates of Hades will not prevail against it.'[284] Christ, the 'living
stone',[285] thus assures his Church, built on Peter, of victory over
the powers of death. Because of the faith he confessed Peter will
remain the unshakeable rock of the Church. His mission will be to *424*
keep this faith from every lapse and to strengthen his brothers in
it.[286]

553 Jesus entrusted a specific authority to Peter: 'I will give you
the keys of the kingdom of heaven, and whatever you bind on
earth shall be bound in heaven, and whatever you loose on earth
shall be loosed in heaven.'[287] The 'power of the keys' designates
authority to govern the house of God, which is the Church. Jesus,
the Good Shepherd, confirmed this mandate after his Resurrection: 'Feed my sheep.'[288] The power to 'bind and loose' connotes *1445*
the authority to absolve sins, to pronounce doctrinal judgements,
and to make disciplinary decisions in the Church. Jesus entrusted
this authority to the Church through the ministry of the apostles[289] and in particular through the ministry of Peter, the only *641*
one to whom he specifically entrusted the keys of the kingdom. *881*

A foretaste of the kingdom: the Transfiguration

554 From the day Peter confessed that Jesus is the Christ, the Son
of the living God, the Master 'began to show his disciples that he
must go to Jerusalem and suffer many things... and be killed, and
on the third day be raised.'[290] Peter scorns this prediction, nor do
the others understand it any better than he.[291] In this context the
mysterious episode of Jesus' Transfiguration takes place on a high *2600, 697*
mountain,[292] before three witnesses chosen by himself: Peter,
James and John. Jesus' face and clothes become dazzling with light,
and Moses and Elijah appear, speaking 'of his departure, which he
was to accomplish at Jerusalem'.[293] A cloud covers him and a voice
from heaven says: 'This is my Son, my Chosen; listen to him!'[294] *440*

555 For a moment Jesus discloses his divine glory, confirming
Peter's confession. He also reveals that he will have to go by the

---

[284] Mt 16:18.
[285] 1 Pt 2:4.
[286] Cf. Lk 22:32.
[287] Mt 16:19.
[288] Jn 21:15–17; cf. 10:11.
[289] Cf. Mt 18:18.

[290] Mt 16:21.
[291] Cf. Mt 16:22–23; 17:23; Lk 9:45.
[292] Cf. Mt 17:1–8 and parallels; 2 Pt
1:16–18.
[293] Lk 9:31.
[294] Lk 9:35.

way of the cross at Jerusalem in order to 'enter into his glory'.[295]
2576, 2583 Moses and Elijah had seen God's glory on the Mountain; the Law
and the Prophets had announced the Messiah's sufferings.[296]
Christ's Passion is the will of the Father: the Son acts as God's
servant;[297] the cloud indicates the presence of the Holy Spirit. 'The
257 whole Trinity appeared: the Father in the voice; the Son in the
man; the Spirit in the shining cloud.'[298]

> You were transfigured on the mountain, and your disciples, as much as
> they were capable of it, beheld your glory, O Christ our God, so that
> when they should see you crucified they would understand that your
> Passion was voluntary, and proclaim to the world that you truly are the
> splendour of the Father.[299]

556 On the threshold of the public life: the baptism; on the threshold of the Passover: the Transfiguration. Jesus' baptism proclaimed 'the mystery of the first regeneration', namely, our
Baptism; the Transfiguration 'is the sacrament of the second
regeneration': our own Resurrection.[300] From now on we share in
the Lord's Resurrection through the Spirit who acts in the sacraments of the Body of Christ. The Transfiguration gives us a fore-
1003 taste of Christ's glorious coming, when he 'will change our lowly
body to be like his glorious body.'[301] But it also recalls that 'it is
through many persecutions that we must enter the kingdom of
God'.[302]

> Peter did not yet understand this when he wanted to remain with Christ
> on the mountain. It has been reserved for you, Peter, but for after death.
> For now, Jesus says: 'Go down to toil on earth, to serve on earth, to be
> scorned and crucified on earth. Life goes down to be killed; Bread
> goes down to suffer hunger; the Way goes down to be exhausted on
> his journey; the Spring goes down to suffer thirst; and you refuse to
> suffer?'[303]

Jesus' ascent to Jerusalem

557 'When the days drew near for him to be taken up [Jesus] set
his face to go to Jerusalem.'[304] By this decision he indicated that he
was going up to Jerusalem prepared to die there. Three times he
had announced his Passion and Resurrection; now, heading

---

[295] Lk 24:26.
[296] Cf. Lk 24:27.
[297] Cf. Is 42:1.
[298] St Thomas Aquinas, STh III, 45, 4, ad 2.
[299] Byzantine Liturgy, Feast of the Transfiguration, Kontakion.
[300] St Thomas Aquinas, STh III, 45, 4, ad 2.
[301] Phil 3:21.
[302] Acts 14:22.
[303] St Augustine, Sermo 78, 6: PL 38, 492–493; cf. Lk 9:33.
[304] Lk 9:51; cf. Jn 13:1.

toward Jerusalem, Jesus says: 'It cannot be that a prophet should perish away from Jerusalem.'[305]

558 Jesus recalls the martyrdom of the prophets who had been put to death in Jerusalem. Nevertheless he persists in calling Jerusalem to gather around him: 'How often would I have gathered your children together as a hen gathers her brood under her wings, and you would not!'[306] When Jerusalem comes into view he weeps over her and expresses once again his heart's desire: 'Would that even today you knew the things that make for peace! But now they are hid from your eyes.'[307]

Jesus' messianic entrance into Jerusalem

559 How will Jerusalem welcome her Messiah? Although Jesus had always refused popular attempts to make him king, he chooses the time and prepares the details for his messianic entry into the city of 'his father David'.[308] Acclaimed as son of David, as the one who brings salvation (*Hosanna* means 'Save!' or 'Give salvation!'), the 'King of glory' enters his City 'riding on an ass'.[309] Jesus conquers the Daughter of Zion, a figure of his Church, neither by ruse nor by violence, but by the humility that bears witness to the truth.[310] And so the subjects of his kingdom on that day are children and God's poor, who acclaim him as had the angels when they announced him to the shepherds.[311] Their acclamation, 'Blessed be he who comes in the name of the LORD',[312] is taken up by the Church in the *Sanctus* of the Eucharistic liturgy that introduces the memorial of the Lord's Passover.

333

1352

560 *Jesus' entry into Jerusalem* manifested the coming of the kingdom that the King-Messiah was going to accomplish by the Passover of his Death and Resurrection. It is with the celebration of that entry on Palm Sunday that the Church's liturgy solemnly opens Holy Week.

550, 2814

IN BRIEF

561 '*The whole of Christ's life was a continual teaching: his silences, his miracles, his gestures, his prayer, his love for people, his special affection for the little and the poor, his acceptance of the total sacrifice on the Cross for the*

---

[305] Lk 13:33; cf. Mk 8:31–33; 9:31–32; 10:32–34.
[306] Mt 23:37.
[307] Lk 19:41–42.
[308] Lk 1:32; cf. Mt 21:1–11; Jn 6:15.

[309] Ps 24:7–10; Zech 9:9.
[310] Cf. Jn 18:37.
[311] Cf. Mt 21:15–16; cf. Ps 8:3; Lk 19:38; 2:14.
[312] Cf. Ps 118:26.

redemption of the world, and his Resurrection are the actualization of his word and the fulfilment of Revelation' (John Paul II, CT 9).

562 Christ's disciples are to conform themselves to him until he is formed in them (cf. Gal 4:19). 'For this reason we, who have been made like to him, who have died with him and risen with him, are taken up into the mysteries of his life, until we reign together with him' (LG 7 §4).

563 No one, whether shepherd or wise man, can approach God here below except by kneeling before the manger at Bethlehem and adoring him hidden in the weakness of a new-born child.

564 By his obedience to Mary and Joseph, as well as by his humble work during the long years in Nazareth, Jesus gives us the example of holiness in the daily life of family and work.

565 From the beginning of his public life, at his baptism, Jesus is the 'Servant', wholly consecrated to the redemptive work that he will accomplish by the 'baptism' of his Passion.

566 The temptation in the desert shows Jesus, the humble Messiah, who triumphs over Satan by his total adherence to the plan of salvation willed by the Father.

567 The kingdom of heaven was inaugurated on earth by Christ. 'This kingdom shone out before men in the word, in the works and in the presence of Christ' (LG 5). The Church is the seed and beginning of this kingdom. Its keys are entrusted to Peter.

568 Christ's Transfiguration aims at strengthening the apostles' faith in anticipation of his Passion: the ascent on to the 'high mountain' prepares for the ascent to Calvary. Christ, Head of the Church, manifests what his Body contains and radiates in the sacraments: 'the hope of glory' (Col 1:27; cf. St Leo the Great, Sermo 51, 3: PL 54, 310C).

569 Jesus went up to Jerusalem voluntarily, knowing well that there he would die a violent death because of the opposition of sinners (cf. Heb 12:3).

570 Jesus' entry into Jerusalem manifests the coming of the kingdom that the Messiah-King, welcomed into his city by children and the humble of heart, is going to accomplish by the Passover of his Death and Resurrection.

Article 4

'JESUS CHRIST SUFFERED UNDER PONTIUS PILATE, WAS CRUCIFIED, DIED AND WAS BURIED'

1067   571 The Paschal mystery of Christ's cross and Resurrection stands at the centre of the Good News that the apostles, and the Church following them, are to proclaim to the world. God's saving plan was accomplished 'once for all'[313] by the redemptive death of his Son Jesus Christ.

572 The Church remains faithful to the interpretation of 'all the Scriptures' that Jesus gave both before and after his Passover: 'Was it not necessary that the Christ should suffer these things and enter into his glory?'[314] Jesus' sufferings took their historical, concrete form from the fact that he was 'rejected by the elders and the chief priests and the scribes', who handed 'him to the Gentiles to be mocked and scourged and crucified'.[315]

599

573 Faith can therefore try to examine the circumstances of Jesus' death, faithfully handed on by the Gospels[316] and illuminated by other historical sources, the better to understand the meaning of the Redemption.

158

Paragraph 1. Jesus and Israel

574 From the beginning of Jesus' public ministry, certain Pharisees and partisans of Herod together with priests and scribes agreed together to destroy him.[317] Because of certain acts of his – expelling demons, forgiving sins, healing on the sabbath day, his novel interpretation of the precepts of the Law regarding purity, and his familiarity with tax collectors and public sinners[318] – some ill-intentioned persons suspected Jesus of demonic possession.[319] He is accused of blasphemy and false prophecy, religious crimes which the Law punished with death by stoning.[320]

530

591

575 Many of Jesus' deeds and words constituted a 'sign of contradiction',[321] but more so for the religious authorities in Jerusalem, whom the Gospel according to John often calls simply 'the Jews',[322] than for the ordinary People of God.[323] To be sure, Christ's relations with the Pharisees were not exclusively polemical. Some Pharisees warn him of the danger he was courting;[324] Jesus praises some of them, like the scribe of Mark 12:34, and dines several times at their homes.[325] Jesus endorses some of the teachings imparted by this religious elite of God's people: the resurrection of the dead,[326] certain forms of piety (almsgiving, fasting and prayer),[327] the custom of addressing God as Father, and the centrality of the commandment to love God and neighbour.[328]

993

[313] Heb 9:26.
[314] Lk 24:26–27, 44–45.
[315] Mk 8:31; Mt 20:19.
[316] Cf. DV 19.
[317] Cf. Mk 3:6; 14:1.
[318] Cf. Mt 12:24; Mk 2:7, 14–17; 3:1–6; 7:14–23.
[319] Cf. Mk 3:22; Jn 8:48; 10:20.
[320] Cf. Mk 2:7; Jn 5:18; 7:12, 52; 8:59; 10:31, 33.
[321] Lk 2:34.
[322] Cf. Jn 1:19; 2:18; 5:10; 7:13; 9:22; 18:12; 19:38; 20:19.
[323] Jn 7:48–49.
[324] Cf. Lk 13:31.
[325] Cf. Lk 7:36; 14:1.
[326] Cf. Mt 22:23–34; Lk 20:39.
[327] Cf. Mt 6:18.
[328] Cf. Mk 12:28–34.

576 In the eyes of many in Israel, Jesus seems to be acting against essential institutions of the Chosen People:
– submission to the whole of the Law in its written commandments and, for the Pharisees, in the interpretation of oral tradition;
– the centrality of the Temple at Jerusalem as the holy place where God's presence dwells in a special way;
– faith in the one God whose glory no man can share.

I. Jesus and the Law

1965 577 At the beginning of the Sermon on the Mount Jesus issued a solemn warning in which he presented God's law, given on Sinai during the first covenant, in light of the grace of the New Covenant:

> 1967 Do not think that I have come to abolish the law or the prophets: I have come not to abolish but to fulfil. For truly I tell you, until heaven and earth pass away, not one letter, not one stroke of a letter, will pass from the law, until all is accomplished. Therefore, whoever breaks one of the least of these commandments, and teaches others to do the same, will be called least in the kingdom of heaven; but whoever does them and teaches them will be called great in the kingdom of heaven.[329]

578 Jesus, Israel's Messiah and therefore the greatest in the king-
1953 dom of heaven, was to fulfil the Law by keeping it in its all-embracing detail – according to his own words, down to 'the least of these commandments'.[330] He is in fact the only one who could keep it perfectly.[331] On their own admission the Jews were never able to observe the Law in its entirety without violating the least of its precepts.[332] This is why every year on the Day of Atonement the children of Israel ask God's forgiveness for their transgressions of the Law. The Law indeed makes up one inseparable whole, and St James recalls, 'Whoever keeps the whole law but fails in one point has become guilty of all of it.'[333]

579 This principle of integral observance of the Law not only in letter but in spirit was dear to the Pharisees. By giving Israel this principle they had led many Jews of Jesus' time to an extreme religious zeal.[334] This zeal, were it not to lapse into 'hypocritical' casuistry,[335] could only prepare the People for the unprecedented intervention of God through the perfect fulfilment of the Law by the only Righteous One in place of all sinners.[336]

580 The perfect fulfilment of the Law could be the work of none

---

[329] Mt 5:17–19.
[330] Mt 5:19.
[331] Cf. Jn 8:46.
[332] Cf. Jn 7:19; Acts 13:38–41; 15:10.

[333] Jas 2:10; cf. Gal 3:10; 5:3.
[334] Cf. Rom 10:2.
[335] Cf. Mt 15:3–7; Lk 11:39–54.
[336] Cf. Is 53:11; Heb 9:15.

but the divine legislator, born subject to the Law in the person of
the Son.[337] In Jesus, the Law no longer appears engraved on tables   527
of stone but 'upon the heart' of the Servant who becomes 'a
covenant to the people', because he will 'faithfully bring forth
justice'.[338] Jesus fulfils the Law to the point of taking upon himself
'the curse of the Law' incurred by those who do not 'abide by the
things written in the book of the Law, and do them', for his death
took place to redeem them 'from the transgressions under the first
covenant'.[339]

581 The Jewish people and their spiritual leaders viewed Jesus as a rabbi.[340] He
often argued within the framework of rabbinical interpretation of the Law.[341]
Yet Jesus could not help but offend the teachers of the Law, for he was not
content to propose his interpretation alongside theirs but taught the people 'as   2054
one who had authority, and not as their scribes'.[342] In Jesus, the same Word of
God that had resounded on Mount Sinai to give the written Law to Moses,
made itself heard anew on the Mount of the Beatitudes.[343] Jesus did not abolish
the Law but fulfilled it by giving its ultimate interpretation in a divine way:
'You have heard that it was said to the men of old. . . But I say to you. . .'[344] With
this same divine authority, he disavowed certain human traditions of the Pharisees that were 'making void the word of God'.[345]

582 Going even further, Jesus perfects the dietary law, so important in Jewish
daily life, by revealing its pedagogical meaning through a divine interpretation:
'Whatever goes into a man from outside cannot defile him. . . (Thus he declared
all foods clean.). . . What comes out of a man is what defiles a man. For from
within, out of the heart of man, come evil thoughts. . .'[346] In presenting with   368
divine authority the definitive interpretation of the Law, Jesus found himself
confronted by certain teachers of the Law who did not accept his interpretation
of the Law, guaranteed though it was by the divine signs that accompanied it.[347]   548
This was the case especially with the sabbath laws, for he recalls, often with
rabbinical arguments, that the sabbath rest is not violated by serving God and   2173
neighbour,[348] which his own healings did.

II. Jesus and the Temple

583 Like the prophets before him Jesus expressed the deepest
respect for the Temple in Jerusalem. It was in the Temple that   529
Joseph and Mary presented him forty days after his birth.[349] At the
age of twelve he decided to remain in the Temple to remind his   534

---

[337] Cf. Gal 4:4.

[338] Jer 31:33; Is 42:3, 6.

[339] Gal 3:13; 3:10; Heb 9:15.

[340] Cf. Jn 11:28; 3:2; Mt 22:23–24, 34–36.

[341] Cf. Mt 12:5; 9:12; Mk 2:23–27; Lk
6:6–9; Jn 7:22–23.

[342] Mt 7:28–29.

[343] Cf. Mt 5:1.

[344] Mt 5:33–34.

[345] Mk 7:13; cf. 3:8.

[346] Mk 7:18–21; cf. Gal 3:24.

[347] Cf. Jn 5:36; 10:25, 37–38; 12:37.

[348] Cf. Num 28:9; Mt 12:5; Mk 2:25–27;
Lk 13:15–16; 14:3–4; Jn 7:22–24.

[349] Lk 2:22–39.

parents that he must be about his Father's business.[350] He went there each year during his hidden life at least for Passover.[351] His public ministry itself was patterned by his pilgrimages to Jerusalem for the great Jewish feasts.[352]

2599 584 Jesus went up to the Temple as the privileged place of encounter with God. For him, the Temple was the dwelling of his Father, a house of prayer, and he was angered that its outer court had become a place of commerce.[353] He drove merchants out of it because of jealous love for his Father: ' "You shall not make my Father's house a house of trade." His disciples remembered that it was written, "Zeal for your house will consume me." '[354] After his Resurrection his apostles retained their reverence for the Temple.[355]

585 On the threshold of his Passion Jesus announced the coming destruction of this splendid building, of which there would not remain 'one stone upon another'.[356] By doing so, he announced a sign of the last days, which were to begin with his own Passover.[357] But this prophecy would be distorted in its telling by false witnesses during his interrogation at the high priest's house, and would be thrown back at him as an insult when he was nailed to the cross.[358]

586 Far from having been hostile to the Temple, where he gave the essential part of his teaching, Jesus was willing to pay the Temple-tax, associating with him Peter, whom he had just made the foundation of his future Church.[359] He even identified himself
797 with the Temple by presenting himself as God's definitive dwelling-place among men.[360] Therefore his being put to bodily
1179 death[361] presaged the destruction of the Temple, which would manifest the dawning of a new age in the history of salvation: 'The hour is coming when neither on this mountain nor in Jerusalem will you worship the Father.'[362]

III. Jesus and Israel's Faith in the One God and Saviour

587 If the Law and the Jerusalem Temple could be occasions of

---

[350] Cf. Lk 2:46–49.
[351] Cf. Lk 2:41.
[352] Cf. Jn 2:13–14; 5:1, 14; 7:1, 10, 14; 8:2; 10:22–23.
[353] Cf. Mt 21:13.
[354] Jn 2:16–17; cf. Ps 69:10.
[355] Cf. Acts 2:46; 3:1; 5:20, 21; etc.
[356] Cf. Mt 24:1–2.

[357] Cf. Mt 24:3; Lk 13:35.
[358] Cf. Mk 14:57–58; Mt 27:39–40.
[359] Cf. Mt 8:4; 16:18; 17:24–27; Lk 17:14; Jn 4:22; 18:20.
[360] Cf. Jn 2:21; Mt 12:6.
[361] Cf. Jn 2:18–22.
[362] Jn 4:21; cf. 4:23–24; Mt 27:51; Heb 9:11; Rev 21:22.

opposition to Jesus by Israel's religious authorities, his role in the redemption of sins, the divine work *par excellence*, was the true stumbling-block for them.[363]

588 Jesus scandalized the Pharisees by eating with tax collectors and sinners as familiarly as with themselves.[364] Against those among them 'who trusted in themselves that they were righteous and despised others', Jesus affirmed: 'I have not come to call the righteous, but sinners to repentance.'[365] He went further by proclaiming before the Pharisees that, since sin is universal, those who pretend not to need salvation are blind to themselves.[366]   545

589 Jesus gave scandal above all when he identified his merciful conduct toward sinners with God's own attitude toward them.[367] He went so far as to hint that by sharing the table of sinners he was admitting them to the messianic banquet.[368] But it was most especially by forgiving sins that Jesus placed the religious authorities of Israel on the horns of a dilemma. Were they not entitled to demand in consternation, 'Who can forgive sins but God   431 alone?'[369] By forgiving sins Jesus either is blaspheming as a man   432 who made himself God's equal, or is speaking the truth and his person really does make present and reveal God's name.[370]   1441

590 Only the divine identity of Jesus' person can justify so absolute a claim as 'He who is not with me is against me'; and his saying that there was in him 'something greater than Jonah, . . . greater than Solomon', something 'greater than the Temple'; his reminder that David had called the Messiah his Lord,[371] and his affirmations, 'Before Abraham was, I AM', and even 'I and the Father are one.'[372]   253

591 Jesus asked the religious authorities of Jerusalem to believe in him because of the Father's works which he accomplished.[373] But such an act of faith must go through a mysterious death to self, for a new 'birth from above' under the influence of divine grace.[374]   526 Such a demand for conversion in the face of so surprising a fulfilment of the promises[375] allows one to understand the Sanhedrin's tragic misunderstanding of Jesus: they judged that he deserved the death sentence as a blasphemer.[376] The members of the Sanhedrin   574

---

[363] Cf. *Lk* 2:34; 20:17–18; *Ps* 118:22.
[364] Cf. *Lk* 5:30; 7:36; 11:37; 14:1.
[365] *Lk* 18:9; 5:32; cf. *Jn* 7:49; 9:34.
[366] Cf. *Jn* 8:33–36; 9:40–41.
[367] Cf. *Mt* 9:13; *Hos* 6:6.
[368] Cf. *Lk* 15:1–2, 22–32.
[369] *Mk* 2:7.

[370] Cf. *Jn* 5:18; 10:33; 17:6, 26.
[371] Cf. *Mt* 12:6, 30, 36, 37, 41–42.
[372] *Jn* 8:58; 10:30.
[373] *Jn* 10:36–38.
[374] Cf. *Jn* 3:7; 6:44.
[375] Cf. *Is* 53:1.
[376] Cf. *Mk* 3:6; *Mt* 26:64–66.

were thus acting at the same time out of 'ignorance' and the 'hardness' of their 'unbelief'.[377]

IN BRIEF

592 Jesus did not abolish the Law of Sinai, but rather fulfilled it (cf. Mt 5:17–19) with such perfection (cf. Jn 8:46) that he revealed its ultimate meaning (cf. Mt 5:33) and redeemed the transgressions against it (cf. Heb 9:15).

593 Jesus venerated the Temple by going up to it for the Jewish feasts of pilgrimage, and with a jealous love he loved this dwelling of God among men. The Temple prefigures his own mystery. When he announces its destruction, it is as a manifestation of his own execution and of the entry into a new age in the history of salvation, when his Body would be the definitive Temple.

594 Jesus performed acts, such as pardoning sins, that manifested him to be the Saviour God himself (cf. Jn 5:16–18). Certain Jews, who did not recognize God made man (cf. Jn 1:14), saw in him only a man who made himself God (Jn 10:33), and judged him as a blasphemer.

Paragraph 2. Jesus Died Crucified

I. The Trial of Jesus

Divisions among the Jewish authorities concerning Jesus

595 Among the religious authorities of Jerusalem, not only were the Pharisee Nicodemus and the prominent Joseph of Arimathea both secret disciples of Jesus, but there was also long-standing dissension about him, so much so that St John says of these authorities on the very eve of Christ's Passion, 'many... believed in him', though very imperfectly.[378] This is not surprising, if one recalls that on the day after Pentecost 'a great many of the priests were obedient to the faith' and 'some believers... belonged to the party of the Pharisees', to the point that St James could tell St Paul, 'How many thousands there are among the Jews of those who have believed; and they are all zealous for the Law.'[379]

596 The religious authorities in Jerusalem were not unanimous about what stance to take towards Jesus.[380] The Pharisees threatened to excommunicate his followers.[381] To those who feared that 'everyone will believe in him, and the Romans will come and destroy both our holy place and our nation', the high priest Caiaphas replied by prophesying: 'It is expedient for you that one man should die for the people, and that the whole nation should not perish.'[382] The Sanhedrin, having declared Jesus deserving of death as a blasphemer but having lost the right to put anyone to death, hands him over to the Romans, accusing him of political revolt, a charge that puts him in the same category as Barabbas

1753

---

[377] Cf. Lk 23:34; Acts 3:17–18; Mk 3:5; Rom 11:25, 20.
[378] Jn 12:42; cf. 7:50; 9:16–17; 10:19–21; 19:38–39.

[379] Acts 6:7; 15:5; 21:20.
[380] Cf. Jn 9:16; 10:19.
[381] Cf. Jn 9:22.
[382] Jn 11:48–50.

who had been accused of sedition.[383] The chief priests also threatened Pilate politically so that he would condemn Jesus to death.[384]

Jews are not collectively responsible for Jesus' death

597 The historical complexity of Jesus' trial is apparent in the Gospel accounts. The personal sin of the participants (Judas, the Sanhedrin, Pilate) is known to God alone. Hence we cannot lay responsibility for the trial on the Jews in Jerusalem as a whole, despite the outcry of a manipulated crowd and the global reproaches contained in the apostles' calls to conversion after Pentecost.[385] Jesus himself, in forgiving them on the cross, and Peter in following suit, both accept 'the ignorance' of the Jews of 1735 Jerusalem and even of their leaders.[386] Still less can we extend responsibility to other Jews of different times and places, based merely on the crowd's cry: 'His blood be on us and on our children!', a formula for ratifying a judicial sentence.[387] As the Church declared at the Second Vatican Council:

> ... neither all Jews indiscriminately at that time, nor Jews today, can be 839
> charged with the crimes committed during his Passion... the Jews should
> not be spoken of as rejected or accursed as if this followed from holy
> Scripture.[388]

All sinners were the authors of Christ's Passion

598 In her Magisterial teaching of the faith and in the witness of her saints, the Church has never forgotten that 'sinners were the authors and the ministers of all the sufferings that the divine Redeemer endured.'[389] Taking into account the fact that our sins affect Christ himself,[390] the Church does not hesitate to impute to Christians the gravest responsibility for the torments inflicted upon Jesus, a responsibility with which they have all too often burdened the Jews alone:

> We must regard as guilty all those who continue to relapse into their sins.
> Since our sins made the Lord Christ suffer the torment of the cross, those 1851
> who plunge themselves into disorders and crimes crucify the Son of God
> anew in their hearts (for he is in them) and hold him up to contempt. And
> it can be seen that our crime in this case is greater in us than in the Jews. As
> for them, according to the witness of the Apostle, 'None of the rulers of
> this age understood this; for if they had, they would not have crucified
> the Lord of glory.' We, however, profess to know him. And when we

---

[383] Cf. Mt 26:66; Jn 18:31; Lk 23:2, 19.
[384] Cf. Jn 19:12, 15, 21.
[385] Cf. Mk 15:11; Acts 2:23, 36; 3:13-14; 4:10; 5:30; 7:52; 10:39; 13:27-28; 1 Th 2:14-15.
[386] Cf. Lk 23:34; Acts 3:17.
[387] Mt 27:25; cf. Acts 5:28; 18:6.
[388] NA 4.
[389] Roman Catechism I, 5, 11; cf. Heb 12:3.
[390] Cf. Mt 25:45; Acts 9:4-5.

deny him by our deeds, we in some way seem to lay violent hands on him.[391]

Nor did demons crucify him; it is you who have crucified him and crucify him still, when you delight in your vices and sins.[392]

II. Christ's Redemptive Death in God's Plan of Salvation

'Jesus handed over according to the definite plan of God'

599 Jesus' violent death was not the result of chance in an unfortunate coincidence of circumstances, but is part of the mystery of God's plan, as St Peter explains to the Jews of Jerusalem in his first sermon on Pentecost: 'This Jesus [was] delivered up according to the definite plan and foreknowledge of God.'[393] This Biblical language does not mean that those who handed him over were merely passive players in a scenario written in advance by God.[394]

600 To God, all moments of time are present in their immediacy. When therefore he establishes his eternal plan of 'predestination', he includes in it each person's free response to his grace: 'In this city, in fact, both Herod and Pontius Pilate, with the Gentiles and the peoples of Israel, gathered together against your holy servant Jesus, whom you anointed, to do whatever your hand and your plan had predestined to take place.'[395] For the sake of accomplishing his plan of salvation, God permitted the acts that flowed from their blindness.[396]

'He died for our sins in accordance with the Scriptures'

601 The Scriptures had foretold this divine plan of salvation through the putting to death of 'the righteous one, my Servant' as a mystery of universal redemption, that is, as the ransom that would free men from the slavery of sin.[397] Citing a confession of faith that he himself had 'received', St Paul professes that 'Christ died for our sins *in accordance with the scriptures*.'[398] In particular Jesus' redemptive death fulfils Isaiah's prophecy of the suffering Servant.[399] Indeed Jesus himself explained the meaning of his life and death in the light of God's suffering Servant.[400] After his Resurrection he gave this interpretation of the Scriptures to the disciples at Emmaus, and then to the apostles.[401]

517

312

652

713

---

[391] *Roman Catechism* I, 5, 11; cf. *Heb* 6:6; 1 *Cor* 2:8.
[392] St Francis of Assisi, *Admonitio* 5, 3.
[393] *Acts* 2:23.
[394] Cf. *Acts* 3:13.
[395] *Acts* 4:27–28; cf. *Ps* 2:1–2.
[396] Cf. *Mt* 26:54; *Jn* 18:36; 19:11; *Acts* 3:17–18.

[397] *Is* 53:11; cf. 53:12; *Jn* 8:34–36; *Acts* 3:14.
[398] 1 *Cor* 15:3; cf. also *Acts* 3:18; 7:52; 13:29; 26:22–23.
[399] Cf. *Is* 53:7–8 and *Acts* 8:32–35.
[400] Cf. *Mt* 20:28.
[401] Cf. *Lk* 24:25–27, 44–45.

'For our sake God made him to be sin'

602 Consequently, St Peter can formulate the apostolic faith in the divine plan of salvation in this way: 'You were ransomed from the futile ways inherited from your fathers... with the precious blood of Christ, like that of a lamb without blemish or spot. He was destined before the foundation of the world but was made manifest at the end of the times for your sake.'[402] Man's sins, following on original sin, are punishable by death.[403] By sending *400* his own Son in the form of a slave, in the form of a fallen humanity, on account of sin, God 'made him to be sin who knew no sin, so that in him we might become the righteousness of God.'[404] *519*

603 Jesus did not experience reprobation as if he himself had sinned.[405] But in the redeeming love that always united him to the Father, he assumed us in the state of our waywardness of sin, to the point that he could say in our name from the cross: 'My God, my God, why have you forsaken me?'[406] Having thus established him in solidarity with us sinners, God 'did not spare his own Son but *2572* gave him up for us all', so that we might be 'reconciled to God by the death of his Son'.[407]

God takes the initiative of universal redeeming love

604 By giving up his own Son for our sins, God manifests that his *211* plan for us is one of benevolent love, prior to any merit on our *2009* part: 'In this is love, not that we loved God but that he loved us and sent his Son to be the expiation for our sins.'[408] God 'shows his love for us in that while we were yet sinners Christ died for us.'[409] *1825*

605 At the end of the parable of the lost sheep Jesus recalled that God's love excludes no one: 'So it is not the will of your Father who is in heaven that one of these little ones should perish.'[410] He affirms that he came 'to give his life as a ransom *for many*'; this last term is not restrictive, but contrasts the whole of humanity with the unique person of the redeemer who hands himself over to save us.[411] The Church, following the apostles, teaches that Christ died for all men without exception: 'There is not, never has been, and *402* never will be a single human being for whom Christ did not *634, 2793* suffer.'[412]

---

[402] 1 *Pt* 1:18–20.
[403] Cf. *Rom* 5:12; 1 *Cor* 15:56.
[404] 2 *Cor* 5:21; cf. *Phil* 2:7; *Rom* 8:3.
[405] Cf. *Jn* 8:46.
[406] *Mk* 15:34; *Ps* 22:2; cf. *Jn* 8:29.
[407] *Rom* 8:32; 5:10.

[408] 1 *John* 4:10; 4:19.
[409] *Rom* 5:8.
[410] *Mt* 18:14.
[411] *Mt* 20:28; cf. *Rom* 5:18–19.
[412] Council of Quiercy (853): DS 624; cf. 2 *Cor* 5:15; 1 *Jn* 2:2.

III. Christ Offered Himself to His Father for Our Sins

Christ's whole life is an offering to the Father

606 The Son of God, who came down 'from heaven, not to do [his] own will, but the will of him who sent [him]',[413] said on coming into the world, 'Lo, I have come to do your will, O God.' *517* 'And by that will we have been sanctified through the offering of the body of Jesus Christ once for all.'[414] From the first moment of his Incarnation the Son embraces the Father's plan of divine salvation in his redemptive mission: 'My food is to do the will of him who sent me, and to accomplish his work.'[415] The sacrifice of Jesus *536* 'for the sins of the whole world'[416] expresses his loving communion with the Father. 'The Father loves me, because I lay down my life', said the Lord, '[for] I do as the Father has commanded me, so that the world may know that I love the Father.'[417]

607 The desire to embrace his Father's plan of redeeming love *457* inspired Jesus' whole life,[418] for his redemptive passion was the very reason for his Incarnation. And so he asked, 'And what shall I say? "Father, save me from this hour"'? No, for this purpose I have come to this hour.'[419] And again, 'Shall I not drink the cup which the Father has given me?'[420] From the cross, just before 'It is finished', he said, 'I thirst.'[421]

'The Lamb who takes away the sin of the world'

523 608 After agreeing to baptize him along with the sinners, John the Baptist looked at Jesus and pointed him out as the 'Lamb of God, who takes away the sin of the world'.[422] By doing so, he reveals that Jesus is at the same time the suffering Servant who silently allows himself to be led to the slaughter and who bears the sin of the multitudes, and also the Paschal Lamb, the symbol of Israel's redemption at the first Passover.[423] Christ's whole life expresses his mission: 'to serve, and to give his life as a ransom for many.'[424]

Jesus freely embraced the Father's redeeming love

609 By embracing in his human heart the Father's love for men, *478* Jesus 'loved them to the end', for 'greater love has no man than

---

[413] *Jn* 6:38.
[414] *Heb* 10:5–10.
[415] *Jn* 4:34.
[416] 1 *Jn* 2:2.
[417] *Jn* 10:17; 14:31.
[418] Cf. *Lk* 12:50; 22:15; *Mt* 16:21–23.
[419] *Jn* 12:27.

[420] *Jn* 18:11.
[421] *Jn* 19:30; 19:28.
[422] *Jn* 1:29; cf. *Lk* 3:21; *Mt* 3:14–15; *Jn* 1:36.
[423] *Is* 53:7, 12; cf. *Jer* 11:19; *Ex* 12:3–14; *Jn* 19:36; 1 *Cor* 5:7.
[424] *Mk* 10:45.

this, that a man lay down his life for his friends.'[425] In suffering and
death his humanity became the free and perfect instrument of his   515
divine love which desires the salvation of men.[426] Indeed, out of   272
love for his Father and for men, whom the Father wants to save,
Jesus freely accepted his Passion and death: 'No one takes [my life]   539
from me, but I lay it down of my own accord.'[427] Hence the
sovereign freedom of God's Son as he went out to his death.[428]

At the Last Supper Jesus anticipated the free offering of his life

610   Jesus gave the supreme expression of his free offering of him-   766
self at the meal shared with the twelve Apostles 'on the night he   1337
was betrayed'.[429] On the eve of his Passion, while still free, Jesus
transformed this Last Supper with the apostles into the memorial
of his voluntary offering to the Father for the salvation of men:
'This is my body which is *given* for you.' 'This is my blood of the
covenant, which is *poured out* for many for the forgiveness of
sins.'[430]

611   The Eucharist that Christ institutes at that moment will be the
memorial of his sacrifice.[431] Jesus includes the apostles in his own   1364
offering and bids them perpetuate it.[432] By doing so, the Lord   1341
institutes his apostles as priests of the New Covenant: 'For their sakes   1566
I sanctify myself, so that they also may be sanctified in
truth.'[433]

The agony at Gethsemani

612   The cup of the New Covenant, which Jesus anticipated when
he offered himself at the Last Supper, is afterwards accepted by
him from his Father's hands in his agony in the garden at Gethsemani,[434] making himself 'obedient unto death'. Jesus prays: 'My   532, 2600
Father, if it be possible, let this cup pass from me...'[435] Thus he
expresses the horror that death represented for his human nature.
Like ours, his human nature is destined for eternal life; but unlike
ours, it is perfectly exempt from sin, the cause of death.[436] Above
all, his human nature has been assumed by the divine person of the
'Author of life', the 'Living One'.[437] By accepting in his human

---

[425] *Jn* 13:1; 15:13.
[426] Cf. *Heb* 2:10, 17–18; 4:15; 5:7–9.
[427] *Jn* 10:18.
[428] Cf. *Jn* 18:4–6; *Mt* 26:53.
[429] *Roman Missal*, EP III,111; cf. *Mt* 26:20; 1 *Cor* 11:23.
[430] *Lk* 22:19; *Mt* 26:28; cf. 1 *Cor* 5:7.
[431] 1 *Cor* 11:25.

[432] Cf. *Lk* 22:19.
[433] *Jn* 17:19; cf. Council of Trent: DS 1752; 1764.
[434] Cf. *Mt* 26:42; *Lk* 22:20.
[435] *Phil* 2:8; *Mt* 26:39; cf. *Heb* 5:7–8.
[436] Cf. *Rom* 5:12; *Heb* 4:15.
[437] Cf. *Acts* 3:15; *Rev* 1:17; *Jn* 1:4; 5:26.

1009 will that the Father's will be done, he accepts his death as redemptive, for 'he himself bore our sins in his body on the tree.'[438]

Christ's death is the unique and definitive sacrifice

1366 613 Christ's death is both the *Paschal sacrifice* that accomplishes the definitive redemption of men, through 'the Lamb of God, who takes away the sin of the world',[439] and the *sacrifice of the New* *2009* *Covenant*, which restores man to communion with God by reconciling him to God through the 'blood of the covenant, which was poured out for many for the forgiveness of sins'.[440]

529, 1330 614 This sacrifice of Christ is unique; it completes and surpasses all other sacrifices.[441] First, it is a gift from God the Father himself, for the Father handed his Son over to sinners in order to reconcile us *2100* with himself. At the same time it is the offering of the Son of God made man, who in freedom and love offered his life to his Father through the Holy Spirit in reparation for our disobedience.[442]

Jesus substitutes his obedience for our disobedience

615 'For as by one man's disobedience many were made sinners, so by one man's obedience many will be made righteous.'[443] By his *1850* obedience unto death, Jesus accomplished the substitution of the *433* suffering Servant, who 'makes himself an *offering for sin*', when 'he bore the sin of many', and who 'shall make many to be accounted *411* righteous', for 'he shall bear their iniquities'.[444] Jesus atoned for our faults and made satisfaction for our sins to the Father.[445]

Jesus consummates his sacrifice on the cross

616 It is love 'to the end'[446] that confers on Christ's sacrifice its value as redemption and reparation, as atonement and satisfaction. He knew and loved us all when he offered his life.[447] Now 'the *478* love of Christ controls us, because we are convinced that one has died for all; therefore all have died.'[448] No man, not even the holiest, was ever able to take on himself the sins of all men and offer himself as a sacrifice for all. The existence in Christ of the *468* divine person of the Son, who at once surpasses and embraces all

---

438 1 *Pt* 2:24; cf. *Mt* 26:42.
439 *Jn* 1:29; cf. 8:34–36; 1 *Cor* 5:7; 1 *Pt* 1:19.
440 *Mt* 26:28; cf. *Ex* 24:8; *Lev* 16:15–16; 1 *Cor* 11:25.
441 Cf. *Heb* 10:10.
442 Cf. *Jn* 10:17–18; 15:13; *Heb* 9:14; 1 *Jn* 4:10.

443 *Rom* 5:19.
444 *Is* 53:10–12.
445 Cf. Council of Trent (1547): DS 1529.
446 *Jn* 13:1.
447 Cf. *Gal* 2:20; *Eph* 5:2, 25.
448 2 *Cor* 5:14.

human persons, and constitutes himself as the Head of all man- *519*
kind, makes possible his redemptive sacrifice *for all*.

617 The Council of Trent emphasizes the unique character of
Christ's sacrifice as 'the source of eternal salvation'[449] and teaches
that 'his most holy Passion on the wood of the cross merited *1992*
justification for us.'[450] And the Church venerates his cross as she *1235*
sings: 'Hail, O Cross, our only hope.'[451]

Our participation in Christ's sacrifice

618 The cross is the unique sacrifice of Christ, the 'one mediator
between God and men'.[452] But because in his incarnate divine
person he has in some way united himself to every man, 'the
possibility of being made partners, in a way known to God, in the
paschal mystery' is offered to all men.[453] He calls his disciples to
'take up [their] cross and follow [him]',[454] for 'Christ also suffered *1368*
for [us], leaving [us] an example so that [we] should follow in his *1460, 307*
steps.'[455] In fact Jesus desires to associate with his redeeming sacri- *2100*
fice those who were to be its first beneficiaries.[456] This is achieved
supremely in the case of his mother, who was associated more *964*
intimately than any other person in the mystery of his redemptive
suffering.[457]

> Apart from the cross there is no other ladder by which we may get to
> heaven.[458]

IN BRIEF

619 *'Christ died for our sins in accordance with the scriptures'* (1 Cor 15:3).

620 *Our salvation flows from God's initiative of love for us, because 'he
loved us and sent his Son to be the expiation for our sins'* (1 Jn 4:10). *'God
was in Christ reconciling the world to himself'* (2 Cor 5:19).

621 *Jesus freely offered himself for our salvation. Beforehand, during the
Last Supper, he both symbolized this offering and made it really present:
'This is my body which is given for you'* (Lk 22:19).

622 *The redemption won by Christ consists in this, that he came 'to give his
life as a ransom for many' (Mt 20:28), that is, he 'loved [his own] to the end'
(Jn 13:1), so that they might be 'ransomed from the futile ways inherited from
[their] fathers'* (1 Pt 1:18).

---

[449] *Heb* 5:9.
[450] Council of Trent: DS 1529.
[451] *LH*, Lent, Holy Week, Evening
Prayer, Hymn *Vexilla Regis*.
[452] 1 *Tim* 2:5.
[453] GS 22 § 5; cf. § 2.

[454] *Mt* 16:24.
[455] 1 *Pt* 2:21.
[456] Cf. *Mk* 10:39; *Jn* 21:18–19; *Col* 1:24.
[457] Cf. *Lk* 2:35.
[458] St Rose of Lima: cf. P. Hansen, *Vita
mirabilis* (Louvain, 1668).

> 623 By his loving obedience to the Father, 'unto death, even death on a cross' (Phil 2:8), Jesus fulfils the atoning mission (cf. Is 53:10) of the suffering Servant, who will 'make many righteous; and he shall bear their iniquities' (Is 53:11; cf. Rom 5:19).

Paragraph 3. Jesus Christ Was Buried

624 'By the grace of God' Jesus tasted death 'for every one'.[459] In his plan of salvation, God ordained that his Son should not only *1005* 'die for our sins'[460] but should also 'taste death', experience the *362* condition of death, the separation of his soul from his body, between the time he expired on the cross and the time he was raised from the dead. The state of the dead Christ is the mystery of the tomb and the descent into hell. It is the mystery of Holy Saturday, when Christ, lying in the tomb,[461] reveals God's great *349* sabbath rest[462] after the fulfilment[463] of man's salvation, which brings peace to the whole universe.[464]

Christ in the tomb in his body

625 Christ's stay in the tomb constitutes the real link between his passible state before Easter and his glorious and risen state today. The same person of the 'Living One' can say, 'I died, and behold I am alive for evermore':[465]

> God [the Son] did not impede death from separating his soul from his body according to the necessary order of nature, but has reunited them to one another in the Resurrection, *so that he himself might be, in his person, the meeting point for death and life*, by arresting in himself the decomposition of nature produced by death and so becoming the source of reunion for the separated parts.[466]

626 Since the 'Author of life' who was killed[467] is the same 'living one [who has] risen',[468] the divine person of the Son of God *470, 650* necessarily continued to possess his human soul and body, separated from each other by death:

> By the fact that at Christ's death his soul was separated from his flesh, his one person is not itself divided into two persons; for the human body and soul of Christ have existed in the same way from the beginning of his earthly existence, in the divine person of the Word; and in death,

---

[459] Heb 2:9.
[460] 1 Cor 15:3.
[461] Cf. Jn 19:42.
[462] Cf. Heb 4:7–9.
[463] Cf. Jn 19:30.
[464] Cf. Col 1:18–20.

[465] Rev 1:18.
[466] St Gregory of Nyssa, Orat. catech. 16: PG 45, 52D.
[467] Acts 3:15.
[468] Lk 24:5–6.

although separated from each other, both remained with one and the same person of the Word.[469]

'You will not let your Holy One see corruption'

627 Christ's death was a real death in that it put an end to his earthly human existence. But because of the union which the person of the Son retained with his body, his was not a mortal corpse like others, for 'it was not possible for death to hold him'[469a] and therefore 'divine power preserved Christ's body from corruption'.[470] Both of these statements can be said of Christ: 'He was cut off out of the land of the living',[471] and 'My flesh will dwell in hope. For you will not abandon my soul to Hades, nor let your Holy One see corruption.'[472] Jesus' Resurrection 'on the third day' was the sign of this, also because bodily decay was held to begin on the fourth day after death.[473]

1009

1683

'Buried with Christ...'

628 Baptism, the original and full sign of which is immersion, efficaciously signifies the descent into the tomb by the Christian who dies to sin with Christ in order to live a new life. 'We were buried therefore with him by baptism into death, so that as Christ was raised from the dead by the glory of the Father, we too might walk in newness of life.'[474]

537

1214

IN BRIEF

629 *To the benefit of every man, Jesus Christ tasted death (cf. Heb 2:9). It is truly the Son of God made man who died and was buried.*

630 *During Christ's period in the tomb, his divine person continued to assume both his soul and his body, although they were separated from each other by death. For this reason the dead Christ's body 'saw no corruption' (Acts 13:37).*

Article 5
'HE DESCENDED INTO HELL. ON THE THIRD DAY HE ROSE AGAIN'

631 Jesus 'descended into the lower parts of the earth. He who descended is he who also ascended far above all the heavens.'[475] The Apostles' Creed confesses in the same article Christ's descent

---

[469] St John Damascene, *De fide orth.* 3, 27: PG 94, 1097.
[469a] *Acts* 2:24.
[470] St Thomas Aquinas, *STh* III, 51, 3.
[471] *Is* 53:8.
[472] *Acts* 2:26–27; cf. *Ps* 16:9–10.
[473] Cf. 1 *Cor* 15:4; *Lk* 24:46; *Mt* 12:40; *Jon* 2:1; *Hos* 6:2; cf. *Jn* 11:39.
[474] *Rom* 6:4; cf. *Col* 2:12; *Eph* 5:26.
[475] *Eph* 4:9–10.

into hell and his Resurrection from the dead on the third day, because in his Passover it was precisely out of the depths of death that he made life spring forth:

> Christ, that Morning Star, who came back from the dead,
> and shed his peaceful light on all mankind,
> your Son who lives and reigns for ever and ever. Amen.[476]

Paragraph 1. Christ Descended into Hell

632 The frequent New Testament affirmations that Jesus was 'raised from the dead' presuppose that the crucified one sojourned in the realm of the dead prior to his resurrection.[477] This was the first meaning given in the apostolic preaching to Christ's descent into hell: that Jesus, like all men, experienced death and in his soul joined the others in the realm of the dead. But he descended there as Saviour, proclaiming the Good News to the spirits imprisoned there.[478]

633 Scripture calls the abode of the dead, to which the dead Christ went down, 'hell' – Sheol in Hebrew or Hades in Greek – because those who are there are deprived of the vision of God.[479] Such is the case for all the dead, whether evil or righteous, while they await the Redeemer: which does not mean that their lot is identical, as Jesus shows through the parable of the poor man Lazarus who was received into 'Abraham's bosom':[480] 'It is precisely these holy souls, who awaited their Saviour in Abraham's bosom, whom Christ the Lord delivered when he descended into hell.'[481] Jesus *1033* did not descend into hell to deliver the damned, nor to destroy the hell of damnation, but to free the just who had gone before him.[482]

634 'The gospel was preached even to the dead.'[483] The descent into hell brings the Gospel message of salvation to complete fulfilment. This is the last phase of Jesus' messianic mission, a phase which is condensed in time but vast in its real significance: the *605* spread of Christ's redemptive work to all men of all times and all places, for all who are saved have been made sharers in the redemption.

635 Christ went down into the depths of death so that 'the dead

---

[476] *Roman Missal*, Easter Vigil 18, *Exsultet*.

[477] *Acts* 3:15; *Rom* 8:11; 1 *Cor* 15:20; cf. *Heb* 13:20.

[478] Cf. 1 *Pt* 3:18–19.

[479] Cf. *Phil* 2:10; *Acts* 2:24; *Rev* 1:18; *Eph* 4:9; *Pss* 6:6; 88:11–13.

[480] Cf. *Ps* 89:49; 1 *Sam* 28:19; *Ezek* 32:17–32; *Lk* 16:22–26.

[481] *Roman Catechism* I, 6, 3.

[482] Cf. Council of Rome (745): DS 587; Benedict XII, *Cum dudum* (1341): DS 1011; Clement VI, *Super quibusdam* (1351): DS 1077; Council of Toledo IV (625): DS 485; *Mt* 27:52–53.

[483] 1 *Pt* 4:6.

will hear the voice of the Son of God, and those who hear will live.'[484] Jesus, 'the Author of life', by dying destroyed 'him who has the power of death, that is, the devil, and [delivered] all those who through fear of death were subject to lifelong bondage.'[485] Henceforth the risen Christ holds 'the keys of Death and Hades', so that 'at the name of Jesus every knee should bow, in heaven and on earth and under the earth.'[486]

> Today a great silence reigns on earth, a great silence and a great stillness. A great silence because the King is asleep. The earth trembled and is still because God has fallen asleep in the flesh and he has raised up all who have slept ever since the world began... He has gone to search for Adam, our first father, as for a lost sheep. Greatly desiring to visit those who live in darkness and in the shadow of death, he has gone to free from sorrow Adam in his bonds and Eve, captive with him – He who is both their God and the son of Eve... 'I am your God, who for your sake have become your son... I order you, O sleeper, to awake. I did not create you to be a prisoner in hell. Rise from the dead, for I am the life of the dead.'[487]

IN BRIEF

636 By the expression 'He descended into hell', the Apostles' Creed confesses that Jesus did really die and through his death for us conquered death and the devil 'who has the power of death' (Heb 2:14).

637 In his human soul united to his divine person, the dead Christ went down to the realm of the dead. He opened heaven's gates for the just who had gone before him.

Paragraph 2. On the Third Day He Rose from the Dead

638 'We bring you the good news that what God promised to the fathers, this day he has fulfilled to us their children by raising Jesus.'[488] The Resurrection of Jesus is the crowning truth of our faith in Christ, a faith believed and lived as the central truth by the first Christian community; handed on as fundamental by Tradition; established by the documents of the New Testament; and preached as an essential part of the Paschal mystery along with the cross: *90* *651, 991*

> Christ is risen from the dead!
> Dying, he conquered death;
> To the dead, he has given life.[489]

---

[484] Jn 5:25; cf. Mt 12:40; Rom 10:7; Eph 4:9.
[485] Heb 2:14–15; cf. Acts 3:15.
[486] Rev 1:18; Phil 2:10.
[487] Ancient Homily for Holy Saturday: PG 43, 440A, 452C; LH, Holy Saturday, OR.
[488] Acts 13:32–33.
[489] Byzantine Liturgy, Troparion of Easter.

I. The Historical and Transcendent Event

639 The mystery of Christ's resurrection is a real event, with manifestations that were historically verified, as the New Testament bears witness. In about A.D. 56 St Paul could already write to the Corinthians: 'I delivered to you as of first importance what I also received, that Christ died for our sins in accordance with the scriptures, and that he was buried, that he was raised on the third day in accordance with the scriptures, and that he appeared to Cephas, then to the Twelve...'[490] The Apostle speaks here of *the living tradition of the Resurrection* which he had learned after his conversion at the gates of Damascus.[491]

The empty tomb

640 'Why do you seek the living among the dead? He is not here, but has risen.'[492] The first element we encounter in the framework of the Easter events is the empty tomb. In itself it is not a direct proof of Resurrection; the absence of Christ's body from the tomb could be explained otherwise.[493] Nonetheless the empty tomb was still an essential sign for all. Its discovery by the disciples was the first step toward recognizing the very fact of the Resurrection. This was the case, first with the holy women, and then with Peter.[494] The disciple 'whom Jesus loved' affirmed that when he entered the empty tomb and discovered 'the linen cloths lying there', 'he saw and believed'.[495] This suggests that he realized from the empty tomb's condition that the absence of Jesus' body could not have been of human doing and that Jesus had not simply returned to earthly life as had been the case with Lazarus.[496]

999

The appearances of the Risen One

641 Mary Magdalene and the holy women who came to finish anointing the body of Jesus, which had been buried in haste because the Sabbath began on the evening of Good Friday, were the first to encounter the Risen One.[497] Thus the women were the first messengers of Christ's Resurrection for the apostles themselves.[498] They were the next to whom Jesus appears: first Peter, then the Twelve. Peter had been called to strengthen the faith of his brothers,[499] and so sees the Risen One before them; it is on the

553

---

[490] 1 *Cor* 15:3–4.
[491] Cf. *Acts* 9:3–18.
[492] *Lk* 24:5–6.
[493] Cf. *Jn* 20:13; *Mt* 28:11–15.
[494] Cf. *Lk* 24:3, 12, 22–23.
[495] *Jn* 20:2, 6, 8.

[496] Cf. *Jn* 11:44; 20:5–7.
[497] *Mk* 16:1; *Lk* 24:1; *Jn* 19:31, 42.
[498] Cf. *Lk* 24:9–10; *Mt* 28:9–10; *Jn* 20:11–18.
[499] Cf. 1 *Cor* 15:5; *Lk* 22:31–32.

basis of his testimony that the community exclaims: 'The Lord has *448* risen indeed, and has appeared to Simon!'[500]

642 Everything that happened during those Paschal days involves each of the apostles – and Peter in particular – in the building of the new era begun on Easter morning. As witnesses of the Risen One, *659* they remain the foundation stones of his Church. The faith of the *881* first community of believers is based on the witness of concrete men known to the Christians and for the most part still living among them. Peter and the Twelve are the primary 'witnesses to *860* his Resurrection', but they are not the only ones – Paul speaks clearly of more than five hundred persons to whom Jesus appeared on a single occasion and also of James and of all the apostles.[501]

643 Given all these testimonies, Christ's Resurrection cannot be interpreted as something outside the physical order, and it is impossible not to acknowledge it as an historical fact. It is clear from the facts that the disciples' faith was drastically put to the test by their master's Passion and death on the cross, which he had foretold.[502] The shock provoked by the Passion was so great that at least some of the disciples did not at once believe in the news of the Resurrection. Far from showing us a community seized by a mystical exaltation, the Gospels present us with disciples demoralized ('looking sad'[503]) and frightened. For they had not believed the holy women returning from the tomb and had regarded their words as an 'idle tale'.[504] When Jesus reveals himself to the Eleven on Easter evening, 'he upbraided them for their unbelief and hardness of heart, because they had not believed those who saw him after he had risen.'[505]

644 Even when faced with the reality of the risen Jesus the disciples are still doubtful, so impossible did the thing seem: they thought they were seeing a ghost. 'In their joy they were still disbelieving and still wondering.'[506] Thomas will also experience the test of doubt and St Matthew relates that during the risen Lord's last appearance in Galilee 'some doubted.'[507] Therefore the hypothesis that the Resurrection was produced by the apostles' faith (or credulity) will not hold up. On the contrary their faith in the Resurrection was born, under the action of divine grace, from their direct experience of the reality of the risen Jesus.

The condition of Christ's risen humanity

645 By means of touch and the sharing of a meal, the risen Jesus establishes direct contact with his disciples. He invites them in this way to recognize that he is not a ghost and above all to verify that the risen body in which he appears to them is the same body that *999* had been tortured and crucified, for it still bears the traces of his

[500] Lk 24:34, 36.
[501] 1 Cor 15:4–8; cf. Acts 1:22.
[502] Cf. Lk 22:31–32.
[503] Lk 24:17; cf. Jn 20:19.
[504] Lk 24:11; cf. Mk 16:11, 13.
[505] Mk 16:14.
[506] Lk 24:38–41.
[507] Cf. Jn 20:24–27; Mt 28:17.

Passion.[508] Yet at the same time this authentic, real body possesses the new properties of a glorious body: not limited by space and time but able to be present how and when he wills; for Christ's humanity can no longer be confined to earth, and belongs henceforth only to the Father's divine realm.[509] For this reason too the risen Jesus enjoys the sovereign freedom of appearing as he wishes: in the guise of a gardener or in other forms familiar to his disciples, precisely to awaken their faith.[510]

646 Christ's Resurrection was not a return to earthly life, as was the case with the raisings from the dead that he had performed before Easter: Jairus' daughter, the young man of Naim, Lazarus. 549 These actions were miraculous events, but the persons miraculously raised returned by Jesus' power to ordinary earthly life. At some particular moment they would die again. Christ's Resurrection is essentially different. In his risen body he passes from the state of death to another life beyond time and space. At Jesus' Resurrection his body is filled with the power of the Holy Spirit: he shares the divine life in his glorious state, so that St Paul can say that Christ is 'the man of heaven'.[511]

The Resurrection as transcendent event

647 O truly blessed Night, sings the *Exsultet* of the Easter Vigil, which alone deserved to know the time and the hour when Christ rose from the realm of the dead![512] But no one was an eyewitness to Christ's Resurrection and no evangelist describes it. No one can 1000 say how it came about physically. Still less was its innermost essence, his passing over to another life, perceptible to the senses. Although the Resurrection was an historical event that could be verified by the sign of the empty tomb and by the reality of the apostles' encounters with the risen Christ, still it remains at the very heart of the mystery of faith as something that transcends and surpasses history. This is why the risen Christ does not reveal himself to the world, but to his disciples, 'to those who came up with him from Galilee to Jerusalem, who are now his witnesses to the people'.[513]

---

508 Cf. *Lk* 24:30, 39–40, 41–43; *Jn* 20:20, 27; 21:9, 13–15.
509 Cf. *Mt* 28:9, 16–17; *Lk* 24:15, 36; *Jn* 20:14, 17, 19, 26; 21:4.
510 Cf. *Mk* 16:12; *Jn* 20:14–16; 21:4, 7.

511 Cf. 1 *Cor* 15:35–50.
512 *O vere beata nox, quae sola meruit scire tempus et horam, in qua Christus ab inferis resurrexit!*
513 *Acts* 13:31; cf. *Jn* 14:22.

II. The Resurrection – A Work of the Holy Trinity

648 Christ's Resurrection is an object of faith in that it is a transcendent intervention of God himself in creation and history. In it the three divine persons act together as one, and manifest their own proper characteristics. The Father's power 'raised up' Christ his Son and by doing so perfectly introduced his Son's humanity, including his body, into the Trinity. Jesus is conclusively revealed as 'Son of God in power according to the Spirit of holiness by his Resurrection from the dead'.[514] St Paul insists on the manifestation of God's power[515] through the working of the Spirit who gave life to Jesus' dead humanity and called it to the glorious state of Lordship. *989, 258 663 445 272*

649 As for the Son, he effects his own Resurrection by virtue of his divine power. Jesus announces that the Son of man will have to suffer much, die, and then rise.[516] Elsewhere he affirms explicitly: 'I lay down my life, that I may take it again. . . I have power to lay it down, and I have power to take it again.'[517] 'We believe that Jesus died and rose again.'[518]

650 The Fathers contemplate the Resurrection from the perspective of the divine person of Christ who remained united to his soul and body, even when these were separated from each other by death: 'By the unity of the divine nature, which remains present in each of the two components of man, these are reunited. For as death is produced by the separation of the human components, so Resurrection is achieved by the union of the two.'[519] *626 1005*

III. The Meaning and Saving Significance of the Resurrection

651 'If Christ has not been raised, then our preaching is in vain and your faith is in vain.'[520] The Resurrection above all constitutes the confirmation of all Christ's works and teachings. All truths, even those most inaccessible to human reason, find their justification if Christ by his Resurrection has given the definitive proof of his divine authority, which he had promised. *129 274*

652 Christ's Resurrection is *the fulfilment of the promises* both of the Old Testament and of Jesus himself during his earthly life.[521] The

---

[514] *Rom* 1:3–4; cf. *Acts* 2:24.
[515] Cf. *Rom* 6:4; 2 *Cor* 13:4; *Phil* 3:10; *Eph* 1:19–22; *Heb* 7:16.
[516] Cf. *Mk* 8:31; 9:9–31; 10:34.
[517] *Jn* 10:17–18.
[518] 1 *Th* 4:14.

[519] St Gregory of Nyssa, *In Christi res. orat.* 1: PG 46, 617B; cf. also DS 325; 359; 369.
[520] 1 *Cor* 15:14.
[521] Cf. *Mt* 28:6; *Mk* 16:7; *Lk* 24:6–7, 26–27, 44–48.

601, 994   phrase 'in accordance with the Scriptures'[522] indicates that Christ's Resurrection fulfilled these predictions.

653 The truth of *Jesus' divinity* is confirmed by his Resurrection. He had said: 'When you have lifted up the Son of man, then you
445   will know that I am he.'[523] The Resurrection of the crucified one shows that he was truly 'I AM', the Son of God and God himself. So St Paul could declare to the Jews: 'What God promised to the fathers, this he has fulfilled to us their children by raising Jesus; as also it is written in the second psalm, "You are my Son, today I have begotten you." '[524] Christ's Resurrection is closely linked to
461, 422   the Incarnation of God's Son, and is its fulfilment in accordance with God's eternal plan.

654 The Paschal mystery has two aspects: by his death, Christ liberates us from sin; by his Resurrection, he opens for us the way
1987   to a new life. This new life is above all *justification* that reinstates us in God's grace, 'so that as Christ was raised from the dead by the glory of the Father, we too might walk in newness of life.'[525] Justification consists in both victory over the death caused by sin
1996   and a new participation in grace.[526] It brings about *filial adoption* so that men become Christ's brethren, as Jesus himself called his disciples after his Resurrection: 'Go and tell my brethren.'[527] We are brethren not by nature, but by the gift of grace, because that adoptive filiation gains us a real share in the life of the only Son, which was fully revealed in his Resurrection.

655 Finally, Christ's Resurrection – and the risen Christ himself –
989   is the principle and source of *our future resurrection*: 'Christ has been raised from the dead, the first fruits of those who have fallen asleep. . . For as in Adam all die, so also in Christ shall all be made alive.'[528] The risen Christ lives in the hearts of his faithful while
1002   they await that fulfilment. In Christ, Christians 'have tasted. . . the powers of the age to come'[529] and their lives are swept up by Christ into the heart of divine life, so that they may 'live no longer for themselves but for him who for their sake died and was raised.'[530]

---

[522] Cf. 1 *Cor* 15:3–4; cf. the Nicene Creed.
[523] *Jn* 8:28.
[524] *Acts* 13:32–33; cf. *Ps* 2:7.
[525] *Rom* 6:4; cf. 4:25.

[526] Cf. *Eph* 2:4–5; 1 *Pt* 1:3.
[527] *Mt* 28:10; *Jn* 20:17.
[528] 1 *Cor* 15:20–22.
[529] *Heb* 6:5.
[530] 2 *Cor* 5:15; cf. *Col* 3:1–3.

IN BRIEF

656 Faith in the Resurrection has as its object an event which is historically attested to by the disciples, who really encountered the Risen One. At the same time, this event is mysteriously transcendent insofar as it is the entry of Christ's humanity into the glory of God.

657 The empty tomb and the linen cloths lying there signify in themselves that by God's power Christ's body had escaped the bonds of death and corruption. They prepared the disciples to encounter the Risen Lord.

658 Christ, 'the first-born from the dead' (Col 1:18), is the principle of our own resurrection, even now by the justification of our souls (cf. Rom 6:4), and one day by the new life he will impart to our bodies (cf. Rom 8:11).

Article 6

'HE ASCENDED INTO HEAVEN AND IS SEATED AT THE RIGHT HAND OF THE FATHER'

659 'So then the Lord Jesus, after he had spoken to them, was taken up into heaven, and sat down at the right hand of God.'[531] Christ's body was glorified at the moment of his Resurrection, as *645* proved by the new and supernatural properties it subsequently and permanently enjoys.[532] But during the forty days when he eats and drinks familiarly with his disciples and teaches them about the kingdom, his glory remains veiled under the appearance of ordinary humanity.[533] Jesus' final apparition ends with the irreversible entry of his humanity into divine glory, symbolized by the cloud *66, 697* and by heaven, where he is seated from that time forward at God's right hand.[534] Only in a wholly exceptional and unique way would Jesus show himself to Paul 'as to one untimely born', in a last apparition that established him as an apostle.[535]   *642*

660 The veiled character of the glory of the Risen One during this time is intimated in his mysterious words to Mary Magdalene: 'I have not yet ascended to the Father; but go to my brethren and say to them, I am ascending to my Father and your Father, to my God and your God.'[536] This indicates a difference in manifestation between the glory of the risen Christ and that of the Christ exalted to the Father's right hand, a transition marked by the historical and transcendent event of the Ascension.

---

[531] Mk 16:19.
[532] Cf. Lk 24:31; Jn 20:19, 26.
[533] Cf. Acts 1:3; 10:41; Mk 16:12; Lk 24:15; Jn 20:14–15; 21:4.

[534] Cf. Acts 1:9; 2:33; 7:56; Lk 9:34–35; 24:51; Ex 13:22; Mk 16:19; Ps 110:1.
[535] 1 Cor 15:8; cf. 9:1; Gal 1:16.
[536] Jn 20:17.

661 This final stage stays closely linked to the first, that is, to his
461 descent from heaven in the Incarnation. Only the one who 'came
from the Father' can return to the Father: Christ Jesus.[537] 'No one
has ascended into heaven but he who descended from heaven, the
Son of man.'[538] Left to its own natural powers humanity does not
have access to the 'Father's house', to God's life and happiness.[539]
Only Christ can open to man such access that we, his members,
792 might have confidence that we too shall go where he, our Head
and our Source, has preceded us.[540]

662 'And I, when I am lifted up from the earth, will draw all men
to myself.'[541] The lifting up of Jesus on the cross signifies and
announces his lifting up by his Ascension into heaven, and indeed
1545 begins it. Jesus Christ, the one priest of the new and eternal Covenant, 'entered, not into a sanctuary made by human hands... but
into heaven itself, now to appear in the presence of God on our
behalf.'[542] There Christ permanently exercises his priesthood, for
he 'always lives to make intercession' for 'those who draw near to
1137 God through him'.[543] As 'high priest of the good things to come'
he is the centre and the principal actor of the liturgy that honours
the Father in heaven.[544]

663 Henceforth Christ is *seated at the right hand of the Father*: 'By
"the Father's right hand" we understand the glory and honour of
divinity, where he who exists as Son of God before all ages, indeed
648 as God, of one being with the Father, is seated bodily after he
became incarnate and his flesh was glorified.'[545]

664 Being seated at the Father's right hand signifies the inaugur-
541 ation of the Messiah's kingdom, the fulfilment of the prophet
Daniel's vision concerning the Son of man: 'To him was given
dominion and glory and kingdom, that all peoples, nations, and
languages should serve him; his dominion is an everlasting dominion, which shall not pass away, and his kingdom one that shall not
be destroyed.'[546] After this event the apostles became witnesses of
the 'kingdom [that] will have no end'.[547]

---

[537] Cf. *Jn* 16:28.
[538] *Jn* 3:13; cf. *Eph* 4:8–10.
[539] *Jn* 14:2.
[540] *Missale Romanum*, Preface of the
Ascension: *sed ut illuc confideremus, sua
membra, nos subsequi quo ipse, caput
nostrum principiumque, praecessit.*
[541] *Jn* 12:32.

[542] *Heb* 9:24.
[543] *Heb* 7:25.
[544] *Heb* 9:11; cf. *Rev* 4:6–11.
[545] St John Damascene, *De fide orth.* 4, 2:
PG 94, 1104C.
[546] *Dan* 7:14.
[547] Nicene Creed.

IN BRIEF

665 *Christ's Ascension marks the definitive entrance of Jesus' humanity into God's heavenly domain, whence he will come again (cf. Acts 1:11); this humanity in the meantime hides him from the eyes of men (cf. Col 3:3).*

666 *Jesus Christ, the head of the Church, precedes us into the Father's glorious kingdom so that we, the members of his Body, may live in the hope of one day being with him for ever.*

667 *Jesus Christ, having entered the sanctuary of heaven once and for all, intercedes constantly for us as the mediator who assures us of the permanent outpouring of the Holy Spirit.*

Article 7

'FROM THENCE HE WILL COME AGAIN TO JUDGE THE LIVING AND THE DEAD'

I. He Will Come Again in Glory

Christ already reigns through the Church...

668 'Christ died and lived again, that he might be Lord both of the dead and of the living.'[548] Christ's Ascension into heaven signifies his participation, in his humanity, in God's power and authority. Jesus Christ is Lord: he possesses all power in heaven and on earth. He is 'far above all rule and authority and power and dominion', for the Father 'has put all things under his feet.'[549] Christ is Lord of the cosmos and of history. In him human history and indeed all creation are 'set forth' and transcendently fulfilled.[550]
450
518

669 As Lord, Christ is also head of the Church, which is his Body.[551] Taken up to heaven and glorified after he had thus fully accomplished his mission, Christ dwells on earth in his Church. The redemption is the source of the authority that Christ, by virtue of the Holy Spirit, exercises over the Church. 'The kingdom of Christ [is] already present in mystery', 'on earth, the seed and the beginning of the kingdom'.[552]
792
1088
541

670 Since the Ascension God's plan has entered into its fulfilment. We are already at 'the last hour'.[553] 'Already the final age of the world is with us, and the renewal of the world is irrevocably under way; it is even now anticipated in a certain real way, for the
1042

---

[548] *Rom* 14:9.
[549] *Eph* 1:20-22.
[550] *Eph* 1:10; cf. 4:10; 1 *Cor* 15:24, 27-28.
[551] Cf. *Eph* 1:22.
[552] *LG* 3; 5; cf. *Eph* 4:11-13.
[553] 1 *Jn* 2:18; cf. 1 *Pt* 4:7.

Church on earth is endowed already with a sanctity that is real but
825, 547 imperfect.'[554] Christ's kingdom already manifests its presence
through the miraculous signs that attend its proclamation by the
Church.[555]

... until all things are subjected to him

671 Though already present in his Church, Christ's reign is
nevertheless yet to be fulfilled 'with power and great glory' by the
King's return to earth.[556] This reign is still under attack by the evil
powers, even though they have been defeated definitively by
Christ's Passover.[557] Until everything is subject to him, 'until
1043 there be realized new heavens and a new earth in which justice
769, 773 dwells, the pilgrim Church, in her sacraments and institutions,
which belong to this present age, carries the mark of this world
which will pass, and she herself takes her place among the creatures
1043 which groan and travail yet and await the revelation of the sons of
God.'[558] That is why Christians pray, above all in the Eucharist, to
1046, 2817 hasten Christ's return by saying to him:[559] Marana tha! 'Our Lord,
come!'[560]

672 Before his Ascension Christ affirmed that the hour had not
yet come for the glorious establishment of the messianic kingdom
awaited by Israel[561] which, according to the prophets, was to
bring all men the definitive order of justice, love and peace.[562]
732 According to the Lord, the present time is the time of the Spirit
and of witness, but also a time still marked by 'distress' and the trial
of evil which does not spare the Church[563] and ushers in the strug-
2612 gles of the last days. It is a time of waiting and watching.[564]

The glorious advent of Christ, the hope of Israel

1040 673 Since the Ascension Christ's coming in glory has been immi-
1048 nent,[565] even though 'it is not for you to know times or seasons
which the Father has fixed by his own authority.'[566]. This eschatological coming could be accomplished at any moment, even if
both it and the final trial that will precede it are 'delayed'.[567]

---

[554] LG 48 § 3; cf. 1 Cor 10:11.
[555] Cf. Mk 16:17–18, 20.
[556] Lk 21:27; cf. Mt 25:31.
[557] Cf. 2 Th 2:7.
[558] LG 48 § 3; cf. 2 Pt 3:13; Rom 8:19–22; 1 Cor 15:28.
[559] Cf. 1 Cor 11:26; 2 Pt 3:11–12.
[560] 1 Cor 16:22; Rev 22:17, 20.
[561] Cf. Acts 1:6–7.

[562] Cf. Is 11:1–9.
[563] Cf. Acts 1:8; 1 Cor 7:26; Eph 5:16; 1 Pt 4:17.
[564] Cf. Mt 25:1, 13; Mk 13:33–37; 1 Jn 2:18; 4:3; 1 Tim 4:1.
[565] Cf. Rev 22:20.
[566] Acts 1:7; cf. Mk 13:32.
[567] Cf. Mt 24:44; 1 Th 5:2; 2 Th 2:3–12.

674 The glorious Messiah's coming is suspended at every moment of history until his recognition by 'all Israel', for 'a hardening has come upon part of Israel' in their 'unbelief' toward Jesus.[568] St Peter says to the Jews of Jerusalem after Pentecost: 'Repent therefore, and turn again, that your sins may be blotted out, that times of refreshing may come from the presence of the Lord, and that he may send the Christ appointed for you, Jesus, whom heaven must receive until the time for establishing all that God spoke by the mouth of his holy prophets from of old.'[569] St Paul echoes him: 'For if their rejection means the reconciliation of the world, what will their acceptance mean but life from the dead?'[570] The 'full inclusion' of the Jews in the Messiah's salvation, in the wake of 'the full number of the Gentiles',[571] will enable the People of God to achieve 'the measure of the stature of the fullness of Christ', in which 'God may be all in all'.[572]

840
58

The Church's ultimate trial

675 Before Christ's second coming the Church must pass through a final trial that will shake the faith of many believers.[573] The persecution that accompanies her pilgrimage on earth[574] will unveil the 'mystery of iniquity' in the form of a religious deception offering men an apparent solution to their problems at the price of apostasy from the truth. The supreme religious deception is that of the Antichrist, a pseudo-messianism by which man glorifies himself in place of God and of his Messiah come in the flesh.[575]

769

676 The Antichrist's deception already begins to take shape in the world every time the claim is made to realize within history that messianic hope which can only be realized beyond history through the eschatological judgement. The Church has rejected even modified forms of this falsification of the kingdom to come under the name of millenarianism,[576] especially the 'intrinsically perverse' political form of a secular messianism.[577]

2425

677 The Church will enter the glory of the kingdom only through this final Passover, when she will follow her Lord in his death and Resurrection.[578] The kingdom will be fulfilled, then,

1340

---

[568] *Rom* 11:20–26; cf. *Mt* 23:39.
[569] *Acts* 3:19–21.
[570] *Rom* 11:15.
[571] *Rom* 11:12, 25; cf. *Lk* 21:24.
[572] *Eph* 4:13; I *Cor* 15:28.
[573] Cf. *Lk* 18:8; *Mt* 24:12.
[574] Cf. *Lk* 21:12; *Jn* 15:19–20.
[575] Cf. 2 *Th* 2:4–12; I *Th* 5:2–3; 2 *Jn* 7; I *Jn* 2:18, 22.

[576] Cf. DS 3839.
[577] Pius XI, *Divini Redemptoris*, condemning the 'false mysticism' of this 'counterfeit of the redemption of the lowly'; cf. *GS* 20–21.
[578] Cf. *Rev* 19:1–9.

not by a historic triumph of the Church through a progressive
2853 ascendancy, but only by God's victory over the final unleashing of
evil, which will cause his Bride to come down from heaven.[579]
God's triumph over the revolt of evil will take the form of the Last
Judgement after the final cosmic upheaval of this passing world.[580]

1038–1041 ## II. To Judge the Living and the Dead

678 Following in the steps of the prophets and John the Baptist,
Jesus announced the judgement of the Last Day in his
preaching.[581] Then will the conduct of each one and the secrets of
hearts be brought to light.[582] Then will the culpable unbelief that
counted the offer of God's grace as nothing be condemned.[583] Our
attitude to our neighbour will disclose acceptance or refusal of
grace and divine love.[584] On the Last Day Jesus will say: 'Truly I
say to you, as you did it to one of the least of these my brethren,
you did it to me.'[585]

679 Christ is Lord of eternal life. Full right to pass definitive
judgement on the works and hearts of men belongs to him as
redeemer of the world. He 'acquired' this right by his cross. The
Father has given 'all judgement to the Son'.[586] Yet the Son did not
come to judge, but to save and to give the life he has in himself.[587]
By rejecting grace in this life, one already judges oneself, receives
1021 according to one's works, and can even condemn oneself for all
eternity by rejecting the Spirit of love.[588]

IN BRIEF

680 *Christ the Lord already reigns through the Church, but all the things of
this world are not yet subjected to him. The triumph of Christ's kingdom will
not come about without one last assault by the powers of evil.*

681 *On Judgement Day at the end of the world, Christ will come in glory to
achieve the definitive triumph of good over evil which, like the wheat and the
tares, have grown up together in the course of history.*

682 *When he comes at the end of time to judge the living and the dead, the
glorious Christ will reveal the secret disposition of hearts and will render to
each man according to his works, and according to his acceptance or refusal of
grace.*

---

[579] Cf. *Rev* 13:8; 20:7–10; 21:2–4.
[580] Cf. *Rev* 20:12; 2 *Pt* 3:12–13.
[581] Cf. *Dan* 7:10; *Joel* 3 – 4; *Mal* 3:19; *Mt*
3:7–12.
[582] Cf. *Mk* 12:38–40; *Lk* 12:1–3; *Jn*
3:20–21; *Rom* 2:16; 1 *Cor* 4:5.
[583] Cf. *Mt* 11:20–24; 12:41–42.
[584] Cf. *Mt* 5:22; 7:1–5.
[585] *Mt* 25:40.
[586] *Jn* 5:22; cf. 5:27; *Mt* 25:31; *Acts* 10:42;
17:31; 2 *Tim* 4:1.
[587] Cf. *Jn* 3:17; 5:26.
[588] Cf. *Jn* 3:18; 12:48; *Mt* 12:32; 1 *Cor*
3:12–15; *Heb* 6:4–6; 10:26–31.

Chapter Three

I BELIEVE IN THE HOLY SPIRIT

683 'No one can say "Jesus is Lord" except by the Holy Spirit.'[1] 152
'God has sent the Spirit of his Son into our hearts, crying, "*Abba!*
Father!"'[2] This knowledge of faith is possible only in the Holy 424, 2670
Spirit: to be in touch with Christ, we must first have been touched
by the Holy Spirit. He comes to meet us and kindles faith in us. By
virtue of our Baptism, the first sacrament of the faith, the Holy
Spirit in the Church communicates to us, intimately and personally, the life that originates in the Father and is offered to us in
the Son.

> Baptism gives us the grace of new birth in God the Father, through his 249
> Son, in the Holy Spirit. For those who bear God's Spirit are led to the
> Word, that is, to the Son, and the Son presents them to the Father, and the
> Father confers incorruptibility on them. And it is impossible to see God's
> Son without the Spirit, and no one can approach the Father without the
> Son, for the knowledge of the Father is the Son, and the knowledge of
> God's Son is obtained through the Holy Spirit.[3]

684 Through his grace, the Holy Spirit is the first to awaken faith
in us and to communicate to us the new life, which is to 'know the
Father and the one whom he has sent, Jesus Christ'.[4] But the Spirit
is the last of the persons of the Holy Trinity to be revealed. St 236
Gregory of Nazianzus, the Theologian, explains this progression
in terms of the pedagogy of divine 'condescension':

> The Old Testament proclaimed the Father clearly, but the Son more
> obscurely. The New Testament revealed the Son, and gave us a glimpse
> of the divinity of the Spirit. Now the Spirit dwells among us and grants
> us a clearer vision of himself. It was not prudent, when the divinity of the
> Father had not yet been confessed, to proclaim the Son openly and, when
> the divinity of the Son was not yet admitted, to add the Holy Spirit as an
> extra burden, to speak somewhat daringly... By advancing and pro-
> gressing 'from glory to glory', the light of the Trinity will shine in ever
> more brilliant rays.[5]

685 To believe in the Holy Spirit is to profess that the Holy Spirit
is one of the persons of the Holy Trinity, consubstantial with the 465
Father and the Son: 'with the Father and the Son he is worshipped
and glorified.'[6] For this reason, the divine mystery of the Holy
Spirit was already treated in the context of Trinitarian 'theology'.

---

[1] 1 *Cor* 12:3.
[2] *Gal* 4:6.
[3] St Irenaeus, *Dem. ap.* 7: SCh 62,
41–42.

[4] *Jn* 17:3.
[5] St Gregory of Nazianzus, *Oratio* 31,
26: PG 36, 161–163.
[6] Nicene Creed.

Here, however, we have to do with the Holy Spirit only in the
236 divine 'economy'.

258 686 The Holy Spirit is at work with the Father and the Son from
the beginning to the completion of the plan for our salvation. But
in these 'end times', ushered in by the Son's redeeming Incarnation, the Spirit is revealed and given, recognized and welcomed as
a person. Now can this divine plan, accomplished in Christ, the
firstborn and head of the new creation, be embodied in mankind
by the outpouring of the Spirit: as the Church, the communion of
saints, the forgiveness of sins, the resurrection of the body, and the
life everlasting.

Article 8
'I BELIEVE IN THE HOLY SPIRIT'

687 'No one comprehends the thoughts of God except the Spirit
243 of God.'[7] Now God's Spirit, who reveals God, makes known to us
Christ, his Word, his living Utterance, but the Spirit does not
speak of himself. The Spirit who 'has spoken through the
prophets' makes us hear the Father's Word, but we do not hear the
Spirit himself. We know him only in the movement by which he
reveals the Word to us and disposes us to welcome him in faith.
The Spirit of truth who 'unveils' Christ to us 'will not speak on his
own.'[8] Such properly divine self-effacement explains why 'the
world cannot receive [him], because it neither sees him nor knows
him', while those who believe in Christ know the Spirit because he
dwells with them.[9]

688 The Church, a communion living in the faith of the apostles
which she transmits, is the place where we know the Holy Spirit:
– in the Scriptures he inspired;
– in the Tradition, to which the Church Fathers are always timely
witnesses;
– in the Church's Magisterium, which he assists;
– in the sacramental liturgy, through its words and symbols, in
which the Holy Spirit puts us into communion with Christ;
– in prayer, wherein he intercedes for us;
– in the charisms and ministries by which the Church is built up;
– in the signs of apostolic and missionary life;

---

[7] 1 Cor 2:11.   [9] Jn 14:17.
[8] Jn 16:13.

– in the witness of saints through whom he manifests his holiness and continues the work of salvation.

I. The Joint Mission of the Son and the Spirit

689 The One whom the Father has sent into our hearts, the Spirit of his Son, is truly God.[10] Consubstantial with the Father and the Son, the Spirit is inseparable from them, in both the inner life of the Trinity and his gift of love for the world. In adoring the Holy Trinity, life-giving, consubstantial and indivisible, the Church's faith also professes the distinction of persons. When the Father sends his Word, he always sends his Breath. In their joint mission, the Son and the Holy Spirit are distinct but inseparable. To be sure, it is Christ who is seen, the visible image of the invisible God, but it is the Spirit who reveals him.   245 254 485

690 Jesus is Christ, 'anointed', because the Spirit is his anointing, and everything that occurs from the Incarnation on derives from this fullness.[11] When Christ is finally glorified,[12] he can in turn send the Spirit from his place with the Father to those who believe in him: he communicates to them his glory,[13] that is, the Holy Spirit who glorifies him.[14] From that time on, this joint mission will be manifested in the children adopted by the Father in the Body of his Son: the mission of the Spirit of adoption is to unite them to Christ and make them live in him: 436 788

> The notion of anointing suggests. . . that there is no distance between the Son and the Spirit. Indeed, just as between the surface of the body and the anointing with oil neither reason nor sensation recognizes any intermediary, so the contact of the Son with the Spirit is immediate, so that anyone who would make contact with the Son by faith must first encounter the oil by contact. In fact there is no part that is not covered by the Holy Spirit. That is why the confession of the Son's Lordship is made in the Holy Spirit by those who receive him, the Spirit coming from all sides to those who approach the Son in faith.[15]   448

II. The Name, Titles and Symbols of the Holy Spirit

The proper name of the Holy Spirit

691 'Holy Spirit' is the proper name of the one whom we adore and glorify with the Father and the Son. The Church has received

---

[10] Cf. Gal 4:6.
[11] Cf. Jn 3:34.
[12] Jn 7:39.
[13] Cf. Jn 17:22.
[14] Cf. Jn 16:14.
[15] St Gregory of Nyssa, De Spiritu Sancto 16: PG 45, 1321A-B.

this name from the Lord and professes it in the Baptism of her new children.[16]

The term 'Spirit' translates the Hebrew word *ruah*, which, in its primary sense, means breath, air, wind. Jesus indeed uses the sensory image of the wind to suggest to Nicodemus the transcendent newness of him who is personally God's breath, the divine Spirit.[17] On the other hand, 'Spirit' and 'Holy' are divine attributes common to the three divine persons. By joining the two terms, Scripture, liturgy and theological language designate the inexpressible person of the Holy Spirit, without any possible equivocation with other uses of the terms 'spirit' and 'holy'.

Titles of the Holy Spirit

692 When he proclaims and promises the coming of the Holy Spirit, Jesus calls him the 'Paraclete', literally, 'he who is called to one's side', *ad-vocatus*.[18] 'Paraclete' is commonly translated by
1433 'consoler', and Jesus is the first consoler.[19] The Lord also called the Holy Spirit 'the Spirit of truth'.[20]

693 Besides the proper name of 'Holy Spirit', which is most frequently used in the *Acts of the Apostles* and in the Epistles, we also find in St Paul the titles: the Spirit of the promise,[21] the Spirit of adoption,[22] the Spirit of Christ,[23] the Spirit of the Lord,[24] and the Spirit of God[25] – and, in St Peter, the Spirit of glory.[26]

Symbols of the Holy Spirit

694 *Water*. The symbolism of water signifies the Holy Spirit's action in Baptism, since after the invocation of the Holy Spirit it becomes the efficacious
1218 sacramental sign of new birth: just as the gestation of our first birth took place in water, so the water of Baptism truly signifies that our birth into the divine life is given to us in the Holy Spirit. As 'by one Spirit we were all baptized', so we are also 'made to drink of one Spirit'.[27] Thus the Spirit is also personally the living
2652 water welling up from Christ crucified[28] as its source and welling up in us to eternal life.[29]

1293 695 *Anointing*. The symbolism of anointing with oil also signifies the Holy Spirit,[30] to the point of becoming a synonym for the Holy Spirit. In Christian initiation, anointing is the sacramental sign of Confirmation, called 'chrismation' in the Churches of the East. Its full force can be grasped only in relation

---

[16] Cf. *Mt* 28:19.
[17] *Jn* 3:5–8.
[18] *Jn* 14:16, 26; 15:26; 16:7.
[19] Cf. 1 *Jn* 2:1.
[20] *Jn* 16:13.
[21] Cf. *Gal* 3:14; *Eph* 1:13.
[22] *Rom* 8:15; *Gal* 4:6.
[23] *Rom* 8:9.
[24] 2 *Cor* 3:17.

[25] *Rom* 8:9, 14; 15:19; 1 *Cor* 6:11; 7:40.
[26] 1 *Pt* 4:14.
[27] 1 *Cor* 12:13.
[28] *Jn* 19:34; 1 *Jn* 5:8.
[29] Cf. *Jn* 4:10–14; 7:38; *Ex* 17:1–6; *Is* 55:1; *Zech* 14:8; 1 *Cor* 10:4; *Rev* 21:6; 22:17.
[30] Cf. 1 *Jn* 2:20, 27; 2 *Cor* 1:21.

to the primary anointing accomplished by the Holy Spirit, that of Jesus. Christ (in Hebrew *messiah*) means the one 'anointed' by God's Spirit. There were several anointed ones of the Lord in the Old Covenant, pre-eminently King David.[31] But Jesus is God's Anointed in a unique way: the humanity the Son assumed was entirely anointed by the Holy Spirit. The Holy Spirit established him as 'Christ'.[32] The Virgin Mary conceived Christ by the Holy Spirit who, through the angel, proclaimed him the Christ at his birth, and prompted Simeon to come to the Temple to see the Christ of the Lord.[33] The Spirit filled Christ and the power of the Spirit went out from him in his acts of healing and of saving.[34] Finally, it was the Spirit who raised Jesus from the dead.[35] Now, fully established as 'Christ' in his humanity victorious over death, Jesus pours out the Holy Spirit abundantly until 'the saints' constitute in their union with the humanity of the Son of God that perfect man 'to the measure of the stature of the fullness of Christ':[36] 'the whole Christ', in St Augustine's expression.

436

794

696 *Fire.* While water signifies birth and the fruitfulness of life given in the Holy Spirit, fire symbolizes the transforming energy of the Holy Spirit's actions. The prayer of the prophet Elijah, who 'arose like fire' and whose 'word burned like a torch', brought down fire from heaven on the sacrifice on Mount Carmel.[37] This event was a 'figure' of the fire of the Holy Spirit, who transforms what he touches. John the Baptist, who goes 'before [the Lord] in the spirit and power of Elijah', proclaims Christ as the one who 'will baptize you with the Holy Spirit and with fire.'[38] Jesus will say of the Spirit: 'I came to cast fire upon the earth; and would that it were already kindled!'[39] In the form of tongues 'as of fire', the Holy Spirit rests on the disciples on the morning of Pentecost and fills them with himself.[40] The spiritual tradition has retained this symbolism of fire as one of the most expressive images of the Holy Spirit's actions.[41] 'Do not quench the Spirit.'[42]

1127

2586

718

697 *Cloud and light.* These two images occur together in the manifestations of the Holy Spirit. In the theophanies of the Old Testament, the cloud, now obscure, now luminous, reveals the living and saving God, while veiling the transcendence of his glory – with Moses on Mount Sinai,[43] at the tent of meeting,[44] and during the wandering in the desert,[45] and with Solomon at the dedication of the Temple.[46] In the Holy Spirit, Christ fulfils these figures. The Spirit comes upon the Virgin Mary and 'overshadows' her, so that she might conceive and give birth to Jesus.[47] On the mountain of Transfiguration, the Spirit in the 'cloud came and overshadowed' Jesus, Moses and Elijah, Peter, James and John, and 'a voice came out of the cloud, saying, "This is my Son, my

484

554

---

[31] Cf. *Ex* 30:22–32; 1 *Sam* 16:13.
[32] Cf. *Lk* 4:18–19; *Is* 61:1.
[33] Cf. *Lk* 2:11, 26–27.
[34] Cf. *Lk* 4:1; 6:19; 8:46.
[35] Cf. *Rom* 1:4; 8:11.
[36] *Eph* 4:13; cf. *Acts* 2:36.
[37] *Sir* 48:1; cf. 1 *Kings* 18:38–39.
[38] *Lk* 1:17; 3:16.
[39] *Lk* 12:49.
[40] *Acts* 2:3–4.
[41] Cf. St John of the Cross, *The Living*

Flame of Love, in *The Collected Works of St John of the Cross,* tr. K. Kavanaugh OCD and O. Rodriguez OCD (Washington DC: Institute of Carmelite Studies, 1979), 577ff.
[42] 1 *Th* 5:19.
[43] Cf. *Ex* 24:15–18.
[44] Cf. *Ex* 33:9–10.
[45] Cf. *Ex* 40:36–38; 1 *Cor* 10:1–2.
[46] Cf. 1 *Kings* 8:10–12.
[47] *Lk* 1:35.

Chosen; listen to him!'' [48] Finally, the cloud took Jesus out of the sight of the
659 disciples on the day of his Ascension, and will reveal him as Son of man in glory
on the day of his final coming. [49]

1295–1296 698 *The seal* is a symbol close to that of anointing. 'The Father has set his seal'
on Christ and also seals us in him. [50] Because this seal indicates the indelible effect
of the anointing with the Holy Spirit in the sacraments of Baptism, Confirmation and Holy Orders, the image of the seal (*sphragis*) has been used in some
1121 theological traditions to express the indelible 'character' imprinted by these
three unrepeatable sacraments.

292 699 *The hand.* Jesus heals the sick and blesses little children by laying hands on
them. [51] In his name the apostles will do the same. [52] Even more pointedly, it is
1288 by the apostles' imposition of hands that the Holy Spirit is given. [53] The *Letter to
the Hebrews* lists the imposition of hands among the 'fundamental elements' of
1300, 1573, its teaching. [54] The Church has kept this sign of the all-powerful outpouring of
1668 the Holy Spirit in her sacramental epicleses.

700 *The finger.* 'It is by the finger of God that [Jesus] cast out demons.' [55] If
2056 God's law was written on tablets of stone 'by the finger of God', then the 'letter
from Christ' entrusted to the care of the apostles is written 'with the Spirit of
the living God, not on tablets of stone, but on tablets of human hearts'. [56] The
hymn *Veni Creator Spiritus* invokes the Holy Spirit as the '*finger of the Father's
right hand*'. [57]

701 *The dove.* At the end of the flood, whose symbolism refers to Baptism, a
dove released by Noah returns with a fresh olive-tree branch in its beak as a sign
1219 that the earth was again habitable. [58] When Christ comes up from the water of
535 his baptism, the Holy Spirit, in the form of a dove, comes down upon him and
remains with him. [59] The Spirit comes down and remains in the purified hearts
of the baptized. In certain churches, the Eucharist is reserved in a metal recep-
tacle in the form of a dove (*columbarium*) suspended above the altar. Christian
iconography traditionally uses a dove to suggest the Spirit.

III. God's Spirit and Word in the Time of the Promises

702 From the beginning until 'the fullness of time', [60] the joint
mission of the Father's Word and Spirit remains *hidden*, but it is at
122 work. God's Spirit prepares for the time of the Messiah. Neither is
fully revealed but both are already promised, to be watched for
and welcomed at their manifestation. So, for this reason, when the
Church reads the Old Testament, she searches there for what the

---

[48] *Lk* 9:34–35.
[49] Cf. *Acts* 1:9; cf. *Lk* 21:27.
[50] *Jn* 6:27; cf. 2 *Cor* 1:22; *Eph* 1:13; 4:30.
[51] Cf. *Mk* 6:5; 8:23; 10:16.
[52] Cf. *Mk* 16:18; *Acts* 5:12; 14:3.
[53] Cf. *Acts* 8:17–19; 13:3; 19:6.
[54] Cf. *Heb* 6:2.
[55] *Lk* 11:20.

[56] *Ex* 31:18; 2 *Cor* 3:3.
[57] LH, Easter Season after Ascension,
Hymn at Vespers: *digitus paternae
dexterae.*
[58] Cf. *Gen* 8:8–12.
[59] Cf. *Mt* 3:16 and parallels.
[60] *Gal* 4:4.

Spirit, 'who has spoken through the prophets', wants to tell us *107* about Christ.[61]

> By 'prophets' the faith of the Church here understands all whom the Holy *243* Spirit inspired in living proclamation and in the composition of the sacred books, both of the Old and the New Testaments. Jewish tradition distinguishes first the Law (the five first books or Pentateuch), then the Prophets (our historical and prophetic books) and finally the Writings (especially the wisdom literature, in particular the Psalms).[62]

In creation

703 The Word of God and his Breath are at the origin of the being *292* and life of every creature:[63]

> It belongs to the Holy Spirit to rule, sanctify and animate creation, for he *291* is God, consubstantial with the Father and the Son... Power over life pertains to the Spirit, for being God he preserves creation in the Father through the Son.[64]

704 'God fashioned man with his own hands [that is, the Son and the Holy Spirit] and impressed his own form on the flesh he had fashioned, in such a way that even what was visible might bear the divine form.'[65]

356

The Spirit of the promise

705 Disfigured by sin and death, man remains 'in the image of God', in the image of the Son, but is deprived 'of the glory of God',[66] of his 'likeness'. The promise made to Abraham inaugurates the economy of salvation, at the culmination of which the *410* Son himself will assume that 'image'[67] and restore it in the Father's 'likeness' by giving it again its Glory, the Spirit who is 'the giver of *2809* life'.

706 Against all human hope, God promises descendants to Abraham, as the fruit of faith and of the power of the Holy Spirit.[68] In Abraham's progeny all the nations of the earth will be blessed. *60* This progeny will be Christ himself,[69] in whom the outpouring of the Holy Spirit will 'gather into one the children of God who are scattered abroad'.[70] God commits himself by his own solemn oath

---

[61] Cf. 2 Cor 3:14; Jn 5:39, 46.
[62] Cf. Lk 24:44.
[63] Cf. Pss 33:6; 104:30; Gen 1:2; 2:7; Eccl 3:20–21; Ezek 37:10.
[64] Byzantine Liturgy, Sundays of the second mode, Troparion of Morning Prayer.
[65] St Irenaeus, Dem. ap. 11: SCh 62, 48–49.

[66] Rom 3:23.
[67] Cf. Jn 1:14; Phil 2:7.
[68] Cf. Gen 18:1–15; Lk 1:26–38, 54–55; Jn 1:12–13; Rom 4:16–21.
[69] Cf. Gen 12:3; Gal 3:16.
[70] Cf. Jn 11:52.

to giving his beloved Son and 'the promised Holy Spirit... [who is] the guarantee of our inheritance until we acquire possession of it'.[71]

In theophanies and the Law

707 Theophanies (manifestations of God) light up the way of the promise, from the patriarchs to Moses and from Joshua to the visions that inaugurated the missions of the great prophets. Christian tradition has always recognized that God's Word allowed himself to be seen and heard in these theophanies, in which the cloud of the Holy Spirit both revealed him and concealed him in its shadow.

1961–1964 708 This divine pedagogy appears especially in the gift of the
122 Law.[72] God gave the Law as a 'pedagogue' to lead his people towards Christ.[73] But the Law's powerlessness to save man deprived of the divine 'likeness', along with the growing awareness of sin that it imparts,[74] enkindles a desire for the Holy
2585 Spirit. The lamentations of the Psalms bear witness to this.

In the Kingdom and the Exile

709 The Law, the sign of God's promise and covenant, ought to have governed the hearts and institutions of that people to whom Abraham's faith gave birth. 'If you will obey my voice and keep my covenant,... you shall be to me a kingdom of priests and a holy nation.'[75] But after David, Israel gave in to the temptation of becoming a kingdom like other nations. The Kingdom, however,
2579 the object of the promise made to David,[76] would be the work of
544 the Holy Spirit; it would belong to the poor according to the Spirit.

710 The forgetting of the Law and the infidelity to the covenant end in death: it is the Exile, apparently the failure of the promises, which is in fact the mysterious fidelity of the Saviour God and the beginning of a promised restoration, but according to the Spirit. The People of God had to suffer this purification.[77] In God's plan, the Exile already stands in the shadow of the Cross, and the Remnant of the poor that returns from the Exile is one of the most transparent prefigurations of the Church.

---

[71] Eph 1:13–14; cf. Gen 22:17–19; Lk 1:73; Jn 3:16; Rom 8:32; Gal 3:14.
[72] Cf. Ex 19 – 20; Dt 1 – 11; 29 – 30.
[73] Gal 3:24.

[74] Cf. Rom 3:20.
[75] Ex 19:5–6; cf. 1 Pt 2:9.
[76] Cf. 2 Sam 7; Ps 89; Lk 1:32–33.
[77] Cf. Lk 24:26.

Expectation of the Messiah and his Spirit

711 'Behold, I am doing a new thing.'[78] Two prophetic lines were
to develop, one leading to the expectation of the Messiah, the 522
other pointing to the announcement of a new Spirit. They con- 64
verge in the small Remnant, the people of the poor, who await in
hope the 'consolation of Israel' and 'the redemption of Jerusalem'.[79]

We have seen earlier how Jesus fulfils the prophecies concerning himself. We
limit ourselves here to those in which the relationship of the Messiah and his
Spirit appears more clearly.

712 The characteristics of the awaited *Messiah* begin to appear in 439
the 'Book of Emmanuel' ('Isaiah said this when he saw his glory',[80]
speaking of Christ), especially in the first two verses of *Isaiah* 11:

There shall come forth a shoot from the stump of Jesse,
and a branch shall grow out of his roots.
And the Spirit of the LORD shall rest upon him,
the spirit of wisdom and understanding,
the spirit of counsel and might,
the spirit of knowledge and the fear of the LORD.[81]

713 The Messiah's characteristics are revealed above all in the
'Servant songs'.[82] These songs proclaim the meaning of Jesus' Pas- 601
sion, and show how he will pour out the Holy Spirit to give life to
the many: not as an outsider, but by embracing our 'form as
slave'.[83] Taking our death upon himself, he can communicate to us
his own Spirit of life.

714 This is why Christ inaugurates the proclamation of the Good
News by making his own the following passage from Isaiah:[84]

The Spirit of the LORD GOD is upon me,
because the LORD has anointed me
to bring good tidings to the afflicted;
he has sent me to bind up the broken hearted,
to proclaim liberty to the captives,
and the opening of the prison to those who are bound;
to proclaim the year of the LORD's favour.

715 The prophetic texts that directly concern the sending of the
Holy Spirit are oracles by which God speaks to the heart of his
people in the language of the promise, with the accents of 'love 214

---

[78] *Is* 43:19.
[79] Cf. *Zeph* 2:3; *Lk* 2:25, 38.
[80] *Jn* 12:41; cf. *Is* 6 – 12.
[81] *Is* 11:1–2.
[82] Cf. *Is* 42:1–9; cf. *Mt* 12:18–21; *Jn*

1:32–34; then cf. *Is* 49:1–6; cf. *Mt*
3:17; *Lk* 2:32; finally cf. *Is* 50:4–10 and
52:13 – 53:12.
[83] *Phil* 2:7.
[84] *Is* 61:1–2; cf. *Lk* 4:18–19.

and fidelity'.[85] St Peter will proclaim their fulfilment on the morning of Pentecost.[86] According to these promises, at the 'end
1965 time' the Lord's Spirit will renew the hearts of men, engraving a new law in them. He will gather and reconcile the scattered and divided peoples; he will transform the first creation, and God will dwell there with men in peace.

716 The People of the 'poor'[87] – those who, humble and meek, rely solely on their God's mysterious plans, who await the justice, not of men but of the Messiah – are in the end the great achievement of the Holy Spirit's hidden mission during the time of the promises that prepare for Christ's coming. It is this quality of
368 heart, purified and enlightened by the Spirit, which is expressed in the Psalms. In these poor, the Spirit is making ready 'a people prepared for the Lord'.[88]

IV. The Spirit of Christ in the Fullness of Time

John, precursor, prophet and baptist

523 717 'There was a man sent from God, whose name was John.'[89] John was 'filled with the Holy Spirit even from his mother's womb'[90] by Christ himself, whom the Virgin Mary had just conceived by the Holy Spirit. Mary's visitation to Elizabeth thus became a visit from God to his people.[91]

718 John is 'Elijah [who] must come'.[92] The fire of the Spirit dwells in him and makes him the forerunner of the coming Lord.
696 In John, the precursor, the Holy Spirit completes the work of '[making] ready a people prepared for the Lord'.[93]

719 John the Baptist is 'more than a prophet'.[94] In him, the Holy Spirit concludes his speaking through the prophets. John com-
2684 pletes the cycle of prophets begun by Elijah.[95] He proclaims the imminence of the consolation of Israel; he is the 'voice' of the Consoler who is coming.[96] As the Spirit of truth will also do, John 'came to bear witness to the light.'[97] In John's sight, the Spirit thus brings to completion the careful search of the prophets and fulfils the longing of the angels.[98] 'He on whom you see the Spirit

---

[85] Cf. Ezek 11:19; 36:25–28; 37:1–14; Jer 31:31–34; and cf. Joel 3:1–5.
[86] Cf. Acts 2:17–21.
[87] Cf. Zeph 2:3; Pss 22:27; 34:3; Is 49:13; 61:1; etc.
[88] Lk 1:17.
[89] Jn 1:6.
[90] Lk 1:15, 41.

[91] Cf. Lk 1:68.
[92] Mt 17:10–13; cf. Lk 1:76.
[93] Lk 1:17.
[94] Lk 7:26.
[95] Cf. Mt 11:13–14.
[96] Jn 1:23; cf. Is 40:1–3.
[97] Jn 1:7; cf. Jn 15:26; 5:35.
[98] Cf. 1 Pt 1:10–12.

descend and remain, this is he who baptizes with the Holy Spirit. 536
And I have seen and have borne witness that this is the Son of
God... Behold, the Lamb of God.'[99]

720 Finally, with John the Baptist, the Holy Spirit begins the
restoration to man of 'the divine likeness', prefiguring what he
would achieve with and in Christ. John's baptism was for
repentance; baptism in water and the Spirit will be a new birth.[100]

'Rejoice, you who are full of grace'

721 Mary, the all-holy ever-virgin Mother of God, is the masterwork of the mission of the Son and the Spirit in the fullness of 484
time. For the first time in the plan of salvation and because his
Spirit had prepared her, the Father found the *dwelling-place* where
his Son and his Spirit could dwell among men. In this sense the
Church's Tradition has often read the most beautiful texts on
wisdom in relation to Mary.[101] Mary is acclaimed and represented
in the liturgy as the 'Seat of Wisdom'.

In her, the 'wonders of God' that the Spirit was to fulfil in
Christ and the Church began to be manifested:

722 The Holy Spirit *prepared* Mary by his grace. It was fitting that 489
the mother of him in whom 'the whole fullness of deity dwells
bodily'[102] should herself be 'full of grace'. She was, by sheer grace,
conceived without sin as the most humble of creatures, the most
capable of welcoming the inexpressible gift of the Almighty. It
was quite correct for the angel Gabriel to greet her as the 'Daugh- 2676
ter of Zion': 'Rejoice.'[103] It is the thanksgiving of the whole People
of God, and thus of the Church, which Mary in her canticle[104] lifts
up to the Father in the Holy Spirit while carrying within her
eternal Son.

723 In Mary, the Holy Spirit *fulfils* the plan of the Father's loving
goodness. Through the Holy Spirit, the Virgin conceives and 485
gives birth to the Son of God. By the Holy Spirit's power and 2619
her faith, her virginity became uniquely fruitful.[105]

724 In Mary, the Holy Spirit *manifests* the Son of the Father, now
become the Son of the Virgin. She is the burning bush of the
definitive theophany. Filled with the Holy Spirit she makes the
Word visible in the humility of his flesh. It is to the poor and the 963

---

[99] Jn 1:33–36.
[100] Cf. Jn 3:5.
[101] Cf. Prov 8:1 – 9:6; Sir 24.
[102] Col 2:9.

[103] Cf. Zeph 3:14; Zech 2:14.
[104] Cf. Lk 1:46–55.
[105] Cf. Lk 1:26–38; Rom 4:18–21; Gal 4:26–28.

first representatives of the gentiles that she makes him known.[106]

963   725 Finally, through Mary, the Holy Spirit begins to bring men, the objects of God's merciful love,[107] *into communion* with Christ. And the humble are always the first to accept him: shepherds, magi, Simeon and Anna, the bride and groom at Cana and the first disciples.

494   726 At the end of this mission of the Spirit, Mary became the
2618 Woman, the new Eve ('mother of the living'), the mother of the 'whole Christ'.[108] As such, she was present with the Twelve, who 'with one accord devoted themselves to prayer',[109] at the dawn of the 'end time' which the Spirit was to inaugurate on the morning of Pentecost with the manifestation of the Church.

Christ Jesus

727 The entire mission of the Son and the Holy Spirit, in the
438, 695 fullness of time, is contained in this: that the Son is the one anoin-
536 ted by the Father's Spirit since his Incarnation – Jesus is the Christ, the Messiah.

Everything in the second chapter of the Creed is to be read in this light. Christ's whole work is in fact a joint mission of the Son and the Holy Spirit. Here, we shall mention only what has to do with Jesus' promise of the Holy Spirit and the gift of him by the glorified Lord.

728 Jesus does not reveal the Holy Spirit fully, until he himself has been glorified through his death and Resurrection. Nevertheless, little by little he alludes to him even in his teaching of the multitudes, as when he reveals that his own flesh will be food for the life of the world.[110] He also alludes to the Spirit in speaking to Nicodemus,[111] to the Samaritan woman,[112] and to those who take part
2615 in the feast of Tabernacles.[113] To his disciples he speaks openly of the Spirit in connection with prayer[114] and with the witness they will have to bear.[115]

729 Only when the hour has arrived for his glorification does Jesus *promise* the coming of the Holy Spirit, since his death and Resurrection will fulfil the promise made to the fathers.[116] The Spirit of truth, the other Paraclete, will be given by the Father in

---

[106] Cf. *Lk* 1:15–19; *Mt* 2:11.
[107] Cf. *Lk* 2:14.
[108] Cf. *Jn* 19:25–27.
[109] *Acts* 1:14.
[110] Cf. *Jn* 6:27, 51, 62–63.
[111] Cf. *Jn* 3:5–8.
[112] Cf. *Jn* 4:10, 14, 23–24.
[113] Cf. *Jn* 7:37–39.
[114] Cf. *Lk* 11:13.
[115] Cf. *Mt* 10:19–20.
[116] Cf. *Jn* 14:16–17, 26; 15:26; 16:7–15; 17:26.

answer to Jesus' prayer; he will be sent by the Father in Jesus' name; and Jesus will send him from the Father's side, since he comes from the Father. The Holy Spirit will come and we shall know him; he will be with us for ever; he will remain with us. The Spirit will teach us everything, remind us of all that Christ said to us and bear witness to him. The Holy Spirit will lead us into all truth and will glorify Christ. He will prove the world wrong *388, 1433* about sin, righteousness and judgement.

730 At last Jesus' hour arrives:[117] he commends his spirit into the Father's hands[118] at the very moment when by his death he conquers death, so that, 'raised from the dead by the glory of the Father',[119] he might immediately *give* the Holy Spirit by 'breathing' on his disciples.[120] From this hour onward, the mission of Christ and the Spirit becomes the mission of the Church: 'As the *850* Father has sent me, even so I send you.'[121]

V. The Spirit and the Church in the Last Days

Pentecost

731 On the day of Pentecost when the seven weeks of Easter had come to an end, Christ's Passover is fulfilled in the outpouring of *2623* the Holy Spirit, manifested, given and communicated as a divine *767* person: of his fullness, Christ, the Lord, pours out the Spirit in *1302* abundance.[122]

732 On that day, the Holy Trinity is fully revealed. Since that day, the Kingdom announced by Christ has been open to those who believe in him: in the humility of the flesh and in faith, they already share in the communion of the Holy Trinity. By his *244* coming, which never ceases, the Holy Spirit causes the world to enter into the 'last days', the time of the Church, the Kingdom *672* already inherited though not yet consummated.

> We have seen the true Light, we have received the heavenly Spirit, we have found the true faith: we adore the indivisible Trinity, who has saved us.[123]

The Holy Spirit – God's gift

733 'God is Love'[124] and love is his first gift, containing all others. *218*

---

[117] Cf. *Jn* 13:1; 17:1.
[118] Cf. *Lk* 23:46; *Jn* 19:30.
[119] *Rom* 6:4.
[120] Cf. *Jn* 20:22.
[121] *Jn* 20:21; cf. *Mt* 28:19; *Lk* 24:47–48; *Acts* 1:8.

[122] Cf. *Acts* 2:33–36.
[123] Byzantine Liturgy, Pentecost, Vespers, Troparion, repeated after communion.
[124] 1 *Jn* 4:8, 16.

'God's love has been poured into our hearts through the Holy Spirit who has been given to us.'[125]

734 Because we are dead or at least wounded through sin, the first effect of the gift of love is the forgiveness of our sins. The communion of the Holy Spirit[126] in the Church restores to the baptized the divine likeness lost through sin.

1987

735 He, then, gives us the 'pledge' or 'first fruits' of our inheritance: the very life of the Holy Trinity, which is to love as 'God [has] loved us'.[127] This love (the 'charity' of 1 *Cor* 13) is the source of the new life in Christ, made possible because we have received 'power' from the Holy Spirit.[128]

1822

736 By this power of the Spirit, God's children can bear much fruit. He who has grafted us on to the true vine will make us bear 'the fruit of the Spirit: ... love, joy, peace, patience, kindness, goodness, faithfulness, gentleness, self-control'.[129] 'We live by the Spirit'; the more we renounce ourselves, the more we 'walk by the Spirit'.[130]

1832

> Through the Holy Spirit we are restored to paradise, led back to the Kingdom of heaven and adopted as children, given confidence to call God 'Father' and to share in Christ's grace, called children of light and given a share in eternal glory.[131]

The Holy Spirit and the Church

737 The mission of Christ and the Holy Spirit is brought to completion in the Church, which is the Body of Christ and the Temple of the Holy Spirit. This joint mission henceforth brings Christ's faithful to share in his communion with the Father in the Holy Spirit. The Spirit *prepares* men and goes out to them with his grace, in order to draw them to Christ. The Spirit *manifests* the risen Lord to them, recalls his word to them and opens their minds to the understanding of his death and Resurrection. He *makes present* the mystery of Christ, supremely in the Eucharist, in order to reconcile them, to *bring them into communion* with God, that they may 'bear much fruit'.[132]

787–798

1093–1109

738 Thus the Church's mission is not an addition to that of Christ and the Holy Spirit, but is its sacrament: in her whole being and in all her members, the Church is sent to announce, bear witness,

850

777

---

[125] *Rom* 5.5.
[126] 2 *Cor* 13:14.
[127] 1 *Jn* 4:11–12; cf. *Rom* 8:23; 2 *Cor* 1:21.
[128] *Acts* 1:8; cf. 1 *Cor* 13.
[129] *Gal* 5:22–23.
[130] *Gal* 5:25; cf. *Mt* 16:24–26.
[131] St Basil, *De Spiritu Sancto* 15, 36: PG 32, 132.
[132] *Jn* 15:8, 16.

make present and spread the mystery of the communion of the Holy Trinity (the topic of the next article):

> All of us who have received one and the same Spirit, that is, the Holy Spirit, are in a sense blended together with one another and with God. For if Christ, together with the Father's and his own Spirit, comes to dwell in each of us, though we are many, still the Spirit is one and undivided. He binds together the spirits of each and every one of us,... and makes all appear as one in him. For just as the power of Christ's sacred flesh unites those in whom it dwells into one body, I think that in the same way the one and undivided Spirit of God, who dwells in all, leads all into spiritual unity.[133]

739 Because the Holy Spirit is the anointing of Christ, it is Christ who, as the head of the Body, pours out the Spirit among his *1076* members to nourish, heal, and organize them in their mutual functions, to give them life, send them to bear witness, and associate them to his self-offering to the Father and to his intercession for the whole world. Through the Church's sacraments, Christ communicates his Holy and sanctifying Spirit to the members of his Body. (This will be the topic of Part Two of the Catechism.)

740 These 'mighty works of God', offered to believers in the sacraments of the Church, bear their fruit in the new life in Christ, according to the Spirit. (This will be the topic of Part Three.)

741 'The Spirit helps us in our weakness; for we do not know how to pray as we ought, but the Spirit himself intercedes with sighs too deep for words.'[134] The Holy Spirit, the artisan of God's works, is the master of prayer. (This will be the topic of Part Four.)

IN BRIEF

742 *'Because you are sons, God has sent the Spirit of his Son into our hearts, crying, "Abba! Father!"' (Gal 4:6).*

743 *From the beginning to the end of time, whenever God sends his Son, he always sends his Spirit: their mission is conjoined and inseparable.*

744 *In the fullness of time the Holy Spirit completes in Mary all the preparations for Christ's coming among the People of God. By the action of the Holy Spirit in her, the Father gives the world Emmanuel, 'God-with-us' (Mt 1:23).*

---

[133] St Cyril of Alexandria, *In Jo. ev.* 11, 11: PG 74, 561.   [134] *Rom* 8:26.

745   *The Son of God was consecrated as Christ (Messiah) by the anointing of the Holy Spirit at his Incarnation (cf. Ps 2:6–7).*

746   *By his death and his Resurrection, Jesus is constituted in glory as Lord and Christ (cf. Acts 2:36). From his fullness, he poured out the Holy Spirit on the apostles and the Church.*

747   *The Holy Spirit, whom Christ the head pours out on his members, builds, animates and sanctifies the Church. She is the sacrament of the Holy Trinity's communion with men.*

Article 9

'I BELIEVE IN THE HOLY CATHOLIC CHURCH'

748   'Christ is the light of humanity; and it is, accordingly, the heart-felt desire of this sacred Council, being gathered together in the Holy Spirit, that, by proclaiming his Gospel to every creature, it may bring to all men that light of Christ which shines out visibly from the Church.'[135] These words open the Second Vatican Council's *Dogmatic Constitution on the Church.* By choosing this starting point, the Council demonstrates that the article of faith about the Church depends entirely on the articles concerning Christ Jesus. The Church has no other light than Christ's; according to a favourite image of the Church Fathers, the Church is like the moon, all its light reflected from the sun.

749   The article concerning the Church also depends entirely on the article about the Holy Spirit, which immediately precedes it. 'Indeed, having shown that the Spirit is the source and giver of all holiness, we now confess that it is he who has endowed the Church with holiness.'[136] The Church is, in a phrase used by the Fathers, the place 'where the Spirit flourishes'.[137]

811   750   To believe that the Church is 'holy' and 'catholic', and that she is 'one' and 'apostolic' (as the Nicene Creed adds), is inseparable from belief in God, the Father, the Son and the Holy Spirit. In the Apostles' Creed we profess 'one Holy Church' (*Credo. . .Eccle-*
169   *siam*), and not to believe *in* the Church, so as not to confuse God with his works and to attribute clearly to God's goodness *all* the gifts he has bestowed on his Church.[138]

---

[135] *LG* 1; cf. *Mk* 16:15.
[136] *Roman Catechism* I, 10, 1.
[137] St Hippolytus, *Trad. ap.* 35: SCh 11, 118.

[138] *Roman Catechism* I, 10, 22.

Paragraph 1. The Church in God's Plan

I. Names and Images of the Church

751 The word 'Church' (Latin *ecclesia*, from the Greek *ek-kalein*, 'to call out of') means a convocation or an assembly. It designates the assemblies of the people, usually for a religious purpose.[139] *Ekklēsia* is used frequently in the Greek Old Testament for the assembly of the Chosen People before God, above all for their assembly on Mount Sinai where Israel received the Law and was established by God as his holy people.[140] By calling itself 'Church', the first community of Christian believers recognized itself as heir to that assembly. In the Church, God is 'calling together' his people from all the ends of the earth. The equivalent Greek term *Kyriakē*, from which the English word *Church* and the German *Kirche* are derived, means 'what belongs to the Lord'.

752 In Christian usage, the word 'church' designates the liturgical assembly,[141] but also the local community[142] or the whole univer- *830* sal community of believers.[143] These three meanings are insepar- *1140* able. 'The Church' is the People that God gathers in the whole *832* world. She exists in local communities and is made real as a liturgical, above all a Eucharistic, assembly. She draws her life from the word and the Body of Christ and so herself becomes Christ's Body.

Symbols of the Church

753 In Scripture, we find a host of interrelated images and figures through which Revelation speaks of the inexhaustible mystery of the Church. The images taken from the Old Testament are varia- tions on a profound theme: the People of God. In the New Testa- *781* ment, all these images find a new centre because Christ has become the head of this people, which henceforth is his Body.[144] Around *789* this centre are grouped images taken 'from the life of the shepherd or from cultivation of the land, from the art of building or from family life and marriage'.[145]

754 'The Church is, accordingly, a *sheepfold*, the sole and necessary gateway to which is Christ. It is also the flock of which God himself foretold that he would be the shepherd, and whose sheep, even though governed by human shepherds,

---

[139] Cf. *Acts* 19:39.
[140] Cf. *Ex* 19.
[141] Cf. 1 *Cor* 11:18; 14:19, 28, 34, 35.
[142] Cf. 1 *Cor* 1:2; 16:1.

[143] Cf. 1 *Cor* 15:9; *Gal* 1:13; *Phil* 3:6.
[144] Cf. *Eph* 1:22; *Col* 1:18; *LG* 9.
[145] *LG* 6.

857   are unfailingly nourished and led by Christ himself, the Good Shepherd and Prince of Shepherds, who gave his life for his sheep.[146]

755   'The Church is a *cultivated field*, the tillage of God. On that land the ancient olive tree grows whose holy roots were the prophets and in which the reconciliation of Jews and Gentiles has been brought about and will be brought about again. That land, like a choice vineyard, has been planted by the heavenly
795   cultivator. Yet the true vine is Christ who gives life and fruitfulness to the branches, that is, to us, who through the Church remain in Christ, without whom we can do nothing.[147]

756   'Often, too, the Church is called the *building* of God. The Lord compared himself to the stone which the builders rejected, but which was made into the
857   corner-stone. On this foundation the Church is built by the apostles and from it the Church receives solidity and unity. This edifice has many names to describe it: the house of God in which his *family* dwells; the household of God in the
797   Spirit; the dwelling-place of God among men; and, especially, the holy *temple*. This temple, symbolized in places of worship built out of stone, is praised by the
1045   Fathers and, not without reason, is compared in the liturgy to the Holy City, the New Jerusalem. As living stones we here on earth are built into it. It is this holy city that is seen by John as it comes down out of heaven from God when the world is made anew, prepared like a bride adorned for her husband.[148]

757   'The Church, further, which is called "that Jerusalem which is above" and
507, 796 "our mother", is described as the spotless spouse of the spotless lamb. It is she whom Christ "loved and for whom he delivered himself up that he might
1616   sanctify her". It is she whom he unites to himself by an unbreakable alliance, and whom he constantly "nourishes and cherishes".'[149]

II. The Church's Origin, Foundation and Mission

758   We begin our investigation of the Church's mystery by med-
257   itating on her origin in the Holy Trinity's plan and her progressive realization in history.

A plan born in the Father's heart

759   'The eternal Father, in accordance with the utterly gratuitous
293   and mysterious design of his wisdom and goodness, created the whole universe, and chose to raise up men to share in his own divine life',[150] to which he calls all men in his Son. 'The Father... determined to call together in a holy Church those who should

---

[146] LG 6; cf. Jn 10:1–10; Is 40:11; Ezek 34:11–31; Jn 10:11; 1 Pt 5:4; Jn 10:11–16.

[147] LG 6; cf. 1 Cor 3:9; Rom 11:13–26; Mt 21:33–43 and parallels; Is 5:1–7; Jn 15:1–5.

[148] LG 6; cf. 1 Cor 3:9; Mt 21:42 and parallels; Acts 4:11; 1 Pt 2:7; Ps 118:22; 1 Cor 3:11; 1 Tim 3:15; Eph 2:19–22; Rev 21:3; 1 Pt 2:5; Rev 21:1–2.

[149] LG 6; cf. Gal 4:26; Rev 12:17; 19:7; 21:2, 9; 22:17; Eph 5:25–26, 29.

[150] LG 2.

believe in Christ.'[151] This 'family of God' is gradually formed and takes shape during the stages of human history, in keeping with the Father's plan. In fact, 'already present in figure at the beginning of the world, this Church was prepared in marvellous fashion in the history of the people of Israel and the old Alliance. Established in this last age of the world, and made manifest in the outpouring of the Spirit, it will be brought to glorious completion at the end of time.'[152]   *1655*

The Church – foreshadowed from the world's beginning

760 Christians of the first centuries said, 'The world was created for the sake of the Church.'[153] God created the world for the sake of communion with his divine life, a communion brought about   *294* by the 'convocation' of men in Christ, and this 'convocation' is the Church. The Church is the goal of all things,[154] and God permitted such painful upheavals as the angels' fall and man's sin only   *309* as occasions and means for displaying all the power of his arm and the whole measure of the love he wanted to give the world:

> Just as God's will is creation and is called 'the world', so his intention is the salvation of men, and it is called 'the Church'.[155]

The Church – prepared for in the Old Covenant

761 The gathering together of the People of God began at the moment when sin destroyed the communion of men with God, and that of men among themselves. The gathering together of the Church is, as it were, God's reaction to the chaos provoked by sin.   *55* This reunification is achieved secretly in the heart of all peoples: 'In every nation anyone who fears him and does what is right is acceptable' to God.[156]

762 The remote *preparation* for this gathering together of the   *122, 522* People of God begins when he calls Abraham and promises that he   *60* will become the father of a great people.[157] Its immediate preparation begins with Israel's election as the People of God. By this election, Israel is to be the sign of the future gathering of all nations.[158] But the prophets accuse Israel of breaking the covenant

---

[151] LG 2.
[152] LG 2.
[153] *Pastor Hermae*, Vision 2, 4, 1: PG 2, 899; cf. Aristides, *Apol.* 16, 6; St Justin, *Apol.* 2, 7: PG 6, 456; Tertullian, *Apol.* 31, 3; 32, 1: PL 1, 508–509.
[154] Cf. St Epiphanius, *Panarion* 1, 1, 5: PG

41, 181C.
[155] Clement of Alexandria, *Paed.* 1, 6, 27: PG 8, 281.
[156] *Acts* 10:35; cf. *LG* 9; 13; 16.
[157] Cf. *Gen* 12:2; 15:5–6.
[158] Cf. *Ex* 19:5–6; *Dt* 7:6; *Is* 2:2–5; *Mic* 4:1–4.

and behaving like a prostitute. They announce a new and eternal
64 covenant. 'Christ instituted this New Covenant.'[159]

The Church – instituted by Christ Jesus

763 It was the Son's task to accomplish the Father's plan of salvation in the fullness of time. Its accomplishment was the reason for his being sent.[160] 'The Lord Jesus inaugurated his Church by preaching the Good News, that is, the coming of the Reign of God, promised over the ages in the scriptures.'[161] To fulfil the
541 Father's will, Christ ushered in the Kingdom of heaven on earth. The Church 'is the Reign of Christ already present in mystery.'[162]

764 'This Kingdom shines out before men in the word, in the
543 works and in the presence of Christ.'[163] To welcome Jesus' word is to welcome 'the Kingdom itself'.[164] The seed and beginning of the Kingdom are the 'little flock' of those whom Jesus came to gather around him, the flock whose shepherd he is.[165] They form Jesus' true family.[166] To those whom he thus gathered around him, he
1691, 2558 taught a new 'way of acting' and a prayer of their own.[167]

765 The Lord Jesus endowed his community with a structure that will remain until the Kingdom is fully achieved. Before all else
551 there is the choice of the Twelve with Peter as their head.[168]
860 Representing the twelve tribes of Israel, they are the foundation stones of the new Jerusalem.[169] The Twelve and the other disciples share in Christ's mission and his power, but also in his lot.[170] By all his actions, Christ prepares and builds his Church.

813 766 The Church is born primarily of Christ's total self-giving for
1340 our salvation, anticipated in the institution of the Eucharist and
860 fulfilled on the cross. 'The origin and growth of the Church are symbolized by the blood and water which flowed from the open side of the crucified Jesus.'[171] 'For it was from the side of Christ as
617 he slept the sleep of death upon the cross that there came forth the
478 "wondrous sacrament of the whole Church".'[172] As Eve was

---

[159] LG 9; cf. Hos 1; Is 1:2–4; Jer 2; 31:31–34; Is 55:3.
[160] Cf. LG 3; AG 3.
[161] LG 5.
[162] LG 3.
[163] LG 5.
[164] LG 5.
[165] Lk 12:32; cf. Mt 10:16; 26:31; Jn 10:1–21.
[166] Cf. Mt 12:49.
[167] Cf. Mt 5 – 6.
[168] Cf. Mk 3:14–15.
[169] Cf. Mt 19:28; Lk 22:30; Rev 21:12–14.
[170] Cf. Mk 6:7; Lk 10:1–2; Mt 10:25; Jn 15:20.
[171] LG 3; cf. Jn 19:34.
[172] SC 5.

formed from the sleeping Adam's side, so the Church was born from the pierced heart of Christ hanging dead on the cross.[173]

The Church – revealed by the Holy Spirit

767 'When the work which the Father gave the Son to do on earth was accomplished, the Holy Spirit was sent on the day of Pentecost in order that he might continually sanctify the Church.'[174] Then 'the Church was openly displayed to the crowds and the spread of the Gospel among the nations, through preaching, was begun.'[175] As the 'convocation' of all men for salvation, the Church in her very nature is missionary, sent by Christ to all the nations to make disciples of them.[176]

768 So that she can fulfil her mission, the Holy Spirit 'bestows upon [the Church] varied hierarchic and charismatic gifts, and in this way directs her.'[177] 'Henceforward the Church, endowed with the gifts of her founder and faithfully observing his precepts of charity, humility and self-denial, receives the mission of proclaiming and establishing among all peoples the Kingdom of Christ and of God, and she is on earth the seed and the beginning of that kingdom.'[178]

The Church – perfected in glory

769 'The Church. . . will receive her perfection only in the glory of heaven',[179] at the time of Christ's glorious return. Until that day, 'the Church progresses on her pilgrimage amidst this world's persecutions and God's consolations.'[180] Here below she knows that she is in exile far from the Lord, and longs for the full coming of the Kingdom, when she will 'be united in glory with her king'.[181] The Church, and through her the world, will not be perfected in glory without great trials. Only then will 'all the just from the time of Adam, "from Abel, the just one, to the last of the elect",. . . be gathered together in the universal Church in the Father's presence.'[182]

III. The Mystery of the Church

770 The Church is in history, but at the same time she transcends

---

[173] Cf. St Ambrose, *In Luc.* 2, 85–89: PL 15, 1583–1586.
[174] LG 4; cf. *Jn* 17:4.
[175] AG 4.
[176] Cf. *Mt* 28:19–20; AG 2; 5–6.
[177] LG 4.
[178] LG 5.
[179] LG 48.
[180] St Augustine, *De civ. Dei* 18, 51: PL 41, 614; cf. LG 8.
[181] LG 5; cf. 6; 2 *Cor* 5:6.
[182] LG 2.

Margin references: 731, 849, 541, 2818, 671, 675, 1045

812 it. It is only 'with the eyes of faith'[183] that one can see her in her visible reality and at the same time in her spiritual reality as bearer of divine life.

The Church – both visible and spiritual

771 'The one mediator, Christ, established and ever sustains here on earth his holy Church, the community of faith, hope and charity, as a visible organization through which he communicates
827 truth and grace to all men.'[184] The Church is at the same time:
1880 – a 'society structured with hierarchical organs and the mystical body of Christ;
– the visible society and the spiritual community;
954 – the earthly Church and the Church endowed with heavenly riches'.[185]

These dimensions together constitute 'one complex reality which comes together from a human and a divine element':[186]

> The Church is essentially both human and divine, visible but endowed with invisible realities, zealous in action and dedicated to contemplation, present in the world, but as a pilgrim, so constituted that in her the human is directed toward and subordinated to the divine, the visible to the invisible, action to contemplation, and this present world to that city yet to come, the object of our quest.[187]

> O humility! O sublimity! Both tabernacle of cedar and sanctuary of God; earthly dwelling and celestial palace; house of clay and royal hall; body of death and temple of light; and at last both object of scorn to the proud and bride of Christ! She is black but beautiful, O daughters of Jerusalem, for even if the labour and pain of her long exile may have discoloured her, yet heaven's beauty has adorned her.[188]

The Church – mystery of men's union with God

772 It is in the Church that Christ fulfils and reveals his own
518 mystery as the purpose of God's plan: 'to unite all things in him.'[189] St Paul calls the nuptial union of Christ and the Church 'a
796 great mystery'. Because she is united to Christ as to her bridegroom, she becomes a mystery in her turn.[190] Contemplating this mystery in her, Paul exclaims: 'Christ in you, the hope of glory.'[191]

---

[183] *Roman Catechism* I, 10, 20.
[184] *LG* 8 § 1.
[185] *LG* 8.
[186] *LG* 8.
[187] *SC* 2; cf. *Heb* 13:14.

[188] St Bernard of Clairvaux, *In Cant. Sermo* 27, 14: PL 183, 920D.
[189] *Eph* 1:10.
[190] *Eph* 5:32; 3:9–11; 5:25–27.
[191] *Col* 1:27.

773 In the Church this communion of men with God, in the 'love [that] never ends', is the purpose which governs everything in her that is a sacramental means, tied to this passing world.[192] '[The 671 Church's] structure is totally ordered to the holiness of Christ's members. And holiness is measured according to the "great mystery" in which the Bride responds with the gift of love to the gift of the Bridegroom.'[193] Mary goes before us all in the holiness that 972 is the Church's mystery as 'the bride without spot or wrinkle'.[194] This is why the 'Marian' dimension of the Church precedes the 'Petrine'.[195]

The universal sacrament of salvation

774 The Greek word *mystērion* was translated into Latin by two terms: *mysterium* and *sacramentum*. In later usage the term *sacramentum* emphasizes the 1075 visible sign of the hidden reality of salvation which was indicated by the term *mysterium*. In this sense, Christ himself is the mystery of salvation: 'For there is no other mystery of God, except Christ.'[196] The saving work of his holy and sanctifying humanity is the sacrament of salvation, which is revealed and active 515 in the Church's sacraments (which the Eastern Churches also call 'the holy mysteries'). The seven sacraments are the signs and instruments by which the 2014 Holy Spirit spreads the grace of Christ the head throughout the Church which 1116 is his Body. The Church, then, both contains and communicates the invisible grace she signifies. It is in this analogical sense that the Church is called a 'sacrament'.

775 'The Church, in Christ, is like a sacrament – a sign and instrument, that is, of communion with God and of unity among all men.'[197] The Church's first purpose is to be the sacrament of the *inner union of men with God*. Because men's communion with one another is rooted in that union with God, the Church is also the sacrament of the *unity of the human race*. In her, this unity is already 360 begun, since she gathers men 'from every nation, from all tribes and peoples and tongues';[198] at the same time, the Church is the 'sign and instrument' of the full realization of the unity yet to come.

776 As sacrament, the Church is Christ's instrument. 'She is taken up by him also as the instrument for the salvation of all', 'the universal sacrament of salvation', by which Christ is 'at once 1088 manifesting and actualizing the mystery of God's love for men'.[199]

---

[192] 1 *Cor* 13:8; cf. *LG* 48.
[193] John Paul II, *MD* 27.
[194] *Eph* 5:27.
[195] Cf. John Paul II, *MD* 27.
[196] St Augustine, *Ep.* 187, 11, 34: PL 33, 846.

[197] *LG* 1.
[198] *Rev* 7:9.
[199] *LG* 9 § 2, 48 § 2; *GS* 45 § 1.

The Church 'is the visible plan of God's love for humanity', because God desires 'that the whole human race may become one People of God, form one Body of Christ, and be built up into one temple of the Holy Spirit'.[200]

IN BRIEF

777   The word 'Church' means 'convocation'. It designates the assembly of those whom God's Word 'convokes', i.e. gathers together to form the People of God. and who themselves, nourished with the Body of Christ, become the Body of Christ.

778   The Church is both the means and the goal of God's plan: prefigured in creation, prepared for in the Old Covenant, founded by the words and actions of Jesus Christ, fulfilled by his redeeming cross and his Resurrection, the Church has been manifested as the mystery of salvation by the outpouring of the Holy Spirit. She will be perfected in the glory of heaven as the assembly of all the redeemed of the earth (cf. Rev 14:4).

779   The Church is both visible and spiritual, a hierarchical society and the Mystical Body of Christ. She is one, yet formed of two components, human and divine. That is her mystery, which only faith can accept.

780   The Church in this world is the sacrament of salvation, the sign and the instrument of the communion of God and men.

Paragraph 2. The Church – People of God, Body of Christ, Temple of the Holy Spirit

I. The Church – People of God

781   'At all times and in every race, anyone who fears God and does what is right has been acceptable to him. He has, however, willed to make men holy and save them, not as individuals without any bond or link between them, but rather to make them into a people who might acknowledge him and serve him in holiness. He therefore chose the Israelite race to be his own people and established a covenant with it. He gradually instructed this people. . . All these things, however, happened as a preparation for and figure of that new and perfect covenant which was to be ratified in Christ. . . the New Covenant in his blood; he called together a race made up of Jews and Gentiles which would be one, not according to the flesh, but in the Spirit.'[201]

---

[200] Paul VI, 22 June 1973; AG 7 § 2; cf. LG 17.

[201] LG 9; cf. Acts 10:35; 1 Cor 11:25.

Characteristics of the People of God

782 The People of God is marked by characteristics that clearly *871* distinguish it from all other religious, ethnic, political or cultural groups found in history:

− It is the People *of God*: God is not the property of any one people. *2787* But he acquired a people for himself from those who previously were not a people: 'a chosen race, a royal priesthood, a holy nation'.[202]

− One becomes a *member* of this people not by a physical birth, but by being 'born anew', a birth 'of water and the Spirit',[203] that is, by faith in Christ, and Baptism. *1267*

− This People has for its *Head* Jesus the Christ (the anointed, the Messiah). Because the same anointing, the Holy Spirit, flows from *695* the head into the body, this is 'the messianic people'.

− 'The *status* of this people is that of the dignity and freedom of the *1741* sons of God, in whose hearts the Holy Spirit dwells as in a temple.'

− 'Its *law* is the new commandment to love as Christ loved us.'[204] This is the 'new' law of the Holy Spirit.[205] *1972*

− Its *mission* is to be salt of the earth and light of the world.[206] This *849* people is 'a most sure seed of unity, hope and salvation for the whole human race'.

− Its *destiny*, finally, 'is the Kingdom of God which has been begun *769* by God himself on earth and which must be further extended until it has been brought to perfection by him at the end of time.'[207]

A priestly, prophetic and royal people

783 Jesus Christ is the one whom the Father anointed with the Holy Spirit and established as priest, prophet and king. The whole *436* People of God participates in these three offices of Christ and bears the responsibilities for mission and service that flow from them.[208] *873*

784 On entering the People of God through faith and Baptism, one receives a share in this people's unique, *priestly* vocation: *1268* 'Christ the Lord, high priest taken from among men, has made this new people "a kingdom of priests to God, his Father". The baptized, by regeneration and the anointing of the Holy Spirit, are *consecrated* to be a spiritual house and a holy priesthood.'[209] *1546*

785 'The holy People of God shares also in Christ's *prophetic* office', above all in the supernatural sense of faith that belongs to *92*

---

[202] 1 *Pt* 2:9.
[203] *Jn* 3:3–5.
[204] Cf. *Jn* 13:34.
[205] *Rom* 8:2; *Gal* 5:25.
[206] Cf. *Mt* 5:13–16.
[207] *LG* 9 § 2.
[208] Cf. John Paul II, *RH* 18–21.
[209] *LG* 10; cf. *Heb* 5:1–5; *Rev* 1:6.

the whole People, lay and clergy, when it 'unfailingly adheres to this faith... once for all delivered to the saints',[210] and when it deepens its understanding and becomes Christ's witness in the midst of this world.

786 Finally, the People of God shares in the *royal* office of Christ. He exercises his kingship by drawing all men to himself through his death and Resurrection.[211] Christ, King and Lord of the universe, made himself the servant of all, for he came 'not to be served but to serve, and to give his life as a ransom for many'.[212] For the Christian, 'to reign is to serve him', particularly when serving 'the poor and the suffering, in whom the Church recognizes the image of her poor and suffering founder'.[213] The People of God fulfils its royal dignity by a life in keeping with its vocation to serve with Christ.

2449
2443

> The sign of the cross makes kings of all those reborn in Christ and the anointing of the Holy Spirit consecrates them as priests, so that, apart from the particular service of our ministry, all spiritual and rational Christians are recognized as members of this royal race and sharers in Christ's priestly office. What, indeed, is as royal for a soul as to govern the body in obedience to God? And what is as priestly as to dedicate a pure conscience to the Lord and to offer the spotless offerings of devotion on the altar of the heart?[214]

II. The Church – Body of Christ

The Church is communion with Jesus

787 From the beginning, Jesus associated his disciples with his own life, revealed the mystery of the Kingdom to them and gave them a share in his mission, joy and sufferings.[215] Jesus spoke of a still more intimate communion between him and those who would follow him: 'Abide in me, and I in you... I am the vine, you are the branches.'[216] And he proclaimed a mysterious and real communion between his own body and ours: 'He who eats my flesh and drinks my blood abides in me, and I in him.'[217]

755

788 When his visible presence was taken from them, Jesus did not leave his disciples orphans. He promised to remain with them until the end of time; he sent them his Spirit.[218] As a result communion

690

---

[210] LG 12; cf. *Jude* 3.
[211] Cf. *Jn* 12:32.
[212] *Mt* 20:28.
[213] LG 8; cf. 36.
[214] St Leo the Great, *Sermo* 4, 1: PL 54, 149.

[215] Cf. *Mk* 1:16–20; 3:13–19; *Mt* 13:10–17; *Lk* 10:17–20; 22:28–30.
[216] *Jn* 15:4–5.
[217] *Jn* 6:56.
[218] Cf. *Jn* 14:18; 20:22; *Mt* 28:20; *Acts* 2:33.

with Jesus has become, in a way, more intense: 'By communicating his Spirit, Christ mystically constitutes as his body those brothers of his who are called together from every nation.'[219]

789 The comparison of the Church with the body casts light on the intimate bond between Christ and his Church. Not only is she gathered *around him*; she is united *in him*, in his body. Three aspects *521* of the Church as the Body of Christ are to be more specifically noted: the unity of all her members with each other as a result of their union with Christ; Christ as head of the Body; and the Church as bride of Christ.

'One Body'

790 Believers who respond to God's word and become members of Christ's Body become intimately united with him: 'In that body the life of Christ is communicated to those who believe, and *947* who, through the sacraments, are united in a hidden and real way to Christ in his Passion and glorification.'[220] This is especially true of Baptism, which unites us to Christ's death and Resurrection, *1227* and the Eucharist, by which 'really sharing in the body of the *1329* Lord,. . . we are taken up into communion with him and with one another.'[221]

791 The body's unity does not do away with the diversity of its *814* members: 'In the building up of Christ's Body there is engaged a diversity of members and functions. There is only one Spirit who, according to his own richness and the needs of the ministries, gives his different gifts for the welfare of the Church.'[222] The unity of *1937* the Mystical Body produces and stimulates charity among the faithful: 'From this it follows that if one member suffers anything, all the members suffer with him, and if one member is honoured, all the members together rejoice.'[223] Finally, the unity of the Mystical Body triumphs over all human divisions: 'For as many of you as were baptized into Christ have put on Christ. There is neither Jew nor Greek, there is neither slave nor free, there is neither male nor female; for you are all one in Christ Jesus.'[224]

'Christ is the Head of this Body'

792 Christ 'is the head of the body, the Church.'[225] He is the *669, 1119* principle of creation and redemption. Raised to the Father's glory,

---

[219] LG 7.
[220] LG 7.
[221] LG 7; cf. Rom 6:4–5; 1 Cor 12:13.
[222] LG 7 § 3.
[223] LG 7 § 3; cf. 1 Cor 12:26.
[224] Gal 3:27–28.
[225] Col 1:18.

'in everything he [is] pre-eminent',[226] especially in the Church, through whom he extends his reign over all things.

519   793   *Christ unites us with his Passover*: all his members must strive to resemble him, 'until Christ be formed' in them.[227] 'For this reason we. . . are taken up into the mysteries of his life,. . . associated with
661   his sufferings as the body with its head, suffering with him, that with him we may be glorified.'[228]

794   *Christ provides for our growth*: to make us grow towards him,
872   our head,[229] he provides in his Body, the Church, the gifts and assistance by which we help one another along the way of salvation.

795   Christ and his Church thus together make up the 'whole
695   *Christ*' (*Christus totus*). The Church is one with Christ. The saints are acutely aware of this unity:

> Let us rejoice then and give thanks that we have become not only Christians, but Christ himself. Do you understand and grasp, brethren, God's grace toward us? Marvel and rejoice: we have become Christ. For if he is the head, we are the members; he and we together are the whole man. . . The fullness of Christ then is the head and the members. But what does 'head and members' mean? Christ and the Church.[230]

> Our redeemer has shown himself to be one person with the holy Church whom he has taken to himself.[231]

1474   Head and members form as it were one and the same mystical person.[232]

> A reply of St Joan of Arc to her judges sums up the faith of the holy doctors and the good sense of the believer: 'About Jesus Christ and the Church, I simply know they're just one thing, and we shouldn't complicate the matter.'[233]

The Church is the Bride of Christ

796   The unity of Christ and the Church, head and members of one Body, also implies the distinction of the two within a personal relationship. This aspect is often expressed by the image of bride-
757, 219   groom and bride. The theme of Christ as Bridegroom of the Church was prepared for by the prophets and announced by John the Baptist.[234] The Lord referred to himself as the 'bride-
772   groom'.[235] The Apostle speaks of the whole Church and of each of the faithful, members of his Body, as a bride 'betrothed' to Christ

---

[226] *Col* 1:18.
[227] *Gal* 4:19.
[228] *LG* 7 § 4; cf. *Phil* 3:21; *Rom* 8:17.
[229] Cf. *Col* 2:19; *Eph* 4:11–16.
[230] St Augustine, *In ev. Jo.* 21, 8: PL 35, 1568.

[231] St Gregory the Great, *Moralia in Job*, praef. 1, 6, 14: PL 75, 525A.
[232] St Thomas Aquinas, *STh* III, 48, 2.
[233] Acts of the Trial of Joan of Arc.
[234] *Jn* 3:29.
[235] *Mk* 2:19.

the Lord so as to become but one spirit with him.[236] The Church is the spotless bride of the spotless Lamb.[237] 'Christ loved the Church   *1602, 1616* and gave himself up for her, that he might sanctify her.'[238] He has joined her with himself in an everlasting covenant, and never stops caring for her as for his own body:[239]

> This is the whole Christ, head and body, one formed from many... whether the head or members speak, it is Christ who speaks. He speaks in his role as the head (*ex persona capitis*) and in his role as body (*ex persona corporis*). What does this mean? 'The two will become one flesh. This is a great mystery, and I am applying it to Christ and the Church.'[240] And the Lord himself says in the Gospel: 'So they are no longer two, but one flesh.'[241] They are, in fact, two different persons, yet they are one in the conjugal union,... *as head, he calls himself the bridegroom, as body, he calls himself 'bride'*.[242]

III. The Church Is the Temple of the Holy Spirit

797 'What the soul is to the human body, the Holy Spirit is to the Body of Christ, which is the Church.'[243] 'To this Spirit of Christ,   *813* as an invisible principle, is to be ascribed the fact that all the parts of the body are joined one with the other and with their exalted head; for the whole Spirit of Christ is in the head, the whole Spirit is in the body, and the whole Spirit is in each of the members.'[244] The Holy Spirit makes the Church 'the temple of the living God':[245]   *586*

> Indeed, it is to the Church herself that the 'Gift of God' has been entrusted... It is in her that communion with Christ has been deposited, that is to say: the Holy Spirit, the pledge of incorruptibility, the strengthening of our faith and the ladder of our ascent to God... For where the Church is, there also is God's Spirit; where God's Spirit is, there is the Church and every grace.[246]

798 The Holy Spirit is 'the principle of every vital and truly saving action in each part of the Body'.[247] He works in many ways   *737* to build up the whole Body in charity:[248] by God's Word 'which is   *1091-1109* able to build you up';[249] by Baptism, through which he forms

---

[236] Cf. *Mt* 22:1–14; 25:1–13; 1 *Cor* 6:15–17; 2 *Cor* 11:2.

[237] Cf. *Rev* 22:17; *Eph* 1:4; 5:27.

[238] *Eph* 5:25–26.

[239] Cf. *Eph* 5:29.

[240] *Eph* 5:31–32.

[241] *Mt* 19:6.

[242] St Augustine, *En. in Ps.* 74, 4: PL 36, 948–949.

[243] St Augustine, *Sermo* 267, 4: PL 38, 1231D.

[244] Pius XII, Enc. *Mystici Corporis*: DS 3808.

[245] 2 *Cor* 6:16; cf. 1 *Cor* 3:16–17; *Eph* 2:21.

[246] St Irenaeus, *Adv. haeres.* 3, 24, 1: PG 7/1, 966.

[247] Pius XII, Enc. *Mystici Corporis*: DS 3808.

[248] Cf. *Eph* 4:16.

[249] *Acts* 20:32.

Christ's Body;[250] by the sacraments, which give growth and healing to Christ's members; by 'the grace of the apostles, which holds first place among his gifts';[251] by the virtues, which make us act according to what is good; finally, by the many special graces (called 'charisms'), by which he makes the faithful 'fit and ready to

791 undertake various tasks and offices for the renewal and building up of the Church'.[252]

Charisms

2003   799   Whether extraordinary or simple and humble, charisms are
951 graces of the Holy Spirit which directly or indirectly benefit the Church, ordered as they are to her building up, to the good of men and to the needs of the world.

800 Charisms are to be accepted with gratitude by the person who receives them, and by all members of the Church as well. They are a wonderfully rich grace for the apostolic vitality and for the holiness of the entire Body of Christ, provided they really are genuine gifts of the Holy Spirit and are used in full conformity with authentic promptings of this same Spirit, that is, in keeping with charity, the true measure of all charisms.[253]

801 It is in this sense that discernment of charisms is always necessary. No charism is exempt from being referred and submitted to

894 the Church's shepherds. 'Their office [is] not indeed to extinguish the Spirit, but to test all things and hold fast to what is good',[254] so that all the diverse and complementary charisms work together

1905 'for the common good'.[255]

IN BRIEF

802   *Christ Jesus 'gave himself for us to redeem us from all iniquity and to purify for himself a people of his own' (Titus 2:14).*

803   *'You are a chosen race, a royal priesthood, a holy nation, God's own people' (1 Pt 2:9).*

804   *One enters into the People of God by faith and Baptism. 'All men are called to belong to the new People of God' (LG 13), so that, in Christ, 'men may form one family and one People of God' (AG 1).*

---

[250] Cf. 1 Cor 12:13.
[251] LG 7 § 2.
[252] LG 12 § 2; cf. AA 3.
[253] Cf. 1 Cor 13.

[254] LG 12; cf. 30; 1 Th 5:12, 19–21; John Paul II, *Christifideles Laici* 24.
[255] 1 Cor 12:7.

805 *The Church is the Body of Christ. Through the Spirit and his action in the sacraments, above all the Eucharist, Christ, who once was dead and is now risen, establishes the community of believers as his own Body.*

806 *In the unity of this Body, there is a diversity of members and functions. All members are linked to one another, especially to those who are suffering, to the poor and persecuted.*

807 *The Church is this Body of which Christ is the head: she lives from him, in him and for him; he lives with her and in her.*

808 *The Church is the Bride of Christ: he loved her and handed himself over for her. He has purified her by his blood and made her the fruitful mother of all God's children.*

809 *The Church is the Temple of the Holy Spirit. The Spirit is the soul, as it were, of the Mystical Body, the source of its life, of its unity in diversity, and of the riches of its gifts and charisms.*

810 *'Hence the universal Church is seen to be "a people brought into unity from the unity of the Father, the Son and the Holy Spirit"' (LG 4, citing St Cyprian, De Dom. orat. 23: PL 4, 553).*

Paragraph 3. The Church Is One, Holy, Catholic and Apostolic

811 'This is the sole Church of Christ, which in the Creed we profess to be one, holy, catholic and apostolic.'[256] These four char- *750* acteristics, inseparably linked with each other,[257] indicate essential features of the Church and her mission. The Church does not possess them of herself; it is Christ who, through the Holy Spirit, makes his Church one, holy, catholic and apostolic, and it is he *832, 865* who calls her to realize each of these qualities.

812 Only faith can recognize that the Church possesses these *770* properties from her divine source. But their historical manifestations are signs that also speak clearly to human reason. As the *156* First Vatican Council noted, the 'Church herself, with her marvellous propagation, eminent holiness and inexhaustible fruitfulness in everything good, her catholic unity and invincible stability, is a great and perpetual motive of credibility and an irrefutable witness of her divine mission.'[258]

---

[256] LG 8.
[257] Cf. DS 2888.

[258] Vatican Council I, *Dei Filius* 3: DS 3013.

I. The Church Is One

'The sacred mystery of the Church's unity' (UR 2)

813 *The Church is one because of her source*: 'the highest exemplar
172 and source of this mystery is the unity, in the Trinity of Persons, of
one God, the Father and the Son in the Holy Spirit.'[259] The
766 Church is one *because of her founder*: for 'the Word made flesh, the
prince of peace, reconciled all men to God by the cross, . . . restoring the unity of all in one people and one body.'[260] The Church is
797 one *because of her 'soul'*: 'It is the Holy Spirit, dwelling in those who
believe and pervading and ruling over the entire Church, who
brings about that wonderful communion of the faithful and joins
them together so intimately in Christ that he is the principle of the
Church's unity.'[261] Unity is of the essence of the Church:

> What an astonishing mystery! There is one Father of the universe, one
> *Logos* of the universe, and also one Holy Spirit, everywhere one and the
> same; there is also one virgin become mother, and I should like to call her
> 'Church'.[262]

814 From the beginning, this one Church has been marked by a
791, 873 great *diversity* which comes from both the variety of God's gifts
and the diversity of those who receive them. Within the unity
of the People of God, a multiplicity of peoples and cultures is
gathered together. Among the Church's members, there are dif-
1202 ferent gifts, offices, conditions and ways of life. 'Holding a rightful
place in the communion of the Church there are also particular
832 Churches that retain their own traditions.'[263] The great richness of
such diversity is not opposed to the Church's unity. Yet sin and the
burden of its consequences constantly threaten the gift of unity.
And so the Apostle has to exhort Christians to 'maintain the unity
of the Spirit in the bond of peace'.[264]

1827 815 What are these bonds of unity? Above all charity 'binds
830 everything together in perfect harmony.'[265] But the unity of the
837 pilgrim Church is also assured by visible bonds of communion:
173 – profession of one faith received from the apostles;
– common celebration of divine worship, especially of the sacraments;
– apostolic succession through the sacrament of Holy Orders,
maintaining the fraternal concord of God's family.[266]

---

[259] UR 2 § 5.
[260] GS 78 § 3.
[261] UR 2 § 2.
[262] Clement of Alexandria, *Paed.* 1, 6, 42:
PG 8, 300.

[263] LG 13 § 2.
[264] Eph 4:3.
[265] Col 3:14.
[266] Cf. UR 2; LG 14; CIC, can. 205.

816 'The sole Church of Christ [is that] which our Saviour, after his Resurrection, entrusted to Peter's pastoral care, commissioning him and the other apostles to extend and rule it... This Church, constituted and organized as a society in the present world, subsists in (*subsistit in*) the Catholic Church, which is governed by the successor of Peter and by the bishops in communion with him.'[267]

> The Second Vatican Council's Decree on Ecumenism explains: 'For it is through Christ's Catholic Church alone, which is the universal help toward salvation, that the fullness of the means of salvation can be obtained. It was to the apostolic college alone, of which Peter is the head, that we believe that our Lord entrusted all the blessings of the New Covenant, in order to establish on earth the one Body of Christ into which all those should be fully incorporated who belong in any way to the People of God.'[268]   *830*

Wounds to unity

817 In fact, 'in this one and only Church of God from its very beginnings there arose certain rifts, which the Apostle strongly censures as damnable. But in subsequent centuries much more serious dissensions appeared and large communities became separated from full communion with the Catholic Church – for which, often enough, men of both sides were to blame.'[269] The ruptures that wound the unity of Christ's Body – here we must distinguish heresy, apostasy and schism[270] – do not occur without human sin: *2089*

> Where there are sins, there are also divisions, schisms, heresies, and disputes. Where there is virtue, however, there also are harmony and unity, from which arise the one heart and one soul of all believers.[271]

818 'However, one cannot charge with the sin of the separation those who at present are born into these communities [that resulted from such separation] and in them are brought up in the faith of Christ, and the Catholic Church accepts them with respect and affection as brothers... All who have been justified by faith in Baptism are incorporated into Christ; they therefore have a right to be called Christians, and with good reason are accepted as brothers in the Lord by the children of the Catholic Church.'[272]   *1271*

819 'Furthermore, many elements of sanctification and of truth'[273] are found outside the visible confines of the Catholic Church: 'the written Word of God; the life of grace; faith, hope

---

[267] LG 8 § 2.
[268] UR 3 § 5.
[269] UR 3 § 1.
[270] Cf. CIC, can. 751.

[271] Origen, *Hom. in Ezech.* 9, 1: PG 13, 732.
[272] UR 3 § 1.
[273] LG 8 § 2.

and charity, with the other interior gifts of the Holy Spirit, as well as visible elements.'[274] Christ's Spirit uses these Churches and ecclesial communities as means of salvation, whose power derives from the fullness of grace and truth that Christ has entrusted to the Catholic Church. All these blessings come from Christ and lead to him,[275] and are in themselves calls to 'Catholic unity'.[276]

Towards unity

820 'Christ bestowed unity on his Church from the beginning. This unity, we believe, subsists in the Catholic Church as something she can never lose, and we hope that it will continue to increase until the end of time.'[277] Christ always gives his Church the gift of unity, but the Church must always pray and work to maintain, reinforce and perfect the unity that Christ wills for her.

2748 This is why Jesus himself prayed at the hour of his Passion, and does not cease praying to his Father, for the unity of his disciples: 'That they may all be one. As you, Father, are in me and I am in you, may they also be one in us,... so that the world may know that you have sent me.'[278] The desire to recover the unity of all Christians is a gift of Christ and a call of the Holy Spirit.[279]

821 Certain things are required in order to respond adequately to this call:

827 – a permanent *renewal* of the Church in greater fidelity to her vocation; such renewal is the driving-force of the movement toward unity;[280]

– *conversion of heart* as the faithful 'try to live holier lives according to the Gospel';[281] for it is the unfaithfulness of the members to Christ's gift which

2751 causes divisions;

– *prayer in common*, because 'change of heart and holiness of life, along with public and private prayer for the unity of Christians, should be regarded as the soul of the whole ecumenical movement, and merits the name "spiritual ecumenism"';[282]

– *fraternal knowledge of each other*;[283]

– *ecumenical formation* of the faithful and especially of priests;[284]

– *dialogue* among theologians, and meetings among Christians of the different churches and communities;[285]

– *collaboration* among Christians in various areas of service to mankind.[286]

822 Concern for achieving unity 'involves the whole Church, faithful and clergy alike.'[287] But we must realize 'that this holy

---

[274] *UR* 3 § 2; cf. *LG* 15.
[275] Cf. *UR* 3.
[276] Cf. *LG* 8.
[277] *UR* 4 § 3.
[278] *Jn* 17:21; cf. *Heb* 7:25.
[279] Cf. *UR* 1.
[280] Cf. *UR* 6.

[281] *UR* 7 § 3.
[282] *UR* 8 § 1.
[283] Cf. *UR* 9.
[284] Cf. *UR* 10.
[285] Cf. *UR* 4; 9; 11.
[286] Cf. *UR* 12.
[287] *UR* 5.

objective – the reconciliation of all Christians in the unity of the one and only Church of Christ – transcends human powers and gifts'. That is why we place all our hope 'in the prayer of Christ for the Church, in the love of the Father for us, and in the power of the Holy Spirit'.[288]

II. The Church Is Holy

823 'The Church... is held, as a matter of faith, to be unfailingly holy. This is because Christ, the Son of God, who with the Father and the Spirit is hailed as "alone holy", loved the Church as his Bride, giving himself up for her so as to sanctify her; he joined her to himself as his body and endowed her with the gift of the Holy Spirit for the glory of God.'[289] The Church, then, is 'the holy People of God',[290] and her members are called 'saints'.[291]

459
796

946

824 United with Christ, the Church is sanctified by him; through him and with him she becomes *sanctifying*. 'All the activities of the Church are directed, as towards their end, to the sanctification of men in Christ and the glorification of God.'[292] It is in the Church that 'the fullness of the means of salvation'[293] has been deposited. It is in her that 'by the grace of God we acquire holiness.'[294]

816

825 'The Church on earth is endowed already with a sanctity that is real though imperfect.'[295] In her members perfect holiness is something yet to be acquired: 'Strengthened by so many and such great means of salvation, all the faithful, whatever their condition or state – though each in his own way – are called by the Lord to that perfection of sanctity by which the Father himself is perfect.'[296]

670

2013

826 *Charity* is the soul of the holiness to which all are called: it 'governs, shapes, and perfects all the means of sanctification.'[297]

1827, 2658

> If the Church was a body composed of different members, it couldn't lack the noblest of all; *it must have a Heart, and a Heart BURNING WITH LOVE.* And I realized that *this love alone* was the true motive force which enabled the other members of the Church to act; if it ceased to function, the Apostles would forget to preach the gospel, the Martyrs would refuse to shed their blood. LOVE, IN FACT, IS THE VOCATION WHICH

864

---

[288] *UR* 24 § 2.
[289] *LG* 39; cf. *Eph* 5:25–26.
[290] *LG* 12.
[291] *Acts* 9:13; 1 *Cor* 6:1; 16:1.
[292] *SC* 10.
[293] *UR* 3 § 5.
[294] *LG* 48.
[295] *LG* 48 § 3.
[296] *LG* 11 § 3.
[297] *LG* 42.

INCLUDES ALL OTHERS; IT'S A UNIVERSE OF ITS OWN, COMPRISING ALL TIME AND SPACE – IT'S ETERNAL![298]

827 'Christ, "holy, innocent and undefiled", knew nothing of sin, but came only to expiate the sins of the people. The Church,

1425–1429 however, clasping sinners to her bosom, at once holy and always in need of purification, follows constantly the path of penance and

821 renewal.'[299] All members of the Church, including her ministers, must acknowledge that they are sinners.[300] In everyone, the weeds of sin will still be mixed with the good wheat of the Gospel until the end of time.[301] Hence the Church gathers sinners already caught up in Christ's salvation but still on the way to holiness:

> The Church is therefore holy, though having sinners in her midst, because she herself has no other life but the life of grace. If they live her life, her members are sanctified; if they move away from her life, they fall into sins and disorders that prevent the radiation of her sanctity. This is why she suffers and does penance for those offences, of which she has the power to free her children through the blood of Christ and the gift of the Holy Spirit.[302]

828 By *canonizing* some of the faithful, i.e., by solemnly proclaiming that they practised heroic virtue and lived in fidelity to God's grace, the Church recognizes the power of the Spirit of holiness within her and sustains the hope of believers by proposing

1173 the saints to them as models and intercessors.[303] 'The saints have always been the source and origin of renewal in the most difficult

2045 moments in the Church's history.'[304] Indeed, 'holiness is the hidden source and infallible measure of her apostolic activity and missionary zeal.'[305]

829 'But while in the most Blessed Virgin the Church has already reached that perfection whereby she exists without spot or wrinkle, the faithful still strive to conquer sin and increase in holi-

1172, 972 ness. And so they turn their eyes to Mary':[306] in her, the Church is already the 'all-holy'.

III. The Church Is Catholic

What does 'catholic' mean?

830 The word 'catholic' means 'universal', in the sense of 'accord-

---

[298] St Thérèse of Lisieux, *Autobiography of a Saint*, tr. Ronald Knox (London: Collins, 1960), 185–186.
[299] *LG* 8 § 3; cf. *UR* 3; 6; *Heb* 2:17; 7:26; 2 *Cor* 5:21.
[300] Cf. 1 *Jn* 1:8–10.
[301] Cf. *Mt* 13:24–30.
[302] Paul VI, *CPG* § 19.
[303] Cf. *LG* 40; 48–51.
[304] John Paul II, *CL* 16, 3.
[305] *CL* 17, 3.
[306] *LG* 65; cf. *Eph* 5:26–27.

ing to the totality' or 'in keeping with the whole'. The Church is catholic in a double sense:

First, the Church is catholic because Christ is present in her. 'Where there is Christ Jesus, there is the Catholic Church.'[307] In her subsists the fullness of Christ's body united with its head; this implies that she receives from him 'the fullness of the means of salvation'[308] which he has willed: correct and complete confession of faith, full sacramental life, and ordained ministry in apostolic succession. The Church was, in this fundamental sense, catholic on the day of Pentecost[309] and will always be so until the day of the Parousia.

795, 815–816

831 Secondly, the Church is catholic because she has been sent out by Christ on a mission to the whole of the human race:[310]

849

> All men are called to belong to the new People of God. This People, therefore, while remaining one and only one, is to be spread throughout the whole world and to all ages in order that the design of God's will may be fulfilled: he made human nature one in the beginning and has decreed that all his children who were scattered should be finally gathered together as one. . . The character of universality which adorns the People of God is a gift from the Lord himself whereby the Catholic Church ceaselessly and efficaciously seeks for the return of all humanity and all its goods, under Christ the Head in the unity of his Spirit.[311]

360

518

Each particular Church is 'catholic'

832 'The Church of Christ is really present in all legitimately organized local groups of the faithful, which, in so far as they are united to their pastors, are also quite appropriately called Churches in the New Testament. . . In them the faithful are gathered together through the preaching of the Gospel of Christ, and the mystery of the Lord's Supper is celebrated. . . In these communities, though they may often be small and poor, or existing in the diaspora, Christ is present, through whose power and influence the One, Holy, Catholic and Apostolic Church is constituted.'[312]

814

811

833 The phrase 'particular Church', which is in the first place the diocese (or eparchy), refers to a community of the Christian faithful in communion of faith and sacraments with their bishop ordained in apostolic succession.[313] These particular Churches 'are constituted after the model of the universal Church; it is in these and formed out of them that the one and unique Catholic

886

---

[307] St Ignatius of Antioch, *Ad Smyrn*. 8, 2: AF II/2, 311.

[308] *UR* 3; *AG* 6; *Eph* 1:22–23.

[398] Cf. *AG* 4.

[310] Cf. *Mt* 28:19.

[311] *LG* 13 §§ 1–2; cf. *Jn* 11:52.

[312] *LG* 26.

[313] Cf. *CD* 11; CIC, cann. 368–369; CCEO, cann. 177 § 1; 178; 311 § 1; 312.

Church exists.'[314]

834 Particular Churches are fully catholic through their commu-
882, 1369 nion with one of them, the Church of Rome 'which presides in
charity'.[315] 'For with this church, by reason of its pre-eminence,
the whole Church, that is the faithful everywhere, must necessarily be in accord.'[316] Indeed, 'from the incarnate Word's descent to
us, all Christian churches everywhere have held and hold the great
Church that is here [at Rome] to be their only basis and foundation
since, according to the Saviour's promise, the gates of hell have
never prevailed against her.'[317]

835 'Let us be very careful not to conceive of the universal Church as the simple
sum, or. . . the more or less anomalous federation of essentially different particular churches. In the mind of the Lord the Church is universal by vocation and
mission, but when she puts down her roots in a variety of cultural, social and
human terrains, she takes on different external expressions and appearances in
each part of the world.'[318] The rich variety of ecclesiastical disciplines, liturgical
rites, and theological and spiritual heritages proper to the local Churches 'uni-
1202 fied in a common effort, shows all the more resplendently the catholicity of the
undivided Church.'[319]

Who belongs to the Catholic Church?

836 'All men are called to this catholic unity of the People of
God. . . And to it, in different ways, belong or are ordered: the
Catholic faithful, others who believe in Christ, and finally all man-
831 kind, called by God's grace to salvation.'[320]

837 'Fully incorporated into the society of the Church are those
who, possessing the Spirit of Christ, accept all the means of salva-
771 tion given to the Church together with her entire organization,
815 and who – by the bonds constituted by the profession of faith, the
sacraments, ecclesiastical government, and communion – are
joined in the visible structure of the Church of Christ, who rules
882 her through the Supreme Pontiff and the bishops. Even though
incorporated into the Church, one who does not however persevere in charity is not saved. He remains indeed in the bosom of
the Church, but "in body" not "in heart".'[321]

838 'The Church knows that she is joined in many ways to the
818 baptized who are honoured by the name of Christian, but do not

---

[314] LG 23.
[315] St Ignatius of Antioch, *Ad Rom.* 1, 1:
AF II/2, 192; cf. LG 13.
[316] St Irenaeus, *Adv. haeres.* 3, 3, 2: PG
7/1, 849; cf. Vatican Council I: DS
3057.
[317] St Maximus the Confessor, *Opuscula
theo.*: PG 91, 137–140.
[318] Paul VI, *EN* 62.
[319] LG 23.
[320] LG 13.
[321] LG 14.

profess the Catholic faith in its entirety or have not preserved unity
or communion under the successor of Peter.'[322] Those 'who believe in Christ and have been properly baptized are put in a certain, *1271*
although imperfect, communion with the Catholic Church.'[323]
With the Orthodox Churches, this communion is so profound 'that *1399*
it lacks little to attain the fullness that would permit a common
celebration of the Lord's Eucharist.'[324]

The Church and non-Christians

839 'Those who have not yet received the Gospel are related to *856*
the People of God in various ways.'[325]

The relationship of the Church with the Jewish People. When she
delves into her own mystery, the Church, the People of God in the
New Covenant, discovers her link with the Jewish People,[326] 'the
first to hear the Word of God'.[327] The Jewish faith, unlike other
non-Christian religions, is already a response to God's revelation *63*
in the Old Covenant. To the Jews 'belong the sonship, the glory, *147*
the covenants, the giving of the law, the worship, and the promises; to them belong the patriarchs, and of their race, according to
the flesh, is the Christ';[328] 'for the gifts and the call of God are
irrevocable.'[329]

840 And when one considers the future, God's People of the Old Covenant and
the new People of God tend towards similar goals: expectation of the coming
(or the return) of the Messiah. But one awaits the return of the Messiah who *674*
died and rose from the dead and is recognized as Lord and Son of God; the other
awaits the coming of a Messiah, whose features remain hidden till the end of
time; and the latter waiting is accompanied by the drama of not knowing or of
misunderstanding Christ Jesus.   *597*

841 *The Church's relationship with the Muslims.* 'The plan of salvation also includes those who acknowledge the Creator, in the first
place amongst whom are the Muslims; these profess to hold the
faith of Abraham, and together with us they adore the one, merciful God, mankind's judge on the last day.'[330]

842 *The Church's bond with non-Christian religions* is in the first
place the common origin and end of the human race: *360*

All nations form but one community. This is so because all stem from the
one stock which God created to people the entire earth, and also because

---

[322] *LG* 15.
[323] *UR* 3.
[324] Paul VI, Discourse, 14 December
1975; cf. *UR* 13–18.
[325] *LG* 16.
[326] Cf. *NA* 4.

[327] *Roman Missal*, Good Friday 13,
General Intercessions, VI.
[328] *Rom* 9:4–5.
[329] *Rom* 11:29.
[330] *LG* 16: cf. *NA* 3.

all share a common destiny, namely God. His providence, evident goodness, and saving designs extend to all against the day when the elect are
gathered together in the holy city...[331]

843 The Catholic Church recognizes in other religions that
28 search, among shadows and images, for the God who is unknown
yet near since he gives life and breath and all things, and wants all
men to be saved. Thus, the Church considers all goodness and
856 truth found in these religions as 'a preparation for the Gospel, and
given by him who enlightens all men that they may at length have
life'.[332]

844 In their religious behaviour, however, men also display the
29 limits and errors that disfigure the image of God in them:

Very often, deceived by the Evil One, men have become vain in their
reasonings, and have exchanged the truth of God for a lie, and served the
creature rather than the Creator. Or else, living and dying in this world
without God, they are exposed to ultimate despair.[333]

845 To reunite all his children, scattered and led astray by sin, the
30 Father willed to call the whole of humanity together into his Son's
Church. The Church is the place where humanity must rediscover
953 its unity and salvation. The Church is 'the world reconciled'. She is
that bark which 'in the full sail of the Lord's cross, by the breath of
the Holy Spirit, navigates safely in this world.' According to
another image dear to the Church Fathers, she is prefigured by
1219 Noah's ark, which alone saves from the flood.[334]

'Outside the Church there is no salvation'

846 How are we to understand this affirmation, often repeated by
the Church Fathers?[335] Re-formulated positively, it means that all
salvation comes from Christ the Head through the Church which
is his Body:

Basing itself on Scripture and Tradition, the Council teaches that the
Church, a pilgrim now on earth, is necessary for salvation: the one Christ
is the mediator and the way of salvation; he is present to us in his body
161   which is the Church. He himself explicitly asserted the necessity of faith
1257   and Baptism, and thereby affirmed at the same time the necessity of the
Church which men enter through Baptism as through a door. Hence
they could not be saved who, knowing that the Catholic Church was

---

[331] NA 1.
[332] LG 16; cf. NA 2; EN 53.
[333] LG 16; cf. Rom 1:21, 25.
[334] St Augustine, Sermo 96, 7, 9: PL 38,

588; St Ambrose, De virg. 18, 118: PL
16, 311; cf. already 1 Pt 3:20–21.
[335] Cf. St Cyprian, Ep. 73, 21: PL 3, 1169;
De unit.: PL 4, 509–536.

founded as necessary by God through Christ, would refuse either to enter it, or to remain in it.[336]

847 This affirmation is not aimed at those who, through no fault of their own, do not know Christ and his Church:

> Those who, through no fault of their own, do not know the Gospel of Christ or his Church, but who nevertheless seek God with a sincere heart, and, moved by grace, try in their actions to do his will as they know it through the dictates of their conscience – those too may achieve eternal salvation.[337]

848 'Although in ways known to himself God can lead those who, through no fault of their own, are ignorant of the Gospel, to *1260* that faith without which it is impossible to please him, the Church still has the obligation and also the sacred right to evangelize all men.'[338]

Mission – a requirement of the Church's catholicity

849 *The missionary mandate.* 'Having been divinely sent to the nations that she might be "the universal sacrament of salvation", the Church, in obedience to the command of her founder and because it is demanded by her own essential universality, strives to preach the Gospel to all men':[339] 'Go therefore and make disciples *738, 767* of all nations, baptizing them in the name of the Father and of the Son and of the Holy Spirit, teaching them to observe all that I have commanded you; and lo, I am with you always, until the close of the age.'[340]

850 *The origin and purpose of mission.* The Lord's missionary mandate is ultimately grounded in the eternal love of the Most Holy Trinity: 'The Church on earth is by her nature missionary since, *257* according to the plan of the Father, she has as her origin the mission of the Son and the Holy Spirit.'[341] The ultimate purpose of mission is none other than to make men share in the communion *730* between the Father and the Son in their Spirit of love.[342]

851 *Missionary motivation.* It is from God's *love* for all men that the Church in every age receives both the obligation and the vigour of her missionary dynamism, 'for the love of Christ urges us on'.[343] *221, 429* Indeed, God 'desires all men to be saved and to come to the know- *74* ledge of the truth';[344] that is, God wills the salvation of everyone *217, 2104*

---

[336] *LG* 14; cf. *Mk* 16:16; *Jn* 3:5.
[337] *LG* 16; cf. DS 3866–3872.
[338] *AG* 7; cf. *Heb* 11:6; 1 *Cor* 9:16.
[339] *AG* 1; cf. *Mt* 16:15.
[340] *Mt* 28:19–20.

[341] *AG* 2.
[342] Cf. John Paul II, *Redemptoris missio* 23.
[343] 2 *Cor* 5:14; cf. *AA* 6; *RMiss* 11.
[344] 1 *Tim* 2:4.

through the knowledge of *the truth*. Salvation is found in the truth. Those who obey the prompting of the Spirit of truth are already on the way of salvation. But the Church, to whom this truth has been entrusted, must go out to meet their desire, so as to bring 890 them the truth. Because she believes in God's universal plan of salvation, the Church must be missionary.

852 *Missionary paths*. The Holy Spirit is the protagonist, 'the principal agent of the whole of the Church's mission'.[345] It is he who leads the Church on her missionary paths. 'This mission continues 2044 and, in the course of history, unfolds the mission of Christ, who was sent to evangelize the poor; so the Church, urged on by the Spirit of Christ, must walk the road Christ himself walked, a way of poverty and obedience, of service and self-sacrifice even to 2473 death, a death from which he emerged victorious by his resurrection.'[346] So it is that 'the blood of martyrs is the seed of Christians.'[347]

853 On her pilgrimage, the Church has also experienced the 'discrepancy existing between the message she proclaims and the human weakness of those to 1428 whom the Gospel has been entrusted'.[348] Only by taking the 'way of penance and renewal', the 'narrow way of the cross', can the People of God extend Christ's reign.[349] For 'just as Christ carried out the work of redemption in 2443 poverty and oppression, so the Church is called to follow the same path if she is to communicate the fruits of salvation to men.'[350]

854 By her very mission, 'the Church... travels the same journey as all humanity and shares the same earthly lot with the world: she is to be a leaven and, as it were, the soul of human society in its renewal by Christ and transformation into the family of God.'[351] Missionary endeavour requires *patience*. It begins with the 2105 proclamation of the Gospel to peoples and groups who do not yet believe in Christ,[352] continues with the establishment of Christian communities that are 'a sign of God's presence in the world',[353] and leads to the foundation of local 1204 churches.[354] It must involve a process of inculturation if the Gospel is to take flesh in each people's culture.[355] There will be times of defeat. 'With regard to individuals, groups and peoples it is only by degrees that [the Church] touches and penetrates them, and so receives them into a fullness which is Catholic.'[356]

821 855 The Church's mission stimulates efforts *towards Christian unity*.[357] Indeed, 'divisions among Christians prevent the Church from realizing in practice the fullness of catholicity proper to her in those of her sons who, though joined to

---

[345] *RMiss* 21.
[346] *AG* 5.
[347] Tertullian, *Apol.* 50, 13: PL 1, 603.
[348] *GS* 43 § 6.
[349] *LG* 8 § 3; 15; *AG* 1 § 3; cf. *RMiss* 12–20.
[350] *LG* 8 § 3.

[351] *GS* 40 § 2.
[352] Cf. *RMiss* 42–47.
[353] *AG* 15 § 1.
[354] Cf. *RMiss* 48–49.
[355] Cf. *RMiss* 52–54.
[356] *AG* 6 § 2.
[357] Cf. *RMiss* 50.

her by Baptism, are yet separated from full communion with her. Furthermore, the Church herself finds it more difficult to express in actual life her full catholicity in all its aspects.'[358]

856 The missionary task implies a *respectful dialogue* with those who do not yet accept the Gospel.[359] Believers can profit from this dialogue by learning to *839* appreciate better 'those elements of truth and grace which are found among peoples, and which are, as it were, a secret presence of God'.[360] They proclaim the Good News to those who do not know it, in order to consolidate, complete *843* and raise up the truth and the goodness that God has distributed among men and nations, and to purify them from error and evil 'for the glory of God, the confusion of the demon, and the happiness of man'.[361]

IV. The Church Is Apostolic

857 The Church is apostolic because she is founded on the *75* apostles, in three ways:
– she was and remains built on 'the foundation of the apostles',[362] the witnesses chosen and sent on mission by Christ himself;[363]
– with the help of the Spirit dwelling in her, the Church keeps and hands on the teaching,[364] the 'good deposit', the salutary words she has heard from the apostles;[365]   *171*
– she continues to be taught, sanctified and guided by the apostles until Christ's return, through their successors in pastoral office: the *880* college of bishops, 'assisted by priests, in union with the successor *1575* of Peter, the Church's supreme pastor':[366]

> You are the eternal Shepherd
> who never leaves his flock untended.
> Through the apostles
> you watch over us and protect us always.
> You made them shepherds of the flock
> to share in the work of your Son. . .[367]

The apostles' mission

858 Jesus is the Father's Emissary. From the beginning of his ministry, he 'called to him those whom he desired;. . . And he appointed twelve, whom also he named apostles, to be with him, *551* and to be sent out to preach.'[368] From then on, they would also be his 'emissaries' (Greek *apostoloi*). In them, Christ continues his own

---

[358] UR 4 § 8.
[359] Cf. RMiss 55.
[360] AG 9.
[361] AG 9.
[362] Eph 2:20; Rev 21:14.
[363] Cf. Mt 28:16–20; Acts 1:8; 1 Cor 9:1; 15:7–8; Gal 1:1; etc.
[364] Cf. Acts 2:42.
[365] Cf. 2 Tim 1:13–14.
[366] AG 5.
[367] Roman Missal, Preface of the Apostles I.
[368] Mk 3:13–14.

1086, 425 mission: 'As the Father has sent me, even so I send you.'[369] The apostles' ministry is the continuation of his mission; Jesus said to the Twelve: 'he who receives you receives me.'[370]

859 Jesus unites them to the mission he received from the Father. As 'the Son can do nothing of his own accord', but receives everything from the Father who sent him, so those whom Jesus sends can do nothing apart from him,[371] from whom they received both the mandate for their mission and the power to carry it out.
876 Christ's apostles knew that they were called by God as 'ministers of a new covenant', 'servants of God', 'ambassadors for Christ', 'servants of Christ and stewards of the mysteries of God'.[372]

860 In the office of the apostles there is one aspect that cannot be
642 transmitted: to be the chosen witnesses of the Lord's Resurrection
765 and so the foundation stones of the Church. But their office also has a permanent aspect. Christ promised to remain *with them* always. The divine mission entrusted by Jesus to them 'will continue to the end of time, since the Gospel they handed on is the lasting source of all life for the Church. Therefore,... the apostles took
1087 care to appoint successors.'[373]

The bishops – successors of the apostles

861 'In order that the mission entrusted to them might be con-
77 tinued after their death, [the apostles] consigned, by will and testament, as it were, to their immediate collaborators the duty of completing and consolidating the work they had begun, urging them to tend to the whole flock, in which the Holy Spirit had appointed them to shepherd the Church of God. They accordingly designated such men and then made the ruling that like-
1087 wise on their death other proven men should take over their ministry.'[374]

862 'Just as the office which the Lord confided to Peter alone, as first of the apostles, destined to be transmitted to his successors, is a
880 permanent one, so also endures the office, which the apostles received, of shepherding the Church, a charge destined to be exercised without interruption by the sacred order of bishops.'[375] Hence the Church teaches that 'the bishops have by divine institu-
1556 tion taken the place of the apostles as pastors of the Church, in such wise that whoever listens to them is listening to Christ and

---

[369] Jn 20:21; cf. 13:20; 17:18.
[370] Mt 10:40; cf. Lk 10:16.
[371] Jn 5:19, 30; cf. 15:5.
[372] 2 Cor 3:6; 6:4; 5:20; 1 Cor 4:1.

[373] LG 20; cf. Mt 28:20.
[374] LG 20; cf. Acts 20:28; St Clement of Rome, Ad Cor. 42–44: PG 1, 291–300.
[375] LG 20 § 2.

whoever despises them despises Christ and him who sent Christ.'[376]

The apostolate

863 The whole Church is apostolic, in that she remains, through the successors of St Peter and the other apostles, in communion of faith and life with her origin; and in that she is 'sent out' into the whole world. All members of the Church share in this mission, *900* though in various ways. 'The Christian vocation is, of its nature, a *2472* vocation to the apostolate as well.' Indeed, we call an apostolate 'every activity of the Mystical Body' that aims 'to spread the Kingdom of Christ over all the earth'.[377]

864 'Christ, sent by the Father, is the source of the Church's whole apostolate'; thus the fruitfulness of apostolate for ordained *828* ministers as well as for lay people clearly depends on their vital union with Christ.[378] In keeping with their vocations, the de- *824* mands of the times and the various gifts of the Holy Spirit, the apostolate assumes the most varied forms. But charity, drawn from the Eucharist above all, is always 'as it were, the soul of the *1324* whole apostolate'.[379]

865 The Church is ultimately *one, holy, catholic and apostolic* in her *811, 541* deepest and ultimate identity, because it is in her that 'the Kingdom of heaven', the 'Reign of God',[380] already exists, and will be fulfilled at the end of time. The kingdom has come in the person of Christ and grows mysteriously in the hearts of those incorporated into him, until its full eschatological manifestation. Then *all* those he has redeemed and made '*holy* and blameless before him in love'[381] will be gathered together as the *one* People of God, the 'Bride of the Lamb',[382] 'the holy city Jerusalem coming down out of heaven from God, having the glory of God'.[383] For 'the wall of the city had twelve foundations, and on them the twelve names of the *twelve apostles of the Lamb*.'[384]

IN BRIEF

866 *The Church is one: she acknowledges one Lord, confesses one faith, is born of one Baptism, forms only one Body, is given life by the one Spirit, for the sake of one hope (cf. Eph 4:3–5), at whose fulfilment all divisions will be overcome.*

---

[376] LG 20 § 2.
[377] AA 2.
[378] AA 4; cf. Jn 15:5.
[379] AA 3.
[380] Rev 19:6.
[381] Eph 1:4.
[382] Rev 21:9.
[383] Rev 21:10–11.
[384] Rev 21:14.

867 The Church is holy: the Most Holy God is her author; Christ, her bridegroom, gave himself up to make her holy; the Spirit of holiness gives her life. Since she still includes sinners, she is 'the sinless one made up of sinners'. Her holiness shines in the saints; in Mary she is already all-holy.

868 The Church is catholic: she proclaims the fullness of the faith. She bears in herself and administers the totality of the means of salvation. She is sent out to all peoples. She speaks to all men. She encompasses all times. She is 'missionary of her very nature' (AG 2).

869 The Church is apostolic. She is built on a lasting foundation: 'the twelve apostles of the Lamb' (Rev 21:14). She is indestructible (cf. Mt 16:18). She is upheld infallibly in the truth: Christ governs her through Peter and the other apostles, who are present in their successors, the Pope and the college of bishops.

870 'The sole Church of Christ which in the Creed we profess to be one, holy, catholic and apostolic,... subsists in the Catholic Church, which is governed by the successor of Peter and by the bishops in communion with him. Nevertheless, many elements of sanctification and of truth are found outside its visible confines' (LG 8).

Paragraph 4. Christ's Faithful – Hierarchy, Laity, Consecrated Life

871 'The Christian faithful are those who, inasmuch as they have been incorporated in Christ through Baptism, have been consti-
1268–1269 tuted as the People of God; for this reason, since they have become
782–786 sharers in Christ's priestly, prophetic and royal office in their own manner, they are called to exercise the mission which God has entrusted to the Church to fulfil in the world, in accord with the condition proper to each one.'[385]

872 'In virtue of their rebirth in Christ there exists among all the Christian faithful a true equality with regard to dignity and the
1934, 794 activity whereby all co-operate in the building up of the Body of Christ in accord with each one's own condition and function.'[386]

873 The very differences which the Lord has willed to put be-tween the members of his Body serve its unity and mission. For 'in
814, 1937 the Church there is diversity of ministry but unity of mission. To the apostles and their successors Christ has entrusted the office of teaching, sanctifying and governing in his name and by his power. But the laity are made to share in the priestly, prophetical and kingly office of Christ; they have therefore, in the Church and in

---

[385] CIC, can. 204 § 1; cf. LG 31.
[386] CIC, can. 208; cf. LG 32.

the world, their own assignment in the mission of the whole People of God.'[387] Finally, 'from both groups [hierarchy and laity] there exist Christian faithful who are consecrated to God in their own special manner and serve the salvific mission of the Church through the profession of the evangelical counsels.'[388]

I. The Hierarchical Constitution of the Church

Why the ecclesial ministry?

874 Christ is himself the source of ministry in the Church. He instituted the Church. He gave her authority and mission, orientation and goal:

> In order to shepherd the People of God and to increase its numbers without cease, Christ the Lord set up in his Church a variety of offices which aim at the good of the whole body. The holders of office, who are invested with a sacred power, are, in fact, dedicated to promoting the interests of their brethren, so that all who belong to the People of God... may attain to salvation.[389]

875 'How are they to believe in him of whom they have never heard? And how are they to hear without a preacher? And how can men preach unless they are sent?'[390] No one – no individual and no community – can proclaim the Gospel to himself: 'Faith comes from what is heard.'[391] No one can give himself the mandate and the mission to proclaim the Gospel. The one sent by the Lord does not speak and act on his own authority, but by virtue of Christ's authority; not as a member of the community, but speaking to it in the name of Christ. No one can bestow grace on himself; it must be given and offered. This fact presupposes ministers of grace, authorized and empowered by Christ. From him, bishops and priests receive the mission and faculty ('the sacred power') to act in persona Christi Capitis; deacons receive the strength to serve the people of God in the diaconia of liturgy, word and charity, in communion with the bishop and his presbyterate. The ministry in which Christ's emissaries do and give by God's grace what they cannot do and give by their own powers, is called a 'sacrament' by the Church's tradition. Indeed, the ministry of the Church is conferred by a special sacrament.

876 Intrinsically linked to the sacramental nature of ecclesial ministry is its character as service. Entirely dependent on Christ who gives mission and authority, ministers are truly 'slaves of Christ',[392] in the image of him who freely took 'the form of a

1544

166

1548

1536

1551

---

[387] AA 2.
[388] CIC, can. 207 § 2.
[389] LG 18.

[390] Rom 10:14–15.
[391] Rom 10:17.
[392] Cf. Rom 1:1.

slave' for us.[393] Because the word and grace of which they are
427 ministers are not their own, but are given to them by Christ for the
sake of others, they must freely become the slaves of all.[394]

877   Likewise, it belongs to the sacramental nature of ecclesial
1559 ministry that it have a *collegial character*. In fact, from the beginning
of his ministry, the Lord Jesus instituted the Twelve as 'the seeds of
the new Israel and the beginning of the sacred hierarchy'.[395]
Chosen together, they were also sent out together, and their fraternal unity would be at the service of the fraternal communion of
all the faithful: they would reflect and witness to the communion
of the divine persons.[396] For this reason every bishop exercises his
ministry from within the episcopal college, in communion with
the bishop of Rome, the successor of St Peter and head of the
college. So also priests exercise their ministry from within the
presbyterium of the diocese, under the direction of their bishop.

878   Finally, it belongs to the sacramental nature of ecclesial ministry that it have a *personal character*. Although Christ's ministers act
in communion with one another, they also always act in a personal
way. Each one is called personally: 'You, follow me',[397] in order to
be a personal witness within the common mission, to bear personal
responsibility before him who gives the mission, acting 'in his
person' and for other persons: 'I baptize you in the name of the
1484 Father and of the Son and of the Holy Spirit. . .'; 'I absolve you. . .'

879   Sacramental ministry in the Church, then, is a service exercised in the name of Christ. It has a personal character and a
collegial form. This is evidenced by the bonds between the episcopal college and its head, the successor of St Peter, and in the
relationship between the bishop's pastoral responsibility for his
particular church and the common solicitude of the episcopal
college for the universal Church.

The episcopal college and its head, the Pope

880   When Christ instituted the Twelve, 'he constituted [them] in
552, 862 the form of a college or permanent assembly, at the head of which
he placed Peter, chosen from among them.'[398] Just as 'by the
Lord's institution, St Peter and the rest of the apostles constitute a
single apostolic college, so in like fashion the Roman Pontiff,

---

[393] Phil 2:7.
[394] Cf. 1 Cor 9:19.
[395] AG 5.
[396] Cf. Jn 17:21–23.
[397] Jn 21:22; cf. Mt 4:19, 21; Jn 1:4.
[398] LG 19; cf. Lk 6:13; Jn 21:15–17.

Peter's successor, and the bishops, the successors of the apostles, are related with and united to one another.'[399]

881 The Lord made Simon alone, whom he named Peter, the 'rock' of his Church. He gave him the keys of his Church, and instituted him shepherd of the whole flock.[400] 'The office of binding and loosing which was given to Peter was also assigned to the college of apostles united to its head.'[401] This pastoral office of Peter and the other apostles belongs to the Church's very foundation and is continued by the bishops under the primacy of the Pope.

553

642

882 The *Pope*, Bishop of Rome and Peter's successor, 'is the perpetual and visible source and foundation of the unity both of the bishops and of the whole company of the faithful.'[402] 'For the Roman Pontiff, by reason of his office as Vicar of Christ, and as pastor of the entire Church has full, supreme and universal power over the whole Church, a power which he can always exercise unhindered.'[403]

1369, 834

837

883 'The *college or body of bishops* has no authority unless united with the Roman Pontiff, Peter's successor, as its head.' As such, this college has 'supreme and full authority over the universal Church; but this power cannot be exercised without the agreement of the Roman Pontiff.'[404]

884 'The college of bishops exercises power over the universal Church in a solemn manner in an ecumenical council.'[405] But 'there never is an ecumenical council which is not confirmed or at least recognized as such by Peter's successor.'[406]

885 'This college, in so far as it is composed of many members, is the expression of the variety and universality of the People of God; and of the unity of the flock of Christ, in so far as it is assembled under one head.'[407]

886 'The individual *bishops* are the visible source and foundation of unity in their own particular Churches.'[408] As such, they 'exercise their pastoral office over the portion of the People of God assigned to them',[409] assisted by priests and deacons. But, as a member of the episcopal college, each bishop shares in the concern for all the Churches.[410] The bishops exercise this care first 'by

1560

833

---

[399] LG 22; cf. CIC, can. 330.
[400] Cf. Mt 16:18–19; Jn 21:15–17.
[401] LG 22 § 2.
[402] LG 23.
[403] LG 22; cf. CD 2, 9.
[404] LG 22; cf. CIC, can. 336.

[405] CIC, can. 337 § 1.
[406] LG 22.
[407] LG 22.
[408] LG 23.
[409] LG 23.
[410] Cf. CD 3.

ruling well their own Churches as portions of the universal Church', and so contributing 'to the welfare of the whole Mystical Body, which, from another point of view, is a corporate body of Churches'.[411] They extend it especially to the poor,[412] to those persecuted for the faith, as well as to missionaries who are working throughout the world.

887 Neighbouring particular Churches who share the same culture form ecclesiastical provinces or larger groupings called patriarchates or regions.[413] The bishops of these groupings can meet in synods or provincial councils. 'In a like fashion, the episcopal conferences at the present time are in a position to contribute in many and fruitful ways to the concrete realization of the collegiate spirit.'[414]

The teaching office

888 Bishops, with priests as co-workers, have as their first task 'to preach the Gospel of God to all men', in keeping with the Lord's command.[415] They are 'heralds of faith, who draw new disciples to Christ; they are authentic teachers' of the apostolic faith 'endowed with the authority of Christ'.[416]

889 In order to preserve the Church in the purity of the faith handed on by the apostles, Christ who is the Truth willed to confer on her a share in his own infallibility. By a 'supernatural sense of faith' the People of God, under the guidance of the Church's living Magisterium, 'unfailingly adheres to this faith'.[417]

890 The mission of the Magisterium is linked to the definitive nature of the covenant established by God with his people in Christ. It is this Magisterium's task to preserve God's people from deviations and defections and to guarantee them the objective possibility of professing the true faith without error. Thus, the pastoral duty of the Magisterium is aimed at seeing to it that the People of God abides in the truth that liberates. To fulfil this service, Christ endowed the Church's shepherds with the charism of infallibility in matters of faith and morals. The exercise of this charism takes several forms:

891 'The Roman Pontiff, head of the college of bishops, enjoys this infallibility in virtue of his office, when, as supreme pastor and teacher of all the faithful – who confirms his brethren in the faith –

---

411 LG 23.
412 Cf. Gal 2:10.
413 Cf. Canon of the Apostles 34.
414 LG 23 § 3.

415 PO 4; cf. Mk 16:15.
416 LG 25.
417 LG 12; cf. DV 10.

he proclaims by a definitive act a doctrine pertaining to faith or morals... The infallibility promised to the Church is also present in the body of bishops when, together with Peter's successor, they exercise the supreme Magisterium', above all in an Ecumenical Council.[418] When the Church through her supreme Magisterium proposes a doctrine 'for belief as being divinely revealed',[419] and as the teaching of Christ, the definitions 'must be adhered to with the obedience of faith.'[420] This infallibility extends as far as the deposit of divine Revelation itself.[421]

892 Divine assistance is also given to the successors of the apostles, teaching in communion with the successor of Peter, and, in a particular way, to the bishop of Rome, pastor of the whole Church, when, without arriving at an infallible definition and without pronouncing in a 'definitive manner', they propose in the exercise of the ordinary Magisterium a teaching that leads to better understanding of Revelation in matters of faith and morals. To this ordinary teaching the faithful 'are to adhere... with religious assent',[422] which, though distinct from the assent of faith, is nonetheless an extension of it.

The sanctifying office

893 The bishop is 'the steward of the grace of the supreme priesthood',[423] especially in the Eucharist which he offers personally or *1561* whose offering he assures through the priests, his co-workers. The Eucharist is the centre of the life of the particular Church. The bishop and priests sanctify the Church by their prayer and work, by their ministry of the word and of the sacraments. They sanctify her by their example, 'not as domineering over those in your charge but being examples to the flock'.[424] Thus, 'together with the flock entrusted to them, they may attain to eternal life.'[425]

The governing office

894 'The bishops, as vicars and legates of Christ, govern the particular Churches assigned to them by their counsels, exhortations and example, but over and above that also by the authority and *801* sacred power' which indeed they ought to exercise so as to edify, in the spirit of service which is that of their Master.[426]

895 'The power which they exercise personally in the name of *1558*

---

[418] LG 25; cf. Vatican Council I: DS 3074.
[419] DV 10 § 2.
[420] LG 25 § 2.
[421] Cf. LG 25.

[422] LG 25.
[423] LG 26.
[424] 1 Pt 5:3.
[425] LG 26 § 3.
[426] LG 27; cf. Lk 22:26–27.

Christ, is proper, ordinary and immediate, although its exercise is ultimately controlled by the supreme authority of the Church.'[427] But the bishops should not be thought of as vicars of the Pope. His ordinary and immediate authority over the whole Church does not annul, but on the contrary confirms and defends that of the bishops. Their authority must be exercised in communion with the whole Church under the guidance of the Pope.

896 The Good Shepherd ought to be the model and 'form' of the bishop's pastoral office. Conscious of his own weaknesses, 'the bishop... can have compassion for those who are ignorant and erring. He should not refuse to listen to his subjects whose welfare he promotes as of his very own children... The faithful... should be closely attached to the bishop as the Church is to Jesus Christ, and as Jesus Christ is to the Father':[428]

1550

> Let all follow the bishop, as Jesus Christ follows his Father, and the college of presbyters as the apostles; respect the deacons as you do God's law. Let no one do anything concerning the Church in separation from the bishop.[429]

II. The Lay Faithful

897 'The term "laity" is here understood to mean all the faithful except those in Holy Orders and those who belong to a religious state approved by the Church. That is, the faithful who by Baptism are incorporated into Christ and integrated into the People of God are made sharers in their particular way in the priestly, prophetic and kingly office of Christ, and have their own part to play in the mission of the whole Christian people in the Church and in the world.'[430]

873

The vocation of lay people

898 'By reason of their special vocation it belongs to the laity to seek the kingdom of God by engaging in temporal affairs and directing them according to God's will... It pertains to them in a special way so to illuminate and order all temporal things with which they are closely associated that these may always be effected and grow according to Christ and may be to the glory of the Creator and Redeemer.'[431]

2105

899 The initiative of lay Christians is necessary especially when

---

[427] LG 27.
[428] LG 27 § 2.
[429] St Ignatius of Antioch, *Ad Smyrn.* 8, 1: AF II/2, 309.

[430] LG 31.
[431] LG 31 § 2.

the matter involves discovering or inventing the means for permeating social, political and economic realities with the demands 2442 of Christian doctrine and life. This initiative is a normal element of the life of the Church:

> Lay believers are in the front line of Church life; for them the Church is the animating principle of human society. Therefore, they in particular ought to have an ever-clearer consciousness not only of belonging to the Church, but of being the Church, that is to say, the community of the faithful on earth under the leadership of the Pope, the common Head, and of the bishops in communion with him. They are the Church.[432]

900 Since, like all the faithful, lay Christians are entrusted by God 863 with the apostolate by virtue of their Baptism and Confirmation, they have the right and duty, individually or grouped in associations, to work so that the divine message of salvation may be known and accepted by all men throughout the earth. This duty is the more pressing when it is only through them that men can hear the Gospel and know Christ. Their activity in ecclesial communities is so necessary that, for the most part, the apostolate of the pastors cannot be fully effective without it.[433]

The participation of lay people in Christ's priestly office

901 'Hence the laity, dedicated as they are to Christ and anointed by the Holy Spirit, are marvellously called and prepared so that 784 even richer fruits of the Spirit may be produced in them. For all 1268 their works, prayers and apostolic undertakings, family and married life, daily work, relaxation of mind and body, if they are accomplished in the Spirit – indeed even the hardships of life if patiently born – all these become spiritual sacrifices acceptable to God through Jesus Christ. In the celebration of the Eucharist these may most fittingly be offered to the Father along with the body of the Lord. And so, worshipping everywhere by their holy actions, the laity consecrate the world itself to God, everywhere offering 358 worship by the holiness of their lives.'[434]

902 In a very special way, parents share in the office of sanctifying 'by leading a conjugal life in the Christian spirit and by seeing to the Christian education of their children'.[435]

903 Lay people who possess the required qualities can be admitted permanently to the ministries of lector and acolyte.[436] 'When the necessity of the Church 1143 warrants it and when ministers are lacking, lay persons, even if they are not

---

[432] Pius XII, Discourse, 20 February 1946: AAS 38 (1946), 149; quoted by John Paul II, CL 9.
[433] Cf. LG 33.
[434] LG 34; cf. LG 10; 1 Pt 2:5.
[435] CIC, can. 835 § 4.
[436] Cf. CIC, can. 230 § 1.

lectors or acolytes, can also supply for certain of their offices, namely, to exercise the ministry of the word, to preside over liturgical prayers, to confer Baptism, and to distribute Holy Communion in accord with the prescriptions of law.'[437]

Participation in Christ's prophetic office

904 'Christ... fulfils this prophetic office, not only by the hierarchy... but also by the laity. He accordingly both establishes
785, 92 them as witnesses and provides them with the sense of the faith (*sensus fidei*) and the grace of the word':[438]

> To teach in order to lead others to faith is the task of every preacher and of each believer.[439]

905 Lay people also fulfil their prophetic mission by evange-
2044 lization, 'that is, the proclamation of Christ by word and the testimony of life'. For lay people, 'this evangelization... acquires a specific property and peculiar efficacy because it is accomplished in the ordinary circumstances of the world.'[440]

2472 This witness of life, however, is not the sole element in the apostolate; the true apostle is on the lookout for occasions of announcing Christ by word, either to unbelievers... or to the faithful.[441]

906 Lay people who are capable and trained may also collaborate in catechetical formation, in teaching the sacred sciences, and in use of the communica-
2495 tions media.[442]

907 'In accord with the knowledge, competence and pre-eminence which they possess, [lay people] have the right and even at times a duty to manifest to the sacred pastors their opinion on matters which pertain to the good of the Church, and they have a right to make their opinion known to the other Christian faithful, with due regard to the integrity of faith and morals and reverence toward their pastors, and with consideration for the common good and the dignity of persons.'[443]

Participation in Christ's kingly office

908 By his obedience unto death,[444] Christ communicated to his
786 disciples the gift of royal freedom, so that they might 'by the self-abnegation of a holy life, overcome the reign of sin in themselves':[445]

> That man is rightly called a king who makes his own body an obedient subject and, by governing himself with suitable rigour, refuses to let his passions breed rebellion in his soul, for he exercises a kind of royal power

---

[437] CIC, can. 230 § 3.
[438] LG 35.
[439] St Thomas Aquinas, STh III, 71, 4, ad 3.
[440] LG 35 §§ 1, 2.
[441] AA 6 § 3; cf. AG 15.

[442] Cf. CIC, cann. 229; 774; 776; 780; 823 § 1.
[443] CIC, can. 212 § 3.
[444] Cf. Phil 2:8–9.
[445] LG 36.

over himself. And because he knows how to rule his own person as king, so too does he sit as its judge. He will not let himself be imprisoned by sin, or thrown headlong into wickedness.[446]

909 'Moreover, by uniting their forces let the laity so remedy the institutions and conditions of the world when the latter are an inducement to sin, that these may be conformed to the norms of justice, favouring rather than hindering the practice of virtue. By so doing they will impregnate culture and human works with a moral value.'[447] 1887

910 'The laity can also feel called, or be in fact called, to co-operate with their pastors in the service of the ecclesial community, for the sake of its growth and life. This can be done through the exercise of different kinds of ministries according to the grace and charisms which the Lord has been pleased to bestow on them.'[448] 799

911 In the Church, 'lay members of the Christian faithful can co-operate in the exercise of this power [of governance] in accord with the norm of law.'[449] And so the Church provides for their presence at particular councils, diocesan synods, pastoral councils; the exercise of the pastoral care of a parish, collaboration in finance committees, and participation in ecclesiastical tribunals, etc.[450]

912 The faithful should 'distinguish carefully between the rights and the duties which they have as belonging to the Church and those which fall to them as members of the human society. They will strive to unite the two harmoniously, remembering that in every temporal affair they are to be guided by a Christian conscience, since no human activity, even of the temporal order, can be withdrawn from God's dominion.'[451] 2245

913 'Thus, every person, through these gifts given to him, is at once the witness and the living instrument of the mission of the Church herself "according to the measure of Christ's bestowal".'[452]

III. The Consecrated Life

914 'The state of life which is constituted by the profession of the evangelical counsels, while not entering into the hierarchical structure of the Church, belongs undeniably to her life and holiness.'[453] 2103

---

[446] St Ambrose, *Psal. 118*, 14, 30: PL 15, 1403A.
[447] *LG* 36 § 3.
[448] Paul VI, *EN* 73.
[449] CIC, can. 129 § 2.

[450] Cf. CIC, cann. 443 § 4; 463 §§ 1, 2; 492 § 1; 511; 517 § 2; 536; 1421 § 2.
[451] *LG* 36 § 4.
[452] *LG* 33 § 2; cf. *Eph* 4:7.
[453] *LG* 44 § 4.

Evangelical counsels, consecrated life

915 Christ proposes the evangelical counsels, in their great
1973–1974 variety, to every disciple. The perfection of charity, to which all
the faithful are called, entails for those who freely follow the call to
consecrated life the obligation of practising chastity in celibacy for
the sake of the Kingdom, poverty and obedience. It is the *profession*
of these counsels, within a permanent state of life recognized by
the Church, that characterizes the life consecrated to God.[454]

916 The state of consecrated life is thus one way of experiencing
a 'more intimate' consecration, rooted in Baptism and dedicated
2687 totally to God.[455] In the consecrated life, Christ's faithful, moved
by the Holy Spirit, propose to follow Christ more nearly, to
give themselves to God who is loved above all and, pursuing the
perfection of charity in the service of the Kingdom, to signify
933 and proclaim in the Church the glory of the world to come.[456]

One great tree, with many branches

917 'From the God-given seed of the counsels a wonderful and
wide-spreading tree has grown up in the field of the Lord, bran-
2684 ching out into various forms of the religious life lived in solitude
or in community. Different religious families have come into
existence in which spiritual resources are multiplied for the progress in holiness of their members and for the good of the entire
Body of Christ.'[457]

918 From the very beginning of the Church there were men and women who
set out to follow Christ with greater liberty, and to imitate him more closely, by
practising the evangelical counsels. They led lives dedicated to God, each in his
own way. Many of them, under the inspiration of the Holy Spirit, became
hermits or founded religious families. These the Church, by virtue of her
authority, gladly accepted and approved.[458]

919 Bishops will always strive to discern new gifts of consecrated
life granted to the Church by the Holy Spirit; the approval of new
forms of consecrated life is reserved to the Apostolic See.[459]

The eremitic life

920 Without always professing the three evangelical counsels
publicly, hermits 'devote their life to the praise of God and salva-

---

454 Cf. *LG* 42–43; *PC* 1.   457 *LG* 43.
455 Cf. *PC* 5.   458 *PC* 1.
456 Cf. CIC, can. 573.   459 Cf. CIC, can. 605.

tion of the world through a stricter separation from the world, the silence of solitude and assiduous prayer and penance.'[460]

921 They manifest to everyone the interior aspect of the mystery of the Church, that is, personal intimacy with Christ. Hidden from the eyes of men, the life of the hermit is a silent preaching of   2719
the Lord, to whom he has surrendered his life simply because he is everything to him. Here is a particular call to find in the desert, in the thick of spiritual battle, the glory of the Crucified One.   2015

Consecrated virgins and widows

922 From apostolic times Christian virgins[460a] and widows,[460b] called by the Lord to cling only to him with greater freedom of heart, body and spirit, have decided with the Church's approval to live in the respective states of virginity or perpetual chastity 'for the sake of the Kingdom of heaven'.[461]   1618–1620

923 'Virgins who, committed to the holy plan of following Christ more closely, are consecrated to God by the diocesan 1537 bishop according to the approved liturgical rite, are betrothed mystically to Christ, the Son of God, and are dedicated to the service of the Church.'[462] By this solemn rite (*consecratio virginum*), 1672 the virgin is 'constituted... a sacred person, a transcendent sign of the Church's love for Christ, and an eschatological image of this heavenly Bride of Christ and of the life to come'.[463]

924 'As with other forms of consecrated life', the order of virgins establishes the woman living in the world (or the nun) in prayer, penance, service of her brethren, and apostolic activity, according to the state of life and spiritual gifts given to her.[464] Consecrated virgins can form themselves into associations to observe their commitment more faithfully.[465]

Religious life

925 Religious life was born in the East during the first centuries of Christianity. Lived within institutes canonically erected by the Church, it is distinguished from other forms of consecrated life by 1672 its liturgical character, public profession of the evangelical counsels, fraternal life led in common, and witness given to the union of Christ with the Church.[466]

---

[460] CIC, can. 603 § 1.
[460a] Cf. 1 *Cor* 7:34–36.
[460b] Cf. John Paul II, *Vita consecrata* 7.
[461] *Mt* 19:12.
[462] CIC, can. 604 § 1.

[463] *Ordo consecrationis virginum, Praenotanda* 1.
[464] Cf. CIC, can. 604 § 1; *OCV, Praenotanda* 2.
[465] Cf. CIC, can. 604 § 2.
[466] Cf. CIC, cann. 607; 573; *UR* 15.

926 Religious life derives from the mystery of the Church. It is a gift she has received from her Lord, a gift she offers as a stable way of life to the faithful called by God to profess the counsels. Thus, the Church can both show forth Christ and acknowledge herself 796 to be the Saviour's bride. Religious life in its various forms is called to signify the very charity of God in the language of our time.

927 All religious, whether exempt or not, take their place among the collaborators of the diocesan bishop in his pastoral duty.[467] 854 From the outset of the work of evangelization, the missionary 'planting' and expansion of the Church require the presence of the religious life in all its forms.[468] 'History witnesses to the outstanding service rendered by religious families in the propagation of the faith and in the formation of new Churches: from the ancient monastic institutions to the medieval orders, all the way to the more recent congregations.'[469]

Secular institutes

928 'A secular institute is an institute of consecrated life in which the Christian faithful living in the world strive for the perfection of charity and work for the sanctification of the world especially from within.'[470]

929 By a 'life perfectly and entirely consecrated to [such] sanctification', the members of these institutes share in the Church's task of evangelization, 'in the world and from within the world', 901 where their presence acts as 'leaven in the world'.[471] 'Their witness of a Christian life' aims 'to order temporal things according to God and inform the world with the power of the gospel'. They commit themselves to the evangelical counsels by sacred bonds and observe among themselves the communion and fellowship appropriate to their 'particular secular way of life'.[472]

Societies of apostolic life

930 Alongside the different forms of consecrated life are 'societies of apostolic life whose members without religious vows pursue the particular apostolic purpose of their society, and lead a life as brothers or sisters in common according to a particular manner of life, strive for the perfection of charity through the observance of the constitutions. Among these there are societies in which the

---

[467] Cf. CD 33–35; CIC, can. 591.
[468] Cf. AG 18; 40.
[469] John Paul II, RMiss 69.

[470] CIC, can. 710.
[471] Pius XII, Provida Mater; cf. PC 11.
[472] Cf. CIC, can. 713 § 2.

members embrace the evangelical counsels' according to their constitutions.[473]

Consecration and mission: proclaiming the King who is coming

931 Already dedicated to him through Baptism, the person who surrenders himself to the God he loves above all else thereby consecrates himself more intimately to God's service and to the good of the Church. By this state of life consecrated to God, the Church manifests Christ and shows us how the Holy Spirit acts so wonderfully in her. And so the first mission of those who profess the evangelical counsels is to live out their consecration. Moreover, 'since members of institutes of consecrated life dedicate themselves through their consecration to the service of the Church they are obliged in a special manner to engage in missionary work, in accord with the character of the institute.'[474]

932 In the Church, which is like the sacrament – the sign and instrument – of God's own life, the consecrated life is seen as a special sign of the mystery of redemption. To follow and imitate Christ more nearly and to manifest more clearly his self-emptying is to be more deeply present to one's contemporaries, in the heart of Christ. For those who are on this 'narrower' path encourage their brethren by their example, and bear striking witness 'that the world cannot be transfigured and offered to God without the spirit of the Beatitudes'.[475]   775

933 Whether their witness is public, as in the religious state, or less public, or even secret, Christ's coming remains for all those consecrated both the origin and rising sun of their life: 672

> For the People of God has here no lasting city, . . . [and this state] reveals more clearly to all believers the heavenly goods which are already present in this age, witnessing to the new and eternal life which we have acquired through the redemptive work of Christ and preluding our future resurrection and the glory of the heavenly kingdom.[476]   769

IN BRIEF

934 *'Among the Christian faithful by divine institution there exist in the Church sacred ministers, who are also called clerics in law, and other Christian faithful who are also called laity.' In both groups there are those Christian faithful who, professing the evangelical counsels, are consecrated to God and so serve the Church's saving mission (cf CIC, can. 207 §§ 1, 2).*

---

[473] Cf. CIC, can. 731 §§ 1, 2.
[474] CIC, can. 783; cf. RMiss 69.
[475] LG 31 § 2.
[476] LG 44 § 3.

935 *To proclaim the faith and to plant his reign, Christ sends his apostles and their successors. He gives them a share in his own mission. From him they receive the power to act in his person.*

936 *The Lord made St Peter the visible foundation of his Church. He entrusted the keys of the Church to him. The bishop of the Church of Rome, successor to St Peter, is 'head of the college of bishops, the Vicar of Christ and Pastor of the universal Church on earth' (CIC, can. 331).*

937 *The Pope enjoys, by divine institution, 'supreme, full, immediate and universal power in the care of souls' (CD 2).*

938 *The bishops, established by the Holy Spirit, succeed the apostles. They are 'the visible source and foundation of unity in their own particular Churches' (LG 23).*

939 *Helped by the priests, their co-workers, and by the deacons, the bishops have the duty of authentically teaching the faith, celebrating divine worship, above all the Eucharist, and guiding their Churches as true pastors. Their responsibility also includes concern for all the Churches, with and under the Pope.*

940 *'The characteristic of the lay state being a life led in the midst of the world and of secular affairs, lay people are called by God to make of their apostolate, through the vigour of their Christian spirit, a leaven in the world' (AA 2 §2).*

941 *Lay people share in Christ's priesthood: ever more united with him, they exhibit the grace of Baptism and Confirmation in all dimensions of their personal, family, social and ecclesial lives, and so fulfil the call to holiness addressed to all the baptized.*

942 *By virtue of their prophetic mission, lay people 'are called... to be witnesses to Christ in all circumstances and at the very heart of the community of mankind' (GS 43 §4).*

943 *By virtue of their kingly mission, lay people have the power to uproot the rule of sin within themselves and in the world, by their self-denial and holiness of life (cf. LG 36).*

944 *The life consecrated to God is characterized by the public profession of the evangelical counsels of poverty, chastity and obedience, in a stable state of life recognized by the Church.*

945 *Already destined for him through Baptism, the person who surrenders himself to the God he loves above all else thereby consecrates himself more intimately to God's service and to the good of the whole Church.*

Paragraph 5. The Communion of Saints

946 After confessing 'the holy catholic Church', the Apostles' Creed adds 'the communion of saints'. In a certain sense this article

is a further explanation of the preceding: 'What is the Church if not the assembly of all the saints?'[477] The communion of saints *is* the Church. 823

947 'Since all the faithful form one body, the good of each is communicated to the others... We must therefore believe that there exists a communion of goods in the Church. But the most important member is Christ, since he is the head... Therefore, the riches of Christ are communicated to all the members, through the sacraments.'[478] 'As this Church is governed by one and the same Spirit, all the goods she has received necessarily become a common fund.'[479] 790

948 The term 'communion of saints' therefore has two closely linked meanings: communion 'in holy things (*sancta*)', and 'among holy persons (*sancti*)'. 1331

Sancta sanctis! ('God's holy gifts for God's holy people') is proclaimed by the celebrant in most Eastern liturgies during the elevation of the holy Gifts before the distribution of communion. The faithful (*sancti*) are fed by Christ's holy body and blood (*sancta*) to grow in the communion of the Holy Spirit (*koinōnia*) and to communicate it to the world.

I. Communion in Spiritual Goods

949 In the primitive community of Jerusalem, the disciples 'devoted themselves to the apostles' teaching and fellowship, to the breaking of the bread and the prayers.'[480]

Communion in the faith. The faith of the faithful is the faith *of the Church*, received from the apostles. Faith is a treasure of life which is enriched by being shared. 185

950 *Communion of the sacraments*. 'The fruit of all the sacraments belongs to all the faithful. All the sacraments are sacred links uniting the faithful with one another and binding them to Jesus Christ, and above all Baptism, the gate by which we enter into the Church. The communion of saints must be understood as the communion of the sacraments... The name "communion" can be applied to all of them, for they unite us to God... But this name is better suited to the Eucharist than to any other, because it is primarily the Eucharist that brings this communion about.'[481] 1130 1331

951 *Communion of charisms*. Within the communion of the Church, the Holy Spirit 'distributes special graces among the

---

[477] Nicetas, *Expl. symb.* 10: PL 52, 871B.
[478] St Thomas Aquinas, *Symb.* 10.
[479] *Roman Catechism* I, 10, 24.
[480] *Acts* 2:42.
[481] *Roman Catechism* I, 10, 24.

799 faithful of every rank' for the building up of the Church.[482] Now, 'to each is given the manifestation of the Spirit for the common good.'[483]

952 *They had everything in common.*'[484] 'Everything the true Christian has is to be regarded as a good possessed in common with everyone else. All Christians should be ready and eager to
2402 come to the help of the needy... and of their neighbours in want.'[485] A Christian is a steward of the Lord's goods.[486]

953 *Communion in charity.* In the *sanctorum communio*, 'None of us lives to himself, and none of us dies to himself.'[487] 'If one member
1827 suffers, all suffer together; if one member is honoured, all rejoice together. Now you are the body of Christ and individually mem-
2011 bers of it.'[488] 'Charity does not insist on its own way.'[489] In this solidarity with all men, living or dead, which is founded on the
845 communion of saints, the least of our acts done in charity redounds
1469 to the profit of all. Every sin harms this communion.

II. The Communion of the Church of Heaven and Earth

771 954 *The three states of the Church.* 'When the Lord comes in glory, and all his angels with him, death will be no more and all things will be subject to him. But at the present time some of his disciples
1031, 1023 are pilgrims on earth. Others have died and are being purified, while still others are in glory, contemplating "in full light, God himself triune and one, exactly as he is:"'[490]

All of us, however, in varying degrees and in different ways share in the same charity towards God and our neighbours, and we all sing the one hymn of glory to our God. All, indeed, who are of Christ and who have his Spirit form one Church and in Christ cleave together.[491]

955 'So it is that the union of the wayfarers with the brethren who sleep in the peace of Christ is in no way interrupted, but on the contrary, according to the constant faith of the Church, this union is reinforced by an exchange of spiritual goods.'[492]

956 *The intercession of the saints.* 'Being more closely united to
1370 Christ, those who dwell in heaven fix the whole Church more
2683 firmly in holiness ... they do not cease to intercede with the Father

[482] LG 12 § 2.
[483] 1 Cor 12:7.
[484] Acts 4:32.
[485] Roman Catechism I, 10, 27.
[486] Cf. Lk 16:1, 3.
[487] Rom 14:7.
[488] 1 Cor 12:26–27.
[489] 1 Cor 13:5; cf. 10:24.
[490] LG 49; cf. Mt 25:31; 1 Cor 15:26–27; Council of Florence (1439): DS 1305.
[491] LG 49; cf. Eph 4:16.
[492] LG 49.

for us, as they proffer the merits which they acquired on earth through the one mediator between God and men, Christ Jesus . . . , So by their fraternal concern is our weakness greatly helped.'[493]

> Do not weep, for I shall be more useful to you after my death and I shall help you then more effectively than during my life.[494]

> I want to spend my heaven in doing good on earth.[495]

957 *Communion with the saints.* 'It is not merely by the title of example that we cherish the memory of those in heaven; we seek, rather, that by this devotion to the exercise of fraternal charity the union of the whole Church in the Spirit may be strengthened. Exactly as Christian communion among our fellow pilgrims brings us closer to Christ, so our communion with the saints joins us to Christ, from whom as from its fountain and head issues all grace, and the life of the People of God itself':[496]   1173

> We worship Christ as God's Son; we love the martyrs as the Lord's disciples and imitators, and rightly so because of their matchless devotion towards their king and master. May we also be their companions and fellow disciples![497]

958 *Communion with the dead.* 'In full consciousness of this communion of the whole Mystical Body of Jesus Christ, the Church in its pilgrim members, from the very earliest days of the Christian religion, has honoured with great respect the memory of the dead;   1371
and "because it is a holy and a wholesome thought to pray for the dead that they may be loosed from their sins" she offers her suf-   1032
frages for them.'[498] Our prayer for them is capable not only of   1689
helping them, but also of making their intercession for us effective.

959 *In the one family of God.* 'For if we continue to love one another and to join in praising the Most Holy Trinity – all of us who are sons of God and form one family in Christ – we will be   1027
faithful to the deepest vocation of the Church.'[499]

IN BRIEF

960 *The Church is a 'communion of saints': this expression refers first to the 'holy things' ('sancta'), above all the Eucharist, by which 'the unity of believers, who form one body in Christ, is both represented and brought about' (LG 3).*

---

[493] LG 49; cf. 1 Tim 2:5.
[494] St Dominic, dying, to his brothers.
[495] St Thérèse of Lisieux, *The Final Conversations*, tr. John Clarke (Washington DC: ICS, 1977), 102.

[496] LG 50; cf. Eph 4:1–6.
[497] *Martyrium Polycarpi* 17: AF II/3, 396.
[498] LG 50; cf. 2 Macc 12:45.
[499] LG 51; cf. Heb 3:6.

> 961 The term 'communion of saints' refers also to the communion of 'holy persons' ('sancti') in Christ who 'died for all', so that what each one does or suffers in and for Christ bears fruit for all.
>
> 962 'We believe in the communion of all the faithful of Christ, those who are pilgrims on earth, the dead who are being purified, and the blessed in heaven, all together forming one Church; and we believe that in this communion, the merciful love of God and his saints is always [attentive] to our prayers' (Paul VI, CPG § 30).

Paragraph 6. Mary – Mother of Christ, Mother of the Church

963 Since the Virgin Mary's role in the mystery of Christ and the Spirit has been treated, it is fitting now to consider her place in the *484–507,* mystery of the Church. 'The Virgin Mary... is acknowledged *721–726* and honoured as being truly the Mother of God and of the redeemer... She is "clearly the mother of the members of Christ"... since she has by her charity joined in bringing about the birth of believers in the Church, who are members of its head.'[500] 'Mary, Mother of Christ, Mother of the Church.'[501]

I. Mary's Motherhood with Regard to the Church

Wholly united with her Son...

964 Mary's role in the Church is inseparable from her union with Christ and flows directly from it. 'This union of the mother with the Son in the work of salvation is made manifest from the time of Christ's virginal conception up to his death';[502] it is made manifest above all at the hour of his Passion:

534   Thus the Blessed Virgin advanced in her pilgrimage of faith, and faith-
       fully persevered in her union with her Son unto the cross. There she
       stood, in keeping with the divine plan, enduring with her only begotten
618   Son the intensity of his suffering, joining herself with his sacrifice in her
       mother's heart, and lovingly consenting to the immolation of this vic-
       tim, born of her: to be given, by the same Christ Jesus dying on the cross,
       as a mother to his disciple, with these words: 'Woman, behold your
       son.'[503]

965 After her Son's Ascension, Mary 'aided the beginnings of the Church by her prayers.'[504] In her association with the apostles and several women, 'we also see Mary by her prayers imploring the

---

[500] LG 53; cf. St Augustine, *De virg.* 6: PL 40, 399.
[501] Paul VI, Discourse, 21 November 1964.
[502] LG 57.
[503] LG 58; cf. Jn 19:26–27.
[504] LG 69.

gift of the Spirit, who had already overshadowed her in the Annunciation.'[505]

... also in her Assumption

966 'Finally the Immaculate Virgin, preserved free from all stain of original sin, when the course of her earthly life was finished, was 491 taken up body and soul into heavenly glory, and exalted by the Lord as Queen over all things, so that she might be the more fully conformed to her Son, the Lord of lords and conqueror of sin and death.'[506] The Assumption of the Blessed Virgin is a singular participation in her Son's Resurrection and an anticipation of the resurrection of other Christians:

> In giving birth you kept your virginity; in your Dormition you did not leave the world, O Mother of God, but were joined to the source of Life. You conceived the living God and, by your prayers, will deliver our souls from death.[507]

... she is our Mother in the order of grace

967 By her complete adherence to the Father's will, to his Son's redemptive work, and to every prompting of the Holy Spirit, the Virgin Mary is the Church's model of faith and charity. Thus she is 2679 a 'pre-eminent and... wholly unique member of the Church'; indeed, she is the 'exemplary realization' (typus)[508] of the Church. 507

968 Her role in relation to the Church and to all humanity goes still further. 'In a wholly singular way she co-operated by her 494 obedience, faith, hope and burning charity in the Saviour's work of restoring supernatural life to souls. For this reason she is a mother to us in the order of grace.'[509]

969 'This motherhood of Mary in the order of grace continues 501 uninterruptedly from the consent which she loyally gave at the 149 Annunciation and which she sustained without wavering beneath the cross, until the eternal fulfilment of all the elect. Taken up to heaven she did not lay aside this saving office but by her manifold intercession continues to bring us the gifts of eternal salvation ... 1370 Therefore the Blessed Virgin is invoked in the Church under the titles of Advocate, Helper, Benefactress, and Mediatrix.'[510]

970 'Mary's function as mother of men in no way obscures or diminishes this unique mediation of Christ, but rather shows its power. But the Blessed

---

[505] LG 59.

[506] LG 59; cf. Pius XII, *Munificentissimus Deus* (1950): DS 3903; cf. *Rev* 19:16.

[507] Byzantine Liturgy, Feast of the Dormition, 15 August, Troparion.

[508] LG 53; 63.

[509] LG 61.

[510] LG 62.

2008 Virgin's salutary influence on men . . . flows forth from the superabundance of the merits of Christ, rests on his mediation, depends entirely on it and draws all its power from it.'[511] 'No creature could ever be counted along with the Incar-
1545 nate Word and Redeemer; but just as the priesthood of Christ is shared in various ways both by his ministers and the faithful, and as the one goodness of God is radiated in different ways among his creatures, so also the unique media-tion of the Redeemer does not exclude but rather gives rise to a manifold
308   co-operation which is but a sharing in this one source.'[512]

2673–2679 ## II. Devotion to the Blessed Virgin

971 '*All generations will call me blessed*': 'The Church's devotion to the Blessed Virgin is intrinsic to Christian worship.'[513] The
1172 Church rightly honours 'the Blessed Virgin with special devotion. From the most ancient times the Blessed Virgin has been honoured with the title of "Mother of God", to whose protection the faith-ful fly in all their dangers and needs. . . This very special devo-tion. . . differs essentially from the adoration which is given to the incarnate Word and equally to the Father and the Holy Spirit, and greatly fosters this adoration.'[514] The liturgical feasts dedicated to
2678 the Mother of God and Marian prayer, such as the rosary, an 'epitome of the whole Gospel', express this devotion to the Virgin Mary.[515]

III. Mary – Eschatological Icon of the Church

972 After speaking of the Church, her origin, mission and des-tiny, we can find no better way to conclude than by looking to
773 Mary. In her we contemplate what the Church already is in her mystery on her own 'pilgrimage of faith', and what she will be in the homeland at the end of her journey. There, 'in the glory of the Most Holy and Undivided Trinity', 'in the communion of all the
829 saints',[516] the Church is awaited by the one she venerates as Mother of her Lord and as her own mother.

2853 In the meantime the Mother of Jesus, in the glory which she possesses in body and soul in heaven, is the image and beginning of the Church as it is to be perfected in the world to come. Likewise she shines forth on earth, until the day of the Lord shall come, a sign of certain hope and comfort to the pilgrim People of God.[517]

---

[511] *LG* 60.
[512] *LG* 62.
[513] *Lk* 1:48; Paul VI, *MC* 56.
[514] *LG* 66.

[515] Cf. Paul VI, *MC* 42; *SC* 103.
[516] *LG* 69.
[517] *LG* 68; cf. 2 *Pt* 3:10.

IN BRIEF

973 By pronouncing her 'fiat' at the Annunciation and giving her consent to the Incarnation, Mary was already collaborating with the whole work her Son was to accomplish. She is mother wherever he is Saviour and head of the Mystical Body.

974 The Most Blessed Virgin Mary, when the course of her earthly life was completed, was taken up body and soul into the glory of heaven, where she already shares in the glory of her Son's Resurrection, anticipating the resurrection of all members of his Body.

975 'We believe that the Holy Mother of God, the new Eve, Mother of the Church, continues in heaven to exercise her maternal role on behalf of the members of Christ' (Paul VI, CPG § 15).

Article 10
'I BELIEVE IN THE FORGIVENESS OF SINS'

976 The Apostles' Creed associates faith in the forgiveness of sins not only with faith in the Holy Spirit, but also with faith in the Church and in the communion of saints. It was when he gave the Holy Spirit to his apostles that the risen Christ conferred on them his own divine power to forgive sins: 'Receive the Holy Spirit. If you forgive the sins of any, they are forgiven; if you retain the sins of any, they are retained.'[518]

(Part Two of the Catechism will deal explicitly with the forgiveness of sins through Baptism, the sacrament of Penance and the other sacraments, especially the Eucharist. Here it will suffice to suggest some basic facts briefly.)

I. One Baptism for the Forgiveness of Sins

1263

977 Our Lord tied the forgiveness of sins to faith and Baptism: 'Go into all the world and preach the gospel to the whole creation. He who believes and is baptized will be saved.'[519] Baptism is the first and chief sacrament of forgiveness of sins because it unites us with Christ, who died for our sins and rose for our justification, so that 'we too might walk in newness of life'.[520]

978 'When we made our first profession of faith while receiving the holy Baptism that cleansed us, the forgiveness we received then was so full and complete that there remained in us absolutely nothing left to efface, neither original sin nor offences committed

---

[518] Jn 20:22–23.
[519] Mk 16:15–16.

[520] Rom 6:4; cf. 4:25.

by our own will, nor was there left any penalty to suffer in order to
expiate them . . . Yet the grace of Baptism delivers no one from all
the weakness of nature. On the contrary, we must still combat the
1264 movements of concupiscence that never cease leading us into
evil.'[521]

979 In this battle against our inclination towards evil, who could
be brave and watchful enough to escape every wound of sin? 'If
the Church has the power to forgive sins, then Baptism cannot be
her only means of using the keys of the Kingdom of heaven re-
1446 ceived from Jesus Christ. The Church must be able to forgive all
penitents their offences, even if they should sin until the last
moment of their lives.'[522]

1422–1484 980 It is through the sacrament of Penance that the baptized can
be reconciled with God and with the Church:

> Penance has rightly been called by the holy Fathers 'a laborious kind of
> baptism'. This sacrament of Penance is necessary for salvation for those
> who have fallen after Baptism, just as Baptism is necessary for salvation
> for those who have not yet been reborn.[523]

II. The Power of the Keys

981 After his Resurrection, Christ sent his apostles 'so that
repentance and forgiveness of sins should be preached in his name
to all nations'.[524] The apostles and their successors carry out this
'ministry of reconciliation', not only by announcing to men God's
forgiveness merited for us by Christ, and calling them to conversion and faith; but also by communicating to them the forgiveness
1444 of sins in Baptism, and reconciling them with God and with the
Church through the power of the keys, received from Christ:[525]

553   [The Church] has received the keys of the Kingdom of heaven so that, in
> her, sins may be forgiven through Christ's blood and the Holy Spirit's
> action. In this Church, the soul dead through sin comes back to life in
> order to live with Christ, whose grace has saved us.[526]

982 There is no offence, however serious, that the Church cannot
forgive. 'There is no one, however wicked and guilty, who may
1463 not confidently hope for forgiveness, provided his repentance is
honest.'[527] Christ who died for all men desires that in his Church

---

[521] *Roman Catechism* I, 11, 3.
[522] *Roman Catechism* I, 11, 4.
[523] Council of Trent (1551): DS 1672; cf.
St Gregory of Nazianzus, *Oratio* 39,
17: PG 36, 356A.

[524] *Lk* 24:47.
[525] 2 *Cor* 5:18.
[526] St Augustine, *Sermo* 214, 11: PL 38,
1071–1072.
[527] *Roman Catechism* I, 11, 5.

the gates of forgiveness should always be open to anyone who 605 turns away from sin.[528]

983 Catechesis strives to awaken and nourish in the faithful faith in the incomparable greatness of the risen Christ's gift to his Church: the mission and the power to forgive sins through the 1442 ministry of the apostles and their successors:

> The Lord wills that his disciples possess a tremendous power: that his lowly servants accomplish in his name all that he did when he was on 1465 earth.[529]

> Priests have received from God a power that he has given neither to angels nor to archangels ... God above confirms what priests do here below.[530]

> Were there no forgiveness of sins in the Church, there would be no hope of life to come or eternal liberation. Let us thank God who has given his Church such a gift.[531]

IN BRIEF

984 *The Creed links 'the forgiveness of sins' with its profession of faith in the Holy Spirit, for the risen Christ entrusted to the apostles the power to forgive sins when he gave them the Holy Spirit.*

985 *Baptism is the first and chief sacrament of the forgiveness of sins: it unites us to Christ, who died and rose, and gives us the Holy Spirit.*

986 *By Christ's will, the Church possesses the power to forgive the sins of the baptized and exercises it through bishops and priests normally in the sacrament of Penance.*

987 *'In the forgiveness of sins, both priests and sacraments are instruments which our Lord Jesus Christ, the only author and liberal giver of salvation, wills to use in order to efface our sins and give us the grace of justification'* (Roman Catechism I, 11, 6).

Article 11
'I BELIEVE IN THE RESURRECTION OF THE BODY'

988 The Christian Creed – the profession of our faith in God, the Father, the Son and the Holy Spirit, and in God's creative, saving and sanctifying action – culminates in the proclamation of the resurrection of the dead on the last day, and in life everlasting.

---

[528] Cf. *Mt* 18:21–22.
[529] St Ambrose, *De poenit.* I, 15: PL 16, 479.
[530] St John Chrysostom, *De sac.* 3, 5: PG 48, 643A.
[531] St Augustine, *Sermo* 213, 8: PL 38, 1064.

989 We firmly believe, and hence we hope that, just as Christ is truly risen from the dead and lives for ever, so after death the
655 righteous will live for ever with the risen Christ and he will raise
648 them up on the last day.[532] Our resurrection, like his own, will be the work of the Most Holy Trinity:

> If the Spirit of him who raised Jesus from the dead dwells in you, he who raised Christ Jesus from the dead will give life to your mortal bodies also through his Spirit who dwells in you.[533]

990 The term 'flesh' refers to man in his state of weakness and mortality.[534] The 'resurrection of the flesh' [the literal formulation of the Apostles' Creed] means not only that the immortal soul will live on after death, but that even our
364 'mortal body' will come to life again.[535]

638 991 Belief in the resurrection of the dead has been an essential element of the Christian faith from its beginnings. 'The confidence of Christians is the resurrection of the dead; believing this we live.'[536]

> How can some of you say that there is no resurrection of the dead? But if there is no resurrection of the dead, then Christ has not been raised; if Christ has not been raised, then our preaching is in vain and your faith is in vain . . . But in fact Christ has been raised from the dead, the first fruits of those who have fallen asleep.[537]

I. Christ's Resurrection and Ours

The progressive revelation of the resurrection

992 God revealed the resurrection of the dead to his people progressively. Hope in the bodily resurrection of the dead established itself as a consequence intrinsic to faith in God as creator of the
297 whole man, soul and body. The creator of heaven and earth is also the one who faithfully maintains his covenant with Abraham and his posterity. It was in this double perspective that faith in the resurrection came to be expressed. In their trials, the Maccabean martyrs confessed:

> The King of the universe will raise us up to an everlasting renewal of life, because we have died for his laws.[538] One cannot but choose to die at the hands of men and to cherish the hope that God gives of being raised again by him.[539]

993 The Pharisees and many of the Lord's contemporaries hoped

---

[532] Cf. Jn 6:39–40.
[533] Rom 8:11; cf. 1 Th 4:14; 1 Cor 6:14; 2 Cor 4:14; Phil 3:10–11.
[534] Cf. Gen 6:3; Ps 56:5; Is 40:6.
[535] Rom 8:11.
[536] Tertullian, De res. 1, 1: PL 2, 841.
[537] 1 Cor 15:12–14, 20.
[538] 2 Macc 7:9.
[539] 2 Macc 7:14; cf. 7:29; Dan 12:1–13.

for the resurrection. Jesus teaches it firmly. To the Sadducees who
deny it he answers, 'Is not this why you are wrong, that you know
neither the scriptures nor the power of God?'[540] Faith in the resurrection rests on faith in God who 'is not God of the dead, but of the
living'.[541]

994 But there is more. Jesus links faith in the resurrection to his
own person: 'I am the Resurrection and the life.'[542] It is Jesus
himself who on the last day will raise up those who have believed
in him, who have eaten his body and drunk his blood.[543] Already
now in this present life he gives a sign and pledge of this by restoring some of the dead to life,[544] announcing thereby his own Resurrection, though it was to be of another order. He speaks of this
unique event as the 'sign of Jonah',[545] the sign of the Temple: he
announces that he will be put to death but rise thereafter on the
third day.[546]

995 To be a witness to Christ is to be a 'witness to his Resurrection', to '[have eaten and drunk] with him after he rose from the
dead'.[547] Encounters with the risen Christ characterize the Christian hope of resurrection. We shall rise like Christ, with him, and
through him.

996 From the beginning, Christian faith in the resurrection has
met with incomprehension and opposition.[548] 'On no point does
the Christian faith encounter more opposition than on the resurrection of the body.'[549] It is very commonly accepted that the life
of the human person continues in a spiritual fashion after death.
But how can we believe that this body, so clearly mortal, could
rise to everlasting life?

How do the dead rise?

997 What is 'rising'? In death, the separation of the soul from the
body, the human body decays and the soul goes to meet God,
while awaiting its reunion with its glorified body. God, in his
almighty power, will definitively grant incorruptible life to our
bodies by reuniting them with our souls, through the power of
Jesus' Resurrection.

998 Who will rise? All the dead will rise, 'those who have done

---

[540] Mk 12:24; cf. Jn 11:24; Acts 23:6.
[541] Mk 12:27.
[542] Jn 11:25.
[543] Cf. Jn 5:24–25; 6:40, 54.
[544] Cf. Mk 5:21–42; Lk 7:11–17; Jn 11.
[545] Mt 12:39.

[546] Cf. Mk 10:34; Jn 2:19–22.
[547] Acts 1:22; 10:41; cf. 4:33.
[548] Cf. Acts 17:32; 1 Cor 15:12–13.
[549] St Augustine, En. in Ps. 88, 2, 5: PL
37, 1134.

good, to the resurrection of life, and those who have done evil, to
1038 the resurrection of judgement'.[550]

999   *How?* Christ is raised with his own body: 'See my hands and
640 my feet, that it is I myself';[551] but he did not return to an earthly
life. So, in him, 'all of them will rise again with their own bodies
which they now bear', but Christ 'will change our lowly body to
645 be like his glorious body', into a 'spiritual body':[552]

> But someone will ask, 'How are the dead raised? With what kind of body
> do they come?' You foolish man! What you sow does not come to life
> unless it dies. And what you sow is not the body which is to be, but a bare
> kernel ... What is sown is perishable, what is raised is imperishable ...
> The dead will be raised imperishable ... For this perishable nature
> must put on the imperishable, and this mortal nature must put on im-
> mortality.[553]

647 1000   This 'how' exceeds our imagination and understanding; it is
accessible only to faith. Yet our participation in the Eucharist already gives us a foretaste of Christ's transfiguration of our bodies:

> Just as bread that comes from the earth, after God's blessing has been
1405 invoked upon it, is no longer ordinary bread, but Eucharist, formed of
> two things, the one earthly and the other heavenly: so too our bodies,
> which partake of the Eucharist, are no longer corruptible, but possess the
> hope of resurrection.[554]

1038 1001   *When?* Definitively 'at the last day', 'at the end of the
world'.[555] Indeed, the resurrection of the dead is closely associated
673 with Christ's *Parousia*:

> For the Lord himself will descend from heaven, with a cry of command,
> with the archangel's call, and with the sound of the trumpet of God. And
> the dead in Christ will rise first.[556]

Risen with Christ

1002   Christ will raise us up 'on the last day'; but it is also true that,
in a certain way, we have already risen with Christ. For, by virtue
655 of the Holy Spirit, Christian life is already now on earth a participation in the death and Resurrection of Christ:

> And you were buried with him in Baptism, in which you were also raised
> with him through faith in the working of God, who raised him from the

---

[550] *Jn* 5:29; cf. *Dan* 12:2.
[551] *Lk* 24:39.
[552] Lateran Council IV (1215): DS 801;
Phil 3:21; 1 *Cor* 15:44.
[553] 1 *Cor* 15:35-37, 42, 52, 53.

[554] St Irenaeus, *Adv. haeres.* 4, 18, 4-5: PG
7/1, 1028-1029.
[555] *Jn* 6:39-40, 44, 54; 11:24; LG 48 § 3.
[556] 1 *Th* 4:16.

dead . . . If then you have been raised with Christ, seek the things that are above, where Christ is, seated at the right hand of God.[557]

1003 United with Christ by Baptism, believers already truly participate in the heavenly life of the risen Christ, but this life remains 'hidden with Christ in God'.[558] The Father has already 'raised us up with him, and made us sit with him in the heavenly places in Christ Jesus.'[559] Nourished with his body in the Eucharist, we already belong to the Body of Christ. When we rise on the last day we 'also will appear with him in glory'.[560]

1227
2796

1004 In expectation of that day, the believer's body and soul already participate in the dignity of belonging to Christ. This dignity entails the demand that he should treat with respect his own body, but also the body of every other person, especially the suffering:

364

1397

> The body [is meant] for the Lord, and the Lord for the body. And God raised the Lord and will also raise us up by his power. Do you not know that your bodies are members of Christ? . . . You are not your own; . . . So glorify God in your body.[561]

II. Dying in Christ Jesus

1005 To rise with Christ, we must die with Christ: we must 'be away from the body and at home with the Lord'.[562] In that 'departure' which is death the soul is separated from the body.[563] It will be reunited with the body on the day of resurrection of the dead.[564]

625, 650

Death

1006 'It is in regard to death that man's condition is most shrouded in doubt.'[565] In a sense bodily death is natural, but for faith it is in fact 'the wages of sin'.[566] For those who die in Christ's grace it is a participation in the death of the Lord, so that they can also share his Resurrection.[567]

164, 1500

1007 *Death is the end of earthly life.* Our lives are measured by time, in the course of which we change, grow old and, as with all living beings on earth, death seems like the normal end of life. That aspect of death lends urgency to our lives: remembering our

---

[557] Col 2:12; 3:1.
[558] Col 3:3; cf. Phil 3:20.
[559] Eph 2:6.
[560] Col 3:4.
[561] 1 Cor 6:13-15, 19-20.
[562] 2 Cor 5:8.

[563] Cf. Phil 1:23.
[564] Cf. Paul VI, CPG § 28.
[565] GS 18.
[566] Rom 6:23; cf. Gen 2:17.
[567] Cf. Rom 6:3-9; Phil 3:10-11.

mortality helps us realize that we have only a limited time in which to bring our lives to fulfilment:

> Remember also your Creator in the days of your youth, ... before the dust returns to the earth as it was, and the spirit returns to God who gave it.[568]

1008 *Death is a consequence of sin.* The Church's Magisterium, as authentic interpreter of the affirmations of Scripture and Tradition, teaches that death entered the world on account of man's 401 sin.[569] Even though man's nature is mortal, God had destined him 376 not to die. Death was therefore contrary to the plans of God the Creator, and entered the world as a consequence of sin.[570] 'Bodily death, from which man would have been immune had he not sinned' is thus 'the last enemy' of man left to be conquered.[571]

1009 *Death is transformed by Christ.* Jesus, the Son of God, also himself suffered the death that is part of the human condition. Yet, 612 despite his anguish as he faced death, he accepted it in an act of complete and free submission to his Father's will.[572] The obedience of Jesus has transformed the curse of death into a blessing.[573]

1681–1690 **The meaning of Christian death**

1010 Because of Christ, Christian death has a positive meaning: 'For to me to live is Christ, and to die is gain.'[574] 'The saying is sure: if we have died with him, we will also live with him.'[575] What is essentially new about Christian death is this: through 376 Baptism, the Christian has already 'died with Christ' sacramentally, in order to live a new life; and if we die in Christ's grace, physical death completes this 'dying with Christ' and so completes our incorporation into him in his redeeming act:

> It is better for me to die in (*eis*) Christ Jesus than to reign over the ends of 612 the earth. Him it is I seek – who died for us. Him it is I desire – who rose for us. I am on the point of giving birth... Let me receive pure light; when I shall have arrived there, then shall I be a man.[576]

1681–1690 1011 In death, God calls man to himself. Therefore the Christian can experience a desire for death like St Paul's: 'My desire is to depart and be with Christ.'[577] He can transform his own death into

---

[568] *Eccl* 12:1, 7.
[569] Cf. *Gen* 2:17; 3:3, 19; *Wis* 1:13; *Rom* 5:12; 6:23; DS 1511.
[570] Cf. *Wis* 2:23–24.
[571] *GS* 18 § 2; cf. 1 *Cor* 15:26.
[572] Cf. *Mk* 14:33–34; *Heb* 5:7–8.

[573] Cf. *Rom* 5:19–21.
[574] *Phil* 1:21.
[575] 2 *Tim* 2:11.
[576] St Ignatius of Antioch, *Ad Rom.* 6, 1–2: AF II/2, 217–220.
[577] *Phil* 1:23.

an act of obedience and love towards the Father, after the example of Christ:[578]

> My earthly desire has been crucified; . . . there is living water in me, water *1220*
> that murmurs and says within me: Come to the Father.[579]

> I want to see God and, in order to see him, I must die.[580]

> I am not dying; I am entering life.[581]

1012 The Christian vision of death receives privileged expression in the liturgy of the Church:[582]

> Lord, for your faithful people life is changed, not ended.
> When the body of our earthly dwelling lies in death
> we gain an everlasting dwelling place in heaven.[583]   *1025*

1013 Death is the end of man's earthly pilgrimage, of the time of grace and mercy which God offers him so as to work out his earthly life in keeping with the divine plan, and to decide his ultimate destiny. When 'the single course of our earthly life' is completed,[584] we shall not return to other earthly lives: 'It is appointed for men to die once.'[585] There is no 'reincarnation' after death.

1014 The Church encourages us to prepare ourselves for the hour of our death: in the ancient litany of the saints, for instance, she has us pray: 'From a sudden and unforeseen death, deliver us, O Lord';[586] to ask the Mother of God to intercede for us 'at the hour of our death' in the *Hail Mary*; and to entrust ourselves to *2676–2677* St Joseph, the patron of a happy death.

> Every action of yours, every thought, should be those of one who expects to die before the day is out. Death would have no great terrors for you if you had a quiet conscience . . . Then why not keep clear of sin instead of running away from death? If you aren't fit to face death today, it's very unlikely you will be tomorrow . . .[587]

> Praised are you, my Lord, for our sister bodily Death,
> from whom no living man can escape.
> Woe on those who will die in mortal sin!
> Blessed are they who will be found
> in your most holy will,
> for the second death will not harm them.[588]

---

[578] Cf. *Lk* 23:46.
[579] St Ignatius of Antioch, *Ad Rom.* 7, 2: AF II/2, 223–224.
[580] St Teresa of Avila, *Life*, chap. 1.
[581] St Thérèse of Lisieux, *The Last Conversations.*
[582] Cf. 1 *Th* 4:13–14.
[583] *Roman Missal*, Preface of Christian Death I.
[584] *LG* 48 § 3.
[585] *Heb* 9:27.
[586] *Roman Missal*, Litany of the Saints.
[587] *The Imitation of Christ* 1, 23, 1.
[588] St Francis of Assisi, *Canticle of the Creatures.*

IN BRIEF

1015 *'The flesh is the hinge of salvation' (Tertullian, De res. 8, 2: PL 2, 852). We believe in God who is creator of the flesh; we believe in the Word made flesh in order to redeem the flesh; we believe in the resurrection of the flesh, the fulfilment of both the creation and the redemption of the flesh.*

1016 *By death the soul is separated from the body, but in the resurrection God will give incorruptible life to our body, transformed by reunion with our soul. Just as Christ is risen and lives for ever, so all of us will rise at the last day.*

1017 *'We believe in the true resurrection of this flesh that we now possess' (Council of Lyons II: DS 854). We sow a corruptible body in the tomb, but he raises up an incorruptible body, a 'spiritual body' (cf. 1 Cor 15:42–44).*

1018 *As a consequence of original sin, man must suffer 'bodily death, from which man would have been immune had he not sinned' (GS 18 § 2).*

1019 *Jesus, the Son of God, freely suffered death for us in complete and free submission to the will of God, his Father. By his death he has conquered death, and so opened the possibility of salvation to all men.*

Article 12
'I BELIEVE IN LIFE EVERLASTING'

1020 The Christian who unites his own death to that of Jesus views it as a step towards him and an entrance into everlasting life. When the Church for the last time speaks Christ's words of pardon and absolution over the dying Christian, seals him for the last time with a strengthening anointing and gives him Christ in viaticum as nourishment for the journey, she speaks with gentle assurance:

1523–1525

> Go forth, Christian soul, from this world
> in the name of God the almighty Father,
> who created you,
> in the name of Jesus Christ, the Son of the living God,
> who suffered for you,
> in the name of the Holy Spirit,
> who was poured out upon you.
> Go forth, faithful Christian!
>
> May you live in peace this day,
> may your home be with God in Zion,
> with Mary, the virgin Mother of God,
> with Joseph, and all the angels and saints . . .
> May you return to [your Creator]
> who formed you from the dust of the earth.

May holy Mary, the angels, and all the saints 2677, 336
come to meet you as you go forth from this life . . .
May you see your Redeemer face to face . . .[589]

I. The Particular Judgement

1021 Death puts an end to human life as the time open to either
accepting or rejecting the divine grace manifested in Christ.[590]
The New Testament speaks of judgement primarily in its aspect of
the final encounter with Christ in his second coming, but also
repeatedly affirms that each will be rewarded immediately after
death in accordance with his works and faith. The parable of the 679
poor man Lazarus and the words of Christ on the cross to the good
thief, as well as other New Testament texts, speak of a final destiny
of the soul – a destiny which can be different for some and for
others.[591]

1022 Each man receives his eternal retribution in his immortal
soul at the very moment of his death, in a particular judgement 393
that refers his life to Christ: either entrance into the blessedness of
heaven – through a purification[592] or immediately[593] – or immediate and everlasting damnation.[594]

At the evening of life, we shall be judged on our love.[595] 1470

II. Heaven

1023 Those who die in God's grace and friendship and are perfectly purified live for ever with Christ. They are like God for 954
ever, for they 'see him as he is', face to face:[596]

By virtue of our apostolic authority, we define the following: According
to the general disposition of God, the souls of all the saints . . . and other
faithful who died after receiving Christ's holy Baptism (provided they
were not in need of purification when they died, . . . or, if they then did
need or will need some purification, when they have been purified after
death, . . .) already before they take up their bodies again and before the
general judgement – and this since the Ascension of our Lord and Saviour Jesus Christ into heaven – have been, are and will be in heaven, in the
heavenly Kingdom and celestial paradise with Christ, joined to the company of the holy angels. Since the Passion and death of our Lord Jesus

---

589 OCF, Prayer of Commendation.
590 Cf. 2 Tim 1:9–10.
591 Cf. Lk 16:22; 23:43; Mt 16:26; 2 Cor
5:8; Phil 1:23; Heb 9:27; 12:23.
592 Cf. Council of Lyons II (1274): DS
857–858; Council of Florence (1439):
DS 1304–1306; Council of Trent
(1563): DS 1820.

593 Cf. Benedict XII, Benedictus Deus
(1336): DS 1000–1001; John XXII, Ne
super his (1334): DS 990.
594 Cf. Benedict XII, Benedictus Deus
(1336): DS 1002.
595 St John of the Cross, Dichos 64.
596 1 Jn 3:2; cf. 1 Cor 13:12; Rev 22:4.

Christ, these souls have seen and do see the divine essence with an intuitive vision, and even face to face, without the mediation of any creature.[597]

260 1024 This perfect life with the Most Holy Trinity – this commu-
326 nion of life and love with the Trinity, with the Virgin Mary, the
2794 angels and all the blessed – is called 'heaven'. Heaven is the ulti-
1718 mate end and fulfilment of the deepest human longings, the state
of supreme, definitive happiness.

1025 To live in heaven is 'to be with Christ'. The elect live 'in
1011 Christ',[598] but they retain, or rather find, their true identity, their own name.[599]

> For life is to be with Christ; where Christ is, there is life, there is the kingdom.[600]

1026 By his death and Resurrection, Jesus Christ has 'opened' heaven to us. The life of the blessed consists in the full and perfect possession of the fruits of the redemption accomplished by Christ. He makes partners in his heavenly glorification those who have believed in him and remained faithful to his will. Heaven is the
793 blessed community of all who are perfectly incorporated into Christ.

959 1027 This mystery of blessed communion with God and all who are in Christ is beyond all understanding and description. Scrip-
1720 ture speaks of it in images: life, light, peace, wedding feast, wine of the kingdom, the Father's house, the heavenly Jerusalem, paradise: 'no eye has seen, nor ear heard, nor the heart of man conceived, what God has prepared for those who love him.'[601]

1028 Because of his transcendence, God cannot be seen as he is,
1722 unless he himself opens up his mystery to man's immediate contemplation and gives him the capacity for it. The Church calls this
163 contemplation of God in his heavenly glory 'the beatific vision':

> How great will your glory and happiness be, to be allowed to see God, to be honoured with sharing the joy of salvation and eternal light with Christ your Lord and God, . . . to delight in the joy of immortality in the Kingdom of heaven with the righteous and God's friends.[602]

956 1029 In the glory of heaven the blessed continue joyfully to fulfil God's will in relation to other men and to all creation. Already

---

[597] Benedict XII, *Benedictus Deus* (1336): DS 1000; cf. *LG* 49.
[598] *Phil* 1:23; cf. *Jn* 14:3; 1 *Th* 4:17.
[599] Cf. *Rev* 2:17.
[600] St Ambrose, *In Luc.* 10, 121: PL 15, 1834A.

[601] 1 *Cor* 2:9.
[602] St Cyprian, *Ep.* 58, 10, 1: CSEL 3/2, 665.

they reign with Christ; with him 'they shall reign for ever and *668*
ever.'[603]

III. The Final Purification, or Purgatory

1030 All who die in God's grace and friendship, but still imperfectly purified, are indeed assured of their eternal salvation; but
after death they undergo purification, so as to achieve the holiness
necessary to enter the joy of heaven.

1031 The Church gives the name *Purgatory* to this final purifica- *954*
tion of the elect, which is entirely different from the punishment of *1472*
the damned.[604] The Church formulated her doctrine of faith on
Purgatory especially at the Councils of Florence and Trent. The
tradition of the Church, by reference to certain texts of Scripture,
speaks of a cleansing fire:[605]

> As for certain lesser faults, we must believe that, before the Final Judge-
> ment, there is a purifying fire. He who is truth says that whoever utters
> blasphemy against the Holy Spirit will be pardoned neither in this age
> nor in the age to come. From this sentence we understand that certain
> offences can be forgiven in this age, but certain others in the age to
> come.[606]

1032 This teaching is also based on the practice of prayer for the
dead, already mentioned in Sacred Scripture: 'Therefore [Judas
Maccabeus] made atonement for the dead, that they might be
delivered from their sin.'[607] From the beginning the Church has *958*
honoured the memory of the dead and offered prayers in suffrage
for them, above all the Eucharistic sacrifice, so that, thus purified, *1371*
they may attain the beatific vision of God.[608] The Church also
commends almsgiving, indulgences and works of penance under- *1479*
taken on behalf of the dead:

> Let us help and commemorate them. If Job's sons were purified by their
> father's sacrifice, why would we doubt that our offerings for the dead
> bring them some consolation? Let us not hesitate to help those who have
> died and to offer our prayers for them.[609]

IV. Hell

1033 We cannot be united with God unless we freely choose to

---

[603] *Rev* 22:5; cf. *Mt* 25:21, 23.

[604] Cf. Council of Florence (1439): DS
1304; Council of Trent (1563): DS
1820; (1547): DS 1580; see also
Benedict XII, *Benedictus Deus* (1336):
DS 1000.

[605] Cf. 1 *Cor* 3:15; 1 *Pt* 1:7.

[606] St Gregory the Great, *Dial.* 4, 39: PL
77, 396; cf. *Mt* 12:31.

[607] 2 *Macc* 12:46.

[608] Cf. Council of Lyons II (1274): DS
856.

[609] St John Chrysostom, *Hom. in 1 Cor.*
41, 5: PG 61, 361C; cf. *Job* 1:5.

love him. But we cannot love God if we sin gravely against him, against our neighbour or against ourselves: 'He who does not love remains in death. Anyone who hates his brother is a murderer, and you know that no murderer has eternal life abiding in him.'[610] Our Lord warns us that we shall be separated from him if we fail to meet the serious needs of the poor and the little ones who are his brethren.[611] To die in mortal sin without repenting and accepting God's merciful love means remaining separated from him for ever by our own free choice. This state of definitive self-exclusion from communion with God and the blessed is called 'hell'.

1034 Jesus often speaks of 'Gehenna', of 'the unquenchable fire' reserved for those who to the end of their lives refuse to believe and be converted, where both soul and body can be lost.[612] Jesus solemnly proclaims that he 'will send his angels, and they will gather . . . all evil doers, and throw them into the furnace of fire',[613] and that he will pronounce the condemnation: 'Depart from me, you cursed, into the eternal fire!'[614]

1035 The teaching of the Church affirms the existence of hell and its eternity. Immediately after death the souls of those who die in a state of mortal sin descend into hell, where they suffer the punishments of hell, 'eternal fire'.[615] The chief punishment of hell is eternal separation from God, in whom alone man can possess the life and happiness for which he was created and for which he longs.

1036 The affirmations of Sacred Scripture and the teachings of the Church on the subject of hell are a *call to the responsibility* incumbent upon man to make use of his freedom in view of his eternal destiny. They are at the same time an urgent *call to conversion*: 'Enter by the narrow gate; for the gate is wide and the way is easy, that leads to destruction, and those who enter by it are many. For the gate is narrow and the way is hard, that leads to life, and those who find it are few.'[616]

> Since we know neither the day nor the hour, we should follow the advice of the Lord and watch constantly so that, when the single course of our earthly life is completed, we may merit to enter with him into the marriage feast and be numbered among the blessed, and not, like the

Marginal references: 1861, 393, 633, 393, 1734, 1428

---

[610] I Jn 3:14–15.
[611] Cf. Mt 25:31–46.
[612] Cf. Mt 5:22, 29; 10:28; 13:42, 50; Mk 9:43–48.
[613] Mt 13:41–42.

[614] Mt 25:41.
[615] Cf. DS 76; 409; 411; 801; 858; 1002; 1351; 1575; Paul VI, CPG § 12.
[616] Mt 7:13–14.

Fragment of a fresco from the catacombs of Priscilla in Rome, dating from the beginning of the third century A.D. It is the most ancient image of the Blessed Virgin.

This image, among the most ancient in Christian art, expresses a theme that lies at the heart of the Christian faith: the mystery of the incarnation of the Son of God born of the Virgin Mary.

– At the left, the figure of a man pointing to a star, located above the Virgin with the child: a prophet, probably Balaam, who announced that 'a star shall come out of Jacob, and a sceptre shall rise out of Israel' (*Num 24:17*). This is the whole expectation of the Old Covenant and the cry of a fallen humanity for a saviour and redeemer (cf. §§ *27;528*).

– This prophecy was fulfilled in the birth of Jesus, the incarnate Son of God, conceived by the power of the Holy Spirit and born of the Virgin Mary (cf. §§ *27: 53: 422: 488*). Mary brought him into the world and gave him to all humanity. For this reason, she is the purest image of the Church (cf. § *967*).

wicked and slothful servants, be ordered to depart into the eternal fire, into the outer darkness where 'men will weep and gnash their teeth'.[617]

1037 God predestines no one to go to hell;[618] for this, a wilful turning away from God (a mortal sin) is necessary, and persistence in it until the end. In the Eucharistic liturgy and in the daily prayers of her faithful, the Church implores the mercy of God, who does not want 'any to perish, but all to come to repentance':[619] 162 1014, 1821

> Father, accept this offering
> from your whole family.
> Grant us your peace in this life,
> save us from final damnation,
> and count us among those you have chosen.[620]

V. The Last Judgement

678–679

1038 The resurrection of all the dead, 'of both the just and the unjust',[621] will precede the Last Judgement. This will be 'the hour when all who are in the tombs will hear [the Son of man's] voice and come forth, those who have done good, to the resurrection of life, and those who have done evil, to the resurrection of judgement.'[622] Then Christ will come 'in his glory, and all the angels with him . . . Before him will be gathered all the nations, and he will separate them one from another as a shepherd separates the sheep from the goats, and he will place the sheep at his right hand, but the goats at the left . . . And they will go away into eternal punishment, but the righteous into eternal life.'[623]

1001, 998

1039 In the presence of Christ, who is Truth itself, the truth of each man's relationship with God will be laid bare.[624] The Last Judgement will reveal even to its furthest consequences the good each person has done or failed to do during his earthly life:

678

> All that the wicked do is recorded, and they do not know. When 'our God comes, he does not keep silence' . . . he will turn towards those at his left hand: . . . 'I placed my poor little ones on earth for you. I as their head was seated in heaven at the right hand of my Father — but on earth my members were suffering, my members on earth were in need. If you gave anything to my members, what you gave would reach their Head. Would that you had known that my little ones were in need when I placed them on earth for you and appointed them your stewards to bring

---

[617] LG 48 § 3; Mt 22:13; cf. Heb 9:27; Mt 25:13, 26, 30, 31–46.

[618] Cf. Council of Orange II (529): DS 397; Council of Trent (1547): DS 1567.

[619] 2 Pt 3:9.

[620] Roman Missal, EP I (Roman Canon), 88.

[621] Acts 24:15.

[622] Jn 5:28–29.

[623] Mt 25:31, 32, 46.

[624] Cf. Jn 12:49.

your good works into my treasury. But you have placed nothing in their hands; therefore you have found nothing in my presence.'[625]

1040 The Last Judgement will come when Christ returns in glory. Only the Father knows the day and the hour; only he deter-
637 mines the moment of its coming. Then through his Son Jesus Christ he will pronounce the final word on all history. We shall know the ultimate meaning of the whole work of creation and of the entire economy of salvation, and understand the marvellous
314 ways by which his Providence led everything towards its final end. The Last Judgement will reveal that God's justice triumphs over all the injustices committed by his creatures and that God's love is stronger than death.[626]

1432 1041 The message of the Last Judgement calls men to conversion while God is still giving them 'the acceptable time, ... the day of salvation'.[627] It inspires a holy fear of God and commits them to the justice of the Kingdom of God. It proclaims the 'blessed hope' of the Lord's return, when he will come 'to be glorified in his saints, and to be marvelled at in all who have believed'.[628]

2854 VI. The Hope of the New Heaven and the New Earth

1042 At the end of time, the Kingdom of God will come in its
769 fullness. After the universal judgement, the righteous will reign for ever with Christ, glorified in body and soul. The universe itself
670 will be renewed:

> The Church ... will receive her perfection only in the glory of heaven, when will come the time of the renewal of all things. At that time,
> 310 together with the human race, the universe itself, which is so closely related to man and which attains its destiny through him, will be per- fectly re-established in Christ.[629]

1043 Sacred Scripture calls this mysterious renewal, which will transform humanity and the world, 'new heavens and a new
671 earth'.[630] It will be the definitive realization of God's plan to bring
518, 280 under a single head 'all things in [Christ], things in heaven and things on earth'.[631]

1044 In this new universe, the heavenly Jerusalem, God will have his dwelling among men.[632] 'He will wipe away every tear from their eyes, and death shall be no more, neither shall there be

---

[625] St Augustine, Sermo 18, 4, 4: PL 38, 130–131; cf. Ps 50:3.
[626] Cf. Song 8:6.
[627] 2 Cor 6:2.
[628] Titus 2:13; 2 Th 1:10.

[629] LG 48; cf. Acts 3:21; Eph 1:10; Col 1:20; 2 Pt 3:10–13.
[630] 2 Pt 3:13; cf. Rev 21:1.
[631] Eph 1:10.
[632] Cf. Rev 21:5.

mourning nor crying nor pain any more, for the former things have passed away.'[633]

1045 *For man*, this consummation will be the final realization of the unity of the human race, which God willed from creation and of which the pilgrim Church has been 'in the nature of sacrament'.[634] Those who are united with Christ will form the community of the redeemed, 'the holy city' of God, 'the Bride, the wife of the Lamb'.[635] She will not be wounded any longer by sin, stains, self-love, that destroy or wound the earthly community.[636] The beatific vision, in which God opens himself in an inexhaustible way to the elect, will be the ever-flowing well-spring of happiness, peace, and mutual communion.

775

1404

1046 *For the cosmos*, Revelation affirms the profound common destiny of the material world and man:

> For the creation waits with eager longing for the revealing of the sons of God ... in hope because the creation itself will be set free from its bondage to decay ... We know that the whole creation has been groaning in travail together until now; and not only the creation, but we ourselves, who have the first fruits of the Spirit, groan inwardly as we wait for adoption as sons, the redemption of our bodies.[637]

349

1047 The visible universe, then, is itself destined to be transformed, 'so that the world itself, restored to its original state, facing no further obstacles, should be at the service of the just', sharing their glorification in the risen Jesus Christ.[638]

1048 '*We know neither the moment of the consummation* of the earth and of man, nor the way in which the universe will be transformed. The form of this world, distorted by sin, is passing away, and we are taught that God is preparing a new dwelling and a new earth in which righteousness dwells, in which happiness will fill and surpass all the desires of peace arising in the hearts of men.'[639]

673

1049 'Far from diminishing our concern to develop this earth, the expectancy of a new earth should spur us on, for it is here that the body of a new human family grows, foreshadowing in some way the age which is to come. That is why, although we must be careful to distinguish earthly progress clearly from the increase of the kingdom of Christ, such progress is of vital concern to the

2820

---

[633] *Rev* 21:4.
[634] Cf. *LG* 1.
[635] *Rev* 21:2, 9.
[636] Cf. *Rev* 21:27.

[637] *Rom* 8:19–23.
[638] St Irenaeus, *Adv. haeres.* 5, 32, 1: PG 7/2, 1210.
[639] *GS* 39 § 1.

kingdom of God, insofar as it can contribute to the better ordering of human society.'[640]

1050 'When we have spread on earth the fruits of our nature and
1709 our enterprise . . . according to the command of the Lord and in his Spirit, we will find them once again, cleansed this time from the stain of sin, illuminated and transfigured, when Christ presents to
260 his Father an eternal and universal kingdom.'[641] God will then be 'all in all' in *eternal life*:[642]

> True and subsistent life consists in this: the Father, through the Son and in the Holy Spirit, pouring out his heavenly gifts on all things without exception. Thanks to his mercy, we too, men that we are, have received the inalienable promise of eternal life.[643]

IN BRIEF

1051 *Every man receives his eternal recompense in his immortal soul from the moment of his death in a particular judgement by Christ, the judge of the living and the dead.*

1052 *'We believe that the souls of all who die in Christ's grace . . . are the People of God beyond death. On the day of resurrection, death will be definitively conquered, when these souls will be reunited with their bodies' (Paul VI, CPG § 28).*

1053 *'We believe that the multitude of those gathered around Jesus and Mary in Paradise forms the Church of heaven, where in eternal blessedness they see God as he is and where they are also, to various degrees, associated with the holy angels in the divine governance exercised by Christ in glory, by interceding for us and helping our weakness by their fraternal concern' (Paul VI, CPG § 29).*

1054 *Those who die in God's grace and friendship imperfectly purified, although they are assured of their eternal salvation, undergo a purification after death, so as to achieve the holiness necessary to enter the joy of God.*

1055 *By virtue of the 'communion of saints', the Church commends the dead to God's mercy and offers her prayers, especially the holy sacrifice of the Eucharist, on their behalf.*

1056 *Following the example of Christ, the Church warns the faithful of the 'sad and lamentable reality of eternal death' (GCD 69), also called 'hell'.*

---

[640] GS 39 § 2.
[641] GS 39 § 3.
[642] 1 *Cor* 15:28.

[643] St Cyril of Jerusalem, *Catech. illum.* 18, 29: PG 33, 1049.

1057 Hell's principal punishment consists of eternal separation from God in whom alone man can have the life and happiness for which he was created and for which he longs.

1058 The Church prays that no one should be lost: 'Lord, let me never be parted from you.' If it is true that no one can save himself, it is also true that God 'desires all men to be saved' (1 Tim 2:4), and that for him 'all things are possible' (Mt 19:26).

1059 'The holy Roman Church firmly believes and confesses that on the Day of Judgement all men will appear in their own bodies before Christ's tribunal to render an account of their own deeds' (Council of Lyons II [1274]: DS 859; cf. DS 1549).

1060 At the end of time, the Kingdom of God will come in its fullness. Then the just will reign with Christ for ever, glorified in body and soul, and the material universe itself will be transformed. God will then be 'all in all' (1 Cor 15:28), in eternal life.

'AMEN'

1061 The Creed, like the last book of the Bible,[644] ends with the Hebrew word *amen*. This word frequently concludes prayers in the New Testament. The Church likewise ends her prayers with 'Amen'. 2856

1062 In Hebrew, *amen* comes from the same root as the word for 'believe'. This root expresses solidity, trustworthiness, faithfulness. And so we can understand why 'Amen' may express both God's faithfulness towards us and our trust in him. 214

1063 In the book of the prophet Isaiah, we find the expression 'God of truth' (literally 'God of the Amen'), that is, the God who is faithful to his promises: 'He who blesses himself in the land shall 215 bless himself by the God of truth (*amen*).'[645] Our Lord often used the word 'Amen', sometimes repeated,[646] to emphasize the trustworthiness of his teaching, his authority founded on God's 156 truth.

1064 Thus the Creed's final 'Amen' repeats and confirms its first words: 'I believe.' To believe is to say 'Amen' to God's words, promises and commandments; to entrust oneself completely to him who is the 'Amen' of infinite love and perfect faithfulness.

---

[644] Cf. Rev 22:21.
[645] Is 65:16.
[646] Cf. Mt 6:2, 5, 16; Jn 5:19.

The Christian's everyday life will then be the 'Amen' to the 'I
197, 2101 believe' of our baptismal profession of faith:

> May your Creed be for you as a mirror. Look at yourself in it, to see if
> you believe everything you say you believe. And rejoice in your faith
> each day.[647]

1065 Jesus Christ himself is the 'Amen'. [648] He is the definitive
'Amen' of the Father's love for us. He takes up and completes our
'Amen' to the Father: 'For all the promises of God find their Yes in
him. That is why we utter the Amen through him, to the glory of
God':[649]

> Through him, with him, in him,
> in the unity of the Holy Spirit,
> all glory and honour is yours,
> almighty Father,
> for ever and ever.
> AMEN.

---

[647] St Augustine, *Sermo* 58, 11, 13: PL 38,   [648] *Rev* 3:14.
399.   [649] 2 *Cor* 1:20.

Part Two

THE CELEBRATION OF THE CHRISTIAN MYSTERY

Why the liturgy?

1066 In the Symbol of the faith the Church confesses the mystery
50 of the Holy Trinity and of the plan of God's 'good pleasure' for all
creation: the Father accomplishes the 'mystery of his will' by giving his beloved Son and his Holy Spirit for the salvation of the
world and for the glory of his name.[1] Such is the mystery of
Christ, revealed and fulfilled in history according to the wisely
236 ordered plan that St Paul calls the 'plan of the mystery'[2] and the
patristic tradition will call the 'economy of the Word incarnate' or
the 'economy of salvation'.

1067 'The wonderful works of God among the people of the Old
Testament were but a prelude to the work of Christ the Lord in
redeeming mankind and giving perfect glory to God. He accomplished this work principally by the Paschal mystery of his blessed
Passion, Resurrection from the dead and glorious Ascension,
whereby "dying he destroyed our death, rising he restored our
life". For it was from the side of Christ as he slept the sleep of death
upon the cross that there came forth "the wondrous sacrament of
the whole Church".'[3] For this reason, the Church celebrates in the
571 liturgy above all the Paschal mystery by which Christ accomplished the work of our salvation.

1068 It is this mystery of Christ that the Church proclaims and
celebrates in her liturgy so that the faithful may live from it and
bear witness to it in the world:

> For it is in the liturgy, especially in the divine sacrifice of the Eucharist,
> that 'the work of our redemption is accomplished', and it is through the
> liturgy especially that the faithful are enabled to express in their lives and
> manifest to others the mystery of Christ and the real nature of the true
> Church.[4]

What does the word liturgy mean?

1069 The word 'liturgy' originally meant a 'public work' or a
'service in the name of/on behalf of the people'. In Christian tradition it means the participation of the People of God in 'the work of
God'.[5] Through the liturgy Christ, our redeemer and high priest,
continues the work of our redemption in, with and through his
Church.

1070 In the New Testament the word 'liturgy' refers not only to

---

[1] *Eph* 1:9.
[2] *Eph* 3:9; cf. 3:4.
[3] SC 5 § 2; cf. St Augustine, *En. in Ps.*

138, 2: PL 37, 1784–1785.
[4] SC 2.
[5] Cf. *Jn* 17:4.

the celebration of divine worship but also to the proclamation of the Gospel and to active charity.[6] In all of these situations it is a question of the service of God and neighbour. In a liturgical celebration the Church is servant in the image of her Lord, the one *leitourgos*[7]; she shares in Christ's priesthood (worship), which is both prophetic (proclamation) and kingly (service of charity):   *783*

> The liturgy then is rightly seen as an exercise of the priestly office of Jesus Christ. It involves the presentation of man's sanctification under the guise of signs perceptible by the senses, and its accomplishment in ways appropriate to each of these signs. In it full public worship is performed by the Mystical Body of Jesus Christ, that is, by the Head and his members. From this it follows that every liturgical celebration, because it is an action of Christ the priest and of his Body which is the Church, is a sacred action surpassing all others. No other action of the Church can equal its efficacy by the same title and to the same degree.[8]

Liturgy as source of life

1071 As the work of Christ liturgy is also an action of his *Church*. It makes the Church present and manifests her as the visible sign of the communion in Christ between God and men. It engages the faithful in the new life of the community and involves the 'con- *1692* scious, active and fruitful participation' of everyone.[9]

1072 'The sacred liturgy does not exhaust the entire activity of the Church':[10] it must be preceded by evangelization, faith and conversion. It can then produce its fruits in the lives of the faithful: new life in the Spirit, involvement in the mission of the Church and service to her unity.

Prayer and liturgy

1073 The liturgy is also a participation in Christ's own prayer addressed to the Father in the Holy Spirit. In the liturgy, all Christian prayer finds its source and goal. Through the liturgy the inner man is rooted and grounded in 'the great love with which [the Father] loved us' in his beloved Son.[11] It is the same 'marvellous work of God' that is lived and internalized by all prayer, 'at all *2558* times in the Spirit'.[12]

Catechesis and liturgy

1074 'The liturgy is the summit towards which the activity of the Church is directed; it is also the fount from which all her power

---

[6] Cf. *Lk* 1:23; *Acts* 13:2; *Rom* 15:16, 27; 2 *Cor* 9:12; *Phil* 2:14–17, 25, 30.
[7] Cf. *Heb* 8:2, 6.
[8] SC 7 §§ 2–3.
[9] SC 11.
[10] SC 9.
[11] *Eph* 2:4; 3:16–17.
[12] *Eph* 6:18.

flows.'[13] It is therefore the privileged place for catechizing the People of God. 'Catechesis is intrinsically linked with the whole of liturgical and sacramental activity, for it is in the sacraments, especially in the Eucharist, that Christ Jesus works in fullness for the transformation of men.'[14]

426   1075   Liturgical catechesis aims to initiate people into the mystery of Christ (it is 'mystagogy') by proceeding from the visible to the invisible, from the sign to the thing signified, from the 'sacra-
774   ments' to the 'mysteries'. Such catechesis is to be presented by local and regional catechisms. This Catechism, which aims to serve the whole Church in all the diversity of her rites and cultures,[15] will present what is fundamental and common to the whole Church in the liturgy as mystery and as celebration (Section One); and then the seven sacraments and the sacramentals (Section Two).

---

[13] SC 10.
[14] John Paul II, CT 23.
[15] Cf. SC 3–4.

Section One

THE SACRAMENTAL ECONOMY

1076 The Church was made manifest to the world on the day of
Pentecost by the outpouring of the Holy Spirit.[1] The gift of the *739*
Spirit ushers in a new era in the 'dispensation of the mystery' – the
age of the Church, during which Christ manifests, makes present
and communicates his work of salvation through the liturgy of his
Church, 'until he comes'.[2] In this age of the Church Christ now
lives and acts in and with his Church, in a new way appropriate to
this new age. He acts through the sacraments in what the common
Tradition of the East and the West calls 'the sacramental
economy'; this is the communication (or 'dispensation') of the
fruits of Christ's Paschal mystery in the celebration of the
Church's 'sacramental' liturgy.

It is therefore important first to explain this 'sacramental
dispensation' (*Chapter One*). The nature and essential features of
liturgical celebration will then appear more clearly (*Chapter Two*).

Chapter One
THE PASCHAL MYSTERY IN THE AGE OF THE CHURCH

Article 1
THE LITURGY – WORK OF THE HOLY TRINITY

I. The Father – Source and Goal of the Liturgy

1077 'Blessed be the God and Father of our Lord Jesus Christ,
who has blessed us in Christ with every spiritual blessing in the *492*
heavenly places, even as he chose us in him before the foundation
of the world, that we should be holy and blameless before him. He
destined us before him in love to be his sons through Jesus Christ,
according to the purpose of his will, to the praise of his glorious
grace which he freely bestowed on us in the Beloved.'[3]

1078 Blessing is a divine and life-giving action, the source of *2626*
which is the Father; his blessing is both word and gift.[4] When
applied to man, the word 'blessing' means adoration, and surrender to his Creator in thanksgiving.

---

[1] Cf. *SC* 6; *LG* 2.
[2] 1 *Cor* 11:26.
[3] *Eph* 1:3–6.
[4] *eu-logia, bene-dictio.*

1079 From the beginning until the end of time the whole of God's work is a *blessing*. From the liturgical poem of the first creation to the canticles of the heavenly Jerusalem, the inspired authors proclaim the plan of salvation as one vast divine blessing.

1080 From the very beginning God blessed all living beings, especially man and woman. The covenant with Noah and with all living things renewed this blessing of fruitfulness despite man's sin which had brought a curse on the ground. But with Abraham, the divine blessing entered into human history which was moving towards death, to redirect it towards life, towards its source. By the faith of 'the father of all believers', who embraced the blessing, the history of salvation is inaugurated.

1081 The divine blessings were made manifest in astonishing and saving events: the birth of Isaac, the escape from Egypt (Passover and Exodus), the gift of the promised land, the election of David, the presence of God in the Temple, the purifying exile and return of a 'small remnant'. The Law, the Prophets and the Psalms, interwoven in the liturgy of the Chosen People, recall these divine blessings and at the same time respond to them with blessings of praise and thanksgiving.

1082 In the Church's liturgy the divine blessing is fully revealed and communicated. The Father is acknowledged and adored as the source and the end of all the blessings of creation and salvation. In his Word who became incarnate, died, and rose for us, he fills us with his blessings. Through his Word, he pours into our hearts the Gift that contains all gifts, the Holy Spirit.

2627 1083 The dual dimension of the Christian liturgy as a response of faith and love to the spiritual blessings the Father bestows on us is thus evident. On the one hand, the Church, united with her Lord and 'in the Holy Spirit',[5] blesses the Father 'for his inexpressible gift'[6] in her adoration, praise and thanksgiving. On the other 1360 hand, until the consummation of God's plan, the Church never ceases to present to the Father the offering of his own gifts, and to beg him to send the Holy Spirit upon that offering, upon herself, upon the faithful and upon the whole world, so that through communion in the death and resurrection of Christ the Priest, and by the power of the Spirit, these divine blessings will bring forth the fruits of life 'to the praise of his glorious grace'.[7]

---

[5] *Lk* 10:21.
[6] 2 *Cor* 9:15.
[7] *Eph* 1:6.

II. Christ's Work in the Liturgy

Christ glorified...

1084 'Seated at the right hand of the Father' and pouring out the *662* Holy Spirit on his Body which is the Church, Christ now acts through the sacraments he instituted to communicate his grace. The sacraments are perceptible signs (words and actions) accessible *1127* to our human nature. By the action of Christ and the power of the Holy Spirit they make present efficaciously the grace that they signify.

1085 In the liturgy of the Church, it is principally his own Paschal mystery that Christ signifies and makes present. During his earthly life Jesus announced his Paschal mystery by his teaching and anticipated it by his actions. When his Hour comes, he lives out the unique event of history which does not pass away: Jesus dies, is buried, rises from the dead and is seated at the right hand of the Father 'once for all'.[8] His Paschal mystery is a real event that occurred in our history, but it is unique: all other historical events happen once, and then they pass away, swallowed up in the past. The Paschal mystery of Christ, by contrast, cannot remain only in the past, because by his death he destroyed death, and all that Christ is – all that he did and suffered for all men – participates in *519* the divine eternity, and so transcends all times while being made present in them all. The event of the Cross and Resurrection *abides* *1165* and draws everything toward life.

... from the time of the Church of the apostles...

1086 'Accordingly, just as Christ was sent by the Father so also he *858* sent the apostles, filled with the Holy Spirit. This he did so that they might preach the Gospel to every creature and proclaim that the Son of God by his death and resurrection had freed us from the power of Satan and from death, and brought us into the Kingdom of his Father. But he also willed that the work of salvation which they preached should be set in train through the sacrifice and sacraments, around which the entire liturgical life revolves.'[9]

1087 Thus the risen Christ, by giving the Holy Spirit to the apostles, entrusted to them his power of sanctifying:[10] they became sacramental signs of Christ. By the power of the same Holy Spirit they entrusted this power to their successors. This 'apostolic *861*

---

[8] *Rom* 6:10; *Heb* 7:27; 9:12; cf. *Jn* 13:1; 17:1.

[9] *SC* 6.

[10] Cf. *Jn* 20:21–23.

succession' structures the whole liturgical life of the Church and is
1536 itself sacramental, handed on by the sacrament of Holy Orders.

... is present in the earthly liturgy ...

1088 'To accomplish so great a work' – the dispensation or com-
776, 669 munication of his work of salvation – 'Christ is always present in
his Church, especially in her liturgical celebrations. He is present in
the Sacrifice of the Mass not only in the person of his minister, "the
same now offering, through the ministry of priests, who formerly
1373 offered himself on the cross", but especially in the Eucharistic
species. By his power he is present in the sacraments so that when
anybody baptizes it is really Christ himself who baptizes. He is
present in his word since it is he himself who speaks when the holy
Scriptures are read in the Church. Lastly, he is present when the
Church prays and sings, for he has promised "where two or three
are gathered together in my name there am I in the midst of
them." '[11]

1089 'Christ, indeed, always associates the Church with himself in
this great work in which God is perfectly glorified and men are
796 sanctified. The Church is his beloved Bride who calls to her Lord,
and through him offers worship to the eternal Father.'[12]

... which participates in the liturgy of heaven

1090 'In the earthly liturgy we share in a foretaste of that heavenly
1137–1139 liturgy which is celebrated in the Holy City of Jerusalem towards
which we journey as pilgrims, where Christ is sitting at the right
hand of God, Minister of the sanctuary and of the true tabernacle.
With all the warriors of the heavenly army we sing a hymn of
glory to the Lord; venerating the memory of the saints, we hope
for some part and fellowship with them; we eagerly await the
Saviour, our Lord Jesus Christ, until he, our life, shall appear and
we too will appear with him in glory.'[13]

III. The Holy Spirit and the Church in the Liturgy

1091 In the liturgy the Holy Spirit is teacher of the faith of the
798 People of God and artisan of 'God's masterpieces', the sacraments
of the New Covenant. The desire and work of the Spirit in the
heart of the Church is that we may live from the life of the risen

---

[11] SC 7; Mt 18:20.
[12] SC 7.
[13] SC 8; cf. LG 50.

Christ. When the Spirit encounters in us the response of faith which he has aroused in us, he brings about genuine co-operation. Through it, the liturgy becomes the common work of the Holy Spirit and the Church.

1092 In this sacramental dispensation of Christ's mystery the Holy Spirit acts in the same way as at other times in the economy of salvation: he prepares the Church to encounter her Lord; he 737 recalls and makes Christ manifest to the faith of the assembly. By his transforming power, he makes the mystery of Christ present here and now. Finally the Spirit of communion unites the Church to the life and mission of Christ.

The Holy Spirit prepares for the reception of Christ

1093 In the sacramental economy the Holy Spirit fulfils what was prefigured in *the Old Covenant*. Since Christ's Church was 'pre- 762 pared in marvellous fashion in the history of the people of Israel and in the Old Covenant',[14] the Church's liturgy has retained certain elements of the worship of the Old Covenant as integral and irreplaceable, adopting them as her own:
– notably, reading the Old Testament; 121
– praying the Psalms; 2585
– above all, recalling the saving events and significant realities 1081 which have found their fulfilment in the mystery of Christ (prom- ise and covenant, Exodus and Passover, kingdom and Temple, exile and return).

1094 It is on this harmony of the two Testaments that the Paschal 128–130 catechesis of the Lord is built,[15] and then that of the apostles and the Fathers of the Church. This catechesis unveils what lay hidden under the letter of the Old Testament: the mystery of Christ. It is called 'typological' because it reveals the newness of Christ on the basis of the 'figures' (types) which announce him in the deeds, words and symbols of the first covenant. By this re-reading in the Spirit of Truth, starting from Christ, the figures are unveiled.[16] Thus the flood and Noah's ark prefigured salvation by Baptism,[17] as did the cloud and the crossing of the Red Sea. Water from the rock was the figure of the spiritual gifts of Christ, and manna in the desert prefigured the Eucharist, 'the true bread from heaven'.[18]

1095 For this reason the Church, especially during Advent and Lent and above all at the Easter Vigil, re-reads and re-lives the

---

[14] *LG* 2.
[15] Cf. *DV* 14–16; *Lk* 24:13–49.
[16] Cf. 2 *Cor* 3:14–16.

[17] Cf. 1 *Pt* 3:21.
[18] *Jn* 6:32; cf. 1 *Cor* 10:1–6.

281 great events of salvation history in the 'today' of her liturgy. But this also demands that catechesis help the faithful to open them-
117 selves to this spiritual understanding of the economy of salvation as the Church's liturgy reveals it and enables us to live it.

1096 *Jewish liturgy and Christian liturgy.* A better knowledge of the Jewish people's faith and religious life as professed and lived even now can help our better understanding of certain aspects of Christian liturgy. For both Jews and Christians sacred Scripture is an essential part of their respective liturgies: in the proclamation of the Word of God, the response to this word, prayer of praise and intercession for the living and the dead, invocation of God's mercy. In its characteristic structure the Liturgy of the Word originates in Jewish prayer. The
1174 Liturgy of the Hours and other liturgical texts and formularies, as well as those of our most venerable prayers, including the Lord's Prayer, have parallels in
1352 Jewish prayer. The Eucharistic Prayers also draw their inspiration from the Jewish tradition. The relationship between Jewish liturgy and Christian liturgy, but also their differences in content, are particularly evident in the great feasts of
840 the liturgical year, such as Passover. Christians and Jews both celebrate the Passover. For Jews, it is the Passover of history, tending toward the future; for Christians, it is the Passover fulfilled in the death and Resurrection of Christ, though always in expectation of its definitive consummation.

1097 In the *liturgy of the New Covenant* every liturgical action, especially the celebration of the Eucharist and the sacraments, is an encounter between Christ and the Church. The liturgical assembly derives its unity from the 'communion of the Holy Spirit' who gathers the children of God into the one Body of Christ. This assembly transcends racial, cultural, social – indeed, all human affinities.

1098 The assembly should *prepare* itself to encounter its Lord and to become 'a people well disposed'. The preparation of hearts is the joint work of the Holy Spirit and the assembly, especially of its ministers. The grace of the Holy Spirit seeks to awaken faith,
1430 conversion of heart and adherence to the Father's will. These dispositions are the precondition both for the reception of other graces conferred in the celebration itself and for the fruits of new life which the celebration is intended to produce afterwards.

The Holy Spirit recalls the mystery of Christ

1099 The Spirit and the Church co-operate to manifest Christ and his work of salvation in the liturgy. Primarily in the Eucharist, and by analogy in the other sacraments, the liturgy is the *memorial* of
91 the mystery of salvation. The Holy Spirit is the Church's living memory.[19]

---

[19] Cf. *Jn* 14:26.

1100 *The Word of God*. The Holy Spirit first recalls the meaning of the salvation event to the liturgical assembly by giving life to the Word of God, which is proclaimed so that it may be received and *1184* lived:

> In the celebration of the liturgy, sacred Scripture is extremely important. *103, 131* From it come the lessons that are read and explained in the homily, and the psalms that are sung. It is from the Scriptures that the prayers, collects and hymns draw their inspiration and their force, and that actions and signs derive their meaning.[20]

1101 The Holy Spirit gives a spiritual understanding of the Word *117* of God to those who read or hear it, according to the dispositions of their hearts. By means of the words, actions and symbols that form the structure of a celebration, the Spirit puts both the faithful and the ministers into a living relationship with Christ, the Word and Image of the Father, so that they can live out the meaning of what they hear, contemplate and do in the celebration.

1102 'By the saving word of God, faith... is nourished in the hearts of believers. By this faith then the congregation of the faithful begins and grows.'[21] The proclamation does not stop with a teaching; it elicits the *response of faith* as consent and commitment, *143* directed at the covenant between God and his people. Once again it is the Holy Spirit who gives the grace of faith, strengthens it and makes it grow in the community. The liturgical assembly is first of all a communion in faith.

1103 *Anamnesis*. The liturgical celebration always refers to God's *1362* saving interventions in history. 'The economy of Revelation is realized by deeds and words which are intrinsically bound up with each other... [T]he words for their part proclaim the works, and bring to light the mystery they contain.'[22] In the Liturgy of the Word the Holy Spirit 'recalls' to the assembly all that Christ has done for us. In keeping with the nature of liturgical actions and the ritual traditions of the churches, the celebration 'makes a remembrance' of the marvellous works of God in an anamnesis which may be more or less developed. The Holy Spirit who thus awakens the memory of the Church then inspires thanksgiving and praise (*doxology*).

The Holy Spirit makes present the mystery of Christ

1104 Christian liturgy not only recalls the events that saved us but

---

[20] SC 24.
[21] PO 4.
[22] DV 2.

1085 actualizes them, makes them present. The Paschal mystery of Christ is celebrated, not repeated. It is the celebrations that are repeated, and in each celebration there is an outpouring of the Holy Spirit that makes the unique mystery present.

1105 The *Epiclesis* ('invocation upon') is the intercession in which
1153 the priest begs the Father to send the Holy Spirit, the Sanctifier, so that the offerings may become the body and blood of Christ and that the faithful, by receiving them, may themselves become a living offering to God.[23]

1106 Together with the anamnesis, the epiclesis is at the heart of each sacramental celebration, most especially of the Eucharist:

1375   You ask how the bread becomes the Body of Christ, and the wine... the Blood of Christ. I shall tell you: the Holy Spirit comes upon them and accomplishes what surpasses every word and thought... Let it be enough for you to understand that it is by the Holy Spirit, just as it was of the Holy Virgin and by the Holy Spirit that the Lord, through and in himself, took flesh.[24]

1107 The Holy Spirit's transforming power in the liturgy hastens
2816 the coming of the kingdom and the consummation of the mystery of salvation. While we wait in hope he causes us really to anticipate the fullness of communion with the Holy Trinity. Sent by the Father who hears the epiclesis of the Church, the Spirit gives life to those who accept him and is, even now, the 'guarantee' of their inheritance.[25]

The communion of the Holy Spirit

1108 In every liturgical action the Holy Spirit is sent in order to
788 bring us into communion with Christ and so to form his Body. The Holy Spirit is like the sap of the Father's vine which bears fruit on its branches.[26] The most intimate co-operation of the Holy
1091 Spirit and the Church is achieved in the liturgy. The Spirit, who is the Spirit of communion, abides indefectibly in the Church. For
775 this reason the Church is the great sacrament of divine communion which gathers God's scattered children together. Communion with the Holy Trinity and fraternal communion are inseparably the fruit of the Spirit in the liturgy.[27]

1109 The epiclesis is also a prayer for the full effect of the assembly's communion with the mystery of Christ. 'The grace of the Lord Jesus Christ and the love of God and the fellowship of the

---

[23] Cf. *Rom* 12:1.
[24] St John Damascene, *De fide orth.* 4, 13: PG 94, 1145A.
[25] Cf. *Eph* 1:14; 2 *Cor* 1:22.
[26] Cf. *Jn* 15:1–17; *Gal* 5:22.
[27] Cf. 1 *Jn* 1:3–7.

Holy Spirit'[28] have to remain with us always and bear fruit beyond the Eucharistic celebration. The Church therefore asks the Father to send the Holy Spirit to make the lives of the faithful a living sacrifice to God by their spiritual transformation into the image of Christ, by concern for the Church's unity, and by taking part in her mission through the witness and service of charity.

1368

IN BRIEF

1110 *In the liturgy of the Church, God the Father is blessed and adored as the source of all the blessings of creation and salvation with which he has blessed us in his Son, in order to give us the Spirit of filial adoption.*

1111 *Christ's work in the liturgy is sacramental: because his mystery of salvation is made present there by the power of his Holy Spirit; because his Body, which is the Church, is like a sacrament (sign and instrument) in which the Holy Spirit dispenses the mystery of salvation; and because through her liturgical actions the pilgrim Church already participates, as by a foretaste, in the heavenly liturgy.*

1112 *The mission of the Holy Spirit in the liturgy of the Church is to prepare the assembly to encounter Christ; to recall and manifest Christ to the faith of the assembly; to make the saving work of Christ present and active by his transforming power; and to make the gift of communion bear fruit in the Church.*

Article 2
THE PASCHAL MYSTERY IN THE CHURCH'S SACRAMENTS

1113 The whole liturgical life of the Church revolves around the Eucharistic sacrifice and the sacraments.[29] There are seven sacraments in the Church: Baptism, Confirmation or Chrismation, Eucharist, Penance, Anointing of the Sick, Holy Orders, and Matrimony.[30] This article will discuss what is common to the Church's seven sacraments from a doctrinal point of view. What is common to them in terms of their celebration will be presented in the second chapter, and what is distinctive about each will be the topic of *Section Two*.

1210

I. The Sacraments of Christ

1114 'Adhering to the teaching of the Holy Scriptures, to the

---

[28] 2 Cor 13:14.
[29] Cf. SC 6.
[30] Cf. Council of Lyons II (1274): DS

860; Council of Florence (1439): DS 1310; Council of Trent (1547): DS 1601.

apostolic traditions and to the consensus... of the Fathers', we profess that 'the sacraments of the new law were... all instituted by Jesus Christ our Lord.'[31]

1115 Jesus' words and actions during his hidden life and public ministry were already salvific, for they anticipated the power of his Paschal mystery. They announced and prepared what he was going to give the Church when all was accomplished. The mys-512–560 teries of Christ's life are the foundations of what he would hence-forth dispense in the sacraments, through the ministers of his Church, for 'what was visible in our Saviour has passed over into his mysteries.'[32]

1504 1116 Sacraments are 'powers that comes forth' from the Body of Christ,[33] which is ever-living and life-giving. They are actions of 774 the Holy Spirit at work in his Body, the Church. They are 'the masterworks of God' in the new and everlasting covenant.

II. The Sacraments of the Church

120 1117 As she has done for the canon of sacred Scripture and for the doctrine of the faith, the Church, by the power of the Spirit who guides her 'into all truth', has gradually recognized this treasure received from Christ and, as the faithful steward of God's mys-teries, has determined its 'dispensation'.[34] Thus the Church has discerned over the centuries that among liturgical celebrations there are seven that are, in the strict sense of the term, sacraments instituted by the Lord.

1118 The sacraments are 'of the Church' in the double sense that they are 'by her' and 'for her'. They are 'by the Church', for she is the sacrament of Christ's action at work in her through the mission 1396 of the Holy Spirit. They are 'for the Church' in the sense that 'the sacraments make the Church',[35] since they manifest and commu-nicate to men, above all in the Eucharist, the mystery of commu-nion with the God who is love, One in three persons.

1119 Forming 'as it were, one mystical person' with Christ the 792 head, the Church acts in the sacraments as 'an organically struc-tured priestly community'.[36] Through Baptism and Confirma-

---

[31] Council of Trent (1547): DS 1600–1601.
[32] St Leo the Great, Sermo 74, 2: PL 54, 398.
[33] Cf. Lk 5:17; 6:19; 8:46.
[34] Jn 16:13; cf. Mt 13:52; 1 Cor 4:1.

[35] St Augustine, De civ. Dei 22, 17: PL 41, 779; cf. St Thomas Aquinas, STh III, 64, 2, ad 3.
[36] LG 11; cf. Pius XII, Mystici Corporis (1943).

tion the priestly people is enabled to celebrate the liturgy, while those of the faithful 'who have received Holy Orders, are appointed to nourish the Church with the word and grace of God in the name of Christ.'[37]

1120 The ordained ministry or *ministerial* priesthood is at the *1547* service of the baptismal priesthood.[38] The ordained priesthood guarantees that it really is Christ who acts in the sacraments through the Holy Spirit for the Church. The saving mission entrusted by the Father to his incarnate Son was committed to the apostles and through them to their successors: they receive the Spirit of Jesus to act in his name and in his person.[39] The ordained minister is the sacramental bond that ties the liturgical action to what the apostles said and did and, through them, to the words and actions of Christ, the source and foundation of the sacraments.

1121 The three sacraments of Baptism, Confirmation and Holy Orders confer, in addition to grace, a sacramental *character* or 'seal' *1272, 1304,* by which the Christian shares in Christ's priesthood and is made a *1582* member of the Church according to different states and functions. This configuration to Christ and to the Church, brought about by the Spirit, is indelible;[40] it remains for ever in the Christian as a positive disposition for grace, a promise and guarantee of divine protection, and as a vocation to divine worship and to the service of the Church. Therefore these sacraments can never be repeated.

III. The Sacraments of Faith

1122 Christ sent his apostles so that 'repentance and forgiveness of sins should be preached in his name to all nations.'[41] 'Go therefore and make disciples of all nations, baptizing them in the name of the Father and of the Son and of the Holy Spirit.'[42] The mission to baptize, and so the sacramental mission, is implied in the mission to evangelize, because the sacrament is prepared for by *the word of* *849* *God and by the faith* which is assent to this word: *1236*

> The People of God is formed into one in the first place by the Word of the living God... The preaching of the Word is required for the sacramental ministry itself, since the sacraments are sacraments of faith, drawing their origin and nourishment from the Word.[43]

1123 'The purpose of the sacraments is to sanctify men, to build

---

[37] *LG* 11 § 2.
[38] Cf. *LG* 10 § 2.
[39] Cf. *Jn* 20:21–23; *Lk* 24:47; *Mt* 28:18–20.
[40] Cf. Council of Trent (1547): DS 1609.
[41] *Lk* 24:47.
[42] *Mt* 28:19.
[43] *PO* 4 §§ 1, 2.

up the Body of Christ and, finally, to give worship to God. Because they are signs they also instruct. They not only presuppose
1154 faith, but by words and objects they also nourish, strengthen, and
express it. That is why they are called "sacraments *of faith*".'[44]

166 1124 The Church's faith precedes the faith of the believer who is
invited to adhere to it. When the Church celebrates the sacra-
1327 ments, she confesses the faith received from the apostles – whence
the ancient saying: *lex orandi, lex credendi* (or: *legem credendi lex
statuat supplicandi*, according to Prosper of Aquitaine [5th cent.]).[45]
The law of prayer is the law of faith: the Church believes as she
prays. Liturgy is a constitutive element of the holy and living
78 Tradition.[46]

1205 1125 For this reason no sacramental rite may be modified or
manipulated at the will of the minister or the community. Even
the supreme authority in the Church may not change the liturgy
arbitrarily, but only in the obedience of faith and with religious
respect for the mystery of the liturgy.

1126 Likewise, since the sacraments express and develop the communion of faith in the Church, the *lex orandi* is one of the essential
815 criteria of the dialogue that seeks to restore the unity of Christians.[47]

IV. The Sacraments of Salvation

1127 Celebrated worthily in faith, the sacraments confer the grace
that they signify.[48] They are *efficacious* because in them Christ
1084 himself is at work: it is he who baptizes, he who acts in his sacraments in order to communicate the grace that each sacrament
signifies. The Father always hears the prayer of his Son's Church
1105 which, in the epiclesis of each sacrament, expresses her faith in the
696 power of the Spirit. As fire transforms into itself everything it
touches, so the Holy Spirit transforms into the divine life whatever
is subjected to his power.

1128 This is the meaning of the Church's affirmation[49] that the
sacraments act *ex opere operato* (literally: 'by the very fact of the
action's being performed'), i.e., by virtue of the saving work of
Christ, accomplished once for all. It follows that 'the sacrament is
1584 not wrought by the righteousness of either the celebrant or the
recipient, but by the power of God.'[50] From the moment that a

[44] SC 59.

[45] Prosper of Aquitaine, *Ep.* 8.

[46] Cf. *DV* 8.

[47] Cf. *UR* 2; 15.

[48] Cf. Council of Trent (1547): DS 1605;
DS 1606.

[49] Cf. Council of Trent (1547): DS 1608.

[50] St Thomas Aquinas, *STh* III, 68, 8.

sacrament is celebrated in accordance with the intention of the Church, the power of Christ and his Spirit acts in and through it, independently of the personal holiness of the minister. Nevertheless, the fruits of the sacraments also depend on the disposition of the one who receives them.

1129 The Church affirms that for believers the sacraments of the New Covenant are *necessary for salvation*.[51] 'Sacramental grace' is the grace of the Holy Spirit, given by Christ and proper to each sacrament. The Spirit heals and transforms those who receive him by conforming them to the Son of God. The fruit of the sacramental life is that the Spirit of adoption makes the faithful partakers in the divine nature[52] by uniting them in a living union with the only Son, the Saviour.

1257
2003

460

V. The Sacraments of Eternal Life

1130 The Church celebrates the mystery of her Lord 'until he comes', when God will be 'everything to everyone'.[53] Since the apostolic age the liturgy has been drawn toward its goal by the Spirit's groaning in the Church: *Marana tha!*[54] The liturgy thus shares in Jesus' desire: 'I have earnestly desired to eat this Passover with you... until it is fulfilled in the kingdom of God.'[55] In the sacraments of Christ the Church already receives the guarantee of her inheritance and even now shares in everlasting life, while 'awaiting our blessed hope, the appearing of the glory of our great God and Saviour Christ Jesus'.[56] The 'Spirit and the Bride say, "Come... Come, Lord Jesus!"'[57]

2817

950

> St Thomas sums up the various aspects of sacramental signs: 'Therefore a sacrament is a sign that commemorates what precedes it – Christ's Passion; demonstrates what is accomplished in us through Christ's Passion – grace; and prefigures what that Passion pledges to us – future glory.'[58]

IN BRIEF

1131 *The sacraments are efficacious signs of grace, instituted by Christ and entrusted to the Church, by which divine life is dispensed to us. The visible rites by which the sacraments are celebrated signify and make present the graces proper to each sacrament. They bear fruit in those who receive them with the required dispositions.*

---

[51] Cf. Council of Trent (1547): DS 1604.
[52] Cf. 2 *Pt* 1:4.
[53] 1 *Cor* 11:26; 15:28.
[54] 1 *Cor* 16:22.
[55] *Lk* 22:15.
[56] *Titus* 2:13.
[57] *Rev* 22:17, 20.
[58] St Thomas Aquinas, *STh* III, 60, 3.

> 1132 *The Church celebrates the sacraments as a priestly community struc-
> tured by the baptismal priesthood and the priesthood of ordained ministers.*
>
> 1133 *The Holy Spirit prepares the faithful for the sacraments by the Word
> of God and the faith which welcomes that word in well-disposed hearts. Thus
> the sacraments strengthen faith and express it.*
>
> 1134 *The fruit of sacramental life is both personal and ecclesial. For every
> one of the faithful on the one hand, this fruit is life for God in Christ Jesus; for
> the Church, on the other, it is an increase in charity and in her mission of
> witness.*

Chapter Two

THE SACRAMENTAL CELEBRATION OF THE PASCHAL MYSTERY

1135 The catechesis of the liturgy entails first of all an understanding of the sacramental economy (*Chapter One*). In this light, the
innovation of its *celebration* is revealed. This chapter will therefore
treat of the celebration of the sacraments of the Church. It will
consider that which, through the diversity of liturgical traditions,
is common to the celebration of the seven sacraments. What is
proper to each will be treated later. This fundamental catechesis on
the sacramental celebrations responds to the first questions posed
by the faithful regarding this subject:

– Who celebrates the liturgy?
– How is the liturgy celebrated?
– When is the liturgy celebrated?
– Where is the liturgy celebrated?

Article 1

CELEBRATING THE CHURCH'S LITURGY

I. Who Celebrates?

795   1136 Liturgy is an 'action' of the *whole Christ* (*Christus totus*).
Those who even now celebrate it without signs are already in the
1090 heavenly liturgy, where celebration is wholly communion and
feast.

2642 **The celebrants of the heavenly liturgy**

1137 The book of *Revelation* of St John, read in the Church's
liturgy, first reveals to us, 'A throne stood in heaven, with one
seated on the throne': 'the Lord God'.[1] It then shows the Lamb,

---

[1] *Rev* 4:2, 8; cf. *Is* 6:1; *Ezek* 1:26–28.

'standing, as though it had been slain': Christ crucified and risen, the one high priest of the true sanctuary, the same one 'who offers and is offered, who gives and is given'.[2] Finally it presents 'the river of the water of life... flowing from the throne of God and of the Lamb', one of most beautiful symbols of the Holy Spirit.[3]   662

1138 'Recapitulated in Christ', these are the ones who take part in the service of the praise of God and the fulfilment of his plan: the heavenly powers, all creation (the four living beings), the servants of the Old and New Covenants (the twenty-four elders), the new People of God (the one hundred and forty-four thousand),[4] especially the martyrs 'slain for the word of God', and the all-holy Mother of God (the Woman), the Bride of the Lamb,[5] and finally 'a great multitude which no one could number, from every nation, from all tribes and peoples and tongues'.[6]   335   1370

1139 It is in this eternal liturgy that the Spirit and the Church enable us to participate whenever we celebrate the mystery of salvation in the sacraments.

The celebrants of the sacramental liturgy

1140 It is the whole *community*, the Body of Christ united with its Head, that celebrates. 'Liturgical services are not private functions but are celebrations of the Church which is "the sacrament of unity", namely, the holy people united and organized under the authority of the bishops. Therefore, liturgical services pertain to the whole Body of the Church. They manifest it, and have effects upon it. But they touch individual members of the Church in different ways, depending on their orders, their role in the liturgical services, and their actual participation in them.'[7] For this reason, 'rites which are meant to be celebrated in common, with the faithful present and actively participating, should as far as possible be celebrated in that way rather than by an individual and quasi-privately.'[8]   752, 1348   1372

1141 The celebrating assembly is the community of the baptized who, 'by regeneration and the anointing of the Holy Spirit, are consecrated to be a spiritual house and a holy priesthood, that through all the works of Christian men they may offer spiritual   1120

---

[2] *Rev* 5:6; Liturgy of St John
  Chrysostom, Anaphora; cf. *Jn* 1:29;
  Heb 4:14–15; 10:19–21.
[3] *Rev* 22:1; cf. 21:6; *Jn* 4:10–14.
[4] Cf. *Rev* 4 – 5; 7:1–8; 14:1; *Is* 6:2–3.
[5] *Rev* 6:9–11; cf. 12; 21:9.

[6] *Rev* 7:9.
[7] *SC* 26.
[8] *SC* 27.
[9] *LG* 10; cf. 1 *Pt* 2:4–5.

sacrifices.'[9] This 'common priesthood' is that of Christ the sole priest, in which all his members participate:[10]

> Mother Church earnestly desires that all the faithful should be led to that full, conscious and active participation in liturgical celebrations which is demanded by the very nature of the liturgy, and to which the Christian people, 'a chosen race, a royal priesthood, a holy nation, a redeemed people', have a right and an obligation by reason of their Baptism.[11]

1268

1142 But 'the members do not all have the same function.'[12] Certain members are called by God, in and through the Church, to a special service of the community. These servants are chosen and consecrated by the sacrament of Holy Orders, by which the Holy Spirit enables them to act in the person of Christ the head, for the service of all the members of the Church.[13] The ordained minister is, as it were, an 'icon' of Christ the priest. Since it is in the Eucharist that the sacrament of the Church is made fully visible, it is in his presiding at the Eucharist that the bishop's ministry is most evident, as well as, in communion with him, the ministry of priests and deacons.

1549

1561

1143 For the purpose of assisting the work of the common priesthood of the faithful, other *particular ministries* also exist, not consecrated by the sacrament of Holy Orders; their functions are determined by the bishops, in accord with liturgical traditions and pastoral needs. 'Servers, readers, commentators, and members of the choir also exercise a genuine liturgical function.'[14]

903

1672

1144 In the celebration of the sacraments it is thus the whole assembly that is *leitourgos*, each according to his function, but in the 'unity of the Spirit' who acts in all. 'In liturgical celebrations each person, minister or layman, who has an office to perform, should carry out *all* and *only* those parts which pertain to his office by the nature of the rite and the norms of the liturgy.'[15]

II. How Is the Liturgy Celebrated?

1333–1340 Signs and symbols

1145 A sacramental celebration is woven from signs and symbols. In keeping with the divine pedagogy of salvation, their meaning is rooted in the work of creation and in human culture, specified by the events of the Old Covenant and fully revealed in the person and work of Christ.

53

---

[9] Cf. LG 10; 34; PO 2.
[10] SC 14; cf. 1 Pt 2:9; 2:4–5.
[11] Rom 12:4.
[13] Cf. PO 2; 15.
[14] SC 29.
[15] SC 28.

1146 *Signs of the human world*. In human life, signs and symbols 362
occupy an important place. As a being at once body and spirit, 2702
man expresses and perceives spiritual realities through physical
signs and symbols. As a social being, man needs signs and symbols
to communicate with others, through language, gestures, and 1879
actions. The same holds true for his relationship with God.

1147 God speaks to man through the visible creation. The material cosmos is so presented to man's intelligence that he can read
there traces of its Creator.[16] Light and darkness, wind and fire, 299
water and earth, the tree and its fruit speak of God and symbolize
both his greatness and his nearness.

1148 Inasmuch as they are creatures, these perceptible realities can
become means of expressing the action of God who sanctifies men,
and the action of men who offer worship to God. The same is true
of signs and symbols taken from the social life of man: washing
and anointing, breaking bread and sharing the cup can express the
sanctifying presence of God and man's gratitude toward his
Creator.

1149 The great religions of mankind witness, often impressively, 843
to this cosmic and symbolic meaning of religious rites. The liturgy
of the Church presupposes, integrates and sanctifies elements from
creation and human culture, conferring on them the dignity of
signs of grace, of the new creation in Jesus Christ.

1150 *Signs of the covenant*. The Chosen People received from God 1334
distinctive signs and symbols that marked its liturgical life. These
are no longer solely celebrations of cosmic cycles and social gestures, but signs of the covenant, symbols of God's mighty deeds
for his people. Among these liturgical signs from the Old Covenant are circumcision, anointing and consecration of kings and
priests, laying on of hands, sacrifices, and above all the Passover.
The Church sees in these signs a prefiguring of the sacraments of
the New Covenant.

1151 *Signs taken up by Christ*. In his preaching the Lord Jesus often 1335
makes use of the signs of creation to make known the mysteries of
the Kingdom of God.[17] He performs healings and illustrates his
preaching with physical signs or symbolic gestures.[18] He gives
new meaning to the deeds and signs of the Old Covenant, above

---

[16] Cf. *Wis* 13:1; *Rom* 1:19–20; *Acts* 14:17.
[17] Cf. *Lk* 8:10.
[18] Cf. *Jn* 9:6; *Mk* 7:33ff.; 8:22ff.

all to the Exodus and the Passover,[19] for he himself is the meaning of all these signs.

1152 *Sacramental signs*. Since Pentecost, it is through the sacramental signs of his Church that the Holy Spirit carries on the work of sanctification. The sacraments of the Church do not abolish but purify and integrate all the richness of the signs and symbols of the cosmos and of social life. Further, they fulfil the types and figures of the Old Covenant, signify and make actively present the salvation wrought by Christ, and prefigure and anticipate the glory of heaven.

Words and actions

1153 A sacramental celebration is a meeting of God's children with their Father, in Christ and the Holy Spirit; this meeting takes
53 the form of a dialogue, through actions and words. Admittedly, the symbolic actions are already a language, but the Word of God and the response of faith have to accompany and give life to them, so that the seed of the Kingdom can bear its fruit in good soil. The liturgical actions signify what the Word of God expresses: both his free initiative and his people's response of faith.

1100 1154 The *liturgy of the Word* is an integral part of sacramental celebrations. To nourish the faith of believers, the signs which accompany the Word of God should be emphasized: the book of
103 the Word (a lectionary or a book of the Gospels), its veneration (procession, incense, candles), the place of its proclamation (lectern or ambo), its audible and intelligible reading, the minister's homily which extends its proclamation, and the responses of the assembly (acclamations, meditation psalms, litanies and profession of faith).

1155 The liturgical word and action are inseparable both insofar as they are signs and instruction and insofar as they accomplish
1127 what they signify. When the Holy Spirit awakens faith, he not only gives an understanding of the Word of God, but through the sacraments also makes present the 'wonders' of God which it proclaims. The Spirit makes present and communicates the Father's work, fulfilled by the beloved Son.

Singing and music

1156 'The musical tradition of the universal Church is a treasure of inestimable value, greater even than that of any other art. The

---

[19] Cf. *Lk* 9:31; 22:7-20.

main reason for this pre-eminence is that, as a combination of sacred music and words, it forms a necessary or integral part of solemn liturgy.'[20] The composition and singing of inspired psalms, often accompanied by musical instruments, were already closely linked to the liturgical celebrations of the Old Covenant. The Church continues and develops this tradition: 'Address. . . one another in psalms and hymns and spiritual songs, singing and making melody to the Lord with all your heart.' 'He who sings prays twice.'[21]

1157 Song and music fulfil their function as signs in a manner all the more significant when they are 'more closely connected. . . with the liturgical action',[22] according to three principal criteria: beauty expressive of prayer, the unanimous participation of the assembly at the designated moments, and the solemn character of the celebration. In this way they participate in the purpose of the liturgical words and actions: the glory of God and the sanctification of the faithful:[23]   2502

> How I wept, deeply moved by your hymns, songs and the voices that echoed through your Church! What emotion I experienced in them! Those sounds flowed into my ears, distilling the truth in my heart. A feeling of devotion surged within me, and tears streamed down my face − tears that did me good.[24]

1158 The harmony of signs (song, music, words and actions) is all the more expressive and fruitful when expressed in the *cultural richness* of the People of God who celebrate.[25] Hence 'religious singing by the faithful is to be intelligently fostered so that in devotions and sacred exercises as well as in liturgical services', in conformity with the Church's norms, 'the voices of the faithful may be heard.' But 'the texts intended to be sung must always be in conformity with Catholic doctrine. Indeed they should be drawn chiefly from the sacred Scripture and from liturgical sources.'[26]   1201

1674

Holy images

1159 The sacred image, the liturgical icon, principally represents *Christ*. It cannot represent the invisible and incomprehensible God, but the incarnation of the Son of God has ushered in a new 'economy' of images: 476–477, 2129–2132

---

[20] SC 112.
[21] *Eph* 5:19; St Augustine, *En. in Ps.* 72, 1: PL 36, 914; cf. *Col* 3:16.
[22] SC 112 § 3.
[23] Cf. SC 112.

[24] St Augustine, *Conf.* 9, 6, 14: PL 32, 769–770.
[25] Cf. SC 119.
[26] SC 118; 121.

Previously God, who has neither a body nor a face, absolutely could not be represented by an image. But now that he has made himself visible in the flesh and has lived with men, I can make an image of what I have seen of God... and contemplate the glory of the Lord, his face unveiled.[27]

1160 Christian iconography expresses in images the same Gospel message that Scripture communicates by words. Image and word illuminate each other:

We declare that we preserve intact all the written and unwritten traditions of the Church which have been entrusted to us. One of these traditions consists in the production of representational artwork, which accords with the history of the preaching of the Gospel. For it confirms that the incarnation of the Word of God was real and not imaginary, and to our benefit as well, for realities that illustrate each other undoubtedly reflect each other's meaning.[28]

1161 All the signs in the liturgical celebrations are related to Christ: as are sacred images of the holy Mother of God and of the saints as well. They truly signify Christ, who is glorified in them. They make manifest the 'cloud of witnesses'[29] who continue to participate in the salvation of the world and to whom we are united, above all in sacramental celebrations. Through their icons, it is man 'in the image of God', finally transfigured 'into his likeness',[30] who is revealed to our faith. So too are the angels, who also are recapitulated in Christ:

Following the divinely inspired teaching of our holy Fathers and the tradition of the Catholic Church (for we know that this tradition comes from the Holy Spirit who dwells in her) we rightly define with full certainty and correctness that, like the figure of the precious and life-giving cross, venerable and holy images of our Lord and God and Saviour, Jesus Christ, our inviolate Lady, the holy Mother of God, and the venerated angels, all the saints and the just, whether painted or made of mosaic or another suitable material, are to be exhibited in the holy churches of God, on sacred vessels and vestments, walls and panels, in houses and on streets.[31]

2502 1162 'The beauty of the images moves me to contemplation, as a meadow delights the eyes and subtly infuses the soul with the glory of God.'[32] Similarly, the contemplation of sacred icons, united with meditation on the Word of God and the singing of liturgical hymns, enters into the harmony of the signs of celebration so that the mystery celebrated is imprinted in the heart's memory and is then expressed in the new life of the faithful.

---

[27] St John Damascene, De imag. 1, 16: PG 96: 1245A.
[28] Council of Nicaea II (787): COD 111.
[29] Heb 12:1.

[30] Cf. Rom 8:29; 1 Jn 3:2.
[31] Council of Nicaea II: DS 600.
[32] St John Damascene, De imag. 1, 27: PG 94, 1268A-B.

III. When Is the Liturgy Celebrated?

Liturgical seasons

1163 'Holy Mother Church believes that she should celebrate the saving work of her divine Spouse in a sacred commemoration on certain days throughout the course of the year. Once each week, on the day which she has called the Lord's Day, she keeps the memory of the Lord's resurrection. She also celebrates it once every year, together with his blessed Passion, at Easter, that most solemn of all feasts. In the course of the year, moreover, she unfolds the whole mystery of Christ... Thus recalling the mysteries of the redemption, she opens up to the faithful the riches of her Lord's powers and merits, so that these are in some way made present in every age; the faithful lay hold of them and are filled with saving grace.'[33]

512

1164 From the time of the Mosaic law, the People of God have observed fixed feasts, beginning with Passover, to commemorate the astonishing actions of the Saviour God, to give him thanks for them, to perpetuate their remembrance and to teach new generations to conform their conduct to them. In the age of the Church, between the Passover of Christ already accomplished once for all, and its consummation in the kingdom of God, the liturgy celebrated on fixed days bears the imprint of the newness of the mystery of Christ.

1165 'When the Church celebrates the mystery of Christ, there is a word that marks her prayer: 'Today!' – a word echoing the prayer her Lord taught her and the call of the Holy Spirit.[34] This 'today' of the living God which man is called to enter is 'the hour' of Jesus' Passover, which reaches across and underlies all history:

2659, 2836

1085

> Life extends over all beings and fills them with unlimited light; the Orient of orients pervades the universe, and he who was 'before the daystar' and before the heavenly bodies, immortal and vast, the great Christ, shines over all beings more brightly than the sun. Therefore a day of long, eternal light is ushered in for us who believe in him, a day which is never blotted out: the mystical Passover.[35]

The Lord's Day

2174–2188

1166 'By a tradition handed down from the apostles which took its origin from the very day of Christ's Resurrection, the Church celebrates the Paschal mystery every seventh day, which day is

---

[33] SC 102.
[34] Cf. *Mt* 6:11; *Heb* 3:7 – 4:11; *Ps* 95:7.
[35] Ps.-Hippolytus, *De pasch.* 1–2: SCh 27, 117.

1343 appropriately called the Lord's Day or Sunday.'[36] The day of Christ's Resurrection is both the first day of the week, the memorial of the first day of creation, and the 'eighth day', on which Christ after his 'rest' on the great sabbath inaugurates the 'day that the Lord has made', the 'day that knows no evening'.[37] The Lord's Supper is its centre, for there the whole community of the faithful encounters the risen Lord who invites them to his banquet:[38]

> The Lord's day, the day of Resurrection, the day of Christians, is our day. It is called the Lord's day because on it the Lord rose victorious to the Father. If pagans call it the 'day of the sun', we willingly agree, for today the light of the world is raised, today is revealed the sun of justice with healing in his rays.[39]

1167 Sunday is the pre-eminent day for the liturgical assembly, when the faithful gather 'to listen to the word of God and take part in the Eucharist, thus calling to mind the Passion, Resurrection, and glory of the Lord Jesus, and giving thanks to God who "has begotten them again, by the resurrection of Jesus Christ from the dead" unto a living hope':[40]

> When we ponder, O Christ, the marvels accomplished on this day, the Sunday of your holy resurrection, we say: 'Blessed is Sunday, for on it began creation... the world's salvation... the renewal of the human race... On Sunday heaven and earth rejoiced and the whole universe was filled with light. Blessed is Sunday, for on it were opened the gates of paradise so that Adam and all the exiles might enter it without fear.'[41]

The liturgical year

1168 Beginning with the Easter Triduum as its source of light, the
2698 new age of the Resurrection fills the whole liturgical year with its brilliance. Gradually, on either side of this source, the year is transfigured by the liturgy. It really is a 'year of the Lord's favour'.[42] The economy of salvation is at work within the framework of time, but since its fulfilment in the Passover of Jesus and the outpouring of the Holy Spirit, the culmination of history is anticipated 'as a foretaste', and the kingdom of God enters into our time.

1169 Therefore *Easter* is not simply one feast among others, but the 'Feast of feasts', the 'Solemnity of solemnities', just as the
1330 Eucharist is the 'Sacrament of sacraments' (the Great Sacrament).

---

[36] *SC* 106.
[37] Byzantine Liturgy.
[38] Cf. *Jn* 21:12; *Lk* 24:30.
[39] St Jerome, *Pasch.*: CCL 78, 550.

[40] *SC* 106.
[41] Fanqîth, Syriac Office of Antioch, vol. VI, first part of summer, 193B.
[42] *Lk* 4:19.

Madonna and Child by Sir Jacob Epstein.

The outstretched arms of the infant Jesus and the supporting gesture of Mary holding the child forth to the world indicate the openness to the world, and service within the world, which are central to the Church's mission. The teaching of the Second Vatican Council calls the Church to a renewed and deeper relationship with the world, in faithfulness to Christ.

The statue was presented to the Society of the Holy Child Jesus, and was placed outside their teaching training college in London. The building later housed Heythrop College, a Jesuit college. In their time both colleges gave a theological and secular education to many lay people and to those preparing for the priesthood and the religious life.

Reproduced by kind permission of the Society of the Holy Child Jesus.

St Athanasius calls Easter 'the Great Sunday'[43] and the Eastern
Churches call Holy Week 'the Great Week'. The mystery of the 560
Resurrection, in which Christ crushed death, permeates with its
powerful energy our old time, until all is subjected to him.

1170 At the Council of Nicaea in 325, all the Churches agreed that Easter,
the Christian Passover, should be celebrated on the Sunday following the first
full moon (14 Nisan) after the vernal equinox. Because of different methods
of calculating the 14th day of the month of Nisan, the date of Easter in the
Western and Eastern Churches is not always the same. For this reason, the
Churches are currently seeking an agreement in order once again to celebrate
the date of the Lord's Resurrection on a common date.

1171 In the liturgical year the various aspects of the one Paschal
mystery unfold. This is also the case with the cycle of feasts surrounding the mystery of the incarnation (Annunciation, Christmas, Epiphany). They commemorate the beginning of our 524
salvation and communicate to us the first fruits of the Paschal
mystery.

The sanctoral in the liturgical year

1172 'In celebrating this annual cycle of the mysteries of Christ,
Holy Church honours the Blessed Mary, Mother of God, with a 971
special love. She is inseparably linked with the saving work of her
Son. In her the Church admires and exalts the most excellent fruit 2030
of redemption, and joyfully contemplates, as in a faultless image,
that which she herself desires and hopes wholly to be.'[44]

1173 When the Church keeps the memorials of martyrs and other 957
saints during the annual cycle, she proclaims the Paschal mystery
in those 'who have suffered and have been glorified with Christ.
She proposes them to the faithful as examples who draw all men to
the Father through Christ, and through their merits she begs for
God's favours.'[45]

The Liturgy of the Hours

1174 The mystery of Christ, his Incarnation and Passover, which
we celebrate in the Eucharist especially at the Sunday assembly,
permeates and transfigures the time of each day, through the celebration of the Liturgy of the Hours, 'the divine office'.[46] This 2698
celebration, faithful to the apostolic exhortations to 'pray constantly', is 'so devised that the whole course of the day and night is
made holy by the praise of God'.[47] In this 'public prayer of the

---

[43] St Athanasius, *Ep. fest.* 1: PG 26, 1366A. [46] Cf. *SC*, ch. IV, 83–101.
[44] *SC* 103. [47] *SC* 84; 1 *Th* 5:17; *Eph* 6:18.
[45] *SC* 104; cf. *SC* 108, 111.

Church',[48] the faithful (clergy, religious and lay people) exercise the royal priesthood of the baptized. Celebrated in 'the form approved' by the Church, the Liturgy of the Hours 'is truly the voice of the Bride herself addressed to her Bridegroom. It is the very prayer which Christ himself together with his Body addresses to the Father.'[49]

1175 The Liturgy of the Hours is intended to become the prayer of the whole People of God. In it Christ himself 'continues his priestly work through his Church.'[50] His members participate according to their own place in the Church and the circumstances of their lives: priests devoted to the pastoral ministry, because they are called to remain diligent in prayer and the service of the word; religious, by the charism of their consecrated lives; all the faithful as much as possible: 'Pastors of souls should see to it that the principal hours, especially Vespers, are celebrated in common in church on Sundays and on the more solemn feasts. The laity, too, are encouraged to recite the divine office, either with the priests, or among themselves, or even individually.'[51]

1176 The celebration of the Liturgy of the Hours demands not
2700 only harmonizing the voice with the praying heart, but also a deeper 'understanding of the liturgy and of the Bible, especially of the Psalms'.[52]

1177 The hymns and litanies of the Liturgy of the Hours integrate
2586 the prayer of the psalms into the age of the Church, expressing the symbolism of the time of day, the liturgical season or the feast being celebrated. Moreover, the reading from the Word of God at each Hour (with the subsequent responses or *troparia*) and readings from the Fathers and spiritual masters at certain Hours, reveal more deeply the meaning of the mystery being celebrated, assist in understanding the psalms, and prepare for silent prayer. The *lectio divina*, where the Word of God is so read and meditated that it becomes prayer, is thus rooted in the liturgical celebration.

1178 The Liturgy of the Hours, which is like an extension of the Eucharistic celebration, does not exclude but rather in a complementary way calls forth the various devotions of the People of
1378 God, especially adoration and worship of the Blessed Sacrament.

IV. Where Is the Liturgy Celebrated?

1179 The worship 'in Spirit and in truth'[53] of the New Covenant is not tied exclusively to any one place. The whole earth is sacred and entrusted to the children of men. What matters above all is

---

[48] *SC* 98.
[49] *SC* 84.
[50] *SC* 83.

[51] *SC* 100; cf. 86; 96; 98; *PO* 5.
[52] *SC* 90.
[53] *Jn* 4:24.

that, when the faithful assemble in the same place, they are the 'living stones', gathered to be 'built into a spiritual house'.[54] For the Body of the risen Christ is the spiritual temple from which the source of living water springs forth: incorporated into Christ by the Holy Spirit, 'we are the temple of the living God.'[55]

586

1180 When the exercise of religious liberty is not thwarted,[56] Christians construct buildings for divine worship. These visible churches are not simply gathering places but signify and make visible the Church living in this place, the dwelling of God with men reconciled and united in Christ.

2106

1181 A church, 'a house of prayer in which the Eucharist is cele- brated and reserved, where the faithful assemble, and where is worshipped the presence of the Son of God our Saviour, offered for us on the sacrificial altar for the help and consolation of the faithful – this house ought to be in good taste and a worthy place for prayer and sacred ceremonial.'[57] In this 'house of God' the truth and the harmony of the signs that make it up should show Christ to be present and active in this place.[58]

2691

1182 The *altar* of the New Covenant is the Lord's Cross,[59] from which the sacraments of the Paschal mystery flow. On the altar, which is the centre of the church, the sacrifice of the Cross is made present under sacramental signs. The altar is also the table of the Lord, to which the People of God are invited.[60] In certain Eastern liturgies, the altar is also the symbol of the tomb (Christ truly died and is truly risen).

617, 1383

1183 The *tabernacle* is to be situated 'in churches in a most worthy place with the greatest honour'.[61] The dignity, placing and security of the Eucharistic tabernacle should foster adoration before the Lord really present in the Blessed Sacrament of the altar.[62]

1379

2120

The *sacred chrism (myron)*, used in anointings as the sacramental sign of the seal of the gift of the Holy Spirit, is traditionally reserved and venerated in a secure place in the sanctuary. The oil of catechumens and the oil of the sick may also be placed there.

1241

1184 The *chair* of the bishop *(cathedra)* or that of the priest 'should express his office of presiding over the assembly and of directing prayer.'[63]

1348

The *lectern (ambo)*: 'The dignity of the Word of God requires the church to have a suitable place for announcing his message so that the attention of the people may be easily directed to that place during the liturgy of the Word.'[64]

103

[54] 1 Pt 2:4–5.
[55] 2 Cor 6:16.
[56] Cf. DH 4.
[57] PO 5; cf. SC 122–127
[57a] CIC, can. 861 § 2.
[58] Cf. 1 Tim 2:4.
[59] Cf. Jn 3:5.

[60] Cf. Mt 28:19–20; cf. Council of Trent (1547): DS 1618; LG 14; AG 5.
[61] Cf. Mk 16:16.
[62] GS 22 § 5; cf. LG 16; AG 7.
[63] GIRM 271.
[64] GIRM 272.

1185   The gathering of the People of God begins with Baptism; a church must have a place for the celebration of *Baptism* (baptistery) and for fostering remembrance of the baptismal promises (holy water font).

The renewal of the baptismal life requires *penance.* A church, then, must lend itself to the expression of repentance and the reception of forgiveness, which requires an appropriate place to receive penitents.

2717   A church must also be a space that invites us to the recollection and silent prayer that extend and internalize the great prayer of the Eucharist.

1186 Finally, the church has an eschatological significance. To
1130 enter into the house of God, we must cross a *threshold,* which symbolizes passing from the world wounded by sin to the world of the new Life to which all men are called. The visible church is a symbol of the Father's house toward which the People of God is journeying and where the Father 'will wipe every tear from their eyes.'[65] Also for this reason, the church is the house of *all* God's children, open and welcoming.

IN BRIEF

1187   *The liturgy is the work of the whole Christ, head and body. Our high priest celebrates it unceasingly in the heavenly liturgy, with the holy Mother of God, the apostles, all the saints and the multitude of those who have already entered the kingdom.*

1188   *In a liturgical celebration, the whole assembly is 'leitourgos', each member according to his own function. The baptismal priesthood is that of the whole Body of Christ. But some of the faithful are ordained through the sacrament of Holy Orders to represent Christ as head of the Body.*

1189   *The liturgical celebration involves signs and symbols relating to creation (candles, water, fire), human life (washing, anointing, breaking bread) and the history of salvation (the rites of the Passover). Integrated into the world of faith and taken up by the power of the Holy Spirit, these cosmic elements, human rituals, and gestures of remembrance of God become bearers of the saving and sanctifying action of Christ.*

1190   *The Liturgy of the Word is an integral part of the celebration. The meaning of the celebration is expressed by the Word of God which is proclaimed and by the response of faith to it.*

1191   *Song and music are closely connected with the liturgical action. The criteria for their proper use are the beauty expressive of prayer, the unanimous participation of the assembly, and the sacred character of the celebration.*

---

[65] *Rev* 21:4.

1192 Sacred images in our churches and homes are intended to awaken and nourish our faith in the mystery of Christ. Through the icon of Christ and his works of salvation it is he whom we adore. Through sacred images of the holy Mother of God, of the angels and of the saints, we venerate the persons represented.

1193 Sunday, the 'Lord's Day', is the principal day for the celebration of the Eucharist because it is the day of the Resurrection. It is the pre-eminent day of the liturgical assembly, the day of the Christian family, and the day of joy and rest from work. Sunday is 'the foundation and kernel of the whole liturgical year' (SC 106).

1194 The Church, 'in the course of the year,... unfolds the whole mystery of Christ from his Incarnation and Nativity through his Ascension, to Pentecost and the expectation of the blessed hope of the coming of the Lord' (SC 102 §2).

1195 By keeping the memorials of the saints – first of all the holy Mother of God, then the apostles, the martyrs and other saints – on fixed days of the liturgical year, the Church on earth shows that she is united with the liturgy of heaven. She gives glory to Christ for having accomplished his salvation in his glorified members; their example encourages her on her way to the Father.

1196 The faithful who celebrate the Liturgy of the Hours are united to Christ our high priest, by the prayer of the Psalms, meditation on the Word of God, and canticles and blessings, in order to be joined with his unceasing and universal prayer that gives glory to the Father and implores the gift of the Holy Spirit on the whole world.

1197 Christ is the true temple of God, 'the place where his glory dwells'; by the grace of God, Christians also become temples of the Holy Spirit, living stones out of which the Church is built.

1198 In her earthly state the Church needs places where the community can gather together. Our visible churches, holy places, are images of the holy city, the heavenly Jerusalem, towards which we are making our way on pilgrimage.

1199 It is in these churches that the Church celebrates public worship to the glory of the Holy Trinity, hears the word of God and sings his praise, lifts up her prayer, and offers the sacrifice of Christ sacramentally present in the midst of the assembly. These churches are also places of recollection and personal prayer.

Article 2

LITURGICAL DIVERSITY AND THE UNITY OF THE MYSTERY

Liturgical traditions and the catholicity of the Church

1200 From the first community of Jerusalem until the Parousia, it is the same Paschal mystery that the Churches of God, faithful to the apostolic faith, celebrate in every place. The mystery celebra-2625 ted in the liturgy is one, but the forms of its celebration are diverse.

1201 The mystery of Christ is so unfathomably rich that it cannot 2663 be exhausted by its expression in any single liturgical tradition. The history of the blossoming and development of these rites witnesses to a remarkable complementarity. When the Churches 1158 lived their respective liturgical traditions in the communion of the faith and the sacraments of the faith, they enriched one another and grew in fidelity to Tradition and to the common mission of the whole Church.[66]

814 1202 The diverse liturgical traditions have arisen by very reason of the Church's mission. Churches of the same geographical and cultural area came to celebrate the mystery of Christ through particular expressions characterized by the culture: in the tradition 1674 of the 'deposit of faith',[67] in liturgical symbolism, in the organi-zation of fraternal communion, in the theological understanding of the mysteries, and in various forms of holiness. Through the liturgical life of a local Church, Christ, the light and salvation of all peoples, is made manifest to the particular people and culture to which that Church is sent and in which she is rooted. The Church 835 is catholic, capable of integrating into her unity, while purifying 1937 them, all the authentic riches of cultures.[68]

1203 The liturgical traditions or rites presently in use in the Church are the Latin (principally the Roman rite, but also the rites of certain local Churches, such as the Ambrosian rite, or those of certain religious orders) and the By-zantine, Alexandrian or Coptic, Syriac, Armenian, Maronite and Chaldean rites. In 'faithful obedience to tradition, the sacred Council declares that Holy Mother Church holds all lawfully recognized rites to be of equal right and dignity, and that she wishes to preserve them in the future and to foster them in every way.'[69]

Liturgy and culture

1204 The celebration of the liturgy, therefore, should correspond 2684 to the genius and culture of the different peoples.[70] In order that the mystery of Christ be 'made known to all the nations... to bring about the obedience of faith',[71] it must be proclaimed, cele-854, 1232 brated and lived in all cultures in such a way that they themselves are not abolished by it, but redeemed and fulfilled.[72] It is with and

---

[66] Cf. Paul VI, EN 63–64.
[67] 2 Tim 1:14 (Vulg.).
[68] Cf. LG 23; UR 4.
[69] SC 4.

[70] Cf. SC 37–40.
[71] Rom 16:26.
[72] Cf. CT 53.

through their own human culture, assumed and transfigured by 2527
Christ, that the multitude of God's children has access to the
Father, in order to glorify him in the one Spirit.

1205 'In the liturgy, above all that of the sacraments, there is an
immutable part, a part that is divinely instituted and of which the 1125
Church is the guardian, and parts that *can be changed*, which the
Church has the power and on occasion also the duty to adapt to the
cultures of recently evangelized peoples.'[73]

1206 'Liturgical diversity can be a source of enrichment, but it can
also provoke tensions, mutual misunderstandings and even
schisms. In this matter it is clear that diversity must not damage
unity. It must express only fidelity to the common faith, to the
sacramental signs that the Church has received from Christ, and to
hierarchical communion. Cultural adaptation also requires a conversion of heart and even, where necessary, a breaking with ances-
tral customs incompatible with the Catholic faith.'[74]

IN BRIEF

1207 It is fitting that liturgical celebration tends to express itself in the culture
of the people where the Church finds herself, though without being submissive to it. Moreover, the liturgy itself generates cultures and shapes them.

1208 The diverse liturgical traditions or rites, legitimately recognized,
manifest the catholicity of the Church, because they signify and communicate
the same mystery of Christ.

1209 The criterion that assures unity amid the diversity of liturgical traditions is fidelity to apostolic Tradition, i.e., the communion in the faith and the
sacraments received from the apostles, a communion that is both signified and
guaranteed by apostolic succession.

---

[73] John Paul II, *Vicesimus quintus annus* 16;
cf. SC 21.
[74] John Paul II, *Vicesimus quintus annus* 16.

Section Two

THE SEVEN SACRAMENTS OF THE CHURCH

1113   1210 Christ instituted the sacraments of the new law. There are seven: Baptism, Confirmation (or Chrismation), the Eucharist, Penance, the Anointing of the Sick, Holy Orders and Matrimony. The seven sacraments touch all the stages and all the important moments of Christian life:[1] they give birth and increase, healing and mission to the Christian's life of faith. There is thus a certain resemblance between the stages of natural life and the stages of the spiritual life.

1211 Following this analogy, the *first chapter* will expound the three sacraments of Christian initiation; the *second*, the sacraments of healing; and the *third*, the sacraments at the service of communion and the mission of the faithful. This order, while not the only one possible, does allow one to see that the sacraments form an organic whole in which each particular sacrament has its own vital place. In this organic whole, the Eucharist occupies a unique place

1374   as the 'Sacrament of sacraments': 'all the other sacraments are ordered to it as to their end.'[2]

Chapter One

THE SACRAMENTS OF CHRISTIAN INITIATION

1212 The sacraments of Christian initiation – Baptism, Confirmation and the Eucharist – lay the *foundations* of every Christian life. 'The sharing in the divine nature given to men through the grace of Christ bears a certain likeness to the origin, development and nourishing of natural life. The faithful are born anew by Baptism, strengthened by the sacrament of Confirmation, and receive in the Eucharist the food of eternal life. By means of these sacraments of Christian initiation, they thus receive in increasing measure the treasures of the divine life and advance toward the perfection of charity.'[3]

Article 1

THE SACRAMENT OF BAPTISM

1213 Holy Baptism is the basis of the whole Christian life, the

---

[1] Cf. St Thomas Aquinas, *STh* III, 65, 1.

[2] St Thomas Aquinas, *STh* III, 65, 3.

[3] Paul VI, Ap. Const. *Divinae consortium naturae*: AAS 63 (1971), 657; cf. RCIA, Introduction 1–2.

gateway to life in the Spirit (*vitae spiritualis ianua*),[4] and the door which gives access to the other sacraments. Through Baptism we are freed from sin and reborn as sons of God; we become members of Christ, are incorporated into the Church and made sharers in her mission: 'Baptism is the sacrament of regeneration through water in the word.'[5]

I. What Is This Sacrament Called?

1214 This sacrament is called *Baptism*, after the central rite by which it is carried out: to baptize (Greek *baptizein*) means to 'plunge' or 'immerse'; the 'plunge' into the water symbolizes the catechumen's burial into Christ's death, from which he rises up by resurrection with him, as 'a new creature'.[6]

628

1215 This sacrament is also called '*the washing of regeneration and renewal by the Holy Spirit*', for it signifies and actually brings about the birth of water and the Spirit without which no one 'can enter the kingdom of God'.[7]

1257

1216 'This bath is called *enlightenment*, because those who receive this [catechetical] instruction are enlightened in their understanding...'[8] Having received in Baptism the Word, 'the true light that enlightens every man', the person baptized has been 'enlightened', he becomes a 'son of light', indeed, he becomes 'light' himself:[9]

1243

> Baptism is God's most beautiful and magnificent gift... We call it gift, grace, anointing, enlightenment, garment of immortality, bath of rebirth, seal and most precious gift. It is called *gift* because it is conferred on those who bring nothing of their own; *grace* since it is given even to the guilty; *Baptism* because sin is buried in the water; *anointing* for it is priestly and royal as are those who are anointed; *enlightenment* because it radiates light; *clothing* since it veils our shame; *bath* because it washes; and *seal* as it is our guard and the sign of God's Lordship.[10]

II. Baptism in the Economy of Salvation

Prefigurations of Baptism in the Old Covenant

1217 In the liturgy of the Easter Vigil, during the *blessing of the baptismal water*, the Church solemnly commemorates the great

---

[4] Cf. Council of Florence: DS 1314: *vitae spiritualis ianua*.
[5] *Roman Catechism* II, 2, 5; cf. Council of Florence: DS 1314; CIC, cann. 204 § 1; 849; CCEO, can. 675 § 1.
[6] 2 *Cor* 5:17; *Gal* 6:15; cf. *Rom* 6:3–4; *Col* 2:12.

[7] *Titus* 3:5; *Jn* 3:5.
[8] St Justin, *Apol.* 1, 61, 12: PG 6, 421.
[9] *Jn* 1:9; 1 *Th* 5:5; *Heb* 10:32; *Eph* 5:8.
[10] St Gregory of Nazianzus, *Oratio* 40, 3–4: PG 36, 361C.

events in salvation history that already prefigured the mystery of Baptism:

> Father, you give us grace through sacramental signs,
>   which tell us of the wonders of your unseen power.

> In Baptism we use your gift of water,
>   which you have made a rich symbol
>   of the grace you give us in this sacrament.[11]

344
694
1218 Since the beginning of the world, water, so humble and wonderful a creature, has been the source of life and fruitfulness. Sacred Scripture sees it as 'overshadowed' by the Spirit of God:[12]

> At the very dawn of creation
>   your Spirit breathed on the waters,
>   making them the wellspring of all holiness.[13]

701, 845
1219 The Church has seen in Noah's ark a prefiguring of salvation by Baptism, for by it 'a few, that is, eight persons, were saved through water':[14]

> The waters of the great flood
>   you made a sign of the waters of Baptism,
>   that make an end of sin and a new beginning of goodness.[15]

1220 If water springing up from the earth symbolizes life, the water of the sea is a symbol of death and so can represent the mystery of the cross. By this symbolism Baptism signifies communion with Christ's death.

1010

1221 But above all, the crossing of the Red Sea, literally the liberation of Israel from the slavery of Egypt, announces the liberation wrought by Baptism:

> You freed the children of Abraham from the slavery of Pharaoh,
>   bringing them dry-shod through the waters of the Red Sea,
>   to be an image of the people set free in Baptism.[16]

1222 Finally, Baptism is prefigured in the crossing of the Jordan River by which the People of God received the gift of the land promised to Abraham's descendants, an image of eternal life. The promise of this blessed inheritance is fulfilled in the New Covenant.

Christ's Baptism

1223 All the Old Covenant prefigurations find their fulfilment in

---

[11] *Roman Missal*, Easter Vigil 42: Blessing of Water.

[12] Cf. *Gen* 1:2.

[13] *Roman Missal*, Easter Vigil 42: Blessing of Water.

[14] I *Pt* 3:20.

[15] *Roman Missal*, Easter Vigil 42:

Blessing of Water.

[16] *Missale Romanum*, Easter Vigil 42: Blessing of Water: *Abrahae filios per mare Rubrum sicco vestigio transire fecisti, ut plebs, a Pharaonis servitute liberata, populum baptizatorum praefiguraret.*

Christ Jesus. He begins his public life after having himself baptized
by St John the Baptist in the Jordan.[17] After his resurrection Christ
gives this mission to his apostles: 'Go therefore and make disciples
of all nations, baptizing them in the name of the Father and of the   *232*
Son and of the Holy Spirit, teaching them to observe all that I have
commanded you.'[18]

1224 Our Lord voluntarily submitted himself to the baptism of St   *536*
John, intended for sinners, in order to 'fulfil all righteousness'.[19]
Jesus' gesture is a manifestation of his self-emptying.[20] The Spirit
who had hovered over the waters of the first creation descended
then on the Christ as a prelude of the new creation, and the Father
revealed Jesus as his 'beloved Son'.[21]

1225 In his Passover Christ opened to all men the fountain of
Baptism. He had already spoken of his Passion, which he was
about to suffer in Jerusalem, as a 'Baptism' with which he had to be
baptized.[22] The blood and water that flowed from the pierced side   *766*
of the crucified Jesus are types of Baptism and the Eucharist, the
sacraments of new life.[23] From then on, it is possible 'to be born of
water and the Spirit'[24] in order to enter the Kingdom of God.

> See where you are baptized, see where Baptism comes from, if not from
> the cross of Christ, from his death. There is the whole mystery: he died
> for you. In him you are redeemed, in him you are saved.[25]

Baptism in the Church

1226 From the very day of Pentecost the Church has celebrated
and administered holy Baptism. Indeed St Peter declares to the
crowd astounded by his preaching: 'Repent, and be baptized every   *849*
one of you in the name of Jesus Christ for the forgiveness of your
sins; and you shall receive the gift of the Holy Spirit.'[26] The
apostles and their collaborators offer Baptism to anyone who
believes in Jesus: Jews, the God-fearing, pagans.[27] Always, Baptism is seen as connected with faith: 'Believe in the Lord Jesus, and
you will be saved, you and your household', St Paul declares to his
jailer in Philippi. And, the narrative continues, the jailer 'was
baptized at once, with all his family.'[28]

1227 According to the Apostle Paul, the believer enters through   *790*

---

[17] Cf. *Mt* 3:13.
[18] *Mt* 28:19–20; cf. *Mk* 16:15–16.
[19] *Mt* 3:15.
[20] Cf. *Phil* 2:7.
[21] *Mt* 3:16–17.
[22] *Mk* 10:38; cf. *Lk* 12:50.
[23] Cf. *Jn* 19:34; 1 *Jn* 5:6–8.
[24] Cf. *Jn* 3:5.
[25] St Ambrose, *De sacr.* 2, 2, 6: PL 16, 444; cf. *Jn* 3:5.
[26] *Acts* 2:38.
[27] Cf. *Acts* 2:41; 8:12–13; 10:48; 16:15.
[28] *Acts* 16:31–33.

Baptism into communion with Christ's death, is buried with him, and rises with him:

> Do you not know that all of us who have been baptized into Christ Jesus were baptized into his death? We were buried therefore with him by baptism into death, so that as Christ was raised from the dead by the glory of the Father, we too might walk in newness of life.[29]

The baptized have 'put on Christ.'[30] Through the Holy Spirit, Baptism is a bath that purifies, justifies and sanctifies.[31]

1228 Hence Baptism is a bath of water in which the 'imperishable seed' of the Word of God produces its life-giving effect.[32] St Augustine says of Baptism: 'The word is brought to the material element, and it becomes a sacrament.'[33]

III. How Is the Sacrament of Baptism Celebrated?

Christian initiation

1229 From the time of the apostles, becoming a Christian has been accomplished by a journey and initiation in several stages. This journey can be covered rapidly or slowly, but certain essential elements will always have to be present: proclamation of the Word, acceptance of the Gospel entailing conversion, profession of faith, Baptism itself, the outpouring of the Holy Spirit, and admission to Eucharistic communion.

1230 This initiation has varied greatly through the centuries according to circumstances. In the first centuries of the Church, Christian initiation saw 1248 considerable development. A long period of *catechumenate* included a series of preparatory rites, which were liturgical landmarks along the path of catechumenal preparation and culminated in the celebration of the sacraments of Christian initiation.

1231 Where infant Baptism has become the form in which this sacrament is usually celebrated, it has become a single act encapsulating the preparatory stages of Christian initiation in a very abridged way. By its very nature infant Baptism requires a *post-baptismal catechumenate*. There is a need not only for 13 instruction after Baptism, but also for the necessary flowering of baptismal grace in personal growth. The *catechism* has its proper place here.

1232 The Second Vatican Council restored for the Latin Church 'the catechumenate for adults, comprising several distinct steps'.[34] The rites for these stages are to be found in the *Rite of Christian Initiation of Adults* (RCIA).[35] The Council also gives permission that: 'In mission countries, in addition to what is

---

[29] Rom 6:3–4; cf. Col 2:12.
[30] Gal 3:27.
[31] Cf. 1 Cor 6:11; 12:13.
[32] 1 Pt 1:23; cf. Eph 5:26.

[33] St Augustine, *In ev. Jo.* 80, 3: PL 35, 1840.
[34] SC 64.
[35] Cf. RCIA (1972).

furnished by the Christian tradition, those elements of initiation rites may be *1204* admitted which are already in use among some peoples insofar as they can be adapted to the Christian ritual.'[36]

1233 Today in all the rites, Latin and Eastern, the Christian initiation of adults begins with their entry into the catechumenate and reaches its culmination in a single celebration of the three sacraments of initiation: Baptism, Confirmation and the Eucharist.[37] In the Eastern rites the Christian initiation of infants also begins with Baptism followed immediately by Confirmation and the Eucharist, *1290* while in the Roman rite it is followed by years of catechesis before being completed later by Confirmation and the Eucharist, the summit of their Christian initiation.[38]

The mystagogy of the celebration

1234 The meaning and grace of the sacrament of Baptism are clearly seen in the rites of its celebration. By following the gestures and words of this celebration with attentive participation, the faithful are initiated into the riches this sacrament signifies and actually brings about in each newly baptized person.

1235 The *sign of the cross*, on the threshold of the celebration, *617* marks with the imprint of Christ the one who is going to belong to him and signifies the grace of the redemption Christ won for us by his cross. *2157*

1236 The *proclamation of the Word of God* enlightens the candidates and the assembly with the revealed truth, and elicits the response of faith, which is inseparable from Baptism. Indeed Baptism is 'the sacrament of faith' in a particular way, since it is the sacramental *1122* entry into the life of faith.

1237 Since Baptism signifies liberation from sin and from its instigator the devil, one or more *exorcisms* are pronounced over the *1673* candidate. The celebrant then anoints him with the oil of catechumens, or lays his hands on him, and he explicitly renounces Satan. Thus prepared, he is able to *confess the faith of the Church*, to *189* which he will be 'entrusted' by Baptism.[39]

1238 The *baptismal water* is consecrated by a prayer of epiclesis *1217* (either at this moment or at the Easter Vigil). The Church asks God that through his Son the power of the Holy Spirit may be sent upon the water, so that those who will be baptized in it may be 'born of water and the Spirit'.[40]

1239 The *essential rite* of the sacrament follows: *Baptism* properly *1214*

---

[36] SC 65; cf. SC 37–40.
[37] Cf. AG 14; CIC, cann. 851; 865; 866.
[38] Cf. CIC, cann. 851, 2°; 868.

[39] Cf. Rom 6:17.
[40] Jn 3:5.

speaking. It signifies and actually brings about death to sin and entry into the life of the Most Holy Trinity through configuration to the Paschal mystery of Christ. Baptism is performed in the most expressive way by triple immersion in the baptismal water. However, from ancient times it has also been able to be conferred by pouring the water three times over the candidate's head.

1240 In the Latin Church this triple infusion is accompanied by the minister's words: 'N., I baptize you in the name of the Father, and of the Son, and of the Holy Spirit.' In the Eastern liturgies the catechumen turns towards the East and the priest says: 'The servant of God, N., is baptized in the name of the Father, and of the Son, and of the Holy Spirit.' At the invocation of each person of the Most Holy Trinity, the priest immerses the candidate in the water and raises him up again.

1294, 1574   1241 The *anointing with sacred chrism*, perfumed oil consecrated by the bishop, signifies the gift of the Holy Spirit to the newly baptized, who has become a Christian, that is, one 'anointed' by the
783   Holy Spirit, incorporated into Christ who is anointed priest, prophet and king.[41]

1242 In the liturgy of the Eastern Churches, the post-baptismal anointing is the sacrament of Chrismation (Confirmation). In the Roman liturgy the post-baptismal anointing announces a second
1291 anointing with sacred chrism to be conferred later by the bishop – Confirmation, which will as it were 'confirm' and complete the baptismal anointing.

1243 The *white garment* symbolizes that the person baptized has 'put on Christ',[42] has risen with Christ. The *candle*, lit from the
1216 Easter candle, signifies that Christ has enlightened the neophyte. In him the baptized are 'the light of the world'.[43]

     The newly baptized is now, in the only Son, a child of God
2769 entitled to say the prayer of the children of God: 'Our Father'.

1244 *First Holy Communion*. Having become a child of God clothed with the wedding garment, the neophyte is admitted 'to the marriage supper of the Lamb'[44] and receives the food of the
1292 new life, the body and blood of Christ. The Eastern Churches maintain a lively awareness of the unity of Christian initiation by giving Holy Communion to all the newly baptized and confirmed, even little children, recalling the Lord's words: 'Let the children come to me, do not hinder them.'[45] The Latin Church, which reserves admission to Holy Communion to those who have

---

[41] Cf. RBC 62.
[42] Gal 3:27.
[43] Mt 5:14; cf. Phil 2:15.

[44] Rev 19:9.
[45] Mk 10:14.

attained the age of reason, expresses the orientation of Baptism to the Eucharist by having the newly baptized child brought to the altar for the praying of the *Our Father*.

1245 The *solemn blessing* concludes the celebration of Baptism. At the Baptism of newborns the blessing of the mother occupies a special place.

IV. Who Can Receive Baptism?

1246 'Every person not yet baptized and only such a person is able to be baptized.'[46]

The Baptism of adults

1247 Since the beginning of the Church, adult Baptism is the common practice where the proclamation of the Gospel is still new. The catechumenate (preparation for Baptism) therefore occupies an important place. This initiation into Christian faith and life should dispose the catechumen to receive the gift of God in Baptism, Confirmation and the Eucharist.

1248 The catechumenate, or formation of catechumens, aims at *1230* bringing their conversion and faith to maturity, in response to the divine initiative and in union with an ecclesial community. The catechumenate is to be 'a formation in the whole Christian life... during which the disciples will be joined to Christ their teacher. The catechumens should be properly initiated into the mystery of salvation and the practice of the evangelical virtues, and they should be introduced into the life of faith, liturgy and charity of the People of God by successive sacred rites.'[47]

1249 Catechumens 'are already joined to the Church, they are *1259* already of the household of Christ, and are quite frequently already living a life of faith, hope and charity.'[48] 'With love and solicitude mother Church already embraces them as her own.'[49]

The Baptism of infants

1250 Born with a fallen human nature and tainted by original sin, children also have need of the new birth in Baptism to be freed *403* from the power of darkness and brought into the realm of the freedom of the children of God, to which all men are called.[50] The sheer gratuitousness of the grace of salvation is particularly *1996*

---

[46] CIC, can. 864; cf. CCEO, can. 679.

[47] *AG* 14; cf. RCIA 19; 98.

[48] *AG* 14 § 5.

[49] *LG* 14 § 3; cf. CIC, cann. 206; 788 § 3.

[50] Cf. Council of Trent (1546): DS 1514; cf. *Col* 1:12–14.

manifest in infant Baptism. The Church and the parents would deny a child the priceless grace of becoming a child of God were they not to confer Baptism shortly after birth.[51]

1251 Christian parents will recognize that this practice also accords with their role as nurturers of the life that God has entrusted to them.[52]

1252 The practice of infant Baptism is an immemorial tradition of the Church. There is explicit testimony to this practice from the second century on, and it is quite possible that, from the beginning of the apostolic preaching, when whole 'households' received Baptism, infants may also have been baptized.[53]

Faith and Baptism

1123 1253 Baptism is the sacrament of faith.[54] But faith needs the community of believers. It is only within the faith of the Church that each of the faithful can believe. The faith required for Baptism is not a perfect and mature faith, but a beginning that is called to develop. The catechumen or the godparent is asked: 'What do you *168* ask of God's Church?' The response is: 'Faith!'

1254 For all the baptized, children or adults, faith must grow *after* Baptism. For this reason the Church celebrates each year at the *2101* Easter Vigil the renewal of baptismal promises. Preparation for Baptism leads only to the threshold of new life. Baptism is the source of that new life in Christ from which the entire Christian life springs forth.

1255 For the grace of Baptism to unfold, the parents' help is *1311* important. So too is the role of the *godfather* and *godmother*, who must be firm believers, able and ready to help the newly baptized – child or adult – on the road of Christian life.[55] Their task is a truly ecclesial function (*officium*).[56] The whole ecclesial community bears some responsibility for the development and safeguarding of the grace given at Baptism.

V. Who Can Baptize?

1256 The ordinary ministers of Baptism are the bishop and priest and, in the Latin Church, also the deacon.[57] In case of necessity,

---

[51] Cf. CIC, can. 867; CCEO, cann. 681; 686, 1.
[52] Cf. *LG* 11; 41; *GS* 48; CIC, can. 868.
[53] Cf. *Acts* 16:15, 33; 18:8; 1 *Cor* 1:16; CDF, Instr. *Pastoralis actio*: AAS 72 (1980), 1137–1156.
[54] Cf. *Mk* 16:16.
[55] Cf. CIC, cann. 872–874.
[56] Cf. *SC* 67.
[57] Cf. CIC, can. 861 § 1; CCEO, can. 677 § 1.

anyone, even a non-baptized person, with the required intention, can baptize,[57a] by using the Trinitarian baptismal formula. The *1239–1240* intention required is to will to do what the Church does when *1752* she baptizes. The Church finds the reason for this possibility in the universal saving will of God and the necessity of Baptism for salvation.[58]

VI. The Necessity of Baptism

1257 The Lord himself affirms that Baptism is necessary for salva- *1129* tion.[59] He also commands his disciples to proclaim the Gospel to all nations and to baptize them.[60] Baptism is necessary for salvation *161, 846* for those to whom the Gospel has been proclaimed and who have had the possibility of asking for this sacrament.[61] The Church does not know of any means other than Baptism that assures entry into eternal beatitude; this is why she takes care not to neglect the mission she has received from the Lord to see that all who can be baptized are 'reborn of water and the Spirit'. *God has bound salvation to the sacrament of Baptism, but he himself is not bound by his sacraments.*

1258 The Church has always held the firm conviction that those who suffer death for the sake of the faith without having received Baptism are baptized by their death for and with Christ. This *2473* *Baptism of blood*, like the *desire for Baptism*, brings about the fruits of Baptism without being a sacrament.

1259 For *catechumens* who die before their Baptism, their explicit *1249* desire to receive it, together with repentance for their sins, and charity, assures them the salvation that they were not able to receive through the sacrament.

1260 'Since Christ died for all, and since all men are in fact called to one and the same destiny, which is divine, we must hold that the Holy Spirit offers to all the possibility of being made partakers, in a way known to God, of the Paschal mystery.'[62] Every man who is ignorant of the Gospel of Christ and of his Church, but seeks the *848* truth and does the will of God in accordance with his understanding of it, can be saved. It may be supposed that such persons would have *desired Baptism explicitly* if they had known its necessity.

1261 As regards *children who have died without Baptism*, the Church can only entrust them to the mercy of God, as she does in her

---

[57a] CIC, can. 861 § 2.
[58] Cf. 1 *Tim* 2:4.
[59] Cf. *Jn* 3:5.

[60] Cf. *Mt* 28:19–20; cf. Council of Trent (1547): DS 1618; *LG* 14; *AG* 5.
[61] Cf. *Mk* 16:16.
[62] *GS* 22 § 5; cf. *LG* 16; *AG* 7.

funeral rites for them. Indeed, the great mercy of God who desires
that all men should be saved, and Jesus' tenderness toward children
which caused him to say: 'Let the children come to me, do not
1257 hinder them',[63] allow us to hope that there is a way of salvation for
children who have died without Baptism. All the more urgent is
1250 the Church's call not to prevent little children coming to Christ
through the gift of holy Baptism.

VII. The Grace of Baptism

1234 1262 The different effects of Baptism are signified by the perceptible elements of the sacramental rite. Immersion in water symbolizes not only death and purification, but also regeneration and
renewal. Thus the two principal effects are purification from sins
and new birth in the Holy Spirit.[64]

For the forgiveness of sins...

977 1263 By Baptism *all sins* are forgiven, original sin and all personal
1425 sins, as well as all punishment for sin.[65] In those who have been
reborn nothing remains that would impede their entry into the
Kingdom of God, neither Adam's sin, nor personal sin, nor the
consequences of sin, the gravest of which is separation from God.

1264 Yet certain temporal consequences of sin remain in the baptized, such as suffering, illness, death, and such frailties inherent in
life as weaknesses of character, and so on, as well as an inclination
976, 2514 to sin that Tradition calls *concupiscence*, or, metaphorically, 'the
1426 tinder for sin' (*fomes peccati*); since concupiscence 'is left for us to
wrestle with, it cannot harm those who do not consent but man-
405 fully resist it by the grace of Jesus Christ.'[66] Indeed, 'an athlete is
not crowned unless he competes according to the rules.'[67]

'A new creature'

1265 Baptism not only purifies from all sins, but also makes the
neophyte 'a new creature', an adopted son of God, who has
505, 460 become a 'partaker of the divine nature',[68] member of Christ and
co-heir with him,[69] and a temple of the Holy Spirit.[70]

1266 The Most Holy Trinity gives the baptized *sanctifying grace*,
1992 the grace of *justification*:

---

[63] *Mk* 10:14; cf. 1 *Tim* 2:4.
[64] Cf. *Acts* 2:38; *Jn* 3:5.
[65] Cf. Council of Florence (1439): DS 1316.
[66] Council of Trent (1546): DS 1515.
[67] 2 *Tim* 2:5.
[68] 2 *Cor* 5:17; 2 *Pt* 1:4; cf. *Gal* 4:5-7.
[69] Cf. 1 *Cor* 6:15; 12:27; *Rom* 8:17.
[70] Cf. 1 *Cor* 6:19.

– enabling them to believe in God, to hope in him and to love him
through the *theological virtues*;   *1812*
– giving them the power to live and act under the prompting of
the Holy Spirit through the *gifts of the Holy Spirit*;   *1831*
– allowing them to grow in goodness through the *moral virtues*.   *1810*
Thus the whole organism of the Christian's supernatural life has its
roots in Baptism.

Incorporated into the Church, the Body of Christ

1267 Baptism makes us members of the Body of Christ: 'There- *782*
fore... we are members one of another.'[71] Baptism incorporates
us *into the Church*. From the baptismal fonts is born the one People
of God of the New Covenant, which transcends all the natural or
human limits of nations, cultures, races and sexes: 'For by one
Spirit we were all baptized into one body.'[72]

1268 The baptized have become 'living stones' to be 'built into a
spiritual house, to be a holy priesthood'.[73] By Baptism they share
in the priesthood of Christ, in his prophetic and royal mission.
They are 'a chosen race, a royal priesthood, a holy nation, God's *1141*
own people, that [they] may declare the wonderful deeds of him
who called [them] out of darkness into his marvellous light'.[74]
Baptism gives a share in the common priesthood of all believers.   *784*

1269 Having become a member of the Church, the person baptized belongs no longer to himself, but to him who died and rose
for us.[75] From now on, he is called to be subject to others, to serve
them in the communion of the Church, and to 'obey and submit'
to the Church's leaders,[76] holding them in respect and affection.[77]
Just as Baptism is the source of responsibilities and duties, the *871*
baptized person also enjoys rights within the Church: to receive
the sacraments, to be nourished with the Word of God and to be
sustained by the other spiritual helps of the Church.[78]

1270 'Reborn as sons of God, [the baptized] must profess before
men the faith they have received from God through the Church'
and participate in the apostolic and missionary activity of the
People of God.[79]

---

[71] *Eph* 4:25.
[72] 1 *Cor* 12:13.
[73] 1 *Pt* 2:5.
[74] 1 *Pt* 2:9.
[75] Cf. 1 *Cor* 6:19; 2 *Cor* 5:15.
[76] *Heb* 13:17.

[77] Cf. *Eph* 5:21; 1 *Cor* 16:15–16; 1 *Th*
5:12–13; *Jn* 13:12–15.
[78] Cf. *LG* 37; CIC, cann. 208–223;
CCEO, can. 675 § 2.
[79] *LG* 11; cf. 17; *AG* 7; 23.

The sacramental bond of the unity of Christians

1271 Baptism constitutes the foundation of communion among all Christians, including those who are not yet in full communion with the Catholic Church: 'For men who believe in Christ and have been properly baptized are put in some, though imperfect, communion with the Catholic Church. Justified by faith in Baptism, [they] are incorporated into Christ; they therefore have a right to be called Christians, and with good reason are accepted as brothers by the children of the Catholic Church.'[80] 'Baptism therefore constitutes *the sacramental bond of unity* existing among all who through it are reborn.'[81]

An indelible spiritual mark...

1272 Incorporated into Christ by Baptism, the person baptized is configured to Christ. Baptism seals the Christian with the indelible spiritual mark (*character*) of his belonging to Christ. No sin can erase this mark, even if sin prevents Baptism from bearing the fruits of salvation.[82] Given once for all, Baptism cannot be repeated.

1273 Incorporated into the Church by Baptism, the faithful have received the sacramental character that consecrates them for Christian religious worship.[83] The baptismal seal enables and commits Christians to serve God by a vital participation in the holy liturgy of the Church and to exercise their baptismal priesthood by the witness of holy lives and practical charity.[84]

1274 The Holy Spirit has marked us with the '*seal of the Lord*' (*Dominicus character*) 'for the day of redemption'.[85] 'Baptism indeed is the seal of eternal life.'[86] The faithful Christian who has 'kept the seal' until the end, remaining faithful to the demands of his Baptism, will be able to depart this life 'marked with the sign of faith',[87] with his baptismal faith, in expectation of the blessed vision of God – the consummation of faith – and in the hope of resurrection.

197
2016

---

[80] *UR* 3.
[81] *UR* 22 § 2.
[82] Cf. *Rom* 8:29; Council of Trent (1547): DS 1609–1619.
[83] Cf. *LG* 11.
[84] Cf. *LG* 10.

[85] St Augustine, *Ep.* 98, 5: PL 33, 362; *Eph* 4:30; cf. 1:13–14; 2 *Cor* 1:21–22.
[86] St Irenaeus, *Dem. ap.* 3: SCh 62, 32.
[87] *Roman Missal*, EP I (Roman Canon), 97.

IN BRIEF

1275 *Christian initiation is accomplished by three sacraments together: Baptism which is the beginning of new life; Confirmation which is its strengthening; and the Eucharist which nourishes the disciple with Christ's Body and Blood for his transformation in Christ.*

1276 *'Go therefore and make disciples of all nations, baptizing them in the name of the Father and of the Son and of the Holy Spirit, teaching them to observe all that I have commanded you' (Mt 28:19–20).*

1277 *Baptism is birth into the new life in Christ. In accordance with the Lord's will, it is necessary for salvation, as is the Church herself, which we enter by Baptism.*

1278 *The essential rite of Baptism consists in immersing the candidate in water or pouring water on his head, while pronouncing the invocation of the Most Holy Trinity: the Father, the Son, and the Holy Spirit.*

1279 *The fruit of Baptism, or baptismal grace, is a rich reality that includes forgiveness of original sin and all personal sins, birth into the new life by which man becomes an adoptive son of the Father, a member of Christ and a temple of the Holy Spirit. By this very fact the person baptized is incorporated into the Church, the Body of Christ, and made a sharer in the priesthood of Christ.*

1280 *Baptism imprints on the soul an indelible spiritual sign, the character, which consecrates the baptized person for Christian worship. Because of the character Baptism cannot be repeated (cf. DS 1609 and DS 1624).*

1281 *Those who die for the faith, those who are catechumens, and all those who, without knowing of the Church but acting under the inspiration of grace, seek God sincerely and strive to fulfil his will, can be saved even if they have not been baptized (cf. LG 16).*

1282 *Since the earliest times, Baptism has been administered to children, for it is a grace and a gift of God that does not presuppose any human merit; children are baptized in the faith of the Church. Entry into Christian life gives access to true freedom.*

1283 *With respect to children who have died without Baptism, the liturgy of the Church invites us to trust in God's mercy and to pray for their salvation.*

1284 *In case of necessity, any person can baptize provided that he have the intention of doing that which the Church does and provided that he pours water on the candidate's head while saying: 'I baptize you in the name of the Father, and of the Son, and of the Holy Spirit.'*

Article 2

THE SACRAMENT OF CONFIRMATION

1285 Baptism, the Eucharist and the sacrament of Confirmation together constitute the 'sacraments of Christian initiation', whose unity must be safeguarded. It must be explained to the faithful that the reception of the sacrament of Confirmation is necessary for the completion of baptismal grace.[88] For 'by the sacrament of Confirmation, [the baptized] are more perfectly bound to the Church and are enriched with a special strength of the Holy Spirit. Hence they are, as true witnesses of Christ, more strictly obliged to spread and defend the faith by word and deed.'[89]

I. Confirmation in the Economy of Salvation

702–716 1286 In the *Old Testament* the prophets announced that the Spirit of the Lord would rest on the hoped-for Messiah for his saving mission.[90] The descent of the Holy Spirit on Jesus at his baptism by John was the sign that this was he who was to come, the Messiah, the Son of God.[91] He was conceived of the Holy Spirit; his whole life and his whole mission are carried out in total communion with the Holy Spirit whom the Father gives him 'without measure'.[92]

1287 This fullness of the Spirit was not to remain uniquely the
739 Messiah's, but was to be communicated to *the whole messianic people*.[93] On several occasions Christ promised this outpouring of the Spirit,[94] a promise which he fulfilled first on Easter Sunday and then more strikingly at Pentecost.[95] Filled with the Holy Spirit the apostles began to proclaim 'the mighty works of God', and Peter declared this outpouring of the Spirit to be the sign of the messianic age.[96] Those who believed in the apostolic preaching and were baptized received the gift of the Holy Spirit in their turn.[97]

1288 'From that time on the apostles, in fulfilment of Christ's
699 will, imparted to the newly baptized by the laying on of hands the gift of the Spirit that completes the grace of Baptism. For this reason in the *Letter to the Hebrews* the doctrine concerning Baptism and the laying on of hands is listed among the first elements of Christian instruction. The imposition of hands is rightly recognized by the Catholic tradition as the origin of the sacrament of Confirmation, which in a certain way perpetuates the grace of Pentecost in the Church.'[98]

---

[88] Cf. *Roman Ritual*, Rite of Confirmation (OC), Introduction 1.
[89] *LG* 11; cf. OC, Introduction 2.
[90] Cf. *Is* 11:2; 61:1; *Lk* 4:16–22.
[91] Cf. *Mt* 3:13–17; *Jn* 1:33–34.
[92] *Jn* 3:34.
[93] Cf. *Ezek* 36:25–27; *Joel* 3:1–2.

[94] Cf. *Lk* 12:12; *Jn* 3:5–8; 7:37–39; 16:7–15; *Acts* 1:8.
[95] Cf. *Jn* 20:22; *Acts* 2:1–4.
[96] *Acts* 2:11; cf. 2:17–18.
[97] Cf. *Acts* 2:38.
[98] Paul VI, *Divinae consortium naturae* 659; cf. *Acts* 8:15–17; 19:5–6; *Heb* 6:2.

1289 Very early, the better to signify the gift of the Holy Spirit, an anointing with perfumed oil (*chrism*) was added to the laying on of *695* hands. This anointing highlights the name 'Christian', which means 'anointed' and derives from that of Christ himself whom *436* God 'anointed with the Holy Spirit.'[99] This rite of anointing has continued ever since, in both East and West. For this reason the Eastern Churches call this sacrament *Chrismation*, anointing with chrism, or *myron* which means 'chrism'. In the West, the term *1297* *Confirmation* suggests that this sacrament both confirms baptism and strengthens baptismal grace.

Two traditions: East and West

1290 In the first centuries Confirmation generally comprised one single celebration with Baptism, forming with it a 'double sacrament', according to the expression of St Cyprian. Among other reasons, the multiplication of infant baptisms all through the year, the increase of rural parishes and the growth of dioceses often prevented the bishop from being present at all baptismal celebrations. In the West the desire to reserve the completion of Baptism to the bishop caused the temporal separation of the two sacraments. The East has kept them *1233* united, so that Confirmation is conferred by the priest who baptizes. But he can do so only with the *myron* consecrated by a bishop.[100]

1291 A custom of the Roman Church facilitated the development of the Western practice: a double anointing with sacred chrism after Baptism. The first *1242* anointing of the neophyte on coming out of the baptismal bath was performed by the priest; it was completed by a second anointing on the forehead of the newly baptized by the bishop.[101] The first anointing with sacred chrism, by the priest, has remained attached to the baptismal rite; it signifies the participation of the one baptized in the prophetic, priestly and kingly offices of Christ. If Baptism is conferred on an adult, there is only one post-baptismal anointing, that of Confirmation.

1292 The practice of the Eastern Churches gives greater emphasis to the unity of Christian initiation. That of the Latin Church more clearly expresses the *1244* communion of the new Christian with the bishop as guarantor and servant of the unity, catholicity and apostolicity of his Church, and hence the connection with the apostolic origins of Christ's Church.

II. The Signs and the Rite of Confirmation

1293 In treating the rite of Confirmation, it is fitting to consider the sign of *anointing* and what it signifies and imprints: a spiritual *seal*.

Anointing, in biblical and other ancient symbolism, is rich in *695*

---

[99] *Acts* 10:38.
[100] Cf. CCEO, cann. 695 § 1; 696 § 1.
[101] Cf. St Hippolytus, *Trad. ap.* 21: SCh 11, 80–95.

meaning: oil is a sign of abundance and joy;[102] it cleanses (anointing before and after a bath) and limbers (the anointing of athletes and wrestlers); oil is a sign of healing, since it is soothing to bruises and wounds;[103] and it makes radiant with beauty, health and strength.

1152 1294 Anointing with oil has all these meanings in the sacramental life. The pre-baptismal anointing with the oil of catechumens signifies cleansing and strengthening; the anointing of the sick expresses healing and comfort. The post-baptismal anointing with sacred chrism in Confirmation and ordination is the sign of consecration. By Confirmation Christians, that is, those who are anointed, share more completely in the mission of Jesus Christ and the fullness of the Holy Spirit with which he is filled, so that their lives may give off 'the aroma of Christ'.[104]

1295 By this anointing the confirmand receives the 'mark', the
698 seal of the Holy Spirit. A seal is a symbol of a person, a sign of personal authority, or ownership of an object.[105] Hence soldiers were marked with their leader's seal and slaves with their master's. A seal authenticates a juridical act or document and occasionally makes it secret.[106]

1296 Christ himself declared that he was marked with his Father's
1121 seal.[107] Christians are also marked with a seal: 'It is God who establishes us with you in Christ and has commissioned us; he has put his seal on us and given us his Spirit in our hearts as a guarantee.'[108] This seal of the Holy Spirit marks our total belonging to Christ, our enrolment in his service for ever, as well as the promise of divine protection in the great eschatological trial.[109]

The celebration of Confirmation

1183 1297 *The consecration of the sacred chrism* is an important action that precedes the celebration of Confirmation, but is in a certain way a part of it. It is the bishop who, in the course of the Chrism Mass of
1241 Holy Thursday, consecrates the sacred chrism for his whole diocese. In some Eastern Churches this consecration is even reserved to the patriarch:

> The liturgy of Antioch expresses the epiclesis for the consecration of the sacred chrism (myron) in this way: '[Father...send your Holy

---

[102] Cf. Dt 11:14; Pss 23:5; 104:15.
[103] Cf. Is 1:6; Lk 10:34.
[104] 2 Cor 2:15.
[105] Cf. Gen 38:18; 41:42; Dt 32:34; Song 8:6.
[106] Cf. 1 Kings 21:8; Jer 32:10; Is 29:11.
[107] Cf. Jn 6:27.
[108] 2 Cor 1:21–22; cf. Eph 1:13; 4:30.
[109] Cf. Rev 7:2–3; 9:4; Ezek 9:4–6.

Spirit] on us and on this oil which is before us and consecrate it, so that it may be for all who are anointed and marked with it holy myron, priestly myron, royal myron, anointing with gladness, clothing with light, a cloak of salvation, a spiritual gift, the sanctification of souls and bodies, imperishable happiness, the indelible seal, a buckler of faith and a fearsome helmet against all the works of the adversary.'

1298 When Confirmation is celebrated separately from Baptism, as is the case in the Roman rite, the Liturgy of Confirmation begins with the renewal of baptismal promises and the profession of faith by the confirmands. This clearly shows that Confirmation follows Baptism.[110] When adults are baptized, they immediately receive Confirmation and participate in the Eucharist.[111]

1299 In the Roman rite the bishop extends his hands over the whole group of the confirmands. Since the time of the apostles this gesture has signified the gift of the Spirit. The bishop invokes the outpouring of the Spirit in these words:

All-powerful God, Father of our Lord Jesus Christ,
by water and the Holy Spirit
you freed your sons and daughters from sin
and gave them new life.
Send your Holy Spirit upon them   *1831*
to be their helper and guide.
Give them the spirit of wisdom and understanding,
the spirit of right judgement and courage,
the spirit of knowledge and reverence.
Fill them with the spirit of wonder and awe in your presence.
We ask this through Christ our Lord.[112]

1300 The *essential rite* of the sacrament follows. In the Latin rite, 'the sacrament of Confirmation is conferred through the anointing with chrism on the forehead, which is done by the laying on of the hand, and through the words: *Accipe signaculum doni Spiritus* *699* *Sancti* [Be sealed with the Gift of the Holy Spirit].'[113] In the Eastern Churches of Byzantine rite, after a prayer of epiclesis, the more significant parts of the body are anointed with myron: forehead, eyes, nose, ears, lips, chest, back, hands and feet. Each anointing is accompanied by the formula *Sphragis doreas Pneumatos Hagiou (Signaculum doni Spiritus Sancti):* 'the seal of the gift of the Holy Spirit.'[113a]

[110] Cf. SC 71.
[111] Cf. CIC, can. 866.
[112] OC 25.
[113] Paul VI, Ap. Const. *Divinae consortium naturae* 663.

[113a] *Rituale per le Chiese orientali di rito bizantino in lingua greca*, Pars Prima (Libreria Editrice Vaticana, 1954), 36.
[114] Cf. St Hippolytus, *Trad. ap.* 21: SCh 11, 80–95.

III. The Effects of Confirmation

1302 It is evident from its celebration that the effect of the sacrament of Confirmation is the special outpouring of the Holy Spirit
731 as once granted to the apostles on the day of Pentecost.

1303 From this fact, Confirmation brings an increase and
1262–1274 deepening of baptismal grace:
– it roots us more deeply in the divine filiation which makes us cry 'Abba! Father!';[115]
– it unites us more firmly to Christ;
– it increases the gifts of the Holy Spirit in us;
– it renders our bond with the Church more perfect;[116]
– it gives us a special strength of the Holy Spirit to spread and
2044 defend the faith by word and action as true witnesses of Christ, to confess the name of Christ boldly, and never to be ashamed of the Cross:[117]

> Recall then that you have received the spiritual seal, the spirit of wisdom and understanding, the spirit of right judgement and courage, the spirit of knowledge and reverence, the spirit of holy fear in God's presence. Guard what you have received. God the Father has marked you with his sign; Christ the Lord has confirmed you and has placed his pledge, the Spirit, in your hearts.[118]

1304 Like Baptism which it completes, Confirmation is given
1121 only once, for it too imprints on the soul an *indelible spiritual mark*, the 'character', which is the sign that Jesus Christ has marked a Christian with the seal of his Spirit by clothing him with power from on high so that he may be his witness.[119]

1268 1305 This 'character' perfects the common priesthood of the faithful, received in Baptism, and 'the confirmed person receives the power to profess faith in Christ publicly and as it were officially (*quasi ex officio*).'[120]

IV. Who Can Receive This Sacrament?

1306 Every baptized person not yet confirmed can and should receive the sacrament of Confirmation.[121] Since Baptism, Con-
1212 firmation and Eucharist form a unity, it follows that 'the faithful are obliged to receive this sacrament at the appropriate time',[122]

---

[115] *Rom* 8:15.
[116] Cf. *LG* 11.
[117] Cf. Council of Florence (1439): DS 1319; *LG* 11; 12.
[118] St Ambrose, *De myst.* 7, 42: PL 16, 419.

[119] Cf. Council of Trent (1547): DS 1609; *Lk* 24:48–49.
[120] St Thomas Aquinas, *STh* III, 72, 5, ad 2.
[121] Cf. CIC, can. 889 § 1.
[122] CIC, can. 890.

for without Confirmation and Eucharist Baptism is certainly valid and efficacious, but Christian initiation remains incomplete.

1307 For centuries, Latin custom has indicated 'the age of discretion' as the reference point for receiving Confirmation. But in danger of death children should be confirmed even if they have not yet attained the age of discretion.[123]

1308 Although Confirmation is sometimes called the 'sacrament of Christian maturity', we must not confuse adult faith with the adult age of natural growth, nor forget that the baptismal grace is a grace of free, unmerited election and does not need 'ratification' to *1250* become effective. St Thomas reminds us of this:

> Age of body does not determine age of soul. Even in childhood man can attain spiritual maturity: as the book of *Wisdom* says: 'For old age is not honoured for length of time, or measured by number of years.' Many children, through the strength of the Holy Spirit they have received, have bravely fought for Christ even to the shedding of their blood.[124]

1309 *Preparation* for Confirmation should aim at leading the Christian toward a more intimate union with Christ and a more lively familiarity with the Holy Spirit – his actions, his gifts, and his biddings – in order to be more capable of assuming the apostolic responsibilities of Christian life. To this end catechesis for Confirmation should strive to awaken a sense of belonging to the Church of Jesus Christ, the universal Church as well as the parish community. The latter bears special responsibility for the preparation of confirmands.[125]

1310 To receive Confirmation one must be in a state of grace. One should receive the sacrament of Penance in order to be cleansed for the gift of the Holy Spirit. More intense prayer should *2670* prepare one to receive the strength and graces of the Holy Spirit with docility and readiness to act.[126]

1311 Candidates for Confirmation, as for Baptism, fittingly seek the spiritual help of a *sponsor*. To emphasize the unity of the two *1255* sacraments, it is appropriate that this be one of the baptismal godparents.[127]

V. The Minister of Confirmation

1312 The *original minister* of Confirmation is the bishop.[128]

In the *East*, ordinarily the priest who baptizes also imme- *1233*

---

[123] Cf. CIC, cann. 891; 883, 3°.
[124] St Thomas Aquinas, *STh* III, 72, 8, ad 2; cf. *Wis* 4:8.
[125] Cf. OC, Introduction 3.

[126] Cf. *Acts* 1:14.
[127] Cf. OC, Introduction 5; 6; CIC, can. 893 §§ 1–2.
[128] Cf. *LG* 26.

diately confers Confirmation in one and the same celebration. But he does so with sacred chrism consecrated by the patriarch or the bishop, thus expressing the apostolic unity of the Church whose bonds are strengthened by the sacrament of Confirmation. In the Latin Church, the same discipline applies to the Baptism of adults or to the reception into full communion with the Church of a person baptized in another Christian community that does not have valid Confirmation.[129]

1290   1313 *In the Latin rite*, the ordinary minister of Confirmation is the bishop.[130] If the need arises, the bishop may grant the faculty of administering Confirmation to priests,[131] although it is fitting that he confer it himself, mindful that the celebration of Confirmation has been temporally separated from Baptism for this reason. Bishops are the successors of the apostles. They have received the fullness of the sacrament of Holy Orders. The administration of this sacrament by them demonstrates clearly that its effect is to unite those who receive it more closely to the Church, to her 1285 apostolic origins and to her mission of bearing witness to Christ.

1307   1314 If a Christian is in danger of death, any priest can give him Confirmation.[132] Indeed the Church desires that none of her children, even the youngest, should depart this world without having been perfected by the Holy Spirit with the gift of Christ's fullness.

IN BRIEF

1315 *'Now when the apostles at Jerusalem heard that Samaria had received the word of God, they sent to them Peter and John, who came down and prayed for them that they might receive the Holy Spirit; for it had not yet fallen on any of them, but they had only been baptized in the name of the Lord Jesus. Then they laid their hands on them and they received the Holy Spirit'* (Acts 8:14–17).

1316 *Confirmation perfects Baptismal grace; it is the sacrament which gives the Holy Spirit in order to root us more deeply in the divine filiation, incorporate us more firmly into Christ, strengthen our bond with the Church, associate us more closely with her mission, and help us bear witness to the Christian faith in words accompanied by deeds.*

1317 *Confirmation, like Baptism, imprints a spiritual mark or indelible character on the Christian's soul; for this reason one can receive this sacrament only once in one's life.*

---

[129] Cf. CIC, can. 883 § 2.
[130] Cf. CIC, can. 882.
[131] Cf. CIC, can. 884 § 2.
[132] Cf. CIC, can. 883 § 3.

1318 *In the East this sacrament is administered immediately after Baptism and is followed by participation in the Eucharist; this tradition highlights the unity of the three sacraments of Christian initiation. In the Latin Church this sacrament is administered when the age of reason has been reached, and its celebration is ordinarily reserved to the bishop, thus signifying that this sacrament strengthens the ecclesial bond.*

1319 *A candidate for Confirmation who has attained the age of reason must profess the faith, be in the state of grace, have the intention of receiving the sacrament, and be prepared to assume the role of disciple and witness to Christ, both within the ecclesial community and in temporal affairs.*

1320 *The essential rite of Confirmation is anointing the forehead of the baptized with sacred chrism (in the East other sense-organs as well), together with the laying on of the minister's hand and the words:* Accipe signaculum doni Spiritus Sancti *[Be sealed with the Gift of the Holy Spirit] in the Roman rite, or:* Signaculum doni Spiritus Sancti *[the seal of the gift of the Holy Spirit] in the Byzantine rite.*

1321 *When Confirmation is celebrated separately from Baptism, its connection with Baptism is expressed, among other ways, by the renewal of baptismal promises. The celebration of Confirmation during the Eucharist helps underline the unity of the sacraments of Christian initiation.*

Article 3
THE SACRAMENT OF THE EUCHARIST

1322 The holy Eucharist completes Christian initiation. Those who have been raised to the dignity of the royal priesthood by Baptism, and configured more deeply to Christ by Confirmation, participate with the whole community in the Lord's own sacrifice by means of the Eucharist. *1212*

1323 'At the Last Supper, on the night he was betrayed, our Saviour instituted the Eucharistic sacrifice of his Body and Blood. This he did in order to perpetuate the sacrifice of the cross throughout the ages until he should come again, and so to entrust to his beloved Spouse, the Church, a memorial of his death and resurrection: a sacrament of love, a sign of unity, a bond of charity, a Paschal banquet "in which Christ is consumed, the mind is filled with grace, and a pledge of future glory is given to us".'[133] *1402*

I. The Eucharist – Source and Summit of Ecclesial Life

1324 The Eucharist is 'the source and summit of the Christian

---

[133] SC 47.

life'.[134] 'The other sacraments, and indeed all ecclesiastical minis-
864 tries and works of the apostolate, are bound up with the Eucharist
and are oriented towards it. For in the blessed Eucharist is contained the whole spiritual good of the Church, namely Christ
himself, our Pasch.'[135]

1325 'The Eucharist is the efficacious sign and sublime cause of
775 that communion in the divine life and that unity of the People of
God by which the Church is kept in being. It is the culmination
both of God's action sanctifying the world in Christ and of the
worship men offer to Christ and through him to the Father in the
Holy Spirit.'[136]

1326 Finally, by the Eucharistic celebration we already unite our-
1090 selves with the heavenly liturgy and anticipate eternal life, when
God will be all in all.[137]

1124 1327 In brief, the Eucharist is the sum and summary of our faith:
'Our way of thinking is attuned to the Eucharist, and the Eucharist
in turn confirms our way of thinking.'[138]

II. What Is This Sacrament Called?

1328 The inexhaustible richness of this sacrament is expressed in
the different names we give it. Each name evokes certain aspects of
it. It is called:

2637   *Eucharist*, because it is an action of thanksgiving to God. The
Greek words *eucharistein*[139] and *eulogein*[140] recall the Jewish bless-
1082, 1359 ings that proclaim – especially during a meal – God's works: creation, redemption and sanctification.

1329 The *Lord's Supper*, because of its connection with the supper
which the Lord took with his disciples on the eve of his Passion,
1382 and because it anticipates the *wedding feast of the Lamb* in the heavenly Jerusalem.[141]

        The *Breaking of Bread*, because Jesus used this rite, part of a
Jewish meal, when as master of the table he blessed and distributed
the bread,[142] above all at the Last Supper.[143] It is by this action that
his disciples will recognize him after his Resurrection,[144] and it is
this expression that the first Christians will use to designate their

---

[134] LG 11.
[135] PO 5.
[136] Congregation of Rites. Instr.
    Eucharisticum mysterium 6.
[137] Cf. 1 *Cor* 15:28.
[138] St Irenaeus. *Adv. haeres*. 4. 18. 5: PG
    7/1. 1028.

[139] Cf. *Lk* 22:19; 1 *Cor* 11:24.
[140] Cf. *Mt* 26:26; *Mk* 14:22.
[141] Cf. 1 *Cor* 11:20; *Rev* 19:9.
[142] Cf. *Mt* 14:19; 15:36; *Mk* 8:6, 19.
[143] Cf. *Mt* 26:26; 1 *Cor* 11:24.
[144] Cf. *Lk* 24:13–35.

Eucharistic assemblies;[145] by doing so they signified that all who eat the one broken bread, Christ, enter into communion with him and form but one body in him.[146]

790

The *Eucharistic assembly* (*synaxis*), because the Eucharist is celebrated amid the assembly of the faithful, the visible expression of the Church.[147]

1348

1330 The *memorial* of the Lord's Passion and Resurrection.

1341

The *Holy Sacrifice*, because it makes present the one sacrifice of Christ the Saviour and includes the Church's offering. The terms *holy sacrifice of the Mass*, '*sacrifice of praise*', *spiritual sacrifice*, *pure and holy sacrifice* are also used,[148] since it completes and surpasses all the sacrifices of the Old Covenant.

2643
614

The *Holy and Divine Liturgy*, because the Church's whole liturgy finds its centre and most intense expression in the celebration of this sacrament; in the same sense we also call its celebration the *Sacred Mysteries*. We speak of the *Most Blessed Sacrament* because it is the Sacrament of sacraments. The Eucharistic species reserved in the tabernacle are designated by this same name.

1169

1331 *Holy Communion*, because by this sacrament we unite ourselves to Christ who makes us sharers in his Body and Blood to form a single body.[149] We also call it: *the holy things* (*ta hagia*; *sancta*)[150] — the first meaning of the phrase 'communion of saints' in the Apostles' Creed — *the bread of angels, bread from heaven, medicine of immortality*,[151] *viaticum*. . .

950
948
1405

1332 *Holy Mass* (*Missa*), because the liturgy in which the mystery of salvation is accomplished concludes with the sending forth (*missio*) of the faithful, so that they may fulfil God's will in their daily lives.

849

III. The Eucharist in the Economy of Salvation

The signs of bread and wine

1333 At the heart of the Eucharistic celebration are the bread and wine that, by the words of Christ and the invocation of the Holy Spirit, become Christ's Body and Blood. Faithful to the Lord's command the Church continues to do, in his memory and until his

1350

---

[145] Cf. *Acts* 2:42, 46; 20:7, 11.
[146] Cf. 1 *Cor* 10:16–17.
[147] Cf. 1 *Cor* 11:17–34.
[148] *Heb* 13:15; cf. 1 *Pt* 2:5; *Ps* 116:13, 17; *Mal* 1:11.
[149] Cf. 1 *Cor* 10:16–17.
[150] *Const. App.* 8, 13, 12: PG 1, 1108; *Didache* 9, 5; 10, 6: SCh 248, 176–178, 180.
[151] St Ignatius of Antioch, *Ad Eph.* 20, 2: SCh 10, 76.

glorious return, what he did on the eve of his Passion: 'He took bread...' 'He took the cup filled with wine...' The signs of bread and wine become, in a way surpassing understanding, the Body

1147 and Blood of Christ; they continue also to signify the goodness of creation. Thus in the Offertory we give thanks to the Creator for

1148 bread and wine,[152] fruit of the 'work of human hands', but above all as 'fruit of the earth' and 'of the vine' – gifts of the Creator. The Church sees in the gesture of the king-priest Melchizedek, who 'brought out bread and wine', a prefiguring of her own offering.[153]

1150 **1334** In the Old Covenant bread and wine were offered in sacrifice among the first fruits of the earth, as a sign of grateful acknowledgement to the Creator. But they also received a new

1363 significance in the context of the Exodus: the unleavened bread that Israel eats every year at Passover commemorates the haste of the departure that liberated them from Egypt; the remembrance of the manna in the desert will always recall to Israel that it lives by the bread of the Word of God;[154] their daily bread is the fruit of the promised land, the pledge of God's faithfulness to his promises. The 'cup of blessing'[155] at the end of the Jewish Passover meal adds to the festive joy of wine an eschatological dimension: the messianic expectation of the rebuilding of Jerusalem. When Jesus instituted the Eucharist, he gave a new and definitive meaning to the blessing of the bread and the cup.

1151 **1335** The miracles of the multiplication of the loaves, when the Lord says the blessing, breaks and distributes the loaves through his disciples to feed the multitude, prefigure the superabundance of this unique bread of his Eucharist.[156] The sign of water turned into wine at Cana already announces the Hour of Jesus' glorification. It makes manifest the fulfilment of the wedding feast in the Father's kingdom, where the faithful will drink the new wine that has become the Blood of Christ.[157]

1336 The first announcement of the Eucharist divided the disciples, just as the announcement of the Passion scandalized them: 'This is a hard saying; who can listen to it?'[158] The Eucharist and the Cross are stumbling blocks. It is the same mystery and it never ceases to be an occasion of division. 'Will you also go away?':[159]

---

[152] Cf. Ps 104:13–15.
[153] Gen 14:18; cf. Roman Missal, EP I (Roman Canon), 95.
[54] Cf. Dt 8:3.
[55] 1 Cor 10:16.

[156] Cf. Mt 14:13–21; 15:32–39.
[157] Cf. Jn 2:11; Mk 14:25.
[158] Jn 6:60.
[159] Jn 6:67.

the Lord's question echoes through the ages, as a loving invitation to discover that only he has 'the words of eternal life'[160] and that to receive in faith the gift of his Eucharist is to receive the Lord *1327* himself.

The institution of the Eucharist

1337 The Lord, having loved those who were his own, loved them to the end. Knowing that the hour had come to leave this world and return to the Father, in the course of a meal he washed *610* their feet and gave them the commandment of love.[161] In order to leave them a pledge of this love, in order never to depart from his own and to make them sharers in his Passover, he instituted the Eucharist as the memorial of his death and Resurrection, and *611* commanded his apostles to celebrate it until his return; 'thereby he constituted them priests of the New Testament.'[162]

1338 The three synoptic Gospels and St Paul have handed on to us the account of the institution of the Eucharist; St John, for his part, reports the words of Jesus in the synagogue of Capernaum that prepare for the institution of the Eucharist: Christ calls himself the bread of life, come down from heaven.[163]

1339 Jesus chose the time of Passover to fulfil what he had *1169* announced at Capernaum: giving his disciples his Body and his Blood:

> Then came the day of Unleavened Bread, on which the passover lamb had to be sacrificed. So Jesus sent Peter and John, saying, 'Go and prepare the passover meal for us, that we may eat it...' They went... and prepared the passover. And when the hour came, he sat at table, and the apostles with him. And he said to them, 'I have earnestly desired to eat this passover with you before I suffer; for I tell you I shall not eat it again until it is fulfilled in the kingdom of God.'... And he took bread, and when he had given thanks he broke it and gave it to them, saying, 'This is my body which is given for you. Do this in remembrance of me.' And likewise the cup after supper, saying, 'This cup which is poured out for you is the New Covenant in my blood.'[164]

1340 By celebrating the Last Supper with his apostles in the course of the Passover meal, Jesus gave the Jewish Passover its definitive meaning. Jesus' passing over to his Father by his death *1151* and Resurrection, the new Passover, is anticipated in the Supper and celebrated in the Eucharist, which fulfils the Jewish Passover and anticipates the final Passover of the Church in the glory of the *677* kingdom.

---

[160] *Jn* 6:68.
[161] Cf. *Jn* 13:1–17, 34–35.
[162] Council of Trent (1562): DS 1740.

[163] Cf. *Jn* 6.
[164] *Lk* 22:7–20; cf. *Mt* 26:17–29; *Mk* 14:12–25; I *Cor* 11:23–26.

'Do this in memory of me'

611   1341 The command of Jesus to repeat his actions and words 'until he comes' does not only ask us to remember Jesus and what he did. It is directed at the liturgical celebration, by the apostles and their
1363   successors, of the *memorial* of Christ, of his life, of his death, of his Resurrection, and of his intercession in the presence of the Father.[165]

2624   1342 From the beginning the Church has been faithful to the Lord's command. Of the Church of Jerusalem it is written:

> They devoted themselves to the apostles' teaching and fellowship, to the breaking of bread and the prayers... Day by day, attending the temple together and breaking bread in their homes, they partook of food with glad and generous hearts.[166]

1166, 2177   1343 It was above all on 'the first day of the week', Sunday, the day of Jesus' Resurrection, that the Christians met 'to break bread'.[167] From that time on down to our own day the celebration of the Eucharist has been continued so that today we encounter it everywhere in the Church with the same fundamental structure. It remains the centre of the Church's life.

1404   1344 Thus from celebration to celebration, as they proclaim the Paschal mystery of Jesus 'until he comes', the pilgrim People of God advances, 'following the narrow way of the cross',[168] toward the heavenly banquet, when all the elect will be seated at the table of the kingdom.

IV. The Liturgical Celebration of the Eucharist

The Mass of all ages

1345 As early as the second century we have the witness of St Justin Martyr for the basic lines of the order of the Eucharistic celebration. They have stayed the same until our own day for all the great liturgical families. St Justin wrote to the pagan emperor Antoninus Pius (138–161) around the year 155, explaining what Christians did:

> On the day we call the day of the sun, all who dwell in the city or country gather in the same place.
>
> The memoirs of the apostles and the writings of the prophets are read, as much as time permits.
>
> When the reader has finished, he who presides over those gathered admonishes and challenges them to imitate these beautiful things.

---

[165] Cf. 1 *Cor* 11:26.
[166] *Acts* 2:42, 46.
[167] *Acts* 20:7.
[168] *AG* 1; cf. 1 *Cor* 11:26.

Then we all rise together and offer prayers* for ourselves. . . and for all others, wherever they may be, so that we may be found righteous by our life and actions, and faithful to the commandments, so as to obtain eternal salvation.

When the prayers are concluded we exchange the kiss.

Then someone brings bread and a cup of water and wine mixed together to him who presides over the brethren.

He takes them and offers praise and glory to the Father of the universe, through the name of the Son and of the Holy Spirit and for a considerable time he gives thanks (in Greek: *eucharistian*) that we have been judged worthy of these gifts.

When he has concluded the prayers and thanksgivings, all present give voice to an acclamation by saying: 'Amen.'

When he who presides has given thanks and the people have responded, those whom we call deacons give to those present the 'eucharisted' bread, wine and water and take them to those who are absent.[169]

1346 The liturgy of the Eucharist unfolds according to a fundamental structure which has been preserved throughout the centuries down to our own day. It displays two great parts that form a fundamental unity:

– the gathering, the *liturgy of the Word*, with readings, homily and general intercessions;

– the *liturgy of the Eucharist*, with the presentation of the bread and wine, the consecratory thanksgiving, and communion.

The liturgy of the Word and liturgy of the Eucharist together form 'one single act of worship';[170] the Eucharistic table   *103* set for us is the table both of the Word of God and of the Body of the Lord.[171]

1347 Is this not the same movement as the Paschal meal of the risen Jesus with his disciples? Walking with them he explained the Scriptures to them; sitting with them at table 'he took bread, blessed and broke it, and gave it to them.'[172]

The movement of the celebration

1348 *All gather together.* Christians come together in one place for the Eucharistic assembly. At its head is Christ himself, the principal   *1140* agent of the Eucharist. He is high priest of the New Covenant; it is he himself who presides invisibly over every Eucharistic celebration. It is in representing him that the bishop or priest acting *in the person of Christ the head* (*in persona Christi capitis*) presides over the   *1548* assembly, speaks after the readings, receives the offerings and says

---

[169] St Justin, *Apol.* 1, 65–67: PG 6, 428–429; the text before the asterisk [*] is from chap. 67.

[170] SC 56.
[171] Cf. *DV* 21.
[172] Cf. *Lk* 24:13–35.

the Eucharistic Prayer. *All* have their own active parts to play in the celebration, each in his own way: readers, those who bring up the offerings, those who give communion and the whole people whose 'Amen' manifests their participation.

1184 1349 The *liturgy of the Word* includes 'the writings of the prophets', that is, the Old Testament, and 'the memoirs of the apostles' (their letters and the Gospels). After the homily, which is an exhortation to accept this Word as what it truly is, the Word of God,[173] and to put it into practice, come the intercessions for all men, according to the Apostle's words: 'I urge that supplications, prayers, intercessions, and thanksgivings be made for all men, for kings and all who are in high positions.'[174]

1350 The *presentation of the offerings* (the Offertory). Then, sometimes in procession, the bread and wine are brought to the altar; they will be offered by the priest in the name of Christ in the Eucharistic sacrifice in which they will become his body and blood. It is the very action of Christ at the Last Supper — 'taking the bread and a cup'. 'The Church alone offers this pure oblation to the Creator, when she offers what comes forth from his creation
1359 with thanksgiving.'[175] The presentation of the offerings at the altar takes up the gesture of Melchizedek and commits the Creator's
614 gifts into the hands of Christ who, in his sacrifice, brings to perfection all human attempts to offer sacrifices.

1351 From the very beginning Christians have brought, along
1397, 2186 with the bread and wine for the Eucharist, gifts to share with those in need. This custom of the *collection*, ever appropriate, is inspired by the example of Christ who became poor to make us rich:[176]

> Those who are well off, and who are also willing, give as each chooses. What is gathered is given to him who presides to assist orphans and widows, those whom illness or any other cause has deprived of resources, prisoners, immigrants and, in a word, all who are in need.[177]

1352 The *anaphora*: with the Eucharistic Prayer — the prayer of thanksgiving and consecration — we come to the heart and summit of the celebration:

> In the *preface*, the Church gives thanks to the Father, through Christ, in the Holy Spirit, for all his works: creation, redemption and sanctification. The
559 whole community thus joins in the unending praise that the Church in heaven, the angels and all the saints, sing to the thrice-holy God.

1105 1353 In the *epiclesis*, the Church asks the Father to send his Holy Spirit (or the

---

[173] Cf. 1 *Th* 2:13.
[174] 1 *Tim* 2:1–2.
[175] St Irenaeus, *Adv. haeres.* 4, 18, 4: PG

7/1, 1027; cf. *Mal* 1:11.
[176] Cf. 1 *Cor* 16:1; 2 *Cor* 8:9.
[177] St Justin, *Apol.* 1, 67, 6: PG 6, 429.

power of his blessing[178]) on the bread and wine, so that by his power they may become the body and blood of Jesus Christ and so that those who take part in the Eucharist may be one body and one spirit (some liturgical traditions put the epiclesis after the anamnesis).

In the *institution narrative*, the power of the words and the action of Christ, and the power of the Holy Spirit, make sacramentally present under the species [1375] of bread and wine Christ's body and blood, his sacrifice offered on the cross once for all.

1354 In the *anamnesis* that follows, the Church calls to mind the Passion, Resur- [1103] rection and glorious return of Christ Jesus; she presents to the Father the offering of his Son which reconciles us with him.

In the *intercessions*, the Church indicates that the Eucharist is celebrated in communion with the whole Church in heaven and on earth, the living and the [954] dead, and in communion with the pastors of the Church, the Pope, the diocesan bishop, his presbyterium and his deacons, and all the bishops of the whole world together with their Churches.

1355 In the *communion*, preceded by the Lord's Prayer and the [1382] breaking of the bread, the faithful receive 'the bread of heaven' and 'the cup of salvation', the body and blood of Christ who offered himself 'for the life of the world':[179]

Because this bread and wine have been made Eucharist ('eucharisted', according to an ancient expression), 'we call this food *Eucharist*, and no [1327] one may take part in it unless he believes that what we teach is true, has received baptism for the forgiveness of sins and new birth, and lives in keeping with what Christ taught.'[180]

V. The Sacramental Sacrifice: Thanksgiving, Memorial, Presence

1356 If Christians have celebrated the Eucharist from the begin- ning and in a form whose substance has not changed despite the great diversity of times and liturgies, it is because we know our- selves to be bound by the command the Lord gave on the eve of his Passion: 'Do this in remembrance of me.'[181]

1357 We carry out this command of the Lord by celebrating the *memorial of his sacrifice*. In so doing, *we offer to the Father* what he has himself given us: the gifts of his creation, bread and wine which, by the power of the Holy Spirit and by the words of Christ, have become the body and blood of Christ. Christ is thus really and mysteriously made *present*.

---

[178] Cf. *Roman Missal*, EP I (Roman Canon), 90.
[179] *Jn* 6:51.
[180] St Justin, *Apol.* 1, 66, 1–2: PG 6, 428.
[181] 1 *Cor* 11:24–25.

1358 We must therefore consider the Eucharist as:
— thanksgiving and praise to the *Father*;
— the sacrificial memorial of *Christ* and his Body;
— the presence of Christ by the power of his word and of his *Spirit*.

Thanksgiving and praise to the Father

1359 The Eucharist, the sacrament of our salvation accomplished by Christ on the cross, is also a sacrifice of praise in thanksgiving
293 for the work of creation. In the Eucharistic sacrifice the whole of creation loved by God is presented to the Father through the death and the Resurrection of Christ. Through Christ the Church can offer the sacrifice of praise in thanksgiving for all that God has made good, beautiful and just in creation and in humanity.

1083 1360 The Eucharist is a sacrifice of thanksgiving to the Father, a blessing by which the Church expresses her gratitude to God for all his benefits, for all that he has accomplished through creation, redemption and sanctification. Eucharist means first of all 'thanksgiving'.

1361 The Eucharist is also the sacrifice of praise by which the Church sings the glory of God in the name of all creation. This
294 sacrifice of praise is possible only through Christ: he unites the faithful to his person, to his praise, and to his intercession, so that the sacrifice of praise to the Father is offered *through* Christ and *with* him, to be accepted *in* him.

The sacrificial memorial of Christ and of his Body, the Church

1362 The Eucharist is the memorial of Christ's Passover, the making present and the sacramental offering of his unique sacrifice, in the liturgy of the Church which is his Body. In all the Eucharistic Prayers we find after the words of institution a prayer
1103 called the *anamnesis* or memorial.

1099 1363 In the sense of Sacred Scripture the *memorial* is not merely the recollection of past events but the proclamation of the mighty works wrought by God for men.[182] In the liturgical celebration of these events, they become in a certain way present and real. This is how Israel understands its liberation from Egypt: every time Passover is celebrated the Exodus events are made present to the memory of believers so that they may conform their lives to them.

611 1364 In the New Testament, the memorial takes on new mean-

---

[182] Cf. *Ex* 13:3.

ing. When the Church celebrates the Eucharist, she commemorates Christ's Passover, and it is made present: the sacrifice Christ offered once for all on the cross remains ever present.[183] 'As often *1085* as the sacrifice of the Cross by which "Christ our Pasch has been sacrificed" is celebrated on the altar, the work of our redemption is carried out.'[184]

1365 Because it is the memorial of Christ's Passover, *the Eucharist is also a sacrifice.* The sacrificial character of the Eucharist is mani- *2100* fested in the very words of institution: 'This is my body which is given for you' and 'This cup which is poured out for you is the New Covenant in my blood.'[185] In the Eucharist Christ gives us *1846* the very body which he gave up for us on the cross, the very blood which he 'poured out for many for the forgiveness of sins'.[186]

1366 The Eucharist is thus a sacrifice because it *re-presents* (makes *613* present) the sacrifice of the cross, because it is its *memorial* and because it *applies* its fruit:

> [Christ], our Lord and God, was once and for all to offer himself to God the Father by his death on the altar of the cross, to accomplish there an everlasting redemption. But because his priesthood was not to end with his death, at the Last Supper 'on the night when he was betrayed', [he wanted] to leave to his beloved spouse the Church a visible sacrifice (as the nature of man demands) by which the bloody sacrifice which he was to accomplish once for all on the cross would be re-presented, its memory perpetuated until the end of the world, and its salutary power be applied to the forgiveness of the sins we daily commit.[187]

1367 The sacrifice of Christ and the sacrifice of the Eucharist are *one single sacrifice:* 'The victim is one and the same: the same now *1545* offers through the ministry of priests, who then offered himself on the cross; only the manner of offering is different.' 'And since in this divine sacrifice which is celebrated in the Mass, the same Christ who offered himself once in a bloody manner on the altar of the cross is contained and is offered in an unbloody manner. . .this sacrifice is truly propitiatory.'[188]

1368 *The Eucharist is also the sacrifice of the Church.* The Church which is the Body of Christ participates in the offering of her Head. With him, she herself is offered whole and entire. She unites herself to his intercession with the Father for all men. In the Eucharist the sacrifice of Christ becomes also the sacrifice of the mem- *618* bers of his Body. The lives of the faithful, their praise, sufferings, *2031*

---

[183] Cf. *Heb* 7:25–27.
[184] *LG* 3; cf. 1 *Cor* 5:7.
[185] *Lk* 22:19–20.
[186] *Mt* 26:28.

[187] Council of Trent (1562): DS 1740; cf. 1 *Cor* 11:23; *Heb* 7:24, 27.
[188] Council of Trent (1562), *Doctrina de SS. Missae sacrificio,* c. 2: DS 1743; cf. *Heb* 9:14, 27.

1109 prayer and work, are united with those of Christ and with his total offering, and so acquire a new value. Christ's sacrifice present on the altar makes it possible for all generations of Christians to be united with his offering.

> In the catacombs the Church is often represented as a woman in prayer, arms outstretched in the praying position. Like Christ who stretched out his arms on the cross, through him, with him and in him, she offers herself and intercedes for all men.

1369 *The whole Church is united with the offering and intercession of* 834, 882 *Christ.* Since he has the ministry of Peter in the Church, the *Pope* is associated with every celebration of the Eucharist, wherein he is named as the sign and servant of the unity of the universal Church. 1561, 1566 The *bishop* of the place is always responsible for the Eucharist, even when a *priest* presides; the bishop's name is mentioned to signify his presidency over the particular Church, in the midst of his presbyterium and with the assistance of *deacons.* The community intercedes also for all ministers who, for it and with it, offer the Eucharistic sacrifice:

> Let only that Eucharist be regarded as legitimate, which is celebrated under [the presidency of] the bishop or him to whom he has entrusted it.[189]

> Through the ministry of priests the spiritual sacrifice of the faithful is completed in union with the sacrifice of Christ the only Mediator, which in the Eucharist is offered through the priests' hands in the name of the whole Church in an unbloody and sacramental manner until the Lord himself comes.[190]

1370 To the offering of Christ are united not only the members 956 still here on earth, but also those already *in the glory of heaven.* In 969 communion with and commemorating the Blessed Virgin Mary and all the saints, the Church offers the Eucharistic sacrifice. In the Eucharist the Church is as it were at the foot of the cross with Mary, united with the offering and intercession of Christ.

958, 1689 1371 The Eucharistic sacrifice is also offered for *the faithful departed* who 'have died in Christ but are not yet wholly purified',[191] so 1032 that they may be able to enter into the light and peace of Christ:

> Put this body anywhere! Don't trouble yourselves about it! I simply ask you to remember me at the Lord's altar wherever you are.[192]

> Then, we pray [in the anaphora] for the holy fathers and bishops who

---

[189] St Ignatius of Antioch. *Ad Smyrn.* 8, 1: SCh 10, 162.

[190] *PO* 2 § 4.

[191] Council of Trent (1562): DS 1743.

[192] St Monica, before her death, to her sons, St Augustine and his brother: St Augustine, *Conf.* 9, 11, 27: PL 32, 775.

have fallen asleep, and in general for all who have fallen asleep before us, in the belief that it is a great benefit to the souls on whose behalf the supplication is offered, while the holy and tremendous Victim is present... By offering to God our supplications for those who have fallen asleep, if they have sinned, we... offer Christ sacrificed for the sins of all, and so render favourable, for them and for us, the God who loves man.[193]

1372 St Augustine admirably summed up this doctrine that moves us to an ever more complete participation in our *1140* Redeemer's sacrifice which we celebrate in the Eucharist:

This wholly redeemed city, the assembly and society of the saints, is offered to God as a universal sacrifice by the high priest who in the form of a slave went so far as to offer himself for us in his Passion, to make us the Body of so great a head... Such is the sacrifice of Christians: 'we who are many are one Body in Christ.' The Church continues to reproduce this sacrifice in the sacrament of the altar so well known to believers wherein it is evident to them that in what she offers she herself is offered.[194]

The presence of Christ by the power of his word and the Holy Spirit

1373 'Christ Jesus, who died, yes, who was raised from the dead, who is at the right hand of God, who indeed intercedes for us', is present in many ways to his Church:[195] in his word, in his Church's prayer, 'where two or three are gathered in my name',[196] in the poor, the sick and the imprisoned,[197] in the sacraments of which he is the author, in the sacrifice of the Mass and in the person of the minister. But 'he is present... most *especially in 1088 the Eucharistic species.*'[198]

1374 The mode of Christ's presence under the Eucharistic species is unique. It raises the Eucharist above all the sacraments as 'the *1211* perfection of the spiritual life and the end to which all the sacraments tend'.[199] In the most blessed sacrament of the Eucharist 'the body and blood, together with the soul and divinity, of our Lord Jesus Christ and, therefore, *the whole Christ is truly, really, and substantially* contained.'[200] 'This presence is called "real" – by which is not intended to exclude the other types of presence as if they could not be "real" too, but because it is presence in the fullest sense: that is to say, it is a *substantial* presence by which Christ, God and man, makes himself wholly and entirely present.'[201]

[193] St Cyril of Jerusalem, *Catech. myst.* 5, 9 and 10: PG 33, 1116–1117.
[194] St Augustine, *De civ. Dei* 10, 6: PL 41, 283; cf. *Rom* 12:5.
[195] *Rom* 8:34; cf. *LG* 48.
[196] *Mt* 18:20.
[197] Cf. *Mt* 25:31–46.
[198] *SC* 7.
[199] St Thomas Aquinas, *STh* III, 73, 3 c.
[200] Council of Trent (1551): DS 1651.
[201] Paul VI, *MF* 39.

1375 It is by the *conversion* of the bread and wine into Christ's body and blood that Christ becomes present in this sacrament. The Church Fathers strongly affirmed the faith of the Church in the efficacy of the Word of Christ and of the action of the Holy Spirit to bring about this conversion. Thus St John Chrysostom declares:

> It is not man that causes the things offered to become the Body and Blood of Christ, but he who was crucified for us, Christ himself. The priest, in the role of Christ, pronounces these words, but their power and grace are God's. *This is my body*, he says. This word transforms the things offered.[202]

And St Ambrose says about this conversion:

> Be convinced that this is not what nature has formed, but what the blessing has consecrated. The power of the blessing prevails over that of nature, because by the blessing nature itself is changed... Could not Christ's word, which can make from nothing what did not exist, change existing things into what they were not before? It is no less a feat to give things their original nature than to change their nature.[203]

1376 The Council of Trent summarizes the Catholic faith by declaring: 'Because Christ our Redeemer said that it was truly his body that he was offering under the species of bread, it has always been the conviction of the Church of God, and this holy Council now declares again, that by the consecration of the bread and wine there takes place a change of the whole substance of the bread into the substance of the body of Christ our Lord and of the whole substance of the wine into the substance of his blood. This change the holy Catholic Church has fittingly and properly called *transubstantiation*.'[204]

1377 The Eucharistic presence of Christ begins at the moment of the consecration and endures as long as the Eucharistic species subsist. Christ is present whole and entire in each of the species and whole and entire in each of their parts, in such a way that the breaking of the bread does not divide Christ.[205]

1378 *Worship of the Eucharist.* In the liturgy of the Mass we express our faith in the real presence of Christ under the species of bread and wine by, among other ways, genuflecting or bowing deeply as a sign of adoration of the Lord. 'The Catholic Church has always offered and still offers to the sacrament of the Eucharist the cult of adoration, not only during Mass, but also outside of it, reserving

Margin references: 1105, 1128, 298, 1178, 103, 2628

---

[202] St John Chrysostom, *De prod. Jud.* 1, 6: PG 49, 380C.
[203] St Ambrose, *De myst.* 9, 50; 52: PL 16, 422–423.
[204] Council of Trent (1551): DS 1642; cf. *Mt* 26:26ff.; *Mk* 14:22ff.; *Lk* 22:19ff.; 1 *Cor* 11:24ff.
[205] Cf. Council of Trent: DS 1641.

the consecrated hosts with the utmost care, exposing them to the solemn veneration of the faithful, and carrying them in procession.'[206]

1379 The tabernacle was first intended for the reservation of the Eucharist in a *1183* worthy place so that it could be brought to the sick and those absent, outside of Mass. As faith in the real presence of Christ in his Eucharist deepened, the Church became conscious of the meaning of silent adoration of the Lord present under the Eucharistic species. It is for this reason that the tabernacle should be located in an especially worthy place in the church, and should be constructed in such a way that it emphasizes and manifests the truth of the real presence of *2691* Christ in the Blessed Sacrament.

1380 It is highly fitting that Christ should have wanted to remain present to his Church in this unique way. Since Christ was about to take his departure from his own in his visible form, he wanted to give us his sacramental presence; since he was about to offer *669* himself on the cross to save us, he wanted us to have the memorial of the love with which he loved us 'to the end',[207] even to the giving of his life. In his Eucharistic presence he remains mysteri- *478* ously in our midst as the one who loved us and gave himself up for us,[208] and he remains under signs that express and communicate this love:

> The Church and the world have a great need for Eucharistic worship. Jesus awaits us in this sacrament of love. Let us not refuse the time to go to meet him in adoration, in contemplation full of faith, and open to *2715* making amends for the serious offences and crimes of the world. Let our adoration never cease.[209]

1381 'That in this sacrament are the true Body of Christ and his true Blood is something that "cannot be apprehended by the senses", says St Thomas, "but *only by faith*, which relies on divine *156* authority." For this reason, in a commentary on Luke 22:19 ("This is my body which is given for you"), St Cyril says: "Do not doubt whether this is true, but rather receive the words of the Saviour in faith, for since he is the truth, he cannot lie." '[210]   *215*

> Godhead here in hiding, whom I do adore
> Masked by these bare shadows, shape and nothing more,
> See, Lord, at thy service low lies here a heart
> Lost, all lost in wonder at the God thou art.
>
> Seeing, touching, tasting are in thee deceived;
> How says trusty hearing? that shall be believed;

---

[206] Paul VI, *MF* 56.
[207] *Jn* 13:1.
[208] Cf. *Gal* 2:20.
[209] John Paul II, *Dominicae cenae* 3.

[210] St Thomas Aquinas, *STh* III, 75, 1; St Cyril of Alexandria, *In Luc.* 22, 19: PG 72, 912; both cited Paul VI, *MF* 18.

What God's Son has told me, take for truth I do;
Truth himself speaks truly or there's nothing true.[211]

VI. The Paschal Banquet

950

1382 The Mass is at the same time, and inseparably, the sacrificial memorial in which the sacrifice of the cross is perpetuated, and the sacred banquet of communion with the Lord's body and blood. But the celebration of the Eucharistic sacrifice is wholly directed toward the intimate union of the faithful with Christ through communion. To receive communion is to receive Christ himself who has offered himself for us.

1182

1383 *The altar*, around which the Church is gathered in the celebration of the Eucharist, represents the two aspects of the same mystery: the altar of the sacrifice and the table of the Lord. This is all the more so since the Christian altar is the symbol of Christ himself, present in the midst of the assembly of his faithful, both as the victim offered for our reconciliation and as food from heaven who is giving himself to us. 'For what is the altar of Christ if not the image of the Body of Christ?'[212] asks St Ambrose. He says elsewhere, 'The altar represents the Body [of Christ] and the Body of Christ is on the altar.'[213] The liturgy expresses this unity of sacrifice and communion in many prayers. Thus the Roman Church prays in her anaphora:

We entreat you, almighty God,
that by the hands of your holy Angel
this offering may be borne to your altar in heaven
in the sight of your divine majesty,
so that as we receive in communion at this altar
the most holy Body and Blood of your Son,
we may be filled with every heavenly blessing and grace.[214]

'Take this and eat it, all of you': communion

2835

1384 The Lord addresses an invitation to us, urging us to receive him in the sacrament of the Eucharist: 'Truly, I say to you, unless

---

[211] St Thomas Aquinas (attr.), *Adoro te devote*; tr. Gerard Manley Hopkins.

[212] St Ambrose, *De sacr.* 5, 2, 7: PL 16, 467.

[213] St Ambrose, *De sacr.* 4, 2, 7: PL 16, 456.

[214] *Missale Romanum*, EP I (Roman Canon), 96: *Supplices te rogamus,*

omnipotens Deus: iube haec perferri per manus sancti Angeli tui in sublime altare tuum, in conspectu divinae maiestatis tuae: ut, quotquot ex hac altaris participatione sacrosanctum Filii tui Corpus et Sanguinem sumpserimus, omni benedictione caelesti et gratia repleamur.

you eat the flesh of the Son of man and drink his blood, you have no life in you.'[215]

1385 To respond to this invitation we must *prepare ourselves* for so great and so holy a moment. St Paul urges us to examine our conscience: 'Whoever, therefore, eats the bread or drinks the cup of the Lord in an unworthy manner will be guilty of profaning the body and blood of the Lord. Let a man examine himself, and so eat of the bread and drink of the cup. For any one who eats and drinks without discerning the body eats and drinks judgement upon himself.'[216] Anyone conscious of a grave sin must receive the sacrament of Reconciliation before coming to communion.

1457

1386 Before so great a sacrament, the faithful can only echo humbly and with ardent faith the words of the Centurion: *Domine, non sum dignus ut intres sub tectum meum, sed tantum dic verbo, et sanabitur anima mea* ('Lord, I am not worthy that you should enter under my roof, but only say the word and my soul will be healed').[217] And in the Divine Liturgy of St John Chrysostom the faithful pray in the same spirit:

> O Son of God, bring me into communion today with your mystical supper. I shall not tell your enemies the secret, nor kiss you with Judas' kiss. But like the good thief I cry, 'Jesus, remember me when you come into your kingdom.'

832

1387 To prepare for worthy reception of this sacrament, the faithful should observe the fast required in their Church.[218] Bodily demeanour (gestures, clothing) ought to convey the respect, solemnity and joy of this moment when Christ becomes our guest.

2043

1388 It is in keeping with the very meaning of the Eucharist that the faithful, if they have the required dispositions,[218a] *receive communion when* they participate in the Mass.[219] As the Second Vatican Council says: 'That more perfect form of participation in the Mass whereby the faithful, after the priest's communion, receive the Lord's Body from the same sacrifice, is warmly recommended.'[220]

1389 The Church obliges the faithful to take part in the Divine Liturgy on Sundays and feast days and, prepared by the sacrament of Reconciliation, to receive the Eucharist at least once a year, if possible during the Easter season.[221] But the Church strongly

2042

[215] *Jn* 6:53.
[216] I *Cor* 11:27-29.
[217] *Missale Romanum*, response to the invitation to communion; cf. *Mt* 8:8.
[218] Cf. CIC, can. 919.
[218a] Cf. CIC, can. 916.
[219] Cf. CIC, can. 917; The faithful may receive the Holy Eucharist only a second time on the same day [cf. Pontificia Commissio Codici Iuris Canonici Authentice Interpretando, *Responsa ad proposita dubia*, 1: AAS 76 (1984), 746].
[220] SC 55.
[221] Cf. OE 15; CIC, can. 920.

2837 encourages the faithful to receive the holy Eucharist on Sundays and feast days, or more often still, even daily.

1390 Since Christ is sacramentally present under each of the species, communion under the species of bread alone makes it possible to receive all the fruit of Eucharistic grace. For pastoral reasons this manner of receiving communion has been legitimately established as the most common form in the Latin rite. But 'the sign of communion is more complete when given under both kinds, since in that form the sign of the Eucharistic meal appears more clearly.'[222] This is the usual form of receiving communion in the Eastern rites.

The fruits of Holy Communion

460 1391 *Holy Communion augments our union with Christ*. The principal fruit of receiving the Eucharist in Holy Communion is an intimate union with Christ Jesus. Indeed, the Lord said: 'He who eats my flesh and drinks my blood abides in me, and I in him.'[223] Life in Christ has its foundation in the Eucharistic banquet: 'As the living Father sent me, and I live because of the Father, so he who 521 eats me will live because of me.'[224]

> On the feasts of the Lord, when the faithful receive the Body of the Son, they proclaim to one another the Good News that the first fruits of life have been given, as when the angel said to Mary Magdalene, 'Christ is risen!' Now too are life and resurrection conferred on whoever receives Christ.[225]

1212 1392 What material food produces in our bodily life, Holy Communion wonderfully achieves in our spiritual life. Communion with the flesh of the risen Christ, a flesh 'given life and giving life through the Holy Spirit',[226] preserves, increases and renews the life of grace received at Baptism. This growth in Christian life needs the nourishment of Eucharistic Communion, the bread for our pilgrimage until the moment of death, when it will be given 1524 to us as viaticum.

1393 *Holy Communion separates us from sin*. The body of Christ we receive in Holy Communion is 'given up for us', and the blood we 613 drink 'shed for the many for the forgiveness of sins'. For this reason the Eucharist cannot unite us to Christ without at the same time cleansing us from past sins and preserving us from future sins:

---

[222] GIRM 240.
[223] Jn 6:56.
[224] Jn 6:57.

[225] Fanqith, Syriac Office of Antioch, vol. I, Commun., 237 A-B.
[226] PO 5.

> For as often as we eat this bread and drink the cup, we proclaim the death
> of the Lord. If we proclaim the Lord's death, we proclaim the forgiveness
> of sins. If, as often as his blood is poured out, it is poured for the forgive-
> ness of sins, I should always receive it, so that it may always forgive my
> sins. Because I always sin, I should always have a remedy.[227]

1394 As bodily nourishment restores lost strength, so the Eucharist strengthens our charity, which tends to be weakened in daily   *1863*
life; and this living charity *wipes away venial sins.*[228] By giving   *1436*
himself to us Christ revives our love and enables us to break our
disordered attachments to creatures and root ourselves in him:

> Since Christ died for us out of love, when we celebrate the memorial of
> his death at the moment of sacrifice we ask that love may be granted to us
> by the coming of the Holy Spirit. We humbly pray that in the strength of
> this love by which Christ willed to die for us, we, by receiving the gift of
> the Holy Spirit, may be able to consider the world as crucified for us, and
> to be ourselves as crucified to the world... Having received the gift of
> love, let us die to sin and live for God.[229]

1395 By the same charity that it enkindles in us, the Eucharist
preserves us from future mortal sins. The more we share the life of   *1855*
Christ and progress in his friendship, the more difficult it is to
break away from him by mortal sin. The Eucharist is not ordered
to the forgiveness of mortal sins – that is proper to the sacrament of   *1446*
Reconciliation. The Eucharist is properly the sacrament of those
who are in full communion with the Church.

1396 *The unity of the Mystical Body: the Eucharist makes the Church.*   *1118*
Those who receive the Eucharist are united more closely to Christ.
Through it Christ unites them to all the faithful in one body – the
Church. Communion renews, strengthens, and deepens this
incorporation into the Church, already achieved by Baptism. In
Baptism we have been called to form but one body.[230] The Euch-   *1267*
arist fulfils this call: 'The cup of blessing which we bless, is it not a
participation in the blood of Christ? The bread which we break, is
it not a participation in the body of Christ? Because there is one
bread, we who are many are one body, for we all partake of the   *790*
one bread':[231]

> If you are the body and members of Christ, then it is your sacrament that
> is placed on the table of the Lord; it is your sacrament that you receive.

---

[227] St Ambrose, *De sacr.* 4, 6, 28: PL 16,
   464; cf. 1 *Cor* 11:26.
[228] Cf. Council of Trent (1551): DS 1638.
[229] St Fulgentius of Ruspe, *Contra Fab.* 28,
   16–19: CCL 19A, 813–814.
[230] Cf. 1 *Cor* 12:13.
[231] 1 *Cor* 10:16–17.

1064   To that which you are you respond 'Amen' ('yes, it is true!') and by responding to it you assent to it. For you hear the words, 'the Body of Christ' and respond 'Amen'. Be then a member of the Body of Christ that your *Amen* may be true.[232]

1397 *The Eucharist commits us to the poor.* To receive in truth the Body and Blood of Christ given up for us, we must recognize *2449* Christ in the poorest, his brethren:

> You have tasted the Blood of the Lord, yet you do not recognize your brother... You dishonour this table when you do not judge worthy of sharing your food someone judged worthy to take part in this meal... God freed you from all your sins and invited you here, but you have not become more merciful.[233]

1398 *The Eucharist and the unity of Christians.* Before the greatness of this mystery St Augustine exclaims, '*O sacrament of devotion! O sign of unity! O bond of charity!*'[234] The more painful the experience *817* of the divisions in the Church which break the common participation in the table of the Lord, the more urgent are our prayers to the Lord that the time of complete unity among all who believe in him may return.

838   1399 The Eastern Churches that are not in full communion with the Catholic Church celebrate the Eucharist with great love. 'These Churches, although separated from us, yet possess true sacraments, above all – by apostolic succession – the priesthood and the Eucharist, whereby they are still joined to us in closest intimacy.' A certain communion *in sacris*, and so in the Eucharist, 'given suitable circumstances and the approval of Church authority, is not merely possible but is encouraged.'[235]

1400 Ecclesial communities derived from the Reformation and separated from the Catholic Church 'have not preserved the proper reality of the Eucharistic mystery in its fullness, especially because of the absence of the sacrament of *1536* Holy Orders.'[236] It is for this reason that, for the Catholic Church, Eucharistic intercommunion with these communities is not possible. However these ecclesial communities, 'when they commemorate the Lord's death and resurrection in the Holy Supper...profess that it signifies life in communion with Christ and await his coming in glory.'[237]

1483   1401 When, in the Ordinary's judgement, a grave necessity arises, Catholic ministers may give the sacraments of Eucharist, Penance, and Anointing of the Sick to other Christians not in full communion with the Catholic Church, who ask for them of their own will, provided they give evidence of holding the *1385* Catholic faith regarding these sacraments, and possess the required dispositions.[238]

---

[232] St Augustine, *Sermo* 272: PL 38, 1247.
[233] St John Chrysostom, *Hom. in 1 Cor.* 27, 5: PG 61, 230–231; cf. *Mt* 25:40.
[234] St Augustine, *In ev. Jo.* 26, 13: PL 35, 1613; cf. *SC* 47.
[235] *UR* 15 § 2; cf. CIC, can. 844 § 3.
[236] *UR* 22 § 3.
[237] *UR* 22 § 3.
[238] Cf. CIC, can. 844 § 4.

VII. The Eucharist – 'Pledge of the Glory to Come'

1402 In an ancient prayer the Church acclaims the mystery of the Eucharist: 'O sacred banquet in which Christ is received as food, *1323* the memory of his Passion is renewed, the soul is filled with grace and a pledge of the life to come is given to us.' If the Eucharist is the memorial of the Passover of the Lord Jesus, if by our communion at the altar we are filled 'with every heavenly blessing and grace',[239] then the Eucharist is also an anticipation of the heavenly *1130* glory.

1403 At the Last Supper the Lord himself directed his disciples' attention toward the fulfilment of the Passover in the kingdom of God: 'I tell you I shall not drink again of this fruit of the vine until that day when I drink it new with you in my Father's kingdom.'[240] Whenever the Church celebrates the Eucharist she remembers this promise and turns her gaze 'to him who is to come'. In her prayer she calls for his coming: *Marana tha!*, 'Come, Lord Jesus!'[241] 'May *671* your grace come and this world pass away!'[242]

1404 The Church knows that the Lord comes even now in his Eucharist and that he is there in our midst. However, his presence is veiled. Therefore we celebrate the Eucharist 'awaiting the blessed hope and the coming of our Saviour, Jesus Christ',[243] *1041* asking 'to share in your glory when every tear will be wiped away. On that day we shall see you, our God, as you are. We shall *1028* become like you and praise you for ever through Christ our Lord.'[244]

1405 There is no surer pledge or clearer sign of this great hope in the new heavens and new earth 'in which righteousness dwells',[245] *1042* than the Eucharist. Every time this mystery is celebrated, 'the work of our redemption is carried on' and we 'break the one bread that provides the medicine of immortality, the antidote for death and the food that makes us live for ever in Jesus Christ.'[246]

1060

---

[239] *Missale Romanum*, EP I (Roman Canon), 96: *Supplices te rogamus*.
[240] Mt 26:29; cf. Lk 22:18; Mk 14:25.
[241] Rev 1:4; 22:20; 1 Cor 16:22.
[242] *Didache* 10, 6: SCh 248 180.
[243] *Missale Romanum* 126, embolism after the *Our Father*: *expectantes beatam spem*

et adventum Salvatoris nostri Jesu Christi; cf. *Titus* 2:13.
[244] EP III, 116: prayer for the dead.
[245] 2 Pt 3:13.
[246] *LG* 3; St Ignatius of Antioch, *Ad Eph.* 20, 2: SCh 10, 76.

IN BRIEF

1406 Jesus said: 'I am the living bread that came down from heaven; if any one eats of this bread, he will live for ever;... he who eats my flesh and drinks my blood has eternal life and... abides in me, and I in him' (Jn 6:51, 54, 56).

1407 The Eucharist is the heart and the summit of the Church's life, for in it Christ associates his Church and all her members with his sacrifice of praise and thanksgiving offered once for all on the cross to his Father; by this sacrifice he pours out the graces of salvation on his Body which is the Church.

1408 The Eucharistic celebration always includes: the proclamation of the Word of God; thanksgiving to God the Father for all his benefits, above all the gift of his Son; the consecration of bread and wine; and participation in the liturgical banquet by receiving the Lord's body and blood. These elements constitute one single act of worship.

1409 The Eucharist is the memorial of Christ's Passover, that is, of the work of salvation accomplished by the life, death and resurrection of Christ, a work made present by the liturgical action.

1410 It is Christ himself, the eternal high priest of the New Covenant who, acting through the ministry of the priests, offers the Eucharistic sacrifice. And it is the same Christ, really present under the species of bread and wine, who is the offering of the Eucharistic sacrifice.

1411 Only validly ordained priests can preside at the Eucharist and consecrate the bread and the wine so that they become the Body and Blood of the Lord.

1412 The essential signs of the Eucharistic sacrament are wheat bread and grape wine, on which the blessing of the Holy Spirit is invoked and the priest pronounces the words of consecration spoken by Jesus during the Last Supper: 'This is my body which will be given up for you... This is the cup of my blood...'

1413 By the consecration the transubstantiation of the bread and wine into the Body and Blood of Christ is brought about. Under the consecrated species of bread and wine Christ himself, living and glorious, is present in a true, real and substantial manner: his Body and his Blood, with his soul and his divinity (cf. Council of Trent: DS 1640; 1651).

1414 As sacrifice, the Eucharist is also offered in reparation for the sins of the living and the dead, and to obtain spiritual or temporal benefits from God.

1415 Anyone who desires to receive Christ in Eucharistic communion must be in the state of grace. Anyone aware of having sinned mortally must not receive communion without having received absolution in the sacrament of Penance.

1416 *Communion with the Body and Blood of Christ increases the communicant's union with the Lord, forgives his venial sins and preserves him from grave sins. Since receiving this sacrament strengthens the bonds of charity between the communicant and Christ, it also reinforces the unity of the Church as the Mystical Body of Christ.*

1417 *The Church warmly recommends that the faithful receive Holy Communion when they participate in the celebration of the Eucharist; she obliges them to do so at least once a year.*

1418 *Because Christ himself is present in the sacrament of the altar, he is to be honoured with the worship of adoration. 'To visit the Blessed Sacrament is... a proof of gratitude, an expression of love, and a duty of adoration toward Christ our Lord' (Paul VI, MF 66).*

1419 *Having passed from this world to the Father, Christ gives us in the Eucharist the pledge of glory with him. Participation in the Holy Sacrifice identifies us with his Heart, sustains our strength along the pilgrimage of this life, makes us long for eternal life and unites us even now to the Church in heaven, the Blessed Virgin Mary and all the saints.*

Chapter Two
THE SACRAMENTS OF HEALING

1420 Through the sacraments of Christian initiation, man receives the new life of Christ. Now we carry this life 'in earthen vessels', and it remains 'hidden with Christ in God'.[1] We are still in our 'earthly tent', subject to suffering, illness and death.[2] This new life as a child of God can be weakened and even lost by sin.

1421 The Lord Jesus Christ, physician of our souls and bodies, who forgave the sins of the paralytic and restored him to bodily health,[3] has willed that his Church continue, in the power of the Holy Spirit, his work of healing and salvation, even among her own members. This is the purpose of the two sacraments of healing: the sacrament of Penance and the sacrament of Anointing of the Sick.

Article 4
THE SACRAMENT OF PENANCE AND RECONCILIATION

1422 'Those who approach the sacrament of Penance obtain par-   *980*

---

[1] 2 Cor 4:7; Col 3:3.
[2] 2 Cor 5:1.
[3] Cf. Mk 2:1–12.

don from God's mercy for the offence committed against him, and are, at the same time, reconciled with the Church which they have wounded by their sins and which by charity, by example and by prayer labours for their conversion.'[4]

I. What Is This Sacrament Called?

1989   1423 It is called the *sacrament of conversion* because it makes sacramentally present Jesus' call to conversion, the first step in returning to the Father[5] from whom one has strayed by sin.

1440   It is called the *sacrament of Penance*, since it consecrates the Christian sinner's personal and ecclesial steps of conversion, penance and satisfaction.

1456   1424 It is called the *sacrament of confession*, since the disclosure or confession of sins to a priest is an essential element of this sacrament. In a profound sense it is also a 'confession' – acknowledgement and praise – of the holiness of God and of his mercy towards sinful man.

1449   It is called the *sacrament of forgiveness*, since by the priest's sacramental absolution God grants the penitent 'pardon and peace'.[6]

1442   It is called the *sacrament of Reconciliation*, because it imparts to the sinner the love of God who reconciles: 'Be reconciled to God.'[7] He who lives by God's merciful love is ready to respond to the Lord's call: 'Go; first be reconciled to your brother.'[8]

II. Why a Sacrament of Reconciliation After Baptism?

1263   1425 'You were washed, you were sanctified, you were justified in the name of the Lord Jesus Christ and in the Spirit of our God.'[9] One must appreciate the magnitude of the gift God has given us in the sacraments of Christian initiation in order to grasp the degree to which sin is excluded for him who has 'put on Christ'.[10] But the apostle John also says: 'If we say we have no sin, we deceive ourselves, and the truth is not in us.'[11] And the Lord himself taught us
2838   to pray: 'Forgive us our trespasses',[12] linking our forgiveness of one another's offences to the forgiveness of our sins that God will grant us.

1426 *Conversion* to Christ, the new birth of Baptism, the gift of

[4] *LG* 11 § 2.
[5] Cf. *Mk* 1:15; *Lk* 15:18.
[6] *OP* 46: formula of absolution.
[7] *2 Cor* 5:20.
[8] *Mt* 5:24.
[9] *1 Cor* 6:11.
[10] *Gal* 3:27.
[11] *1 Jn* 1:8.
[12] Cf. *Lk* 11:4; *Mt* 6:12.

the Holy Spirit and the Body and Blood of Christ received as food
have made us 'holy and without blemish', just as the Church herself, the Bride of Christ, is 'holy and without blemish'.[13] Nevertheless the new life received in Christian initiation has not
abolished the frailty and weakness of human nature, nor the inclination to sin that tradition calls *concupiscence*, which remains in the
baptized such that with the help of the grace of Christ they may
prove themselves in the struggle of Christian life.[14] This is the
struggle of *conversion* directed toward holiness and eternal life to
which the Lord never ceases to call us.[15]

405, 978
1264

III. The Conversion of the Baptized

1427 Jesus calls to conversion. This call is an essential part of the
proclamation of the kingdom: 'The time is fulfilled, and the kingdom of God is at hand; repent, and believe in the gospel.'[16] In the
Church's preaching this call is addressed first to those who do not
yet know Christ and his Gospel. Also, Baptism is the principal
place for the first and fundamental conversion. It is by faith in the
Gospel and by Baptism[17] that one renounces evil and gains salvation, that is, the forgiveness of all sins and the gift of new life.

541

1226

1428 Christ's call to conversion continues to resound in the lives
of Christians. This *second conversion* is an uninterrupted task for the
whole Church who, 'clasping sinners to her bosom, [is] at once
holy and always in need of purification, [and] follows constantly
the path of penance and renewal.'[18] This endeavour of conversion
is not just a human work. It is the movement of a 'contrite heart',
drawn and moved by grace to respond to the merciful love of God
who loved us first.[19]

1036

853

1996

1429 St Peter's conversion after he had denied his master three
times bears witness to this. Jesus' look of infinite mercy drew tears
of repentance from Peter and, after the Lord's Resurrection, a
threefold affirmation of love for him.[20] The second conversion
also has a *communitarian* dimension, as is clear in the Lord's call to a
whole Church: 'Repent!'[21]

> St Ambrose says of the two conversions that, in the Church, 'there are
> water and tears: the water of Baptism and the tears of repentance.'[22]

---

[13] *Eph* 1:4; 5:27.
[14] Cf. Council of Trent (1546): DS 1515.
[15] Cf. Council of Trent (1547): DS 1545; *LG* 40.
[16] *Mk* 1:15.
[17] Cf. *Acts* 2:38.

[18] *LG* 8 § 3.
[19] *Ps* 51:17; cf. *Jn* 6:44; 12:32; 1 *Jn* 4:10.
[20] Cf. *Lk* 22:61; *Jn* 21:15–17.
[21] *Rev* 2:5, 16.
[22] St Ambrose, *Ep.* 41, 12: PL 16, 1116B.

IV. Interior Penance

1430 Jesus' call to conversion and penance, like that of the prophets before him, does not aim first at outward works, 'sackcloth and ashes', fasting and mortification, but at the *conversion of the heart, interior conversion*. Without this, such penances remain sterile and false; however, interior conversion urges expression in visible signs, gestures and works of penance.[23]

1098

1431 Interior repentance is a radical reorientation of our whole life, a return, a conversion to God with all our heart, an end of sin, a turning away from evil, with repugnance toward the evil actions we have committed. At the same time it entails the desire and resolution to change one's life, with hope in God's mercy and trust in the help of his grace. This conversion of heart is accompanied by a salutary pain and sadness which the Fathers called *animi cruciatus* (affliction of spirit) and *compunctio cordis* (repentance of heart).[24]

1451

368

1432 The human heart is heavy and hardened. God must give man a new heart.[25] Conversion is first of all a work of the grace of God who makes our hearts return to him: 'Restore us to thyself, O LORD, that we may be restored!'[26] God gives us the strength to begin anew. It is in discovering the greatness of God's love that our heart is shaken by the horror and weight of sin and begins to fear offending God by sin and being separated from him. The human heart is converted by looking upon him whom our sins have pierced:[27]

1989

> Let us fix our eyes on Christ's blood and understand how precious it is to his Father, for, poured out for our salvation, it has brought to the whole world the grace of repentance.[28]

1433 Since Easter, the Holy Spirit has proved 'the world wrong about sin',[29] i.e. proved that the world has not believed in him whom the Father has sent. But this same Spirit who brings sin to light is also the Consoler who gives the human heart grace for repentance and conversion.[30]

729

692

1848

V. The Many Forms of Penance in Christian Life

1434 The interior penance of the Christian can be expressed in many and

---

[23] Cf. *Joel* 2:12–13; *Is* 1:16–17; *Mt* 6:1–6, 16–18.
[24] Cf. Council of Trent (1551): DS 1676–1678; 1705; cf. *Roman Catechism* II, 5, 4.
[25] Cf. *Ezek* 36:26–27.
[26] *Lam* 5:21.

[27] Cf. *Jn* 19:37; *Zech* 12:10.
[28] St Clement of Rome, *Ad Cor.* 7, 4: PG 1, 224.
[29] Cf. *Jn* 16:8–9.
[30] Cf. *Jn* 15:26; *Acts* 2:36–38; John Paul II, *DeV* 27–48.

various ways. Scripture and the Fathers insist above all on three forms, *fasting, prayer* and *almsgiving*,[31] which express conversion in relation to oneself, to God and to others. Alongside the radical purification brought about by Baptism or martyrdom they cite as means of obtaining forgiveness of sins: efforts at reconciliation with one's neighbour, tears of repentance, concern for the salvation of one's neighbour, the intercession of the saints and the practice of charity 'which covers a multitude of sins'.[32]

1969

1435 Conversion is accomplished in daily life by gestures of reconciliation, concern for the poor, the exercise and defence of justice and right[33] by the admission of faults to one's brethren, fraternal correction, revision of life, examination of conscience, spiritual direction, acceptance of suffering, endurance of persecution for the sake of righteousness. Taking up one's cross each day and following Jesus is the surest way of penance.[34]

1436 *Eucharist and penance.* Daily conversion and penance find their source and nourishment in the Eucharist, for in it is made present the sacrifice of Christ which has reconciled us with God. Through the Eucharist those who live from the life of Christ are fed and strengthened. 'It is a remedy to free us from our daily faults and to preserve us from mortal sins.'[35]

1394

1437 Reading Sacred Scripture, praying the Liturgy of the Hours and the *Our Father* – every sincere act of worship or devotion revives the spirit of conversion and repentance within us and contributes to the forgiveness of our sins.

1438 *The seasons and days of penance* in the course of the liturgical year (Lent, and each Friday in memory of the death of the Lord) are intense moments of the Church's penitential practice.[36] These times are particularly appropriate for spiritual exercises, penitential liturgies, pilgrimages as signs of penance, voluntary self-denial such as fasting and almsgiving, and fraternal sharing (charitable and missionary works).

540

2043

1439 *The process of conversion and repentance* was described by Jesus in the parable of the prodigal son, the centre of which is the merciful father:[37] the fascination of illusory freedom, the abandonment of the father's house; the extreme misery in which the son finds himself after squandering his fortune; his deep humiliation at finding himself obliged to feed swine, and still worse, at wanting to feed on the husks the pigs ate; his reflection on all he has lost; his repentance and decision to declare himself guilty before his father; the journey back; the father's generous welcome; the father's joy – all these are characteristic of the process of conversion. The beautiful robe, the ring and the festive banquet are symbols of that new life – pure, worthy and joyful – of anyone who returns to God and to the bosom of his family, which is the Church. Only the heart of Christ who knows the depths of his Father's love could reveal to us the abyss of his mercy in so simple and beautiful a way.

545

---

[31] Cf. *Tob* 12:8; *Mt* 6:1–18.
[32] 1 *Pt* 4:8; cf. *Jas* 5:20.
[33] Cf. *Am* 5:24; *Is* 1:17.
[34] Cf. *Lk* 9:23.

[35] Council of Trent (1551): DS 1638.
[36] Cf. *SC* 109–110; CIC, cann. 1249–1253; CCEO, cann. 880–883.
[37] Cf. *Lk* 15:11–24.

VI. The Sacrament of Penance and Reconciliation

1850   1440 Sin is before all else an offence against God, a rupture of communion with him. At the same time it damages communion with the Church. For this reason conversion entails both God's forgiveness and reconciliation with the Church, which are expressed and accomplished liturgically by the sacrament of Penance and Reconciliation.[38]

Only God forgives sin

270, 431   1441 Only God forgives sins.[39] Since he is the Son of God, Jesus says of himself, 'The Son of man has authority on earth to forgive sins', and exercises this divine power: 'Your sins are forgiven.'[40] Further, by virtue of his divine authority he gives this power to
589   men to exercise in his name.[41]

1442 Christ has willed that in her prayer and life and action his whole Church should be the sign and instrument of the forgiveness and reconciliation that he acquired for us at the price of his
983   blood. But he entrusted the exercise of the power of absolution to the apostolic ministry which he charged with the 'ministry of reconciliation'.[42] The apostle is sent out 'on behalf of Christ' with 'God making his appeal' through him and pleading: 'Be reconciled to God.'[43]

Reconciliation with the Church

1443 During his public life Jesus not only forgave sins, but also made plain the effect of this forgiveness: he reintegrated forgiven sinners into the community of the People of God from which sin had alienated or even excluded them. A remarkable sign of this
545   is the fact that Jesus receives sinners at his table, a gesture that expresses in an astonishing way both God's forgiveness and the return to the bosom of the People of God.[44]

981   1444 In imparting to his apostles his own power to forgive sins the Lord also gives them the authority to reconcile sinners with the Church. This ecclesial dimension of their task is expressed most notably in Christ's solemn words to Simon Peter: 'I will give you the keys of the kingdom of heaven, and whatever you bind on earth shall be bound in heaven, and whatever you loose on earth shall be loosed in heaven.'[45] 'The office of binding and loosing

---

[38] Cf. LG 11.
[39] Cf. Mk 2:7.
[40] Mk 2:5, 10; Lk 7:48.
[41] Cf. Jn 20:21–23.

[42] 2 Cor 5:18.
[43] 2 Cor 5:20.
[44] Cf. Lk 15; 19:9.
[45] Mt 16:19; cf. Mt 18:18; 28:16–20.

which was given to Peter was also assigned to the college of the
apostles united to its head.'[46]

1445 The words *bind and loose* mean: whomever you exclude 553
from your communion, will be excluded from communion with
God; whomever you receive anew into your communion, God
will welcome back into his. *Reconciliation with the Church is inseparable from reconciliation with God.*

The sacrament of forgiveness

1446 Christ instituted the sacrament of Penance for all sinful 979
members of his Church: above all for those who, since Baptism,
have fallen into grave sin, and have thus lost their baptismal grace 1856
and wounded ecclesial communion. It is to them that the sacrament of Penance offers a new possibility to convert and to recover
the grace of justification. The Fathers of the Church present this 1990
sacrament as 'the second plank [of salvation] after the shipwreck
which is the loss of grace'.[47]

1447 Over the centuries the concrete form in which the Church has exercised
this power received from the Lord has varied considerably. During the first
centuries the reconciliation of Christians who had committed particularly grave
sins after their Baptism (for example, idolatry, murder or adultery) was tied to a
very rigorous discipline, according to which penitents had to do public penance
for their sins, often for years, before receiving reconciliation. To this 'order of
penitents' (which concerned only certain grave sins), one was only rarely
admitted and in certain regions only once in a lifetime. During the seventh
century Irish missionaries, inspired by the Eastern monastic tradition, took to
continental Europe the 'private' practice of penance, which does not require
public and prolonged completion of penitential works before reconciliation
with the Church. From that time on, the sacrament has been performed in
secret between penitent and priest. This new practice envisioned the possibility
of repetition and so opened the way to a regular frequenting of this sacrament. It
allowed the forgiveness of grave sins and venial sins to be integrated into one
sacramental celebration. In its main lines this is the form of penance that the
Church has practised down to our day.

1448 Beneath the changes in discipline and celebration that this
sacrament has undergone over the centuries, the same *fundamental
structure* is to be discerned. It comprises two equally essential elements: on the one hand, the acts of the man who undergoes conversion through the action of the Holy Spirit: namely, contrition,
confession and satisfaction; on the other, God's action through the
intervention of the Church. The Church, who through the bishop

---

[46] *LG* 22 § 2.
[47] Tertullian, *De paenit.* 4, 2: PL 1, 1343;
    cf. Council of Trent (1547): DS 1542.

and his priests forgives sins in the name of Jesus Christ and determines the manner of satisfaction, also prays for the sinner and does penance with him. Thus the sinner is healed and re-established in ecclesial communion.

1481 1449 The formula of absolution used in the Latin Church expresses the essential elements of this sacrament: the Father of mercies is the source of all forgiveness. He effects the reconciliation of *234* sinners through the Passover of his Son and the gift of his Spirit, through the prayer and ministry of the Church:

> God, the Father of mercies,
> through the death and the resurrection of his Son
> has reconciled the world to himself
> and sent the Holy Spirit among us
> for the forgiveness of sins;
> through the ministry of the Church
> may God give you pardon and peace,
> and I absolve you from your sins
> in the name of the Father, and of the Son, and of the Holy Spirit.[48]

VII. The Acts of the Penitent

1450 'Penance requires... the sinner to endure all things willingly, be contrite of heart, confess with the lips, and practise complete humility and fruitful satisfaction.'[49]

Contrition

1451 Among the penitent's acts contrition occupies first place. *431* Contrition is 'sorrow of the soul and detestation for the sin committed, together with the resolution not to sin again'.[50]

1822 1452 When it arises from a love by which God is loved above all else, contrition is called 'perfect' (contrition of charity). Such contrition remits venial sins; it also obtains forgiveness of mortal sins if it includes the firm resolution to have recourse to sacramental confession as soon as possible.[51]

1453 The contrition called 'imperfect' (or 'attrition') is also a gift of God, a prompting of the Holy Spirit. It is born of the consideration of sin's ugliness or the fear of eternal damnation and the other penalties threatening the sinner (contrition of fear). Such a stirring of conscience can initiate an interior process which, under the prompting of grace, will be brought to completion by sacra-

---

[48] *OP* 46: formula of absolution.
[49] *Roman Catechism* II, 5, 21; cf. Council of Trent (1551): DS 1673.

[50] Council of Trent (1551): DS 1676.
[51] Cf. Council of Trent (1551): DS 1677.

mental absolution. By itself however, imperfect contrition cannot obtain the forgiveness of grave sins, but it disposes one to obtain forgiveness in the sacrament of Penance.[52]

1454 The reception of this sacrament ought to be prepared for by an *examination of conscience* made in the light of the Word of God. The passages best suited to this can be found in the Ten Commandments, and the moral catechesis of the Gospels and the apostolic Letters, such as the Sermon on the Mount and the apostolic teachings.[53]

The confession of sins

1455 The confession (or disclosure) of sins, even from a simply human point of view, frees us and facilitates our reconciliation with others. Through such an admission man looks squarely at the sins he is guilty of, takes responsibility for them, and thereby opens himself again to God and to the communion of the Church in order to make a new future possible. *1424* *1734*

1456 Confession to a priest is an essential part of the sacrament of Penance: 'All mortal sins of which penitents after a diligent self-examination are conscious must be recounted by them in confession, even if they are most secret and have been committed against the last two precepts of the Decalogue; for these sins sometimes wound the soul more grievously and are more dangerous than those which are committed openly.'[54] *1855*

> When Christ's faithful strive to confess all the sins that they can remember, they undoubtedly place all of them before the divine mercy for pardon. But those who fail to do so and knowingly withhold some, place nothing before the divine goodness for remission through the mediation of the priest, 'for if the sick person is too ashamed to show his wound to the doctor, the medicine cannot heal what it does not know.'[55]

1457 According to the Church's command, 'after having attained the age of discretion, each of the faithful is bound by an obligation faithfully to confess serious sins at least once a year.'[56] Anyone who is aware of having committed a mortal sin must not receive Holy Communion, even if he experiences deep contrition, without having first received sacramental absolution, unless he has a grave reason for receiving Communion and there is no possibility of going to confession.[57] Children must go to the sacrament of Penance before receiving Holy Communion for the first time.[58] *2042* *1385*

1458 Without being strictly necessary, confession of everyday

---

[52] Cf. Council of Trent (1551): DS 1678; 1705.

[53] Cf. *Mt* 5 – 7; *Rom* 12 – 15; 1 *Cor* 12 – 13; *Gal* 5; *Eph* 4 – 6; etc.

[54] Council of Trent (1551): DS 1680 (ND 1626); cf. *Ex* 20:17; *Mt* 5:28.

[55] Council of Trent (1551): DS 1680 (ND 1626); cf. St Jerome, *In Eccl.* 10, 11: PL 23, 1096.

[56] Cf. CIC, can. 989; Council of Trent (1551): DS 1683; 1708.

[57] Cf. Council of Trent (1551): DS 1647; 1661; CIC, can. 916; CCEO, can. 711.

[58] Cf. CIC, can. 914.

faults (venial sins) is nevertheless strongly recommended by the
Church.[59] Indeed the regular confession of our venial sins helps us
1783 form our conscience, fight against evil tendencies, let ourselves be
healed by Christ and progress in the life of the Spirit. By receiving
more frequently through this sacrament the gift of the Father's
mercy, we are spurred to be merciful as he is merciful:[60]

> Whoever confesses his sins... is already working with God. God indicts
> your sins; if you also indict them, you are joined with God. Man and
> sinner are, so to speak, two realities: when you hear 'man' – this is what
> God has made; when you hear 'sinner' – this is what man himself has
> made. Destroy what you have made, so that God may save what he has
> made... When you begin to abhor what you have made, it is then that
> your good works are beginning, since you are accusing yourself of your
2468 evil works. The beginning of good works is the confession of evil works.
> You do the truth and come to the light.[61]

Satisfaction

1459 Many sins wrong our neighbour. One must do what is pos-
2412 sible in order to repair the harm (e.g., return stolen goods, restore
the reputation of someone slandered, pay compensation for inju-
2487 ries). Simple justice requires as much. But sin also injures and
weakens the sinner himself, as well as his relationships with God
and neighbour. Absolution takes away sin, but it does not remedy
all the disorders sin has caused.[62] Raised up from sin, the sinner
must still recover his full spiritual health by doing something more
to make amends for the sin: he must 'make satisfaction for' or
1473 'expiate' his sins. This satisfaction is also called 'penance'.

1460 The *penance* the confessor imposes must take into account
the penitent's personal situation and must seek his spiritual good. It
must correspond as far as possible with the gravity and nature of
the sins committed. It can consist of prayer, an offering, works of
2447 mercy, service of neighbour, voluntary self-denial, sacrifices, and
above all the patient acceptance of the cross we must bear. Such
618 penances help configure us to Christ, who alone expiated our sins
once for all. They allow us to become co-heirs with the risen
Christ, 'provided we suffer with him'.[63]

> The satisfaction that we make for our sins, however, is not so much ours
> as though it were not done through Jesus Christ. We who can do

---

[59] Cf. Council of Trent: DS 1680; CIC.
can. 988 § 2.
[60] Cf. Lk 6:36.
[61] St Augustine, *In ev. Jo.* 12, 13: PL 35,
1491.

[62] Cf. Council of Trent (1551): DS 1712.
[63] *Rom* 8:17; 3:25; 1 *Jn* 2:1–2; cf. Council
of Trent (1551): DS 1690.

nothing ourselves, as if just by ourselves, can do all things with the co-operation of 'him who strengthens' us. Thus man has nothing of which to boast, but all our boasting is in Christ... in whom we make *2011* satisfaction by bringing forth 'fruits that befit repentance'. These fruits have their efficacy from him, by him they are offered to the Father, and through him they are accepted by the Father.[64]

VIII. The Minister of This Sacrament

1461 Since Christ entrusted to his apostles the ministry of recon- *981* ciliation,[65] bishops who are their successors, and priests, the bishops' collaborators, continue to exercise this ministry. Indeed bishops and priests, by virtue of the sacrament of Holy Orders, have the power to forgive all sins 'in the name of the Father, and of the Son, and of the Holy Spirit'.

1462 Forgiveness of sins brings reconciliation with God, but also with the Church. Since ancient times the bishop, visible head of a *886* particular Church, has thus rightfully been considered to be the one who principally has the power and ministry of reconciliation: he is the moderator of the penitential discipline.[66] Priests, his col- *1567* laborators, exercise it to the extent that they have received the commission either from their bishop (or religious superior) or the Pope, according to the law of the Church.[67]

1463 Certain particularly grave sins incur excommunication, the most severe ecclesiastical penalty, which impedes the reception of the sacraments and the exercise of certain ecclesiastical acts, and for which absolution consequently cannot be granted, according to canon law, except by the Pope, the bishop of the place or priests authorized by them.[68] In danger of death any priest, even if deprived of faculties for hearing confessions, can absolve from every sin and *982* excommunication.[69]

1464 Priests must encourage the faithful to come to the sacrament of Penance, and must make themselves available to celebrate this sacrament each time Christians reasonably ask for it.[70]

1465 When he celebrates the sacrament of Penance, the priest is *983* fulfilling the ministry of the Good Shepherd who seeks the lost sheep, of the Good Samaritan who binds up wounds, of the Father who awaits the prodigal son and welcomes him on his return, and of the just and impartial judge whose judgement is both just and

---

[64] Council of Trent (1551): DS 1691; cf. Phil 4:13; 1 Cor 1:31; 2 Cor 10:17; Gal 6:14; Lk 3:8.
[65] Cf. Jn 20:23; 2 Cor 5:18.
[66] Cf. LG 26 § 3.
[67] Cf. CIC, cann. 844; 967–969; 972; CCEO, can. 722 §§ 3–4.
[68] Cf. CIC, cann. 1331; 1354–1357; CCEO, can. 1431; 1434; 1420.
[69] Cf. CIC, can. 976; CCEO, can. 725.
[70] Cf. CIC, can. 986; CCEO, can. 735; PO 13.

merciful. The priest is the sign and the instrument of God's merciful love for the sinner.

1466 The confessor is not the master of God's forgiveness, but its 1551 servant. The minister of this sacrament should unite himself to the intention and charity of Christ.[71] He should have a proven know- 2690 ledge of Christian behaviour, experience of human affairs, respect and sensitivity toward the one who has fallen; he must love the truth, be faithful to the Magisterium of the Church, and lead the penitent with patience toward healing and full maturity. He must pray and do penance for his penitent, entrusting him to the Lord's mercy.

1467 Given the delicacy and greatness of this ministry and the respect due to persons, the Church declares that every priest who hears confessions is bound under very severe penalties to keep 2490 absolute secrecy regarding the sins that his penitents have confessed to him. He can make no use of knowledge that confession gives him about penitents' lives.[72] This secrecy, which admits of no exceptions, is called the 'sacramental seal', because what the penitent has made known to the priest remains 'sealed' by the sacrament.

IX. The Effects of This Sacrament

1468 'The whole power of the sacrament of Penance consists in restoring us to God's grace, and joining us with him in an intimate friendship.'[73] *Reconciliation with God* is thus the purpose and effect of this sacrament. For those who receive the sacrament of Penance with contrite heart and religious disposition, reconciliation 'is usu- 2305 ally followed by peace and serenity of conscience with strong spiritual consolation.'[74] Indeed the sacrament of Reconciliation with God brings about a true 'spiritual resurrection', restoration of the dignity and blessings of the life of the children of God, of which the most precious is friendship with God.[75]

953 1469 This sacrament *reconciles us with the Church*. Sin damages or even breaks fraternal communion. The sacrament of Penance repairs or restores it. In this sense it does not simply heal the one restored to ecclesial communion, but has also a revitalizing effect on the life of the Church which suffered from the sin of one of her members.[76] Re-established or strengthened in the communion of

[71] Cf. PO 13.
[72] Cf. CIC, can. 1388 § 1; CCEO, can. 1456.
[73] Roman Catechism, II, 5, 18.
[74] Council of Trent (1551): DS 1674.
[75] Cf. Lk 15:32.
[76] Cf. 1 Cor 12:26.

saints, the sinner is made stronger by the exchange of spiritual *949* goods among all the living members of the Body of Christ, whether still on pilgrimage or already in the heavenly home-land:[77]

> It must be recalled that. . . this reconciliation with God leads, as it were, to other reconciliations, which repair the other breaches caused by sin. The forgiven penitent is reconciled with himself in his inmost being, where he regains his innermost truth. He is reconciled with his brethren whom he has in some way offended and wounded. He is reconciled with the Church. He is reconciled with all creation.[78]

1470 In this sacrament, the sinner, placing himself before the merciful judgement of God, *anticipates* in a certain way *the judgement* to *678, 1039* which he will be subjected at the end of his earthly life. For it is now, in this life, that we are offered the choice between life and death, and it is only by the road of conversion that we can enter the Kingdom, from which one is excluded by grave sin.[79] In converting to Christ through penance and faith, the sinner passes from death to life and 'does not come into judgement.'[80]

X. Indulgences

1471 The doctrine and practice of indulgences in the Church are closely linked to the effects of the sacrament of Penance.

What is an indulgence?

'An indulgence is a remission before God of the temporal punishment due to sins whose guilt has already been forgiven, which the faithful Christian who is duly disposed gains under certain prescribed conditions through the action of the Church which, as the minister of redemption, dispenses and applies with authority the treasury of the satisfactions of Christ and the saints.'[81]

'An indulgence is partial or plenary according as it removes either part or all of the temporal punishment due to sin.'[82] The faithful can gain indulgences for themselves or apply them to the dead.[82a]

The punishments of sin

1472 To understand this doctrine and practice of the Church it is necessary to understand that sin has *a double consequence*. Grave sin deprives us of communion with God, and therefore makes us incapable of eternal life, the privation of *1861* which is called the 'eternal punishment' of sin. On the other hand every sin, even venial, entails an unhealthy attachment to creatures, which must be purified either here on earth, or after death in the state called Purgatory. This *1031*

---

[77] Cf. *LG* 48–50.
[78] John Paul II, *RP* 31, V.
[79] Cf. 1 *Cor* 5:11; *Gal* 5:19–21; *Rev* 22:15.
[80] *Jn* 5:24.

[81] Paul VI, Ap. Const. *Indulgentiarum doctrina*, Norm 1.
[82] *Indulgentiarum doctrina*, Norm 2; cf. Norm 3.
[82a] CIC, can. 994.

purification frees one from what is called the 'temporal punishment' of sin. These two punishments must not be conceived of as a kind of vengeance inflicted by God from without, but as following from the very nature of sin. A conversion which proceeds from a fervent charity can attain the complete purification of the sinner in such a way that no punishment would remain.[83]

1473 The forgiveness of sin and restoration of communion with God entail the remission of the eternal punishment of sin, but temporal punishment of sin remains. While patiently bearing sufferings and trials of all kinds and, when the day comes, serenely facing death, the Christian must strive to accept this tem-
2447 poral punishment of sin as a grace. He should strive by works of mercy and charity, as well as by prayer and the various practices of penance, to put off completely the 'old man' and to put on the 'new man'.[84]

In the communion of saints

1474 The Christian who seeks to purify himself of his sin and to become holy with the help of God's grace is not alone. 'The life of each of God's children is joined in Christ and through Christ in a wonderful way to the life of all the
946-959 other Christian brethren in the supernatural unity of the Mystical Body of
795 Christ, as in a single mystical person.'[85]

1475 In the communion of saints, 'a perennial link of charity exists between the faithful who have already reached their heavenly home, those who are ex-piating their sins in purgatory and those who are still pilgrims on earth. Be-tween them there is, too, an abundant exchange of all good things.'[86] In this wonderful exchange, the holiness of one profits others, well beyond the harm that the sin of one could cause others. Thus recourse to the communion of saints lets the contrite sinner be more promptly and efficaciously purified of the punishments for sin.

1476 We also call these spiritual goods of the communion of saints the *Church's treasury*, which is 'not the sum total of the material goods which have accumu-lated during the course of the centuries. On the contrary the "treasury of the Church" is the infinite value, which can never be exhausted, which Christ's
617 merits have before God. They were offered so that the whole of mankind could be set free from sin and attain communion with the Father. In Christ, the Redeemer himself, the satisfactions and merits of his Redemption exist and find their efficacy.'[87]

1477 'This treasury includes as well the prayers and good works of the Blessed
969 Virgin Mary. They are truly immense, unfathomable and even pristine in their value before God. In the treasury, too, are the prayers and good works of all the saints, all those who have followed in the footsteps of Christ the Lord and by his grace have made their lives holy and carried out the mission the Father entrusted to them. In this way they attained their own salvation and at the same time co-operated in saving their brothers in the unity of the Mystical Body.'[88]

---

[83] Cf. Council of Trent (1551): DS 1712-1713; (1563): DS 1820.
[84] Eph 4:22, 24.
[85] Indulgentiarum doctrina 5.

[86] Indulgentiarum doctrina 5.
[87] Indulgentiarum doctrina 5.
[88] Indulgentiarum doctrina 5.

Obtaining indulgence from God through the Church

1478 An indulgence is obtained through the Church who, by virtue of the power of binding and loosing granted her by Christ Jesus, intervenes in favour of individual Christians and opens for them the treasury of the merits of Christ and the saints to obtain from the Father of mercies the remission of the temporal *981* punishments due for their sins. Thus the Church does not want simply to come to the aid of these Christians, but also to spur them to works of devotion, penance and charity.[89]

1479 Since the faithful departed now being purified are also members of the *1032* same communion of saints, one way we can help them is to obtain indulgences for them, so that the temporal punishments due for their sins may be remitted.

XI. The Celebration of the Sacrament of Penance

1480 Like all the sacraments, Penance is a liturgical action. The elements of the celebration are ordinarily these: a greeting and blessing from the priest, reading the Word of God to illuminate the conscience and elicit contrition, and an exhortation to repentance; the confession, which acknowledges sins and makes them known to the priest; the imposition and acceptance of a penance; the priest's absolution; a prayer of thanksgiving and praise and dismissal with the blessing of the priest.

1481 The Byzantine Liturgy recognizes several formulas of absolution, in the *1449* form of invocation, which admirably express the mystery of forgiveness: 'May the same God, who through the Prophet Nathan forgave David when he confessed his sins, who forgave Peter when he wept bitterly, the prostitute when she washed his feet with her tears, the publican, and the prodigal son, through me, a sinner, forgive you both in this life and in the next and enable you to appear before his awe-inspiring tribunal without condemnation, he who is blessed for ever and ever. Amen.'

1482 The sacrament of Penance can also take place in the framework of a *communal celebration* in which we prepare ourselves together for confession and give thanks together for the forgiveness received. Here, the personal confession of sins and individual absolution are inserted into a liturgy of the Word of God with readings and a homily, an examination of conscience conducted in common, a communal request for forgiveness, the *Our Father* and a thanksgiving in common. This communal celebration expresses more clearly the ecclesial character of penance. However, regardless of its manner of celebration the sacrament of Penance is always, by its very nature, a liturgical action, and therefore *1140* an ecclesial and public action.[90]

1483 In case of grave necessity recourse may be had to a *communal celebration of 1401 reconciliation with general confession and general absolution*. Grave necessity of this sort can arise when there is imminent danger of death without sufficient time for

---

[89] Cf. *Indulgentiarum doctrina* 5.
[90] Cf. SC 26–27.

the priest or priests to hear each penitent's confession. Grave necessity can also exist when, given the number of penitents, there are not enough confessors to hear individual confessions properly in a reasonable time, so that the penitents through no fault of their own would be deprived of sacramental grace or Holy Communion for a long time. In this case, for the absolution to be valid the faithful must have the intention of individually confessing their grave sins in the time required.[91] The diocesan bishop is the judge of whether or not the conditions required for general absolution exist.[92] A large gathering of the faithful on the occasion of major feasts or pilgrimages does not constitute a case of grave necessity.[93]

1484 'Individual, integral confession and absolution remain the only ordinary way for the faithful to reconcile themselves with God and the Church, unless physical or moral impossibility excuses from this kind of confession.'[94] There are profound reasons for this. Christ is at work in each of the sacraments. He personally addresses every sinner: 'My son, your sins are forgiven.'[95] He is the physician tending each one of the sick who need him to cure them.[96] He raises them up and reintegrates them into fraternal communion. Personal confession is thus the form most expressive of reconciliation with God and with the Church.

878

IN BRIEF

1485 *'On the evening of that day, the first day of the week', Jesus showed himself to his apostles. 'He breathed on them, and said to them: "Receive the Holy Spirit. If you forgive the sins of any, they are forgiven; if you retain the sins of any, they are retained"' (Jn 20:19, 22–23).*

1486 *The forgiveness of sins committed after Baptism is conferred by a particular sacrament called the sacrament of conversion, confession, Penance or Reconciliation.*

1487 *The sinner wounds God's honour and love, his own human dignity as a man called to be a son of God, and the spiritual well-being of the Church, of which each Christian ought to be a living stone.*

1488 *To the eyes of faith no evil is graver than sin and nothing has worse consequences for sinners themselves, for the Church and for the whole world.*

1489 *To return to communion with God after having lost it through sin is a process born of the grace of God who is rich in mercy and solicitous for the salvation of men. One must ask for this precious gift for oneself and for others.*

---

[91] Cf. CIC, can. 962 § 1.
[92] Cf. CIC, can. 961 § 2.
[93] Cf. CIC, can. 961 § 1.
[94] OP-31.
[95] Mk 2:5.
[96] Cf. Mk 2:17.

1490 *The movement of return to God, called conversion and repentance, entails sorrow for and abhorrence of sins committed, and the firm purpose of sinning no more in the future. Conversion touches the past and the future, and is nourished by hope in God's mercy.*

1491 *The sacrament of Penance is a whole consisting in three actions of the penitent and the priest's absolution. The penitent's acts are repentance, confession or disclosure of sins to the priest, and the intention to make reparation and do works of reparation.*

1492 *Repentance (also called contrition) must be inspired by motives that arise from faith. If repentance arises from love of charity for God, it is called 'perfect' contrition; if it is founded on other motives, it is called 'imperfect'.*

1493 *One who desires to obtain reconciliation with God and with the Church must confess to a priest all the unconfessed grave sins he remembers after having carefully examined his conscience. The confession of venial faults, without being necessary in itself, is nevertheless strongly recommended by the Church.*

1494 *The confessor proposes the performance of certain acts of 'satisfaction' or 'penance' to be performed by the penitent in order to repair the harm caused by sin and to re-establish habits befitting a disciple of Christ.*

1495 *Only priests who have received the faculty of absolving from the authority of the Church can forgive sins in the name of Christ.*

1496 *The spiritual effects of the sacrament of Penance are:*
– reconciliation with God by which the penitent recovers grace;
– reconciliation with the Church;
– remission of the eternal punishment incurred by mortal sins;
– remission, at least in part, of temporal punishments resulting from sin;
– peace and serenity of conscience, and spiritual consolation;
– an increase of spiritual strength for the Christian battle.

1497 *Individual and integral confession of grave sins followed by absolution remains the only ordinary means of reconciliation with God and with the Church.*

1498 *Through indulgences the faithful can obtain the remission of temporal punishment resulting from sin for themselves and also for the souls in Purgatory.*

Article 5

THE ANOINTING OF THE SICK

1499 'By the sacred anointing of the sick and the prayer of the priests the whole Church commends those who are ill to the suffering and glorified Lord, that he may raise them up and save them. And indeed she exhorts them to contribute to the good of the People of God by freely uniting themselves to the Passion and death of Christ.'[97]

I. Its Foundations in the Economy of Salvation

Illness in human life

1500 Illness and suffering have always been among the gravest problems confronted in human life. In illness, man experiences his powerlessness, his limitations and his finitude. Every illness can make us glimpse death.

1006

1501 Illness can lead to anguish, self-absorption, sometimes even despair and revolt against God. It can also make a person more mature, helping him discern in his life what is not essential so that he can turn toward that which is. Very often illness provokes a search for God and a return to him.

The sick person before God

1502 The man of the Old Testament lives his sickness in the presence of God. It is before God that he laments his illness, and it is of God, Master of life and death, that he implores healing.[98] Illness becomes a way to conversion; God's forgiveness initiates the healing.[99] It is the experience of Israel that illness is mysteriously linked to sin and evil, and that faithfulness to God according to his law restores life: 'For I am the LORD, your healer.'[100] The prophet intuits that suffering can also have a redemptive meaning for the sins of others.[101] Finally Isaiah announces that God will usher in a time for Zion when he will pardon every offence and heal every illness.[102]

164
376

Christ the physician

549
1503 Christ's compassion toward the sick and his many healings of every kind of infirmity are a resplendent sign that 'God has visited his people'[103] and that the Kingdom of God is close at hand. Jesus has the power not only to heal, but also to forgive sins;[104] he has come to heal the whole man, soul and body; he is the physician the sick have need of.[105] His compassion toward all who suffer goes so far that he identifies himself with them: 'I was sick and you

1421

---

97 *LG* 11; cf. *Jas* 5:14–16; *Rom* 8:17; *Col* 1:24; 2 *Tim* 2:11–12; 1 *Pt* 4:13.
98 Cf. *Pss* 6:3; 38; *Is* 38.
99 Cf. *Pss* 32:5; 38:5; 39:9, 12; 107:20; cf. *Mk* 2:5–12.
100 *Ex* 15:26.
101 Cf. *Is* 53:11.
102 Cf. *Is* 33:24.
103 *Lk* 7:16; cf. *Mt* 4:24.
104 Cf. *Mk* 2:5–12.
105 Cf. *Mk* 2:17.

visited me.'[106] His preferential love for the sick has not ceased through the centuries to draw the very special attention of Christians toward all those who suffer in body and soul. It is the source of tireless efforts to comfort them.   2288

1504 Often Jesus asks the sick to believe.[107] He makes use of signs to heal: spittle and the laying on of hands,[108] mud and washing.[109] The sick try to touch him, 'for power came forth from him and 695, 1116 healed them all.'[110] And so in the sacraments Christ continues to 'touch' us in order to heal us.

1505 Moved by so much suffering Christ not only allows himself to be touched by the sick, but he makes their miseries his own: 'He took our infirmities and bore our diseases.'[111] But he did not heal all the sick. His healings were signs of the coming of the Kingdom of God. They announced a more radical healing: the victory over sin and death through his Passover. On the cross Christ took upon 440 himself the whole weight of evil and took away the 'sin of the world',[112] of which illness is only a consequence. By his Passion and death on the cross Christ has given a new meaning to suffering: it can henceforth configure us to him and unite us with his 307 redemptive Passion.

'Heal the sick...'

1506 Christ invites his disciples to follow him by taking up their cross in their turn.[113] By following him they acquire a new outlook on illness and the sick. Jesus associates them with his own life of poverty and service. He makes them share in his ministry of 859 compassion and healing: 'So they went out and preached that men should repent. And they cast out many demons, and anointed with oil many that were sick and healed them.'[114]

1507 The risen Lord renews this mission ('In my name... they will lay their hands on the sick, and they will recover'[115]) and confirms it through the signs that the Church performs by invoking his name.[116] These signs demonstrate in a special way that Jesus is truly 'God who saves'.[117]   430

1508 The Holy Spirit gives to some a special charism of healing[118]   798

---

[106] Mt 25:36.
[107] Cf. Mk 5:34, 36; 9:23.
[108] Cf. Mk 7:32–36; 8:22–25.
[109] Cf. Jn 9:6–7.
[110] Lk 6:19; cf. Mk 1:41; 3:10; 6:56.
[111] Mt 8:17; cf. Is 53:4.
[112] Jn 1:29; cf. Is 53:4–6.
[113] Cf. Mt 10:38.
[114] Mk 6:12–13.
[115] Mk 16:17–18.
[116] Cf. Acts 9:34; 14:3.
[117] Cf. Mt 1:21; Acts 4:12.
[118] Cf. 1 Cor 12:9, 28, 30.

so as to make manifest the power of the grace of the risen Lord. But even the most intense prayers do not always obtain the healing of all illnesses. Thus St Paul must learn from the Lord that 'my grace is sufficient for you, for my power is made perfect in weakness', and that the sufferings to be endured can mean that 'in my 618 flesh I complete what is lacking in Christ's afflictions for the sake of his Body, that is, the Church.'[119]

1509 'Heal the sick!'[120] The Church has received this charge from the Lord and strives to carry it out by taking care of the sick as well as by accompanying them with her prayer of intercession. She believes in the life-giving presence of Christ, the physician of souls and bodies. This presence is particularly active through the sacra-1405 ments, and in an altogether special way through the Eucharist, the bread that gives eternal life and that St Paul suggests is connected with bodily health.[121]

1510 However, the apostolic Church has its own rite for the sick, attested to by St James: 'Is any among you sick? Let him call for the elders [presbyters] of the Church and let them pray over him, anointing him with oil in the name of the Lord; and the prayer of faith will save the sick man, and the Lord will raise him up; and if he has committed sins, he will be forgiven.'[122] Tradition has 1117 recognized in this rite one of the seven sacraments.[123]

A sacrament of the sick

1511 The Church believes and confesses that among the seven sacraments there is one especially intended to strengthen those who are being tried by illness, the Anointing of the Sick:

> This sacred anointing of the sick was instituted by Christ our Lord as a true and proper sacrament of the New Testament. It is alluded to indeed by Mark, but is recommended to the faithful and promulgated by James the apostle and brother of the Lord.[124]

1512 From ancient times in the liturgical traditions of both East and West, we have testimonies to the practice of anointings of the sick with blessed oil. Over the centuries the Anointing of the Sick was conferred more and more exclusively on those at the point of death. Because of this it received the name 'Extreme Unction'. Notwithstanding this evolution the liturgy has never failed to beg the

---

[119] 2 Cor 12:9; Col 1:24.
[120] Mt 10:8.
[121] Cf. Jn 6:54, 58; 1 Cor 11:30.
[122] Jas 5:14–15.
[123] Cf. St Innocent I, Letter Si instituta ecclesiastica: DS 216; Council of

Florence (1439): DS 1324–1325; Council of Trent (1551): DS 1695–1696; 1716–1717.
[124] Council of Trent (1551): DS 1695; cf. Mk 6:13; Jas 5:14–15.

Lord that the sick person may recover his health if it would be conducive to his salvation.[125]

1513 The Apostolic Constitution *Sacram unctionem infirmorum*,[126] following upon the Second Vatican Council,[127] established that henceforth, in the Roman Rite, the following be observed:

> The sacrament of Anointing of the Sick is given to those who are seriously ill by anointing them on the forehead and hands with duly blessed oil – pressed from olives or from other plants – saying, only once: 'Through this holy anointing may the Lord in his love and mercy help you with the grace of the Holy Spirit. May the Lord who frees you from sin save you and raise you up.'[128]

II. Who Receives and Who Administers This Sacrament?

In case of grave illness. . .

1514 The Anointing of the Sick 'is not a sacrament for those only who are at the point of death. Hence, as soon as anyone of the faithful begins to be in danger of death from sickness or old age, the fitting time for him to receive this sacrament has certainly already arrived.'[129]

1515 If a sick person who received this anointing recovers his health, he can in the case of another grave illness receive this sacrament again. If during the same illness the person's condition becomes more serious, the sacrament may be repeated. It is fitting to receive the Anointing of the Sick just prior to a serious operation. The same holds for the elderly whose frailty becomes more pronounced.

'. . . let him call for the presbyters of the Church'

1516 Only priests (bishops and presbyters) are ministers of the Anointing of the Sick.[130] It is the duty of pastors to instruct the faithful on the benefits of this sacrament. The faithful should encourage the sick to call for a priest to receive this sacrament. The sick should prepare themselves to receive it with good dispositions, assisted by their pastor and the whole ecclesial community, which is invited to surround the sick in a special way through their prayers and fraternal attention.

---

[125] Cf. Council of Trent (1551): DS 1696.
[126] Paul VI, Ap. Const. *Sacram unctionem infirmorum*, 30 November 1972.
[127] Cf. *SC* 73.
[128] Cf. CIC, can. 847 § 1.

[129] *SC* 73; cf. CIC, cann. 1004 § 1; 1005; 1007; CCEO, can. 738.
[130] Cf. Council of Trent (1551): DS 1697; 1719; CIC, can. 1003; CCEO, can. 739 § 1.

III. How Is This Sacrament Celebrated?

1517 Like all the sacraments the Anointing of the Sick is a liturgi-
1140 cal and communal celebration,[131] whether it takes place in the
family home, a hospital or church, for a single sick person or a
whole group of sick persons. It is very fitting to celebrate it within
the Eucharist, the memorial of the Lord's Passover. If circumstances suggest it, the celebration of the sacrament can be preceded
by the sacrament of Penance and followed by the sacrament of the
Eucharist. As the sacrament of Christ's Passover the Eucharist
should always be the last sacrament of the earthly journey, the
1524 'viaticum' for 'passing over' to eternal life.

1518 Word and sacrament form an indivisible whole. The
Liturgy of the Word, preceded by an act of repentance, opens the
celebration. The words of Christ, the witness of the apostles,
awaken the faith of the sick person and of the community to ask
the Lord for the strength of his Spirit.

1519 The celebration of the sacrament includes the following
principal elements: the 'priests of the Church'[132] – in silence – lay
hands on the sick; they pray over them in the faith of the
Church[133] – this is the epiclesis proper to this sacrament; they then
anoint them with oil blessed, if possible, by the bishop.

These liturgical actions indicate what grace this sacrament confers
upon the sick.

IV. The Effects of the Celebration of This Sacrament

733 1520 A *particular gift of the Holy Spirit*. The first grace of this
sacrament is one of strengthening, peace and courage to overcome
the difficulties that go with the condition of serious illness or the
frailty of old age. This grace is a gift of the Holy Spirit, who
renews trust and faith in God and strengthens against the temptations of the evil one, the temptation to discouragement and
anguish in the face of death.[134] This assistance from the Lord by the
power of his Spirit is meant to lead the sick person to healing of the
soul, but also of the body if such is God's will.[135] Furthermore, 'if
he has committed sins, he will be forgiven.'[136]

1521 *Union with the Passion of Christ*. By the grace of this sacra-

---

[131] Cf. SC 27.
[132] Jas 5:14.
[133] Cf. Jas 5:15.
[134] Cf. Heb 2:15.

[135] Cf. Council of Florence (1439): DS 1325.
[136] Jas 5:15; cf. Council of Trent (1551): DS 1717.

ment the sick person receives the strength and the gift of uniting himself more closely to Christ's Passion: in a certain way he is *consecrated* to bear fruit by configuration to the Saviour's *1535* redemptive Passion. Suffering, a consequence of original sin, acquires a new meaning; it becomes a participation in the saving *1499* work of Jesus.

1522 An *ecclesial grace*. The sick who receive this sacrament, 'by freely uniting themselves to the Passion and death of Christ', 'contribute to the good of the People of God.'[137] By celebrating this sacrament the Church, in the communion of saints, intercedes for the benefit of the sick person, and he, for his part, though the grace of this sacrament, contributes to the sanctification of the Church *953* and to the good of all men for whom the Church suffers and offers herself through Christ to God the Father.

1523 A *preparation for the final journey*. If the sacrament of Anointing of the Sick is given to all who suffer from serious illness and infirmity, even more rightly is it given to those at the point of departing this life; so it is also called *sacramentum exeuntium* (the sacrament of those departing).[138] The Anointing of the Sick completes our conformity to the death and Resurrection of Christ, just as Baptism began it. It completes the holy anointings that mark the *1294* whole Christian life: that of Baptism which sealed the new life in us, and that of Confirmation which strengthened us for the combat of this life. This last anointing fortifies the end of our earthly *1020* life like a solid rampart for the final struggles before entering the Father's house.[139]

V. Viaticum, the Last Sacrament of the Christian

1524 In addition to the Anointing of the Sick, the Church offers those who are about to leave this life the Eucharist as viaticum. *1392* Communion in the body and blood of Christ, received at this moment of 'passing over' to the Father, has a particular significance and importance. It is the seed of eternal life and the power of resurrection, according to the words of the Lord: 'He who eats my flesh and drinks my blood has eternal life, and I will raise him up at the last day.'[140] The sacrament of Christ once dead and now risen, the Eucharist is here the sacrament of passing over from death to life, from this world to the Father.[141]

---

[137] LG 11 § 2.
[138] Council of Trent (1551): DS 1698.
[139] Council of Trent (1551): DS 1694.
[140] Jn 6:54.
[141] Cf. Jn 13:1.

1680 1525 Thus, just as the sacraments of Baptism, Confirmation and the Eucharist form a unity called 'the sacraments of Christian initiation', so too it can be said that Penance, the Anointing of the Sick and the Eucharist as viaticum constitute at the end of Christian life 'the sacraments that prepare for our heavenly homeland' *2299* or the sacraments that complete the earthly pilgrimage.

IN BRIEF

1526 *'Is any among you sick? Let him call for the presbyters of the Church, and let them pray over him, anointing him with oil in the name of the Lord; and the prayer of faith will save the sick man, and the Lord will raise him up; and if he has committed sins, he will be forgiven' (Jas 5:14–15).*

1527 *The sacrament of Anointing of the Sick has as its purpose the conferral of a special grace on the Christian experiencing the difficulties inherent in the condition of grave illness or old age.*

1528 *The proper time for receiving this holy anointing has certainly arrived when the believer begins to be in danger of death because of illness or old age.*

1529 *Each time a Christian falls seriously ill, he may receive the Anointing of the Sick, and also when, after he has received it, the illness worsens.*

1530 *Only priests (presbyters and bishops) can give the sacrament of the Anointing of the Sick, using oil blessed by the bishop, or if necessary by the celebrating presbyter himself.*

1531 *The celebration of the Anointing of the Sick consists essentially in the anointing of the forehead and hands of the sick person (in the Roman rite) or of other parts of the body (in the Eastern rite), the anointing being accompanied by the liturgical prayer of the celebrant asking for the special grace of this sacrament.*

1532 *The special grace of the sacrament of the Anointing the Sick has as its effects:*
– the uniting of the sick person to the Passion of Christ, for his own good and that of the whole Church;
– the strengthening, peace and courage to endure in a Christian manner the sufferings of illness or old age;
– the forgiveness of sins, if the sick person was not able to obtain it through the sacrament of Penance;
– the restoration of health, if it is conducive to the salvation of his soul;
– the preparation for passing over to eternal life.

Chapter Three

THE SACRAMENTS AT THE SERVICE OF COMMUNION

1533 Baptism, Confirmation and Eucharist are sacraments of *1212* Christian initiation. They ground the common vocation of all Christ's disciples, a vocation to holiness and to the mission of evangelizing the world. They confer the graces needed for the life according to the Spirit during this life as pilgrims on the march towards the homeland.

1534 Two other sacraments, Holy Orders and Matrimony, are directed towards the salvation of others; if they contribute as well to personal salvation, it is through service to others that they do so. They confer a particular mission in the Church and serve to build up the People of God.

1535 Through these sacraments those already *consecrated* by Baptism and Confirmation[1] for the common priesthood of all the *784* faithful can receive particular *consecrations*. Those who receive the sacrament of Holy Orders are *consecrated* in Christ's name 'to feed the Church by the word and grace of God'.[2] On their part, 'Christian spouses are fortified and, as it were, *consecrated* for the duties and dignity of their state by a special sacrament.'[3]

Article 6

THE SACRAMENT OF HOLY ORDERS

1536 Holy Orders is the sacrament through which the mission entrusted by Christ to his apostles continues to be exercised in the *860* Church until the end of time: thus it is the sacrament of apostolic ministry. It includes three degrees: episcopate, presbyterate and diaconate.

(On the institution and mission of the apostolic ministry by Christ, see above, §§ 874ff. Here only the sacramental means by which this ministry is handed on will be treated.)

I. Why Is This Sacrament Called 'Orders'?

1537 The word *order* in Roman antiquity designated an established civil body, especially a governing body. *Ordinatio* means incorporation into an *ordo*. In the Church there are established bodies which Tradition, not without a basis in Sacred Scripture,[4]

---

[1] Cf. *LG* 10.
[2] *LG* 11 § 2.
[3] *GS* 48 § 2.
[4] Cf. *Heb* 5:6; 7:11; *Ps* 110:4.

has since ancient times called *taxeis* (Greek) or *ordines*. And so the liturgy speaks of the *ordo episcoporum*, the *ordo presbyterorum*, the *ordo diaconorum*. Other groups also receive this name of *ordo*: catechumens, virgins, spouses, widows. . .

922, 923, 1631

1538 Integration into one of these bodies in the Church was accomplished by a rite called *ordinatio*, a religious and liturgical act which was a consecration, a blessing or a sacrament. Today the word '*ordination*' is reserved for the sacramental act which integrates a man into the order of bishops, presbyters or deacons, and goes beyond a simple *election*, *designation*, *delegation* or *institution* by the community, for it confers a gift of the Holy Spirit that permits the exercise of a 'sacred power' (*sacra potestas*)[5] which can come only from Christ himself through his Church. Ordination is also called *consecratio*, for it is a setting apart and an investiture by Christ himself for his Church. The *laying on of hands* by the bishop, with the consecratory prayer, constitutes the visible sign of this ordination.

875

699

II. The Sacrament of Holy Orders in the Economy of Salvation

The priesthood of the Old Covenant

1539 The chosen people was constituted by God as 'a kingdom of priests and a holy nation'.[6] But within the people of Israel, God chose one of the twelve tribes, that of Levi, and set it apart for liturgical service; God himself is its inheritance.[7] A special rite consecrated the beginnings of the priesthood of the Old Covenant. The priests are 'appointed to act on behalf of men in relation to God, to offer gifts and sacrifices for sins'.[8]

1540 Instituted to proclaim the Word of God and to restore communion with God by sacrifices and prayer,[9] this priesthood nevertheless remains powerless to bring about salvation, needing to repeat its sacrifices ceaselessly and being unable to achieve a definitive sanctification, which only the sacrifice of Christ would accomplish.[10]

2099

1541 The liturgy of the Church, however, sees in the priesthood of Aaron and the service of the Levites, as in the institution of the seventy elders,[11] a prefiguring of the ordained ministry of the

---

[5] Cf. *LG* 10.
[6] *Ex* 19:6; cf. *Is* 61:6.
[7] Cf. *Num* 1:48–53; *Josh* 13:33.
[8] *Heb* 5:1; cf. *Ex* 29:1–30; *Lev* 8.
[9] Cf. *Mal* 2:7–9.
[10] Cf. *Heb* 5:3; 7:27; 10:1–4
[11] Cf. *Num* 11:24–25.

New Covenant. Thus in the Latin rite the Church prays in the consecratory preface of the ordination of bishops:

> God the Father of our Lord Jesus Christ,...
> by your gracious word
> you have established the plan of your Church.
>
> From the beginning,
> you chose the descendants of Abraham to be your holy nation.
> You established rulers and priests,
> and did not leave your sanctuary without ministers to serve you...[12]

1542 At the ordination of priests, the Church prays:

> Lord, holy Father,...
> when you had appointed high priests to rule your people,
> you chose other men next to them in rank and dignity
> to be with them and to help them in their task...
>
> you extended the spirit of Moses to seventy wise men...
> You shared among the sons of Aaron
> the fullness of their father's power.[13]

1543 In the consecratory prayer for ordination of deacons, the Church confesses:

> Almighty God...,
> You make the Church, Christ's body,
> grow to its full stature as a new and greater temple.
> You enrich it with every kind of grace
> and perfect it with a diversity of members
> to serve the whole body in a wonderful pattern of unity.
>
> You established a threefold ministry of worship and service,
> for the glory of your name.
> As ministers of your tabernacle you chose the sons of Levi
> and gave them your blessing as their everlasting inheritance.[14]

The one priesthood of Christ

1544 Everything that the priesthood of the Old Covenant prefigured finds its fulfilment in Christ Jesus, the 'one mediator between God and men'.[15] The Christian tradition considers Melchizedek, 'priest of God Most High', as a prefiguration of the priesthood of Christ, the unique 'high priest after the order of *874* Melchizedek';[16] 'holy, blameless, unstained',[17] 'by a single offering he has perfected for all time those who are sanctified',[18] that is, by the unique sacrifice of the cross.

---

[12] *Roman Pontifical*, Ordination of Bishops 26, Prayer of Consecration.

[13] *Roman Pontifical*, Ordination of Priests 22, Prayer of Consecration.

[14] *Roman Pontifical*, Ordination of Deacons 21, Prayer of Consecration.

[15] 1 *Tim* 2:5.

[16] *Heb* 5:10; cf. 6:20; *Gen* 14:18.

[17] *Heb* 7:26.

[18] *Heb* 10:14.

1545 The redemptive sacrifice of Christ is unique, accomplished
1367 once for all; yet it is made present in the Eucharistic sacrifice of
the Church. The same is true of the one priesthood of Christ; it
is made present through the ministerial priesthood without
662 diminishing the uniqueness of Christ's priesthood: 'Only Christ
is the true priest, the others being only his ministers.'[19]

Two participations in the one priesthood of Christ

1546 Christ, high priest and unique mediator, has made of the
Church 'a kingdom, priests for his God and Father'.[20] The whole
community of believers is, as such, priestly. The faithful exercise
1268 their baptismal priesthood through their participation, each according to his own vocation, in Christ's mission as priest, prophet
and king. Through the sacraments of Baptism and Confirmation
the faithful are 'consecrated to be... a holy priesthood'.[21]

1142 1547 The ministerial or hierarchical priesthood of bishops and
priests, and the common priesthood of all the faithful participate,
'each in its own proper way, in the one priesthood of Christ'.
While being 'ordered one to another', they differ essentially.[22] In
what sense? While the common priesthood of the faithful is exercised by the unfolding of baptismal grace – a life of faith, hope and
1120 charity, a life according to the Spirit, the ministerial priesthood is
at the service of the common priesthood. It is directed at the unfolding of the baptismal grace of all Christians. The ministerial
priesthood is a *means* by which Christ unceasingly builds up and
leads his Church. For this reason it is transmitted by its own sacrament, the sacrament of Holy Orders.

In the person of Christ the Head...

875 1548 In the ecclesial service of the ordained minister, it is Christ
792 himself who is present to his Church as Head of his Body, Shepherd of his flock, high priest of the redemptive sacrifice, Teacher of
Truth. This is what the Church means by saying that the priest, by
virtue of the sacrament of Holy Orders, acts *in persona Christi
Capitis*:[23]

> It is the same priest, Christ Jesus, whose sacred person his minister truly
> represents. Now the minister, by reason of the sacerdotal consecration
> which he has received, is truly made like to the high priest and possesses

---

[19] St Thomas Aquinas, *Hebr.* 8, 4.   [22] *LG* 10 § 2.
[20] *Rev* 1:6; cf. 5:9–10; 1 *Pt* 2:5, 9.   [23] Cf. *LG* 10; 28; *SC* 33; *CD* 11; *PO* 2;
[21] *LG* 10 § 1.   6.

the authority to act in the power and place of the person of Christ himself (*virtute ac persona ipsius Christi*).[24]

Christ is the source of all priesthood: the priest of the old law was a figure of Christ, and the priest of the new law acts in the person of Christ.[25]

1549 Through the ordained ministry, especially that of bishops and priests, the presence of Christ as head of the Church is made *1142* visible in the midst of the community of believers.[26] In the beautiful expression of St Ignatius of Antioch, the bishop is *typos tou Patros*: he is like the living image of God the Father.[27]

1550 This presence of Christ in the minister is not to be understood as if the latter were preserved from all human weaknesses, *896* the spirit of domination, error, even sin. The power of the Holy Spirit does not guarantee all acts of ministers in the same way. While this guarantee extends to the sacraments, so that even the *1128* minister's sin cannot impede the fruit of grace, in many other acts *1584* the minister leaves human traces that are not always signs of fidelity to the Gospel and consequently can harm the apostolic fruitfulness of the Church.

1551 This priesthood is *ministerial*. 'That office... which the Lord committed to the pastors of his people, is in the strict sense of the term a *service*.'[28] It is entirely related to Christ and to men. It *876* depends entirely on Christ and on his unique priesthood; it has been instituted for the good of men and the communion of the Church. The sacrament of Holy Orders communicates a 'sacred *1538* power' which is none other than that of Christ. The exercise of this authority must therefore be measured against the model of Christ, who by love made himself the least and the servant of all.[29] 'The *608* Lord said clearly that concern for his flock was proof of love for him.'[30]

... 'in the name of the whole Church'

1552 The ministerial priesthood has the task not only of representing Christ – Head of the Church – before the assembly of the faithful, but also of acting in the name of the whole Church when presenting to God the prayer of the Church, and above all when offering the Eucharistic sacrifice.[31]

---

[24] Pius XII, Enc. *Mediator Dei*: AAS 39 (1947), 548.
[25] St Thomas Aquinas, *STh* III, 22, 4 c.
[26] Cf. *LG* 21.
[27] St Ignatius of Antioch, *Ad Trall.* 3, 1: SCh 10, 112; cf. *Ad Magn.* 6, 1: SCh 10, 124.

[28] *LG* 24.
[29] Cf. *Mk* 10:43–45; 1 *Pt* 5:3.
[30] St John Chrysostom, *De sac.* 2, 4: PG 48, 636; cf. *Jn* 21:15–17.
[31] Cf. *SC* 33; *LG* 10.

1553 'In the name of the *whole* Church' does not mean that priests are the delegates of the community. The prayer and offering of the Church are inseparable from the prayer and offering of Christ, her head; it is always the case that Christ worships in and through his
795 Church. The whole Church, the Body of Christ, prays and offers herself 'through him, with him, in him', in the unity of the Holy Spirit, to God the Father. The whole Body, *caput et membra*, prays and offers itself, and therefore those who in the Body are especially his ministers are called ministers not only of Christ, but also of the Church. It is because the ministerial priesthood represents Christ that it can represent the Church.

III. The Three Degrees of the Sacrament of Holy Orders

1554 'The divinely instituted ecclesiastical ministry is exercised in different degrees by those who even from ancient times have been
1536 called bishops, priests and deacons.'[32] Catholic doctrine, expressed in the liturgy, the Magisterium and the constant practice of the Church, recognizes that there are two degrees of ministerial participation in the priesthood of Christ: the episcopacy and the presbyterate. The diaconate is intended to help and serve them. For this reason the term *sacerdos* in current usage denotes bishops and priests but not deacons. Yet Catholic doctrine teaches that the degrees of priestly participation (episcopate and presbyterate) and the degree of service (diaconate) are all three conferred by a sacra-
1538 mental act called 'ordination', that is, by the sacrament of Holy Orders:

> Let everyone revere the deacons as Jesus Christ, the bishop as the image of the Father, and the presbyters as the senate of God and the assembly of the apostles. For without them one cannot speak of the Church.[33]

Episcopal ordination – fullness of the sacrament of Holy Orders

1555 'Amongst those various offices which have been exercised in the Church from the earliest times the chief place, according to the witness of tradition, is held by the function of those who, through their appointment to the dignity and responsibility of bishop, and
861 in virtue consequently of the unbroken succession going back to the beginning, are regarded as transmitters of the apostolic line.'[34]

862 1556 To fulfil their exalted mission, 'the apostles were endowed by Christ with a special outpouring of the Holy Spirit coming upon them, and by the imposition of hands they passed on to their

---

[32] LG 28.   SCh 10, 112.
[33] St Ignatius of Antioch, *Ad Trall.* 3, 1:   [34] LG 20.

auxiliaries the gift of the Spirit, which is transmitted down to our day through episcopal consecration.'[35]

1557 The Second Vatican Council 'teaches... that *the fullness of the sacrament of Holy Orders* is conferred by episcopal consecration, that fullness namely which, both in the liturgical tradition of the Church and the language of the Fathers of the Church, is called the high priesthood, the acme (*summa*) of the sacred ministry.'[36]

1558 'Episcopal consecration confers, together with the office of sanctifying, also the offices of teaching and ruling... In fact... by the imposition of hands and through the words of the consecration, the grace of the Holy Spirit is given, and a sacred character is impressed in such wise that bishops, in an eminent and visible manner, take the place of Christ himself, teacher, shepherd, and priest, and act as his representative (*in Eius persona agant*).'[37] 'By virtue, therefore, of the Holy Spirit who has been given to them, bishops have been constituted true and authentic teachers of the faith and have been made pontiffs and pastors.'[38]   895   1121

1559 'One is constituted a member of the episcopal body in virtue of the sacramental consecration and by the hierarchical communion with the head and members of the college.'[39] The character and *collegial nature* of the episcopal order are evidenced among other ways by the Church's ancient practice which calls for several bishops to participate in the consecration of a new bishop.[40] In our day, the lawful ordination of a bishop requires a special intervention of the Bishop of Rome, because he is the supreme visible bond of the communion of the particular Churches in the one Church and the guarantor of their freedom.   877   882

1560 As Christ's vicar, each bishop has the pastoral care of the particular Church entrusted to him, but at the same time he bears collegially with all his brothers in the episcopacy the *solicitude for all the Churches*: 'Though each bishop is the lawful pastor only of the portion of the flock entrusted to his care, as a legitimate successor of the apostles he is, by divine institution and precept, responsible with the other bishops for the apostolic mission of the Church.'[41]   833   886

1561 The above considerations explain why the Eucharist cele-

---

[35] LG 21; cf. *Acts* 1:8; 2:4; *Jn* 20:22–23; 1 *Tim* 4:14; 2 *Tim* 1:6–7.
[36] LG 21 § 2.
[37] LG 21.
[38] CD 2 § 2.

[39] LG 22.
[40] Cf. LG 22.
[41] Pius XII, *Fidei donum*: AAS 49 (1957). 237; cf. LG 23; CD 4; 36; 37; AG 5; 6; 38.

1369 brated by the bishop has a quite special significance as an expression of the Church gathered around the altar, with the one who represents Christ, the Good Shepherd and Head of his Church, presiding.[42]

The ordination of priests – co-workers of the bishops

1562 'Christ, whom the Father hallowed and sent into the world, has, through his apostles, made their successors, the bishops namely, sharers in his consecration and mission; and these, in their turn, duly entrusted in varying degrees various members of the Church with the office of their ministry.'[43] 'The function of the bishops' ministry was handed over in a subordinate degree to priests so that they might be appointed in the order of the priesthood and be *co-workers of the episcopal order* for the proper fulfilment of the apostolic mission that had been entrusted to it by Christ.'[44]

1563 'Because it is joined with the episcopal order the office of priests shares in the authority by which Christ himself builds up and sanctifies and rules his Body. Hence the priesthood of priests, while presupposing the sacraments of initiation, is nevertheless conferred by its own particular sacrament. Through that sacrament priests by the anointing of the Holy Spirit are signed with a *1121* special character and so are configured to Christ the priest in such a way that they are able to act in the person of Christ the head.'[45]

1564 'Whilst not having the supreme degree of the pontifical office, and notwithstanding the fact that they depend on the bishops in the exercise of their own proper power, the priests are for all that associated with them by reason of their sacerdotal dignity; and in virtue of the sacrament of Holy Orders, after the image of Christ, the supreme and eternal priest, they are consecrated in order to preach the Gospel and shepherd the faithful as *611* well as to celebrate divine worship *as true priests of the New Testament*.'[46]

1565 Through the sacrament of Holy Orders priests share in the *849* universal dimensions of the mission that Christ entrusted to the apostles. The spiritual gift they have received in ordination prepares them, not for a limited and restricted mission, 'but for the

---

[42] Cf. *SC* 41; *LG* 26.
[43] *LG* 28; cf. *Jn* 10:36.
[44] *PO* 2 § 2.
[45] *PO* 2.

[46] *LG* 28; cf. *Heb* 5:1–10; 7:24; 9:11–28; St Innocent I, Letter *Si instituta ecclesiastica*: DS 215; St Gregory of Nazianzus, *Oratio* 2, 22: PG 35, 432B.

fullest, in fact the universal mission of salvation "to the end of the earth'",[47] 'prepared in spirit to preach the Gospel everywhere'.[48]

1566 'It is in the Eucharistic cult or in the *Eucharistic assembly* of the *1369* faithful (*synaxis*) that they exercise in a supreme degree their sacred office; there, acting in the person of Christ and proclaiming his mystery, they unite the votive offerings of the faithful to the sacrifice of Christ their head, and in the sacrifice of the Mass they make present again and apply, until the coming of the Lord, the unique sacrifice of the New Testament, that namely of Christ offering *611* himself once for all a spotless victim to the Father.'[49] From this unique sacrifice their whole priestly ministry draws its strength.[50]

1567 'The priests, prudent co-operators of the episcopal college *1462* and its support and instrument, called to the service of the People of God, constitute, together with their bishop, a unique sacerdotal college (*presbyterium*) dedicated it is true to a variety of distinct duties. In each local assembly of the faithful they represent, in a *2179* certain sense, the bishop, with whom they are associated in all trust and generosity; in part they take upon themselves his duties and solicitude and in their daily toils discharge them.'[51] Priests can exercise their ministry only in dependence on the bishop and in communion with him. The promise of obedience they make to the bishop at the moment of ordination and the kiss of peace from him at the end of the ordination liturgy mean that the bishop considers them his co-workers, his sons, his brothers and his friends, and that they in return owe him love and obedience.

1568 'All priests, who are constituted in the order of priesthood by the sacrament of Order, are bound together by an intimate *1537* sacramental brotherhood, but in a special way they form one priestly body in the diocese to which they are attached under their own bishop...'[52] The unity of the presbyterium finds liturgical expression in the custom of the presbyters' imposing hands, after the bishop, during the rite of ordination.

The ordination of deacons – 'in order to serve'

1569 'At a lower level of the hierarchy are to be found deacons, who receive the imposition of hands "not unto the priesthood, but unto the ministry".'[53] At an ordination to the diaconate only the

---

[47] *PO* 10; *OT* 20; cf. *Acts* 1:8.
[48] *OT* 20.
[49] *LG* 28; cf. 1 *Cor* 11:26.
[50] Cf. *PO* 2.

[51] *LG* 28 § 2.
[52] *PO* 8.
[53] *LG* 29; cf. *CD* 15.

bishop lays hands on the candidate, thus signifying the deacon's special attachment to the bishop in the tasks of his *diakonia*.[54]

1570 Deacons share in Christ's mission and grace in a special way.[55] The sacrament of Holy Orders marks them with an *imprint* 1121 ('character') which cannot be removed and which configures them to Christ, who made himself the 'deacon' or servant of all.[56] Among other tasks, it is the task of deacons to assist the bishop and priests in the celebration of the divine mysteries, above all the Eucharist, in the distribution of Holy Communion, in assisting at and blessing marriages, in the proclamation of the Gospel and preaching, in presiding over funerals, and in dedicating themselves to the various ministries of charity.[57]

1571 Since the Second Vatican Council the Latin Church has restored the diaconate 'as a proper and permanent rank of the hierarchy',[58] while the Chur-1579 ches of the East had always maintained it. This *permanent diaconate*, which can be conferred on married men, constitutes an important enrichment for the Church's mission. Indeed it is appropriate and useful that men who carry out a truly diaconal ministry in the Church, whether in its liturgical and pastoral life or whether in its social and charitable works, should 'be strengthened by the imposition of hands which has come down from the apostles. They would be more closely bound to the altar and their ministry would be made more fruitful through the sacramental grace of the diaconate.'[59]

IV. The Celebration of This Sacrament

1572 Given the importance that the ordination of a bishop, a priest or a deacon has for the life of the particular Church, its celebration calls for as many of the faithful as possible to take part. It should take place preferably on Sunday, in the cathedral, with solemnity appropriate to the occasion. All three ordinations, of the bishop, of the priest, and of the deacon, follow the same movement. Their proper place is within the Eucharistic liturgy.

1573 The *essential rite* of the sacrament of Holy Orders for all 699 three degrees consists in the bishop's imposition of hands on the head of the ordinand and in the bishop's specific consecratory 1585 prayer asking God for the outpouring of the Holy Spirit and his gifts proper to the ministry to which the candidate is being ordained.[60]

---

[54] Cf. St Hippolytus, *Trad. ap.* 8: SCh 11, 58–62.

[55] Cf. *LG* 41; *AG* 16.

[56] Cf. *Mk* 10:45; *Lk* 22:27; St Polycarp, *Ad Phil.* 52: SCh 10, 210.

[57] Cf. *LG* 29; *SC* 35 § 4; *AG* 16.

[58] *LG* 29 § 2.

[59] *AG* 16 § 6.

[60] Cf. Pius XII, Ap. Const. *Sacramentum Ordinis*: DS 3858.

1574 As in all the sacraments additional rites surround the celebration. Varying greatly among the different liturgical traditions, these rites have in common the expression of the multiple aspects of sacramental grace. Thus in the Latin Church, the initial rites – presentation and election of the ordinand, instruction by the bishop, examination of the candidate, litany of the saints – attest that the choice of the candidate is made in keeping with the practice of the Church and prepare for the solemn act of consecration, after which several rites symbolically express and complete the mystery accomplished: for bishop and priest, an anointing with holy chrism, a sign of the special anointing of the Holy Spirit *1294* who makes their ministry fruitful; giving the book of the Gospels, the ring, the mitre and the crosier to the bishop as the sign of his apostolic mission to proclaim the Word of God, of his fidelity to the Church, the bride of Christ, and his *796* office as shepherd of the Lord's flock; presentation to the priest of the paten and chalice, 'the offering of the holy people' which he is called to present to God; giving the book of the Gospels to the deacon who has just received the mission to proclaim the Gospel of Christ.

V. Who Can Confer This Sacrament?

1575 Christ himself chose the apostles and gave them a share in his mission and authority. Raised to the Father's right hand, he has not forsaken his flock but he keeps it under his constant protection through the apostles, and guides it still through these same pastors *857* who continue his work today.[61] Thus, it is Christ whose gift it is that some be apostles, others pastors. He continues to act through the bishops.[62]

1576 Since the sacrament of Holy Orders is the sacrament of the *1536* apostolic ministry, it is for the bishops as the successors of the apostles to hand on the 'gift of the Spirit',[63] the 'apostolic line'.[64] Validly ordained bishops, i.e. those who are in the line of apostolic succession, validly confer the three degrees of the sacrament of Holy Orders.[65]

VI. Who Can Receive This Sacrament?

1577 'Only a baptized man (vir) validly receives sacred ordination.'[66] The Lord Jesus chose men (viri) to form the college of the twelve apostles, and the apostles did the same when they chose *551* collaborators to succeed them in their ministry.[67] The college of bishops, with whom the priests are united in the priesthood, makes *861*

---

[61] Cf. *Roman Missal*, Preface of the Apostles I.
[62] Cf. *LG* 21; *Eph* 4:11.
[63] *LG* 21 § 2.
[64] *LG* 20.
[65] Cf. DS 794 and 802; CIC, can. 1012;

CCEO, can. 744; 747.
[66] CIC, can. 1024.
[67] Cf. *Mk* 3:14–19; *Lk* 6:12–16; 1 *Tim* 3:1–13; 2 *Tim* 1:6; *Titus* 1:5–9; St Clement of Rome, *Ad Cor.* 42, 4; 44, 3: PG 1, 292–293; 300.

862 the college of the twelve an ever-present and ever-active reality until Christ's return. The Church recognizes herself to be bound by this choice made by the Lord himself. For this reason the ordination of women is not possible.[68]

2121 1578 No one has a *right* to receive the sacrament of Holy Orders. Indeed no one claims this office for himself; he is called to it by God.[69] Anyone who thinks he recognizes the signs of God's call to the ordained ministry must humbly submit his desire to the authority of the Church, who has the responsibility and right to call someone to receive orders. Like every grace this sacrament can be *received* only as an unmerited gift.

1579 All the ordained ministers of the Latin Church, with the exception of permanent deacons, are normally chosen from among men of faith who live a celibate life and who intend to
1618 remain *celibate* 'for the sake of the kingdom of heaven'.[70] Called to consecrate themselves with undivided heart to the Lord and to 'the affairs of the Lord',[71] they give themselves entirely to God and to men. Celibacy is a sign of this new life to the service of which the Church's minister is consecrated; accepted with a joyous heart
2233 celibacy radiantly proclaims the Reign of God.[72]

1580 In the Eastern Churches a different discipline has been in force for many centuries: while bishops are chosen solely from among celibates, married men can be ordained as deacons and priests. This practice has long been considered legitimate; these priests exercise a fruitful ministry within their communities.[73] Moreover, priestly celibacy is held in great honour in the Eastern Churches and many priests have freely chosen it for the sake of the Kingdom of God. In the East as in the West a man who has already received the sacrament of Holy Orders can no longer marry.

VII. The Effects of the Sacrament of Holy Orders

The indelible character

1581 This sacrament configures the recipient to Christ by a special grace of the Holy Spirit, so that he may serve as Christ's instrument for his Church. By ordination one is enabled to act as a
1548 representative of Christ, Head of the Church, in his triple office of priest, prophet and king.

---

[68] Cf. John Paul II, *MD* 26–27; CDF, Decl. *Inter insigniores*: AAS 69 (1977), 98–116.
[69] Cf. *Heb* 5:4.
[70] *Mt* 19:12.
[71] 1 *Cor* 7:32.
[72] Cf. *PO* 16.
[73] Cf. *PO* 16.

1582 As in the case of Baptism and Confirmation this share in Christ's office is granted once for all. The sacrament of Holy Orders, like the other two, confers an *indelible spiritual character* and cannot be repeated or conferred temporarily.[74]   *1121*

1583 It is true that someone validly ordained can, for grave reasons, be discharged from the obligations and functions linked to ordination, or can be forbidden to exercise them; but he cannot become a layman again in the strict sense,[75] because the character imprinted by ordination is for ever. The vocation and mission received on the day of his ordination mark him permanently.

1584 Since it is ultimately Christ who acts and effects salvation through the ordained minister, the unworthiness of the latter does not prevent Christ from acting.[76] St Augustine states this forcefully: *1128*

> As for the proud minister, he is to be ranked with the devil. Christ's gift is not thereby profaned: what flows through him keeps its purity, and what passes through him remains clear and reaches the fertile earth... The spiritual power of the sacrament is indeed comparable to light: those to be enlightened receive it in its purity, and if it should pass through defiled beings, it is not itself defiled.[77]   *1550*

The grace of the Holy Spirit

1585 The grace of the Holy Spirit proper to this sacrament is configuration to Christ as Priest, Teacher and Pastor, of whom the ordained is made a minister.

1586 For the bishop, this is first of all a grace of strength ('the governing spirit': Prayer of Episcopal Consecration in the Latin rite[78]): the grace to guide and defend his Church with strength and prudence as a father and pastor, with gratuitous love for all and a preferential love for the poor, the sick and the needy. This grace impels him to proclaim the Gospel to all, to be the model for his flock, to go before it on the way of sanctification by identifying himself in the Eucharist with Christ the priest and victim, not fearing to give his life for his sheep: *2448*

> Father, you know all hearts.
> You have chosen your servant for the office of bishop.   *1558*
> May he be a shepherd to your holy flock,
> and a high priest blameless in your sight,

[74] Cf. Council of Trent: DS 1767; *LG* 21; 28; 29; *PO* 2.
[75] Cf. CIC, cann. 290–293; 1336 § 1, 3°, 5°; 1338 § 2; Council of Trent: DS 1774.
[76] Cf. Council of Trent: DS 1612; 1154.
[77] St Augustine, *In ev. Jo.* 5, 15: PL 35. 1422.
[78] Cf. *Roman Pontifical*. Ordination of Bishops 26, Prayer of Consecration; cf. *CD* 13; 16.

ministering to you night and day;
may he always gain the blessing of your favour
and offer the gifts of your holy Church.
Through the Spirit who gives the grace of high priesthood
grant him the power
to forgive sins as you have commanded,
to assign ministries as you have decreed,
and to loose from every bond by the authority which you gave to your
    apostles.
May he be pleasing to you by his gentleness and purity of heart,
presenting a fragrant offering to you,
through Jesus Christ, your Son. . .[79]

1564 1587 The spiritual gift conferred by presbyteral ordination is expressed by this prayer of the Byzantine rite. The bishop, while
laying on his hand, says among other things:

Lord, fill with the gift of the Holy Spirit
him whom you have deigned to raise to the rank of the priesthood,
that he may be worthy to stand without reproach before your altar,
to proclaim the Gospel of your kingdom,
to fulfil the ministry of your word of truth,
to offer you spiritual gifts and sacrifices,
to renew your people by the bath of rebirth;
so that he may go out to meet
our great God and Saviour Jesus Christ, your only Son,
on the day of his second coming,
and may receive from your vast goodness
the recompense for a faithful administration of his order.[80]

1569 1588 With regard to deacons, 'strengthened by sacramental grace
they are dedicated to the People of God, in conjunction with the
bishop and his body of priests, in the service (diakonia) of the
liturgy, of the Gospel and of works of charity.'[81]

1589 Before the grandeur of the priestly grace and office, the holy
doctors felt an urgent call to conversion in order to conform their
whole lives to him whose sacrament had made them ministers.
Thus St Gregory of Nazianzus, as a very young priest, exclaimed:

We must begin by purifying ourselves before purifying others; we must
be instructed to be able to instruct, become light to illuminate, draw close
to God to bring him close to others, be sanctified to sanctify, lead by the
hand and counsel prudently. I know whose ministers we are, where we
find ourselves and to where we strive. I know God's greatness and man's

---

[79] Roman Pontifical, Ordination of
Bishops 26, Prayer of Consecration;
cf. St Hippolytus, Trad. ap. 3: SCh 11,
44–46.

[80] Byzantine Liturgy, Euchologion.
[81] LG 29.

weakness, but also his potential. [Who then is the priest? He is] the defender of truth, who stands with angels, gives glory with archangels, causes sacrifices to rise to the altar on high, shares Christ's priesthood, refashions creation, restores it in God's image, recreates it for the world on high and, even greater, is divinized and divinizes.[82]   460

And the holy Curé of Ars: 'The priest continues the work of redemption on earth... If we really understood the priest on earth, we would die not of fright but of love... The Priesthood is the love of the heart of Jesus.'[83]   1551

IN BRIEF

1590 St Paul said to his disciple Timothy: 'I remind you to rekindle the gift of God that is within you through the laying on of my hands' (2 Tim 1:6), and 'If any one aspires to the office of bishop, he desires a noble task' (1 Tim 3:1). To Titus he said: 'This is why I left you in Crete, that you amend what was defective, and appoint presbyters in every town, as I directed you' (Titus 1:5).

1591 The whole Church is a priestly people. Through Baptism all the faithful share in the priesthood of Christ. This participation is called the 'common priesthood of the faithful'. Based on this common priesthood and ordered to its service, there exists another participation in the mission of Christ: the ministry conferred by the sacrament of Holy Orders, where the task is to serve in the name and in the person of Christ the Head in the midst of the community.

1592 The ministerial priesthood differs in essence from the common priesthood of the faithful because it confers a sacred power for the service of the faithful. The ordained ministers exercise their service for the People of God by teaching (munus docendi), divine worship (munus liturgicum) and pastoral governance (munus regendi).

1593 Since the beginning, the ordained ministry has been conferred and exercised in three degrees: that of bishops, that of presbyters and that of deacons. The ministries conferred by ordination are irreplaceable for the organic structure of the Church: without the bishop, presbyters and deacons, one cannot speak of the Church (cf. St Ignatius of Antioch, Ad Trall. 3, 1).

1594 The bishop receives the fullness of the sacrament of Holy Orders, which integrates him into the episcopal college and makes him the visible head of the particular Church entrusted to him. As successors of the apostles and members of the college, the bishops share in the apostolic responsibility and mission of the whole Church under the authority of the Pope, successor of St Peter.

---

[82] St Gregory of Nazianzus, Oratio 2, 71, 74, 73: PG 35, 480–481.

[83] St John Vianney, quoted in B. Nodet. Jean-Marie Vianney, Curé d'Ars. 100.

1595 *Priests are united with the bishops in sacerdotal dignity and at the same time depend on them in the exercise of their pastoral functions; they are called to be the bishops' prudent co-workers. They form around their bishop the presbyterium which bears responsibility with him for the particular Church. They receive from the bishop the charge of a parish community or a determinate ecclesial office.*

1596 *Deacons are ministers ordained for tasks of service of the Church; they do not receive the ministerial priesthood, but ordination confers on them important functions in the ministry of the word, divine worship, pastoral governance and the service of charity, tasks which they must carry out under the pastoral authority of their bishop.*

1597 *The sacrament of Holy Orders is conferred by the laying on of hands followed by a solemn prayer of consecration asking God to grant the ordinand the graces of the Holy Spirit required for his ministry. Ordination imprints an indelible sacramental character.*

1598 *The Church confers the sacrament of Holy Orders only on baptized men* (viri) *whose suitability for the exercise of the ministry has been duly recognized. Church authority alone has the responsibility and right to call someone to receive the sacrament of Holy Orders.*

1599 *In the Latin Church the sacrament of Holy Orders for the presbyterate is normally conferred only on candidates who are ready to embrace celibacy freely and who publicly manifest their intention of staying celibate for the love of God's kingdom and the service of men.*

1600 *It is bishops who confer the sacrament of Holy Orders in the three degrees.*

Article 7
THE SACRAMENT OF MATRIMONY

1601 'The matrimonial covenant, by which a man and a woman establish between themselves a partnership of the whole of life, is by its nature ordered toward the good of the spouses and the procreation and education of offspring; this covenant between baptized persons has been raised by Christ the Lord to the dignity of a sacrament.'[84]

I. Marriage in God's Plan

369 1602 Sacred Scripture begins with the creation of man and woman in the image and likeness of God and concludes with a

---

[84] CIC. can. 1055 § 1; cf. GS 48 § 1.

vision of 'the wedding-feast of the Lamb'.[85] Scripture speaks *796*
throughout of marriage and its 'mystery', its institution and the
meaning God has given it, its origin and its end, its various real-
izations throughout the history of salvation, the difficulties arising
from sin and its renewal 'in the Lord' in the New Covenant of
Christ and the Church.[86]

Marriage in the order of creation

1603 'The intimate community of life and love which constitutes
the married state has been established by the Creator and endowed
by him with its own proper laws... God himself is the author of *371*
marriage.'[87] The vocation to marriage is written in the very nature
of man and woman as they came from the hand of the Creator. *2331*
Marriage is not a purely human institution despite the many variations it may have undergone through the centuries in different
cultures, social structures and spiritual attitudes. These differences
should not cause us to forget its common and permanent characteristics. Although the dignity of this institution is not transparent
everywhere with the same clarity,[88] some sense of the greatness of
the matrimonial union exists in all cultures. 'The well-being of the
individual person and of both human and Christian society is *2210*
closely bound up with the healthy state of conjugal and family
life.'[89]

1604 God who created man out of love also calls him to love – the
fundamental and innate vocation of every human being. For man
is created in the image and likeness of God who is himself love.[90]
Since God created him man and woman, their mutual love be- *355*
comes an image of the absolute and unfailing love with which God
loves man. It is good, very good, in the Creator's eyes. And this
love which God blesses is intended to be fruitful and to be realized
in the common work of watching over creation: 'And God blessed
them, and God said to them: "Be fruitful and multiply, and fill the
earth and subdue it." '[91]

1605 Holy Scripture affirms that man and woman were created *372*
for one another: 'It is not good that the man should be alone.'[92]
The woman, 'flesh of his flesh', his equal, his nearest in all things,
is given to him by God as a 'helpmate'; she thus represents God

---

[85] Rev 19:7, 9; cf. Gen 1:26–27.
[86] 1 Cor 7:39; cf. Eph 5:31–32.
[87] GS 48 § 1.
[88] Cf. GS 47 § 2.

[89] GS 47 § 1.
[90] Cf. Gen 1:27; 1 Jn 4:8, 16.
[91] Gen 1:28; cf. 1:31.
[92] Gen 2:18.

from whom comes our help.[93] 'Therefore a man leaves his father and his mother and cleaves to his wife, and they become one flesh.'[94] The Lord himself shows that this signifies an unbreakable
1614 union of their two lives by recalling what the plan of the Creator had been 'in the beginning': 'So they are no longer two, but one flesh.'[95]

Marriage under the regime of sin

1606 Every man experiences evil around him and within himself. This experience makes itself felt in the relationships between man and woman. Their union has always been threatened by discord, a spirit of domination, infidelity, jealousy and conflicts that can escalate into hatred and separation. This disorder can manifest itself more or less acutely, and can be more or less overcome according to the circumstances of cultures, eras and individuals, but it does seem to have a universal character.

1607 According to faith the disorder we notice so painfully does not stem from the *nature* of man and woman, nor from the nature
1849 of their relations, but from *sin*. As a break with God, the first sin
400 had for its first consequence the rupture of the original communion between man and woman. Their relations were distorted by mutual recriminations;[96] their mutual attraction, the Creator's own gift, changed into a relationship of domination and lust;[97] and the beautiful vocation of man and woman to be fruitful, multiply and subdue the earth was burdened by the pain of childbirth and the toil of work.[98]

55 1608 Nevertheless, the order of creation persists, though seriously disturbed. To heal the wounds of sin, man and woman need the help of the grace that God in his infinite mercy never refuses them.[99] Without his help man and woman cannot achieve the union of their lives for which God created them 'in the beginning'.

Marriage under the pedagogy of the Law

1609 In his mercy God has not forsaken sinful man. The punish-
410 ments consequent upon sin, 'pain in childbearing' and toil 'in the sweat of your brow',[100] also embody remedies that limit the damaging effects of sin. After the fall, marriage helps to overcome

---

[93] Cf. *Gen* 2:18–25.
[94] *Gen* 2:24.
[95] *Mt* 19:6.
[96] Cf. *Gen* 3:12.

[97] Cf. *Gen* 2:22; 3:16b.
[98] Cf. *Gen* 1:28; 3:16–19.
[99] Cf. *Gen* 3:21.
[100] *Gen* 3:16, 19.

self-absorption, egoism, pursuit of one's own pleasure, and to open oneself to the other, to mutual aid and to self-giving.

1610 Moral conscience concerning the unity and indissolubility of marriage developed under the pedagogy of the old law. In the Old Testament the polygamy of patriarchs and kings is not yet explicitly rejected. Nevertheless, the law given to Moses aims at protecting the wife from arbitrary domination by the husband, even though according to the Lord's words it still carries traces of man's 'hardness of heart' which was the reason Moses permitted men to divorce their wives.[101]

1611 Seeing God's covenant with Israel in the image of exclusive and faithful married love, the prophets prepared the Chosen People's conscience for a deepened understanding of the unity and indissolubility of marriage.[102] The books of *Ruth* and *Tobit* bear moving witness to an elevated sense of marriage, and to the fidelity and tenderness of spouses. Tradition has always seen in the *Song of Solomon* a unique expression of human love, insofar as it is a reflection of God's love – a love 'strong as death' that 'many waters cannot quench.'[103]

Marriage in the Lord

1612 The nuptial covenant between God and his people Israel had prepared the way for the new and everlasting covenant in which the Son of God, by becoming incarnate and giving his life, has united to himself in a certain way all mankind saved by him, thus preparing for 'the wedding-feast of the Lamb'.[104]

1613 On the threshold of his public life Jesus performs his first sign – at his mother's request – during a wedding feast.[105] The Church attaches great importance to Jesus' presence at the wedding at Cana. She sees in it the confirmation of the goodness of marriage and the proclamation that thenceforth marriage will be an efficacious sign of Christ's presence.

1614 In his preaching Jesus unequivocally taught the original meaning of the union of man and woman as the Creator willed it from the beginning: permission given by Moses to divorce one's wife was a concession to the hardness of hearts.[106] The matrimonial union of man and woman is indissoluble: God himself has

1963
2387

219, 2380

2361

521

2336
2382

---

[101] Cf. *Mt* 19:8; *Dt* 24:1.
[102] Cf. *Hos* 1 – 3; *Is* 54; 62; *Jer* 2 – 3; 31; *Ezek* 16; 23; *Mal* 2:13–17.
[103] *Song* 8:6–7.

[104] *Rev* 19:7, 9; cf. *GS* 22.
[105] Cf. *Jn* 2:1–11.
[106] Cf. *Mt* 19:8.

determined it: 'what therefore God has joined together, let no man put asunder.'[107]

2364 1615 This unequivocal insistence on the indissolubility of the marriage bond may have left some perplexed and could seem to be a demand impossible to realize. However, Jesus has not placed on spouses a burden impossible to bear, or too heavy – heavier than the Law of Moses.[108] By coming to restore the original order of creation disturbed by sin, he himself gives the strength and grace to live marriage in the new dimension of the Reign of God. It is by following Christ, renouncing themselves, and taking up their crosses that spouses will be able to 'receive' the original meaning of marriage and live it with the help of Christ.[109] This grace of Chris-
1642 tian marriage is a fruit of Christ's cross, the source of all Christian life.

1616 This is what the Apostle Paul makes clear when he says: 'Husbands, love your wives, as Christ loved the church and gave himself up for her, that he might sanctify her', adding at once: 'For this reason a man shall leave his father and mother and be joined to his wife, and the two shall become one. This is a great mystery, and I mean in reference to Christ and the Church.'[110]

796 1617 The entire Christian life bears the mark of the spousal love of Christ and the Church. Already Baptism, the entry into the People of God, is a nuptial mystery; it is so to speak the nuptial bath[111] which precedes the wedding feast, the Eucharist. Christian marriage in its turn becomes an efficacious sign, the sacrament of the covenant of Christ and the Church. Since it signifies and communicates grace, marriage between baptized persons is a true sacrament of the New Covenant.[112]

Virginity for the sake of the Kingdom

1618 Christ is the centre of all Christian life. The bond with him
2232 takes precedence over all other bonds, familial or social.[113] From the very beginning of the Church there have been men and
1579 women who have renounced the great good of marriage to follow the Lamb wherever he goes, to be intent on the things of the Lord, to seek to please him, and to go out to meet the Bridegroom who is coming.[114] Christ himself has invited certain persons to follow him in this way of life, of which he remains the model:

---

[107] Mt 19:6.
[108] Cf. Mk 8:34; Mt 11:29–30.
[109] Cf. Mt 19:11.
[110] Eph 5:25–26, 31–32; cf. Gen 2:24.
[111] Cf. Eph 5:26–27.
[112] Cf. DS 1800; CIC, can. 1055 § 2.
[113] Cf. Lk 14:26; Mk 10:28–31.
[114] Cf. Rev 14:4; 1 Cor 7:32; Mt 25:6.

> For there are eunuchs who have been so from birth, and there are
> eunuchs who have been made eunuchs by men, and there are eunuchs
> who have made themselves eunuchs for the sake of the kingdom of
> heaven. He who is able to receive this, let him receive it.[115]

1619 Virginity for the sake of the Kingdom of heaven is an un- 922–924
folding of baptismal grace, a powerful sign of the supremacy of
the bond with Christ and of the ardent expectation of his return, a
sign which also recalls that marriage is a reality of this present age
which is passing away.[116]

1620 Both the sacrament of Matrimony and virginity for the
Kingdom of God come from the Lord himself. It is he who gives
them meaning and grants them the grace which is indispensable
for living them out in conformity with his will.[117] Esteem of
virginity for the sake of the kingdom[118] and the Christian under- 2349
standing of marriage are inseparable, and they reinforce each
other:

> Whoever denigrates marriage also diminishes the glory of virginity.
> Whoever praises it makes virginity more admirable and resplendent.
> What appears good only in comparison with evil would not be truly
> good. The most excellent good is something even better than what is
> admitted to be good.[119]

II. The Celebration of Marriage

1621 In the Latin rite the celebration of marriage between two
Catholic faithful normally takes place during Holy Mass, because
of the connection of all the sacraments with the Paschal mystery of
Christ.[120] In the Eucharist the memorial of the New Covenant is 1323
realized, the New Covenant in which Christ has united himself for
ever to the Church, his beloved bride for whom he gave himself
up.[121] It is therefore fitting that the spouses should seal their consent to give themselves to each other through the offering of their
own lives by uniting it to the offering of Christ for his Church
made present in the Eucharistic sacrifice, and by receiving the 1368
Eucharist so that, communicating in the same Body and the same
Blood of Christ, they may form but 'one body' in Christ.[122]

1622 'Inasmuch as it is a sacramental action of sanctification, the
liturgical celebration of marriage. . . must be, per se, valid, worthy
and fruitful.'[123] It is therefore appropriate for the bride and groom

---

[115] Mt 19:12.
[116] Cf. Mk 12:25; 1 Cor 7:31.
[117] Cf. Mt 19:3–12.
[118] Cf. LG 42; PC 12; OT 10.
[119] St John Chrysostom, De virg. 10, 1:

PG 48, 540; cf. John Paul II, FC 16.
[120] Cf. SC 61.
[121] Cf. LG 6.
[122] Cf. 1 Cor 10:17.
[123] FC 67.

to prepare themselves for the celebration of their marriage by
1422 receiving the sacrament of Penance.

1623 According to the Latin tradition, the spouses as ministers
of Christ's grace mutually confer upon each other the sacrament
of Matrimony by expressing their consent before the Church. In
the traditions of the Eastern Churches, the priests (bishops or
presbyters) are witnesses to the mutual consent given by the
spouses,[123a] but for the validity of the sacrament their blessing is
also necessary.[123b]

1624 The various liturgies abound in prayers of blessing and
epiclesis asking God's grace and blessing on the new couple, especially the bride. In the epiclesis of this sacrament the spouses
736 receive the Holy Spirit as the communion of love of Christ and the
Church.[124] The Holy Spirit is the seal of their covenant, the ever-
available source of their love and the strength to renew their
fidelity.

III. Matrimonial Consent

1625 The parties to a marriage covenant are a baptized man and
woman, free to contract marriage, who freely express their con-
1734 sent. 'To be free' means:
– not being under constraint;
– not impeded by any natural or ecclesiastical law.

1626 The Church holds the exchange of consent between the
spouses to be the indispensable element that 'makes the marri-
2201 age'.[125] If consent is lacking there is no marriage.

1627 The consent consists in a 'human act by which the partners
mutually give themselves to each other': 'I take you to be my wife'
– 'I take you to be my husband.'[126] This consent that binds the
spouses to each other finds its fulfilment in the two 'becoming one
flesh'.[127]

1628 The consent must be an act of the will of each of the con-
1735 tracting parties, free of coercion or grave external fear.[128] No
human power can substitute for this consent.[129] If this freedom is
lacking the marriage is invalid.

[123a] Cf. CCEO, can. 817.
[123b] Cf. CCEO, can. 828.
[124] Cf. *Eph* 5:32.
[125] CIC, can. 1057 § 1.

[126] *GS* 48 § 1; *OCM* 45; cf. CIC, can.
1057 § 2.
[127] *Gen* 2:24; cf. *Mk* 10:8; *Eph* 5:31.
[128] Cf. CIC, can. 1103.
[129] Cf. CIC, can. 1057 § 1.

Miniature from the Monastery of Dionysius on Mount Athos (codex 587), painted in Constantinople about the year 1059.

Christ turns in prayer towards the Father (cf. § 2599). He prays alone, in a deserted place. His disciples look on from a respectful distance. St Peter, the chief apostle, turns towards the others and points to him who is the Master and the Way of Christian prayer (cf. § 2607): 'Lord, teach us to pray' (Lk 11:1).

1629 For this reason (or for other reasons that render the marriage null and void) the Church, after an examination of the situation by the competent ecclesiastical tribunal, can declare the nullity of a marriage, i.e. that the marriage never existed.[130] In this case the contracting parties are free to marry, provided the natural obligations of a previous union are discharged.[131]

1630 The priest (or deacon) who assists at the celebration of a marriage receives the consent of the spouses in the name of the Church and gives the blessing of the Church. The presence of the Church's minister (and also of the witnesses) visibly expresses the fact that marriage is an ecclesial reality.

1631 This is the reason why the Church normally requires that the faithful contract marriage according to the *ecclesiastical form*. Several reasons converge to explain this requirement:[132]
– Sacramental marriage is a *liturgical* act. It is therefore appropriate 1069 that it should be celebrated in the public liturgy of the Church;
– Marriage introduces one into an ecclesial *order*, and creates rights 1537 and duties in the Church between the spouses and towards their children;
– Since marriage is a state of life in the Church, certainty about it is necessary (hence the obligation to have witnesses);
– The public character of the consent protects the 'I do' once 2365 given, and helps the spouses remain faithful to it.

1632 So that the 'I do' of the spouses may be a free and responsible act, and so that the marriage covenant may have solid and lasting human and Christian foundations, *preparation for marriage* is of prime importance.

The example and teaching given by parents and families remain the 2206 special form of this preparation.

The role of pastors and of the Christian community as the 'family of God' is indispensable for the transmission of the human and Christian values of marriage and family,[133] and much more so in our era when many young people experience broken homes which no longer sufficiently assure this initiation:

It is imperative to give suitable and timely instruction to young people, above all in the heart of their own families, about the dignity of married love, its role and its exercise, so that, having learned the value of chastity, 2350 they will be able at a suitable age to engage in honourable courtship and enter upon a marriage of their own.[134]

Mixed marriages and disparity of cult

1633 In many countries the situation of a *mixed marriage* (marriage between a

---

[130] Cf. CIC, cann. 1095–1107.   CIC, can. 1108.
[131] Cf. CIC, can. 1071.   [133] Cf. CIC, can 1063.
[132] Cf. Council of Trent: DS 1813–1816;   [134] GS 49 § 3.

Catholic and a baptized non-Catholic) often arises. It requires particular attention on the part of couples and their pastors. A case of marriage with *disparity of cult* (between a Catholic and a non-baptized person) requires even greater circumspection.

1634 Difference of confession between the spouses does not constitute an insurmountable obstacle for marriage, when they succeed in placing in common what they have received from their respective communities, and learn from each other the way in which each lives in fidelity to Christ. But the difficulties of mixed marriages must not be underestimated. They arise from the fact that the separation of Christians has not yet been overcome. The spouses risk experiencing the tragedy of Christian disunity even in the heart of their own home. Disparity of cult can further aggravate these difficulties. Differences about faith and the very notion of marriage, but also different religious mentalities, can become sources of tension in marriage, especially as regards the education of children. The temptation to religious indifference can then arise.

817

1635 According to the law in force in the Latin Church, a mixed marriage needs for liceity the *express permission* of ecclesiastical authority.[135] In case of disparity of cult an *express dispensation* from this impediment is required for the validity of the marriage.[136] This permission or dispensation presupposes that both parties know and do not exclude the essential ends and properties of marriage; and furthermore that the Catholic party confirms the obligations, which have been made known to the non-Catholic party, of preserving his or her own faith and ensuring the baptism and education of the children in the Catholic Church.[137]

821

1636 Through ecumenical dialogue Christian communities in many regions have been able to put into effect a *common pastoral practice for mixed marriages*. Its task is to help such couples live out their particular situation in the light of faith, overcome the tensions between the couple's obligations to each other and towards their ecclesial communities, and encourage the flowering of what is common to them in faith and respect for what separates them.

1637 In marriages with disparity of cult the Catholic spouse has a particular task: 'For the unbelieving husband is consecrated through his wife, and the unbelieving wife is consecrated through her husband.'[138] It is a great joy for the Christian spouse and for the Church if this 'consecration' should lead to the free conversion of the other spouse to the Christian faith.[139] Sincere married love, the humble and patient practice of the family virtues, and perseverance in prayer can prepare the non-believing spouse to accept the grace of conversion.

IV. The Effects of the Sacrament of Matrimony

1638 'From a valid marriage arises *a bond* between the spouses which by its very nature is perpetual and exclusive; furthermore, in a Christian marriage the spouses are strengthened and, as it were, consecrated for the duties and the dignity of their state *by a special sacrament*.'[140]

---

[135] Cf. CIC, can. 1124.
[136] Cf. CIC, can. 1086.
[137] Cf. CIC, can. 1125.

[138] 1 *Cor* 7:14.
[139] Cf. 1 *Cor* 7:16.
[140] Cf. CIC, can. 1134.

The marriage bond

1639 The consent by which the spouses mutually give and receive one another is sealed by God himself.[141] From their covenant arises 'an institution, confirmed by the divine law,... even in the eyes of society'.[142] The covenant between the spouses is integrated into God's covenant with man: 'Authentic married love is caught up into divine love.'[143]

1640 Thus *the marriage bond* has been established by God himself in such a way that a marriage concluded and consummated between baptized persons can never be dissolved. This bond, which results from the free human act of the spouses and their consummation of the marriage, is a reality, henceforth irrevocable, and gives rise to a covenant guaranteed by God's fidelity. The Church does not have the power to contravene this disposition of divine wisdom.[144]   2365

The grace of the sacrament of Matrimony

1641 'By reason of their state in life and of their order, [Christian spouses] have their own special gifts in the People of God.'[145] This grace proper to the sacrament of Matrimony is intended to perfect the couple's love and to strengthen their indissoluble unity. By this grace they 'help one another to attain holiness in their married life and in welcoming and educating their children.'[146]

1642 *Christ is the source of this grace*. 'Just as of old God encountered   1615
his people with a covenant of love and fidelity, so our Saviour, the spouse of the Church, now encounters Christian spouses through   796
the sacrament of Matrimony.'[147] Christ dwells with them, gives them the strength to take up their crosses and so follow him, to rise again after they have fallen, to forgive one another, to bear one another's burdens, to 'be subject to one another out of reverence for Christ'[148] and to love one another with supernatural, tender and fruitful love. In the joys of their love and family life he gives them here on earth a foretaste of the wedding feast of the Lamb:

> How can I ever express the happiness of a marriage joined by the Church, strengthened by an offering, sealed by a blessing, announced by angels and ratified by the Father?... How wonderful the bond between two believers, now one in hope, one in desire, one in discipline, one in the same service! They are both children of one Father and servants of the

---

[141] Cf. *Mk* 10:9.
[142] *GS* 48 § 1.
[143] *GS* 48 § 2.
[144] Cf. CIC, can. 1141.

[145] *LG* 11 § 2.
[146] *LG* 11 § 2; cf. *LG* 41.
[147] *GS* 48 § 2.
[148] *Eph* 5:21; cf. *Gal* 6:2.

same Master, undivided in spirit and flesh, truly two in one flesh. Where the flesh is one, one also is the spirit.[149]

V. The Goods and Requirements of Conjugal Love

2361 1643 'Conjugal love involves a totality, in which all the elements of the person enter – appeal of the body and instinct, power of feeling and affectivity, aspiration of the spirit and of will. It aims at a deeply personal unity, a unity that, beyond union in one flesh, leads to forming one heart and soul; it demands *indissolubility* and *faithfulness* in definitive mutual giving; and it is open to *fertility*. In a word it is a question of the normal characteristics of all natural conjugal love, but with a new significance which not only purifies and strengthens them, but raises them to the extent of making them the expression of specifically Christian values.'[150]

The unity and indissolubility of marriage

1644 The love of the spouses requires, of its very nature, the unity and indissolubility of the spouses' community of persons, which embraces their entire life: 'so they are no longer two, but one flesh.'[151] They 'are called to grow continually in their communion through day-to-day fidelity to their marriage promise of total mutual self-giving.'[152] This human communion is confirmed, purified and completed by communion in Jesus Christ, given through the sacrament of Matrimony. It is deepened by lives of the common faith and by the Eucharist received together.

1645 'The unity of marriage, distinctly recognized by our Lord, is
369 made clear in the equal personal dignity which must be accorded to man and wife in mutual and unreserved affection.'[153] *Polygamy* is contrary to conjugal love which is undivided and exclusive.[154]

2364–2365 The fidelity of conjugal love

1646 By its very nature conjugal love requires the inviolable fidelity of the spouses. This is the consequence of the gift of themselves which they make to each other. Love seeks to be definitive; it cannot be an arrangement 'until further notice'. The 'intimate union of marriage, as a mutual giving of two persons, and the good of the children, demand total fidelity from the spouses and require an unbreakable union between them.'[155]

---

[149] Tertullian, *Ad uxorem* 2, 8, 6–7: PL 1, 1412–1413; cf. *FC* 13.
[150] *FC* 13.
[151] *Mt* 19:6; cf. *Gen* 2:24.
[152] *FC* 19.
[153] *GS* 49 § 2.
[154] Cf. *FC* 19.
[155] *GS* 48 § 1.

1647 The deepest reason is found in the fidelity of God to his covenant, in that of Christ to his Church. Through the sacrament of Matrimony the spouses are enabled to represent this fidelity and witness to it. Through the sacrament, the indissolubility of marriage receives a new and deeper meaning.

1648 It can seem difficult, even impossible, to bind oneself for life to another human being. This makes it all the more important to proclaim the Good News that God loves us with a definitive and irrevocable love, that married couples share in this love, that it supports and sustains them, and that by their own faithfulness they can be witnesses to God's faithful love. Spouses who with God's grace give this witness, often in very difficult conditions, deserve the gratitude and support of the ecclesial community.[156]

1649 Yet there are some situations in which living together becomes practically impossible for a variety of reasons. In such cases the Church permits the physical *separation* of the couple and their living apart. The spouses do not cease to be   2383 husband and wife before God and so are not free to contract a new union. In this difficult situation, the best solution would be, if possible, reconciliation. The Christian community is called to help these persons live out their situation in a Christian manner, and in fidelity to their marriage bond which remains indissoluble.[157]

1650 Today there are numerous Catholics in many countries who have recourse to civil *divorce* and contract new civil unions. In fidelity to the words of   2384 Jesus Christ – 'Whoever divorces his wife and marries another, commits adultery against her; and if she divorces her husband and marries another, she commits adultery'[158] – the Church maintains that a new union cannot be recognized as valid, if the first marriage was. If the divorced are remarried civilly, they find themselves in a situation that objectively contravenes God's law. Consequently, they cannot receive Eucharistic communion as long as this situation persists. For the same reason, they cannot exercise certain ecclesial responsibilities. Reconciliation through the sacrament of Penance can be granted only to those who have repented for having violated the sign of the covenant and of fidelity to Christ, and who are committed to living in complete continence.

1651 Towards Christians who live in this situation, and who often keep the faith and desire to bring up their children in a Christian manner, priests and the whole community must manifest an attentive solicitude, so that they do not consider themselves separated from the Church, in whose life they can and must participate as baptized persons:

> They should be encouraged to listen to the Word of God, to attend the Sacrifice of the Mass, to persevere in prayer, to contribute to works of charity and to community efforts for justice, to bring up their children in

---

[156] Cf. FC 20.
[157] Cf. FC 83; CIC, cann. 1151–1155.
[158] Mk 10:11–12.

the Christian faith, to cultivate the spirit and practice of penance and thus implore, day by day, God's grace.[159]

2366–2367 **The openness to fertility**

1652 'By its very nature the institution of marriage and married
372 love is ordered to the procreation and education of the offspring and it is in them that it finds its crowning glory.'[160]

> Children are the supreme gift of marriage and contribute greatly to the good of the parents themselves. God himself said: 'It is not good that man should be alone', and 'from the beginning [he] made them male and female'; wishing to associate them in a special way in his own creative work, God blessed man and woman with the words: 'Be fruitful and multiply.' Hence, true married love and the whole structure of family life which results from it, without diminishment of the other ends of marriage, are directed to disposing the spouses to co-operate valiantly with the love of the Creator and Saviour, who through them will increase and enrich his family from day to day.[161]

1653 The fruitfulness of conjugal love extends to the fruits of the moral, spiritual and supernatural life that parents hand on to their children by education. Parents are the principal and first educators of their children.[162] In this sense the fundamental task of marriage
2231 and family is to be at the service of life.[163]

1654 Spouses to whom God has not granted children can nevertheless have a conjugal life full of meaning, in both human and Christian terms. Their marriage can radiate a fruitfulness of charity, of hospitality and of sacrifice.

VI. The Domestic Church

1655 Christ chose to be born and grow up in the bosom of the holy family of Joseph and Mary. The Church is nothing other than
759 'the family of God'. From the beginning, the core of the Church was often constituted by those who had become believers 'together with all [their] household'.[164] When they were converted, they desired that 'their whole household' should also be saved.[165] These families who became believers were islands of Christian life in an unbelieving world.

1656 In our own time, in a world often alien and even hostile to faith, believing families are of primary importance as centres of

---

[159] FC 84.
[160] GS 48 § 1; 50.
[161] GS 50 § 1; cf. Gen 2:18; Mt 19:4; Gen 1:28.

[162] Cf. GE 3.
[163] Cf. FC 28.
[164] Cf. Acts 18:8.
[165] Cf. Acts 16:31; 11:14.

living, radiant faith. For this reason the Second Vatican Council, using an ancient expression, calls the family the *Ecclesia domestica*.[166] It is in the bosom of the family that parents are 'by word and example... the first heralds of the faith with regard to their children. They should encourage them in the vocation which is proper to each child, fostering with special care any religious vocation.'[167]   2204

1657 It is here that the father of the family, the mother, children, and all members of the family exercise the *priesthood of the baptized* in a privileged way 'by the reception of the sacraments, prayer and thanksgiving, the witness of a holy life, and self-denial and active charity'.[168] Thus the home is the first school of Christian life and 'a school for human enrichment'.[169] Here one learns endurance and the joy of work, fraternal love, generous – even repeated – forgiveness, and above all divine worship in prayer and the offering of one's life.   1268   2214–2231   2685

1658 We must also remember the great number of *single persons* who, because of the particular circumstances in which they have to live – often not of their choosing – are especially close to Jesus' heart and therefore deserve the special affection and active solicitude of the Church, especially of pastors. Many remain *without a human family*, often due to conditions of poverty. Some live their situation in the spirit of the Beatitudes, serving God and neighbour in exemplary fashion. The doors of homes, the 'domestic churches', and of the great family which is the Church must be open to all of them. 'No one is without a family in this world: the Church is a home and family for everyone, especially those who "labour and are heavy laden".'[170]   2231   2233

IN BRIEF

1659 St Paul said: 'Husbands, love your wives, as Christ loved the Church... This is a great mystery, and I mean in reference to Christ and the Church' (Eph 5:25, 32).

1660 The marriage covenant, by which a man and a woman form with each other an intimate communion of life and love, has been founded and endowed with its own special laws by the Creator. By its very nature it is ordered to the good of the couple, as well as to the generation and education of children. Christ the Lord raised marriage between the baptized to the dignity of a sacrament (cf. CIC, can. 1055 § 1; cf. GS 48 § 1).

---

[166] LG 11; cf. FC 21.
[167] LG 11.
[168] LG 10.

[169] GS 52 § 1.
[170] FC 85; cf. Mt 11:28.

1661 The sacrament of Matrimony signifies the union of Christ and the Church. It gives spouses the grace to love each other with the love with which Christ has loved his Church; the grace of the sacrament thus perfects the human love of the spouses, strengthens their indissoluble unity and sanctifies them on the way to eternal life (cf. Council of Trent: DS 1799).

1662 Marriage is based on the consent of the contracting parties, that is, on their will to give themselves, each to the other, mutually and definitively, in order to live a covenant of faithful and fruitful love.

1663 Since marriage establishes the couple in a public state of life in the Church, it is fitting that its celebration be public, in the framework of a liturgical celebration, before the priest (or a witness authorized by the Church), the witnesses, and the assembly of the faithful.

1664 Unity, indissolubility and openness to fertility are essential to marriage. Polygamy is incompatible with the unity of marriage; divorce separates what God has joined together; the refusal of fertility turns married life away from its 'supreme gift', the child (GS 50 § 1).

1665 The remarriage of persons divorced from a living, lawful spouse contravenes the plan and law of God as taught by Christ. They are not separated from the Church, but they cannot receive Eucharistic communion. They will lead Christian lives especially by educating their children in the faith.

1666 The Christian home is the place where children receive the first proclamation of the faith. For this reason the family home is rightly called 'the domestic church', a community of grace and prayer, a school of human virtues and of Christian charity.

Chapter Four
OTHER LITURGICAL CELEBRATIONS

Article 1
SACRAMENTALS

1667 'Holy Mother Church has, moreover, instituted sacramentals. These are sacred signs which bear a resemblance to the sacraments. They signify effects, particularly of a spiritual nature, which are obtained through the intercession of the Church. By them men are disposed to receive the chief effect of the sacraments, and various occasions in life are rendered holy.'[1]

The characteristics of sacramentals

1668 Sacramentals are instituted for the sanctification of certain

[1] SC 60; cf. CIC, can. 1166; CCEO, can. 867.

ministries of the Church, certain states of life, a great variety of circumstances in Christian life, and the use of many things helpful to man. In accordance with bishops' pastoral decisions, they can also respond to the needs, culture and special history of the Christian people of a particular region or time. They always include a prayer, often accompanied by a specific sign, such as the laying on 699 of hands, the sign of the cross, or the sprinkling of holy water 2157 (which recalls Baptism).

1669 Sacramentals derive from the baptismal priesthood: every 784 baptized person is called to be a 'blessing', and to bless:[2] Hence lay 2626 people may preside at certain blessings; the more a blessing concerns ecclesial and sacramental life, the more is its administration reserved to the ordained ministry (bishops, priests or deacons).[3]

1670 Sacramentals do not confer the grace of the Holy Spirit in 1128 the way that the sacraments do, but by the Church's prayer they prepare us to receive grace and dispose us to co-operate with it. 2001 'For well-disposed members of the faithful, the liturgy of the sacraments and sacramentals sanctifies almost every event of their lives with the divine grace which flows from the Paschal mystery of the Passion, Death and Resurrection of Christ. From this source all sacraments and sacramentals draw their power. There is scarcely any proper use of material things which cannot be thus directed towards the sanctification of men and the praise of God.'[4]

Various forms of sacramentals

1671 Among sacramentals *blessings* (of persons, meals, objects, and places) 1078 come first. Every blessing praises God and prays for his gifts. In Christ, Christians are blessed by God the Father 'with every spiritual blessing'.[5] This is why the Church imparts blessings by invoking the name of Jesus, usually while making the holy sign of the cross of Christ.

1672 Certain blessings have a lasting importance because they *consecrate* persons to God, or reserve objects and places for liturgical use. Among those blessings which are intended for persons – not to be confused with sacramental ordination – are the blessing of the abbot or abbess of a monastery, the consecration of virgins and widows, the rite of religious profession and the blessing of certain 923, 925 ministries of the Church (readers, acolytes, catechists, etc.). The dedication 903 or blessing of a church or an altar, the blessing of holy oils, vessels and vestments, bells, etc. can be mentioned as examples of blessings that concern objects.

1673 When the Church asks publicly and authoritatively in the name of Jesus

---

[2] Cf. *Gen* 12:2; *Lk* 6:28; *Rom* 12:14; 1 *Pt* 3:9.
[3] Cf. SC 79; CIC, can. 1168; *De Ben.* 16, 18.
[4] SC 61.
[5] *Eph* 1:3.

395 Christ that a person or object be protected against the power of the Evil One
550 and withdrawn from his dominion, it is called *exorcism*. Jesus performed exor-
     cisms and from him the Church has received the power and office of exor-
1237 cizing.[6] In a simple form, exorcism is performed at the celebration of Baptism.
     The solemn exorcism, called 'a major exorcism', can be performed only by a
     priest and with the permission of the bishop. The priest must proceed with
     prudence, strictly observing the rules established by the Church. Exorcism is
     directed at the expulsion of demons or to the liberation from demonic posses-
     sion through the spiritual authority which Jesus entrusted to his Church. Illness,
     especially psychological illness, is a very different matter; treating this is the
     concern of medical science. Therefore, before an exorcism is performed, it is
     important to ascertain that one is dealing with the presence of the Evil One, and
     not an illness.[7]

Popular piety

1674 Besides sacramental liturgy and sacramentals, catechesis
must take into account the forms of piety and popular devotions
among the faithful. The religious sense of the Christian people has
2688 always found expression in various forms of piety surrounding the
Church's sacramental life, such as the veneration of relics, visits
2669 to sanctuaries, pilgrimages, processions, the stations of the cross,
2678 religious dances, the rosary, medals,[8] etc.

1675 These expressions of piety extend the liturgical life of the Church, but do
not replace it. They 'should be so drawn up that they harmonize with the
liturgical seasons, accord with the sacred liturgy, are in some way derived from
it and lead the people to it, since in fact the liturgy by its very nature is far
superior to any of them.'[9]

1676 Pastoral discernment is needed to sustain and support popular piety and, if
necessary, to purify and correct the religious sense which underlies these devo-
426 tions so that the faithful may advance in knowledge of the mystery of Christ.[10]
Their exercise is subject to the care and judgement of the bishops and to the
general norms of the Church.

At its core the piety of the people is a storehouse of values that offers
answers of Christian wisdom to the great questions of life. The Catholic
wisdom of the people is capable of fashioning a vital synthesis... It crea-
tively combines the divine and the human, Christ and Mary, spirit and
body, communion and institution, person and community, faith and
homeland, intelligence and emotion. This wisdom is a Christian humanism that radically affirms the dignity of every person as a child of God,
establishes a basic fraternity, teaches people to encounter nature and
understand work, provides reasons for joy and humour even in the midst
of a very hard life. For the people this wisdom is also a principle of

[6] Cf. *Mk* 1:25–26; 3:15; 6:7, 13; 16:17.   Council of Trent: DS 1822.
[7] Cf. CIC, can. 1172.   [9] *SC* 13 § 3.
[8] Cf. Council of Nicaea II: DS 601; 603;   [10] Cf. John Paul II, *CT* 54.

discernment and an evangelical instinct through which they spontaneously sense when the Gospel is served in the Church, and when it is emptied of its content and stifled by other interests.[11]

IN BRIEF

1677 *Sacramentals are sacred signs instituted by the Church. They prepare men to receive the fruit of the sacraments and sanctify different circumstances of life.*

1678 *Among the sacramentals blessings occupy an important place. They include both praise of God for his works and gifts, and the Church's intercession for men that they may be able to use God's gifts according to the spirit of the Gospel.*

1679 *In addition to the liturgy, Christian life is nourished by various forms of popular piety, rooted in the different cultures. While carefully clarifying them in the light of faith, the Church fosters the forms of popular piety that express an evangelical instinct and a human wisdom and that enrich Christian life.*

Article 2
CHRISTIAN FUNERALS

1680 All the sacraments, and principally those of Christian initiation, have as their goal the last Passover of the child of God which, through death, leads him into the life of the Kingdom. Then what he confessed in faith and hope will be fulfilled: 'I look for the resurrection of the dead, and the life of the world to come.'[12] *1525*

I. The Christian's Last Passover

1681 The Christian meaning of death is revealed in the light of the *Paschal mystery* of the death and Resurrection of Christ in whom resides our only hope. The Christian who dies in Christ Jesus is 'away from the body and at home with the Lord'.[13] *1010–1014*

1682 For the Christian the day of death inaugurates, *at the end of his sacramental life*, the fulfilment of his new birth begun at Baptism, the definitive 'conformity' to 'the image of the Son' conferred by the anointing of the Holy Spirit, and participation in the feast of the Kingdom which was anticipated in the Eucharist –

---

[11] CELAM, Third General Conference (Puebla, 1979), Final Document, § 448 (tr. NCCB, 1979); cf. Paul VI, *EN* 48.

[12] Niceno-Constantinopolitan Creed.
[13] 2 *Cor* 5:8.

even if final purifications are still necessary for him in order to be clothed with the nuptial garment.

1683 The Church who, as Mother, has borne the Christian sacramentally in her womb during his earthly pilgrimage, accompanies him at his journey's end, in order to surrender him 'into the Father's hands'. She offers to the Father, in Christ, the child of his grace, and she commits to the earth, in hope, the seed of the body that will rise in glory.[14] This offering is fully celebrated in the Eucharistic sacrifice; the blessings before and after Mass are sacramentals.

1020
627

II. The Celebration of Funerals

1684 The Christian funeral is a liturgical celebration of the Church. The ministry of the Church in this instance aims at expressing efficacious communion with *the deceased*, at the participation in that communion of *the community* gathered for the funeral, and at the proclamation of eternal life to the community.

1685 The different funeral rites express the *Paschal character* of Christian death and are in keeping with the situations and traditions of each region, even as to the colour of the liturgical vestments worn.[16]

1686 The *Order of Christian Funerals* (*Ordo exsequiarum*) of the Roman liturgy gives three types of funeral celebrations, corresponding to the three places in which they are conducted (the home, the church and the cemetery), and according to the importance attached to them by the family, local customs, the culture and popular piety. This order of celebration is common to all the liturgical traditions, and comprises four principal elements:

1687 *The greeting of the community.* A greeting of faith begins the celebration. Relatives and friends of the deceased are welcomed with a word of 'consolation' (in the New Testament sense of the Holy Spirit's power in hope).[17] The community assembling in prayer also awaits the 'words of eternal life'. The death of a member of the community (or the anniversary of a death, or the seventh or thirtieth day after death) is an event that should lead beyond the perspectives of 'this world' and should draw the faithful into the true perspective of faith in the risen Christ.

1688 *The liturgy of the Word* during funerals demands very careful preparation because the assembly present for the funeral may include some faithful who rarely attend the liturgy, and friends of the deceased who are not Christians. The homily in particular must 'avoid the literary genre of funeral eulogy'[18] and illumine the mystery of Christian death in the light of the risen Christ.

---

[14] Cf. 1 *Cor* 15:42–44.
[15] [No note]
[16] Cf. *SC* 81.

[17] Cf. 1 *Th* 4:18.
[18] OCF 41.

1689 *The Eucharistic Sacrifice.* When the celebration takes place in church, the *1371* Eucharist is the heart of the Paschal reality of Christian death.[19] In the Eucharist, the Church expresses her efficacious communion with the departed: offering to the Father in the Holy Spirit the sacrifice of the death and Resurrection of Christ, she asks Him to purify his child of his sins and their consequences, and to admit him to the Paschal fullness of the table of the Kingdom.[20] It is by the Eucharist thus celebrated that the community of the faithful, especially the family of the deceased, learn to live in communion with the one who 'has fallen *958* asleep in the Lord', by communicating in the Body of Christ of which he is a living member and, then, by praying for him and with him.

1690 A *farewell* to the deceased is his final 'commendation to God' by the Church. It is 'the last farewell by which the Christian community greets one of its members before his body is brought to its tomb'.[21] The Byzantine tradition *2300* expresses this by the kiss of farewell to the deceased:

By this final greeting 'we sing for his departure from this life and separation from us, but also because there is a communion and a reunion. For even dead, we are not at all separated from one another, because we all run the same course and we will find one another again in the same place. We shall never be separated, for we live for Christ, and now we are united with Christ as we go toward him... we shall all be together in Christ.'[22]

---

[19] Cf. OCF 1.
[20] Cf. OCF 57.
[21] OCF 10.

[22] St Symeon of Thessalonica, *De ordine sepulturae* 336: PG 155, 684.

Part Three

LIFE IN CHRIST

1691 'Christian, recognize your dignity and, now that you share in God's own nature, do not return to your former base condition
790 by sinning. Remember who is your head and of whose body you are a member. Never forget that you have been rescued from the power of darkness and brought into the light of the Kingdom of God.'[1]

1692 The Symbol of the faith confesses the greatness of God's gifts to man in his work of creation, and even more in redemption and sanctification. What faith confesses, the sacraments communicate: by the sacraments of rebirth, Christians have become 'children of God',[2] 'partakers of the divine nature'.[3] Coming to see in the faith their new dignity, Christians are called to lead henceforth a life 'worthy of the gospel of Christ'.[4] They are made capable of doing so by the grace of Christ and the gifts of his Spirit, which they receive through the sacraments and through prayer.

1693 Christ Jesus always did what was pleasing to the *Father*,[5] and always lived in perfect communion with him. Likewise Christ's disciples are invited to live in the sight of the Father 'who sees in secret',[6] in order to become 'perfect as your heavenly Father is perfect'.[7]

1267 1694 Incorporated into *Christ* by Baptism, Christians are 'dead to sin and alive to God in Christ Jesus' and so participate in the life of the Risen Lord.[8] Following Christ and united with him,[9] Christians can strive to be 'imitators of God as beloved children, and walk in love'[10] by conforming their thoughts, words and actions to the 'mind... which is yours in Christ Jesus',[11] and by following his example.[12]

1695 'Justified in the name of the Lord Jesus Christ and in the Spirit of our God',[13] 'sanctified... [and] called to be saints',[14] Christians have become the temple of the *Holy Spirit*.[15] This 'Spirit of the Son' teaches them to pray to the Father[16] and, having become their life, prompts them to act so as to bear 'the fruit of the Spirit'[17] by charity in action. Healing the wounds of sin, the Holy

---

[1] St Leo the Great, *Sermo 21 in nat. Dom.* 3: PL 54, 192C.
[2] *Jn* 1:12; 1 *Jn* 3:1.
[3] 2 *Pt* 1:4.
[4] *Phil* 1:27.
[5] Cf. *Jn* 8:29.
[6] *Mt* 6:6.
[7] *Mt* 5:48.
[8] *Rom* 6:11 and cf. 6:5; cf. *Col* 2:12.
[9] Cf. *Jn* 15:5.
[10] *Eph* 5:1–2.
[11] *Phil* 2:5.
[12] Cf. *Jn* 13:12–16.
[13] 1 *Cor* 6:11.
[14] 1 *Cor* 1:2.
[15] Cf. 1 *Cor* 6:19.
[16] Cf. *Gal* 4:6.
[17] *Gal* 5:22, 25.

Spirit renews us interiorly through a spiritual transformation.[18] He enlightens and strengthens us to live as 'children of light' through 'all that is good and right and true'.[19]

1696 The way of Christ 'leads to life'; a contrary way 'leads to destruction'.[20] The Gospel parable of the *two ways* remains ever present in the catechesis of the Church; it shows the importance of moral decisions for our salvation: 'There are two ways, the one of life, the other of death; but between the two, there is a great difference.'[21]

1970

1697 *Catechesis* has to reveal in all clarity the joy and the demands of the way of Christ.[22] Catechesis for the 'newness of life'[23] in him should be:

– *a catechesis of the Holy Spirit*, the interior Master of life according to Christ, a gentle guest and friend who inspires, guides, corrects and strengthens this life;

737ff.

– *a catechesis of grace*, for it is by grace that we are saved and again it is by grace that our works can bear fruit for eternal life;

1988ff.

– *a catechesis of the Beatitudes*, for the way of Christ is summed up in the Beatitudes, the only path that leads to the eternal beatitude for which the human heart longs;

1716ff.

– *a catechesis of sin and forgiveness*, for unless man acknowledges that he is a sinner he cannot know the truth about himself, which is a condition for acting justly; and without the offer of forgiveness he would not be able to bear this truth;

1846ff.

– *a catechesis of the human virtues* which causes one to grasp the beauty and attraction of right dispositions towards goodness;

1803ff.

– *a catechesis of the Christian virtues* of faith, hope and charity, generously inspired by the example of the saints;

1812ff.

– *a catechesis of the twofold commandment of charity* set forth in the Decalogue;

2067

– *an ecclesial catechesis*, for it is through the manifold exchanges of 'spiritual goods' in the 'communion of saints' that Christian life can grow, develop and be communicated.

946ff.

1698 The first and last point of reference of this catechesis will always be Jesus Christ himself, who is 'the way, and the truth, and the life'.[24] It is by looking to him in faith that Christ's faithful can hope that he himself fulfils his promises in them, and that, by

426

---

[18] Cf. *Eph* 4:23.
[19] *Eph* 5:8, 9.
[20] *Mt* 7:13; cf. *Dt* 30:15–20.
[21] *Didache* 1, 1: SCh 248, 140.

[22] Cf. John Paul II, *CT* 29.
[23] *Rom* 6:4.
[24] *Jn* 14:6.

loving him with the same love with which he has loved them, they may perform works in keeping with their dignity:

> I ask you to consider that our Lord Jesus Christ is your true head, and that you are one of his members. He belongs to you as the head belongs to its members; all that is his is yours: his spirit, his heart, his body and soul and all his faculties. You must make use of all these as of your own, to serve, praise, love and glorify God. You belong to him, as members belong to their head. And so he longs for you to use all that is in you, as if it were his own, for the service and glory of the Father.[25]

For to me, to live is Christ.[26]

---

[25] St John Eudes, *Tract. de admirabili corde Jesu* 1, 5.   [26] *Phil* 1:21.

Section One

MAN'S VOCATION: LIFE IN THE SPIRIT

1699 Life in the Holy Spirit fulfils the vocation of man (*Chapter One*). This life is made up of divine charity and human solidarity (*Chapter Two*). It is graciously offered as salvation (*Chapter Three*).

Chapter One

THE DIGNITY OF THE HUMAN PERSON

1700 The dignity of the human person is rooted in his creation in the image and likeness of God (*article 1*); it is fulfilled in his voca- 356 tion to divine beatitude (*article 2*). It is essential to a human being freely to direct himself to this fulfilment (*article 3*). By his deliber- ate actions (*article 4*), the human person does, or does not, conform to the good promised by God (*article 5*) and attested by moral conscience (*article 6*). Human beings make their own contribution to their interior growth; they make their whole sentient and spiri- tual lives into means of this growth. With the help of grace they grow in virtue (*article 7*), avoid sin, and if they sin they entrust themselves as did the prodigal son[1] to the mercy of our Father in 1439 heaven (*article 8*). In this way they attain to the perfection of charity.

Article 1

MAN: THE IMAGE OF GOD

1701 'Christ,... in the very revelation of the mystery of the 359 Father and of his love, makes man fully manifest to himself and brings to light his exalted vocation.'[2] It is in Christ, 'the image of the invisible God',[3] that man has been created 'in the image and likeness' of the Creator. It is in Christ, Redeemer and Saviour, that the divine image, disfigured in man by the first sin, has been restored to its original beauty and ennobled by the grace of God.[4]

1702 The divine image is present in every man. It shines forth in the communion of persons, in the likeness of the unity of the divine persons among themselves (cf. *Chapter Two*).   1878

---

[1] *Lk* 15:11–32.　　　　　　　[3] *Col* 1:15; cf. 2 *Cor* 4:4.
[2] *GS* 22.　　　　　　　　　　[4] Cf. *GS* 22.

363   1703   Endowed with 'a spiritual and immortal' soul,[5] the human
person is 'the only creature on earth that God has willed for its
2258   own sake'.[6] From his conception, he is destined for eternal
beatitude.

1704   The human person participates in the light and power of the
divine Spirit. By his reason, he is capable of understanding the
order of things established by the Creator. By free will, he is
339   capable of directing himself toward his true good. He finds his
30   perfection 'in seeking and loving what is true and good'.[7]

1705   By virtue of his soul and his spiritual powers of intellect and
1730   will, man is endowed with freedom, an 'outstanding manifestation of the divine image'.[8]

1706   By his reason, man recognizes the voice of God which urges
him 'to do what is good and avoid what is evil'.[9] Everyone is
1776   obliged to follow this law, which makes itself heard in conscience
and is fulfilled in the love of God and of neighbour. Living a moral
life bears witness to the dignity of the person.

1707   'Man, enticed by the Evil One, abused his freedom at the
very beginning of history.'[10] He succumbed to temptation and did
what was evil. He still desires the good, but his nature bears the
397   wound of original sin. He is now inclined to evil and subject to
error:

> Man is divided in himself. As a result, the whole life of men, both
> individual and social, shows itself to be a struggle, and a dramatic one,
> between good and evil, between light and darkness.[11]

1708   By his Passion, Christ delivered us from Satan and from sin.
617   He merited for us the new life in the Holy Spirit. His grace restores
what sin had damaged in us.

1709   He who believes in Christ becomes a son of God. This filial
1265   adoption transforms him by giving him the ability to follow the
example of Christ. It makes him capable of acting rightly and
doing good. In union with his Saviour, the disciple attains the
perfection of charity which is holiness. Having matured in grace,
1050   the moral life blossoms into eternal life in the glory of heaven.

---

[5] GS 14 § 2.
[6] GS 24 § 3.
[7] GS 15 § 2.
[8] GS 17.

[9] GS 16.
[10] GS 13 § 1.
[11] GS 13 § 2.

IN BRIEF

1710 *'Christ... makes man fully manifest to man himself and brings to light his exalted vocation' (GS 22 § 1).*

1711 *Endowed with a spiritual soul, with intellect and with free will, the human person is from his very conception ordered to God and destined for eternal beatitude. He pursues his perfection in 'seeking and loving what is true and good' (GS 15 § 2).*

1712 *In man, true freedom is an 'outstanding manifestation of the divine image' (GS 17).*

1713 *Man is obliged to follow the moral law, which urges him 'to do what is good and avoid what is evil' (cf. GS 16). This law makes itself heard in his conscience.*

1714 *Man, having been wounded in his nature by original sin, is subject to error and inclined to evil in exercising his freedom.*

1715 *He who believes in Christ has new life in the Holy Spirit. The moral life, increased and brought to maturity in grace, is to reach its fulfilment in the glory of heaven.*

Article 2
OUR VOCATION TO BEATITUDE

I. The Beatitudes

1716 The Beatitudes are at the heart of Jesus' preaching. They take up the promises made to the chosen people since Abraham. The Beatitudes fulfil the promises by ordering them no longer merely to the possession of a territory, but to the Kingdom of heaven:

> Blessed are the poor in spirit, for theirs is the kingdom of heaven.   2546
>
> Blessed are those who mourn, for they shall be comforted.
>
> Blessed are the meek, for they shall inherit the earth.
>
> Blessed are those who hunger and thirst for righteousness,
>   for they shall be satisfied.
>
> Blessed are the merciful, for they shall obtain mercy.
>
> Blessed are the pure in heart, for they shall see God.
>
> Blessed are the peacemakers, for they shall be called sons of God.
>
> Blessed are those who are persecuted for righteousness' sake,
>   for theirs is the kingdom of heaven.

> Blessed are you when men revile you and persecute you
>> and utter all kinds of evil against you falsely on my account.
>> Rejoice and be glad, for your reward is great in heaven.[12]

1717 The Beatitudes depict the countenance of Jesus Christ and
459 portray his charity. They express the vocation of the faithful associated with the glory of his Passion and Resurrection; they shed
light on the actions and attitudes characteristic of the Christian life;
1820 they are the paradoxical promises that sustain hope in the midst of
tribulations; they proclaim the blessings and rewards already
secured, however dimly, for Christ's disciples; they have begun in
the lives of the Virgin Mary and all the saints.

II. The Desire for Happiness

27, 1024 **1718** The Beatitudes respond to the natural desire for happiness.
This desire is of divine origin: God has placed it in the human heart
in order to draw man to the One who alone can fulfil it:

> We all want to live happily; in the whole human race there is no one who
> does not assent to this proposition, even before it is fully articulated.[13]

2541
> How is it, then, that I seek you, Lord? Since in seeking you, my God, I
> seek a happy life, let me seek you so that my soul may live, for my body
> draws life from my soul and my soul draws life from you.[14]

> God alone satisfies.[15]

1719 The Beatitudes reveal the goal of human existence, the ulti-
1950 mate end of human acts: God calls us to his own beatitude. This
vocation is addressed to each individual personally, but also to the
Church as a whole, the new people made up of those who have
accepted the promise and live from it in faith.

III. Christian Beatitude

1027 **1720** The New Testament uses several expressions to characterize
the beatitude to which God calls man:
– the coming of the Kingdom of God;[16]
– the vision of God: 'Blessed are the pure in heart, for they shall see
God';[17]
– entering into the joy of the Lord;[18]

---

[12] Mt 5:3–12.
[13] St Augustine, De moribus eccl. 1, 3, 4:
PL 32, 1312.
[14] St Augustine, Conf. 10, 20, 29: PL 32,
791.
[15] St Thomas Aquinas, Expos. in symb.
apost. 1.
[16] Cf. Mt 4:17.
[17] Mt 5:8; cf. 1 Jn 3:2; 1 Cor 13:12.
[18] Mt 25:21–23.

– entering into God's rest:[19]

> There we shall rest and see, we shall see and love, we shall love and praise. Behold what will be at the end without end. For what other end do we have, if not to reach the kingdom which has no end?[20]

1721 God put us in the world to know, to love, and to serve him, and so to come to paradise. Beatitude makes us 'partakers of the divine nature' and of eternal life.[21] With beatitude, man enters into the glory of Christ[22] and into the joy of the Trinitarian life.   *260*

1722 Such beatitude surpasses the understanding and powers of *1028* man. It comes from an entirely free gift of God: whence it is called supernatural, as is the grace that disposes man to enter into the divine joy.

> 'Blessed are the pure in heart, for they shall see God.' It is true, because of the greatness and inexpressible glory of God, that 'man shall not see me and live', for the Father cannot be grasped. But because of God's love and goodness toward us, and because he can do all things, he goes so far as to grant those who love him the privilege of seeing him. . . For 'what is *294* impossible for men is possible for God.'[23]

1723 The beatitude we are promised confronts us with decisive moral choices. It invites us to purify our hearts of bad instincts and *2519* to seek the love of God above all else. It teaches us that true happiness is not found in riches or well-being, in human fame or power, or in any human achievement – however beneficial it may be – such as science, technology and art, or indeed in any creature, but in God alone, the source of every good and of all love: *227*

> All bow down before wealth. Wealth is that to which the multitude of men pay an instinctive homage. They measure happiness by wealth; and by wealth they measure respectability. . . It is a homage resulting from a profound faith. . . that with wealth he may do all things. Wealth is one idol of the day and notoriety is a second. . . Notoriety, or the making of a noise in the world – it may be called 'newspaper fame' – has come to be considered a great good in itself, and a ground of veneration.[24]

1724 The Decalogue, the Sermon on the Mount, and the apostolic catechesis describe for us the paths that lead to the Kingdom of heaven. Sustained by the grace of the Holy Spirit, we tread them,

---

[19] Cf. *Heb* 4:7–11.
[20] St Augustine, *De civ. Dei* 22, 30, 5: PL 41, 804.
[21] 2 *Pt* 1:4; cf. *Jn* 17:3.
[22] Cf. *Rom* 8:18.
[23] St Irenaeus, *Adv. haeres.* 4, 20, 5: PG

7/1, 1034–1035.
[24] John Henry Cardinal Newman, 'Saintliness the Standard of Christian Principle' in *Discourses to Mixed Congregations* (London: Longmans, Green and Co., 1906) V, 89–90.

step by step, by everyday acts. By the working of the Word of Christ, we slowly bear fruit in the Church to the glory of God.[25]

IN BRIEF

1725 The Beatitudes take up and fulfil God's promises from Abraham on by ordering them to the Kingdom of heaven. They respond to the desire for happiness that God has placed in the human heart.

1726 The Beatitudes teach us the final end to which God calls us: the Kingdom, the vision of God, participation in the divine nature, eternal life, filiation, rest in God.

1727 The beatitude of eternal life is a gratuitous gift of God. It is supernatural, as is the grace that leads us there.

1728 The Beatitudes confront us with decisive choices concerning earthly goods; they purify our hearts in order to teach us to love God above all things.

1729 The beatitude of heaven sets the standards for discernment in the use of earthly goods in keeping with the law of God.

Article 3
MAN'S FREEDOM

1730 God created man a rational being, conferring on him the dignity of a person who can initiate and control his own actions. 'God willed that man should be "left in the hand of his own counsel", so that he might of his own accord seek his Creator and freely attain his full and blessed perfection by cleaving to him.'[26]

> Man is rational and therefore like God; he is created with free will and is master over his acts.[27]

I. Freedom and Responsibility

1731 Freedom is the power, rooted in reason and will, to act or not to act, to do this or that, and so to perform deliberate actions on one's own responsibility. By free will one shapes one's own life. Human freedom is a force for growth and maturity in truth and goodness; it attains its perfection when directed toward God, our beatitude.

---

[25] Cf. the parable of the sower: Mt 13:3–23.
[26] GS 17; Sir 15:14.

[27] St Irenaeus, Adv. haeres. 4, 4, 3: PG 7/1, 983.

1732   As long as freedom has not bound itself definitively to its ultimate good which is God, there is the possibility of *choosing between good and evil*, and thus of growing in perfection or of failing and sinning. This freedom characterizes properly human acts. It is the basis of praise or blame, merit or reproach.   *396 1849 2006*

1733   The more one does what is good, the freer one becomes. There is no true freedom except in the service of what is good and just. The choice to disobey and do evil is an abuse of freedom and leads to 'the slavery of sin'.[28]   *1803*

1734   Freedom makes man *responsible* for his acts to the extent that they are voluntary. Progress in virtue, knowledge of the good, and ascesis enhance the mastery of the will over its acts.   *1036 1804*

1735   *Imputability* and responsibility for an action can be diminished or even nullified by ignorance, inadvertence, duress, fear, habit, inordinate attachments and other psychological or social factors.   *597*

1736   Every act directly willed is imputable to its author:

> Thus the Lord asked Eve after the sin in the garden: 'What is this that you have done?'[29] He asked Cain the same question.[30] The prophet Nathan questioned David in the same way after he committed adultery with the wife of Uriah and had him murdered.[31]   *2568*

> An action can be indirectly voluntary when it results from negligence regarding something one should have known or done: for example, an accident arising from ignorance of traffic laws.

1737   An effect can be tolerated without being willed by its agent; for instance, a mother's exhaustion from tending her sick child. A bad effect is not imputable if it was not willed either as an end or as a means of an action, e.g., a death a person incurs in aiding someone in danger. For a bad effect to be imputable it must be foreseeable and the agent must have the possibility of avoiding it, as in the case of manslaughter caused by a drunken driver.   *2263*

1738   Freedom is exercised in relationships between human beings. Every human person, created in the image of God, has the natural right to be recognized as a free and responsible being. All owe to each other this duty of respect. The *right to the exercise of freedom*, especially in moral and religious matters, is an inalienable requirement of the dignity of the human person. This right must be recognized and protected by civil authority within the limits of the common good and public order.[32]   *2106 2109*

---

[28] Cf. *Rom* 6:17.
[29] *Gen* 3:13.
[30] Cf. *Gen* 4:10.
[31] Cf. 2 *Sam* 12:7–15.
[32] Cf. *DH* 2 § 7.

II. Human Freedom in the Economy of Salvation

387   1739 *Freedom and sin*. Man's freedom is limited and fallible. In fact,
man failed. He freely sinned. By refusing God's plan of love, he
deceived himself and became a slave to sin. This first alienation
401   engendered a multitude of others. From its outset, human history
attests the wretchedness and oppression born of the human heart in
consequence of the abuse of freedom.

1740 *Threats to freedom*. The exercise of freedom does not imply a
2108   right to say or do everything. It is false to maintain that man, 'the
subject of this freedom', is 'an individual who is fully self-sufficient
and whose finality is the satisfaction of his own interests in the
enjoyment of earthly goods'.[33] Moreover, the economic, social,
political and cultural conditions that are needed for a just exercise
1887   of freedom are too often disregarded or violated. Such situations
of blindness and injustice injure the moral life and involve the
strong as well as the weak in the temptation to sin against charity.
By deviating from the moral law man violates his own freedom,
becomes imprisoned within himself, disrupts neighbourly fellowship, and rebels against divine truth.

1741 *Liberation and salvation*. By his glorious Cross Christ has won
salvation for all men. He redeemed them from the sin that held
them in bondage. 'For freedom Christ has set us free.'[34] In him we
have communion with the 'truth that makes us free'.[35] The Holy
782   Spirit has been given to us and, as the Apostle teaches, 'where the
Spirit of the Lord is, there is freedom.'[36] Already we glory in the
'liberty of the children of God'.[37]

2002   1742 *Freedom and grace*. The grace of Christ is not in the slightest
way a rival of our freedom when this freedom accords with the
sense of the true and the good that God has put in the human heart.
On the contrary, as Christian experience attests especially in
prayer, the more docile we are to the promptings of grace, the
1784   more we grow in inner freedom and confidence during trials, such
as those we face in the pressures and constraints of the outer world.
By the working of grace the Holy Spirit educates us in spiritual
freedom in order to make us free collaborators in his work in the
Church and in the world:

---

[33] CDF, Instr. *Libertatis conscientia* 13.   [36] 2 *Cor* 3:17.
[34] *Gal* 5:1.   [37] *Rom* 8:21.
[35] Cf. *Jn* 8:32.

Almighty and merciful God,
in your goodness take away from us all that is harmful,
so that, made ready both in mind and body,
we may freely accomplish your will.[38]

IN BRIEF

1743 'God willed that man should be left in the hand of his own counsel (cf.
Sir 15:14), so that he might of his own accord seek his creator and freely attain
his full and blessed perfection by cleaving to him' (GS 17 § 1).

1744 Freedom is the power to act or not to act, and so to perform deliberate
acts of one's own. Freedom attains perfection in its acts when directed towards
God, the sovereign Good.

1745 Freedom characterizes properly human acts. It makes the human being
responsible for acts of which he is the voluntary agent. His deliberate acts
properly belong to him.

1746 The imputability or responsibility for an action can be diminished or
nullified by ignorance, duress, fear and other psychological or social factors.

1747 The right to the exercise of freedom, especially in religious and moral
matters, is an inalienable requirement of the dignity of man. But the exercise
of freedom does not entail the putative right to say or do anything.

1748 'For freedom Christ has set us free' (Gal 5:1).

Article 4
THE MORALITY OF HUMAN ACTS

1749 Freedom makes man a moral subject. When he acts deliberately man is, so to speak, the *father of his acts*. Human acts, that is,
acts that are freely chosen in consequence of a judgement of con-   1732
science, can be morally evaluated. They are either good or evil.

I. The Sources of Morality

1750 The morality of human acts depends on:
– the object chosen;
– the end in view or the intention;
– the circumstances of the action.

The object, the intention and the circumstances make up the
'sources', or constitutive elements, of the morality of human acts.

---

[38] *Missale Romanum*, 32nd Sunday,
Opening Prayer: *Omnipotens et
misericors Deus, universa nobis*

*adversantia propitiatus exclude, ut, mente
et corpore pariter expediti, quae tua sunt
liberis mentibus exsequamur.*

1751   The *object* chosen is a good towards which the will deliberately directs itself. It is the matter of a human act. The object chosen morally specifies the act of the will, insofar as reason recognizes and judges it to be or not to be in conformity with the true 1794   good. Objective norms of morality express the rational order of good and evil, attested to by conscience.

1752   In contrast to the object, the *intention* resides in the acting subject. Because it lies at the voluntary source of an action and determines it by its end, intention is an element essential to the 2520   moral evaluation of an action. The end is the first goal of the intention and indicates the purpose pursued in the action. The intention is a movement of the will toward the end: it is concerned with the goal of the activity. It aims at the good anticipated from the action undertaken. Intention is not limited to directing individual actions, but can guide several actions towards one and the same purpose; it can orient one's whole life toward its ultimate end. For example, a service done with the end of helping one's 1731   neighbour can at the same time be inspired by the love of God as the ultimate end of all our actions. One and the same action can also be inspired by several intentions, such as performing a service in order to obtain a favour or to boast about it.

1753   A good intention (for example, that of helping one's neighbour) does not make behaviour that is intrinsically disordered, 1731   such as lying and calumny, good or just. The end does not justify 596   the means. Thus the condemnation of an innocent person cannot be justified as a legitimate means of saving the nation. On the other hand, an added bad intention (such as vainglory) makes an act evil that, in and of itself, can be good (such as almsgiving).[39]

1754   The *circumstances*, including the consequences, are secondary elements of a moral act. They contribute to increasing or diminishing the moral goodness or evil of human acts (for example, the amount of a theft). They can also diminish or increase the 1735   agent's responsibility (such as acting out of a fear of death). Circumstances of themselves cannot change the moral quality of acts themselves; they can make neither good nor right an action that is in itself evil.

II. Good Acts and Evil Acts

1755   A *morally good* act requires the goodness of the object, of the end, and of the circumstances together. An evil end corrupts the

---

[39] Cf. *Mt* 6:2–4.

action, even if the object is good in itself (such as praying and fasting 'in order to be seen by men').

The *object of the choice* can by itself vitiate an act in its entirety. There are some concrete acts — such as fornication — that it is always wrong to choose, because choosing them entails a disorder of the will, that is, a moral evil.

1756 It is therefore an error to judge the morality of human acts by considering only the intention that inspires them or the circumstances (environment, social pressure, duress or emergency, etc.) which supply their context. There are acts which, in and of themselves, independently of circumstances and intentions, are always gravely illicit by reason of their object; such as blasphemy and perjury, murder and adultery. One may not do evil so that good *1789* may result from it.

IN BRIEF

1757 *The object, the intention and the circumstances make up the three 'sources' of the morality of human acts.*

1758 *The object chosen morally specifies the act of willing accordingly as reason recognizes and judges it good or evil.*

1759 *'An evil action cannot be justified by reference to a good intention' (cf. St Thomas Aquinas, Dec. praec. 6). The end does not justify the means.*

1760 *A morally good act requires the goodness of its object, of its end, and of its circumstances together.*

1761 *There are concrete acts that it is always wrong to choose, because their choice entails a disorder of the will, i.e., a moral evil. One may not do evil so that good may result from it.*

Article 5

THE MORALITY OF THE PASSIONS

1762 The human person is ordered to beatitude by his deliberate acts: the passions or feelings he experiences can dispose him to it and contribute to it.

I. Passions

1763 The term 'passions' belongs to the Christian patrimony. Feelings or passions are emotions or movements of the sensitive appetite that incline us to act or not to act in regard to something felt or imagined to be good or evil.

1764 The passions are natural components of the human psyche; they form the passageway and ensure the connection between the life of the senses and the life of the mind. Our Lord called man's heart the source from which the passions spring.[40]

368

1765 There are many passions. The most fundamental passion is love, aroused by the attraction of the good. Love causes a desire for the absent good and the hope of obtaining it; this movement finds completion in the pleasure and joy of the good possessed. The apprehension of evil causes hatred, aversion, and fear of the impending evil; this movement ends in sadness at some present evil, or in the anger that resists it.

1766 'To love is to will the good of another.'[41] All other affections have their source in this first movement of the human heart toward the good. Only the good can be loved.[42] Passions 'are evil if love is evil and good if it is good.'[43]

1704

II. Passions and Moral Life

1767 In themselves passions are neither good nor evil. They are morally qualified only to the extent that they effectively engage reason and will. Passions are said to be voluntary, 'either because they are commanded by the will or because the will does not place obstacles in their way.'[44] It belongs to the perfection of the moral or human good that the passions be governed by reason.[45]

1860

1768 Strong feelings are not decisive for the morality or the holiness of persons; they are simply the inexhaustible reservoir of images and affections in which the moral life is expressed. Passions are morally good when they contribute to a good action, evil in the opposite case. The upright will orders the movements of the senses it appropriates to the good and to beatitude; an evil will succumbs to disordered passions and exacerbates them. Emotions and feelings can be taken up into the *virtues*, or perverted by the *vices*.

1803
1865

1769 In the Christian life, the Holy Spirit himself accomplishes his work by mobilizing the whole being, with all its sorrows, fears

---

[40] Cf. *Mk* 7:21.
[41] St Thomas Aquinas, *STh* I–II, 26, 4, corp. art.
[42] Cf. St Augustine, *De Trin.* 8, 3, 4: PL 42, 949–950.
[43] St Augustine, *De civ. Dei* 14, 7, 2: PL

41, 410.
[44] St Thomas Aquinas, *STh* I–II, 24, 1, corp. art.
[45] Cf. St Thomas Aquinas, *STh* I–II, 24, 3.

and sadness, as is visible in the Lord's agony and passion. In Christ human feelings are able to reach their consummation in charity and divine beatitude.

1770 Moral perfection consists in man's being moved to the good not by his will alone, but also by his sensitive appetite, as in the words of the psalm: 'My heart and flesh sing for joy to the living *30* God.'[46]

IN BRIEF

1771 *The term 'passions' refers to the affections or the feelings. By his emotions man intuits the good and suspects evil.*

1772 *The principal passions are love and hatred, desire and fear, joy, sadness and anger.*

1773 *In the passions, as movements of the sensitive appetite, there is neither moral good nor evil. But insofar as they engage reason and will, there is moral good or evil in them.*

1774 *Emotions and feelings can be taken up in the virtues or perverted by the vices.*

1775 *The perfection of the moral good consists in man's being moved to the good not only by his will but also by his 'heart'.*

Article 6
MORAL CONSCIENCE

1776 'Deep within his conscience man discovers a law which he *1954* has not laid upon himself but which he must obey. Its voice, ever calling him to love and to do what is good and to avoid evil, sounds in his heart at the right moment. . . For man has in his heart a law inscribed by God. . . His conscience is man's most secret core and his sanctuary. There he is alone with God whose voice echoes in his depths.'[47]

I. The Judgement of Conscience

1777 Moral conscience,[48] present at the heart of the person, enjoins him at the appropriate moment to do good and to avoid evil. It also judges particular choices, approving those that are good and denouncing those that are evil.[49] It bears witness to the

---

[46] *Ps* 84:2.
[47] *GS* 16.
[48] Cf. *Rom* 2:14–16.
[49] Cf. *Rom* 1:32.

1766
2071
authority of truth in reference to the supreme Good to which the human person is drawn, and it welcomes the commandments. When he listens to his conscience, the prudent man can hear God speaking.

1778 Conscience is a judgement of reason whereby the human
1749 person recognizes the moral quality of a concrete act that he is going to perform, is in the process of performing, or has already completed. In all he says and does, man is obliged to follow faithfully what he knows to be just and right. It is by the judgement of his conscience that man perceives and recognizes the prescriptions of the divine law:

> Conscience is a law of the mind; yet [Christians] would not grant that it is nothing more; I mean that it was not a dictate, nor conveyed the notion of responsibility, of duty, of a threat and a promise... [Conscience] is a messenger of him, who, both in nature and in grace, speaks to us behind a veil, and teaches and rules us by his representatives. Conscience is the aboriginal Vicar of Christ.[50]

1779 It is important for every person to be sufficiently present to himself in order to hear and follow the voice of his conscience.
1886 This requirement of *interiority* is all the more necessary as life often distracts us from any reflection, self-examination or introspection:

> Return to your conscience, question it... Turn inward, brethren, and in everything you do, see God as your witness.[51]

1780 The dignity of the human person implies and requires *uprightness of moral conscience*. Conscience includes the perception of the principles of morality (synderesis); their application in the given circumstances by practical discernment of reasons and goods; and finally judgement about concrete acts yet to be performed or already performed. The truth about the moral good, stated in the law of reason, is recognized practically and concretely
1806 by the *prudent judgement* of conscience. We call that man prudent who chooses in conformity with this judgement.

1731 1781 Conscience enables one to assume *responsibility* for the acts performed. If man commits evil, the just judgement of conscience can remain within him as the witness to the universal truth of the good, at the same time as the evil of his particular choice. The

---

[50] John Henry Cardinal Newman, 'Letter to the Duke of Norfolk' V in *Certain Difficulties felt by Anglicans in Catholic Teaching* II (London:

Longmans Green, 1885), 248.
[51] St Augustine, *In ep. Jo.* 8, 9: PL 35, 2041.

The Passover: a crucifixion and panels showing events from the Last Supper through to Pentecost. This work of art comes from the Mua mission in Malawi, and was installed at the Missionary Institute London in 1992.

The corpus is carved in ebony by James Chikasasa; the panels are carved in ntangatanga wood by James Samikwa.

Photograph by Diana Klein

The crucifixion reflects the troubled and destructive aspects of the history of every age, and the search for meaning and life, particularly through religious faith and prayer.

verdict of the judgement of conscience remains a pledge of hope and mercy. In attesting to the fault committed, it calls to mind the forgiveness that must be asked, the good that must still be practised, and the virtue that must be constantly cultivated with the grace of God:

> We shall. . . reassure our hearts before him whenever our hearts condemn us; for God is greater than our hearts, and he knows everything.[52]

1782 Man has the right to act in conscience and in freedom so as personally to make moral decisions. 'He must not be forced to act contrary to his conscience. Nor must he be prevented from acting according to his conscience, especially in religious matters.'[53]   2106

II. The Formation of Conscience

1783 Conscience must be informed and moral judgement enlightened. A well-formed conscience is upright and truthful. It formulates its judgements according to reason, in conformity with the true good willed by the wisdom of the Creator. The education of conscience is indispensable for human beings who are subjected to negative influences and tempted by sin to prefer their own judgement and to reject authoritative teachings.   2039

1784 The education of the conscience is a lifelong task. From the earliest years, it awakens the child to the knowledge and practice of the interior law recognized by conscience. Prudent education teaches virtue; it prevents or cures fear, selfishness and pride, resentment arising from guilt, and feelings of complacency, born of human weakness and faults. The education of the conscience guarantees freedom and engenders peace of heart.   1742

1785 In the formation of conscience the Word of God is the light for our path;[54] we must assimilate it in faith and prayer, and put it into practice. We must also examine our conscience before the Lord's Cross. We are assisted by the gifts of the Holy Spirit, aided by the witness or advice of others and guided by the authoritative teaching of the Church.[55]   890

III. To Choose in Accord with Conscience

1786 Faced with a moral choice, conscience can make either a right judgement in accordance with reason and the divine law or, on the contrary, an erroneous judgement that departs from them.

---

[52] 1 Jn 3:19–20.   [54] Cf. Ps 119:105.
[53] DH 3 § 2.   [55] Cf. DH 14.

1787 Man is sometimes confronted by situations that make moral judgements less assured and decision difficult. But he must always seriously seek what is right and good and discern the will of God expressed in divine law.

1955

1788 To this purpose, man strives to interpret the data of experience and the signs of the times assisted by the virtue of prudence, by the advice of competent people, and by the help of the Holy Spirit and his gifts.

1806

1789 Some rules apply in every case:

1756 — one may never do evil so that good may result from it;

1970 — the Golden Rule: 'Whatever you wish that men would do to you, do so to them';[56]

1827 — charity always proceeds by way of respect for one's neighbour and his conscience: 'Thus sinning against your brethren and wounding their conscience. . . you sin against Christ.'[57] Therefore 'it is right not to. . .do anything that makes your brother stumble.'[58]

1971

IV. Erroneous Judgement

1790 A human being must always obey the certain judgement of his conscience. If he were deliberately to act against it, he would condemn himself. Yet it can happen that moral conscience remains in ignorance and makes erroneous judgements about acts to be performed or already committed.

1791 This ignorance can often be imputed to personal responsibility. This is the case when a man 'takes little trouble to find out what is true and good, or when conscience is by degrees almost blinded through the habit of committing sin.'[59] In such cases, the person is culpable for the evil he commits.

1704

1792 Ignorance of Christ and his Gospel, bad example given by others, enslavement to one's passions, assertion of a mistaken notion of autonomy of conscience, rejection of the Church's authority and her teaching, lack of conversion and of charity: these can be at the source of errors of judgement in moral conduct.

133

1793 If — on the contrary — the ignorance is invincible, or the moral subject is not responsible for his erroneous judgement, the evil committed by the person cannot be imputed to him. It

1860

---

[56] *Mt* 7:12; cf. *Lk* 6:31; *Tob* 4:15.   [58] *Rom* 14:21.
[57] 1 *Cor* 8:12.   [59] *GS* 16.

remains no less an evil, a privation, a disorder. One must therefore work to correct the errors of moral conscience.

1794 A good and pure conscience is enlightened by true faith, for charity proceeds at the same time 'from a pure heart and a good conscience and sincere faith'.[60]

The more a correct conscience prevails, the more do persons and groups turn aside from blind choice and try to be guided by objective standards *1751* of moral conduct.[61]

IN BRIEF

1795 *'Conscience is man's most secret core and his sanctuary. There he is alone with God whose voice echoes in his depths' (GS 16).*

1796 *Conscience is a judgement of reason by which the human person recognizes the moral quality of a concrete act.*

1797 *For the man who has committed evil, the verdict of his conscience remains a pledge of conversion and of hope.*

1798 *A well-formed conscience is upright and truthful. It formulates its judgements according to reason, in conformity with the true good willed by the wisdom of the Creator. Everyone must avail himself of the means to form his conscience.*

1799 *Faced with a moral choice, conscience can make either a right judgement in accordance with reason and the divine law or, on the contrary, an erroneous judgement that departs from them.*

1800 *A human being must always obey the certain judgement of his conscience.*

1801 *Conscience can remain in ignorance, or make erroneous judgements. Such ignorance and errors are not always free of guilt.*

1802 *The Word of God is a light for our path. We must assimilate it in faith and prayer, and put it into practice. This is how moral conscience is formed.*

Article 7
THE VIRTUES

1803 'Whatever is true, whatever is honourable, whatever is just, whatever is pure, whatever is lovely, whatever is gracious, if there is any excellence, if there is anything worthy of praise, think about these things.'[62]

---

[60] 1 *Tim* 1:5; cf. 3:9; 2 *Tim* 1:3; 1 *Pt* 3:21; *Acts* 24:16.

[61] *GS* 16.

[62] *Phil* 4:8.

1733   A virtue is an habitual and firm disposition to do the good. It
allows the person not only to perform good acts, but to give the
best of himself. The virtuous person tends toward the good with
1768 all his sensory and spiritual powers; he pursues the good and
chooses it in concrete actions.

The goal of a virtuous life is to become like God.[63]

I. The Human Virtues

1804 *Human virtues* are firm attitudes, stable dispositions, habitual
perfections of intellect and will that govern our actions, order our
passions and guide our conduct according to reason and faith.
2500 They make possible ease, self-mastery and joy in leading a morally
good life. The virtuous man is he who freely practises the good.

The moral virtues are acquired by human effort. They are
the fruit and seed of morally good acts; they dispose all the powers
1827 of the human being for communion with divine love.

The cardinal virtues

1805 Four virtues play a pivotal role and accordingly are called
'cardinal'; all the others are grouped around them. They are:
prudence, justice, fortitude and temperance. 'If anyone loves
righteousness, [Wisdom's] labours are virtues; for she teaches temperance and prudence, justice and courage.'[64] These virtues are
praised under other names in many passages of Scripture.

1806 *Prudence* is the virtue that disposes practical reason to discern
our true good in every circumstance and to choose the right means
of achieving it; 'the prudent man looks where he is going.'[65] 'Keep
1788 sane and sober for your prayers.'[66] Prudence is 'right reason in
action', writes St Thomas Aquinas, following Aristotle.[67] It is not
to be confused with timidity or fear, nor with duplicity or dissimulation. It is called *auriga virtutum* (the charioteer of the virtues); it guides the other virtues by setting rule and measure. It is
1780 prudence that immediately guides the judgement of conscience.
The prudent man determines and directs his conduct in accordance with this judgement. With the help of this virtue we apply
moral principles to particular cases without error and overcome
doubts about the good to achieve and the evil to avoid.

1807 *Justice* is the moral virtue that consists in the constant and

---

[63] St Gregory of Nyssa, *De beatitudinibus*
  1: PG 44, 1200D.
[64] *Wis* 8:7.

[65] *Prov* 14:15.
[66] 1 *Pt* 4:7.
[67] St Thomas Aquinas, *STh* II–II, 47, 2.

firm will to give their due to God and neighbour. Justice toward God is called the 'virtue of religion'. Justice toward men disposes one to respect the rights of each and to establish in human relation- ships the harmony that promotes equity with regard to persons and to the common good. The just man, often mentioned in the Sacred Scriptures, is distinguished by habitual right thinking and the uprightness of his conduct toward his neighbour. 'You shall not be partial to the poor or defer to the great, but in righteousness shall you judge your neighbour.'[68] 'Masters, treat your slaves justly and fairly, knowing that you also have a Master in heaven.'[69]

1808 *Fortitude* is the moral virtue that ensures firmness in diffi- culties and constancy in the pursuit of the good. It strengthens the resolve to resist temptations and to overcome obstacles in the moral life. The virtue of fortitude enables one to conquer fear, even fear of death, and to face trials and persecutions. It disposes one even to renounce and sacrifice one's life in defence of a just cause. 'The LORD is my strength and my song.'[70] 'In the world you have tribulation; but be of good cheer, I have overcome the world.'[71]

1809 *Temperance* is the moral virtue that moderates the attraction of pleasures and provides balance in the use of created goods. It ensures the will's mastery over instincts and keeps desires within the limits of what is honourable. The temperate person directs the sensitive appetites toward what is good, and maintains a healthy discretion: 'Do not follow your inclination and strength, walking according to the desires of your heart.'[72] Temperance is often praised in the Old Testament: 'Do not follow your base desires, but restrain your appetites.'[73] In the New Testament it is called 'moderation' or 'sobriety'. We ought 'to live sober, upright, and godly lives in this world'.[74]

> To live well is nothing other than to love God with all one's heart, with all one's soul and with all one's efforts; from this it comes about that love is kept whole and uncorrupted (through temperance). No misfortune can disturb it (and this is fortitude). It obeys only [God] (and this is justice), and is careful in discerning things, so as not to be surprised by deceit or trickery (and this is prudence).[75]

*(marginal numbers: 2095, 2401, 2848, 2473, 2341, 2517)*

[68] *Lev* 19:15.
[69] *Col* 4:1.
[70] *Ps* 118:14.
[71] *Jn* 16:33.
[72] *Sir* 5:2; cf. 37:27–31.

[73] *Sir* 18:30.
[74] *Titus* 2:12.
[75] St Augustine, *De moribus eccl.* 1, 25. 46: PL 32, 1330–1331.

The virtues and grace

1810 Human virtues acquired by education, by deliberate acts and by a perseverance ever-renewed in repeated efforts are purified and elevated by divine grace. With God's help, they forge charac- *1266* ter and give facility in the practice of the good. The virtuous man is happy to practise them.

1811 It is not easy for man, wounded by sin, to maintain moral balance. Christ's gift of salvation offers us the grace necessary to *2015* persevere in the pursuit of the virtues. Everyone should always ask for this grace of light and strength, frequent the sacraments, co-operate with the Holy Spirit, and follow his calls to love what is good and shun evil.

2086–2094, ## II. The Theological Virtues

2656–2658
1812 The human virtues are rooted in the theological virtues, which adapt man's faculties for participation in the divine *1266* nature:[76] for the theological virtues relate directly to God. They dispose Christians to live in a relationship with the Holy Trinity. They have the One and Triune God for their origin, motive and object.

1813 The theological virtues are the foundation of Christian moral activity; they animate it and give it its special character. They inform and give life to all the moral virtues. They are infused by God into the souls of the faithful to make them capable of *2008* acting as his children and of meriting eternal life. They are the pledge of the presence and action of the Holy Spirit in the faculties of the human being. There are three theological virtues: faith, hope and charity.[77]

142–175 ### Faith

1814 Faith is the theological virtue by which we believe in God and believe all that he has said and revealed to us, and that Holy Church proposes for our belief, because he is truth itself. By faith *506* 'man freely commits his entire self to God.'[78] For this reason the believer seeks to know and do God's will. 'The righteous shall live by faith.' Living faith 'work[s] through charity'.[79]

1815 The gift of faith remains in one who has not sinned against it.[80] But 'faith apart from works is dead':[81] when it is deprived of

---

[76] Cf. 2 Pt 1:4.
[77] Cf. 1 Cor 13:13.
[78] DV 5.

[79] Rom 1:17; Gal 5:6.
[80] Cf. Council of Trent (1547): DS 1545.
[81] Jas 2:26.

hope and love, faith does not fully unite the believer to Christ and does not make him a living member of his Body.

1816 The disciple of Christ must not only keep the faith and live on it, but also profess it, confidently bear witness to it and spread it: 'All however must be prepared to confess Christ before men and to follow him along the way of the Cross, amidst the persecutions which the Church never lacks.'[82] Service of and witness to the faith are necessary for salvation: 'So every one who acknowledges me before men, I also will acknowledge before my Father who is in heaven; but whoever denies me before men, I also will deny before my Father who is in heaven.'[83]

2471

Hope

1817 Hope is the theological virtue by which we desire the Kingdom of heaven and eternal life as our happiness, placing our trust in Christ's promises and relying not on our own strength, but on the help of the grace of the Holy Spirit. 'Let us hold fast the confession of our hope without wavering, for he who promised is faithful.'[84] 'The Holy Spirit... he poured out upon us richly through Jesus Christ our Saviour, so that we might be justified by his grace and become heirs in hope of eternal life.'[85]

1024

1818 The virtue of hope responds to the aspiration to happiness which God has placed in the heart of every man; it takes up the hopes that inspire men's activities and purifies them so as to order them to the Kingdom of heaven; it keeps man from discouragement; it sustains him during times of abandonment; it opens up his heart in expectation of eternal beatitude. Buoyed up by hope, he is preserved from selfishness and led to the happiness that flows from charity.

27

1819 Christian hope takes up and fulfils the hope of the chosen people which has its origin and model in the *hope of Abraham*, who was blessed abundantly by the promises of God fulfilled in Isaac, and who was purified by the test of the sacrifice.[86] 'Hoping against hope, he believed, and thus became the father of many nations.'[87]

146

1820 Christian hope unfolds from the beginning of Jesus' preaching in the proclamation of the Beatitudes. The *Beatitudes* raise our hope toward heaven as the new Promised Land; they

1716

---

[82] LG 42; cf. DH 14.
[83] Mt 10:32–33.
[84] Heb 10:23.
[85] Titus 3:6–7.
[86] Cf. Gen 17:4–8; 22:1–18.
[87] Rom 4:18.

trace the path that leads through the trials that await the disciples of Jesus. But through the merits of Jesus Christ and of his Passion, God keeps us in the 'hope that does not disappoint'.[88] Hope is the 'sure and steadfast anchor of the soul... that enters... where Jesus has gone as a forerunner on our behalf'.[89] Hope is also a weapon that protects us in the struggle of salvation: 'Let us... put on the breastplate of faith and charity, and for a helmet the hope of salvation.'[90] It affords us joy even under trial: 'Rejoice in your hope, be patient in tribulation.'[91] Hope is expressed and nourished in 2772 prayer, especially in the *Our Father*, the summary of everything that hope leads us to desire.

1821 We can therefore hope in the glory of heaven promised by God to those who love him and do his will.[92] In every circumstance, each one of us should hope, with the grace of God, to 2016 persevere 'to the end'[93] and to obtain the joy of heaven, as God's eternal reward for the good works accomplished with the grace of 1037 Christ. In hope, the Church prays for 'all men to be saved'.[94] She longs to be united with Christ, her Bridegroom, in the glory of heaven:

> Hope, O my soul, hope. You know neither the day nor the hour. Watch carefully, for everything passes quickly, even though your impatience makes doubtful what is certain, and turns a very short time into a long one. Dream that the more you struggle, the more you prove the love that you bear your God, and the more you will rejoice one day with your Beloved, in a happiness and rapture that can never end.[95]

Charity

1822 Charity is the theological virtue by which we love God 1723 above all things for his own sake, and our neighbour as ourselves for the love of God.

1970 1823 Jesus makes charity the *new commandment*.[96] By loving his own 'to the end',[97] he makes manifest the Father's love which he receives. By loving one another, the disciples imitate the love of Jesus which they themselves receive. Whence Jesus says: 'As the Father has loved me, so have I loved you; abide in my love.' And again: 'This is my commandment, that you love one another as I have loved you.'[98]

---

[88] *Rom* 5:5.
[89] *Heb* 6:19–20.
[90] 1 *Th* 5:8.
[91] *Rom* 12:12.
[92] Cf. *Rom* 8:28–30; *Mt* 7:21.
[93] *Mt* 10:22; cf. Council of Trent: DS 1541.
[94] 1 *Tim* 2:4.
[95] St Teresa of Avila, *Excl.* 15, 3.
[96] Cf. *Jn* 13:34.
[97] *Jn* 13:1.
[98] *Jn* 15:9, 12.

1824 Fruit of the Spirit and fullness of the Law, charity keeps the *commandments* of God and his Christ: 'Abide in my love. If you keep my commandments, you will abide in my love.'[99] *735*

1825 Christ died out of love for us, while we were still 'enemies'.[100] The Lord asks us to love as he does, even our *enemies*, to make ourselves the neighbour of those furthest away, and to love children and the poor as Christ himself.[101] *604*

> The Apostle Paul has given an incomparable depiction of charity: 'charity is patient and kind, charity is not jealous or boastful; it is not arrogant or rude. Charity does not insist on its own way; it is not irritable or resentful; it does not rejoice at wrong, but rejoices in the right. Charity bears all things, believes all things, hopes all things, endures all things.'[102]

1826 'If I... have not charity', says the Apostle, 'I am nothing.' Whatever my privilege, service, or even virtue, 'if I... have not charity, I gain nothing.'[103] Charity is superior to all the virtues. It is the first of the theological virtues: 'So faith, hope, charity abide, these three. But *the greatest of these is charity*.'[104]

1827 The practice of all the virtues is animated and inspired by charity, which 'binds everything together in perfect harmony';[105] it is the *form of the virtues*; it articulates and orders them among themselves; it is the source and the goal of their Christian practice. Charity upholds and purifies our human ability to love, and raises it to the supernatural perfection of divine love. *815* *826*

1828 The practice of the moral life animated by charity gives to the Christian the spiritual freedom of the children of God. He no longer stands before God as a slave, in servile fear, or as a mercenary looking for wages, but as a son responding to the love of him who 'first loved us':[106] *1972*

> If we turn away from evil out of fear of punishment, we are in the position of slaves. If we pursue the enticement of wages... we resemble mercenaries. Finally if we obey for the sake of the good itself and out of love for him who commands... we are in the position of children.[107]

1829 The *fruits* of charity are joy, peace and mercy; charity demands beneficence and fraternal correction; it is benevolence; it

[99] Jn 15:9–10; cf. Mt 22:40; Rom 13:8–10.
[100] Rom 5:10.
[101] Cf. Mt 5:44; Lk 10:27–37; Mk 9:37; Mt 25:40, 45.
[102] 1 Cor 13:4–7.
[103] 1 Cor 13:1–3.
[104] 1 Cor 13:13.
[105] Col 3:14.
[106] Cf. 1 Jn 4:19.
[107] St Basil, Reg. fus. tract., prol. 3: PG 31, 896B.

2540 fosters reciprocity and remains disinterested and generous; it is friendship and communion:

> Love is itself the fulfilment of all our works. There is the goal; that is why we run: we run toward it, and once we reach it, in it we shall find rest.[108]

III. The Gifts and Fruits of the Holy Spirit

1830 The moral life of Christians is sustained by the gifts of the Holy Spirit. These are permanent dispositions which make man docile in following the promptings of the Holy Spirit.

1266 1831 The seven *gifts* of the Holy Spirit are wisdom, understanding, counsel, fortitude, knowledge, piety and fear of the Lord.
1299 They belong in their fullness to Christ, Son of David.[109] They complete and perfect the virtues of those who receive them. They make the faithful docile in readily obeying divine inspirations.

> Let your good spirit lead me on a level path.[110]

> For all who are led by the Spirit of God are sons of God... If children, then heirs, heirs of God and fellow heirs with Christ.[111]

1832 The *fruits* of the Spirit are perfections that the Holy Spirit
736 forms in us as the first fruits of eternal glory. The tradition of the Church lists twelve of them: 'charity, joy, peace, patience, kindness, goodness, generosity, gentleness, faithfulness, modesty, self-control, chastity'.[112]

IN BRIEF

1833 *Virtue is a habitual and firm disposition to do good.*

1834 *The human virtues are stable dispositions of the intellect and the will that govern our acts, order our passions and guide our conduct in accordance with reason and faith. They can be grouped around the four cardinal virtues: prudence, justice, fortitude and temperance.*

1835 *Prudence disposes the practical reason to discern, in every circumstance, our true good and to choose the right means for achieving it.*

1836 *Justice consists in the firm and constant will to give God and neighbour their due.*

1837 *Fortitude ensures firmness in difficulties and constancy in the pursuit of the good.*

---

[108] St Augustine, *In ep. Jo.* 10, 4: PL 35, 2057.
[109] Cf. *Is* 11:1–2.
[110] *Ps* 143:10.
[111] *Rom* 8:14, 17.
[112] *Gal* 5:22–23 (Vulg.).

1838 *Temperance moderates the attraction of the pleasures of the senses and provides balance in the use of created goods.*

1839 *The moral virtues grow through education, deliberate acts and perseverance in struggle. Divine grace purifies and elevates them.*

1840 *The theological virtues dispose Christians to live in a relationship with the Holy Trinity. They have God for their origin, their motive and their object – God known by faith, God hoped in and loved for his own sake.*

1841 *There are three theological virtues: faith, hope and charity. They inform all the moral virtues and give life to them.*

1842 *By faith, we believe in God and believe all that he has revealed to us and that Holy Church proposes for our belief.*

1843 *By hope we desire, and with steadfast trust await from God, eternal life and the graces to merit it.*

1844 *By charity, we love God above all things and our neighbour as ourselves for love of God. Charity, the form of all the virtues, 'binds everything together in perfect harmony' (Col 3:14).*

1845 *The seven gifts of the Holy Spirit bestowed upon Christians are wisdom, understanding, counsel, fortitude, knowledge, piety and fear of the Lord.*

Article 8
SIN

I. Mercy and Sin

1846 The Gospel is the revelation in Jesus Christ of God's mercy to sinners.[113] The angel announced to Joseph: 'You shall call his name Jesus, for he will save his people from their sins.'[114] The same is true of the Eucharist, the sacrament of redemption: 'This is my blood of the covenant, which is poured out for many for the forgiveness of sins.'[115]

1847 'God created us without us: but he did not will to save us without us.'[116] To receive his mercy, we must admit our faults. 'If we say we have no sin, we deceive ourselves, and the truth is not in us. If we confess our sins, he is faithful and just, and will forgive our sins and cleanse us from all unrighteousness.'[117]

1848 As St Paul affirms, 'Where sin increased, grace abounded all the more.'[118] But to do its work grace must uncover sin so as to

430

1365

387, 1455

[113] Cf. *Lk* 15.
[114] *Mt* 1:21.
[115] *Mt* 26:28.
[116] St Augustine, *Sermo* 169, 11, 13: PL
38, 923.
[117] 1 *Jn* 1:8–9.
[118] *Rom* 5:20.

385 convert our hearts and bestow on us 'righteousness to eternal life through Jesus Christ our Lord'.[119] Like a physician who probes the wound before treating it, God, by his Word and by his Spirit, casts a living light on sin:

> Conversion *requires convincing of sin*; it includes the interior judgement of conscience, and this, being a proof of the action of the Spirit of truth in man's inmost being becomes at the same time the start of a new grant of grace and love: 'Receive the Holy Spirit.' Thus in this 'convincing concerning sin' we discover *a double gift*: the gift of the truth of conscience and the gift of the certainty of redemption. The Spirit of truth is the
1433 Consoler.[120]

II. The Definition of Sin

311 1849 Sin is an offence against reason, truth and right conscience; it is failure in genuine love for God and neighbour caused by a perverse attachment to certain goods. It wounds the nature of man and injures human solidarity. It has been defined as 'an utterance, a 1952 deed or a desire contrary to the eternal law'.[121]

1440 1850 Sin is an offence against God: 'Against you, you alone, have I sinned, and done that which is evil in your sight.'[122] Sin sets itself against God's love for us and turns our hearts away from it. Like 397 the first sin, it is disobedience, a revolt against God through the will to become 'like gods',[123] knowing and determining good and evil. Sin is thus 'love of oneself even to contempt of God'.[124] In this proud self-exaltation, sin is diametrically opposed to the obedi-615 ence of Jesus, which achieves our salvation.[125]

1851 It is precisely in the Passion, when the mercy of Christ is 598 about to vanquish it, that sin most clearly manifests its violence and its many forms: unbelief, murderous hatred, shunning and mockery by the leaders and the people, Pilate's cowardice and the cruelty of the soldiers, Judas' betrayal – so bitter to Jesus, Peter's 2746 denial and the disciples' flight. However, at the very hour of dark-616 ness, the hour of the prince of this world,[126] the sacrifice of Christ secretly becomes the source from which the forgiveness of our sins will pour forth inexhaustibly.

---

[119] *Rom* 5:21.
[120] John Paul II, *DeV* 31 § 2.
[121] St Augustine, *Contra Faustum* 22: PL 42, 418; St Thomas Aquinas, *STh* I–II, 71, 6.
[122] *Ps* 51:4.
[123] *Gen* 3:5.
[124] St Augustine, *De civ. Dei* 14, 28: PL 41, 436.
[125] Cf. *Phil* 2:6–9.
[126] Cf. *Jn* 14:30.

III. The Different Kinds of Sins

1852 There are a great many kinds of sins. Scripture provides several lists of them. The *Letter to the Galatians* contrasts the works of the flesh with the fruit of the Spirit: 'Now the works of the flesh are plain: fornication, impurity, licentiousness, idolatry, sorcery, enmity, strife, jealousy, anger, selfishness, dissension, factions, envy, drunkenness, carousing, and the like. I warn you, as I warned you before, that those who do such things shall not inherit the Kingdom of God.'[127]

1853 Sins can be distinguished according to their objects, as can every human *1751* act; or according to the virtues they oppose, by excess or defect; or according to the commandments they violate. They can also be classed according to whether they concern God, neighbour or oneself; they can be divided into spiritual and *2067* carnal sins, or again as sins in thought, word, deed or omission. The root of sin is in the heart of man, in his free will, according to the teaching of the Lord: 'For *368* out of the heart come evil thoughts, murder, adultery, fornication, theft, false witness, slander. These are what defile a man.'[128] But in the heart also resides charity, the source of the good and pure works, which sin wounds.

IV. The Gravity of Sin: Mortal and Venial Sin

1854 Sins are rightly evaluated according to their gravity. The distinction between mortal and venial sin, already evident in Scripture,[129] became part of the tradition of the Church. It is corroborated by human experience.

1855 *Mortal sin* destroys charity in the heart of man by a grave *1395* violation of God's law; it turns man away from God, who is his ultimate end and his beatitude, by preferring an inferior good to him.

Venial sin allows charity to subsist, even though it offends and wounds it.

1856 Mortal sin, by attacking the vital principle within us – that is, charity – necessitates a new initiative of God's mercy and a conversion of heart which is normally accomplished within the setting of the sacrament of Reconciliation: *1446*

> When the will sets itself upon something that is of its nature incompatible with the charity that orients man toward his ultimate end, then the sin is mortal by its very object... whether it contradicts the love of God, such

---

[127] *Gal* 5:19–21; cf. *Rom* 1:28–32; 1 *Cor* 6:9–10; *Eph* 5:3–5; *Col* 3:5–8; 1 *Tim* 1:9–10; 2 *Tim* 3:2–5.

[128] *Mt* 15:19–20.
[129] Cf. 1 *Jn* 5:16–17.

as blasphemy or perjury, or the love of neighbour, such as homicide or adultery... But when the sinner's will is set upon something that of its nature involves a disorder, but is not opposed to the love of God and neighbour, such as thoughtless chatter or immoderate laughter and the like, such sins are venial.[130]

1857 For a *sin* to be *mortal*, three conditions must together be met: 'Mortal sin is sin whose object is grave matter and which is also committed with full knowledge and deliberate consent.'[131]

2072 1858 *Grave matter* is specified by the Ten Commandments, corresponding to the answer of Jesus to the rich young man: 'Do not kill, Do not commit adultery, Do not steal, Do not bear false witness, Do not defraud, Honour your father and your mother.'[132] The gravity of sins is more or less great: murder is graver than theft. One must also take into account who is 2214 wronged: violence against parents is in itself graver than violence against a stranger.

1734 1859 Mortal sin requires *full knowledge* and *complete consent*. It presupposes knowledge of the sinful character of the act, of its opposition to God's law. It also implies a consent sufficiently deliberate to be a personal choice. Feigned ignorance and hardness of heart[133] do not diminish, but rather increase, the voluntary character of a sin.

1735 1860 *Unintentional ignorance* can diminish or even remove the imputability of a grave offence. But no one is deemed to be ignorant of the principles of the moral law, which are written in the 1767 conscience of every man. The promptings of feelings and passions can also diminish the voluntary and free character of the offence, as can external pressures or pathological disorders. Sin committed through malice, by deliberate choice of evil, is the gravest.

1742 1861 Mortal sin is a radical possibility of human freedom, as is love itself. It results in the loss of charity and the privation of sanctifying grace, that is, of the state of grace. If it is not redeemed by repentance and God's forgiveness, it causes exclusion from 1033 Christ's kingdom and the eternal death of hell, for our freedom has the power to make choices for ever, with no turning back. However, although we can judge that an act is in itself a grave offence, we must entrust judgement of persons to the justice and mercy of God.

---

[130] St Thomas Aquinas, *STh* I–II, 88, 2, corp. art.
[131] John Paul II, *RP* 17 § 12.

[132] *Mk* 10:19.
[133] Cf. *Mk* 3:5–6; *Lk* 16:19–31.

1862 One commits *venial sin* when, in a less serious matter, one does not observe the standard prescribed by the moral law, or when one disobeys the moral law in a grave matter, but without full knowledge or without complete consent.

1863 Venial sin weakens charity; it manifests a disordered affec- 1394 tion for created goods; it impedes the soul's progress in the exercise of the virtues and the practice of the moral good; it merits temporal punishment. Deliberate and unrepented venial sin disposes 1472 us little by little to commit mortal sin. However venial sin does not break the covenant with God. With God's grace it is humanly reparable. 'Venial sin does not deprive the sinner of sanctifying grace, friendship with God, charity, and consequently external happiness.'[134]

> While he is in the flesh, man cannot help but have at least some light sins. But do not despise these sins which we call 'light': if you take them for light when you weigh them, tremble when you count them. A number of light objects makes a great mass; a number of drops fills a river; a number of grains makes a heap. What then is our hope? Above all, confession...[135]

1864 'Therefore I tell you, every sin and blasphemy will be forgiven men, but the *blasphemy against the Spirit* will not be forgiven.'[136] There are no limits to the mercy of God, but anyone who deliberately refuses to accept his mercy by repenting, rejects 2091 the forgiveness of his sins and the salvation offered by the Holy Spirit.[137] Such hardness of heart can lead to final impenitence and 1037 eternal loss.

V. The Proliferation of Sin

1865 Sin creates a proclivity to sin; it engenders vice by repetition 401 of the same acts. This results in perverse inclinations which cloud conscience and corrupt the concrete judgement of good and evil. Thus sin tends to reproduce itself and reinforce itself, but it cannot 1768 destroy the moral sense at its root.

1866 Vices can be classified according to the virtues they oppose, or also be linked to the *capital sins* which Christian experience has distinguished, following St John Cassian and St Gregory the Great. They are called 'capital' because they engender other sins,

---

[134] RP 17 § 9.
[135] St Augustine, *In ep. Jo.* 1, 6: PL 35, 1982.
[136] *Mt* 12:31; cf. *Mk* 3:29; *Lk* 12:10.
[137] Cf. John Paul II, *DeV* 46.

2539   other vices.[138] They are pride, avarice, envy, wrath, lust, gluttony, and sloth or acedia.

1867   The catechetical tradition also recalls that there are '*sins that*
2268   *cry to heaven*': the blood of Abel,[139] the sin of the Sodomites,[140] the cry of the people oppressed in Egypt,[141] the cry of the foreigner, the widow and the orphan,[142] injustice to the wage earner.[143]

1868   Sin is a personal act. Moreover, we have a responsibility for the sins committed by others when *we co-operate in them*:
1736   – by participating directly and voluntarily in them;

     – by ordering, advising, praising, or approving them;

     – by not disclosing or not hindering them when we have an obligation to do so;

     – by protecting evil-doers.

1869   Thus sin makes men accomplices of one another and causes concupiscence, violence and injustice to reign among them. Sins give rise to social situations and institutions that are contrary to the
408   divine goodness. 'Structures of sin' are the expression and effect of
1887   personal sins. They lead their victims to do evil in their turn. In an analogous sense, they constitute a 'social sin'.[144]

IN BRIEF

1870   '*God has consigned all men to disobedience, that he may have mercy upon all*' (*Rom* 11:32).

1871   *Sin is an utterance, a deed, or a desire contrary to the eternal law* (*St Augustine, Contra Faustum 22: PL 42, 418*). *It is an offence against God. It rises up against God in a disobedience contrary to the obedience of Christ.*

1872   *Sin is an act contrary to reason. It wounds man's nature and injures human solidarity.*

1873   *The root of all sins lies in man's heart. The kinds and the gravity of sins are determined principally by their objects.*

1874   *To choose deliberately – that is, both knowing it and willing it – something gravely contrary to the divine law and to the ultimate end of man is to commit a mortal sin. This destroys in us the charity without which eternal beatitude is impossible. Unrepented, it brings eternal death.*

---

[138] Cf. St Gregory the Great, *Moralia in Job* 31, 45: PL 76, 621A.
[139] Cf. *Gen* 4:10.
[140] Cf. *Gen* 18:20; 19:13.
[141] Cf. *Ex* 3:7–10.
[142] Cf. *Ex* 20:20–22.
[143] Cf. *Dt* 24:14–15; *Jas* 5:4.
[144] *RP* 16.

> 1875 *Venial sin constitutes a moral disorder that is reparable by charity,*
> *which it allows to subsist in us.*
>
> 1876 *The repetition of sins – even venial ones – engenders vices, among*
> *which are the capital sins.*

Chapter Two

THE HUMAN COMMUNITY

1877 The vocation of humanity is to show forth the image of God *355* and to be transformed into the image of the Father's only Son. This vocation takes a personal form since each of us is called to enter into the divine beatitude; it also concerns the human community as a whole.

Article 1
THE PERSON AND SOCIETY

I. The Communal Character of the Human Vocation

1878 All men are called to the same end: God himself. There is a certain resemblance between the unity of the divine persons and *1702* the fraternity that men are to establish among themselves in truth and love.[1] Love of neighbour is inseparable from love for God.

1879 The human person needs to live in society. Society is not for *1936* him an extraneous addition but a requirement of his nature. Through the exchange with others, mutual service and dialogue with his brethren, man develops his potential; he thus responds to his vocation.[2]

1880 A *society* is a group of persons bound together organically by *771* a principle of unity that goes beyond each one of them. As an assembly that is at once visible and spiritual, a society endures through time: it gathers up the past and prepares for the future. By means of society, each man is established as an 'heir' and receives certain 'talents' that enrich his identity and whose fruits he must develop.[3] He rightly owes loyalty to the communities of which he is part, and respect to those in authority who have charge of the common good.

---

[1] Cf. *GS* 24 § 3.
[2] Cf. *GS* 25 § 1.
[3] Cf. *Lk* 19:13-15.

1881 Each community is defined by its purpose and consequently
1929 obeys specific rules; but 'the *human person*... is and ought to be the
principle, the subject and the end of every social organization.'[4]

1882 Certain societies, such as the family and the state, correspond
more directly to the nature of man; they are necessary to him. To
1913 promote the participation of the greatest number in the life of a
society, the creation of voluntary associations and institutions
must be encouraged 'on both national and international levels,
which relate to economic and social goals, to cultural and recrea-
tional activities, to sport, to various professions, and to political
affairs'.[5] This '*socialization*' also expresses the natural tendency for
human beings to associate with one another for the sake of
attaining objectives that exceed individual capacities. It develops
the qualities of the person, especially the sense of initiative and
responsibility, and helps guarantee his rights.[6]

1883 Socialization also presents dangers. Excessive intervention
by the state can threaten personal freedom and initiative. The
teaching of the Church has elaborated the principle of *subsidiarity*,
according to which 'a community of a higher order should not
interfere in the internal life of a community of a lower order,
2431 depriving the latter of its functions, but rather should support it in
case of need and help to co-ordinate its activity with the activities
of the rest of society, always with a view to the common good.'[7]

1884 God has not willed to reserve to himself all exercise of
307 power. He entrusts to every creature the functions it is capable of
performing, according to the capacities of its own nature. This
mode of governance ought to be followed in social life. The way
God acts in governing the world, which bears witness to such
great regard for human freedom, should inspire the wisdom of
those who govern human communities. They should behave as
302 ministers of divine providence.

1885 The principle of subsidiarity is opposed to all forms of
collectivism. It sets limits for state intervention. It aims at harmonizing the relationships between individuals and societies. It
tends toward the establishment of true international order.

II. Conversion and Society

1886 Society is essential to the fulfilment of the human vocation.

---

[4] *GS* 25 § 1.
[5] John XXIII, *MM* 60.
[6] Cf. *GS* 25 § 2; John Paul II, *CA* 12.

[7] *CA* 48 § 4; cf. Pius XI, *Quadragesimo anno* I, 184–186.

To attain this aim, respect must be accorded to the just hierarchy of values, which 'subordinates physical and instinctual dimensions to interior and spiritual ones':[8]

1779

> Human society must primarily be considered something pertaining to the spiritual. Through it, in the bright light of truth, men should share their knowledge, be able to exercise their rights and fulfil their obligations, be inspired to seek spiritual values; mutually derive genuine pleasure from the beautiful, of whatever order it be; always be readily disposed to pass on to others the best of their own cultural heritage; and eagerly strive to make their own the spiritual achievements of others. These benefits not only influence, but at the same time give aim and scope to all that has bearing on cultural expressions, economic and social institutions, political movements and forms, laws, and all other structures by which society is outwardly established and constantly developed.[9]

2500

1887 The inversion of means and ends,[10] which results in giving the value of ultimate end to what is only a means for attaining it, or in viewing persons as mere means to that end, engenders unjust structures which 'make Christian conduct in keeping with the commandments of the divine Law-giver difficult and almost impossible.'[11]

909, 1869

1888 It is necessary, then, to appeal to the spiritual and moral capacities of the human person and to the permanent need for his *inner conversion*, so as to obtain social changes that will really serve him. The acknowledged priority of the conversion of heart in no way eliminates but on the contrary imposes the obligation of bringing the appropriate remedies to institutions and living conditions when they are an inducement to sin, so that they conform to the norms of justice and advance the good rather than hinder it.[12]

407

1430

1889 Without the help of grace, men would not know how 'to discern the often narrow path between the cowardice which gives in to evil, and the violence which under the illusion of fighting evil only makes it worse'.[13] This is the path of charity, that is, of the love of God and of neighbour. Charity is the greatest social commandment. It respects others and their rights. It requires the practice of justice, and it alone makes us capable of it. Charity inspires a life of self-giving: 'Whoever seeks to gain his life will lose it, but whoever loses his life will preserve it.'[14]

1825

---

[8] *CA* 36 § 2.
[9] John XXIII, *PT* 36.
[10] Cf. *CA* 41.
[11] Pius XII, Address at Pentecost, 1 June 1941.

[12] Cf. *LG* 36.
[13] *CA* 25.
[14] *Lk* 17:33.

IN BRIEF

1890 *There is a certain resemblance between the unity of the divine persons and the fraternity that men ought to establish among themselves.*

1891 *The human person needs life in society in order to develop in accordance with his nature. Certain societies, such as the family and the state, correspond more directly to the nature of man.*

1892 *'The human person. . . is and ought to be the principle, the subject, and the object of every social organization' (GS 25 § 1).*

1893 *Widespread participation in voluntary associations and institutions is to be encouraged.*

1894 *In accordance with the principle of subsidiarity, neither the state nor any larger society should substitute itself for the initiative and responsibility of individuals and intermediary bodies.*

1895 *Society ought to promote the exercise of virtue, not obstruct it. It should be animated by a just hierarchy of values.*

1896 *Where sin has perverted the social climate, it is necessary to call for the conversion of hearts and appeal to the grace of God. Charity urges just reforms. There is no solution to the social question apart from the Gospel (cf. CA 3, 5).*

Article 2
PARTICIPATION IN SOCIAL LIFE

I. Authority

1897 'Human society can be neither well-ordered nor prosperous
2334 unless it has some people invested with legitimate authority to preserve its institutions and to devote themselves as far as is necessary to work and care for the good of all.'[15]

By 'authority' one means the quality by virtue of which persons or institutions make laws and give orders to men, and expect obedience from them.

1898 Every human community needs an authority to govern it.[16] The foundation of such authority lies in human nature. It is necessary for the unity of the state. Its role is to ensure as far as possible the common good of the society.

2235 1899 The authority required by the moral order derives from God: 'Let every person be subject to the governing authorities. For

---

[15] John XXIII, *PT* 46.
[16] Cf. Leo XIII, *Immortale Dei*; *Diuturnum illud.*

there is no authority except from God, and those that exist have been instituted by God. Therefore he who resists the authorities resists what God has appointed, and those who resist will incur judgement.'[17]

1900 The duty of obedience requires all to give due honour to authority, and to treat those who are charged to exercise it with respect, and, insofar as it is deserved, with gratitude and good-will. *2238*

> Pope St Clement of Rome provides the Church's most ancient prayer for political authorities:[18] 'Grant to them, Lord, health, peace, concord and stability, so that they may exercise without offence the sovereignty that you have given them. Master, heavenly King of the ages, you give glory, honour and power over the things of earth to the sons of men. Direct, Lord, their counsel, following what is pleasing and acceptable in your sight, so that by exercising with devotion and in peace and gentleness the power that you have given to them, they may find favour with you.'[19] *2240*

1901 If authority belongs to the order established by God, 'the choice of the political regime and the appointment of rulers are left to the free decision of the citizens.'[20]

The diversity of political regimes is morally acceptable, provided they serve the legitimate good of the communities that adopt them. Regimes whose nature is contrary to the natural law, to the public order and to the fundamental rights of persons cannot achieve the common good of the nations on which they have been imposed. *2242*

1902 Authority does not derive its moral legitimacy from itself. It must not behave in a despotic manner, but must act for the common good as a 'moral force based on freedom and a sense of responsibility':[21] *1930*

> A human law has the character of law to the extent that it accords with right reason, and thus derives from the eternal law. Insofar as it falls short of right reason it is said to be an unjust law, and thus has not so much the nature of law as of a kind of violence.[22] *1951*

1903 Authority is exercised legitimately only when it seeks the common good of the group concerned and if it employs morally licit means to attain it. If rulers were to enact unjust laws or take measures contrary to the moral order, such arrangements would *2242*

---

[17] *Rom* 13:1–2; cf. 1 *Pt* 2:13–17.
[18] Cf. as early as 1 *Tim* 2:1–2.
[19] St Clement of Rome, *Ad Cor.* 61: SCh 167, 198–200.

[20] *GS* 74 § 3.
[21] *GS* 74 § 2.
[22] St Thomas Aquinas, *STh* I–II, 93, 3, ad 2.

not be binding in conscience. In such a case, 'authority breaks down completely and results in shameful abuse.'[23]

1904 'It is preferable that each power be balanced by other powers and by other spheres of responsibility which keep it within proper bounds. This is the principle of the "rule of law", in which the law is sovereign, and not the arbitrary will of men.'[24]

II. The Common Good

1905 In keeping with the social nature of man, the good of each *801* individual is necessarily related to the common good, which in *1881* turn can be defined only in reference to the human person:

> Do not live entirely isolated, having retreated into yourselves, as if you were already justified, but gather instead to seek the common good together.[25]

1906 By common good is to be understood 'the sum total of social conditions which allow people, either as groups or as individuals, to reach their fulfilment more fully and more easily'.[26] The common good concerns the life of all. It calls for prudence from each, and even more from those who exercise the office of authority. It consists of *three essential elements*:

1929 1907 First, the common good presupposes *respect for the person* as such. In the name of the common good, public authorities are bound to respect the fundamental and inalienable rights of the human person. Society should permit each of its members to fulfil his vocation. In particular, the common good resides in the conditions for the exercise of the natural freedoms indispensable for the development of the human vocation, such as 'the right to act according to a sound norm of conscience and to safeguard...pri-*2106* vacy, and rightful freedom also in matters of religion'.[27]

1908 Second, the common good requires the *social well-being* and *2441* *development* of the group itself. Development is the epitome of all social duties. Certainly, it is the proper function of authority to arbitrate, in the name of the common good, between various particular interests; but it should make accessible to each what is needed to lead a truly human life: food, clothing, health, work, education and culture, suitable information, the right to establish a family, and so on.[28]

---

[23] *PT* 51.
[24] *CA* 44.
[25] *Ep. Barnabae* 4, 10: PG 2, 734.

[26] *GS* 26 § 1; cf. 74 § 1.
[27] *GS* 26 § 2.
[28] Cf. *GS* 26 § 2.

1909 Finally, the common good requires *peace*, that is, the stabil-   *2304*
ity and security of a just order. It presupposes that authority should
ensure by morally acceptable means the *security* of society and its
members. It is the basis of the right to legitimate personal and   *2310*
collective defence.

1910 Each human community possesses a common good which
permits it to be recognized as such; it is in the *political community*   *2244*
that its most complete realization is found. It is the role of the state
to defend and promote the common good of civil society, its
citizens and intermediate bodies.

1911 Human interdependence is increasing and gradually spreading throughout the world. The unity of the human family,   *2438*
embracing people who enjoy equal natural dignity, implies a *universal common good*. This good calls for an organization of the community of nations able to 'provide for the different needs of men;
this will involve the sphere of social life to which belong questions
of food, hygiene, education... and certain situations arising here
and there, as for example... alleviating the miseries of refugees
dispersed throughout the world, and assisting migrants and their
families.'[29]

1912 The common good is always oriented towards the progress
of persons: 'The order of things must be subordinate to the order   *1881*
of persons, and not the other way around.'[30] This order is founded
on truth, built up in justice, and animated by love.

III. Responsibility and Participation

1913 'Participation' is the voluntary and generous engagement of
a person in social interchange. It is necessary that all participate,
each according to his position and role, in promoting the common
good. This obligation is inherent in the dignity of the human
person.

1914 Participation is achieved first of all by taking charge of the
areas for which one assumes *personal responsibility*: by the care   *1734*
taken for the education of his family, by conscientious work, and
so forth, man participates in the good of others and of society.[31]

1915 As far as possible citizens should take an active part in *public*   *2239*
life. The manner of this participation may vary from one country

---

[29] *GS* 84 § 2.   [31] Cf. *CA* 43.
[30] *GS* 26 § 3.

or culture to another. 'One must pay tribute to those nations whose systems permit the largest possible number of the citizens to take part in public life in a climate of genuine freedom.'[32]

1916 As with any ethical obligation, the participation of all in
1888 realizing the common good calls for a continually renewed *conversion* of the social partners. Fraud and other subterfuges, by which some people evade the constraints of the law and the prescriptions of societal obligation, must be firmly condemned because they are
2409 incompatible with the requirements of justice. Much care should be taken to promote institutions that improve the conditions of human life.[33]

1917 It is incumbent on those who exercise authority to strengthen the values that inspire the confidence of the members of the group and encourage them to put themselves at the service of others. Participation begins with education and culture. 'One is entitled to think that the future of humanity is in the hands of those who are capable of providing the generations to come with
1818 reasons for life and optimism.'[34]

IN BRIEF

1918 *'There is no authority except from God, and those authorities that exist have been instituted by God' (Rom 13:1).*

1919 *Every human community needs an authority in order to endure and develop.*

1920 *'The political community and public authority are based on human nature and therefore. . . belong to an order established by God' (GS 74 § 3).*

1921 *Authority is exercised legitimately if it is committed to the common good of society. To attain this it must employ morally acceptable means.*

1922 *The diversity of political regimes is legitimate, provided they contribute to the good of the community.*

1923 *Political authority must be exercised within the limits of the moral order and must guarantee the conditions for the exercise of freedom.*

1924 *The common good comprises 'the sum total of social conditions which allow people, either as groups or as individuals, to reach their fulfilment more fully and more easily' (GS 26 § 1).*

---

[32] GS 31 § 3.   [34] GS 31 § 3.
[33] Cf. GS 30 § 1.

1925 *The common good consists of three essential elements: respect for and promotion of the fundamental rights of the person; prosperity, or the development of the spiritual and temporal goods of society; the peace and security of the group and of its members.*

1926 *The dignity of the human person requires the pursuit of the common good. Everyone should be concerned to create and support institutions that improve the conditions of human life.*

1927 *It is the role of the state to defend and promote the common good of civil society. The common good of the whole human family calls for an organization of society on the international level.*

Article 3
SOCIAL JUSTICE

1928 Society ensures social justice when it provides the conditions that allow associations or individuals to obtain what is their due, according to their nature and their vocation. Social justice is linked to the common good and the exercise of authority. *2832*

I. Respect for the Human Person

1929 Social justice can be obtained only in respecting the transcendent dignity of man. The person represents the ultimate end of society, which is ordered to him: *1881*

> What is at stake is the dignity of the human person, whose defence and promotion have been entrusted to us by the Creator, and to whom the men and women at every moment of history are strictly and responsibly in debt.[35]

1930 Respect for the human person entails respect for the rights that flow from his dignity as a creature. These rights are prior to society and must be recognized by it. They are the basis of the moral legitimacy of every authority: by flouting them, or refusing to recognize them in its positive legislation, a society undermines its own moral legitimacy.[36] If it does not respect them, authority can rely only on force or violence to obtain obedience from its subjects. It is the Church's role to remind men of good will of these rights, and to distinguish them from unwarranted or false claims. *1700* *1902*

1931 Respect for the human person proceeds by way of respect for the principle that 'everyone should look upon his neighbour (without any exception) as "another self", above all bearing in *2212*

---

[35] John Paul II, *SRS* 47. [36] Cf. John XXIII, *PT* 65.

mind his life and the means necessary for living it with dignity.'[37]
No legislation could by itself do away with the fears, prejudices,
and attitudes of pride and selfishness which obstruct the establishment of truly fraternal societies. Such behaviour will cease only
1825 through the charity that finds in every man a 'neighbour', a
brother.

1932 The duty of making oneself a neighbour to others and
actively serving them becomes even more urgent when it involves
2449 the disadvantaged, in whatever area this may be. 'As you did it to
one of the least of these my brethren, you did it to me.'[38]

1933 This same duty extends to those who think or act differently
from us. The teaching of Christ goes so far as to require the forgiveness of offences. He extends the commandment of love, which
is that of the New Law, to all enemies.[39] Liberation in the spirit of
2303 the Gospel is incompatible with hatred of one's enemy as a person,
but not with hatred of the evil that he does as an enemy.

II. Equality and Differences Among Men

1934 Created in the image of the one God and equally endowed
with rational souls, all men have the same nature and the same
origin. Redeemed by the sacrifice of Christ, all are called to participate in the same divine beatitude: all therefore enjoy an equal
225 dignity.

1935 The equality of men rests essentially on their dignity as
357 persons and the rights that flow from it:

> Every form of social or cultural discrimination in fundamental personal
> rights on the grounds of sex, race, colour, social conditions, language or
> religion, must be curbed and eradicated as incompatible with God's
> design.[40]

1936 On coming into the world, man is not equipped with everything he needs for developing his bodily and spiritual life. He
1879 needs others. Differences appear tied to age, physical abilities,
intellectual or moral aptitudes, the benefits derived from social
commerce, and the distribution of wealth.[41] The 'talents' are not
distributed equally.[42]

---

[37] GS 27 § 1.
[38] Mt 25:40.
[39] Cf. Mt 5:43–44.

[40] GS 29 § 2.
[41] Cf. GS 29 § 2.
[42] Cf. Mt 25:14–30; Lk 19:11–27.

1937 These differences belong to God's plan, who wills that each   *340*
receive what he needs from others, and that those endowed with
particular 'talents' share the benefits with those who need them.
These differences encourage and often oblige persons to practise   *791*
generosity, kindness and sharing of goods; they foster the mutual
enrichment of cultures: *1202*

> I distribute the virtues quite diversely; I do not give all of them to each
> person, but some to one, some to others. . . I shall give principally charity
> to one; justice to another; humility to this one, a living faith to that one. . .
> And so I have given many gifts and graces, both spiritual and temporal,
> with such diversity that I have not given everything to one single person,
> so that you may be constrained to practise charity towards one
> another. . . I have willed that one should need another and that all should
> be my ministers in distributing the graces and gifts they have received
> from me.[43]

1938 There exist also *sinful inequalities* that affect millions of men   *2437*
and women. These are in open contradiction of the Gospel:

> Their equal dignity as persons demands that we strive for fairer and more
> humane conditions. Excessive economic and social disparity between   *2317*
> individuals and peoples of the one human race is a source of scandal and
> militates against social justice, equity, human dignity, as well as social and
> international peace.[44]

III. Human Solidarity

1939 The principle of solidarity, also articulated in terms of
'friendship' or 'social charity', is a direct demand of human and
Christian brotherhood.[45]   *2213*

> An error, 'today abundantly widespread, is disregard for the law of
> human solidarity and charity, dictated and imposed both by our
> common origin and by the equality in rational nature of all men, what-   *360*
> ever nation they belong to. This law is sealed by the sacrifice of redemp-
> tion offered by Jesus Christ on the altar of the Cross to his heavenly
> Father, on behalf of sinful humanity.'[46]

1940 Solidarity is manifested in the first place by the distribution   *2402*
of goods and remuneration for work. It also presupposes the effort
for a more just social order where tensions are better able to be
reduced and conflicts more readily settled by negotiation.

---

[43] St Catherine of Siena, *Dial.* I, 7.   [46] Pius XII, *Summi pontificatus*,
[44] GS 29 § 3.   20 October 1939: AAS 31 (1939), 423ff.
[45] Cf. *SRS* 38–40; *CA* 10.

2317 1941 Socio-economic problems can be resolved only with the help of all the forms of solidarity: solidarity of the poor among themselves, between rich and poor, of workers among themselves, between employers and employees in a business, solidarity among nations and peoples. International solidarity is a requirement of the moral order; world peace depends in part upon this.

1942 The virtue of solidarity goes beyond material goods. In *1886* spreading the spiritual goods of the faith, the Church has promoted, and often opened new paths for, the development of temporal goods as well. And so throughout the centuries has the *2632* Lord's saying been verified: 'Seek first his kingdom and his righteousness, and all these things shall be yours as well':[47]

> For two thousand years this sentiment has lived and endured in the soul of the Church, impelling souls then and now to the heroic charity of monastic farmers, liberators of slaves, healers of the sick, and messengers of faith, civilization, and science to all generations and all peoples for the sake of creating the social conditions capable of offering to everyone possible a life worthy of man and of a Christian.[48]

IN BRIEF

1943 *Society ensures social justice by providing the conditions that allow associations and individuals to obtain their due.*

1944 *Respect for the human person considers the other 'another self'. It presupposes respect for the fundamental rights that flow from the intrinsic dignity of the person.*

1945 *The equality of men concerns their dignity as persons and the rights that flow from it.*

1946 *The differences among persons belong to God's plan, who wills that we should need one another. These differences should encourage charity.*

1947 *The equal dignity of human persons requires the effort to reduce excessive social and economic inequalities. It gives urgency to the elimination of sinful inequalities.*

1948 *Solidarity is an eminently Christian virtue. It practises the sharing of spiritual goods even more than material ones.*

---

[47] Mt 6:33.   [48] Pius XII, Discourse, 1 June 1941.

Chapter Three
GOD'S SALVATION: LAW AND GRACE

1949 Called to beatitude but wounded by sin, man stands in need of salvation from God. Divine help comes to him in Christ through the law that guides him and the grace that sustains him:

> Work out your own salvation with fear and trembling; for God is at work in you, both to will and to work for his good pleasure.[1]

Article 1
THE MORAL LAW

1950 The moral law is the work of divine Wisdom. Its biblical meaning can be defined as fatherly instruction, God's pedagogy. It *53* prescribes for man the ways, the rules of conduct that lead to the promised beatitude; it proscribes the ways of evil which turn him *1719* away from God and his love. It is at once firm in its precepts and, in its promises, worthy of love.

1951 Law is a rule of conduct enacted by competent authority for the sake of the common good. The moral law presupposes the rational order, established among creatures for their good and to serve their final end, by the power, wisdom and goodness of the *295* Creator. All law finds its first and ultimate truth in the eternal law. Law is declared and established by reason as a participation in the providence of the living God, Creator and Redeemer of all. 'Such *306* an ordinance of reason is what one calls law.'[2]

> Alone among all animate beings, man can boast of having been counted worthy to receive a law from God: as an animal endowed with reason, capable of understanding and discernment, he is to govern his conduct by using his freedom and reason, in obedience to the One who has entrusted *301* everything to him.[3]

1952 There are different expressions of the moral law, all of them interrelated: eternal law – the source, in God, of all law; natural law; revealed law, comprising the Old Law and the New Law, or Law of the Gospel; finally, civil and ecclesiastical laws.

1953 The moral law finds its fullness and its unity in Christ. Jesus *578* Christ is in person the way of perfection. He is the end of the law, for only he teaches and bestows the justice of God: 'For Christ is the end of the law, that every one who has faith may be justified.'[4]

---

[1] *Phil* 2:12–13.
[2] Leo XIII, *Libertas praestantissimum*: AAS 20 (1887/88), 597; cf. St Thomas Aquinas, *STh* I–II, 90, 1.
[3] Tertullian, *Adv. Marc.* 2, 4: PL 2, 288–289.
[4] *Rom* 10:4.

I. The Natural Moral Law

1954 Man participates in the wisdom and goodness of the Creator
307 who gives him mastery over his acts and the ability to govern
himself with a view to the true and the good. The natural law
1776 expresses the original moral sense which enables man to discern by
reason the good and the evil, the truth and the lie:

> The natural law is written and engraved in the soul of each and every
> man, because it is human reason ordaining him to do good and forbid-
> ding him to sin... But this command of human reason would not have
> the force of law if it were not the voice and interpreter of a higher reason
> to which our spirit and our freedom must be submitted.[5]

1787 1955 The 'divine and natural' law[6] shows man the way to follow
so as to practise the good and attain his end. The natural law states
396 the first and essential precepts which govern the moral life. It
hinges upon the desire for God and submission to him, who is the
source and judge of all that is good, as well as upon the sense that
the other is one's equal. Its principal precepts are expressed in the
2070 Decalogue. This law is called 'natural', not in reference to the
nature of irrational beings, but because reason which decrees it
properly belongs to human nature:

> Where then are these rules written, if not in the book of that light we call
> the truth? In it is written every just law; from it the law passes into the
> heart of the man who does justice, not that it migrates into it, but that it
> places its imprint on it, like a seal on a ring that passes onto wax, without
> leaving the ring.[7]

> The natural law is nothing other than the light of understanding placed in
> us by God; through it we know what we must do and what we must
> avoid. God has given this light or law at the creation.[8]

1956 The natural law, present in the heart of each man and estab-
2261 lished by reason, is universal in its precepts and its authority
extends to all men. It expresses the dignity of the person and determines the basis for his fundamental rights and duties:

> For there is a true law: right reason. It is in conformity with nature, is
> diffused among all men and is immutable and eternal; its orders summon
> to duty; its prohibitions turn away from offence... To replace it with a
> contrary law is a sacrilege; failure to apply even one of its provisions is
> forbidden; no one can abrogate it entirely.[9]

1957 Application of the natural law varies greatly; it can demand
reflection that takes account of various conditions of life according

---

[5] Leo XIII, Libertas praestantissimum 597.
[6] GS 89 § 1.
[7] St Augustine, De Trin. 14, 15, 21: PL
42, 1052.
[8] St Thomas Aquinas, Dec. praec. 1.
[9] Cicero, Rep. III, 22, 33.

to places, times, and circumstances. Nevertheless, in the diversity of cultures, the natural law remains as a rule that binds men among themselves and imposes on them, beyond the inevitable differences, common principles.

1958 The natural law is *immutable* and permanent throughout the variations of history;[10] it subsists under the flux of ideas and customs and supports their progress. The rules that express it remain substantially valid. Even when it is rejected in its very principles, it cannot be destroyed or removed from the heart of man. It always rises again in the life of individuals and societies: *2072*

> Theft is surely punished by your law, O Lord, and by the law that is written in the human heart, the law that iniquity itself does not efface.[11]

1959 The natural law, the Creator's very good work, provides the solid foundation on which man can build the structure of moral rules to guide his choices. It also provides the indispensable moral foundation for building the human community. Finally, it provides the necessary basis for the civil law with which it is connected, whether by a reflection that draws conclusions from its principles, or by additions of a positive and juridical nature. *1879*

1960 The precepts of natural law are not perceived by everyone clearly and immediately. In the present situation sinful man needs grace and revelation so moral and religious truths may be known 'by everyone with facility, with firm certainty and with no admixture of error'.[12] The natural law provides revealed law and grace with a foundation prepared by God and in accordance with the work of the Spirit. *2071* *37*

II. The Old Law

1961 God, our Creator and Redeemer, chose Israel for himself to be his people and revealed his Law to them, thus preparing for the coming of Christ. The Law of Moses expresses many truths naturally accessible to reason. These are stated and authenticated within the covenant of salvation. *62*

1962 The Old Law is the first stage of revealed law. Its moral prescriptions are summed up in the Ten Commandments. The precepts of the Decalogue lay the foundations for the vocation of man fashioned in the image of God; they prohibit what is contrary to the love of God and neighbour, and prescribe what is essential *2058*

---

[10] Cf. GS 10.
[11] St Augustine, *Conf.* 2, 4, 9: PL 32, 678.

[12] Pius XII, *Humani generis*: DS 3876; cf. *Dei Filius* 2: DS 3005.

to it. The Decalogue is a light offered to the conscience of every man to make God's call and ways known to him, and to protect him against evil:

> God wrote on the tables of the Law what men did not read in their hearts.[13]

1963 According to Christian tradition, the Law is holy, spiritual and good,[14] yet still imperfect. Like a tutor[15] it shows what must be done, but does not of itself give the strength, the grace of the Spirit, to fulfil it. Because of sin, which it cannot remove, it remains a law of bondage. According to St Paul, its special function is to denounce and *disclose sin*, which constitutes a 'law of concupiscence' in the human heart.[16] However, the Law remains the first stage on the way to the Kingdom. It prepares and disposes the chosen people and each Christian for conversion and faith in the Saviour God. It provides a teaching which endures for ever, like the Word of God.

1964 The Old Law is a *preparation for the Gospel*. 'The Law is a pedagogy and a prophecy of things to come.'[17] It prophesies and presages the work of liberation from sin which will be fulfilled in Christ: it provides the New Testament with images, 'types', and symbols for expressing the life according to the Spirit. Finally, the Law is completed by the teaching of the sapiential books and the prophets which set its course toward the New Covenant and the Kingdom of heaven.

> There were..., under the regimen of the Old Covenant, people who possessed the charity and grace of the Holy Spirit and longed above all for the spiritual and eternal promises by which they were associated with the New Law. Conversely, there exist carnal men under the New Covenant, still distanced from the perfection of the New Law: the fear of punishment and certain temporal promises have been necessary, even under the New Covenant, to incite them to virtuous works. In any case, even though the Old Law prescribed charity, it did not give the Holy Spirit, through whom 'God's charity has been poured into our hearts.'[18]

III. The New Law or the Law of the Gospel

1965 The New Law or the Law of the Gospel is the perfection here on earth of the divine law, natural and revealed. It is the work

*Margin references: 1610, 2542, 2515, 122, 1828, 459*

---

[13] St Augustine, *En. in Ps.* 57, 1: PL 36, 673.
[14] Cf. *Rom* 7:12, 14, 16.
[15] Cf. *Gal* 3:24.
[16] Cf. *Rom* 7.
[17] St Irenaeus, *Adv. haeres.* 4, 15, 1: PG 7/1, 1012.
[18] St Thomas Aquinas, *STh* I–II, 107, 1, ad 2; cf. *Rom* 5:5.

of Christ and is expressed particularly in the Sermon on the 581 Mount. It is also the work of the Holy Spirit and through him it becomes the interior law of charity: 'I will establish a New Covenant with the house of Israel. . . I will put my laws into their minds, and write them on their hearts, and I will be their God, and they shall be my people.'[19]

715

1966 The New Law is the *grace of the Holy Spirit* given to the 1999 faithful through faith in Christ. It works through charity; it uses the Sermon on the Mount to teach us what must be done and makes use of the sacraments to give us the grace to do it:

> If anyone should meditate with devotion and perspicacity on the sermon our Lord gave on the mount, as we read in the Gospel of Saint Matthew, he will doubtless find there. . . the perfect way of the Christian life. . . This sermon contains. . . all the precepts needed to shape one's life.[20]

1967 The Law of the Gospel 'fulfils', refines, surpasses and leads the Old Law to its perfection.[21] In the Beatitudes, the New Law 577 *fulfils the divine promises* by elevating and orienting them toward the 'kingdom of heaven'. It is addressed to those open to accepting this new hope with faith – the poor, the humble, the afflicted, the pure of heart, those persecuted on account of Christ – and so marks out the surprising ways of the Kingdom.

1968 The Law of the Gospel *fulfils the commandments* of the Law. The Lord's Sermon on the Mount, far from abolishing or devaluing the moral prescriptions of the Old Law, releases their hidden 129 potential and has new demands arise from them: it reveals their entire divine and human truth. It does not add new external precepts, but proceeds to reform the heart, the root of human acts, 582 where man chooses between the pure and the impure,[22] where faith, hope and charity are formed, and with them the other virtues. The Gospel thus brings the Law to its fullness through imitation of the perfection of the heavenly Father, through forgiveness of enemies and prayer for persecutors, in emulation of the divine generosity.[23]

1969 The New Law *practises the acts of religion*: almsgiving, prayer 1434 and fasting, directing them to the 'Father who sees in secret', in contrast with the desire to 'be seen by men'.[24] Its prayer is the *Our Father*.[25]

---

[19] *Heb* 8:8, 10; cf. *Jer* 31:31–34.
[20] St Augustine, *De serm. Dom.* 1, 1: PL 34, 1229–1231.
[21] Cf. *Mt* 5:17–19.

[22] Cf. *Mt* 15:18–19.
[23] Cf. *Mt* 5:44, 48.
[24] Cf. *Mt* 6:1–6, 16–18.
[25] Cf. *Mt* 6:9–13; *Lk* 11:2–4.

1970   The Law of the Gospel requires us to make the decisive
1696 choice between 'the two ways' and to put into practice the words
1789 of the Lord.[26] It is summed up in the *Golden Rule*, 'Whatever you
wish that men would do to you, do so to them; this is the law and
the prophets.'[27]

1823   The entire Law of the Gospel is contained in the '*new commandment*' of Jesus, to love one another as he has loved us.[28]

1971   To the Lord's Sermon on the Mount it is fitting to add the
moral catechesis of the apostolic teachings, such as *Romans* 12 – 15, 1
Corinthians 12 – 13, *Colossians* 3 – 4, *Ephesians* 4 – 5, etc. This
doctrine hands on the Lord's teaching with the authority of the
apostles, particularly in the presentation of the virtues that flow
from faith in Christ and are animated by charity, the principal gift
of the Holy Spirit. 'Let charity be genuine... Love one another
with brotherly affection... Rejoice in your hope, be patient in
tribulation, be constant in prayer. Contribute to the needs of the
saints, practise hospitality.'[29] This catechesis also teaches us to deal
1789 with cases of conscience in the light of our relationship to Christ
and to the Church.[30]

782 1972   The New Law is called a *law of love* because it makes us act
out of the love infused by the Holy Spirit, rather than from fear; a
law of grace, because it confers the strength of grace to act, by
means of faith and the sacraments; a *law of freedom*, because it sets us
free from the ritual and juridical observances of the Old Law,
1828 inclines us to act spontaneously by the prompting of charity and,
finally, lets us pass from the condition of a servant who 'does not
know what his master is doing' to that of a friend of Christ – 'For
all that I have heard from my Father I have made known to
you' – or even to the status of son and heir.[31]

2053 1973   Besides its precepts, the New Law also includes the *evangeli-
915 cal counsels*. The traditional distinction between God's commandments and the evangelical counsels is drawn in relation to charity,
the perfection of Christian life. The precepts are intended to
remove whatever is incompatible with charity. The aim of the
counsels is to remove whatever might hinder the development of
charity, even if it is not contrary to it.[32]

---

[26] Cf. *Mt* 7:13–14, 21–27.
[27] *Mt* 7:12; cf. *Lk* 6:31.
[28] Cf. *Jn* 15:12; 13:34.
[29] *Rom* 12:9–13.
[30] Cf. *Rom* 14; 1 *Cor* 5–10.

[31] *Jn* 15:15; cf. *Jas* 1:25; 2:12; *Gal* 4:1–7,
21–31; *Rom* 8:15.
[32] Cf. St Thomas Aquinas, *STh* II–II,
184, 3.

1974 The evangelical counsels manifest the living fullness of charity, which is never satisfied with not giving more. They attest its vitality and call forth our spiritual readiness. The perfection of the *2013* New Law consists essentially in the precepts of love of God and neighbour. The counsels point out the more direct ways, the readier means, and are to be practised in keeping with the vocation of each:

> [God] does not want each person to keep all the counsels, but only those appropriate to the diversity of persons, times, opportunities and strengths, as charity requires; for it is charity, as queen of all virtues, all commandments, all counsels, and, in short, of all laws and all Christian actions, that gives to all of them their rank, order, time and value.[33]

IN BRIEF

1975 *According to Scripture the Law is a fatherly instruction by God which prescribes for man the ways that lead to the promised beatitude, and proscribes the ways of evil.*

1976 *'Law is an ordinance of reason for the common good, promulgated by the one who is in charge of the community' (St Thomas Aquinas, STh I–II, 90, 4).*

1977 *Christ is the end of the law (cf. Rom 10:4); only he teaches and bestows the justice of God.*

1978 *The natural law is a participation in God's wisdom and goodness by man formed in the image of his Creator. It expresses the dignity of the human person and forms the basis of his fundamental rights and duties.*

1979 *The natural law is immutable, permanent throughout history. The rules that express it remain substantially valid. It is a necessary foundation for the erection of moral rules and civil law.*

1980 *The Old Law is the first stage of revealed law. Its moral prescriptions are summed up in the Ten Commandments.*

1981 *The Law of Moses contains many truths naturally accessible to reason. God has revealed them because men did not read them in their hearts.*

1982 *The Old Law is a preparation for the Gospel.*

1983 *The New Law is the grace of the Holy Spirit received by faith in Christ, operating through charity. It finds expression above all in the Lord's Sermon on the Mount and uses the sacraments to communicate grace to us.*

---

[33] St Francis de Sales, *Love of God* 8, 6.

1984 *The Law of the Gospel fulfils and surpasses the Old Law and brings it to perfection: its promises, through the Beatitudes of the Kingdom of heaven; its commandments, by reforming the heart, the root of human acts.*

1985 *The New Law is a law of love, a law of grace, a law of freedom.*

1986 *Besides its precepts the New Law includes the evangelical counsels. 'The Church's holiness is fostered in a special way by the manifold counsels which the Lord proposes to his disciples in the Gospel' (LG 42 § 2).*

Article 2
GRACE AND JUSTIFICATION

I. Justification

1987 The grace of the Holy Spirit has the power to justify us, that
734 is, to cleanse us from our sins and to communicate to us 'the righteousness of God through faith in Jesus Christ' and through Baptism:[34]

> But if we have died with Christ, we believe that we shall also live with him. For we know that Christ being raised from the dead will never die again; death no longer has dominion over him. The death he died he died to sin, once for all, but the life he lives he lives to God. So you also must consider yourselves as dead to sin and alive to God in Christ Jesus.[35]

1988 Through the power of the Holy Spirit we take part in
654 Christ's Passion by dying to sin, and in his Resurrection by being born to a new life; we are members of his Body which is the Church, branches grafted onto the vine which is himself:[36]

> [God] gave himself to us through his Spirit. By the participation of the
460 Spirit, we become communicants in the divine nature... For this reason, those in whom the Spirit dwells are divinized.[37]

1427 1989 The first work of the grace of the Holy Spirit is *conversion*, effecting justification in accordance with Jesus' proclamation at the beginning of the Gospel: 'Repent, for the kingdom of heaven is at hand.'[38] Moved by grace, man turns towards God and away from sin, thus accepting forgiveness and righteousness from on high. 'Justification is not only the remission of sins, but also the sanctification and renewal of the interior man.'[39]

---

[34] *Rom* 3:22; cf. 6:3–4.
[35] *Rom* 6:8–11.
[36] Cf. 1 *Cor* 12; *Jn* 15:1–4.
[37] St Athanasius, *Ep. Serap.* 1, 24: PG 26,

585 and 588.
[38] *Mt* 4:17.
[39] Council of Trent (1547): DS 1528.

1990 Justification *detaches man from sin* which contradicts the love of God, and purifies his heart of sin. Justification follows upon God's merciful initiative of offering forgiveness. It reconciles man with God. It frees from the enslavement to sin, and it heals.

1446

1733

1991 Justification is at the same time *the acceptance of God's right-eousness* through faith in Jesus Christ. Righteousness (or 'justice') here means the rectitude of divine love. With justification, faith, hope and charity are poured into our hearts, and obedience to the divine will is granted us.

1812

1992 Justification has been *merited for us by the Passion of Christ* who offered himself on the cross as a living victim, holy and pleasing to God, and whose blood has become the instrument of atonement for the sins of all men. Justification is conferred in Baptism, the sacrament of faith. It conforms us to the righteousness of God, who makes us inwardly just by the power of his mercy. Its purpose is the glory of God and of Christ, and the gift of eternal life:[40]

617

1266

294

> But now the righteousness of God has been manifested apart from law, although the law and the prophets bear witness to it, the righteousness of God through faith in Jesus Christ for all who believe. For there is no distinction: since all have sinned and fall short of the glory of God, they are justified by his grace as a gift, through the redemption which is in Christ Jesus, whom God put forward as an expiation by his blood, to be received by faith. This was to show God's righteousness, because in his divine forbearance he had passed over former sins; it was to prove at the present time that he himself is righteous and that he justifies him who has faith in Jesus.[41]

1993 Justification establishes *co-operation between God's grace and man's freedom*. On man's part it is expressed by the assent of faith to the Word of God, which invites him to conversion, and in the co-operation of charity with the prompting of the Holy Spirit who precedes and preserves his assent:

2008

> When God touches man's heart through the illumination of the Holy Spirit, man himself is not inactive while receiving that inspiration, since he could reject it; and yet, without God's grace, he cannot by his own free will move himself toward justice in God's sight.[42]

2068

1994 Justification is the *most excellent work of God's love* made manifest in Christ Jesus and granted by the Holy Spirit. It is the opinion of St Augustine that 'the justification of the wicked is a greater work than the creation of heaven and earth', because

312

---

[40] Cf. Council of Trent (1547): DS 1529.   [42] Council of Trent (1547): DS 1525.
[41] *Rom* 3:21–26.

'heaven and earth will pass away but the salvation and justification
of the elect... will not pass away.'[43] He holds also that the justification of sinners surpasses the creation of the angels in justice, in
412   that it bears witness to a greater mercy.

741   1995   The Holy Spirit is the master of the interior life. By giving
birth to the 'inner man',[44] justification entails the *sanctification* of
his whole being:

> Just as you once yielded your members to impurity and to greater and
> greater iniquity, so now yield your members to righteousness for sancti-
> fication... But now that you have been set free from sin and have
> become slaves of God, the return you get is sanctification and its end,
> eternal life.[45]

II. Grace

1996   Our justification comes from the grace of God. Grace is
153   *favour*, the *free and undeserved help* that God gives us to respond to
his call to become children of God, adoptive sons, partakers of the
divine nature and of eternal life.[46]

375   1997   Grace is a *participation in the life of God*. It introduces us into
260   the intimacy of Trinitarian life: by Baptism the Christian participates in the grace of Christ, the Head of his Body. As an 'adopted
son' he can henceforth call God 'Father', in union with the only
Son. He receives the life of the Spirit who breathes charity into
him and who forms the Church.

1719   1998   This vocation to eternal life is *supernatural*. It depends
entirely on God's gratuitous initiative, for he alone can reveal and
give himself. It surpasses the power of human intellect and will, as
that of every other creature.[47]

1966   1999   The grace of Christ is the gratuitous gift that God makes to
us of his own life, infused by the Holy Spirit into our soul to heal it
of sin and to sanctify it. It is the *sanctifying* or *deifying grace* received
in Baptism. It is in us the source of the work of sanctification:[48]

> Therefore if any one is in Christ, he is a new creation; the old has passed
> away, behold, the new has come. All this is from God, who through
> Christ reconciled us to himself.[49]

---

[43] St Augustine, *In ev. Jo.* 72, 3: PL 35,
1823.
[44] Cf. *Rom* 7:22; *Eph* 3:16.
[45] *Rom* 6:19, 22.
[46] Cf. *Jn* 1:12–18; 17:3; *Rom* 8:14–17;

2 *Pt* 1:3–4.
[47] Cf. 1 *Cor* 2:7–9.
[48] Cf. *Jn* 4:14; 7:38–39.
[49] 2 *Cor* 5:17–18.

2000 Sanctifying grace is an habitual gift, a stable and supernatural disposition that perfects the soul itself to enable it to live with God, to act by his love. *Habitual grace*, the permanent disposition to live and act in keeping with God's call, is distinguished from *actual graces* which refer to God's interventions, whether at the beginning of conversion or in the course of the work of sanctification.

2001 The *preparation of man* for the reception of grace is already a work of grace. This latter is needed to arouse and sustain our collaboration in justification through faith, and in sanctification through charity. God brings to completion in us what he has begun, 'since he who completes his work by co-operating with our will began by working so that we might will it':[50]

> Indeed we also work, but we are only collaborating with God who works, for his mercy has gone before us. It has gone before us so that we may be healed, and follows us so that once healed, we may be given life; it goes before us so that we may be called, and follows us so that we may be glorified; it goes before us so that we may live devoutly, and follows us so that we may always live with God: for without him we can do nothing.[51]

2002 God's free initiative demands *man's free response*, for God has created man in his image by conferring on him, along with freedom, the power to know him and love him. The soul only enters freely into the communion of love. God immediately touches and directly moves the heart of man. He has placed in man a longing for truth and goodness that only he can satisfy. The promises of 'eternal life' respond, beyond all hope, to this desire:

> If at the end of your very good works. . . you rested on the seventh day, it was to foretell by the voice of your book that at the end of our works, which are indeed 'very good' since you have given them to us, we shall also rest in you on the sabbath of eternal life.[52]

2003 Grace is first and foremost the gift of the Spirit who justifies and sanctifies us. But grace also includes the gifts that the Spirit grants us to associate us with his work, to enable us to collaborate in the salvation of others and in the growth of the Body of Christ, the Church. There are *sacramental graces*, gifts proper to the different sacraments. There are furthermore *special graces*, also called *charisms* after the Greek term used by St Paul and meaning 'favour', 'gratuitous gift', 'benefit'.[53] Whatever their character –

490

1742

2550

1108

1127

---

[50] St Augustine, *De gratia et libero arbitrio* 17: PL 44, 901.
[51] St Augustine, *De natura et gratia* 31: PL 44, 264.
[52] St Augustine, *Conf.* 13, 36, 51: PL 32, 868; cf. *Gen* 1:31.
[53] Cf. *LG* 12.

sometimes it is extraordinary, such as the gift of miracles or of
799–801 tongues – charisms are oriented toward sanctifying grace, and are
intended for the common good of the Church. They are at the
service of charity which builds up the Church.[54]

2004 Among the special graces ought to be mentioned the *graces
of state* that accompany the exercise of the responsibilities of the
Christian life and of the ministries within the Church:

> Having gifts that differ according to the grace given to us, let us use them:
> if prophecy, in proportion to our faith; if service, in our serving; he who
> teaches, in his teaching; he who exhorts, in his exhortation; he who
> contributes, in liberality; he who gives aid, with zeal; he who does acts of
> mercy, with cheerfulness.[55]

2005 Since it belongs to the supernatural order, grace *escapes our
experience* and cannot be known except by faith. We cannot therefore rely on our feelings or our works to conclude that we are
justified and saved.[56] However, according to the Lord's words –
'Thus you will know them by their fruits'[57] – reflection on God's
blessings in our life and in the lives of the saints offers us a guarantee that grace is at work in us and spurs us on to an ever greater
faith and an attitude of trustful poverty.

> A pleasing illustration of this attitude is found in the reply of St Joan of
> Arc to a question posed as a trap by her ecclesiastical judges: 'Asked if she
> knew that she was in God's grace, she replied: "If I am not, may it please
> God to put me in it; if I am, may it please God to keep me there." '[58]

III. Merit

> You are glorified in the assembly of your Holy Ones,
> for in crowning their merits you are crowning your own gifts.[59]

1723 2006 The term 'merit' refers in general to the *recompense owed* by a
community or a society for the action of one of its members,
experienced either as beneficial or harmful, deserving reward or
1807 punishment. Merit is relative to the virtue of justice, in conformity
with the principle of equality which governs it.

2007 With regard to God, there is no strict right to any merit on
the part of man. Between God and us there is an immeasurable

---

[54] Cf. 1 Cor 12.
[55] Rom 12:6–8.
[56] Cf. Council of Trent (1547): DS
1533–1534.
[57] Mt 7:20.
[58] Acts of the Trial of St Joan of Arc.

[59] *Missale Romanum*, Preface of Holy
Men and Women I: *Qui in Sanctorum
concilio celebraris, et eorum coronando
merita tua dona coronas*, citing the
'Doctor of grace', St Augustine, *En. in
Ps.* 102, 7: PL 37, 1321–1322.

inequality, for we have received everything from him, our 42
Creator.

2008 The merit of man before God in the Christian life arises
from the fact that *God has freely chosen to associate man with the work* 306
of his grace. The fatherly action of God is first on his own initiative,
and then follows man's free acting through his collaboration, so 155
that the merit of good works is to be attributed in the first place to
the grace of God, then to the faithful. Man's merit, moreover, 970
itself is due to God, for his good actions proceed in Christ, from
the predispositions and assistance given by the Holy Spirit.

2009 Filial adoption, in making us partakers by grace in the divine
nature, can bestow *true merit* on us as a result of God's gratuitous
justice. This is our right by grace, the full right of love, making us
'co-heirs' with Christ and worthy of obtaining 'the promised
inheritance of eternal life'.[60] The merits of our good works are
gifts of the divine goodness.[61] 'Grace has gone before us; now we 604
are given what is due... Our merits are God's gifts.'[62]

2010 Since the initiative belongs to God in the order of grace, 1998
no one can merit the initial grace of forgiveness and justification, at
the beginning of conversion. Moved by the Holy Spirit and by
charity, *we can then merit* for ourselves and for others the graces
needed for our sanctification, for the increase of grace and charity,
and for the attainment of eternal life. Even temporal goods like
health and friendship can be merited in accordance with God's
wisdom. These graces and goods are the object of Christian
prayer. Prayer attends to the grace we need for meritorious
actions.

2011 *The charity of Christ is the source in us of all our merits* before 492
God. Grace, by uniting us to Christ in active love, ensures the
supernatural quality of our acts and consequently their merit
before God and before men. The saints have always had a lively
awareness that their merits were pure grace.

> After earth's exile, I hope to go and enjoy you in the fatherland, but I do
> not want to lay up merits for heaven. I want to work for your *love
> alone*... In the evening of this life, I shall appear before you with empty
> hands, for I do not ask you, Lord, to count my works. All our justice is
> blemished in your eyes. I wish, then, to be clothed in your own *justice* and 1460
> to receive from your *love* the eternal possession of *yourself*.[63]

---

[60] Council of Trent (1547): DS 1546.
[61] Cf. Council of Trent (1547): DS 1548.
[62] St Augustine, *Sermo* 298, 4–5: PL 38, 1367.

[63] St Thérèse of Lisieux, 'Act of Offering' in *Story of a Soul*, tr. John Clarke (Washington DC: ICS, 1981), 277.

IV. Christian Holiness

2012 'We know that in everything God works for good with
459 those who love him... For those whom he foreknew he also predestined to be conformed to the image of his Son, in order that he
might be the first-born among many brethren. And those whom
he predestined he also called; and those whom he called he also
justified; and those whom he justified he also glorified.'[64]

2013 'All Christians in any state or walk of life are called to the
915, 2545 fullness of Christian life and to the perfection of charity.'[65] All are
825 called to holiness: 'Be perfect, as your heavenly Father is perfect.'[66]

> In order to reach this perfection the faithful should use the strength dealt
> out to them by Christ's gift, so that... doing the will of the Father in
> everything, they may wholeheartedly devote themselves to the glory of
> God and to the service of their neighbour. Thus the holiness of the People
> of God will grow in fruitful abundance, as is clearly shown in the history
> of the Church through the lives of so many saints.[67]

2014 Spiritual progress tends towards ever more intimate union
with Christ. This union is called 'mystical' because it participates
744 in the mystery of Christ through the sacraments – 'the holy mysteries' – and, in him, in the mystery of the Holy Trinity. God calls
us all to this intimate union with him, even if the special graces or
extraordinary signs of this mystical life are granted only to some
for the sake of manifesting the gratuitous gift given to all.

2015 The way of perfection passes by way of the Cross. There is
407, 2725 no holiness without renunciation and spiritual battle.[68] Spiritual
progress entails the ascesis and mortification that gradually lead to
1438 living in the peace and joy of the Beatitudes:

> He who climbs never stops going from beginning to beginning, through
> beginnings that have no end. He never stops desiring what he already
> knows.[69]

1821 2016 The children of our holy mother the Church rightly hope
162 for *the grace of final perseverance and the recompense* of God their
Father for the good works accomplished with his grace in communion with Jesus.[70] Keeping the same rule of life, believers share
1274 the 'blessed hope' of those whom the divine mercy gathers into the
'holy city, the new Jerusalem, coming down out of heaven from
God, prepared as a bride adorned for her husband'.[71]

---

[64] *Rom* 8:28–30.
[65] *LG* 40 § 2.
[66] *Mt* 5:48.
[67] *LG* 40 § 2.
[68] Cf. 2 *Tim* 4.

[69] St Gregory of Nyssa, *Hom. in Cant.* 8:
PG 44, 941C.
[70] Cf. Council of Trent (1547): DS 1576.
[71] *Rev* 21:2.

IN BRIEF

2017 *The grace of the Holy Spirit confers upon us the righteousness of God. Uniting us by faith and Baptism to the Passion and Resurrection of Christ, the Spirit makes us sharers in his life.*

2018 *Like conversion, justification has two aspects. Moved by grace, man turns towards God and away from sin, and so accepts forgiveness and righteousness from on high.*

2019 *Justification includes the remission of sins, sanctification and the renewal of the inner man.*

2020 *Justification has been merited for us by the Passion of Christ. It is granted us through Baptism. It conforms us to the righteousness of God, who justifies us. It has for its goal the glory of God and of Christ, and the gift of eternal life. It is the most excellent work of God's mercy.*

2021 *Grace is the help God gives us to respond to our vocation of becoming his adopted sons. It introduces us into the intimacy of the Trinitarian life.*

2022 *The divine initiative in the work of grace precedes, prepares and elicits the free response of man. Grace responds to the deepest yearnings of human freedom, calls freedom to co-operate with it and perfects freedom.*

2023 *Sanctifying grace is the gratuitous gift of his life that God makes to us; it is infused by the Holy Spirit into the soul to heal it of sin and to sanctify it.*

2024 *Sanctifying grace makes us 'pleasing to God'. Charisms, special graces of the Holy Spirit, are oriented to sanctifying grace and are intended for the common good of the Church. God also acts through many actual graces, to be distinguished from habitual grace which is permanent in us.*

2025 *We can have merit in God's sight only because of God's free plan to associate man with the work of his grace. Merit is to be ascribed in the first place to the grace of God, and secondly to man's collaboration. Man's merit is due to God.*

2026 *The grace of the Holy Spirit can confer true merit on us, by virtue of our adoptive filiation, and in accordance with God's gratuitous justice. Charity is the principal source of merit in us before God.*

2027 *No one can merit the initial grace which is at the origin of conversion. Moved by the Holy Spirit, we can merit for ourselves and for others all the graces needed to attain eternal life, as well as necessary temporal goods.*

2028 *'All Christians. . . are called to the fullness of Christian life and to the perfection of charity' (LG 40 §2). 'Christian perfection has but one limit, that of having none' (St Gregory of Nyssa, De vita Mos.: PG 44, 300D).*

2029 *'If any man would come after me, let him deny himself and take up his cross and follow me' (Mt 16:24).*

Article 3
THE CHURCH, MOTHER AND TEACHER

2030 It is in the Church, in communion with all the baptized, that the Christian fulfils his vocation. From the Church he receives the Word of God containing the teachings of 'the law of Christ'.[72] From the Church he receives the grace of the sacraments that sustains him on the 'way'. From the Church he learns the *example of holiness* and recognizes its model and source in the all-holy Virgin Mary; he discerns it in the authentic witness of those who

828 live it; he discovers it in the spiritual tradition and long history of the saints who have gone before him and whom the liturgy cele-

1172 brates in the rhythms of the sanctoral cycle.

2031 *The moral life is spiritual worship.* We 'present [our] bodies as a living sacrifice, holy and acceptable to God',[73] within the Body

1368 of Christ that we form and in communion with the offering of his Eucharist. In the liturgy and the celebration of the sacraments, prayer and teaching are conjoined with the grace of Christ to enlighten and nourish Christian activity. As does the whole of the Christian life, the moral life finds its source and summit in the Eucharistic sacrifice.

85–87, **I. Moral Life and the Magisterium of the Church**

888–892 2032 The Church, the 'pillar and bulwark of the truth', 'has received this solemn command of Christ from the apostles to announce the saving truth.'[74] 'To the Church belongs the right

2246 always and everywhere to announce moral principles, including

2420 those pertaining to the social order, and to make judgements on any human affairs to the extent that they are required by the fundamental rights of the human person or the salvation of souls.'[75]

2033 The *Magisterium of the Pastors of the Church* in moral matters is ordinarily exercised in catechesis and preaching, with the help of the works of theologians and spiritual authors. Thus from generation to generation, under the aegis and vigilance of the pastors, the

84 'deposit' of Christian moral teaching has been handed on, a deposit composed of a characteristic body of rules, commandments and virtues proceeding from faith in Christ and animated by charity. Alongside the Creed and the *Our Father*, the basis for this catechesis

---

[72] *Gal* 6:2.
[73] *Rom* 12:1.

[74] 1 *Tim* 3:15; *LG* 17.
[75] CIC, can. 747 § 2.

has traditionally been the Decalogue which sets out the principles of moral life valid for all men.

2034 The Roman Pontiff and the bishops are 'authentic teachers, that is, teachers endowed with the authority of Christ, who preach the faith to the people entrusted to them, the faith to be believed and put into practice'.[76] The *ordinary* and universal *Magisterium* of the Pope and the bishops in communion with him teaches the faithful the truth to believe, the charity to practise, the beatitude to hope for.

2035 The supreme degree of participation in the authority of Christ is ensured by the charism of *infallibility*. This infallibility extends as far as does the deposit of divine Revelation; it also extends to all those elements of doctrine, including morals, without which the saving truths of the faith cannot be preserved, explained, or observed.[77]

2036 The authority of the Magisterium extends also to the specific precepts of the *natural law*, because their observance, demanded by the Creator, is necessary for salvation. In recalling the prescriptions of the natural law, the Magisterium of the Church exercises an essential part of its prophetic office of proclaiming to men what they truly are and reminding them of what they should be before God.[78]   *1960*

2037 The law of God entrusted to the Church is taught to the faithful as the way of life and truth. The faithful therefore have the *right* to be instructed in the divine saving precepts that purify judgement and, with grace, heal wounded human reason.[79] They have the *duty* of observing the constitutions and decrees conveyed by the legitimate authority of the Church. Even if they concern disciplinary matters, these determinations call for docility in charity.   *2041*

2038 In the work of teaching and applying Christian morality, the Church needs the dedication of pastors, the knowledge of theologians and the contribution of all Christians and men of good will. Faith and the practice of the Gospel provide each person with an experience of life 'in Christ', who enlightens him and makes him able to evaluate the divine and human realities according to the Spirit of God.[80] Thus the Holy Spirit can use the humblest to enlighten the learned and those in the highest positions.   *2442*

---

[76] LG 25.
[77] Cf. LG 25; CDF, Decl. *Mysterium Ecclesiae* 3.
[78] Cf. DH 14.
[79] Cf. CIC, can. 213.
[80] Cf. 1 Cor 2:10-15.

2039 Ministries should be exercised in a spirit of fraternal service and dedication to the Church, in the name of the Lord.[81] At the same time the conscience of each person should avoid confining itself to individualistic considerations in its moral judgements of the person's own acts. As far as possible conscience should take account of the good of all, as expressed in the moral law, natural and revealed, and consequently in the law of the Church and in the authoritative teaching of the Magisterium on moral questions.

1783 Personal conscience and reason should not be set in opposition to the moral law or the Magisterium of the Church.

2040 Thus a true *filial spirit towards the Church* can develop among Christians. It is the normal flowering of the baptismal grace which has begotten us in the womb of the Church and made us members of the Body of Christ. In her motherly care, the Church grants us the mercy of God which prevails over all our sins, and is especially

167 at work in the sacrament of Reconciliation. With a mother's foresight, she also lavishes on us day after day in her liturgy the nourishment of the Word and Eucharist of the Lord.

II. The Precepts of the Church

2041 The precepts of the Church are set in the context of a moral life bound to and nourished by liturgical life. The obligatory character of these positive laws decreed by the pastoral authorities is meant to guarantee to the faithful the very necessary minimum in the spirit of prayer and moral effort, in the growth in love of God and neighbour:

2180 2042 The first precept ('You shall attend Mass on Sundays and on holy days
1389 of obligation and rest from servile labour') requires the faithful to sanctify the day commemorating the Resurrection of the Lord, the Blessed Virgin Mary and the saints; in the first place, by participating in the Eucharistic celebration, in which the Christian community is gathered, and by resting from these works and activities which could impede such a sanctification of these days.[82]

1457 The second precept ('You shall confess your sins at least once a year') ensures preparation for the Eucharist by the reception of the sacrament of Reconciliation, which continues Baptism's work of conversion and forgiveness.[83]

1389 The third precept ('You shall receive the sacrament of the Eucharist at least during the Easter season') guarantees as a minimum the reception of the Lord's Body and Blood in connection with the Paschal feasts, the origin and
2177 centre of the Christian liturgy.[84]

---

[81] Cf. *Rom* 12:8, 11.
[82] Cf. CIC, cann. 1246–1248; CCEO, cann. 880 § 3, 881 §§ 1, 2, 4.
[83] Cf. CIC, can. 989; CCEO, can. 719.
[84] Cf. CIC, can. 920; CCEO, cann. 708; 881 § 3.

2043 The fourth precept ('You shall observe the days of fasting and abstinence *1387* established by the Church') ensures the times of ascesis and penance which *1438* prepare us for the liturgical feasts and help us acquire mastery over our instincts and freedom of heart.[86]

The fifth precept ('You shall help to provide for the needs of the Church') *1351* means that the faithful are obliged to assist with the material needs of the Church, each according to his own ability.[87]

III. Moral Life and Missionary Witness

2044 The fidelity of the baptized is a primordial condition for the proclamation of the Gospel and for the *Church's mission in the* *852, 905* *world*. In order that the message of salvation can show the power of its truth and radiance before men, it must be authenticated by the witness of the life of Christians. 'The witness of a Christian life and good works done in a supernatural spirit have great power to draw men to the faith and to God.'[88]

2045 Because they are members of the Body whose Head is *753* Christ,[89] Christians contribute to *building up the Church* by the constancy of their convictions and their moral lives. The Church increases, grows and develops through the holiness of her faithful, *828* until 'we all attain to the unity of the faith and of the knowledge of the Son of God, to mature manhood, to the measure of the stature of the fullness of Christ.'[90]

2046 By living with the mind of Christ, Christians *hasten the coming of the Reign of God*, 'a kingdom of justice, love and peace'.[91] *671, 2819* They do not, for all that, abandon their earthly tasks; faithful to their master, they fulfil them with uprightness, patience and love.

IN BRIEF

2047 *The moral life is a spiritual worship. Christian activity finds its nourishment in the liturgy and the celebration of the sacraments.*

---

[85] [No note]
[86] Cf. CIC, cann. 1249–1251; CCEO, can. 882.
[87] Cf. CIC, can. 222; CCEO, can. 25. Furthermore, episcopal conferences can establish other ecclesiastical precepts for their own territories (cf. CIC, can. 455).

[88] *AA* 6 § 2.
[89] Cf. *Eph* 1:22.
[90] *Eph* 4:13; cf. *LG* 39.
[91] *Roman Missal*, Preface of Christ the King.

2048   The precepts of the Church concern the moral and Christian life united with the liturgy and nourished by it.

2049   The Magisterium of the Pastors of the Church in moral matters is ordinarily exercised in catechesis and preaching, on the basis of the Decalogue which states the principles of moral life valid for every man.

2050   The Roman Pontiff and the bishops, as authentic teachers, preach to the People of God the faith which is to be believed and applied in moral life. It is also incumbent on them to pronounce on moral questions that fall within the natural law and reason.

2051   The infallibility of the Magisterium of the Pastors extends to all the elements of doctrine, including moral doctrine, without which the saving truths of the faith cannot be preserved, expounded or observed.

THE TEN COMMANDMENTS

Exodus 20:2–17	**Deuteronomy 5:6–21**	**A Traditional Catechetical Formula**
I am the LORD your God, who brought you out of the land of Egypt, out of the house of bondage.	I am the LORD your God, who brought you out of the land of Egypt, out of the house of bondage.	1. I am the LORD your God:
You shall have no other gods before me. You shall not make for yourself a graven image, or any likeness of anything that is in heaven above, or that is in the earth beneath, or that is in the water under the earth; you shall not bow down to them or serve them; for I the LORD your God am a jealous God, visiting the iniquity of the fathers upon the children to the third and the fourth generation of those who hate me, but showing steadfast love to thousands of those who love me and keep my commandments.	You shall have no other gods before me...	you shall not have strange gods before me.
You shall not take the name of the LORD your God in vain; for the LORD will not hold him guiltless who takes his name in vain.	You shall not take the name of the LORD your God in vain:...	2. You shall not take the name of the LORD your God in vain.
Remember the sabbath day, to keep it holy. Six days you shall labour, and do all your work; but the seventh day is a sabbath to the LORD your God; in it you shall not do any work, you, or your son, or your daughter, your manservant, or your maidservant, or	Observe the sabbath day, to keep it holy...	3. Remember to keep holy the Lord's Day.

your cattle, or the sojourner
who is within your gates;
for in six days the LORD
made heaven and earth, the
sea, and all that is in them,
and rested the seventh day;
therefore the LORD blessed
the sabbath day and
hallowed it.

Honour your father and your mother, that your days may be long in the land which the LORD your God gives you.	Honour your father and your mother. . .	4. Honour your father and your mother.
You shall not kill.	You shall not kill.	5. You shall not kill.
You shall not commit adultery.	Neither shall you commit adultery.	6. You shall not commit adultery.
You shall not steal.	Neither shall you steal.	7. You shall not steal.
You shall not bear false witness against your neighbour.	Neither shall you bear false witness against your neighbour.	8. You shall not bear false witness against your neighbour.
You shall not covet your neighbour's house; you shall not covet your neighbour's wife, or his manservant, or his maidservant, or his ox, or his ass, or anything that is your neighbour's.	Neither shall you covet your neighbour's wife. . . You shall not desire. . . anything that is your neighbour's.	9. You shall not covet your neighbour's wife. 10. You shall not covet your neighbour's goods.

Section Two

THE TEN COMMANDMENTS

'Teacher, what must I do...?'

2052 'Teacher, what good deed must I do, to have eternal life?' To the young man who asked this question, Jesus answers first by invoking the necessity to recognize God as the 'One there is who is good', as the supreme Good and the source of all good. Then Jesus tells him: 'If you would enter life, keep the commandments.' And he cites for his questioner the precepts that concern love of neigh- 1858 bour: 'You shall not kill, You shall not commit adultery, You shall not steal, You shall not bear false witness, Honour your father and mother.' Finally Jesus sums up these commandments positively: 'You shall love your neighbour as yourself.'[1]

2053 To this first reply Jesus adds a second: 'If you would be perfect, go, sell what you possess and give to the poor, and you will have treasure in heaven; and come, follow me.'[2] This reply does not do away with the first: following Jesus Christ involves keeping the Commandments. The Law has not been abolished,[3] but rather man is invited to rediscover it in the person of his Master who is its perfect fulfilment. In the three synoptic Gospels, Jesus' 1968 call to the rich young man to follow him, in the obedience of a disciple and in the observance of the Commandments, is joined to the call to poverty and chastity.[4] The evangelical counsels are 1973 inseparable from the Commandments.

2054 Jesus acknowledged the Ten Commandments, but he also showed the power of the Spirit at work in their letter. He preached a 'righteousness [which] exceeds that of the scribes and Pharisees'[5] 581 as well as that of the Gentiles.[6] He unfolded all the demands of the Commandments. 'You have heard that it was said to the men of old, "You shall not kill"... But I say to you that every one who is angry with his brother shall be liable to judgement.'[7]

2055 When someone asks him, 'Which commandment in the Law is the greatest?'[8] Jesus replies: 'You shall love the Lord your 129 God with all your heart, and with all your soul, and with all your

---

[1] Mt 19:16-19.
[2] Mt 19:21.
[3] Cf. Mt 5:17.
[4] Cf. Mt 19:6-12, 21, 23-29.

[5] Mt 5:20.
[6] Cf. Mt 5:46-47.
[7] Mt 5:21-22.
[8] Mt 22:36.

mind. This is the greatest and first commandment. And a second is like it: You shall love your neighbour as yourself. On these two commandments hang all the Law and the prophets.'[9] The Decalogue must be interpreted in light of this twofold yet single commandment of love, the fullness of the Law:

> The commandments: 'You shall not commit adultery, You shall not kill, You shall not steal, You shall not covet', and any other commandment, are summed up in this sentence: 'You shall love your neighbour as yourself.' Love does no wrong to a neighbour; therefore love is the fulfilling of the law.[10]

The Decalogue in Sacred Scripture

2056 The word 'Decalogue' means literally 'ten words'.[11] God revealed these 'ten words' to his people on the holy mountain.
700 They were written 'with the finger of God',[12] unlike the other commandments written by Moses.[13] They are pre-eminently the
62 words of God. They are handed on to us in the books of *Exodus*[14] and *Deuteronomy*.[15] Beginning with the Old Testament, the sacred books refer to the 'ten words',[16] but it is in the New Covenant in Jesus Christ that their full meaning will be revealed.

2057 The Decalogue must first be understood in the context of
2084 the Exodus, God's great liberating event at the centre of the Old Covenant. Whether formulated as negative commandments, prohibitions, or as positive precepts such as: 'Honour your father and mother', the 'ten words' point out the conditions of a life freed from the slavery of sin. The Decalogue is a path of life:

> If you love the LORD your God, by walking in his ways, and by keeping his commandments and his statutes and his ordinances, then you shall live and multiply.[17]

2170   This liberating power of the Decalogue appears, for example, in the commandment about the sabbath rest, directed also to foreigners and slaves:

> You shall remember that you were a servant in the land of Egypt, and the LORD your God brought you out thence with a mighty hand and an outstretched arm.[18]

---

[9] Mt 22:37–40; cf. Dt 6:5; Lev 19:18.
[10] Rom 13:9–10.
[11] Ex 34:28; Dt 4:13; 10:4.
[12] Ex 31:18; Dt 5:22.
[13] Cf. Dt 31:9, 24.
[14] Cf. Ex 20:1–17.

[15] Cf. Dt 5:6–22.
[16] Cf. for example Hos 4:2; Jer 7:9; Ezek 18:5–9.
[17] Dt 30:16.
[18] Dt 5:15.

2058 The 'ten words' sum up and proclaim God's law: 'These 1962
words the LORD spoke to all your assembly at the mountain out of
the midst of the fire, the cloud, and the thick darkness, with a loud
voice; and he added no more. And he wrote them upon two tables
of stone, and gave them to me.'[19] For this reason these two tables
are called 'the Testimony'. In fact, they contain the terms of the
covenant concluded between God and his people. These 'tables of
the Testimony' were to be deposited in 'the ark'.[20]

2059 The 'ten words' are pronounced by God in the midst of a
theophany ('The LORD spoke with you face to face at the moun- 707
tain, out of the midst of the fire'[21]). They belong to God's revelation of himself and his glory The gift of the Commandments is
the gift of God himself and his holy will. In making his will 2823
known, God reveals himself to his people.

2060 The gift of the Commandments and of the Law is part of the
covenant God sealed with his own. In *Exodus*, the revelation of the
'ten words' is granted between the proposal of the covenant[22] and
its conclusion — after the people had committed themselves to 'do'
all that the Lord had said, and to 'obey' it.[23] The Decalogue is
never handed on without first recalling the covenant ('The LORD 62
our God made a covenant with us in Horeb').[24]

2061 The Commandments take on their full meaning within the
covenant. According to Scripture, man's moral life has all its
meaning in and through the covenant. The first of the 'ten words'
recalls that God loved his people first:

> Since there was a passing from the paradise of freedom to the slavery of
> this world, in punishment for sin, the first phrase of the Decalogue, the
> first word of God's commandments, bears on freedom: 'I am the LORD 2086
> your God, who brought you out of the land of Egypt, out of the house of
> slavery.'[25]

2062 The Commandments properly so-called come in the second
place: they express the implications of belonging to God through
the establishment of the covenant. Moral existence is a *response* to 142
the Lord's loving initiative. It is the acknowledgement and
homage given to God and a worship of thanksgiving. It is co-
operation with the plan God pursues in history.   2002

---

[19] *Dt* 5:22.
[20] *Ex* 25:16; 31:18; 32:15; 34:29; 40:1–2.
[21] *Dt* 5:4.
[22] Cf. *Ex* 19.
[23] Cf. *Ex* 24:7.
[24] *Dt* 5:2.
[25] Origen, *Hom. in Ex.* 8, 1: PG 12, 350;
cf. *Ex* 20:2; *Dt* 5:6.

2063　The covenant and dialogue between God and man are also attested to by the fact that all the obligations are stated in the first person ('I am the Lord') and addressed by God to another personal subject ('you'). In all God's commandments, the *singular* personal pronoun designates the recipient. God makes his will known to 878　each person in particular, at the same time as he makes it known to the whole people:

> The Lord prescribed love towards God and taught justice towards neighbour, so that man would be neither unjust, nor unworthy of God. Thus, through the Decalogue, God prepared man to become his friend and to live in harmony with his neighbour... The words of the Decalogue remain likewise for us Christians. Far from being abolished, they have received amplification and development from the fact of the coming of the Lord in the flesh.[26]

The Decalogue in the Church's Tradition

2064　In fidelity to Scripture and in conformity with the example of Jesus, the Tradition of the Church has acknowledged the primordial importance and significance of the Decalogue.

2065　Ever since St Augustine, the Ten Commandments have occupied a predominant place in the catechesis of baptismal candidates and the faithful. In the fifteenth century, the custom arose of expressing the commandments of the Decalogue in rhymed formulae, easy to memorize and in positive form. They are still in use today. The catechisms of the Church have often expounded Christian morality by following the order of the Ten Commandments.

2066　The division and numbering of the Commandments have varied in the course of history. The present catechism follows the division of the Commandments established by St Augustine, which has become traditional in the Catholic Church. It is also that of the Lutheran confessions. The Greek Fathers worked out a slightly different division, which is found in the Orthodox Churches and Reformed communities.

2067　The Ten Commandments state what is required in the love 1853　of God and love of neighbour. The first three concern love of God, and the other seven love of neighbour.

> As charity comprises the two commandments to which the Lord related the whole Law and the prophets... so the Ten Commandments were themselves given on two tablets. Three were written on one tablet and seven on the other.[27]

2068　The Council of Trent teaches that the Ten Commandments 1993　are obligatory for Christians and that the justified man is still bound to keep them;[28] the Second Vatican Council confirms: 'The

---

[26] St Irenaeus, *Adv. haeres.* 4, 16, 3–4: PG 7/1, 1017–1018.
[27] St Augustine, *Sermo* 33, 2, 2: PL 38.
[28] Cf. DS 1569–1570.

bishops, successors of the apostles, receive from the Lord... the
mission of teaching all peoples, and of preaching the Gospel to *888*
every creature, so that all men may attain salvation through faith,
Baptism and the observance of the Commandments.'[29]

The unity of the Decalogue

2069 The Decalogue forms a coherent whole. Each 'word' refers
to each of the others and to all of them; they reciprocally condition
one another. The two tables shed light on one another; they form *2534*
an organic unity. To transgress one commandment is to infringe
all the others.[30] One cannot honour another person without blessing God his Creator. One cannot adore God without loving all
men, his creatures. The Decalogue brings man's religious and
social life into unity.

The Decalogue and the natural law

2070 The Ten Commandments belong to God's revelation. At *1955*
the same time they teach us the true humanity of man. They bring
to light the essential duties, and therefore, indirectly, the fundamental rights inherent in the nature of the human person. The
Decalogue contains a privileged expression of the natural law:

> From the beginning, God had implanted in the heart of man the precepts
> of the natural law. Then he was content to remind him of them. This was
> the Decalogue.[31]

2071 The commandments of the Decalogue, although accessible
to reason alone, have been revealed. To attain a complete and
certain understanding of the requirements of the natural law,
sinful humanity needed this revelation: *1960*

> A full explanation of the commandments of the Decalogue became
> necessary in the state of sin because the light of reason was obscured and
> the will had gone astray.[32]

We know God's commandments through the divine revelation proposed to us in the Church, and through the voice of
moral conscience. *1777*

The obligation of the Decalogue

2072 Since they express man's fundamental duties towards God
and towards his neighbour, the Ten Commandments reveal, in
their primordial content, *grave* obligations. They are fundamen- *1858*
tally immutable, and they oblige always and everywhere. No one *1958*

[29] LG 24.
[30] Cf. Jas 2:10–11.
[31] St Irenaeus, *Adv. haeres.* 4, 15, 1: PG
7/I, 1012.
[32] St Bonaventure, *In IV sent.* 37, 1, 3.

can dispense from them. The Ten Commandments are engraved by God in the human heart.

2073 Obedience to the Commandments also implies obligations in matter which is, in itself, light. Thus abusive language is forbidden by the fifth commandment, but would be a grave offence only as a result of circumstances or the offender's intention.

'Apart from me you can do nothing'

2074 Jesus says: 'I am the vine, you are the branches. He who abides in me, and I in him, he it is that bears much fruit, for apart *2732* from me you can do nothing.'[33] The fruit referred to in this saying is the holiness of a life made fruitful by union with Christ. When *521* we believe in Jesus Christ, partake of his mysteries and keep his commandments, the Saviour himself comes to love, in us, his Father and his brethren, our Father and our brethren. His person becomes, through the Spirit, the living and interior rule of our activity. 'This is my commandment, that you love one another as I have loved you.'[34]

IN BRIEF

2075 *'What good deed must I do, to have eternal life?' – 'If you would enter into life, keep the commandments' (Mt 19:16–17).*

2076 *By his life and by his preaching Jesus attested to the permanent validity of the Decalogue.*

2077 *The gift of the Decalogue is bestowed from within the covenant concluded by God with his people. God's commandments take on their true meaning in and through this covenant.*

2078 *In fidelity to Scripture and in conformity with Jesus' example, the tradition of the Church has always acknowledged the primordial importance and significance of the Decalogue.*

2079 *The Decalogue forms an organic unity in which each 'word' or 'commandment' refers to all the others taken together. To transgress one commandment is to infringe the whole Law (cf. Jas 2:10–11).*

2080 *The Decalogue contains a privileged expression of the natural law. It is made known to us by divine revelation and by human reason.*

2081 *The Ten Commandments, in their fundamental content, state grave obligations. However, obedience to these precepts also implies obligations in matter which is, in itself, light.*

2082 *What God commands he makes possible by his grace.*

---

[33] Jn 15:5.   [34] Jn 15:12.

Chapter One

'YOU SHALL LOVE THE LORD YOUR GOD WITH ALL YOUR HEART, AND WITH ALL YOUR SOUL, AND WITH ALL YOUR MIND'

2083 Jesus summed up man's duties toward God in this saying: 'You shall love the Lord your God with all your heart, and with all *367* your soul, and with all your mind.'[1] This immediately echoes the solemn call: 'Hear, O Israel: the LORD our God is one LORD.'[2]

God has loved us first. The love of the One God is recalled in the first of the 'ten words'. The Commandments then make expli- *199* cit the response of love that man is called to give to his God.

Article 1
THE FIRST COMMANDMENT

> I am the LORD your God, who brought you out of the land of Egypt, out of the house of bondage. You shall have no other gods before me. You shall not make for yourself a graven image, or any likeness of anything that is in heaven above, or that is in the earth beneath, or that is in the water under the earth; you shall not bow down to them or serve them.[3]
>
> It is written: 'You shall worship the Lord your God and him only shall you serve.'[4]

I. 'You Shall Worship the Lord Your God and Him Only Shall You Serve'

2084 God makes himself known by recalling his all-powerful, loving and liberating action in the history of the one he addresses: 'I brought you out of the land of Egypt, out of the house of bondage.' The first word contains the first commandment of the *2057* Law: 'You shall fear the LORD your God; you shall serve him... You shall not go after other gods.'[5] God's first call and just demand *398* is that man accept him and worship him.

2085 The one and true God first reveals his glory to Israel.[6] The revelation of the vocation and truth of man is linked to the revel- *200* ation of God. Man's vocation is to make God manifest by acting in conformity with his creation 'in the image and likeness of God': *1701*

---

[1] *Mt* 22:37; cf. *Lk* 10:27: '... and with all your strength'.
[2] *Dt* 6:4.
[3] *Ex* 20:2–5; cf. *Dt* 5:6–9.
[4] *Mt* 4:10.
[5] *Dt* 6:13–14.
[6] Cf. *Ex* 19:16–25; 24:15–18.

There will never be another God, Trypho, and there has been no other since the world began... than he who made and ordered the universe. We do not think that our God is different from yours. He is the same who brought your fathers out of Egypt 'by his powerful hand and his outstretched arm'. We do not place our hope in some other god, for there is none, but in the same God as you do: the God of Abraham, Isaac and Jacob.[7]

2086 'The first commandment embraces faith, hope and charity.
212 When we say "God" we confess a constant, unchangeable being, always the same, faithful and just, without any evil. It follows that we must necessarily accept his words and have complete faith in him, and acknowledge his authority. He is almighty, merciful and infinitely beneficent... Who could not place all hope in him? Who could not love him when contemplating the treasures of goodness and love he has poured out on us? Hence the formula God employs in the Scripture at the beginning and end of his
2061 commandments: "I am the LORD".'[8]

1814–1816 **Faith**

2087 Our moral life has its source in faith in God who reveals his
143 love to us. St Paul speaks of the 'obedience of faith'[9] as our first obligation. He shows that 'ignorance of God' is the principle and explanation of all moral deviations.[10] Our duty toward God is to believe in him and to bear witness to him.

2088 The first commandment requires us to nourish and protect our faith with prudence and vigilance, and to reject everything that is opposed to it. There are various ways of sinning against faith:
157   *Voluntary doubt* about the faith disregards or refuses to hold as true what God has revealed and the Church proposes for belief. *Involuntary doubt* refers to hesitation in believing, difficulty in overcoming objections connected with the faith, or also anxiety aroused by its obscurity. If deliberately cultivated, doubt can lead to spiritual blindness.

162 2089 *Incredulity* is the neglect of revealed truth or the wilful refu-
817 sal to assent to it. '*Heresy* is the obstinate post-baptismal denial of some truth which must be believed with divine and catholic faith, or it is likewise an obstinate doubt concerning the same; *apostasy* is the total repudiation of the Christian faith; *schism* is the refusal of

---

[7] St Justin, *Dial. cum Tryphone Judaeo*
II, I: PG 6, 497.
[8] *Roman Catechism* III, 2, 4.

[9] *Rom* 1:5; 16:26.
[10] Cf. *Rom* 1:18–32.

submission to the Roman Pontiff or of communion with the members of the Church subject to him.'[11]

Hope

1817–1821

2090 When God reveals Himself and calls him, man cannot fully respond to the divine love by his own powers. He must hope that God will give him the capacity to love Him in return and to act in *1996* conformity with the commandments of charity. Hope is the confident expectation of divine blessing and the beatific vision of God; it is also the fear of offending God's love and of incurring punishment.

2091 The first commandment is also concerned with sins against hope, namely, despair and presumption:

By *despair*, man ceases to hope for his personal salvation from God, for help in attaining it or for the forgiveness of his sins. *1864* Despair is contrary to God's goodness, to his justice – for the Lord is faithful to his promises – and to his mercy.

2092 There are two kinds of *presumption*. Either man presumes upon his own capacities (hoping to be able to save himself without help from on high), or he presumes upon God's almighty *2732* power or his mercy (hoping to obtain his forgiveness without conversion, and glory without merit).

Charity

1822–1829

2093 Faith in God's love encompasses the call and the obligation to respond with sincere love to divine charity. The first commandment enjoins us to love God above everything and all creatures for him and because of him.[12]

2094 One can sin against God's love in various ways:
– *indifference* neglects or refuses to reflect on divine charity; it fails to consider its prevenient goodness and denies its power;
– *ingratitude* fails or refuses to acknowledge divine charity and to return him love for love;
– *lukewarmness* is hesitation or negligence in responding to divine love; it can imply refusal to give oneself over to the prompting of charity;
– *acedia* or spiritual sloth goes so far as to refuse the joy that comes *2733* from God and to be repelled by divine goodness;
– *hatred of God* comes from pride. It is contrary to love of God, *2303*

---

[11] CIC, can. 751: emphasis added.   [12] Cf. *Dt* 6:4–5.

whose goodness it denies, and whom it presumes to curse as the one who forbids sins and inflicts punishments.

II. 'Him Only Shall You Serve'

2095   The theological virtues of faith, hope and charity inform and give life to the moral virtues. Thus charity leads us to render to God what we as creatures owe him in all justice. The *virtue of* 1807 *religion* disposes us to have this attitude.

2628 Adoration

2096   Adoration is the first act of the virtue of religion. To adore God is to acknowledge him as God, as the Creator and Saviour, the Lord and Master of everything that exists, as infinite and merciful Love. 'You shall worship the Lord your God, and him only shall you serve', says Jesus, citing *Deuteronomy*.[13]

2807   2097   To adore God is to acknowledge, in respect and absolute submission, the 'nothingness of the creature' who would not exist but for God. To adore God is to praise and exalt him and to humble oneself, as Mary did in the *Magnificat*, confessing with gratitude that he has done great things and holy is his name.[14] The worship of the one God sets man free from turning in on himself, from the slavery of sin and the idolatry of the world.

2558 Prayer

2098   The acts of faith, hope and charity enjoined by the first commandment are accomplished in prayer. Lifting up the mind towards God is an expression of our adoration of God: prayer of praise and thanksgiving, intercession and petition. Prayer is an indispensable condition for being able to obey God's command-
2742   ments. '[We] ought always to pray and not lose heart.'[15]

Sacrifice

2099   It is right to offer sacrifice to God as a sign of adoration and gratitude, supplication and communion: 'Every action done so as to cling to God in communion of holiness, and thus achieve bless-
613   edness, is a true sacrifice.'[16]

2100   Outward sacrifice, to be genuine, must be the expression of 2711 spiritual sacrifice: 'The sacrifice acceptable to God is a broken spirit...'[17] The prophets of the Old Covenant often denounced

---

[13] *Lk* 4:8; cf. *Dt* 6:13.
[14] Cf. *Lk* 1:46–49.
[15] *Lk* 18:1.

[16] St Augustine, *De civ. Dei* 10, 6: PL 41, 283.
[17] *Ps* 51:17.

sacrifices that were not from the heart or not coupled with love of neighbour.[18] Jesus recalls the words of the prophet Hosea: 'I desire mercy, and not sacrifice.'[19] The only perfect sacrifice is the one that Christ offered on the cross as a total offering to the Father's *614, 618* love and for our salvation.[20] By uniting ourselves with his sacrifice we can make our lives a sacrifice to God.

Promises and vows

2101 In many circumstances, the Christian is called to make *promises* to God. Baptism and Confirmation, Matrimony and Holy *1237* Orders always entail promises. Out of personal devotion, the Christian may also promise to God this action, that prayer, this alms-giving, that pilgrimage, and so forth. Fidelity to promises *1064* made to God is a sign of the respect owed to the divine majesty and of love for a faithful God.

2102 'A *vow* is a deliberate and free promise made to God concerning a possible and better good which must be fulfilled by reason of the virtue of religion.'[21] A vow is an act of *devotion* in which the Christian dedicates himself to God or promises him some good work. By fulfilling his vows he renders to God what has been promised and consecrated to Him. The *Acts of the Apostles* shows us St Paul concerned to fulfil the vows he had made.[22]

2103 The Church recognizes an exemplary value in the vows to practise the *evangelical counsels*:[23]

1973

> Mother Church rejoices that she has within herself many men and women who pursue the Saviour's self-emptying more closely and show it forth more clearly, by undertaking poverty with the freedom of the children of God, and renouncing their own will: they submit themselves *914* to man for the sake of God, thus going beyond what is of precept in the matter of perfection, so as to conform themselves more fully to the obedient Christ.[24]

> The Church can, in certain cases and for proportionate reasons, dispense from vows and promises.[25]

The social duty of religion and the right to religious freedom

2104 'All men are bound to seek the truth, especially in what *2467* concerns God and his Church, and to embrace it and hold on to it

---

[18] Cf. *Am* 5:21–25; *Is* 1:10–20.
[19] *Mt* 9:13; 12:7; cf. *Hos* 6:6.
[20] Cf. *Heb* 9:13–14.
[21] CIC, can. 1191 § 1.

[22] Cf. *Acts* 18:18; 21:23–24.
[23] Cf. CIC, can. 654.
[24] *LG* 42 § 2.
[25] Cf. CIC, cann. 692; 1196–1197.

as they come to know it.'[26] This duty derives from 'the very dignity of the human person'.[27] It does not contradict a 'sincere

851 respect' for different religions which frequently 'reflect a ray of that truth which enlightens all men',[28] nor the requirement of charity, which urges Christians 'to treat with love, prudence and patience those who are in error or ignorance with regard to the faith'.[29]

2105 The duty of offering God genuine worship concerns man both individually and socially. This is 'the traditional Catholic teaching on the moral duty of individuals and societies toward the true religion and the one Church of Christ'.[30] By constantly evangelizing men, the Church works toward enabling them 'to

854 infuse the Christian spirit into the mentality and mores, laws and structures of the communities in which [they] live'.[31] The social

898 duty of Christians is to respect and awaken in each man the love of the true and the good. It requires them to make known the worship of the one true religion which subsists in the Catholic and apostolic Church.[32] Christians are called to be the light of the world. Thus, the Church shows forth the kingship of Christ over all creation and in particular over human societies.[33]

160 2106 'Nobody may be forced to act against his convictions, nor is anyone to be restrained from acting in accordance with his con-
1782, 1738 science in religious matters in private or in public, alone or in association with others, within due limits.'[34] This right is based on the very nature of the human person, whose dignity enables him freely to assent to the divine truth which transcends the temporal order. For this reason it 'continues to exist even in those who do not live up to their obligation of seeking the truth and adhering to it.'[35]

2107 'If because of the circumstances of a particular people special civil recognition is given to one religious community in the constitutional organization of a state, the right of all citizens and religious communities to religious freedom must be recognized and respected as well.'[36]

1740 2108 The right to religious liberty is neither a moral licence to

---

[26] DH 1 § 2.
[27] DH 2 § 1.
[28] NA 2 § 2.
[29] DH 14 § 4.
[30] DH 1 § 3.
[31] AA 13 § 1.

[32] Cf. DH 1.
[33] Cf. AA 13; Leo XIII, Immortale Dei 3.
       17; Pius XI, Quas primas 8, 20.
[34] DH 2 § 1.
[35] DH 2 § 2.
[36] DH 6 § 3.

adhere to error, nor a supposed right to error,[37] but rather a natural right of the human person to civil liberty, i.e., immunity, within just limits, from external constraint in religious matters by political authorities. This natural right ought to be acknowledged in the juridical order of society in such a way that it constitutes a civil right.[38]

2109 The right to religious liberty can of itself be neither unlimited nor limited   2244
only by a 'public order' conceived in a positivist or naturalist manner.[39] The
'due limits' which are inherent in it must be determined for each social situation
by political prudence, according to the requirements of the common good, and   1906
ratified by the civil authority in accordance with 'legal principles which are in
conformity with the objective moral order'.[40]

III. 'You Shall Have No Other Gods Before Me'

2110 The first commandment forbids honouring gods other than the one Lord who has revealed himself to his people. It proscribes superstition and irreligion. Superstition in some sense represents a perverse excess of religion; irreligion is the vice contrary by defect to the virtue of religion.

Superstition

2111 Superstition is the deviation of religious feeling and of the practices this feeling imposes. It can even affect the worship we offer the true God, e.g., when one attributes an importance in some way magical to certain practices otherwise lawful or necessary. To attribute the efficacy of prayers or of sacramental signs to their mere external performance, apart from the interior dispositions that they demand, is to fall into superstition.[41]

Idolatry

2112 The first commandment condemns polytheism. It requires man neither to believe in, nor to venerate, other divinities than the one true God. Scripture constantly recalls this rejection of 'idols,   210
[of] silver and gold, the work of men's hands. They have mouths, but do not speak; eyes, but do not see.' These empty idols make their worshippers empty: 'Those who make them are like them; so

---

[37] Cf. Leo XIII, Libertas praestantissimum
    18; Pius XII, Discourse, 6 December
    1953: AAS 1953, 799.
[38] Cf. DH 2.

[39] Cf. Pius VI, Quod aliquantum (1791)
    10; Pius IX, Quanta cura 3.
[40] DH 7 § 3.
[41] Cf. Mt 23:16–22.

are all who trust in them.'[42] God, however, is the 'living God'[43] who gives life and intervenes in history.

2113 Idolatry not only refers to false pagan worship. It remains a constant temptation to faith. Idolatry consists in divinizing what is *398, 2534* not God. Man commits idolatry whenever he honours and reveres *2289* a creature in place of God, whether this be gods or demons (for example, satanism), power, pleasure, race, ancestors, the state, money, etc. Jesus says, 'You cannot serve God and mammon.'[44] *2473* Many martyrs died for not adoring 'the Beast',[45] refusing even to simulate such worship. Idolatry rejects the unique Lordship of God; it is therefore incompatible with communion with God.[46]

2114 Human life finds its unity in the adoration of the one God. The commandment to worship the Lord alone integrates man and saves him from an endless disintegration. Idolatry is a perversion of man's innate religious sense. An idolater is someone who 'transfers his indestructible notion of God to anything other than God'.[47]

Divination and magic

2115 God can reveal the future to his prophets or to other saints. Still, a sound Christian attitude consists in putting oneself confi-*305* dently into the hands of Providence for whatever concerns the future, and giving up all unhealthy curiosity about it. Improvidence, however, can constitute a lack of responsibility.

2116 All forms of *divination* are to be rejected: recourse to Satan or demons, conjuring up the dead or other practices falsely supposed to 'unveil' the future.[48] Consulting horoscopes, astrology, palm reading, interpretation of omens and lots, the phenomena of clairvoyance, and recourse to mediums all conceal a desire for power over time, history and, in the last analysis, other human beings, as well as a wish to conciliate hidden powers. They contradict the honour, respect and loving fear that we owe to God alone.

2117 All practices of *magic* or *sorcery*, by which one attempts to tame occult powers, so as to place them at one's service and have a supernatural power over others – even if this were for the sake of restoring their health – are gravely contrary to the virtue of religion. These practices are even more to be condemned when

---

[42] *Ps* 115:4–5, 8; cf. *Is* 44:9–20; *Jer* 10:1–16; *Dan* 14:1–30; *Bar* 6; *Wis* 13:1 – 15:19.
[43] *Josh* 3:10; *Ps* 42:3; etc.
[44] *Mt* 6:24.

[45] Cf. *Rev* 13 – 14.
[46] Cf. *Gal* 5:20; *Eph* 5:5.
[47] Origen, *Contra Celsum* 2, 40: PG 11, 861.
[48] Cf. *Dt* 18:10; *Jer* 29:8.

accompanied by the intention of harming someone, or when they
have recourse to the intervention of demons. Wearing charms is
also reprehensible. *Spiritism* often implies divination or magical
practices; the Church for her part warns the faithful against it.
Recourse to so-called traditional cures does not justify either
the invocation of evil powers, or the exploitation of another's
credulity.

Irreligion

2118 God's first commandment condemns the main sins of irreligion: tempting God, in words or deeds, sacrilege and simony.

2119 *Tempting God* consists in putting his goodness and almighty
power to the test by word or deed. Thus Satan tried to induce Jesus *394*
to throw himself down from the Temple and, by this gesture,
force God to act.[49] Jesus opposed Satan with the word of God:
'You shall not put the LORD your God to the test.'[50] The challenge
contained in such tempting of God wounds the respect and trust
we owe our Creator and Lord. It always harbours doubt about his *2088*
love, his providence and his power.[51]

2120 *Sacrilege* consists in profaning or treating unworthily the
sacraments and other liturgical actions, as well as persons, things or
places consecrated to God. Sacrilege is a grave sin especially when
committed against the Eucharist, for in this sacrament the true *1374*
Body of Christ is made substantially present for us.[52]

2121 *Simony* is defined as the buying or selling of spiritual
things.[53] To Simon the magician, who wanted to buy the spiritual
power he saw at work in the apostles, St Peter responded: 'Your
silver perish with you, because you thought you could obtain
God's gift with money!'[54] Peter thus held to the words of Jesus:
'You received without pay, give without pay.'[55] It is impossible to
appropriate to oneself spiritual goods and behave towards them as *1578*
their owner or master, for they have their source in God. One can
receive them only from him, without payment.

2122 'The minister should ask nothing for the administration of the sacraments
beyond the offerings defined by the competent authority, always being careful
that the needy are not deprived of the help of the sacraments because of their
poverty.'[56] The competent authority determines these 'offerings' in accordance

---

[49] Cf. *Lk* 4:9.
[50] *Dt* 6:16.
[51] Cf. 1 *Cor* 10:9; *Ex* 17:2–7; *Ps* 95:9.
[52] Cf. CIC, cann. 1367; 1376.

[53] Cf. *Acts* 8:9–24.
[54] *Acts* 8:20.
[55] *Mt* 10:8; cf. already *Is* 55:1.
[56] CIC, can. 848.

with the principle that the Christian people ought to contribute to the support of the Church's ministers. 'The labourer deserves his food.'[57]

Atheism

2123 'Many... of our contemporaries either do not at all per-
29 ceive, or explicitly reject, this intimate and vital bond of man to God. Atheism must therefore be regarded as one of the most serious problems of our time.'[58]

2124 The name 'atheism' covers many very different phenomena. One common form is the practical materialism which restricts its needs and aspirations to space and time. Atheistic humanism falsely considers man to be 'an end to himself, and the sole maker, with supreme control, of his own history'.[59] Another form of contemporary atheism looks for the liberation of man through economic and social liberation. 'It holds that religion, of its very nature, thwarts such emancipation by raising man's hopes in a future life, thus both deceiving him and discouraging him from working for a better form of life on earth.'[60]

2125 Since it rejects or denies the existence of God, atheism is a sin
1735 against the virtue of religion.[61] The imputability of this offence can be significantly diminished in virtue of the intentions and the circumstances. 'Believers can have more than a little to do with the rise of atheism. To the extent that they are careless about their instruction in the faith, or present its teaching falsely, or even fail in their religious, moral, or social life, they must be said to conceal rather than to reveal the true nature of God and of religion.'[62]

2126 Atheism is often based on a false conception of human
396 autonomy, exaggerated to the point of refusing any dependence
154 on God.[63] Yet, 'to acknowledge God is in no way to oppose the dignity of man, since such dignity is grounded and brought to perfection in God...'[64] 'For the Church knows full well that her message is in harmony with the most secret desires of the human heart.'[65]

Agnosticism

2127 Agnosticism assumes a number of forms. In certain cases the agnostic refrains from denying God; instead he postulates the

---

[57] Mt 10:10; cf. Lk 10:7; 1 Cor 9:5–18; 1 Tim 5:17–18.
[58] GS 19 § 1.
[59] GS 20 § 1.
[60] GS 20 § 2.
[61] Cf. Rom 1:18.
[62] GS 19 § 3.
[63] Cf. GS 20 § 1.
[64] GS 21 § 3.
[65] GS 21 § 7.

existence of a transcendent being which is incapable of revealing itself, and about which nothing can be said. In other cases, the agnostic makes no judgement about God's existence, declaring it *36* impossible to prove, or even to affirm or deny.

2128 Agnosticism can sometimes include a certain search for God, but it can equally express indifferentism, a flight from the ultimate *1036* question of existence, and a sluggish moral conscience. Agnosticism is all too often equivalent to practical atheism.

IV. 'You Shall Not Make for Yourself a Graven Image...' *1159–1162*

2129 The divine injunction included the prohibition of every representation of God by the hand of man. *Deuteronomy* explains: 'Since you saw no form on the day that the LORD spoke to you at Horeb out of the midst of the fire, beware lest you act corruptly by making a graven image for yourselves, in the form of any figure...'[66] It is the absolutely transcendent God who revealed himself to Israel. 'He is the all', but at the same time 'he is greater *300* than all his works.'[67] He is 'the author of beauty'.[68] *2500*

2130 Nevertheless, already in the Old Testament, God ordained or permitted the making of images that pointed symbolically toward salvation by the incarnate Word: so it was with the bronze serpent, the ark of the covenant and the cherubim.[69]

2131 Basing itself on the mystery of the incarnate Word the seventh ecumenical council, at Nicaea (787), justified against the iconoclasts the veneration of icons – of Christ, but also of the *476* Mother of God, the angels, and all the saints. By becoming incarnate, the Son of God introduced a new 'economy' of images.

2132 The Christian veneration of images is not contrary to the first commandment, which proscribes idols. Indeed, 'the honour rendered to an image passes to its prototype', and 'whoever venerates an image venerates the person portrayed in it.'[70] The honour paid to sacred images is a 'respectful veneration', not the adoration due to God alone:

> Religious worship is not directed to images in themselves, considered as mere things, but under their distinctive aspect as images leading us on to

---

[66] Dt 4:15–16.
[67] Sir 43:27–28.
[68] Wis 13:3.
[69] Cf. Num 21:4–9; Wis 16:5–14; Jn 3:14–15; Ex 25:10–22; 1 Kings 6:23–28; 7:23–26.

[70] St Basil, *De Spiritu Sancto* 18, 45: PG 32, 149C; Council of Nicaea II: DS 601; cf. Council of Trent: DS 1821–1825; Vatican Council II: SC 126; LG 67.

God incarnate. The movement towards the image does not terminate in it as image, but tends towards that whose image it is.[71]

IN BRIEF

2133   '*You shall love the LORD your God with all your heart, and with all your soul and with all your strength*' *(Dt 6:5).*

2134   *The first commandment summons man to believe in God, to hope in him and to love him above all else.*

2135   '*You shall worship the Lord your God*' *(Mt 4:10). Adoring God, praying to him, offering him the worship that belongs to him, fulfilling the promises and vows made to him, are acts of the virtue of religion which fall under obedience to the first commandment.*

2136   *The duty to offer God authentic worship concerns man both as an individual and as a social being.*

2137   '*Men of the present day want to profess their religion freely in private and in public*' *(DH 15).*

2138   *Superstition is a departure from the worship that we give to the true God. It is manifested in idolatry, as well as in various forms of divination and magic.*

2139   *Tempting God in words or deeds, sacrilege and simony are sins of irreligion forbidden by the first commandment.*

2140   *Since it rejects or denies the existence of God, atheism is a sin against the first commandment.*

2141   *The veneration of sacred images is based on the mystery of the Incarnation of the Word of God. It is not contrary to the first commandment.*

Article 2
THE SECOND COMMANDMENT

You shall not take the name of the LORD your God in vain.[72]

You have heard that it was said to the men of old, 'You shall not swear falsely...' But I say to you, Do not swear at all.[73]

2807–2815   ## I. The Name of the Lord Is Holy

2142   The second commandment *prescribes respect for the Lord's name*. Like the first commandment, it belongs to the virtue of religion and more particularly it governs our use of speech in sacred matters.

---

[71] St Thomas Aquinas, *STh* II–II, 81, 3, ad 3.

[72] *Ex* 20:7; *Dt* 5:11.

[73] *Mt* 5:33–34.

2143 Among all the words of Revelation, there is one which is unique: the revealed name of God. God confides his name to those who believe in him; he reveals himself to them in his personal *203* mystery. The gift of a name belongs to the order of trust and intimacy. 'The Lord's name is holy.' For this reason man must not *435* abuse it. He must keep it in mind in silent, loving adoration. He will not introduce it into his own speech except to bless, praise and glorify it.[74]

2144 Respect for his name is an expression of the respect owed to the mystery of God himself and to the whole sacred reality it evokes. The *sense of the sacred* is part of the virtue of religion:

> Are these feelings of fear and awe Christian feelings or not?... I say this, then, which I think no one can reasonably dispute. They are the class of feelings we *should* have – yes, have to an intense degree – if we literally had the sight of Almighty God; therefore they are the class of feelings which we shall have, *if* we realize His presence. In proportion as we believe that He is present, we shall have them; and not to have them, is not to realize, not to believe that He is present.[75]

2145 The faithful should bear witness to the Lord's name by con- *2472* fessing the faith without giving way to fear.[76] Preaching and *427* catechizing should be permeated with adoration and respect for the name of our Lord Jesus Christ.

2146 The second commandment *forbids the abuse of God's name*, i.e., every improper use of the names of God, of Jesus Christ, but also of the Virgin Mary and all the saints.

2147 *Promises* made to others in God's name engage the divine *2101* honour, fidelity, truthfulness and authority. They must be respected in justice. To be unfaithful to them is to misuse God's name and in some way to make God out to be a liar.[77]

2148 *Blasphemy* is directly opposed to the second commandment. *1756* It consists in uttering against God – inwardly or outwardly – words of hatred, reproach, or defiance, in speaking ill of God, in failing in respect toward him in one's speech, in misusing God's name. St James condemns those 'who blaspheme that honourable name [of Jesus] by which you are called'.[78] The prohibition of blasphemy extends to language against Christ's Church, the saints, and sacred things. It is also blasphemous to make use of God's

---

[74] Cf. *Zech* 2:13; *Pss* 29:2; 96:2; 113:1–2.
[75] John Henry Cardinal Newman, *Parochial and Plain Sermons* V, 2 (London: Longmans, Green and Co., 1907), 21–22.
[76] Cf. *Mt* 10:32; 1 *Tim* 6:12.
[77] Cf. 1 *Jn* 1:10.
[78] *Jas* 2:7.

name to cover up criminal practices, to reduce peoples to servitude, to torture persons or put them to death. The misuse of God's name to commit a crime can provoke others to repudiate religion.

Blasphemy is contrary to the respect due to God and his holy name. It is in itself a grave sin.[79]

2149 *Oaths* which misuse God's name, though without the intention of blasphemy, show lack of respect for the Lord. The second commandment also forbids *magical use* of the divine name.

> [God's] name is great when spoken with respect for the greatness of his majesty. God's name is holy when said with veneration and fear of offending him.[80]

II. Taking the Name of the Lord in Vain

2150 The second commandment *forbids false oaths*. Taking an oath or swearing is to take God as witness to what one affirms. It is to invoke the divine truthfulness as a pledge of one's own truthfulness. An oath engages the Lord's name. 'You shall fear the LORD your God; you shall serve him, and swear by his name.'[81]

2151 Rejection of false oaths is a duty toward God. As Creator
215 and Lord, God is the norm of all truth. Human speech is either in accord with or in opposition to God who is Truth itself. When it is truthful and legitimate, an oath highlights the relationship of human speech with God's truth. A false oath calls on God to be witness to a lie.

2476 2152 A person commits *perjury* when he makes a promise under oath with no intention of keeping it, or when after promising on oath he does not keep it. Perjury is a grave lack of respect for the
1756 Lord of all speech. Pledging oneself by oath to commit an evil deed is contrary to the holiness of the divine name.

2153 In the Sermon on the Mount, Jesus explained the second commandment: 'You have heard that it was said to the men of old, "You shall not swear falsely, but shall perform to the Lord what you have sworn." But I say to you, Do not swear at all. . . Let what you say be simply "Yes" or "No"; anything more than this comes from the evil one.'[82] Jesus teaches that every oath involves a refer-
2466 ence to God and that God's presence and his truth must be honoured in all speech. Discretion in calling upon God is allied with a respectful awareness of his presence, which all our assertions either witness to or mock.

---

[79] Cf. CIC, can. 1369.
[80] St Augustine, *De serm. Dom. in monte*
    2, 5, 19: PL 34, 1278.

[81] *Dt* 6:13.
[82] *Mt* 5:33–34, 37; cf. *Jas* 5:12.

2154 Following St Paul,[83] the tradition of the Church has understood Jesus' words as not excluding oaths made for grave and right reasons (for example, in court). 'An oath, that is the invocation of the divine name as a witness to truth, cannot be taken unless in truth, in judgement and in justice.'[84]

2155 The holiness of the divine name demands that we neither use it for trivial matters, nor take an oath which on the basis of the circumstances could be interpreted as approval of an authority unjustly requiring it. When an oath is required by illegitimate civil authorities, it may be refused. It must be refused when it is *1903* required for purposes contrary to the dignity of persons or to ecclesial communion.

III. The Christian Name

2156 The sacrament of Baptism is conferred 'in the name of the *232* Father and of the Son and of the Holy Spirit'.[85] In Baptism, the *1267* Lord's name sanctifies man, and the Christian receives his name in the Church. This can be the name of a saint, that is, of a disciple who has lived a life of exemplary fidelity to the Lord. The patron saint provides a model of charity; we are assured of his intercession. The 'baptismal name' can also express a Christian mystery or Christian virtue. 'Parents, sponsors and the pastor are to see that a name is not given which is foreign to Christian sentiment.'[86]

2157 The Christian begins his day, his prayers and his activities with the Sign of the Cross: 'in the name of the Father and of the *1235* Son and of the Holy Spirit. Amen.' The baptized person dedicates the day to the glory of God and calls on the Saviour's grace which lets him act in the Spirit as a child of the Father. The Sign of the *1668* Cross strengthens us in temptations and difficulties.

2158 God calls each one by name.[87] Everyone's name is sacred. The name is the icon of the person. It demands respect as a sign of the dignity of the one who bears it.

2159 The name one receives is a name for eternity. In the kingdom, the mysterious and unique character of each person marked with God's name will shine forth in splendour. 'To him who conquers... I will give a white stone, with a new name written on the stone which no one knows except him who receives it.'[88] 'Then I looked, and lo, on Mount Zion stood the Lamb, and with

---

[83] Cf. 2 *Cor* 1:23; *Gal* 1:20.
[84] CIC, can. 1199 § 1.
[85] *Mt* 28:19.
[86] CIC, can. 855.
[87] Cf. *Is* 43:1; *Jn* 10:3.
[88] *Rev* 2:17.

him a hundred and forty-four thousand who had his name and his Father's name written on their foreheads.'[89]

IN BRIEF

2160 'O LORD, our Lord, how majestic is your name in all the earth!' (Ps 8:1).

2161 The second commandment enjoins respect for the Lord's name. The name of the Lord is holy.

2162 The second commandment forbids every improper use of God's name. Blasphemy is the use of the name of God, of Jesus Christ, of the Virgin Mary, and of the saints in an offensive way.

2163 False oaths call on God to be witness to a lie. Perjury is a grave offence against the Lord who is always faithful to his promises.

2164 'Do not swear whether by the Creator, or any creature, except truthfully, of necessity and with reverence' (St Ignatius of Loyola, Spiritual Exercises 38).

2165 In Baptism, the Christian receives his name in the Church. Parents, godparents and the pastor are to see that he be given a Christian name. The patron saint provides a model of charity and the assurance of his prayer.

2166 The Christian begins his prayers and activities with the Sign of the Cross: 'in the name of the Father and of the Son and of the Holy Spirit. Amen.'

2167 God calls each one by name (cf. Is 43:1).

Article 3
THE THIRD COMMANDMENT

Remember the sabbath day, to keep it holy. Six days you shall labour, and do all your work; but the seventh day is a sabbath to the LORD your God; in it you shall not do any work.[90]

The sabbath was made for man, not man for the sabbath; so the Son of Man is lord even of the sabbath.[91]

346–348 ## I. The Sabbath Day

2168 The third commandment of the Decalogue recalls the holiness of the sabbath: 'The seventh day is a sabbath of solemn rest, holy to the LORD.'[92]

---

[89] Rev 14:1.
[90] Ex 20:8–10; cf. Dt 5:12–15.
[91] Mk 2:27–28.
[92] Ex 31:15.

2169 In speaking of the sabbath Scripture *recalls creation*: 'For in six days the LORD made heaven and earth, the sea, and all that is in them, and rested the seventh day; therefore the LORD blessed the sabbath day and hallowed it.'[93]

2170 Scripture also reveals in the Lord's day a *memorial of Israel's liberation* from bondage in Egypt: 'You shall remember that you were a servant in the land of Egypt, and the LORD your God brought you out thence with mighty hand and outstretched arm; therefore the LORD your God commanded you to keep the sabbath day.'[94] *2057*

2171 God entrusted the sabbath to Israel to keep as a *sign of the irrevocable covenant*.[95] The sabbath is for the Lord, holy and set apart for the praise of God, his work of creation and his saving actions on behalf of Israel.

2172 God's action is the model for human action. If God 'rested and was refreshed' on the seventh day, man too ought to 'rest' and should let others, especially the poor, 'be refreshed'.[96] The sabbath brings everyday work to a halt and provides a respite. It is a day of protest against the servitude of work and the worship of money.[97] *2184*

2173 The Gospel reports many incidents when Jesus was accused of violating the sabbath law. But Jesus never fails to respect the holiness of this day.[98] He gives this law its authentic and authoritative interpretation: 'The sabbath was made for man, not man for the sabbath.'[99] With compassion, Christ declares the sabbath for doing good rather than harm, for saving life rather than killing.[100] The sabbath is the day of the Lord of mercies and a day to honour God.[101] 'The Son of Man is lord even of the sabbath.'[102] *582*

II. The Lord's Day

This is the day which the LORD has made; let us rejoice and be glad in it.[103]

The day of the Resurrection: the new creation

2174 Jesus rose from the dead 'on the first day of the week'.[104] Because it is the 'first day', the day of Christ's Resurrection recalls *638*

---

[93] *Ex* 20:11.
[94] *Dt* 5:15.
[95] Cf. *Ex* 31:16.
[96] *Ex* 31:17; cf. 23:12.
[97] Cf. *Neh* 13:15–22; 2 *Chr* 36:21.
[98] Cf. *Mk* 1:21; *Jn* 9:16.
[99] *Mk* 2:27.
[100] Cf. *Mk* 3:4.
[101] Cf. *Mt* 12:5; *Jn* 7:23.
[102] *Mk* 2:28.
[103] *Ps* 118:24.
[104] Cf. *Mt* 28:1; *Mk* 16:2; *Lk* 24:1; *Jn* 20:1.

the first creation. Because it is the 'eighth day' following the sab-
349 bath,[105] it symbolizes the new creation ushered in by Christ's
Resurrection. For Christians it has become the first of all days,
the first of all feasts, the Lord's Day (*hē kuriakē hēmera, dies
dominica*) − Sunday:

> We all gather on the day of the sun, for it is the first day [after the Jewish
> sabbath, but also the first day] when God, separating matter from dark-
> ness, made the world; and on this same day Jesus Christ our Saviour rose
> from the dead.[106]

Sunday − fulfilment of the sabbath

2175 Sunday is expressly distinguished from the sabbath which it
follows chronologically every week; for Christians its ceremonial
observance replaces that of the sabbath. In Christ's Passover,
1166 Sunday fulfils the spiritual truth of the Jewish sabbath and announces man's eternal rest in God. For worship under the Law prepared
for the mystery of Christ, and what was done there prefigured
some aspects of Christ:[107]

> Those who lived according to the old order of things have come to a new
> hope, no longer keeping the sabbath, but the Lord's Day, in which our
> life is blessed by him and by his death.[108]

2176 The celebration of Sunday observes the moral commandment inscribed by nature in the human heart to render to God an
outward, visible, public and regular worship 'as a sign of his universal beneficence to all'.[109] Sunday worship fulfils the moral
command of the Old Covenant, taking up its rhythm and spirit in
the weekly celebration of the Creator and Redeemer of his people.

The Sunday Eucharist

1167 2177 The Sunday celebration of the Lord's Day and his Eucharist
is at the heart of the Church's life. 'Sunday is the day on which the
paschal mystery is celebrated in light of the apostolic tradition and
is to be observed as the foremost holy day of obligation in the
universal Church.'[110]

2043   'Also to be observed are the day of the Nativity of Our Lord Jesus Christ,
the Epiphany, the Ascension of Christ, the feast of the Body and Blood of
Christ, the feast of Mary the Mother of God, her Immaculate Conception, her

---

[105] Cf. *Mk* 16:1; *Mt* 28:1.
[106] St Justin, *Apol.* 1, 67: PG 6, 429 and
432.
[107] Cf. 1 *Cor* 10:11.

[108] St Ignatius of Antioch, *Ad Magn.* 9, 1:
SCh 10, 88.
[109] St Thomas Aquinas, *STh* II–II, 122, 4.
[110] CIC, can. 1246 § 1.

Assumption, the feast of Saint Joseph, the feast of the Apostles Saints Peter and Paul, and the feast of All Saints.'[111]

2178 This practice of the Christian assembly dates from the beginnings of the apostolic age.[112] The *Letter to the Hebrews* reminds the faithful 'not to neglect to meet together, as is the habit of some, but to encourage one another'.[113] *1343*

> Tradition preserves the memory of an ever-timely exhortation: Come to Church early, approach the Lord and confess your sins, repent in prayer... Be present at the sacred and divine liturgy, conclude its prayer and do not leave before the dismissal... We have often said: 'This day is given to you for prayer and rest. This is the day that the Lord has made, let us rejoice and be glad in it.'[114]

2179 'A *parish* is a definite community of the Christian faithful established on a stable basis within a particular church; the pastoral care of the parish is entrusted to a pastor as its own shepherd under the authority of the diocesan bishop.'[115] It is the place where all the faithful can be gathered together for the Sunday celebration of the Eucharist. The parish initiates the Christian people into the ordinary expression of the liturgical life: it gathers them together in this celebration; it teaches Christ's saving doctrine; it practises the charity of the Lord in good works and brotherly love: *1567* *2691* *2226*

> You cannot pray at home as at church, where there is a great multitude, where exclamations are cried out to God as from one great heart, and where there is something more: the union of minds, the accord of souls, the bond of charity, the prayers of the priests.[116]

The Sunday obligation

2180 The precept of the Church specifies the law of the Lord more precisely: 'On Sundays and other holy days of obligation the faithful are bound to participate in the Mass.'[117] 'The precept of participating in the Mass is satisfied by assistance at a Mass which is celebrated anywhere in a Catholic rite either on the holy day or on the evening of the preceding day.'[118] *2042* *1389*

2181 The Sunday Eucharist is the foundation and confirmation of all Christian practice. For this reason the faithful are obliged to participate in the Eucharist on days of obligation, unless excused for a serious reason (for example, illness, the care of infants) or

---

[111] CIC, can. 1246 § 2: 'The conference of bishops can abolish certain holy days of obligation or transfer them to a Sunday with prior approval of the Apostolic See.'
[112] Cf. *Acts* 2:42–46; 1 *Cor* 11:17.
[113] *Heb* 10:25.
[114] *Sermo de die dominica* 2 and 6: PG 86/1, 416C and 421C.
[115] CIC, can. 515 § 1.
[116] St John Chrysostom, *De incomprehensibili* 3, 6: PG 48, 725.
[117] CIC, can. 1247.
[118] CIC, can. 1248 § 1.

dispensed by their own pastor.[119] Those who deliberately fail in this obligation commit a grave sin.

2182 Participation in the communal celebration of the Sunday Eucharist is a testimony of belonging and of being faithful to Christ and to his Church. The faithful give witness by this to their *815* communion in faith and charity. Together they testify to God's holiness and their hope of salvation. They strengthen one another under the guidance of the Holy Spirit.

2183 'If because of lack of a sacred minister or for other grave cause participation in the celebration of the Eucharist is impossible, it is specially recommended that the faithful take part in the Liturgy of the Word if it is celebrated in the parish church or in another sacred place according to the prescriptions of the diocesan bishop, or engage in prayer for an appropriate amount of time personally or in a family or, as occasion offers, in groups of families.'[120]

A day of grace and rest from work

2184 Just as God 'rested on the seventh day from all his work *2172* which he had done',[121] human life has a rhythm of work and rest. The institution of the Lord's Day helps everyone enjoy adequate rest and leisure to cultivate their familial, cultural, social and religious lives.[122]

2185 On Sundays and other holy days of obligation, the faithful *2428* are to refrain from engaging in work or activities that hinder the worship owed to God, the joy proper to the Lord's Day, the performance of the works of mercy, and the appropriate relaxation of mind and body.[123] Family needs or important social service can legitimately excuse from the obligation of Sunday rest. The faithful should see to it that legitimate excuses do not lead to habits prejudicial to religion, family life and health.

The charity of truth seeks holy leisure; the necessity of charity accepts just work.[124]

2186 Those Christians who have leisure should be mindful of their brethren who have the same needs and the same rights, yet cannot rest from work because of poverty and misery. Sunday is *2447* traditionally consecrated by Christian piety to good works and humble service of the sick, the infirm and the elderly. Christians will also sanctify Sunday by devoting time and care to their families and relatives, often difficult to do on other days of the

---

[119] Cf. CIC, can. 1245.
[120] CIC, can. 1248 § 2.
[121] *Gen* 2:2.
[122] Cf. *GS* 67 § 3.

[123] Cf. CIC, can. 1247.
[124] St Augustine, *De civ. Dei* 19, 19: PL 41, 647.

week. Sunday is a time for reflection, silence, cultivation of the mind and meditation which furthers the growth of the Christian interior life.

2187 Sanctifying Sundays and holy days requires a common effort. Every Christian should avoid making unnecessary demands on others that would hinder them from observing the Lord's Day. Traditional activities (sport, res- *2289* taurants, etc.), and social necessities (public services, etc.), require some people to work on Sundays, but everyone should still take care to set aside sufficient time for leisure. With temperance and charity the faithful will see to it that they avoid the excesses and violence sometimes associated with popular leisure activities. In spite of economic constraints, public authorities should ensure citizens a time intended for rest and divine worship. Employers have a similar obligation toward their employees.

2188 In respecting religious liberty and the common good of all, *2105* Christians should seek recognition of Sundays and the Church's holy days as legal holidays. They have to give everyone a public example of prayer, respect and joy, and defend their traditions as a precious contribution to the spiritual life of society. If a country's legislation or other reasons require work on Sunday, the day should nevertheless be lived as the day of our deliverance which lets us share in this 'festal gathering', this 'assembly of the firstborn who are enrolled in heaven'.[125]

IN BRIEF

2189 'Observe the sabbath day, to keep it holy' (Dt 5:12). 'The seventh day is a sabbath of solemn rest, holy to the LORD' (Ex 31:15).

2190 The sabbath, which represented the completion of the first creation, has been replaced by Sunday, which recalls the new creation inaugurated by the Resurrection of Christ.

2191 The Church celebrates the day of Christ's Resurrection on the 'eighth day', Sunday, which is rightly called the Lord's Day (cf. SC 106).

2192 'Sunday... is to be observed as the foremost holy day of obligation in the universal Church' (CIC, can. 1246 § 1). 'On Sundays and other holy days of obligation the faithful are bound to participate in the Mass' (CIC, can. 1247).

2193 'On Sundays and other holy days of obligation the faithful are bound... to abstain from those labours and business concerns which impede the worship to be rendered to God, the joy which is proper to the Lord's Day, or the proper relaxation of mind and body' (CIC, can. 1247).

---

[125] Heb 12:22–23.

> 2194 *The institution of Sunday helps all 'to be allowed sufficient rest and leisure to cultivate their familial, cultural, social and religious lives' (GS 67 § 3).*
>
> 2195 *Every Christian should avoid making unnecessary demands on others that would hinder them from observing the Lord's Day.*

Chapter Two
'YOU SHALL LOVE YOUR NEIGHBOUR AS YOURSELF'

Jesus said to his disciples: 'Love one another even as I have loved you.'[1]

2196 In response to the question about the first of the commandments, Jesus says: 'The first is, "Hear, O Israel: The Lord our God, the Lord is one; and you shall love the Lord your God with all your heart, and with all your soul, and with all your mind, and with all your strength." The second is this, "You shall love your neighbour as yourself." There is no other commandment greater than these.'[2]

2822   The apostle St Paul reminds us of this: 'He who loves his neighbour has fulfilled the law. The commandments, "*You shall not commit adultery, You shall not kill, You shall not steal, You shall not covet*", and any other commandment, are summed up in this sentence, "You shall love your neighbour as yourself." Love does no wrong to a neighbour; therefore love is the fulfilling of the law.'[3]

Article 4
THE FOURTH COMMANDMENT

Honour your father and your mother, that your days may be long in the land which the LORD your God gives you.[4]

He was obedient to them.[5]

The Lord Jesus himself recalled the force of this 'commandment of God'.[6] The Apostle teaches: 'Children, obey your parents in the Lord, for this is right. "Honour your father and mother" (this is the first commandment with a promise) "that it may be well with you and that you may live long on the earth." '[7]

2197 The fourth commandment opens the second table of the Decalogue. It shows us the order of charity. God has willed that,

---

[1] *Jn* 13:34.
[2] *Mk* 12:29–31; cf. *Dt* 6:4–5; *Lev* 19:18;
   Mt 22:34–40; *Lk* 10:25–28.
[3] *Rom* 13:8–10.

[4] *Ex* 20:12; cf. *Dt* 5:16.
[5] *Lk* 2:51.
[6] *Mk* 7:8–13.
[7] *Eph* 6:1–3; cf. *Dt* 5:16.

after him, we should honour our parents to whom we owe life and who have handed on to us the knowledge of God. We are obliged to honour and respect all those whom God, for our good, has vested with his authority.

1897

2198 This commandment is expressed in positive terms of duties to be fulfilled. It introduces the subsequent commandments which are concerned with particular respect for life, marriage, earthly goods, and speech. It constitutes one of the foundations of the social doctrine of the Church.

2419

2199 The fourth commandment is addressed expressly to children in their relationship to their father and mother, because this relationship is the most universal. It likewise concerns the ties of kinship between members of the extended family. It requires honour, affection and gratitude toward elders and ancestors. Finally, it extends to the duties of pupils to teachers, employees to employers, subordinates to leaders, citizens to their country and to those who administer or govern it.

This commandment includes and presupposes the duties of parents, instructors, teachers, leaders, magistrates, those who govern, all who exercise authority over others or over a community of persons.

2200 Observing the fourth commandment brings its reward: 'Honour your father and your mother, that your days may be long in the land which the LORD your God gives you.'[8] Respecting this commandment provides, along with spiritual fruits, temporal fruits of peace and prosperity. Conversely, failure to observe it brings great harm to communities and to individuals.

2304

I. The Family in God's Plan

The nature of the family

2201 The conjugal community is established upon the consent of the spouses. Marriage and the family are ordered to the good of the spouses and to the procreation and education of children. The love of the spouses and the begetting of children create among members of the same family personal relationships and primordial responsibilities.

1625

2202 A man and a woman united in marriage, together with their children, form a family. This institution is prior to any recognition by public authority, which has an obligation to recognize it. It

1882

---

[8] *Ex* 10:12; cf. *Dt* 5:16.

should be considered the normal reference point by which the different forms of family relationship are to be evaluated.

2203 In creating man and woman, God instituted the human family and endowed it with its fundamental constitution. Its
369 members are persons equal in dignity. For the common good of its members and of society, the family necessarily has manifold responsibilities, rights and duties.

1655–1658 **The Christian family**

533 2204 'The Christian family constitutes a specific revelation and realization of ecclesial communion, and for this reason it can and should be called a *domestic church*.'[9] It is a community of faith, hope and charity; it assumes singular importance in the Church, as is evident in the New Testament.[10]

2205 The Christian family is a communion of persons, a sign and
1702 image of the communion of the Father and the Son in the Holy Spirit. In the procreation and education of children it reflects the Father's work of creation. It is called to partake of the prayer and sacrifice of Christ. Daily prayer and the reading of the Word of God strengthen it in charity. The Christian family has an evangelizing and missionary task.

2206 The relationships within the family bring an affinity of feelings, affections and interests, arising above all from the members' respect for one another. The family is a *privileged community* called to achieve a 'sharing of thought and common deliberation by the spouses as well as their eager co-operation as parents in the children's upbringing'.[11]

II. The Family and Society

2207 The family is the *original cell of social life*. It is the natural
1880 society in which husband and wife are called to give themselves in
372 love and in the gift of life. Authority, stability and a life of relationships within the family constitute the foundations for freedom, security and fraternity within society. The family is the community in which, from childhood, one can learn moral values, begin to honour God and make good use of freedom.
1603 Family life is an initiation into life in society.

2208 The family should live in such a way that its members learn

---

[9] John Paul II, *FC* 21; cf. *LG* 11.   [11] *GS* 52 § 1.
[10] Cf. *Eph* 5:21 – 6:4; *Col* 3:18–21; 1 *Pt* 3:1–7.

to care and take responsibility for the young, the old, the sick, the handicapped, and the poor. There are many families who are at times incapable of providing this help. It devolves then on other persons, other families and, in a subsidiary way, society to provide for their needs: 'Religion that is pure and undefiled before God and the Father is this: to visit orphans and widows in their affliction, and to keep oneself unstained from the world.'[12]

2209 The family must be helped and defended by appropriate social measures. Where families cannot fulfil their responsibilities, other social bodies have the duty of helping them and of supporting the institution of the family. Following the principle of subsidiarity, larger communities should take care not to usurp the family's prerogatives or interfere in its life.   *1883*

2210 The importance of the family for the life and well-being of society[13] entails a particular responsibility for society to support and strengthen marriage and the family. Civil authority should consider it a grave duty 'to acknowledge the true nature of marriage and the family, to protect and foster them, to safeguard public morality and promote domestic prosperity'.[14]

2211 The political community has a duty to honour the family, to assist it, and to ensure especially:
– the freedom to establish a family, have children and bring them up in keeping with the family's own moral and religious convictions;
– the protection of the stability of the marriage bond and the institution of the family;
– the freedom to profess one's faith, to hand it on and raise one's children in it, with the necessary means and institutions;
– the right to private property, to free enterprise, to obtain work and housing, and the right to emigrate;
– in keeping with the country's institutions, the right to medical care, assistance for the aged, and family benefits;
– the protection of security and health, especially with respect to dangers like drugs, pornography, alcoholism, etc.;
– the freedom to form associations with other families and so to have representation before civil authority.[15]

2212 The fourth commandment *illuminates other relationships in society*. In our brothers and sisters we see the children of our parents; in our cousins, the descendants of our ancestors; in our fellow citizens, the children of our country; in the baptized, the children of our mother the Church; in every human person, a son   *225* or daughter of the One who wants to be called 'our Father'. In this

---

[12] Jas 1:27.
[13] Cf. GS 47 § 1.
[14] GS 52 § 2.
[15] Cf. FC 46.

way our relationships with our neighbours are recognized as per-
1931 sonal in character. The neighbour is not a 'unit' in the human
collective; he is 'someone' who by his known origins deserves
particular attention and respect.

2213 Human communities are *made up of persons*. Governing
them well is not limited to guaranteeing rights and fulfilling duties
such as honouring contracts. Right relations between employers
and employees, between those who govern and citizens, presuppose a natural good will in keeping with the dignity of human
1939 persons concerned for justice and fraternity.

III. The Duties of Family Members

The duties of children

2214 The divine fatherhood is the source of human fatherhood;[16]
this is the foundation of the honour owed to parents. The respect
of children, whether minors or adults, for their father and
1858 mother[17] is nourished by the natural affection born of the bond
uniting them. It is required by God's commandment.[18]

2215 Respect for parents (*filial piety*) derives from *gratitude* toward
those who, by the gift of life, their love and their work, have
brought their children into the world and enabled them to grow in
stature, wisdom and grace. 'With all your heart honour your
father, and do not forget the birth pangs of your mother. Remember that through your parents you were born; what can you give
back to them that equals their gift to you?'[19]

532 2216 Filial respect is shown by true docility and *obedience*. 'My
son, keep your father's commandment, and forsake not your
mother's teaching... When you walk, they will lead you; when
you lie down, they will watch over you; and when you awake,
they will talk with you.'[20] 'A wise son hears his father's instruction, but a scoffer does not listen to rebuke.'[21]

2217 As long as a child lives at home with his parents, the child should obey his
parents in all that they ask of him when it is for his good or that of the family.
'Children, obey your parents in everything, for this pleases the Lord.'[22] Children should also obey the reasonable directions of their teachers and all to
whom their parents have entrusted them. But if a child is convinced in conscience that it would be morally wrong to obey a particular order, he must not
do so.

---

[16] Cf. *Eph* 3:14.
[17] Cf. *Prov* 1:8; *Tob* 4:3–4.
[18] Cf. *Ex* 20:12.
[19] *Sir* 7:27–28.

[20] *Prov* 6:20–22.
[21] *Prov* 13:1.
[22] *Col* 3:20; cf. *Eph* 6:1.

As they grow up, children should continue to respect their parents. They should anticipate their wishes, willingly seek their advice and accept their just admonitions. Obedience toward parents ceases with the emancipation of the children; not so respect, which is always owed to them. This respect has its roots in the fear of God, one of the gifts of the Holy Spirit.

1831

2218 The fourth commandment reminds grown children of their *responsibilities toward their parents*. As much as they can, they must give them material and moral support in old age and in times of illness, loneliness or distress. Jesus recalls this duty of gratitude.[23]

> For the Lord honoured the father above the children, and he confirmed the right of the mother over her sons. Whoever honours his father atones for sins, and whoever glorifies his mother is like one who lays up treasure. Whoever honours his father will be gladdened by his own children, and when he prays he will be heard. Whoever glorifies his father will have long life, and whoever obeys the Lord will refresh his mother.[24]

> O son, help your father in his old age, and do not grieve him as long as he lives; even if he is lacking in understanding, show forbearance; in all your strength do not despise him... Whoever forsakes his father is like a blasphemer, and whoever angers his mother is cursed by the Lord.[25]

2219 Filial respect promotes harmony in all of family life; it also concerns *relationships between brothers and sisters*. Respect toward parents fills the home with light and warmth. 'Grandchildren are the crown of the aged.'[26] 'With all humility and meekness, with patience, [support] one another in charity.'[27]

2220 For Christians a special gratitude is due to those from whom they have received the gift of faith, the grace of Baptism and life in the Church. These may include parents, grandparents, other members of the family, pastors, catechists, and other teachers or friends. 'I am reminded of your sincere faith, a faith that dwelt first in your grandmother Lois and your mother Eunice and now, I am sure, dwells in you.'[28]

The duties of parents

2221 The fecundity of conjugal love cannot be reduced solely to the procreation of children, but must extend to their moral education and their spiritual formation. 'The *role of parents in education* is of such importance that it is almost impossible to provide an adequate substitute.'[29] The right and the duty of parents to educate their children are primordial and inalienable.[30]

1653

---

[23] Cf. *Mk* 7:10–12.
[24] *Sir* 3:2–6.
[25] *Sir* 3:12–13, 16.
[26] *Prov* 17:6.

[27] *Eph* 4:2.
[28] *2 Tim* 1:5.
[29] *GE* 3.
[30] Cf. *FC* 36.

2222 Parents must regard their children as *children of God* and
494 respect them as *human persons*. Showing themselves obedient to
the will of the Father in heaven, they educate their children to fulfil
God's law.

2223 Parents have the first responsibility for the education of their
children. They bear witness to this responsibility first by *creating a
home* where tenderness, forgiveness, respect, fidelity and disinterested service are the rule. The home is well suited for *education in
1804 the virtues*. This requires an apprenticeship in self-denial, sound
judgement and self-mastery – the preconditions of all true freedom. Parents should teach their children to subordinate the 'material and instinctual dimensions to interior and spiritual ones'.[31]
Parents have a grave responsibility to give good example to their
children. By knowing how to acknowledge their own failings to
their children, parents will be better able to guide and correct
them:

> He who loves his son will not spare the rod. . . He who disciplines his son
> will profit by him.[32]

> Fathers, do not provoke your children to anger, but bring them up in the
> discipline and instruction of the Lord.[33]

2224 The home is the natural environment for initiating a human
1939 being into solidarity and communal responsibilities. Parents
should teach children to avoid the compromising and degrading
influences which threaten human societies.

2225 Through the grace of the sacrament of marriage, parents
1656 receive the responsibility and privilege of *evangelizing their children*. Parents should initiate their children at an early age into the
mysteries of the faith of which they are the 'first heralds' for their
children. They should associate them from their tenderest years
with the life of the Church.[34] A wholesome family life can foster
interior dispositions that are a genuine preparation for a living
faith and remain a support for it throughout one's life.

2226 *Education in the faith* by the parents should begin in the child's
earliest years. This already happens when family members help
one another to grow in faith by the witness of a Christian life in
keeping with the Gospel. Family catechesis precedes, accompanies
and enriches other forms of instruction in the faith. Parents have
the mission of teaching their children to pray and to discover their

---

[31] John Paul II, *CA* 36 § 2.   [33] *Eph* 6:4.
[32] *Sir* 30:1–2.   [34] *LG* 11 § 2.

vocation as children of God.[35] The parish is the Eucharistic com-   *2179*
munity and the heart of the liturgical life of Christian families; it is
a privileged place for the catechesis of children and parents.

2227 Children in turn contribute to the *growth in holiness* of their   *2013*
parents.[36] Each and every one should be generous and tireless in
forgiving one another for offences, quarrels, injustices and neglect.
Mutual affection suggests this. The charity of Christ demands it.[37]

2228 Parents' respect and affection are expressed by the care and
attention they devote to bringing up their young children and
providing for their physical and spiritual needs. As the children grow
up, the same respect and devotion lead parents to educate them in
the right use of their reason and freedom.

2229 As those first responsible for the education of their children,
parents have the right to *choose a school for them* which corresponds
to their own convictions. This right is fundamental. As far as
possible parents have the duty of choosing schools that will best
help them in their task as Christian educators.[38] Public authorities
have the duty of guaranteeing this parental right and of ensuring
the concrete conditions for its exercise.

2230 When they become adults, children have the right and duty
to *choose their profession and state of life*. They should assume their
new responsibilities within a trusting relationship with their
parents, willingly asking and receiving their advice and counsel.
Parents should be careful not to exert pressure on their children
either in the choice of a profession or in that of a spouse. This   *1625*
necessary restraint does not prevent them – quite the contrary –
from giving their children judicious advice, particularly when
they are planning to start a family.

2231 Some forgo marriage in order to care for their parents or
brothers and sisters, to give themselves more completely to a profession, or to serve other honourable ends. They can contribute
greatly to the good of the human family.

IV. The Family and the Kingdom

2232 Family ties are important but not absolute. Just as the child
grows to maturity and human and spiritual autonomy, so his
unique vocation which comes from God asserts itself more clearly
and forcefully. Parents should respect this call and encourage their

---

[35] Cf. *LG* 11.
[36] Cf. *GS* 48 § 4.
[37] Cf. *Mt* 18:21–22; *Lk* 17:4.
[38] Cf. *GE* 6.

children to follow it. They must be convinced that the first voca-
1618 tion of the Christian is to *follow Jesus*: 'He who loves father or
mother more than me is not worthy of me; and he who loves son
or daughter more than me is not worthy of me.'[39]

2233 Becoming a disciple of Jesus means accepting the invitation
542 to belong to *God's family*, to live in conformity with His way of
life: 'For whoever does the will of my Father in heaven is my
brother, and sister, and mother.'[40]

Parents should welcome and respect with joy and
thanksgiving the Lord's call to one of their children to follow him
in virginity for the sake of the Kingdom in the consecrated life or
in priestly ministry.

V. The Authorities in Civil Society

2234 God's fourth commandment also enjoins us to honour all
1897 who for our good have received authority in society from God. It
clarifies the duties of those who exercise authority as well as those
who benefit from it.

Duties of civil authorities

2235 Those who exercise authority should do so as a service.
'Whoever would be great among you must be your servant.'[41]
1899 The exercise of authority is measured morally in terms of its divine
origin, its reasonable nature and its specific object. No one can
command or establish what is contrary to the dignity of persons
and the natural law.

2236 The exercise of authority is meant to give outward expression to a just hierarchy of values in order to facilitate the exercise of
freedom and responsibility by all. Those in authority should prac-
2411 tise distributive justice wisely, taking account of the needs and
contribution of each, with a view to harmony and peace. They
should take care that the regulations and measures they adopt are
not a source of temptation by setting personal interest against that
of the community.[42]

2237 *Political authorities* are obliged to respect the fundamental
357 rights of the human person. They will dispense justice humanely
by respecting the rights of everyone, especially of families and the
disadvantaged.

The political rights attached to citizenship can and should be

---

[39] Mt 10:37; cf. 16:25.   [41] Mt 20:26.
[40] Mt 12:49.   [42] Cf. CA 25.

granted according to the requirements of the common good. They cannot be suspended by public authorities without legitimate and proportionate reasons. Political rights are meant to be exercised for the common good of the nation and the human community.

The duties of citizens

2238 Those subject to authority should regard those in authority as representatives of God, who has made them stewards of his gifts:[43] 'Be subject for the Lord's sake to every human institution... Live as free men, yet without using your freedom as a pretext for evil; but live as servants of God.'[44] Their loyal collaboration includes the right, and at times the duty, to voice their just criticisms of that which seems harmful to the dignity of persons and to the good of the community. *1900*

2239 It is the *duty of citizens* to contribute along with the civil authorities to the good of society in a spirit of truth, justice, solidarity and freedom. The love and service of *one's country* follow from the duty of gratitude and belong to the order of charity. Submission to legitimate authorities and service of the common good require citizens to fulfil their roles in the life of the political community. *1915 2310*

2240 Submission to authority and co-responsibility for the common good make it morally obligatory to pay taxes, to exercise the right to vote, and to defend one's country: *2265*

> Pay to all of them their dues, taxes to whom taxes are due, revenue to whom revenue is due, respect to whom respect is due, honour to whom honour is due.[45]

> [Christians] reside in their own nations, but as resident aliens. They participate in all things as citizens and endure all things as foreigners... They obey the established laws and their way of life surpasses the laws... So noble is the position to which God has assigned them that they are not allowed to desert it.[46]

> The Apostle exhorts us to offer prayers and thanksgiving for kings and all who exercise authority, 'that we may lead a quiet and peaceable life, godly and respectful in every way'.[47] *1900*

2241 The more prosperous nations are obliged, to the extent they are able, to welcome the *foreigner* in search of the security and the means of livelihood which he cannot find in his country of origin.

---

[43] Cf. *Rom* 13:1–2.
[44] 1 *Pt* 2:13, 16.
[45] *Rom* 13:7.
[46] *Ad Diognetum* 5, 5 and 10; 6, 10: PG 2, 1173 and 1176.
[47] 1 *Tim* 2:2.

Public authorities should see to it that the natural right is respected that places a guest under the protection of those who receive him.

> Political authorities, for the sake of the common good for which they are responsible, may make the exercise of the right to immigrate subject to various juridical conditions, especially with regard to the immigrants' duties toward their country of adoption. Immigrants are obliged to respect with gratitude the material and spiritual heritage of the country that receives them, to obey its laws and to assist in carrying civic burdens.

1903
2313
450
2242 The citizen is obliged in conscience not to follow the directives of civil authorities when they are contrary to the demands of the moral order, to the fundamental rights of persons or the teachings of the Gospel. *Refusing obedience* to civil authorities, when their demands are contrary to those of an upright conscience, finds its justification in the distinction between serving God and serving the political community. 'Render therefore to Caesar the things that are Caesar's, and to God the things that are God's.'[48] 'We must obey God rather than men':[49]

1901
> When citizens are under the oppression of a public authority which oversteps its competence, they should still not refuse to give or to do what is objectively demanded of them by the common good; but it is legitimate for them to defend their own rights and those of their fellow citizens against the abuse of this authority within the limits of the natural law and the Law of the Gospel.[50]

2309
2243 Armed *resistance* to oppression by political authority is not legitimate, unless all the following conditions are met: (1) there is certain, grave and prolonged violation of fundamental rights; (2) all other means of redress have been exhausted; (3) such resistance will not provoke worse disorders; (4) there is well-founded hope of success; and (5) it is impossible reasonably to foresee any better solution.

The political community and the Church

1910
1881
2109
2244 Every institution is inspired, at least implicitly, by a vision of man and his destiny, from which it derives the point of reference for its judgement, its hierarchy of values, its line of conduct. Most societies have formed their institutions in the recognition of a certain pre-eminence of man over things. Only the divinely revealed religion has clearly recognized man's origin and destiny in God, the Creator and Redeemer. The Church invites political authorities to measure their judgements and decisions against this inspired truth about God and man:

---

[48] *Mt* 22:21.   [50] *GS* 74 § 5.
[49] *Acts* 5:29.

Societies not recognizing this vision or rejecting it in the name of their independence from God are brought to seek their criteria and goal in themselves or to borrow them from some ideology. Since they do not admit that one can defend an objective criterion of good and evil, they arrogate to themselves an explicit or implicit totalitarian power over man and his destiny, as history shows.[51]

2245 The Church, because of her commission and competence, is not to be confused in any way with the political community. She *912* is both the sign and the safeguard of the transcendent character of the human person. 'The Church respects and encourages the political freedom and responsibility of the citizen.'[52]

2246 It is a part of the Church's mission 'to pass moral judgements *2420* even in matters related to politics, whenever the fundamental rights of man or the salvation of souls requires it. The means, the *2032* only means, she may use are those which are in accord with the Gospel and the welfare of all men according to the diversity of times and circumstances.'[53]

IN BRIEF

2247 *'Honour your father and your mother' (Dt 5:16; Mk 7:10).*

2248 *According to the fourth commandment, God has willed that, after him, we should honour our parents and those whom he has vested with authority for our good.*

2249 *The conjugal community is established upon the covenant and consent of the spouses. Marriage and family are ordered to the good of the spouses, to the procreation and the education of children.*

2250 *'The well-being of the individual person and of both human and Christian society is closely bound up with the healthy state of conjugal and family life' (GS 47 § 1).*

2251 *Children owe their parents respect, gratitude, just obedience and assistance. Filial respect fosters harmony in all of family life.*

2252 *Parents have the first responsibility for the education of their children in the faith, prayer and all the virtues. They have the duty to provide as far as possible for the physical and spiritual needs of their children.*

2253 *Parents should respect and encourage their children's vocations. They should remember and teach that the first calling of the Christian is to follow Jesus.*

---

[51] Cf. CA 45; 46.
[52] GS 76 § 3.
[53] GS 76 § 5.

> 2254 *Public authority is obliged to respect the fundamental rights of the human person and the conditions for the exercise of his freedom.*
>
> 2255 *It is the duty of citizens to work with civil authority for building up society in a spirit of truth, justice, solidarity and freedom.*
>
> 2256 *Citizens are obliged in conscience not to follow the directives of civil authorities when they are contrary to the demands of the moral order. 'We must obey God rather than men' (Acts 5:29).*
>
> 2257 *Every society's judgements and conduct reflect a vision of man and his destiny. Without the light the Gospel sheds on God and man, societies easily become totalitarian.*

Article 5
THE FIFTH COMMANDMENT

You shall not kill.[54]

> You have heard that it was said to the men of old, 'You shall not kill: and whoever kills shall be liable to judgement.' But I say to you that every one who is angry with his brother shall be liable to judgement.[55]

2258 'Human life is sacred because from its beginning it involves 356 the creative action of God and it remains for ever in a special relationship with the Creator, who is its sole end. God alone is the Lord of life from its beginning until its end: no one can under any circumstance claim for himself the right directly to destroy an innocent human being.'[56]

I. Respect for Human Life

The witness of sacred history

2259 In the account of Abel's murder by his brother Cain,[57] Scripture reveals the presence of anger and envy in man, conse- 401 quences of original sin, from the beginning of human history. Man has become the enemy of his fellow man. God declares the wickedness of this fratricide: 'What have you done? The voice of your brother's blood is crying to me from the ground. And now you are cursed from the ground, which has opened its mouth to receive your brother's blood from your hand.'[58]

2260 The covenant between God and mankind is interwoven

---

[54] *Ex* 20:13; *Dt* 5:17.
[55] *Mt* 5:21–22.
[56] CDF, Instruction *Donum vitae*.

intro. 5.
[57] Cf. *Gen* 4:8–12.
[58] *Gen* 4:10–11.

with reminders of God's gift of human life and man's murderous violence:

> For your lifeblood I will surely require a reckoning... Whoever sheds the blood of man, by man shall his blood be shed; for God made man in his own image.[59]

The Old Testament always considered blood a sacred sign of life.[60] This teaching remains necessary for all time.

2261 Scripture specifies the prohibition contained in the fifth commandment: 'Do not slay the innocent and the righteous.'[61] The deliberate murder of an innocent person is gravely contrary to the dignity of the human being, to the golden rule and to the holiness of the Creator. The law forbidding it is universally valid: it obliges each and everyone, always and everywhere.   *1756*   *1956*

2262 In the Sermon on the Mount, the Lord recalls the commandment, 'You shall not kill',[62] and adds to it the proscription of anger, hatred and vengeance. Going further, Christ asks his disciples to turn the other cheek, to love their enemies.[63] He did not defend himself and told Peter to leave his sword in its sheath.[64]   *2844*

Legitimate defence

2263 The legitimate defence of persons and societies is not an exception to the prohibition against the murder of the innocent that constitutes intentional killing. 'The act of self-defence can have a double effect: the preservation of one's own life; and the killing of the aggressor... The one is intended, the other is not.'[65]   *1737*

2264 Love toward oneself remains a fundamental principle of morality. Therefore it is legitimate to insist on respect for one's own right to life. Someone who defends his life is not guilty of murder even if he is forced to deal his aggressor a lethal blow: *2196*

> If a man in self-defence uses more than necessary violence, it will be unlawful: whereas if he repel force with moderation, his defence will be lawful... Nor is it necessary for salvation that a man omit the act of moderate self-defence to avoid killing the other man, since one is bound to take more care of one's own life than of another's.[66]

2265 Legitimate defence can be not only a right but a grave duty for one who is responsible for the lives of others. The defence of the common good requires that an unjust aggressor be rendered unable to cause harm. For this reason, those who legitimately hold authority also have the right to use arms to repel aggressors against the civil community entrusted to their responsibility.   *2240*

---

[59] Gen 9:5–6.
[60] Cf. Lev 17:14.
[61] Ex 23:7.
[62] Mt 5:21.
[63] Cf. Mt 5:22–39, 44.

[64] Cf. Mt 26:52.
[65] St Thomas Aquinas, STh II–II, 64, 7, corp. art.
[66] St Thomas Aquinas, STh II–II, 64, 7, corp. art.

2266 The efforts of the state to curb the spread of behaviour harmful to people's rights and to the basic rules of civil society correspond to the requirement of safeguarding the common good.
1897–1899 Legitimate public authority has the right and the duty to inflict
2308 *punishment* proportionate to the gravity of the offence. Punishment has the primary aim of redressing the disorder introduced by the offence. When it is willingly accepted by the guilty party,
1449 it assumes the value of expiation. Punishment then, in addition to defending public order and protecting people's safety, has a medicinal purpose: as far as possible, it must contribute to the correction of the guilty party.[67]

2267 Assuming that the guilty party's identity and responsibility have been fully determined, the traditional teaching of the Church does not exclude recourse to the death penalty, if this is the only possible way of effectively defending human lives against the unjust aggressor.

2306   If, however, non-lethal means are sufficient to defend and protect people's safety from the aggressor, authority will limit itself to such means, as these are more in keeping with the concrete conditions of the common good and more in conformity with the dignity of the human person.

       Today, in fact, as a consequence of the possibilities which the state has for effectively preventing crime, by rendering one who has committed an offence incapable of doing harm – without definitively taking away from him the possibility of redeeming himself – the cases in which the execution of the offender is an absolute necessity 'are very rare, if not practically non-existent'.[67a]

Intentional homicide

2268 The fifth commandment forbids *direct and intentional killing* as gravely sinful. The murderer and those who co-operate
1867 voluntarily in murder commit a sin that cries out to heaven for vengeance.[68]

       Infanticide,[69] fratricide, parricide and the murder of a spouse are especially grave crimes by reason of the natural bonds which they break. Concern for eugenics or public health cannot justify any murder, even if commanded by public authority.

2269 The fifth commandment forbids doing anything with the intention of *indirectly* bringing about a person's death. The moral law prohibits exposing someone to mortal danger without grave reason, as well as refusing assistance to a person in danger.

       The acceptance by human society of murderous famines, without efforts to remedy them, is a scandalous injustice and a grave offence. Those whose

---

[67] *Lk* 23:40–43.
[67a] John Paul II, *Evangelium vitae* 56.
[68] Cf. *Gen* 4:10.
[69] Cf. *GS* 51 § 3.
[70] Cf. *Am* 8:4–10.

usurious and avaricious dealings lead to the hunger and death of their brethren in the human family indirectly commit homicide, which is imputable to them.[70]

Unintentional killing is not morally imputable. But one is not exonerated from grave offence if, without proportionate reasons, one has acted in a way that brings about someone's death, even without the intention to do so. **2290**

Abortion

2270 Human life must be respected and protected absolutely from the moment of conception. From the first moment of his exist- **1703** ence, a human being must be recognized as having the rights of a **357** person — among which is the inviolable right of every innocent being to life.[71]

> Before I formed you in the womb I knew you, and before you were born I consecrated you.[72]

> My frame was not hidden from you, when I was being made in secret, intricately wrought in the depths of the earth.[73]

2271 Since the first century the Church has affirmed the moral evil of every procured abortion. This teaching has not changed and remains unchangeable. Direct abortion, that is to say, abortion willed either as an end or a means, is gravely contrary to the moral law:

> You shall not kill the embryo by abortion and shall not cause the new-born to perish.[74]

> God, the Lord of life, has entrusted to men the noble mission of safe-guarding life, and men must carry it out in a manner worthy of themselves. Life must be protected with the utmost care from the moment of conception: abortion and infanticide are abominable crimes.[75]

2272 Formal co-operation in an abortion constitutes a grave offence. The Church attaches the canonical penalty of excommunication to this crime against human life. 'A person who procures a completed abortion incurs excommunication *latae sententiae*',[76] **1463** 'by the very commission of the offence',[77] and subject to the conditions provided by Canon Law.[78] The Church does not thereby intend to restrict the scope of mercy. Rather, she makes clear the gravity of the crime committed, the irreparable harm done to the innocent who is put to death, as well as to the parents and the whole of society.

2273 The inalienable right to life of every innocent human individual is a *constitutive element of a civil society and its legislation*: **1930**

---

[71] Cf. CDF, *Donum vitae* I, 1.
[72] Jer 1:5; cf. Job 10:8–12; Ps 22:10–11.
[73] Ps 139:15.
[74] *Didache* 2, 2: SCh 248, 148; cf. *Ep. Barnabae* 19, 5: PG 2, 777; *Ad Diognetum* 5, 6: PG 2, 1173; Tertullian,

Apol. 9: PL 1, 371.
[75] *GS* 51 § 3.
[76] CIC, can. 1398.
[77] CIC, can. 1314.
[78] Cf. CIC, cann. 1323–1324.

'The inalienable rights of the person must be recognized and respected by civil society and the political authority. These human rights depend neither on single individuals nor on parents; nor do they represent a concession made by society and the state; they belong to human nature and are inherent in the person by virtue of the creative act from which the person took his origin. Among such fundamental rights one should mention in this regard every human being's right to life and physical integrity from the moment of conception until death.'[79]

'The moment a positive law deprives a category of human beings of the protection which civil legislation ought to accord them, the state is denying the equality of all before the law. When the state does not place its power at the service of the rights of each citizen, and in particular of the more vulnerable, the very foundations of a state based on law are undermined... As a consequence of the respect and protection which must be ensured for the unborn child from the moment of conception, the law must provide appropriate penal sanctions for every deliberate violation of the child's rights.'[80]

2274 Since it must be treated from conception as a person, the embryo must be defended in its integrity, cared for, and healed, as far as possible, like any other human being.

Prenatal diagnosis is morally licit, 'if it respects the life and integrity of the embryo and the human foetus and is directed toward its safeguarding or healing as an individual... It is gravely opposed to the moral law when this is done with the thought of possibly inducing an abortion, depending upon the results: a diagnosis must not be the equivalent of a death sentence.'[81]

2275 'One must hold as licit procedures carried out on the human embryo which respect the life and integrity of the embryo and do not involve disproportionate risks for it, but are directed toward its healing, the improvement of its condition of health, or its individual survival.'[82]

'It is immoral to produce human embryos intended for exploitation as disposable biological material.'[83]

'Certain attempts to *influence chromosomic or genetic inheritance* are not therapeutic but are aimed at producing human beings selected according to sex or other predetermined qualities. Such manipulations are contrary to the personal dignity of the human being and his integrity and identity'[84] which are unique and unrepeatable.

Euthanasia

2276 Those whose lives are diminished or weakened deserve *1503* special respect. Sick or handicapped persons should be helped to lead lives as normal as possible.

2277 Whatever its motives and means, direct euthanasia consists

---

[79] CDF, *Donum vitae* III.
[80] CDF, *Donum vitae* III.
[81] CDF, *Donum vitae* I, 2.

[82] CDF, *Donum vitae* I, 3.
[83] CDF, *Donum vitae* I, 5.
[84] CDF, *Donum vitae* I, 6.

in putting an end to the lives of handicapped, sick or dying persons. It is morally unacceptable.

Thus an act or omission which, of itself or by intention, causes death in order to eliminate suffering constitutes a murder gravely contrary to the dignity of the human person and to the respect due to the living God, his Creator. The error of judgement into which one can fall in good faith does not change the nature of this murderous act, which must always be forbidden and excluded.

2278 Discontinuing medical procedures that are burdensome, dangerous, extraordinary, or disproportionate to the expected outcome can be legitimate; it is the refusal of 'over-zealous' treatment. Here one does not will to cause death; one's inability to impede it is merely accepted. The decisions should be *1007* made by the patient if he is competent and able or, if not, by those legally entitled to act for the patient, whose reasonable will and legitimate interests must always be respected.

2279 Even if death is thought imminent, the ordinary care owed to a sick person cannot be legitimately interrupted. The use of painkillers to alleviate the sufferings of the dying, even at the risk of shortening their days, can be morally in conformity with human dignity if death is not willed as either an end or a means, but only foreseen and tolerated as inevitable. Palliative care is a special form of disinterested charity. As such it should be encouraged.

Suicide

2280 Everyone is responsible for his life before God who has given it to him. It is God who remains the sovereign Master of life. We are obliged to accept life gratefully and preserve it for his *2258* honour and the salvation of our souls. We are stewards, not owners, of the life God has entrusted to us. It is not ours to dispose of.

2281 Suicide contradicts the natural inclination of the human being to preserve and perpetuate his life. It is gravely contrary to the just love of self. It likewise offends love of neighbour because it unjustly breaks the ties of solidarity with family, nation and other *2212* human societies to which we continue to have obligations. Suicide is contrary to love for the living God.

2282 If suicide is committed with the intention of setting an example, especially to the young, it also takes on the gravity of scandal. Voluntary co-operation in suicide is contrary to the moral law.

Grave psychological disturbances, anguish or grave fear of hardship, suffering or torture can diminish the responsibility of the one committing suicide.   *1735*

2283 We should not despair of the eternal salvation of persons who have taken their own lives. By ways known to him alone,

1037 God can provide the opportunity for salutary repentance. The Church prays for persons who have taken their own lives.

II. Respect for the Dignity of Persons

Respect for the souls of others: scandal

2284 Scandal is an attitude or behaviour which leads another to do evil. The person who gives scandal becomes his neighbour's *2847* tempter. He damages virtue and integrity; he may even draw his brother into spiritual death. Scandal is a grave offence if by deed or omission another is deliberately led into a grave offence.

1903 2285 Scandal takes on a particular gravity by reason of the authority of those who cause it or the weakness of those who are scandalized. It prompted our Lord to utter this curse: 'Whoever causes one of these little ones who believe in me to sin, it would be better for him to have a great millstone fastened round his neck and to be drowned in the depth of the sea.'[85] Scandal is grave when given by those who by nature or office are obliged to teach and educate others. Jesus reproaches the scribes and Pharisees on this account: he likens them to wolves in sheep's clothing.[86]

2286 Scandal can be provoked by laws or institutions, by fashion or opinion.

Therefore, they are guilty of scandal who establish laws or social struc-*1887* tures leading to the decline of morals and the corruption of religious practice, or to 'social conditions that, intentionally or not, make Christian conduct and obedience to the Commandments difficult and practically impossible'.[87] This is also true of business leaders who make rules encouraging fraud, teachers who *2498* provoke their children to anger,[88] or manipulators of public opinion who turn it away from moral values.

2287 Anyone who uses the power at his disposal in such a way that it leads others to do wrong becomes guilty of scandal and responsible for the evil that he has directly or indirectly encouraged. 'Temptations to sin are sure to come; but woe to him by whom they come!'[89]

Respect for health

1503 2288 Life and physical health are precious gifts entrusted to us by God. We must take reasonable care of them, taking into account the needs of others and the common good.

---

[85] *Mt* 18:6; cf. 1 *Cor* 8:10–13.   [88] Cf. *Eph* 6:4; *Col* 3:21.
[86] Cf. *Mt* 7:15.   [89] *Lk* 17:1.
[87] Pius XII, Discourse, 1 June 1941.

Concern for the health of its citizens requires that society help   1509
in the attainment of living conditions that allow them to grow and
reach maturity: food and clothing, housing, health care, basic education, employment and social assistance.

2289 If morality requires respect for the life of the body, it does   364
not make it an absolute value. It rejects a neo-pagan notion that
tends to promote the *cult of the body*, to sacrifice everything for its
sake, to idolize physical perfection and success at sports. By its   2113
selective preference of the strong over the weak, such a conception
can lead to the perversion of human relationships.

2290 The virtue of temperance disposes us to *avoid every kind of*   1809
excess: the abuse of food, alcohol, tobacco or medicine. Those
incur grave guilt who, by drunkenness or a love of speed, endan-
ger their own and others' safety on the road, at sea or in the air.

2291 The *use of drugs* inflicts very grave damage on human health
and life. Their use, except on strictly therapeutic grounds, is a
grave offence. Clandestine production of and trafficking in drugs
are scandalous practices. They constitute direct co-operation in
evil, since they encourage people to practices gravely contrary to
the moral law.

Respect for the person and scientific research

2292 Scientific, medical or psychological experiments on human
individuals or groups can contribute to healing the sick and the
advancement of public health.

2293 Basic scientific research, as well as applied research, is a significant expres-   159
sion of man's dominion over creation. Science and technology are precious
resources when placed at the service of man and promote his integral development for the benefit of all. By themselves however they cannot disclose the
meaning of existence and of human progress. Science and technology are
ordered to man, from whom they take their origin and development; hence   1703
they find in the person and in his moral values both evidence of their purpose
and awareness of their limits.

2294 It is an illusion to claim moral neutrality in scientific research and its
applications. On the other hand, guiding principles cannot be inferred from
simple technical efficiency, or from the usefulness accruing to some at the
expense of others or, even worse, from prevailing ideologies. Science and technology by their very nature require unconditional respect for fundamental
moral criteria. They must be at the service of the human person, of his inalien-   2375
able rights, of his true and integral good, in conformity with the plan and the
will of God.

2295 Research or experimentation on the human being cannot legitimate acts that are in themselves contrary to the dignity of
1753 persons and to the moral law. The subjects' potential consent does not justify such acts. Experimentation on human beings is not morally legitimate if it exposes the subject's life or physical and psychological integrity to disproportionate or avoidable risks. Experimentation on human beings does not conform to the dignity of the person if it takes place without the informed consent of the subject or those who legitimately speak for him.

2296 *Organ transplants* are in conformity with the moral law if the physical and psychological danger and risks to the donor are proportionate to the good
2301 that is sought for the recipient. Organ donation after death is a noble and meritorious act and is to be encouraged as an expression of generous solidarity. It is not morally acceptable if the donor or his proxy has not given explicit consent. Moreover, it is not morally admissible directly to bring about the disabling mutilation or death of a human being, even in order to delay the death of other persons.

Respect for bodily integrity

2297 *Kidnapping* and *hostage taking* bring on a reign of terror; by means of threats they subject their victims to intolerable pressures. They are morally wrong. *Terrorism* threatens, wounds and kills indiscriminately; it is gravely against justice and charity. *Torture* which uses physical or moral violence to extract confessions, punish the guilty, frighten opponents, or satisfy hatred is contrary to respect for the person and for human dignity. Except when performed for strictly therapeutic medical reasons, directly intended *amputations*, *mutilations* and *sterilizations* performed on innocent persons are against the moral law.[90]

2298 In times past, cruel practices were commonly used by legitimate governments to maintain law and order, often without protest from the Pastors of the Church, who themselves adopted in their own tribunals the prescriptions of Roman law concerning torture. Regrettable as these facts are, the Church always taught the duty of clemency and mercy. She forbade clerics to shed blood. In recent times it has become evident that these cruel practices were
2267 neither necessary for public order, nor in conformity with the legitimate rights of the human person. On the contrary, these practices led to ones even more degrading. It is necessary to work for their abolition. We must pray for the victims and their tormentors.

Respect for the dead

2299 The dying should be given attention and care to help them live their last moments in dignity and peace. They will be helped by the prayer of their relatives, who must see to it that the sick

---

[90] Cf. DS 3722.

receive at the proper time the sacraments that prepare them to 1525
meet the living God.

2300 The bodies of the dead must be treated with respect and
charity, in faith and hope of the Resurrection. The burial of the 1681-1690
dead is a corporal work of mercy;[91] it honours the children of
God, who are temples of the Holy Spirit.

2301 Autopsies can be morally permitted for legal inquests or scientific
research. The free gift of organs after death is legitimate and can be meritorious.

The Church permits cremation, provided that it does not demonstrate a
denial of faith in the resurrection of the body.[92]

III. Safeguarding Peace

Peace

2302 By recalling the commandment, 'You shall not kill',[93] our
Lord asked for peace of heart, and denounced murderous anger 1765
and hatred as immoral.

Anger is a desire for revenge. 'To desire vengeance in order
to do evil to someone who should be punished is illicit', but it is
praiseworthy to impose restitution 'to correct vices and maintain
justice'.[94] If anger reaches the point of a deliberate desire to kill or
seriously wound a neighbour it is gravely against charity; it is a
mortal sin. The Lord says, 'Everyone who is angry with his
brother shall be liable to judgement.'[95]

2303 Deliberate *hatred* is contrary to charity. Hatred of the neigh- 2094
bour is a sin when one deliberately wishes him evil. Hatred of the 1933
neighbour is a grave sin when one deliberately desires him grave
harm. 'But I say to you, Love your enemies and pray for those
who persecute you, so that you may be sons of your Father who is
in heaven.'[96]

2304 Respect for and development of human life require *peace*. 1909
Peace is not merely the absence of war, and it is not limited to
maintaining a balance of powers between adversaries. Peace
cannot be attained on earth without safeguarding the goods of
persons, free communication among men, respect for the dignity
of persons and peoples, and the assiduous practice of fraternity.
Peace is 'the tranquillity of order'.[97] Peace is the work of justice 1807
and the effect of charity.[98]

---

[91] Cf. *Tob* 1:16-18.
[92] Cf. CIC, can. 1176 § 3.
[93] *Mt* 5:21.
[94] St Thomas Aquinas, *STh* II-II, 158, 1,
ad 3.
[95] *Mt* 5:22.
[96] *Mt* 5:44-45.
[97] St Augustine, *De civ. Dei* 19, 13, 1:
PL 41, 640.
[98] Cf. *Is* 32:17; GS 78 §§ 1-2.

2305 Earthly peace is the image and fruit of the *peace of Christ*, the messianic 'Prince of Peace'.[99] By the blood of his Cross, 'in his own
1468 person he killed the hostility',[100] he reconciled men with God and made his Church the sacrament of the unity of the human race and of its union with God. 'He is our peace.'[101] He has declared: 'Blessed are the peacemakers.'[102]

2306 Those who renounce violence and bloodshed and, in order
2267 to safeguard human rights, make use of those means of defence available to the weakest, bear witness to evangelical charity, provided they do so without harming the rights and obligations of other men and societies. They bear legitimate witness to the gravity of the physical and moral risks of recourse to violence, with all its destruction and death.[103]

Avoiding war

2307 The fifth commandment forbids the intentional destruction of human life. Because of the evils and injustices that accompany all war, the Church insistently urges everyone to prayer and to action so that the divine Goodness may free us from the ancient bondage of war.[104]

2308 All citizens and all governments are obliged to work for the avoidance of war.

However, 'as long as the danger of war persists and there is no international authority with the necessary competence and
2266 power, governments cannot be denied the right of lawful self-defence, once all peace efforts have failed.'[105]

2243 2309 The strict conditions for *legitimate defence by military force* require rigorous consideration. The gravity of such a decision makes it subject to rigorous conditions of moral legitimacy. At one and the same time:
— the damage inflicted by the aggressor on the nation or community of nations must be lasting, grave and certain;
— all other means of putting an end to it must have been shown to be impractical or ineffective;
— there must be serious prospects of success;
— the use of arms must not produce evils and disorders graver than the evil to be eliminated. The power of modern means of destruction weighs very heavily in evaluating this condition.

---

[99] *Is* 9:5.
[100] *Eph* 2:16 JB; cf. *Col* 1:20–22.
[101] *Eph* 2:14.
[102] *Mt* 5:9.
[103] Cf. *GS* 78 § 5.
[104] Cf. *GS* 81 § 4.
[105] *GS* 79 § 4.

These are the traditional elements enumerated in what is called the 'just war' doctrine.

The evaluation of these conditions for moral legitimacy belongs to the prudential judgement of those who have responsi- *1897* bility for the common good.

2310 Public authorities, in this case, have the right and duty to impose on citizens the *obligations necessary for national defence*.

Those who are sworn to serve their country in the armed *2239* forces are servants of the security and freedom of nations. If they carry out their duty honourably, they truly contribute to the common good of the nation and the maintenance of peace.[106]   *1909*

2311 Public authorities should make equitable provision for those who for reasons of conscience refuse to bear arms; these are none- *1782, 1790* theless obliged to serve the human community in some other way.[107]

2312 The Church and human reason both assert the permanent validity of the *moral law during armed conflict*. 'The mere fact that war has regrettably broken out does not mean that everything becomes licit between the warring parties.'[108]

2313 Non-combatants, wounded soldiers, and prisoners must be respected and treated humanely.

Actions deliberately contrary to the law of nations and to its universal principles are crimes, as are the orders that command such actions. Blind obedience does not suffice to excuse those who carry them out. Thus the extermination of a people, nation or ethnic minority must be condemned as a mortal sin. One is mor- ally bound to resist orders that command genocide.   *2242*

2314 'Every act of war directed to the indiscriminate destruction of whole cities or vast areas with their inhabitants is a crime against God and man, which merits firm and unequivocal condemna- tion.'[109] A danger of modern warfare is that it provides the oppor- tunity to those who possess modern scientific weapons – especially atomic, biological or chemical weapons – to commit such crimes.

2315 The *accumulation of arms* strikes many as a paradoxically suit- able way of deterring potential adversaries from war. They see it as the most effective means of ensuring peace among nations. This method of deterrence gives rise to strong moral reservations. The *arms race* does not ensure peace. Far from eliminating the causes of

---

[106] Cf. GS 79 § 5.   [108] GS 79 § 4.
[107] Cf. GS 79 § 3.   [109] GS 80 § 3.

war, it risks aggravating them. Spending enormous sums to produce ever new types of weapons impedes efforts to aid needy populations;[110] it thwarts the development of peoples. *Over-armament* multiplies reasons for conflict and increases the danger of escalation.

1906 2316 *The production and the sale of arms* affect the common good of nations and of the international community. Hence public authorities have the right and duty to regulate them. The short-term pursuit of private or collective interests cannot legitimate undertakings that promote violence and conflict among nations and compromise the international juridical order.

2538, 1938 2317 Injustice, excessive economic or social inequalities, envy, distrust and pride raging among men and nations constantly threaten peace and cause wars. Everything done to overcome these *1941* disorders contributes to building up peace and avoiding war:

> Insofar as men are sinners, the threat of war hangs over them and will so continue until Christ comes again; but insofar as they can vanquish sin by coming together in charity, violence itself will be vanquished and these words will be fulfilled: 'they shall beat their swords into ploughshares, and their spears into pruning hooks; nation shall not lift up sword against nation, neither shall they learn war any more.'[111]

IN BRIEF

2318 *'In [God's] hand is the life of every living thing and the breath of all mankind' (Job 12:10).*

2319 *Every human life, from the moment of conception until death, is sacred because the human person has been willed for its own sake in the image and likeness of the living and holy God.*

2320 *The murder of a human being is gravely contrary to the dignity of the person and the holiness of the Creator.*

2321 *The prohibition of murder does not abrogate the right to render an unjust aggressor unable to inflict harm. Legitimate defence is a grave duty for whoever is responsible for the lives of others or the common good.*

2322 *From its conception, the child has the right to life. Direct abortion, that is, abortion willed as an end or as a means, is a 'criminal' practice (GS 27 § 3), gravely contrary to the moral law. The Church imposes the canonical penalty of excommunication for this crime against human life.*

---

[110] Cf. Paul VI, *PP* 53.   [111] *GS* 78 § 6; cf. *Is* 2:4.

2323 *Because it should be treated as a person from conception, the embryo must be defended in its integrity, cared for and healed like every other human being.*

2324 *Intentional euthanasia, whatever its forms or motives, is murder. It is gravely contrary to the dignity of the human person and to the respect due to the living God, his Creator.*

2325 *Suicide is seriously contrary to justice, hope and charity. It is forbidden by the fifth commandment.*

2326 *Scandal is a grave offence when by deed or omission it deliberately leads others to sin gravely.*

2327 *Because of the evils and injustices that all war brings with it, we must do everything reasonably possible to avoid it. The Church prays: 'From famine, pestilence and war, O Lord, deliver us.'*

2328 *The Church and human reason assert the permanent validity of the moral law during armed conflicts. Practices deliberately contrary to the law of nations and to its universal principles are crimes.*

2329 *'The arms race is one of the greatest curses on the human race and the harm it inflicts on the poor is more than can be endured' (GS 81 § 3).*

2330 *'Blessed are the peacemakers, for they shall be called sons of God' (Mt 5:9).*

Article 6

THE SIXTH COMMANDMENT

You shall not commit adultery.[112]

You have heard that it was said, 'You shall not commit adultery.' But I say to you that every one who looks at a woman lustfully has already committed adultery with her in his heart.[113]

I. 'Male and Female He Created Them...'

369–373

2331 'God is love and in himself he lives a mystery of personal loving communion. Creating the human race in his own image..., God inscribed in the humanity of man and woman the *vocation*, and thus the capacity and responsibility, *of love* and communion.'[114]

1604

'God created man in his own image... male and female he created them';[115] he blessed them and said, 'Be fruitful and

---

[112] *Ex* 10:14; cf. *Dt* 5:18.
[113] *Mt* 5:27–28.

[114] *FC* 11.
[115] *Gen* 1:27.

multiply';[116] 'When God created man, he made him in the likeness of God. Male and female he created them, and he blessed them and named them Man when they were created.'[117]

2332 *Sequality* affects all aspects of the human person in the unity
362 of his body and soul. It especially concerns affectivity, the capacity to love and to procreate, and in a more general way the aptitude for forming bonds of communion with others.

2333 Everyone, man and woman, should acknowledge and accept his sexual *identity*. Physical, moral and spiritual *difference* and *complementarity* are oriented toward the goods of marriage and
1603 the flourishing of family life. The harmony of the couple and of society depends in part on the way in which the complementarity, needs and mutual support between the sexes are lived out.

2334 'In creating men "male and female", God gives man and woman an equal personal dignity.'[118] 'Man is a person, man and
357 woman equally so, since both were created in the image and likeness of the personal God.'[119]

2335 Each of the two sexes is an image of the power and tenderness of God, with equal dignity though in a different way. The *union of man and woman* in marriage is a way of imitating in the
2205 flesh the Creator's generosity and fecundity: 'Therefore a man leaves his father and his mother and cleaves to his wife, and they become one flesh.'[120] All human generations proceed from this union.[121]

2336 Jesus came to restore creation to the purity of its origins. In
1614 the Sermon on the Mount, he interprets God's plan strictly: 'You have heard that it was said, "You shall not commit adultery." But I say to you that every one who looks at a woman lustfully has already committed adultery with her in his heart.'[122] What God has joined together, let not man put asunder.[123]

The tradition of the Church has understood the sixth commandment as encompassing the whole of human sexuality.

II. The Vocation to Chastity

2520 2337 Chastity means the successful integration of sexuality within
2349 the person and thus the inner unity of man in his bodily and spiritual being. Sexuality, in which man's belonging to the bodily

---

[116] *Gen* 1:28.
[117] *Gen* 5:1–2.
[118] *FC* 22; cf. *GS* 49 § 2.
[119] John Paul II, *MD* 6.

[120] *Gen* 2:24.
[121] Cf. *Gen* 4:1–2, 25–26; 5:1.
[122] *Mt* 5:27–28.
[123] Cf. *Mt* 19:6.

and biological world is expressed, becomes personal and truly human when it is integrated into the relationship of one person to another, in the complete and lifelong mutual gift of a man and a woman.

The virtue of chastity therefore involves the integrity of the person and the integrality of the gift.

The integrity of the person

2338 The chaste person maintains the integrity of the powers of life and love placed in him. This integrity ensures the unity of the person; it is opposed to any behaviour that would impair it. It tolerates neither a double life nor duplicity in speech.[124]

2339 Chastity includes an *apprenticeship in self-mastery* which is a training in human freedom. The alternative is clear: either man governs his passions and finds peace, or he lets himself be dominated by them and becomes unhappy.[125] 'Man's dignity therefore requires him to act out of conscious and free choice, as moved and drawn in a personal way from within, and not by blind impulses in himself or by mere external constraint. Man gains such dignity when, ridding himself of all slavery to the passions, he presses *1767* forward to his goal by freely choosing what is good and, by his diligence and skill, effectively secures for himself the means suited to this end.'[126]

2340 Whoever wants to remain faithful to his baptismal promises and resist temptations will want to adopt the *means* for doing so: self-knowledge, practice of an ascesis adapted to the situations that *2015* confront him, obedience to God's commandments, exercise of the moral virtues and fidelity to prayer. 'Indeed it is through chastity that we are gathered together and led back to the unity from which we were fragmented into multiplicity.'[127]

2341 The virtue of chastity comes under the cardinal virtue of *temperance*, which seeks to permeate the passions and appetites of *1809* the senses with reason.

2342 Self-mastery is a *long and exacting work*. One can never consider it acquired once and for all. It presupposes renewed effort at *409* all stages of life.[128] The effort required can be more intense in certain periods, such as when the personality is being formed during childhood and adolescence.

---

[124] Cf. *Mt* 5:37.
[125] Cf. *Sir* 1:22.
[126] GS 17.

[127] St Augustine, *Conf.* 10, 29, 40: PL 32, 796.
[128] Cf. *Titus* 2:1–6.

2343 Chastity has *laws of growth* which progress through stages marked by imperfection and too often by sin. 'Man... day by day builds himself up through his many free decisions; and so he 2223 knows, loves and accomplishes moral good by stages of growth.'[129]

2344 Chastity represents an eminently personal task; it also involves a *cultural effort*, for there is 'an interdependence between 2525 personal betterment and the improvement of society'.[130] Chastity presupposes respect for the rights of the person, in particular the right to receive information and an education that respect the moral and spiritual dimensions of human life.

1810 2345 Chastity is a moral virtue. It is also a gift from God, a *grace*, a fruit of spiritual effort.[131] The Holy Spirit enables one whom the water of Baptism has regenerated to imitate the purity of Christ.[132]

The integrality of the gift of self

1827 2346 Charity is the *form* of all the virtues. Under its influence, chastity appears as a school of the gift of the person. Self-mastery is ordered to the gift of self. Chastity leads him who practises it to 210 become a witness to his neighbour of God's fidelity and loving kindness.

374 2347 The virtue of chastity blossoms in *friendship*. It shows the disciple how to follow and imitate him who has chosen us as his friends,[133] who has given himself totally to us and allows us to participate in his divine estate. Chastity is a promise of immortality.

Chastity is expressed notably in *friendship with one's neighbour*. Whether it develops between persons of the same or opposite sex, friendship represents a great good for all. It leads to spiritual communion.

The various forms of chastity

2348 All the baptized are called to chastity. The Christian has 'put on Christ',[134] the model for all chastity. All Christ's faithful are called to lead a chaste life in keeping with their particular states of life. At the moment of his Baptism, the Christian is pledged to lead his affective life in chastity.

---

[129] *FC* 34.
[130] *GS* 25 § 1.
[131] Cf. *Gal* 5:22.

[132] Cf. 1 *Jn* 3:3.
[133] Cf. *Jn* 15:15.
[134] *Gal* 3:27.

2349 'People should cultivate [chastity] in the way that is suited to their state of life. Some profess virginity or consecrated celibacy *1620* which enables them to give themselves to God alone with an undivided heart in a remarkable manner. Others live in the way prescribed for all by the moral law, whether they are married or single.'[135] Married people are called to live conjugal chastity; others practise chastity in continence:

> There are three forms of the virtue of chastity: the first is that of spouses, the second that of widows and the third that of virgins. We do not praise any one of them to the exclusion of the others. . . This is what makes for the richness of the discipline of the Church.[136]

2350 Those who are *engaged to marry* are called to live chastity in *1632* continence. They should see in this time of testing a discovery of mutual respect, an apprenticeship in fidelity and the hope of receiving one another from God. They should reserve for marriage the expressions of affection that belong to married love. They will help each other grow in chastity.

Offences against chastity

2351 *Lust* is disordered desire for or inordinate enjoyment of *2528* sexual pleasure. Sexual pleasure is morally disordered when sought for itself, isolated from its procreative and unitive purposes.

2352 By *masturbation* is to be understood the deliberate stimulation of the genital organs in order to derive sexual pleasure. 'Both the Magisterium of the Church, in the course of a constant tradition, and the moral sense of the faithful have been in no doubt and have firmly maintained that masturbation is an intrinsically and gravely disordered action.'[137] 'The deliberate use of the sexual faculty, for whatever reason, outside of marriage is essentially contrary to its purpose.' For here sexual pleasure is sought outside of 'the sexual relationship which is demanded by the moral order and in which the total meaning of mutual self-giving and human procreation in the context of true love is achieved.'[138]

To form an equitable judgement about the subjects' moral responsibility and to guide pastoral action, one must take into account the affective immaturity, force of acquired habit, conditions of anxiety or other psychological or social factors that can *1735* lessen, if not reduce to a minimum, moral culpability.

---

[135] CDF, *Persona humana* 11.
[136] St Ambrose, *De viduis* 4, 23: PL 16, 255A.
[137] CDF, *Persona humana* 9.
[138] CDF, *Persona humana* 9.

2353 *Fornication* is carnal union between an unmarried man and an unmarried woman. It is gravely contrary to the dignity of persons and of human sexuality which is naturally ordered to the good of spouses and the generation and education of children. Moreover, it is a grave scandal when there is corruption of the young.

2354 *Pornography* consists in removing real or simulated sexual
2523 acts from the intimacy of the partners, in order to display them deliberately to third parties. It offends against chastity because it perverts the conjugal act, the intimate giving of spouses to each other. It does grave injury to the dignity of its participants (actors, vendors, the public), since each one becomes an object of base pleasure and illicit profit for others. It immerses all who are involved in the illusion of a fantasy world. It is a grave offence. Civil authorities should prevent the production and distribution of pornographic materials.

2355 *Prostitution* does injury to the dignity of the person who engages in it, reducing the person to an instrument of sexual pleasure. The one who pays sins gravely against himself: he violates the chastity to which his Baptism pledged him and defiles his body, the temple of the Holy Spirit.[139] Prostitution is a social scourge. It usually involves women, but also men, children and adolescents (the latter two cases involve the added sin of scandal). While it is always gravely sinful to engage in prostitution, the imputability of
1735 the offence can be attenuated by destitution, blackmail or social pressure.

2356 *Rape* is the forcible violation of the sexual intimacy of another person. It does injury to justice and charity. Rape deeply
2297 wounds the respect, freedom and physical and moral integrity to which every person has a right. It causes grave damage that can
1756 mark the victim for life. It is always an intrinsically evil act. Graver
2388 still is the rape of children committed by parents (incest) or those responsible for the education of the children entrusted to them.

Chastity and homosexuality

2357 Homosexuality refers to relations between men or between women who experience an exclusive or predominant sexual attraction toward persons of the same sex. It has taken a great variety of forms through the centuries and in different cultures. Its psychological genesis remains largely unexplained. Basing itself

---

[139] Cf. 1 *Cor* 6:15-20.

on Sacred Scripture, which presents homosexual acts as acts of grave depravity,[140] Tradition has always declared that 'homosexual acts are intrinsically disordered.'[141] They are contrary to the natural law. They close the sexual act to the gift of life. They do not proceed from a genuine affective and sexual complementarity. *2333* Under no circumstances can they be approved.

2358 The number of men and women who have deep-seated homosexual tendencies is not negligible. This inclination, which is objectively disordered, constitutes for most of them a trial. They must be accepted with respect, compassion and sensitivity. Every sign of unjust discrimination in their regard should be avoided. These persons are called to fulfil God's will in their lives and, if they are Christians, to unite to the sacrifice of the Lord's Cross the difficulties they may encounter from their condition.

2359 Homosexual persons are called to chastity. By the virtues of self-mastery that teach them inner freedom, at times by the support of disinterested friendship, by prayer and sacramental grace, *2347* they can and should gradually and resolutely approach Christian perfection.

III. The Love of Husband and Wife

2360 Sexuality is ordered to the conjugal love of man and woman. In marriage the physical intimacy of the spouses becomes a sign and pledge of spiritual communion. Marriage bonds between baptized persons are sanctified by the sacrament. *1601*

2361 'Sexuality, by means of which man and woman give themselves to one another through the acts which are proper and exclusive to spouses, is not something simply biological, but concerns the innermost being of the human person as such. It is realized in a *1643* truly human way only if it is an integral part of the love by which a *2332* man and woman commit themselves totally to one another until death.'[142]

> Tobias got out of bed and said to Sarah, 'Sister, get up, and let us pray and *1611* implore our Lord that he grant us mercy and safety.' So she got up, and they began to pray and implore that they might be kept safe. Tobias began by saying, 'Blessed are you, O God of our fathers... You made Adam, and for him you made his wife Eve as a helper and support. From the two of them the race of mankind has sprung. You said, "It is not good that the man should be alone; let us make a helper for him like himself." I now am taking this kinswoman of mine, not because of lust, but with

---

[140] Cf. *Gen* 19:1–29; *Rom* 1:24–27; 1 *Cor* 6:10; 1 *Tim* 1:10.

[141] CDF, *Persona humana* 8.

[142] *FC* 11.

sincerity. Grant that she and I may find mercy and that we may grow old together.' And they both said, 'Amen, Amen.' Then they went to sleep for the night.[143]

2362 'The acts in marriage by which the intimate and chaste union of the spouses takes place are noble and honourable; the truly human performance of these acts fosters the self-giving they signify, and enriches the spouses in joy and gratitude.'[144] Sexuality is a source of joy and pleasure:

> The Creator himself... established that in the [generative] function, spouses should experience pleasure and enjoyment of body and spirit. Therefore, the spouses do nothing evil in seeking this pleasure and enjoyment. They accept what the Creator has intended for them. At the same time, spouses should know how to keep themselves within the limits of just moderation.[145]

2363 The spouses' union achieves the twofold end of marriage: the good of the spouses themselves, and the transmission of life. These two meanings or values of marriage cannot be separated without altering the couple's spiritual life and compromising the goods of marriage and the future of the family.

The conjugal love of man and woman thus stands under the twofold obligation of fidelity and fecundity.

1646–1648 Conjugal fidelity

2364 The married couple forms 'the intimate partnership of life 1603 and love established by the Creator and governed by his laws; it is rooted in the conjugal covenant, that is, in their irrevocable personal consent.'[146] Both give themselves definitively and totally to one another. They are no longer two; from now on they form one flesh. The covenant they freely contracted imposes on the spouses 1615 the obligation to preserve it as unique and indissoluble.[147] 'What therefore God has joined together, let not man put asunder.'[148]

2365 Fidelity expresses constancy in keeping one's given word. God is faithful. The sacrament of Matrimony enables man and 1640 woman to enter into Christ's fidelity for his Church. Through conjugal chastity, they bear witness to this mystery before the world.

> St John Chrysostom suggests that young husbands should say to their wives: I have taken you in my arms, and I love you, and I prefer you to my life itself. For the present life is nothing, and my most ardent dream is

[143] Tob 8:4–9.
[144] GS 49 § 2.
[145] Pius XII, Discourse, 29 October 1951.
[146] GS 48 § 1.
[147] Cf. CIC, can. 1056.
[148] Mk 10:9; cf. Mt 19:1–12; 1 Cor 7:10–11.

to spend it with you in such a way that we may be assured of not being separated in the life reserved for us... I place your love above all things, and nothing would be more bitter or painful to me than to be of a different mind than you.[149]

The fecundity of marriage

1652–1653

2366 Fecundity is a gift, an *end of marriage*, for conjugal love naturally tends to be fruitful. A child does not come from outside as something added on to the mutual love of the spouses, but springs from the very heart of that mutual giving, as its fruit and fulfilment. So the Church, which 'is on the side of life',[150] teaches that 'it is necessary that each and every marriage act remain ordered *per se* in the procreation of human life.'[151] 'This particular doctrine, expounded on numerous occasions by the Magisterium, is based on the inseparable connection, established by God, which man on his own initiative may not break, between the unitive significance and the procreative significance which are both inherent to the marriage act.'[152]

2367 Called to give life, spouses share in the creative power and 2205 fatherhood of God.[153] 'Married couples should regard it as their proper mission to transmit human life, and to educate their children; they should realize that they are thereby *co-operating with* the love of *God the Creator* and are, in a certain sense, its interpreters. They will fulfil this duty with a sense of human and Christian responsibility.'[154]

2368 A particular aspect of this responsibility concerns the *regulation of procreation*. For just reasons, spouses may wish to space the births of their children. It is their duty to make certain that their desire is not motivated by selfishness but is in conformity with the generosity appropriate to responsible parenthood. Moreover, they should conform their behaviour to the objective criteria of morality:

> When it is a question of harmonizing married love with the responsible transmission of life, the morality of the behaviour does not depend on sincere intention and evaluation of motives alone; but it must be determined by objective criteria, criteria drawn from the nature of the person and his acts, criteria that respect the total meaning of mutual self-giving and human procreation in the context of true love; this is possible only if the virtue of married chastity is practised with sincerity of heart.[155]

---

[149] St John Chrysostom, *Hom. in Eph.* 20, 8: PG 62, 146–147.
[150] FC 30.
[151] Paul VI, *HV* 11.
[152] *HV* 12; cf. Pius XI, Enc. *Casti connubii.*
[153] Cf. *Eph* 3:14; *Mt* 23:9.
[154] GS 50 § 2.
[155] GS 51 § 3.

2369 'By safeguarding both these essential aspects, the unitive and the procreative, the conjugal act preserves in its fullness the sense of true mutual love and its orientation toward man's exalted vocation to parenthood.'[156]

2370 Periodic continence, that is, the methods of birth regulation based on self-observation and the use of infertile periods, is in conformity with the objective criteria of morality.[157] These methods respect the bodies of the spouses, encourage tenderness between them and favour the education of an authentic freedom. In contrast, 'every action which, whether in anticipation of the conjugal act, or in its accomplishment, or in the development of its natural consequences, proposes, whether as an end or as a means, to render procreation impossible' is intrinsically evil:[158]

> Thus the innate language that expresses the total reciprocal self-giving of husband and wife is overlaid, through contraception, by an objectively contradictory language, namely, that of not giving oneself totally to the other. This leads not only to a positive refusal to be open to life but also to a falsification of the inner truth of conjugal love, which is called upon to give itself in personal totality... The difference, both anthropological and moral, between contraception and recourse to the rhythm of the cycle... involves in the final analysis two irreconcilable concepts of the human person and of human sexuality.[159]

2371 'Let all be convinced that human life and the duty of transmitting it are not limited by the horizons of this life only: their true evaluation and full significance can be understood only in reference to man's eternal destiny.'[160]

1703

2372 The state has a responsibility for its citizens' well-being. In this capacity it is legitimate for it to intervene to orient the demography of the population. This can be done by means of objective and respectful information, but certainly not by authoritarian, coercive measures. The state may not legitimately usurp the initiative of spouses, who have the primary responsibility for the procreation and education of their children.[161] In this area, it is not authorized to employ means contrary to the moral law.

2209

The gift of a child

2373 Sacred Scripture and the Church's traditional practice see in *large families* a sign of God's blessing and the parents' generosity.[162]

---

[156] HV 12.
[157] Cf. HV 16.
[158] HV 14.
[159] FC 32.

[160] GS 51 § 4.
[161] Cf. HV 23; PP 37.
[162] Cf. GS 50 § 2.

2374 Couples who discover that they are sterile suffer greatly. *1654* 'What will you give me', asks Abraham of God, 'for I continue childless?'[163] And Rachel cries to her husband Jacob, 'Give me children, or I shall die!'[164]

2375 Research aimed at reducing human sterility is to be encouraged, on condition that it is placed 'at the service of the human person, of his inalienable rights and his true and integral good *2293* according to the design and will of God'.[165]

2376 Techniques that entail the dissociation of husband and wife, by the intrusion of a person other than the couple (donation of sperm or ovum, surrogate uterus), are gravely immoral. These techniques (heterologous artificial insemination and fertilization) infringe the child's right to be born of a father and mother known to him and bound to each other by marriage. They betray the spouses' 'right to become a father and a mother only through each other'.[166]

2377 Techniques involving only the married couple (homologous artificial insemination and fertilization) are perhaps less reprehensible, yet remain morally unacceptable. They dissociate the sexual act from the procreative act. The act which brings the child into existence is no longer an act by which two persons give themselves to one another, but one that 'entrusts the life and identity of the embryo into the power of doctors and biologists and establishes the domination of technology over the origin and destiny of the human person. Such a relationship of domination is in itself contrary to the dignity and equality that must be common to parents and children.'[167] 'Under the moral aspect procreation is deprived of its proper perfection when it is not willed as the fruit of the conjugal act, that is to say, of the specific act of the spouses' union... Only respect for the link between the meanings of the conjugal act and respect for the unity of the human being make possible procreation in conformity with the dignity of the person.'[168]

2378 A child is not something *owed* to one, but is a *gift*. The 'supreme gift of marriage' is a human person. A child may not be considered a piece of property, an idea to which an alleged 'right to a child' would lead. In this area, only the child possesses genuine rights: the right 'to be the fruit of the specific act of the conjugal love of his parents', and 'the right to be respected as a person from the moment of his conception'.[169]

2379 The Gospel shows that physical sterility is not an absolute evil. Spouses who still suffer from infertility after exhausting legit-

---

[163] *Gen* 15:2.
[164] *Gen* 30:1.
[165] CDF, *Donum vitae*, intro. 2.
[166] CDF, *Donum vitae* II, 1.

[167] CDF, *Donum vitae* II, 5.
[168] CDF, *Donum vitae* II, 4.
[169] CDF, *Donum vitae* II, 8.

imate medical procedures should unite themselves with the Lord's Cross, the source of all spiritual fecundity. They can give expression to their generosity by adopting abandoned children or performing demanding services for others.

IV. Offences Against the Dignity of Marriage

Adultery

2380 *Adultery* refers to marital infidelity. When two partners, of whom at least one is married to another party, have sexual relations – even transient ones – they commit adultery. Christ condemns even adultery of mere desire.[170] The sixth commandment and the New Testament forbid adultery absolutely.[171] The prophets denounce the gravity of adultery; they see it as an image of the sin of idolatry.[172]

1611

2381 Adultery is an injustice. He who commits adultery fails in his commitment. He does injury to the sign of the covenant which the marriage bond is, transgresses the rights of the other spouse and undermines the institution of marriage by breaking the contract on which it is based. He compromises the good of human generation and the welfare of children who need their parents' stable union.

1640

Divorce

2382 The Lord Jesus insisted on the original intention of the Creator who willed that marriage be indissoluble.[173] He abrogates the accommodations that had slipped into the Old Law.[174]

1614

Between the baptized, 'a ratified and consummated marriage cannot be dissolved by any human power or for any reason other than death.'[175]

2383 The *separation* of spouses while maintaining the marriage bond can be legitimate in certain cases provided for by canon law.[176]

1649

If civil divorce remains the only possible way of ensuring certain legal rights, the care of the children, or the protection of inheritance, it can be tolerated and does not constitute a moral offence.

2384 *Divorce* is a grave offence against the natural law. It claims to break the contract, to which the spouses freely consented, to live

1650

---

[170] Cf. *Mt* 5:27–28.
[171] Cf. *Mt* 5:32; 19:6; *Mk* 10:11; 1 *Cor* 6:9–10.
[172] Cf. *Hos* 2:7; *Jer* 5:7; 13:27.
[173] Cf. *Mt* 5:31–32; 19:3–9; *Mk* 10:9; *Lk* 16:18; 1 *Cor* 7:10–11.
[174] Cf. *Mt* 19:7–9.
[175] CIC, can. 1141.
[176] Cf. CIC, cann. 1151–1155.

with each other till death. Divorce does injury to the covenant of salvation, of which sacramental marriage is the sign. Contracting a new union, even if it is recognized by civil law, adds to the gravity of the rupture: the remarried spouse is then in a situation of public and permanent adultery:

> If a husband, separated from his wife, approaches another woman, he is an adulterer because he makes that woman commit adultery; and the woman who lives with him is an adulteress, because she has drawn another's husband to herself.[177]

2385 Divorce is immoral also because it introduces disorder into the family and into society. This disorder brings grave harm to the deserted spouse, to children traumatized by the separation of their parents and often torn between them, and because of its contagious effect which makes it truly a plague on society.

2386 It can happen that one of the spouses is the innocent victim of a divorce decreed by civil law; this spouse therefore has not contravened the moral law. There is a considerable difference between a spouse who has sincerely tried to be faithful to the sacrament of marriage and is unjustly abandoned, and one who through his own grave fault destroys a canonically valid marriage.[178] *1640*

Other offences against the dignity of marriage

2387 The predicament of a man who, desiring to convert to the Gospel, is obliged to repudiate one or more wives with whom he has shared years of conjugal life, is understandable. However *polygamy* is not in accord with the moral law. '[Conjugal] commu- *1610*
nion is radically contradicted by polygamy; this, in fact, directly negates the plan of God which was revealed from the beginning, because it is contrary to the equal personal dignity of men and women who in matrimony give themselves with a love that is total and therefore unique and exclusive.'[179] The Christian who has previously lived in polygamy has a grave duty in justice to honour the obligations contracted in regard to his former wives and his children.

2388 *Incest* designates intimate relations between relatives or *2356*
in-laws within a degree that prohibits marriage between them.[180]
St Paul stigmatizes this especially grave offence: 'It is actually reported that there is immorality among you. . . for a man is living

---

[177] St Basil, *Moralia* 73, 1: PG 31, 849–852.
[178] Cf. FC 84.
[179] FC 19; cf. GS 47 § 2.
[180] Cf. *Lev* 18:7–20.

with his father's wife... In the name of the Lord Jesus... you are to deliver this man to Satan for the destruction of the flesh...'[181]

2207 Incest corrupts family relationships and marks a regression toward animality.

2389 Connected to incest is any sexual abuse perpetrated by adults on children or adolescents entrusted to their care. The offence is
2285 compounded by the scandalous harm done to the physical and moral integrity of the young, who will remain scarred by it all their lives; and the violation of responsibility for their upbringing.

2390 In a so-called *free union*, a man and a woman refuse to give
1631 juridical and public form to a liaison involving sexual intimacy.

The expression 'free union' is fallacious: what can 'union' mean when the partners make no commitment to one another, each exhibiting a lack of trust in the other, in himself, or in the future?

The expression covers a number of different situations: concubinage, rejection of marriage as such, or inability to make long-term commitments.[182] All these situations offend against the dignity of marriage; they destroy the very idea of the family; they weaken the sense of fidelity. They are contrary to the moral law.
2353 The sexual act must take place exclusively within marriage. Outside of marriage it always constitutes a grave sin and excludes one
1385 from sacramental communion.

2391 Some today claim a '*right to a trial marriage*' where there is an intention of getting married later. However firm the purpose of those who engage in premature sexual relations may be, 'the fact is that such liaisons can scarcely ensure mutual sincerity and fidelity in a relationship between a man and a woman, nor, especially, can they protect it from inconstancy of desires or whim.'[183] Carnal union is morally legitimate only when a definitive community of
2364 life between a man and woman has been established. Human love does not tolerate 'trial marriages'. It demands a total and definitive gift of persons to one another.[184]

IN BRIEF

2392 '*Love is the fundamental and innate vocation of every human being*' (FC 11).

---

[181] 1 *Cor* 5:1, 4–5.   [183] CDF, *Persona humana* 7.
[182] Cf. *FC* 81.   [184] Cf. *FC* 80.

2393 *By creating the human being man and woman, God gives personal dignity equally to the one and the other. Each of them, man and woman, should acknowledge and accept his sexual identity.*

2394 *Christ is the model of chastity. Every baptized person is called to lead a chaste life, each according to his particular state of life.*

2395 *Chastity means the integration of sexuality within the person. It includes an apprenticeship in self-mastery.*

2396 *Among the sins gravely contrary to chastity are masturbation, fornication, pornography, and homosexual practices.*

2397 *The covenant which spouses have freely entered into entails faithful love. It imposes on them the obligation to keep their marriage indissoluble.*

2398 *Fecundity is a good, a gift and an end of marriage. By giving life, spouses participate in God's fatherhood.*

2399 *The regulation of births represents one of the aspects of responsible fatherhood and motherhood. Legitimate intentions on the part of the spouses do not justify recourse to morally unacceptable means (for example, direct sterilization or contraception).*

2400 *Adultery, divorce, polygamy and free union are grave offences against the dignity of marriage.*

Article 7
THE SEVENTH COMMANDMENT

You shall not steal.[185]

2401 The seventh commandment forbids unjustly taking or keeping the goods of one's neighbour and wronging him in any way with respect to his goods. It commands justice and charity in *1807* the care of earthly goods and the fruits of men's labour. For the sake of the common good, it requires respect for the universal destination of goods and respect for the right to private property. Christian life strives to order this world's goods to God and to *952* fraternal charity.

I. The Universal Destination and the Private Ownership of Goods

2402 In the beginning God entrusted the earth and its resources to the common stewardship of mankind to take care of them, master *226* them by labour and enjoy their fruits.[186] The goods of creation are destined for the whole human race. However, the earth is divided

---

[185] *Ex* 20:15; cf. *Dt* 5:19; *Mt* 19:18. [186] Cf. *Gen* 1:26–29.

up among men to assure the security of their lives, endangered by poverty and threatened by violence. The appropriation of property is legitimate for guaranteeing the freedom and dignity of persons, and for helping each of them to meet his basic needs and the needs of those in his charge. It should allow for a natural *1939* solidarity to develop between men.

2403 The *right to private property*, acquired or received in a just way, does not do away with the original gift of the earth to the whole of mankind. The *universal destination of goods* remains primordial, even if the promotion of the common good requires respect for the right to private property and its exercise.

2404 'In his use of things man should regard the external goods he legitimately owns not merely as exclusive to himself but common to others also, in the sense that they can benefit others as well as himself.'[187] The ownership of any property makes its holder a *307* steward of Providence, with the task of making it fruitful and communicating its benefits to others, first of all his family.

2405 Goods of production – material or immaterial – such as land, factories, practical or artistic skills, oblige their possessors to employ them in ways that will benefit the greatest number. Those who hold goods for use and consumption should use them with moderation, reserving the better part for guests, for the sick and the poor.

1903 2406 *Political authority* has the right and duty to regulate the legitimate exercise of the right to ownership for the sake of the common good.[188]

II. Respect for Persons and Their Goods

2407 In economic matters, respect for human dignity requires the *1809* practice of the virtue of *temperance*, so as to moderate attachment *1807* to this world's goods; the practice of the virtue of *justice*, to preserve our neighbour's rights and render him what is his due; and *1939* the practice of *solidarity*, in accordance with the golden rule and in keeping with the generosity of the Lord, who 'though he was rich, yet for your sake... became poor so that by his poverty, you might become rich.'[189]

Respect for the goods of others

2408 The seventh commandment forbids *theft*, that is, usurping

---

[187] GS 69 § 1.
[188] Cf. GS 71 § 4; John Paul II, *SRS* 42;

CA 40; 48.
[189] 2 Cor 8:9.

another's property against the reasonable will of the owner. There is no theft if consent can be presumed or if refusal is contrary to reason and the universal destination of goods. This is the case in obvious and urgent necessity when the only way to provide for immediate, essential needs (food, shelter, clothing...) is to put at one's disposal and use the property of others.[190]

2409 Even if it does not contradict the provisions of civil law, any form of unjustly taking and keeping the property of others is against the seventh commandment: thus, deliberate retention of goods lent or of objects lost; business fraud; paying unjust wages; *1867* forcing up prices by taking advantage of the ignorance or hardship of another.[191]

The following are also morally illicit: speculation in which one contrives to manipulate the price of goods artificially, in order to gain an advantage to the detriment of others; corruption in which one influences the judgement of those who must make decisions according to law; appropriation and use for private purposes of the common goods of an enterprise; work poorly done; tax evasion; forgery of cheques and invoices; excessive expenses and waste. Wilfully damaging private or public property is contrary to the moral law and requires reparation.

2410 *Promises* must be kept and *contracts* strictly observed to the *2101* extent that the commitments made in them are morally just. A significant part of economic and social life depends on the honouring of contracts between physical or moral persons – commercial contracts of purchase or sale, rental or labour contracts. All contracts must be agreed to and executed in good faith.

2411 Contracts are subject to *commutative justice* which regulates *1807* exchanges between persons and between institutions in accordance with a strict respect for their rights. Commutative justice obliges strictly; it requires safeguarding property rights, paying debts and fulfilling obligations freely contracted. Without commutative justice, no other form of justice is possible.

One distinguishes *commutative* justice from *legal* justice which concerns what the citizen owes in fairness to the community, and from *distributive* justice which regulates what the community owes its citizens in proportion to their contributions and needs.

2412 In virtue of commutative justice, *reparation for injustice* com- *1459* mitted requires the restitution of stolen goods to their owner:

Jesus blesses Zacchaeus for his pledge: 'If I have defrauded anyone of anything, I restore it fourfold.'[192] Those who, directly or indirectly, have taken possession of the goods of another are obliged to make restitution of them, or *2487*

---

[190] Cf. GS 69 § 1.   Am 8:4–6.
[191] Cf. Dt 25:13–16; 24:14–15; Jas 5:4;   [192] Lk 19:8.

to return the equivalent in kind or in money, if the goods have disappeared, as well as the profit or advantages their owner would have legitimately obtained from them. Likewise, all who in some manner have taken part in a theft or who have knowingly benefited from it – for example, those who ordered it, assisted in it or received the stolen goods – are obliged to make restitution in proportion to their responsibility and to their share of what was stolen.

2413 *Games of chance* (card games, etc.) or *wagers* are not in themselves contrary to justice. They become morally unacceptable when they deprive someone of what is necessary to provide for his needs and those of others. The passion for gambling risks becoming an enslavement. Unfair wagers and cheating at games constitute grave matter, unless the damage inflicted is so slight that the one who suffers it cannot reasonably consider it significant.

2414 The seventh commandment forbids acts or enterprises that for any reason – selfish or ideological, commercial or totalitarian – 2297 lead to the *enslavement of human beings*, to their being bought, sold and exchanged like merchandise, in disregard for their personal dignity. It is a sin against the dignity of persons and their fundamental rights to reduce them by violence to their productive value or to a source of profit. St Paul directed a Christian master to treat his Christian slave 'no longer as a slave but more than a slave, as a beloved brother . . . both in the flesh and in the Lord'.[193]

Respect for the integrity of creation

2415 The seventh commandment enjoins respect for the integrity 226, 358 of creation. Animals, like plants and inanimate beings, are by nature destined for the common good of past, present and future humanity.[194] Use of the mineral, vegetable and animal resources of the universe cannot be divorced from respect for moral impera- 373 tives. Man's dominion over inanimate and other living beings granted by the Creator is not absolute; it is limited by concern for the quality of life of his neighbour, including generations to come; 378 it requires a religious respect for the integrity of creation.[195]

2416 *Animals* are God's creatures. He surrounds them with his providential care. By their mere existence they bless him and give him glory.[196] Thus men owe them kindness. We should recall the gentleness with which saints like St Francis of Assisi or St Philip 344 Neri treated animals.

2417 God entrusted animals to the stewardship of those whom he created in his own image.[197] Hence it is legitimate to use animals for food and clothing. They may be domesticated to help man in 2294 his work and leisure. Medical and scientific experimentation on

---

[193] *Philem* 16.
[194] Cf. *Gen* 1:28–31.
[195] Cf. *CA* 37–38.

[196] Cf. *Mt* 6:26; *Dan* 3:79–81.
[197] Cf. *Gen* 2:19–20; 9:1–4.

animals is a morally acceptable practice if it remains within reasonable limits and contributes to caring for or saving human lives.

2418 It is contrary to human dignity to cause animals to suffer or die needlessly. It is likewise unworthy to spend money on them that should as a priority go to the relief of human misery. One can love animals; one should not direct to them the affection due only to persons.   *2446*

III. The Social Doctrine of the Church

2419 'Christian revelation... promotes deeper understanding of the laws of social living.'[198] The Church receives from the Gospel *1960* the full revelation of the truth about man. When she fulfils her mission of proclaiming the Gospel, she bears witness to man, in the name of Christ, to his dignity and his vocation to the communion *359* of persons. She teaches him the demands of justice and peace in conformity with divine wisdom.

2420 The Church makes a moral judgement about economic and *2032* social matters, 'when the fundamental rights of the person or the salvation of souls requires it'.[199] In the moral order she bears a mission distinct from that of political authorities: the Church is *2246* concerned with the temporal aspects of the common good because they are ordered to the sovereign Good, our ultimate end. She strives to inspire right attitudes with respect to earthly goods and in socio-economic relationships.

2421 The social doctrine of the Church developed in the nineteenth century when the Gospel encountered modern industrial society with its new structures for the production of consumer goods, its new concept of society, the state and authority, and its new forms of labour and ownership. The development of the doctrine of the Church on economic and social matters attests the permanent value of the Church's teaching at the same time as it attests the true meaning of her Tradition, always living and active.[200]

2422 The Church's social teaching comprises a body of doctrine, which is articulated as the Church interprets events in the course of history, with the assistance of the Holy Spirit, in the light of the whole of what has been revealed by Jesus Christ.[201] This teaching can be more easily accepted by men of good will, the more the faithful let themselves be guided by it.   *2044*

2423 The Church's social teaching proposes principles for

---

[198] GS 23 § 1.   [200] Cf. CA 3.
[199] GS 76 § 5.   [201] Cf. SRS 1; 41.

reflection; it provides criteria for judgement; it gives guidelines for action:

> Any system in which social relationships are determined entirely by economic factors is contrary to the nature of the human person and his acts.[202]

2317 2424 A theory that makes profit the exclusive norm and ultimate end of economic activity is morally unacceptable. The disordered desire for money cannot but produce perverse effects. It is one of the causes of the many conflicts which disturb the social order.[203]

A system that 'subordinates the basic rights of individuals and of groups to the collective organization of production' is contrary to human dignity.[204] Every practice that reduces persons to nothing more than a means of profit enslaves man, leads to idolizing money and contributes to the spread of atheism. 'You cannot serve God and mammon.'[205]

676 2425 The Church has rejected the totalitarian and atheistic ideologies associated in modern times with 'communism' or 'socialism'. She has likewise refused to accept, in the practice of 'capitalism', individualism and the absolute primacy of the law of the marketplace over human labour.[206] Regulating the economy solely by centralized planning perverts the basis of social bonds; regulating it solely by the law of the marketplace fails social justice, for 'there are many human needs which cannot be satisfied by the market.'[207] Reasonable regulation of the marketplace and economic initiatives, in keeping with a just hier-
1886 archy of values and a view to the common good, is to be commended.

IV. Economic Activity and Social Justice

2426 The development of economic activity and growth in production are meant to provide for the needs of human beings. Economic life is not meant solely to multiply goods produced and increase profit or power; it is ordered first of all to the service of persons, of the whole man, and of the entire human community. Economic activity, conducted according to its own proper methods, is to be exercised within the limits of the moral order, in
1928 keeping with social justice so as to correspond to God's plan for man.[208]

307 2427 *Human work* proceeds directly from persons created in the
378 image of God and called to prolong the work of creation by subduing the earth, both with and for one another.[209] Hence work is a duty: 'If any one will not work, let him not eat.'[210] Work honours the Creator's gifts and the talents received from him. It can also be
531 redemptive. By enduring the hardship of work[211] in union with

---

[202] Cf. *CA* 24.
[203] Cf. *GS* 63 § 3; John Paul II, *LE* 7; 20; *CA* 35.
[204] *GS* 65 § 2.
[205] *Mt* 6:24; *Lk* 16:13.
[206] Cf. *CA* 10; 13; 44.

[207] *CA* 34.
[208] Cf. *GS* 64.
[209] Cf. *Gen* 1:28; *GS* 34; *CA* 31.
[210] 2 *Th* 3:10; cf. 1 *Th* 4:11.
[211] Cf. *Gen* 3:14–19.

Jesus, the carpenter of Nazareth and the one crucified on Calvary, man collaborates in a certain fashion with the Son of God in his redemptive work. He shows himself to be a disciple of Christ by carrying the cross, daily, in the work he is called to accomplish.[212] Work can be a means of sanctification and a way of animating earthly realities with the Spirit of Christ.

2428 In work, the person exercises and fulfils in part the potential *2834* inscribed in his nature. The primordial value of labour stems from man himself, its author and its beneficiary. Work is for man, not *2185* man for work.[213]

    Everyone should be able to draw from work the means of providing for his life and that of his family, and of serving the human community.

2429 Everyone has the *right of economic initiative*; everyone should make legitimate use of his talents to contribute to the abundance that will benefit all, and to harvest the just fruits of his labour. He should seek to observe regulations issued by legitimate authority for the sake of the common good.[214]

2430 *Economic life* brings into play different interests, often opposed to one another. This explains why the conflicts that characterize it arise.[215] Efforts should be made to reduce these conflicts by negotiation that respects the rights and duties of each social partner: those responsible for business enterprises, representatives of wage-earners – for example, trade unions – and public authorities when appropriate.

2431 The *responsibility of the state*. 'Economic activity, especially the activity of a market economy, cannot be conducted in an institutional, juridical or political vacuum. On the contrary, it presupposes sure guarantees of individual freedom and private property, as well as a stable currency and efficient public services. Hence the principal task of the state is to guarantee this security, so *1908* that those who work and produce can enjoy the fruits of their labours and thus feel encouraged to work efficiently and honestly... Another task of the state is that of overseeing and directing the exercise of human rights in the economic sector. However, primary responsibility in this area belongs not to the state but to individuals and to the various groups and associations *1883* which make up society.'[216]

---

[212] Cf. *LE* 27.
[213] Cf. *LE* 6.
[214] Cf. *CA* 32; 34.

[215] Cf. *LE* 11.
[216] *CA* 48.

2432 Those *responsible for business enterprises* are responsible to
2415 society for the economic and ecological effects of their operations.[217] They have an obligation to consider the good of persons
and not only the increase of *profits*. Profits are necessary, however.
They make possible the investments that ensure the future of a
business and they guarantee employment.

2433 *Access to employment* and to professions must be open to all
without unjust discrimination: men and women, healthy and dis-
abled, natives and immigrants.[218] For its part society should,
according to circumstances, help citizens find work and employment.[219]

1867 2434 A *just wage* is the legitimate fruit of work. To refuse or
withhold it can be a grave injustice.[220] In determining fair pay
both the needs and the contributions of each person must be taken
into account. 'Remuneration for work should guarantee man the
opportunity to provide a dignified livelihood for himself and his
family on the material, social, cultural and spiritual level, taking
into account the role and the productivity of each, the state of the
business, and the common good.'[221] Agreement between the
parties is not sufficient to justify morally the amount to be received
in wages.

2435 Recourse to a *strike* is morally legitimate when it cannot be
avoided, or at least when it is necessary to obtain a proportionate
benefit. It becomes morally unacceptable when accompanied by
violence, or when objectives are included that are not directly
linked to working conditions or are contrary to the common
good.

2436 It is unjust not to pay the social security *contributions* required
by legitimate authority.

Unemployment almost always wounds its victim's dignity
and threatens the equilibrium of his life. Besides the harm done to
him personally, it entails many risks for his family.[222]

V. Justice and Solidarity Among Nations

1938 2437 On the international level, inequality of resources and
economic capability is such that it creates a real 'gap' between
nations.[223] On the one side there are those nations possessing and

---

[217] Cf. *CA* 37.
[218] Cf. *LE* 19; 22–23.
[219] Cf. *CA* 48.
[220] Cf. *Lev* 19:13; *Dt* 24:14–15; *Jas* 5:4.
[221] *GS* 67 § 2.
[222] Cf. *LE* 18.
[223] Cf. *SRS* 14.

developing the means of growth and, on the other, those accumulating debts.

2438 Various causes of a religious, political, economic and financial nature today give 'the social question a worldwide dimension'.[224] There must be solidarity among nations which are already politically interdependent. It is even more essential when it is a question of dismantling the 'perverse mechanisms' that impede the development of the less advanced countries.[225] In place of abusive if not usurious financial systems, iniquitous commercial relations among nations, and the arms race, there must be substituted a common effort to mobilize resources toward objectives of moral, cultural and economic development, 'redefining the priorities and hierarchies of values'.[226]   *1911*   *2315*

2439 *Rich nations* have a grave moral responsibility towards those which are unable to ensure the means of their development by themselves or have been prevented from doing so by tragic historical events. It is a duty in solidarity and charity; it is also an obligation in justice if the prosperity of the rich nations has come from resources that have not been paid for fairly.

2440 *Direct aid* is an appropriate response to immediate, extraordinary needs caused by natural catastrophes, epidemics, and the like. But it does not suffice to repair the grave damage resulting from destitution or to provide a lasting solution to a country's needs. It is also necessary to *reform* international economic and financial *institutions* so that they will better promote equitable relationships with less advanced countries.[227] The efforts of poor countries working for growth and liberation must be supported.[228] This doctrine must be applied especially in the area of agricultural labour. Peasants, especially in the Third World, form the overwhelming majority of the poor.

2441 An increased sense of God and increased self-awareness are fundamental to any *full development of human society*. This development multiplies material goods and puts them at the service of the person and his freedom. It reduces dire poverty and economic exploitation. It makes for growth in respect for cultural identities and openness to the transcendent.[229]   *1908*

2442 It is not the role of the Pastors of the Church to intervene directly in the political structuring and organization of social life.

---

[224] SRS 9.
[225] Cf. SRS 17; 45.
[226] CA 28; cf. 35.
[227] Cf. SRS 16.
[228] Cf. CA 26.
[229] Cf. SRS 32; CA 51.

899 This task is part of the vocation of the *lay faithful*, acting on their own initiative with their fellow citizens. Social action can assume various concrete forms. It should always have the common good in view and be in conformity with the message of the Gospel and the teaching of the Church. It is the role of the laity 'to animate temporal realities with Christian commitment, by which they show that they are witnesses and agents of peace and justice.'[230]

2544–2547 VI. Love for the Poor

2443 God blesses those who come to the aid of the poor and rebukes those who turn away from them: 'Give to him who begs from you, do not refuse him who would borrow from you'; 'you received without pay, give without pay.'[231] It is by what they have *786, 525* done for the poor that Jesus Christ will recognize his chosen *544, 853* ones.[232] When 'the poor have the good news preached to them' it is the sign of Christ's presence.[233]

2444 'The Church's love for the poor. . . is a part of her constant *1716* tradition.' This love is inspired by the Gospel of the Beatitudes, of the poverty of Jesus and of his concern for the poor.[234] Love for the poor is even one of the motives for the duty of working so as to 'be able to give to those in need'.[235] It extends not only to material poverty but also to the many forms of cultural and religious poverty.[236]

2536 2445 Love for the poor is incompatible with immoderate love of riches or their selfish use:

2547 Come now, you rich, weep and howl for the miseries that are coming upon you. Your riches have rotted and your garments are moth-eaten. Your gold and silver have rusted, and their rust will be evidence against you and will eat your flesh like fire. You have laid up treasure for the last days. Behold, the wages of the labourers who mowed your fields, which you kept back by fraud, cry out; and the cries of the harvesters have reached the ears of the Lord of hosts. You have lived on the earth in luxury and in pleasure; you have fattened your hearts in a day of slaughter. You have condemned, you have killed the righteous man; he does not resist you.[237]

2446 St John Chrysostom vigorously recalls this: 'Not to enable the poor to share in our goods is to steal from them and deprive

---

[230] *SRS* 47 § 6; cf. 42.
[231] *Mt* 5:42; 10:8.
[232] Cf. *Mt* 25:31–36.
[233] *Mt* 11:5; cf. *Lk* 4:18.
[234] *CA* 57; cf. *Lk* 6:20–22; *Mt* 8:20; *Mk*

[235] *Eph* 4:28.
[236] Cf. *CA* 57.
[237] *Jas* 5:1–6.

12:41–44.

them of life. The goods we possess are not ours, but theirs.'[238] 'The 2402
demands of justice must be satisfied first of all; that which is
already due in justice is not to be offered as a gift of charity':[239]

> When we attend to the needs of those in want, we give them what is
> theirs, not ours. More than performing works of mercy, we are paying a
> debt of justice.[240]

2447 The *works of mercy* are charitable actions by which we come 1460
to the aid of our neighbour in his spiritual and bodily necessities.[241]
Instructing, advising, consoling, comforting, are spiritual works
of mercy, as are forgiving and bearing wrongs patiently. The
corporal works of mercy consist especially in feeding the hungry,
sheltering the homeless, clothing the naked, visiting the sick and
imprisoned, and burying the dead.[242] Among all these, giving 1038
alms to the poor is one of the chief witnesses to fraternal charity: it 1969
is also a work of justice pleasing to God:[243]

> He who has two coats, let him share with him who has none; and he who
> has food must do likewise.[244] But give for alms those things which are
> within; and behold, everything is clean for you.[245] If a brother or sister is
> ill-clad and in lack of daily food, and one of you says to them, 'Go in
> peace, be warmed and filled', without giving them the things needed for
> the body, what does it profit?[246] 1004

2448 'In its various forms – material deprivation, unjust oppression, physical and psychological illness and death – *human misery* is
the obvious sign of the inherited condition of frailty and need for
salvation in which man finds himself as a consequence of original 386
sin. This misery elicited the compassion of Christ the Saviour,
who willingly took it upon himself and identified himself with the
least of his brethren. Hence, those who are oppressed by poverty
are the object of *a preferential love* on the part of the Church which, 1586
since her origin and in spite of the failings of many of her members, has not ceased to work for their relief, defence and liberation,
through numerous works of charity which remain indispensable
always and everywhere.'[247]

2449 Beginning with the Old Testament, all kinds of juridical
measures (the jubilee year of forgiveness of debts, prohibition of
loans at interest and the keeping of collateral, the obligation to
tithe, the daily payment of the day-labourer, the right to glean

[238] St John Chrysostom, *Hom. in Lazarum*
 2, 5: PG 48, 992.
[239] *AA* 8 § 5.
[240] St Gregory the Great, *Regula Pastoralis*
 3, 21: PL 77, 87.
[241] Cf. *Is* 58:6–7; *Heb* 13:3.
[242] Cf. *Mt* 25:31–46.
[243] Cf. *Tob* 4:5–11; *Sir* 17:22; *Mt* 6:2–4.
[244] *Lk* 3:11.
[245] *Lk* 11:41.
[246] *Jas* 2:15–16; cf. 1 *Jn* 3:17.
[247] CDF, Instr. *Libertatis conscientia* 68.

vines and fields) answer the exhortation of *Deuteronomy*: 'For the poor will never cease out of the land; therefore I command you, "You shall open wide your hand to your brother, to the needy and to the poor in the land." '[248] Jesus makes these words his own: 'The poor you always have with you, but you do not always have me.'[249] In so doing he does not soften the vehemence of former oracles against 'buying the poor for silver and the needy for a pair of sandals. . .', but invites us to recognize his own presence in the poor who are his brethren:[250]

1397

When her mother reproached her for caring for the poor and the sick at home, St Rose of Lima said to her: 'When we serve the poor and the sick, we serve Jesus. We must not fail to help our neighbours, because in them we serve Jesus.'[251]

786

IN BRIEF

2450 'You shall not steal' (Ex 20:15; Dt 5:19). 'Neither thieves, nor the greedy. . ., nor robbers will inherit the kingdom of God' (1 Cor 6:10).

2451 The seventh commandment enjoins the practice of justice and charity in the administration of earthly goods and the fruits of men's labour.

2452 The goods of creation are destined for the entire human race. The right to private property does not abolish the universal destination of goods.

2453 The seventh commandment forbids theft. Theft is the usurpation of another's goods against the reasonable will of the owner.

2454 Every manner of taking and using another's property unjustly is contrary to the seventh commandment. The injustice committed requires reparation. Commutative justice requires the restitution of stolen goods.

2455 The moral law forbids acts which, for commercial or totalitarian purposes, lead to the enslavement of human beings, or to their being bought, sold or exchanged like merchandise.

2456 The dominion granted by the Creator over the mineral, vegetable and animal resources of the universe cannot be separated from respect for moral obligations, including those towards generations to come.

2457 Animals are entrusted to man's stewardship; he must show them kindness. They may be used to serve the just satisfaction of man's needs.

---

[248] Dt 15:11.
[249] Jn 12:8.
[250] Am 8:6; cf. Mt 25:40.

[251] P. Hansen, *Vita mirabilis* (Louvain, 1668).

Fresco from the catacombs of Sts Marcellinus and Peter, Rome, from the beginning of the fourth century A.D.

The scene depicts the encounter of Jesus with the woman with the haemorrhage. This woman, who had suffered for many years, was healed by touching the cloak of Jesus through the power that 'had gone forth from him' (cf. *Mk 5:25–34*).

The Church's sacraments now continue the works which Christ performed during his earthly life (cf. § *1115*). The sacraments are as it were 'powers that go forth' from the Body of Christ to heal the wounds of sin and to give us the new life of Christ (cf. § *1116*).

This image thus symbolizes the divine and saving power of the Son of God who heals the whole person, soul and body, through the sacramental life.

2458 The Church makes a judgement about economic and social matters when the fundamental rights of the person or the salvation of souls requires it. She is concerned with the temporal common good of men because they are ordered to the sovereign Good, their ultimate end.

2459 Man is himself the author, centre and goal of all economic and social life. The decisive point of the social question is that goods created by God for everyone should in fact reach everyone in accordance with justice and with the help of charity.

2460 The primordial value of labour stems from man himself, its author and beneficiary. By means of his labour man participates in the work of creation. Work united to Christ can be redemptive.

2461 True development concerns the whole man. It is concerned with increasing each person's ability to respond to his vocation and hence to God's call (cf. CA 29).

2462 Giving alms to the poor is a witness to fraternal charity: it is also a work of justice pleasing to God.

2463 How can we not recognize Lazarus, the hungry beggar in the parable (cf. Lk 17:19–31), in the multitude of human beings without bread, a roof or a place to stay? How can we fail to hear Jesus: 'As you did it not to one of the least of these, you did it not to me' (Mt 25:45)?

Article 8
THE EIGHTH COMMANDMENT

You shall not bear false witness against your neighbour.[252]

It was said to the men of old, 'You shall not swear falsely, but shall perform to the Lord what you have sworn.'[253]

2464 The eighth commandment forbids misrepresenting the truth in our relations with others. This moral prescription flows from the vocation of the holy people to bear witness to their God who is the truth and wills the truth. Offences against the truth express by word or deed a refusal to commit oneself to moral uprightness: they are fundamental infidelities to God and, in this sense, they undermine the foundations of the covenant.

I. Living in the Truth

2465 The Old Testament attests that God is the source of all truth. His Word is truth. His Law is truth. His 'faithfulness endures to all
215

---

[252] Ex 20:16; cf. Dt 5:20.   [253] Mt 5:33.

generations.'[254] Since God is 'true', the members of his people are called to live in the truth.[255]

2466 In Jesus Christ, the whole of God's truth has been made manifest. 'Full of grace and truth', he came as the 'light of the world', he *is the Truth*.[256] 'Whoever believes in me may not remain in darkness.'[257] The disciple of Jesus continues in his word so as to know 'the truth [that] will make you free' and that sanctifies.[258] To follow Jesus is to live in 'the Spirit of truth', whom the Father sends in his name and who leads 'into all the truth'.[259] To his disciples Jesus teaches the unconditional love of truth: 'Let what you say be simply "Yes" or "No".'[260]

2153

2467 Man tends by nature towards the truth. He is obliged to honour and bear witness to it: 'It is in accordance with their dignity that all men, because they are persons... are both impelled by their nature and bound by a moral obligation to seek the truth, especially religious truth. They are also bound to adhere to the truth once they come to know it and direct their whole lives in accordance with the demands of truth.'[261]

2104

2468 Truth as uprightness in human action and speech is called *truthfulness*, sincerity or candour. Truth or truthfulness is the virtue which consists in showing oneself true in deeds and truthful in words, and in guarding against duplicity, dissimulation and hypocrisy.

1458

2469 'Men could not live with one another if there were not mutual confidence that they were being truthful to one another.'[262] The virtue of truth gives another his just due. Truthfulness keeps to the just mean between what ought to be expressed and what ought to be kept secret: it entails honesty and discretion. In justice, 'as a matter of honour, one man owes it to another to manifest the truth.'[263]

1807

2470 The disciple of Christ consents to 'live in the truth', that is, in the simplicity of a life in conformity with the Lord's example, abiding in his truth. 'If we say we have fellowship with him while we walk in darkness, we lie and do not live according to the truth.'[264]

[254] Ps 119:90; cf. Prov 8:7; 2 Sam 7:28; Ps 119:142; Lk 1:50.
[255] Rom 3:4; cf. Ps 119:30.
[256] Jn 1:14; 8:12; cf. 14:6.
[257] Jn 12:46.
[258] Jn 8:32; cf. 17:17.
[259] Jn 16:13.
[260] Mt 5:37.
[261] DH 2 § 2.
[262] St Thomas Aquinas, STh II–II, 109, 3, ad 1.
[263] St Thomas Aquinas, STh II–II, 109, 3, corp. art.
[264] 1 Jn 1:6.

II. To Bear Witness to the Truth

2471 Before Pilate, Christ proclaims that he 'has come into the world, to bear witness to the truth.'[265] The Christian is not to 'be ashamed then of testifying to our Lord'.[266] In situations that require witness to the faith, the Christian must profess it without *1816* equivocation, after the example of St Paul before his judges. We must keep 'a clear conscience towards God and towards men'.[267]

2472 The duty of Christians to take part in the life of the Church impels them to act as *witnesses of the Gospel* and of the obligations that flow from it. This witness is a transmission of the faith in *863, 905* words and deeds. Witness is an act of justice that establishes the *1807* truth or makes it known.[268]

> All Christians by the example of their lives and the witness of their word, wherever they live, have an obligation to manifest the new man which they have put on in Baptism, and to reveal the power of the Holy Spirit by whom they were strengthened at Confirmation.[269]

2473 *Martyrdom* is the supreme witness given to the truth of the faith: it means bearing witness even unto death. The martyr bears *852* witness to Christ who died and rose, to whom he is united by charity. He bears witness to the truth of the faith and of Christian doctrine. He endures death through an act of fortitude. 'Let me *1808* become the food of the beasts, through whom it will be given me *1258* to reach God.'[270]

2474 The Church has painstakingly collected the records of those who persevered to the end in witnessing to their faith. These are the acts of the martyrs. They form the archives of truth written in letters of blood:

> Neither the pleasures of the world nor the kingdoms of this age will be of any use to me. It is better for me to die [in order to unite myself] to Christ *1011* Jesus than to reign over the ends of the earth. I seek him who died for us; I desire him who rose for us. My birth is approaching...[271]

> I bless you for having judged me worthy from this day and this hour to be counted among your martyrs... You have kept your promise, God of faithfulness and truth. For this reason and for everything, I praise you, I bless you, I glorify you through the eternal and heavenly High Priest, Jesus Christ, your beloved Son. Through him, who is with you and the

---

[265] *Jn* 18:37.
[266] 2 *Tim* 1:8.
[267] *Acts* 24:16.
[268] Cf. *Mt* 18:16.
[269] *AG* 11.

[270] St Ignatius of Antioch, *Ad Rom.* 4, 1: SCh 10, 130.
[271] St Ignatius of Antioch, *Ad Rom.* 6, 1–2: SCh 10, 132–134.

Holy Spirit, may glory be given to you, now and in the ages to come. Amen.[272]

III. Offences Against Truth

2475 Christ's disciples have 'put on the new man, created after the likeness of God in true righteousness and holiness.'[273] By 'putting away falsehood', they are to 'put away all malice and all guile and insincerity and envy and all slander.'[274]

2152 2476 *False witness and perjury*. When it is made publicly, a statement contrary to the truth takes on a particular gravity. In court it becomes false witness.[275] When it is under oath, it is perjury. Acts such as these contribute to condemnation of the innocent, exoneration of the guilty or the increased punishment of the accused.[276] They gravely compromise the exercise of justice and the fairness of judicial decisions.

2477 *Respect for the reputation* of persons forbids every attitude and word likely to cause them unjust injury.[277] He becomes guilty:
– of *rash judgement* who, even tacitly, assumes as true, without sufficient foundation, the moral fault of a neighbour;
– of *detraction* who, without objectively valid reason, discloses another's faults and failings to persons who did not know them;[278]
– of *calumny* who, by remarks contrary to the truth, harms the reputation of others and gives occasion for false judgements concerning them.

2478 To avoid rash judgement, everyone should be careful to interpret insofar as is possible his neighbour's thoughts, words and deeds in a favourable way:

> Every good Christian ought to be more ready to give a favourable interpretation to another's statement than to condemn it. But if he cannot do so, let him ask how the other understands it. And if the latter understands it badly, let the former correct him with love. If that does not suffice, let the Christian try all suitable ways to bring the other to a correct interpretation so that he may be saved.[279]

2479 Detraction and calumny destroy the *reputation and honour of one's neighbour*. Honour is the social witness given to human dignity, and everyone enjoys a natural right to the honour of his name

---

[272] *Martyrium Polycarpi* 14, 2–3: PG 5, 1040; SCh 10, 262.
[273] *Eph* 4:24.
[274] *Eph* 4:25; 1 *Pt* 2:1.
[275] Cf. *Prov* 19:9.

[276] Cf. *Prov* 18:5.
[277] Cf. CIC, can. 220.
[278] Cf. *Sir* 21:28.
[279] St Ignatius of Loyola, *Spiritual Exercises* 22.

and reputation and to respect. Thus, detraction and calumny *1753* offend against the virtues of justice and charity.

2480 Every word or attitude is forbidden which by *flattery, adulation or complaisance* encourages and confirms another in malicious acts and perverse conduct. Adulation is a grave fault if it makes one an accomplice in another's vices or grave sins. Neither the desire to be of service nor friendship justifies duplicitous speech. Adulation is a venial sin when it only seeks to be agreeable, to avoid evil, to meet a need or to obtain legitimate advantages.

2481 *Boasting* or bragging is an offence against truth. So is *irony* aimed at disparaging someone by maliciously caricaturing some aspect of his behaviour.

2482 'A *lie* consists in speaking a falsehood with the intention of deceiving.'[280] The Lord denounces lying as the work of the devil: 'You are of your father the devil,. . . there is no truth in him. When he lies, he speaks according to his own nature, for he is a liar and *392* the father of lies.'[281]

2483 Lying is the most direct offence against the truth. To lie is to speak or act against the truth in order to lead someone into error. By injuring man's relation to truth and to his neighbour, a lie offends against the fundamental relation of man and of his word to the Lord.

2484 The *gravity of a lie* is measured against the nature of the truth it deforms, the circumstances, the intentions of the one who lies, *1750* and the harm suffered by its victims. If a lie in itself only constitutes a venial sin, it becomes mortal when it does grave injury to the virtues of justice and charity.

2485 By its very nature, lying is to be condemned. It is a profa- *1756* nation of speech, whereas the purpose of speech is to communicate known truth to others. The deliberate intention of leading a neighbour into error by saying things contrary to the truth constitutes a failure in justice and charity. The culpability is greater when the intention of deceiving entails the risk of deadly consequences for those who are led astray.

2486 Since it violates the virtue of truthfulness, a lie does real violence to another. It affects his ability to know, which is a condition of every judgement and decision. It contains the seed of discord and all consequent evils. Lying is destructive of society; it

---

[280] St Augustine, *De mendacio* 4, 5: PL 40, 491.   [281] *Jn* 8:44.

1607 undermines trust among men and tears apart the fabric of social relationships.

2487 Every offence committed against justice and truth entails the
1459 *duty of reparation*, even if its author has been forgiven. When it is impossible publicly to make reparation for a wrong, it must be made secretly. If someone who has suffered harm cannot be directly compensated, he must be given moral satisfaction in the
2412 name of charity. This duty of reparation also concerns offences against another's reputation. This reparation, moral and sometimes material, must be evaluated in terms of the extent of the damage inflicted. It obliges in conscience.

IV. Respect for the Truth

1740 2488 The *right to the communication* of the truth is not unconditional. Everyone must conform his life to the Gospel precept of fraternal love. This requires us in concrete situations to judge whether or not it is appropriate to reveal the truth to someone who asks for it.

2489 Charity and respect for the truth should dictate the response to every *request for information or communication*. The good and safety of others, respect for privacy, and the common good are sufficient reasons for being silent about what ought not be known,
2284 or for making use of a discreet language. The duty to avoid scandal often commands strict discretion. No one is bound to reveal the truth to someone who does not have the right to know it.[282]

1467 2490 The *secret of the sacrament of Reconciliation* is sacred, and cannot be violated under any pretext. 'The sacramental seal is inviolable; therefore, it is a crime for a confessor in any way to betray a penitent by word or in any other manner or for any reason.'[283]

2491 *Professional secrets* – for example, those of political office-holders, soldiers, physicians and lawyers – or confidential information given under the seal of secrecy, must be kept, save in exceptional cases where keeping the secret is bound to cause very grave harm to the one who confided it, to the one who received it or to a third party, and where the very grave harm can be avoided only by divulging the truth. Even if not confided under the seal of secrecy, private information prejudicial to another is not to be divulged without a grave and proportionate reason.

---

[282] Cf. *Sir* 27:16; *Prov* 25:9–10.   [283] CIC, can. 983 § 1.

2492 Everyone should observe an appropriate reserve concerning persons' private lives. Those in charge of communications should maintain a fair balance between the requirements of the common good and respect for individual rights. Interference by the media in the private lives of persons engaged in political or public activity is to be condemned to the extent that it infringes upon their privacy and freedom.

2522

V. The Use of the Social Communications Media

2493 Within modern society the communications media play a major role in information, cultural promotion and formation. This role is increasing, as a result of technological progress, the extent and diversity of the news transmitted, and the influence exercised on public opinion.

2494 The information provided by the media is at the service of the common good.[284] Society has a right to information based on truth, freedom, justice, and solidarity:

1906

> The proper exercise of this right demands that the content of the communication be true and — within the limits set by justice and charity — complete. Further, it should be communicated honestly and properly. This means that in the gathering and in the publication of news, the moral law and the legitimate rights and dignity of man should be upheld.[285]

2495 'It is necessary that all members of society meet the demands of justice and charity in this domain. They should help, through the means of social communication, in the formation and diffusion of sound public opinion.'[286] Solidarity is a consequence of genuine and right communication and the free circulation of ideas that further knowledge and respect for others.

906

2496 The means of social communication (especially the mass media) can give rise to a certain passivity among users, making them less than vigilant consumers of what is said or shown. Users should practise moderation and discipline in their approach to the mass media. They will want to form enlightened and correct consciences the more easily to resist unwholesome influences.

2525

2497 By the very nature of their profession, journalists have an obligation to serve the truth and not offend against charity in disseminating information. They should strive to respect, with equal care, the nature of the facts and the limits of critical judgement concerning individuals. They should not stoop to defamation.

2498 'Civil authorities have particular responsibilities in this field because of the common good... It is for the civil authority... to defend and safeguard a true

2237

---

[284] Cf. *IM* 11.
[285] *IM* 5 § 2.

[286] *IM* 8.

and just freedom of information.'[287] By promulgating laws and overseeing their application, public authorities should ensure that 'public morality and

2286 social progress are not gravely endangered' through misuse of the media.[288] Civil authorities should punish any violation of the rights of individuals to their reputation and privacy. They should give timely and reliable reports concerning the general good or respond to the well-founded concerns of the people. Nothing can justify recourse to disinformation for manipulating public opinion through the media. Interventions by public authority should avoid injuring the freedom of individuals or groups.

2499 Moral judgement must condemn the plague of totalitarian states which systematically falsify the truth, exercise political control of opinion through the media, manipulate defendants and witnesses at public trials, and imagine that

1903 they secure their tyranny by strangling and repressing everything they consider 'thought crimes'.

VI. Truth, Beauty and Sacred Art

1804 2500 The practice of goodness is accompanied by spontaneous spiritual joy and moral beauty. Likewise, truth carries with it the joy and splendour of spiritual beauty. Truth is beautiful in itself. Truth in words, the rational expression of the knowledge of created and uncreated reality, is necessary to man, who is endowed with intellect. But truth can also find other complementary forms of human expression, above all when it is a matter of evoking what is beyond words: the depths of the human heart, the exaltations of the soul, the mystery of God. Even before revealing himself to man in words of truth, God reveals himself to him through

341 the universal language of creation, the work of his Word, of his wisdom: the order and harmony of the cosmos – which both the child and the scientist discover – 'from the greatness and beauty of created things comes a corresponding perception of their Creator',

2129 'for the author of beauty created them'.[289]

> [Wisdom] is a breath of the power of God, and a pure emanation of the glory of the Almighty; therefore nothing defiled gains entrance into her. For she is a reflection of eternal light, a spotless mirror of the working of God, and an image of his goodness.[290] For [wisdom] is more beautiful than the sun, and excels every constellation of the stars. Compared with the light she is found to be superior, for it is succeeded by the night, but against wisdom evil does not prevail.[291] I became enamoured of her beauty.[292]

---

[287] IM 12.
[288] IM 12 § 2.
[289] Wis 13:3, 5.

[290] Wis 7:25–26.
[291] Wis 7:29–30.
[292] Wis 8:2.

2501 Created 'in the image of God',[293] man also expresses the truth of his relationship with God the Creator by the beauty of his artistic works. Indeed, *art* is a distinctively human form of expression; beyond the search for the necessities of life which is common to all living creatures, art is a freely given superabundance of the human being's inner riches. Arising from talent given by the Creator and from man's own effort, art is a form of practical wisdom, uniting knowledge and skill,[294] to give form to the truth of reality in a language accessible to sight or hearing. To the extent that it is inspired by truth and love of beings, art bears a certain likeness to God's activity in what he has created. Like any other human *339* activity, art is not an absolute end in itself, but is ordered to and ennobled by the ultimate end of man.[295]

2502 *Sacred art* is true and beautiful when its form corresponds to *1156–1162* its particular vocation: evoking and glorifying, in faith and adoration, the transcendent mystery of God – the surpassing invisible beauty of truth and love visible in Christ, who 'reflects the glory of God and bears the very stamp of his nature', in whom 'the whole fullness of deity dwells bodily.'[296] This spiritual beauty of God is reflected in the most holy Virgin Mother of God, the angels and saints. Genuine sacred art draws man to adoration, to prayer and to the love of God, Creator and Saviour, the Holy One and Sanctifier.

2503 For this reason bishops, personally or through delegates, should see to the promotion of sacred art, old and new, in all its forms and, with the same religious care, remove from the liturgy and from places of worship everything which is not in conformity with the truth of faith and the authentic beauty of sacred art.[297]

IN BRIEF

2504 'You shall not bear false witness against your neighbour' (Ex 20:16). Christ's disciples have 'put on the new man, created after the likeness of God in true righteousness and holiness' (Eph 4:24).

---

[293] *Gen* 1:26.
[294] Cf. *Wis* 7:16–17.
[295] Cf. Pius XII, *Musicae sacrae disciplina*; Discourses of 3 September 1950 and

25 December 1955.
[296] *Heb* 1:3; *Col* 2:9.
[297] Cf. *SC* 122–127.

2505 *Truth or truthfulness is the virtue which consists in showing oneself true in deeds and truthful in words, and guarding against duplicity, dissimulation and hypocrisy.*

2506 *The Christian is not to 'be ashamed of testifying to our Lord' (2 Tim 1:8) in deed and word. Martyrdom is the supreme witness given to the truth of the faith.*

2507 *Respect for the reputation and honour of persons forbids all detraction and calumny in word or attitude.*

2508 *Lying consists in saying what is false with the intention of deceiving one's neighbour.*

2509 *An offence committed against the truth requires reparation.*

2510 *The golden rule helps one discern, in concrete situations, whether or not it would be appropriate to reveal the truth to someone who asks for it.*

2511 *'The sacramental seal is inviolable' (CIC, can. 983 § 1). Professional secrets must be kept. Confidences prejudicial to another are not to be divulged.*

2512 *Society has a right to information based on truth, freedom and justice. One should practise moderation and discipline in the use of the social communications media.*

2513 *The fine arts, but above all sacred art, 'of their nature are directed toward expressing in some way the infinite beauty of God in works made by human hands. Their dedication to the increase of God's praise and of his glory is more complete, the more exclusively they are devoted to turning men's minds devoutly toward God' (SC 122).*

Article 9
THE NINTH COMMANDMENT

You shall not covet your neighbour's house; you shall not covet your neighbour's wife, or his manservant, or his maidservant, or his ox, or his ass, or anything that is your neighbour's.[298]

Every one who looks at a woman lustfully has already committed adultery with her in his heart.[299]

377, 400 2514 St John distinguishes three kinds of covetousness or concupiscence: lust of the flesh, lust of the eyes and pride of life.[300] In the Catholic catechetical tradition, the ninth commandment forbids carnal concupiscence; the tenth forbids coveting another's goods.

405 2515 Etymologically, 'concupiscence' can refer to any intense

[298] Ex 20:17.
[299] Mt 5:28.

[300] Cf. 1 Jn 2:16.

form of human desire. Christian theology has given it a particular meaning: the movement of the sensitive appetite contrary to the operation of the human reason. The apostle St Paul identifies it with the rebellion of the 'flesh' against the 'spirit'.[301] Concupiscence stems from the disobedience of the first sin. It unsettles man's moral faculties and, without being in itself an offence, inclines man to commit sins.[302]

2516 Because man is a *composite being, spirit and body*, there already *362* exists a certa n tension in him; a certain struggle of tendencies between 'spirit' and 'flesh' develops. But in fact this struggle belongs to the heritage of sin. It is a consequence of sin and at the same time a confirmation of it. It is part of the daily experience of the spiritual battle: *407*

> For the Apostle it is not a matter of despising and condemning the body which with the spiritual soul constitutes man's nature and personal subjectivity. Rather, he is concerned with the morally *good or bad* works, or better, the permanent dispositions – virtues and vices – which are the fruit of *submission* (in the first case) or of *resistance* (in the second case) to *the saving action of the Holy Spirit*. For this reason the Apostle writes: 'If we live by the Spirit, let us also walk by the Spirit.'[303]

I. Purification of the Heart

2517 The heart is the seat of moral p. rsonality: 'Out of the heart *368* come evil thoughts, murder, adultery, fornication...'[304] The struggle against carnal covetousness entails purifying the heart and practising temperance: *1809*

> Remain simple and innocent, and you will be like little children who do not know the evil that destroys man's life.[305]

2518 The sixth Beatitude proclaims, 'Blessed are the pure in heart, for they shall see God.'[306] 'Pure in heart' refers to those who have attuned their intellects and wills to the demands of God's holiness, *94* chiefly in three areas: charity;[307] chastity or sexual rectitude;[308] love of truth and orthodoxy of faith.[309] There is a connection between purity of heart, of body and of faith:

> The faithful must believe the articles of the Creed 'so that by believing they may obey God, by obeying may live well, by living well may

---

[301] Cf. *Gal* 5:16, 17, 24; *Eph* 2:3.
[302] Cf. *Gen* 3:11; Council of Trent: DS 1515.
[303] John Paul II, *DeV* 55; cf. *Gal* 5:25.
[304] *Mt* 15:19.
[305] *Pastor Hermae*, Mandate 2, 1: PG 2, 916.

[306] *Mt* 5:8.
[307] Cf. 1 *Tim* 4:3–9; 2 *Tim* 2:22.
[308] Cf. 1 *Th* 4:7; *Col* 3:5; *Eph* 4:19.
[309] Cf. *Titus* 1:15; 1 *Tim* 1:3–4; 2 *Tim* 2:23–26.

158   purify their hearts, and with pure hearts may understand what they
           believe.'[310]

2548 2519 The 'pure in heart' are promised that they will see God face
2819 to face and be like him.[311] Purity of heart is the precondition of the
      vision of God. Even now it enables us to see *according to* God, to
      accept others as 'neighbours'; it lets us perceive the human body –
      ours and our neighbour's – as a temple of the Holy Spirit, a mani-
2501 festation of divine beauty.

II. The Battle for Purity

1264 2520 Baptism confers on its recipient the grace of purification
      from all sins. But the baptized must continue to struggle against
      concupiscence of the flesh and disordered desires. With God's
      grace he will prevail

2337 – by the *virtue* and *gift of chastity*, for chastity lets us love with
      upright and undivided heart;

1752 – by *purity of intention* which consists in seeking the true end of
      man: with simplicity of vision, the baptized person seeks to find
      and to fulfil God's will in everything;[312]

1762 – by *purity of vision*, external and internal; by discipline of feelings
      and imagination; by refusing all complicity in impure thoughts
      that incline us to turn aside from the path of God's command-
      ments: 'appearance arouses yearning in fools';[313]

2846 – by *prayer*:

> I thought that continence arose from one's own powers, which I did not
> recognize in myself. I was foolish enough not to know. . . that no one can
> be continent unless you grant it. For you would surely have granted it if
> my inner groaning had reached your ears and I with firm faith had cast
> my cares on you.[314]

2521 Purity requires *modesty*, an integral part of temperance.
Modesty protects the intimate centre of the person. It means refusing to unveil what should remain hidden. It is ordered to chastity
to whose sensitivity it bears witness. It guides how one looks at
others and behaves toward them in conformity with the dignity of
persons and their solidarity.

2492 2522 Modesty protects the mystery of persons and their love. It
encourages patience and moderation in loving relationships; it
requires that the conditions for the definitive giving and commit-

---

[310] St Augustine, *De fide et symbolo* 10, 25:
      PL 40, 196.
[311] Cf. 1 *Cor* 13:12; 1 *Jn* 3:2.
[312] Cf. *Rom* 12:2; *Col* 1:10.
[313] *Wis* 15:5.
[314] St Augustine, *Conf.* 6, 11, 20: PL 32,
      729–730.

ment of man and woman to one another be fulfilled. Modesty is decency. It inspires one's choice of clothing. It keeps silence or reserve where there is evident risk of unhealthy curiosity. It is discreet.

2523 There is a modesty of the feelings as well as of the body. It protests, for example, against the voyeuristic explorations of the human body in certain *2354* advertisements, or against the solicitations of certain media that go too far in the exhibition of intimate things. Modesty inspires a way of life which makes it possible to resist the allurements of fashion and the pressures of prevailing ideologies.

2524 The forms taken by modesty vary from one culture to another. Everywhere, however, modesty exists as an intuition of the spiritual dignity proper to man. It is born with the awakening consciousness of being a subject. Teaching modesty to children and adolescents means awakening in them respect for the human person.

2525 Christian purity requires a *purification of the social climate*. It *2344* requires of the communications media that their presentations show concern for respect and restraint. Purity of heart brings freedom from widespread eroticism and avoids entertainment inclined to voyeurism and illusion.

2526 So-called *moral permissiveness* rests on an erroneous conception of human freedom; the necessary precondition for the devel- *1740* opment of true freedom is to let oneself be educated in the moral law. Those in charge of education can reasonably be expected to give young people instruction respectful of the truth, the qualities of the heart, and the moral and spiritual dignity of man.

2527 'The Good News of Christ continually renews the life and *1204* culture of fallen man; it combats and removes the error and evil which flow from the ever-present attraction of sin. It never ceases to purify and elevate the morality of peoples. It takes the spiritual qualities and endowments of every age and nation, and with supernatural riches it causes them to blossom, as it were, from within; it fortifies, completes and restores them in Christ.'[315]

IN BRIEF

2528 'Every one who looks at a woman lustfully has already committed adultery with her in his heart' (Mt 5:28).

2529 The ninth commandment warns against lust or carnal concupiscence.

---

[315] GS 58 § 4.

> 2530 The struggle against carnal lust involves purifying the heart and prac-
> tising temperance.
>
> 2531 Purity of heart will enable us to see God: it enables us even now to see
> things according to God.
>
> 2532 Purification of the heart demands prayer, the practice of chastity, purity
> of intention and of vision.
>
> 2533 Purity of heart requires the modesty which is patience, decency and
> discretion. Modesty protects the intimate centre of the person.

Article 10
THE TENTH COMMANDMENT

You shall not covet... anything that is your neighbour's. You shall not
desire your neighbour's house, his field, or his manservant, or his maidservant, or his ox, or his ass, or anything that is your neighbour's.[316]

For where your treasure is, there will your heart be also.[317]

2534 The tenth commandment unfolds and completes the ninth,
which is concerned with concupiscence of the flesh. It forbids
coveting the goods of another, as the root of theft, robbery and
fraud, which the seventh commandment forbids. 'Lust of the eyes'
leads to the violence and injustice forbidden by the fifth com-
2112 mandment.[318] Avarice, like fornication, originates in the idolatry
prohibited by the first three prescriptions of the Law.[319] The tenth
commandment concerns the intentions of the heart; with the
2069 ninth, it summarizes all the precepts of the Law.

I. The Disorder of Covetous Desires

2535 The sensitive appetite leads us to desire pleasant things we do
not have, e.g., the desire to eat when we are hungry, or to warm
ourselves when we are cold. These desires are good in themselves;
1767 but often they exceed the limits of reason and drive us to covet
unjustly what is not ours and belongs to another or is owed to him.

2536 The tenth commandment forbids greed and the desire to
amass earthly goods without limit. It forbids avarice arising from a
2445 passion for riches and their attendant power. It also forbids the
desire to commit injustice by harming our neighbour in his
temporal goods:

When the Law says, 'You shall not covet', these words mean that we

---

[316] Ex 20:17; Dt 5:21.
[317] Mt 6:21.

[318] Cf. 1 Jn 2:16; Mic 2:2.
[319] Cf. Wis 14:12.

should banish our desires for whatever does not belong to us. Our thirst for another's goods is immense, infinite, never quenched. Thus it is written: 'He who loves money never has money enough.'[320]

2537 It is not a violation of this commandment to desire to obtain things that belong to one's neighbour, provided this is done by just means. Traditional catechesis realistically mentions 'those who have a harder struggle against their criminal desires' and so who 'must be urged the more to keep this commandment':

> ... merchants who desire scarcity and rising prices, who cannot bear not to be the only ones buying and selling so that they themselves can sell more dearly and buy more cheaply; those who hope that their peers will be impoverished, in order to realize a profit either by selling to them or buying from them... physicians who wish disease to spread; lawyers who are eager for many important cases and trials.[321]

2538 The tenth commandment requires that *envy* be banished from the human heart. When the prophet Nathan wanted to spur King David to repentance, he told him the story about the poor man who had only one ewe lamb that he treated like his own daughter and the rich man who, despite the great number of his flocks, envied the poor man and ended by stealing his lamb.[322] Envy can lead to the worst crimes.[323] 'Through the devil's envy death entered the world':[324] *2317* *391*

> We fight one another, and envy arms us against one another... If everyone strives to unsettle the Body of Christ, where shall we end up? We are engaged in making Christ's Body a corpse... We declare ourselves members of one and the same organism, yet we devour one another like beasts.[325]

2539 Envy is a capital sin. It refers to the sadness at the sight of another's goods and the immoderate desire to acquire them for oneself, even unjustly. When it wishes grave harm to a neighbour it is a mortal sin: *1866*

> St Augustine saw envy as '*the* diabolical sin'.[326] 'From envy are born hatred, detraction, calumny, joy caused by the misfortune of a neighbour, and displeasure caused by his prosperity.'[327]

2540 Envy represents a form of sadness and therefore a refusal of charity; the baptized person should struggle against it by exercis- *1829*

---

[320] *Roman Catechism* III, 37; cf. *Sir* 5:8.
[321] *Roman Catechism* III, 37.
[322] Cf. 2 *Sam* 12:1–4.
[323] Cf. *Gen* 4:3–7; 1 *Kings* 21:1–29.
[324] *Wis* 2:24.
[325] St John Chrysostom, *Hom. in 2 Cor.*
27, 3–4: PG 61, 588.
[326] Cf. St Augustine, *De catechizandis rudibus* 4, 8: PL 40, 315–316.
[327] St Gregory the Great, *Moralia in Job* 31, 45: PL 76, 621.

ing good will. Envy often comes from pride; the baptized person should train himself to live in humility:

> Would you like to see God glorified by you? Then rejoice in your brother's progress and you will immediately give glory to God. Because his servant could conquer envy by rejoicing in the merits of others, God will be praised.[328]

II. The Desires of the Spirit

2541 The economy of law and grace turns men's hearts away from avarice and envy. It initiates them into desire for the
1718 Sovereign Good; it instructs them in the desires of the Holy Spirit
2764 who satisfies man's heart.

397   The God of the promises always warned man against seduction by what from the beginning has seemed 'good for food... a delight to the eyes... to be desired to make one wise'.[329]

1963 2542 The Law entrusted to Israel never sufficed to justify those subject to it; it even became the instrument of 'lust'.[330] The gap between wanting and doing points to the conflict between God's Law which is the 'law of my mind', and another law 'making me captive to the law of sin which dwells in my members'.[331]

1992 2543 'But now the righteousness of God has been manifested apart from law, although the law and the prophets bear witness to it, the righteousness of God through faith in Jesus Christ for all who believe.'[332] Henceforth, Christ's faithful 'have crucified the flesh with its passions and desires'; they are led by the Spirit, and follow the desires of the Spirit.[333]

2443–2449 ## III. Poverty of Heart

2544 Jesus enjoins his disciples to prefer him to everything and everyone, and bids them 'renounce all that [they have]' for his sake and that of the Gospel.[334] Shortly before his Passion he gave them the example of the poor widow of Jerusalem who, out of her poverty, gave all that she had to live on.[335] The precept of detach-
544 ment from riches is obligatory for entrance into the Kingdom of heaven.

2545 All Christ's faithful are to 'direct their affections rightly, lest
2013 they be hindered in their pursuit of perfect charity by the use of

---

328 St John Chrysostom, Hom. in Rom.
   71, 5: PG 60, 448.
329 Gen 3:6.
330 Cf. Rom 7:7.
331 Rom 7:23; cf. 7:10

332 Rom 3:21–22.
333 Gal 5:24; cf. Rom 8:14, 27.
334 Lk 14:33; cf. Mk 8:35.
335 Cf. Lk 21:4.

worldly things and by an adherence to riches which is contrary to the spirit of evangelical poverty.'[336]

2546 'Blessed are the poor in spirit.'[337] The Beatitudes reveal an *1716* order of happiness and grace, of beauty and peace. Jesus celebrates the joy of the poor, to whom the Kingdom already belongs:[338]

> The Word speaks of voluntary humility as 'poverty in spirit'; the Apostle gives an example of God's poverty when he says: 'For your sakes he became poor.'[339]

2547 The Lord grieves over the rich, because they find their consolation in the abundance of goods.[340] 'Let the proud seek and love earthly kingdoms, but blessed are the poor in spirit for theirs is the Kingdom of heaven.'[341] Abandonment to the providence of the *305* Father in heaven frees us from anxiety about tomorrow.[342] Trust in God is a preparation for the blessedness of the poor. They shall see God.

IV. 'I Want to See God'

2548 Desire for true happiness frees man from his immoderate attachment to the goods of this world so that he can find his fulfilment in the vision and beatitude of God. 'The promise [of seeing God] surpasses all beatitude... In Scripture, to see is to *2519* possess... Whoever sees God has obtained all the goods of which he can conceive.'[343]

2549 It remains for the holy people to struggle, with grace from on high, to obtain the good things God promises. In order to possess and contemplate God, Christ's faithful mortify their crav- *2015* ings and, with the grace of God, prevail over the seductions of pleasure and power.

2550 On this way of perfection, the Spirit and the Bride call whoever hears them[344] to perfect communion with God:

> There will true glory be, where no one will be praised by mistake or flattery; true honour will not be refused to the worthy, nor granted to the unworthy; likewise, no one unworthy will pretend to be worthy, where only those who are worthy will be admitted. There true peace will reign, where no one will experience opposition either from self or others. God

---

[336] LG 42 § 3.
[337] Mt 5:3.
[338] Cf. Lk 6:20.
[339] St Gregory of Nyssa, De beatitudinibus 1: PG 44, 1200D; cf. 2 Cor 8:9.
[340] Lk 6:24.

[341] St Augustine, De serm. Dom. in monte 1, 1, 3: PL 34, 1232.
[342] Cf. Mt 6:25–34.
[343] St Gregory of Nyssa, De beatitudinibus 6: PG 44, 1265A.
[344] Cf. Rev 22:17.

himself will be virtue's reward; he gives virtue and has promised to give himself as the best and greatest reward that could exist... 'I shall be their God and they will be my people...' This is also the meaning of the Apostle's words: 'So that God may be all in all.' God himself will be the goal of our desires; we shall contemplate him without end, love him without surfeit, praise him without weariness. This gift, this state, this act, like eternal life itself, will assuredly be common to all.[345]

314

IN BRIEF

2551 *'Where your treasure is, there will your heart be also' (Mt 6:21).*

2552 *The tenth commandment forbids avarice arising from a passion for riches and their attendant power.*

2553 *Envy is sadness at the sight of another's goods and the immoderate desire to have them for oneself. It is a capital sin.*

2554 *The baptized person combats envy through good will, humility and abandonment to the providence of God.*

2555 *Christ's faithful 'have crucified the flesh with its passions and desires' (Gal 5:24); they are led by the Spirit and follow his desires.*

2556 *Detachment from riches is necessary for entering the Kingdom of heaven. 'Blessed are the poor in spirit.'*

2557 *'I want to see God' expresses the true desire of man. Thirst for God is quenched by the water of eternal life (cf. Jn 4:14).*

---

[345] St Augustine, *De civ. Dei* 22, 30: PL
41, 801–802; cf. *Lev* 26:12; 1 *Cor*
15:28.

Part Four

CHRISTIAN PRAYER

Section One

PRAYER IN THE CHRISTIAN LIFE

2558 'Great is the mystery of the faith!' The Church professes this mystery in the Apostles' Creed (*Part One*) and celebrates it in the sacramental liturgy (*Part Two*), so that the life of the faithful may be conformed to Christ in the Holy Spirit to the glory of God the Father (*Part Three*). This mystery, then, requires that the faithful believe in it, that they celebrate it, and that they live from it in a vital and personal relationship with the living and true God. This relationship is prayer.

WHAT IS PRAYER?

For me, prayer is a surge of the heart; it is a simple look turned toward heaven, it is a cry of recognition and of love, embracing both trial and joy.[1]

Prayer as God's gift

2559 'Prayer is the raising of one's mind and heart to God or the requesting of good things from God.'[2] But when we pray, do we speak from the height of our pride and will, or 'out of the depths' of a humble and contrite heart?[3] He who humbles himself will be exalted;[4] *humility* is the foundation of prayer. Only when we humbly acknowledge that 'we do not know how to pray as we ought'[5] are we ready to receive freely the gift of prayer. 'Man is a beggar before God.'[6]

2613
2736

2560 'If you knew the gift of God!'[7] The wonder of prayer is revealed beside the well where we come seeking water: there, Christ comes to meet every human being. It is he who first seeks us and asks us for a drink. Jesus thirsts; his asking arises from the depths of God's desire for us. Whether we realize it or not, prayer is the encounter of God's thirst with ours. God thirsts that we may thirst for him.[8]

2561 'You would have asked him, and he would have given you living water.'[9] Paradoxically our prayer of petition is a response to the plea of the living God: 'They have forsaken me, the fountain of

---

[1] St Thérèse of Lisieux, *Manuscrits autobiographiques* C 25r.
[2] St John Damascene, *De fide orth.* 3, 24: PG 94, 1089C.
[3] Ps 130:1.
[4] Cf. Lk 18:9–14.
[5] Rom 8:26.

[6] St Augustine, *Sermo* 56, 6, 9: PL 38, 381.
[7] Jn 4:10.
[8] Cf. St Augustine, *De diversis quaestionibus octoginta tribus* 64, 4: PL 40, 56.
[9] Jn 4:10.

living waters and hewn out cisterns for themselves, broken cisterns that can hold no water!'[10] Prayer is the response of faith to the free promise of salvation and also a response of love to the thirst of the only Son of God.[11]

Prayer as covenant

2562 Where does prayer come from? Whether prayer is expressed in words or gestures, it is the whole man who prays. But in naming the source of prayer, Scripture speaks sometimes of the soul or the spirit, but most often of the heart (more than a thousand times). According to Scripture, it is the *heart* that prays. If our heart is far from God, the words of prayer are in vain.

2563 The heart is the dwelling-place where I am, where I live; according to the Semitic or biblical expression, the heart is the place 'to which I withdraw'. The heart is our hidden centre, beyond the grasp of our reason and of others; only the Spirit of God can fathom the human heart and know it fully. The heart is the place of decision, deeper than our psychic drives. It is the place of truth, where we choose life or death. It is the place of encounter, *1696, 2699* because as image of God we live in relation: it is the place of covenant.

2564 Christian prayer is a covenant relationship between God and man in Christ. It is the action of God and of man, springing forth from both the Holy Spirit and ourselves, wholly directed to the Father, in union with the human will of the Son of God made man.

Prayer as communion

2565 In the New Covenant, prayer is the living relationship of the children of God with their Father who is good beyond measure, with his Son Jesus Christ and with the Holy Spirit. The grace of the Kingdom is 'the union of the entire holy and royal Trinity... *260* with the whole human spirit'.[12] Thus, the life of prayer is the habit of being in the presence of the thrice-holy God and in communion with him. This communion of life is always possible because, through Baptism, we have already been united with Christ.[13] Prayer is *Christian* insofar as it is communion with Christ and extends throughout the Church, which is his Body. Its dimensions *792* are those of Christ's love.[14]

---

[10] Jer 2:13.
[11] Cf. Jn 7:37-39; 19:28; Is 12:3; 51:1; Zech 12:10; 13:1.
[12] St Gregory of Nazianzus, *Oratio* 16, 9:

PG 35, 945.
[13] Cf. Rom 6:5.
[14] Cf. Eph 3:18-21.

Chapter One

THE REVELATION OF PRAYER
THE UNIVERSAL CALL TO PRAYER

2566 *Man is in search of God.* In the act of creation, God calls every
being from nothingness into existence. 'Crowned with glory and
honour', man is, after the angels, capable of acknowledging 'how
majestic is the name of the Lord in all the earth.'[1] Even after losing
through his sin his likeness to God, man remains an image of his
Creator, and retains the desire for the one who calls him into
existence. All religions bear witness to men's essential search for
God.[2]

2567 *God calls man first.* Man may forget his Creator or hide far
from his face; he may run after idols or accuse the deity of having
abandoned him; yet the living and true God tirelessly calls each
person to that mysterious encounter known as prayer. In prayer,
the faithful God's initiative of love always comes first; our own
first step is always a response. As God gradually reveals himself and
reveals man to himself, prayer appears as a reciprocal call, a covenant drama. Through words and actions, this drama engages the
heart. It unfolds throughout the whole history of salvation.

Article 1

IN THE OLD TESTAMENT

2568 In the Old Testament, the revelation of prayer comes
between the fall and the restoration of man, that is, between God's
sorrowful call to his first children: 'Where are you?... What is this
that you have done?'[3] and the response of God's only Son on
coming into the world: 'Lo, I have come to do your will, O God.'[4]
Prayer is bound up with human history, for it is the relationship
with God in historical events.

Creation – source of prayer

2569 Prayer is lived in the first place beginning with the realities
of *creation*. The first nine chapters of *Genesis* describe this relationship with God as an offering of the first-born of Abel's flock, as the
invocation of the divine name at the time of Enosh, and as 'walking with God'.[5] Noah's offering is pleasing to God, who blesses
him and through him all creation, because his heart was upright

*Margin references:* 296, 355, 28, 30, 142, 410, 1736, 2738, 288, 58

---

[1] *Ps* 8:5, 1.
[2] Cf. *Acts* 17:27.
[3] *Gen* 3:9, 13.

[4] *Heb* 10:5–7.
[5] Cf. *Gen* 4:4, 26; 5:24.

and undivided; Noah, like Enoch before him, 'walks with God'.[6] This kind of prayer is lived by many righteous people in all religions.

In his indefectible covenant with every living creature,[7] God has always called people to prayer. But it is above all beginning with our father Abraham that prayer is revealed in the Old Testament. — 59

God's promise and the prayer of faith

2570 When God calls him, Abraham goes forth 'as the Lord had told him';[8] Abraham's heart is entirely submissive to the Word and — 145 so he obeys. Such attentiveness of the heart, whose decisions are made according to God's will, is essential to prayer, while the words used count only in relation to it. Abraham's prayer is expressed first by deeds: a man of silence, he constructs an altar to the Lord at each stage of his journey. Only later does Abraham's first prayer in words appear: a veiled complaint reminding God of his promises which seem unfulfilled.[9] Thus one aspect of the drama of prayer appears from the beginning: the test of faith in the fidelity of God.

2571 Because Abraham believed in God and walked in his presence and in covenant with him,[10] the patriarch is ready to welcome a mysterious Guest into his tent. Abraham's remarkable hospitality at Mamre foreshadows the annunciation of the true — 494 Son of the promise.[11] After that, once God has confided his plan, Abraham's heart is attuned to his Lord's compassion for men and he dares to intercede for them with bold confidence.[12] — 2635

2572 As a final stage in the purification of his faith, Abraham, 'who had received the promises',[13] is asked to sacrifice the son God had given him. Abraham's faith does not weaken ('God himself will provide the lamb for a burnt offering'), for he 'considered that God was able to raise men even from the dead.'[14] And so the father of believers is conformed to the likeness of the Father who will not — 603 spare his own Son but will deliver him up for us all.[15] Prayer restores man to God's likeness and enables him to share in the power of God's love that saves the multitude.[16]

---

[6] Gen 6:9; 8:20 – 9:17.
[7] Gen 9:8–16.
[8] Gen 12:4.
[9] Cf. Gen 15:2–3.
[10] Cf. Gen 15:6; 17:1–2.
[11] Cf. Gen 18:1–15; Lk 1:26–38.
[12] Cf. Gen 18:16–33.
[13] Heb 11:17.
[14] Gen 22:8; Heb 11:19.
[15] Rom 8:32.
[16] Cf. Rom 8:16–21.

2573 God renews his promise to Jacob, the ancestor of the twelve tribes of Israel.[17] Before confronting his elder brother Esau, Jacob wrestles all night with a mysterious figure who refuses to reveal his name, but who blesses him before leaving him at dawn. From this account, the spiritual tradition of the Church has retained the 162 symbol of prayer as a battle of faith and as the triumph of perseverance.[18]

Moses and the prayer of the mediator

2574 Once the promise begins to be fulfilled (Passover, the 62 Exodus, the gift of the Law and the ratification of the covenant), the prayer of Moses becomes the most striking example of intercessory prayer, which will be fulfilled in 'the one mediator between God and men, the man Christ Jesus .[19]

2575 Here again the initiative is God's. From the midst of the 205 burning bush he calls Moses.[20] This event will remain one of the primordial images of prayer in the spiritual tradition of Jews and Christians alike. When 'the God of Abraham, of Isaac and of Jacob' calls Moses to be his servant, it is because he is the living God who wants men to live. God reveals himself in order to save them, though he does not do this alone or despite them: he calls Moses to be his messenger, an associate in his compassion, his work of salvation. There is something of a divine plea in this mission, and only after long debate does Moses attune his own will to that of the Saviour God. But in the dialogue in which God confides in him, Moses also learns how to pray: he balks, makes excuses, above all questions: and it is in response to his question that the Lord confides his ineffable name, which will be revealed through his mighty deeds.

555 2576 'Thus the LORD used to speak to Moses face to face, as a man speaks to his friend.'[21] Moses' prayer is characteristic of contemplative prayer by which God's servant remains faithful to his mission. Moses converses with God often and at length, climbing the mountain to hear and entreat him and coming down to the people to repeat the words of his God for their guidance. Moses 'is entrusted with all my house. With him I speak face to face, clearly, not in riddles', for 'Moses was very humble, more so than anyone else on the face of the earth.'[22]

---

[17] Cf. Gen 28:10–22.
[18] Cf. Gen 32:24–30; Lk 18:1–8.
[19] 1 Tim 2:5.
[20] Ex 3:1–10.
[21] Ex 33:11.
[22] Num 12:3, 7–8.

2577 From this intimacy with the faithful God, slow to anger and abounding in steadfast love,[23] Moses drew strength and determination for his intercession. He does not pray for himself but for *210* the people whom God made his own. Moses already intercedes for them during the battle with the Amalekites and prays to obtain *2635* healing for Miriam.[24] But it is chiefly after their apostasy that Moses 'stands in the breach' before God in order to save the people.[25] The arguments of his prayer – for intercession is also a mysterious battle – will inspire the boldness of the great intercessors among the Jewish people and in the Church: God is love; he is *214* therefore righteous and faithful; he cannot contradict himself; he must remember his marvellous deeds, since his glory is at stake, and he cannot forsake this people that bears his name.

David and the prayer of the king

2578 The prayer of the People of God flourishes in the shadow of God's dwelling place, first the ark of the covenant and later the Temple. At first the leaders of the people – the shepherds and the prophets – teach them to pray. The infant Samuel must have learned from his mother Hannah how 'to stand before the LORD' and from the priest Eli how to listen to his word: 'Speak, LORD, for your servant is listening.'[26] Later, he will also know the cost and consequence of intercession: 'Moreover, as for me, far be it from me that I should sin against the LORD by ceasing to pray for you; and I will instruct you in the good and the right way.'[27]

2579 David is *par excellence* the king 'after God's own heart', the *709* shepherd who prays for his people and prays in their name. His submission to the will of God, his praise and his repentance, will be a model for the prayer of the people. His prayer, the prayer of God's Anointed, is a faithful adherence to the divine promise and *436* expresses a loving and joyful trust in God, the only King and Lord.[28] In the Psalms David, inspired by the Holy Spirit, is the first prophet of Jewish and Christian prayer. The prayer of Christ, the true Messiah and Son of David, will reveal and fulfil the meaning of this prayer.

2580 The Temple of Jerusalem, the house of prayer that David *583* wanted to build, will be the work of his son, Solomon. The prayer at the dedication of the Temple relies on God's promise and covenant, on the active presence of his name among his People,

---

[23] Cf. *Ex* 34:6.
[24] Cf. *Ex* 17:8–12; *Num* 12:13–14.
[25] *Ps* 106:23; cf. *Ex* 32:1 – 34:9.
[26] 1 *Sam* 3:9–10; cf. 1:9–18.
[27] 1 *Sam* 12:23.
[28] Cf. 2 *Sam* 7:18–29.

recalling his mighty deeds at the Exodus.[29] The king lifts his hands toward heaven and begs the Lord, on his own behalf, on behalf of the entire people and of the generations yet to come, for the forgiveness of their sins and for their daily needs, so that the nations may know that He is the only God and that the heart of his people may belong wholly and entirely to him.

Elijah, the prophets and conversion of heart

2581 For the People of God, the Temple was to be the place of their education in prayer: pilgrimages, feasts and sacrifices, the evening offering, the incense, and the bread of the Presence
1150 ('shewbread') – all these signs of the holiness and glory of God Most High and Most Near were appeals to and ways of prayer. But ritualism often encouraged an excessively external worship. The people needed education in faith and conversion of heart; this was the mission of the prophets, both before and after the Exile.

2582 Elijah is the 'father' of the prophets, 'the generation of those who seek him, who seek the face of the God of Jacob'.[30] Elijah's name, 'The Lord is my God', foretells the people's cry in response to his prayer on Mount Carmel.[31] St James refers to Elijah in order to encourage us to pray: 'The prayer of the righteous is powerful and effective.'[32]

2583 After Elijah had learned mercy during his retreat at the Wadi Cherith, he teaches the widow of Zarephath to believe in the Word of God and confirms her faith by his urgent prayer: God brings the widow's child back to life.[33]

The sacrifice on Mount Carmel is a decisive test for the faith of the People of God. In response to Elijah's plea, 'Answer me, O
696 LORD, answer me', the Lord's fire consumes the holocaust, at the time of the evening oblation. The Eastern liturgies repeat Elijah's plea in the Eucharistic *epiclesis*.

Finally, taking the desert road that leads to the place where the living and true God reveals himself to his people, Elijah, like Moses before him, hides 'in a cleft of the rock' until the mysterious presence of God has passed by.[34] But only on the mountain of the
555 Transfiguration will Moses and Elijah behold the unveiled face of him whom they sought; 'the light of the knowledge of the glory of God [shines] in the face of Christ', crucified and risen.[35]

---

[29] 1 Kings 8:10–61.
[30] Ps 24:6.
[31] 1 Kings 18:39.
[32] Jas 5:16b–18.

[33] Cf. 1 Kings 17:7–24.
[34] Cf. 1 Kings 19:1–14; cf. Ex 33:19–23.
[35] 2 Cor 4:6; cf. Lk 9:30–35.

2584 In their 'one to one' encounters with God, the prophets 2709
draw light and strength for their mission. Their prayer is not flight
from this unfaithful world, but rather attentiveness to the Word of
God. At times their prayer is an argument or a complaint, but it is
always an intercession that awaits and prepares for the intervention of the Saviour God, the Lord of history.[36]

The Psalms, the prayer of the assembly

2585 From the time of David to the coming of the Messiah texts
appearing in these sacred books show a deepening in prayer for
oneself and in prayer for others.[37] Thus the Psalms were gradually 1093
collected into the five books of the Psalter (or 'Praises'), the
masterwork of prayer in the Old Testament.

2586 The Psalms both nourished and expressed the prayer of the
People of God gathered during the great feasts at Jerusalem and
each Sabbath in the synagogues. Their prayer is inseparably personal and communal; it concerns both those who are praying, and
all men. The Psalms arose from the communities of the Holy Land
and the Diaspora, but embrace all creation. Their prayer recalls the
saving events of the past, yet extends into the future, even to the
end of history; it commemorates the promises God has already
kept, and awaits the Messiah who will fulfil them definitively.
Prayed by Christ and fulfilled in him, the Psalms remain essential 1177
to the prayer of the Church.[38]

2587 The Psalter is the book in which the Word of God becomes
man's prayer. In other books of the Old Testament, 'the words
proclaim [God's] works and bring to light the mystery they contain.'[39] The words of the Psalmist, sung for God, both express and
acclaim the Lord's saving works; the same Spirit inspires both
God's work and man's response. Christ will unite the two. In him,
the Psalms continue to teach us how to pray.   2641

2588 The Psalter's many forms of prayer take shape both in the
liturgy of the Temple and in the human heart. Whether hymns or
prayers of lamentation or thanksgiving, whether individual or
communal, whether royal chants, songs of pilgrimage or wisdom-
meditations, the Psalms are a mirror of God's marvellous deeds in
the history of his people, as well as reflections of the human experiences of the Psalmist. Though a given psalm may reflect an event

---

[36] Cf. Am 7:2, 5; Is 6:5, 8, 11; Jer 1:6;
    15:15–18; 20:7–18.
[37] Ezra 9:6–15; Neh 1:4–11; Jon 2:3–10;

Tob 3:11–16; Jdt 9:2–14.
[38] Cf. GILH, nn. 100–109.
[39] DV 2.

of the past, it still possesses such direct simplicity that it can be prayed in truth by men of all times and conditions.

2589 Certain constant characteristics appear throughout the Psalms: simplicity and spontaneity of prayer; the desire for God himself through and with all that is good in his creation; the distraught situation of the believer who, in his preferential love for the Lord, is exposed to a host of enemies and temptations, but who waits upon what the faithful God will do, in the certitude of his love and in submission to his will. The prayer of the Psalms is always sustained by praise; that is why the title of this collection as handed down to us is so fitting: 'The Praises'. Collected for the assembly's worship, the Psalter both sounds the call to prayer and sings the response to that call: *Hallelu-Yah!* ('Alleluia'), 'Praise the Lord!'

304

> What is more pleasing than a psalm? David expresses it well: 'Praise the Lord, for a psalm is good: let there be praise of our God with gladness and grace!' Yes, a psalm is a blessing on the lips of the people, praise of God, the assembly's homage, a general acclamation, a word that speaks for all, the voice of the Church, a confession of faith in song.[40]

IN BRIEF

2590 *'Prayer is the raising of one's mind and heart to God or the requesting of good things from God' (St John Damascene, De fide orth. 3, 24: PG 94, 1089C).*

2591 *God tirelessly calls each person to this mysterious encounter with Himself. Prayer unfolds throughout the whole history of salvation as a reciprocal call between God and man.*

2592 *The prayer of Abraham and Jacob is presented as a battle of faith marked by trust in God's faithfulness and by certitude in the victory promised to perseverance.*

2593 *The prayer of Moses responds to the living God's initiative for the salvation of his people. It foreshadows the prayer of intercession of the unique mediator, Christ Jesus.*

2594 *The prayer of the People of God flourished in the shadow of the dwelling place of God's presence on earth, the ark of the covenant and the Temple, under the guidance of their shepherds, especially King David, and of the prophets.*

---

[40] St Ambrose, *En. in Ps.* 1, 9: PL 14, 924; *LH*, week 10, Saturday, OR.

> 2595 *The prophets summoned the people to conversion of heart and, while zealously seeking the face of God, like Elijah, they interceded for the people.*
>
> 2596 *The Psalms constitute the masterwork of prayer in the Old Testament. They present two inseparable qualities: the personal, and the communal. They extend to all dimensions of history, recalling God's promises already fulfilled, and looking for the coming of the Messiah.*
>
> 2597 *Prayed and fulfilled in Christ, the Psalms are an essential and permanent element of the prayer of the Church. They are suitable for men of every condition and time.*

Article 2
IN THE FULLNESS OF TIME

2598 The drama of prayer is fully revealed to us in the Word who became flesh and dwells among us. To seek to understand his prayer through what his witnesses proclaim to us in the Gospel is to approach the holy Lord Jesus as Moses approached the burning bush: first to contemplate him in prayer, then to hear how he teaches us to pray, in order to know how he hears our prayer.

Jesus prays

2599 The Son of God who became Son of the Virgin also learned *470–473* to pray according to his human heart. He learns the formulas of prayer from his mother, who kept in her heart and meditated upon all the 'great things' done by the Almighty.[41] He learns to pray in the words and rhythms of the prayer of his people, in the synagogue at Nazareth and the Temple at Jerusalem. But his prayer *584* springs from an otherwise secret source, as he intimates at the age of twelve: 'I must be in my Father's house.'[42] Here the newness of *534* prayer in the fullness of time begins to be revealed; his *filial prayer*, which the Father awaits from his children, is finally going to be lived out by the only Son in his humanity, with and for men.

2600 The Gospel according to St Luke emphasizes the action of the Holy Spirit and the meaning of prayer in Christ's ministry. Jesus prays *before* the decisive moments of his mission: before his Father's witness to him during his baptism and Transfiguration, *535, 554* and before his own fulfilment of the Father's plan of love by his Passion.[43] He also prays before the decisive moments involving *612* the mission of his apostles: at his election and call of the Twelve, *858*

---

[41] Cf. *Lk* 1:49; 2:19; 2:51.   [43] Cf. *Lk* 3:21; 9:28; 22:41–44.
[42] *Lk* 2:49.

442 before Peter's confession of him as 'the Christ of God', and again that the faith of the chief of the apostles may not fail when tempted.[44] Jesus' prayer before the events of salvation that the Father has asked him to fulfil is a humble and trusting commitment of his human will to the loving will of the Father.

2601 'He was praying in a certain place and when he had ceased, one of his disciples said to him, "Lord, teach us to pray." '[45] In seeing the Master at prayer the disciple of Christ also wants to pray. By *contemplating* and hearing the Son, the master of prayer, 2765 the children learn to pray to the Father.

2602 Jesus often draws apart to pray *in solitude*, on a mountain, 616 preferably at night.[46] *He includes all men* in his prayer, for he has taken on humanity in his incarnation, and he offers them to the Father when he offers himself. Jesus, the Word who has become flesh, shares by his human prayer in all that 'his brethren' experience; he sympathizes with their weaknesses in order to free them.[47] It was for this that the Father sent him. His words and works are the visible manifestation of his prayer in secret.

2603 The evangelists have preserved two more explicit prayers offered by Christ during his public ministry. Each begins with 2637 thanksgiving. In the first, Jesus confesses the Father, acknowledges and blesses him because he has hidden the mysteries of the Kingdom from those who think themselves learned and has revealed 2546 them to infants, the poor of the Beatitudes.[48] His exclamation, 'Yes, Father!' expresses the depth of his heart, his adherence to the 494 Father's 'good pleasure', echoing his mother's *Fiat* at the time of his conception and prefiguring what he will say to the Father in his agony. The whole prayer of Jesus is contained in this loving adherence of his human heart to the mystery of the will of the Father.[49]

2604 The second prayer, before the raising of Lazarus, is recorded by St John.[50] Thanksgiving precedes the event: 'Father, I thank you for having heard me', which implies that the Father always hears his petitions. Jesus immediately adds: 'I know that you always hear me', which implies that Jesus, on his part, *constantly made such petitions*. Jesus' prayer, characterized by thanksgiving, reveals to us how to ask: *before* the gift is given, Jesus commits

---

[44] Cf. *Lk* 6:12; 9:18–20; 22:32.
[45] *Lk* 11:1.
[46] Cf. *Mk* 1:35; 6:46; *Lk* 5:16.
[47] Cf. *Heb* 2:12, 15; 4:15.

[48] Cf. *Mt* 11:25–27; *Lk* 10:21–23.
[49] Cf. *Eph* 1:9.
[50] Cf. *Jn* 11:41–42.

himself to the One who in giving gives himself. The Giver is more precious than the gift; he is the 'treasure'; in him abides his Son's heart; the gift is given 'as well'.[51]

478

The priestly prayer of Jesus holds a unique place in the economy of salvation.[52] A meditation on it will conclude Section One. It reveals the ever present prayer of our High Priest and, at the same time, contains what he teaches us about our prayer to our Father, which will be developed in Section Two.

2746

2605 When the hour has come for him to fulfil the Father's plan of love, Jesus allows a glimpse of the boundless depth of his filial prayer, not only before he freely delivered himself up ('*Abba*... not my will, but yours'),[53] but even in *his last words* on the Cross, where prayer and the gift of self are but one: 'Father, forgive them, for they know not what they do';[54] 'Truly, I say to you, today you will be with me in Paradise';[55] 'Woman, behold your son' – 'Behold your mother';[56] 'I thirst';[57] 'My God, my God, why have you forsaken me?';[58] 'It is finished';[59] 'Father, into your hands I commit my spirit!'[60] until the 'loud cry' as he expires, giving up his spirit.[61]

614

2606 All the troubles, for all time, of humanity enslaved by sin and death, all the petitions and intercessions of salvation history are summed up in this cry of the incarnate Word. Here the Father accepts them and, beyond all hope, answers them by raising his Son. Thus is fulfilled and brought to completion the drama of prayer in the economy of creation and salvation. The Psalter gives us the key to prayer in Christ. In the 'today' of the Resurrection the Father says: 'You are my Son, today I have begotten you. Ask of me, and I will make the nations your heritage, and the ends of the earth your possession.'[62]

403

653

2587

The *Letter to the Hebrews* expresses in dramatic terms how the prayer of Jesus accomplished the victory of salvation: 'In the days of his flesh, Jesus offered up prayers and supplications, with loud cries and tears, to him who was able to save him from death, and he was heard for his godly fear. Although he was a Son, he learned obedience through what he suffered, and being made perfect, he became the source of eternal salvation to all who obey him.'[63]

---

[51] Mt 6:21, 33.
[52] Cf. Jn 17.
[53] Lk 22:42.
[54] Lk 23:34.
[55] Lk 23:43.
[56] Jn 19:26–27.
[57] Jn 19:28.
[58] Mk 15:34; cf. Ps 22:2.
[59] Jn 19:30.
[60] Lk 23:46.
[61] Cf. Mk 15:37; Jn 19:30b.
[62] Ps 2:7–8; cf. Acts 13:33.
[63] Heb 5:7–9.

Jesus teaches us how to pray

520 2607 When Jesus prays he is already teaching us how to pray. His prayer to his Father is the theologal path [the path of faith, hope and charity] of our prayer to God. But the Gospel also gives us Jesus' explicit teaching on prayer. Like a wise teacher he takes hold of us where we are and leads us progressively toward the Father. Addressing the crowds following him, Jesus builds on what they already know of prayer from the Old Covenant and opens to them the newness of the coming Kingdom. Then he reveals this newness to them in parables. Finally, he will speak openly of the Father and the Holy Spirit to his disciples who will be the teachers of prayer in his Church.

541 2608 From the *Sermon on the Mount* onwards, Jesus insists on *con-*
1430 *version of heart*: reconciliation with one's brother before presenting an offering on the altar, love of enemies and prayer for persecutors, prayer to the Father in secret, not heaping up empty phrases, prayerful forgiveness from the depths of the heart, purity of heart and seeking the Kingdom before all else.[64] This filial conversion is entirely directed to the Father.

2609 Once committed to conversion, the heart learns to pray in
153, 1814 *faith*. Faith is a filial adherence to God beyond what we feel and understand. It is possible because the beloved Son gives us access to the Father. He can ask us to 'seek' and to 'knock', since he himself is the door and the way.[65]

2610 Just as Jesus prays to the Father and gives thanks before receiving his gifts, so he teaches us *filial boldness*: 'Whatever you ask in prayer, believe that you receive it, and you will.'[66] Such is the power of prayer and of faith that does not doubt: 'all things are possible to him who believes.'[67] Jesus is as saddened by the 'lack of
165 faith' of his own neighbours and the 'little faith' of his own disciples[68] as he is struck with admiration at the great faith of the Roman centurion and the Canaanite woman.[69]

2611 The prayer of faith consists not only in saying 'Lord, Lord',
2827 but in disposing the heart to do the will of the Father.[70] Jesus calls his disciples to bring into their prayer this concern for co-operating with the divine plan.[71]

---

[64] Cf. *Mt* 5:23–24, 44–45; 6:7, 14–15, 21, 25, 33.
[65] Cf. *Mt* 7:7–11, 13–14.
[66] *Mk* 11:24.
[67] *Mk* 9:23; cf. *Mt* 21:22.
[68] Cf. *Mk* 6:6; *Mt* 8:26.
[69] Cf. *Mt* 8:10; 15:28.
[70] Cf. *Mt* 7:21.
[71] Cf. *Mt* 9:38; *Lk* 10:2; *Jn* 4:34.

Mary by George Mung Mung: wood carving of Mary carrying the infant Jesus in her womb.

This major work of art and devotion is the fruit of the meeting of Catholic and Aboriginal cultures in Australia. The unusual style invites reflection on the search for contemporary images which express the central mysteries of faith anew, drawing from all cultural traditions and renewing them.

2612 In Jesus 'the Kingdom of God is at hand.'[72] He calls his
hearers to conversion and faith, but also to *watchfulness*. In prayer 672
the disciple keeps watch, attentive to Him Who Is and Him Who
Comes, in memory of his first coming in the lowliness of the flesh,
and in the hope of his second coming in glory.[73] In communion
with their Master, the disciples' prayer is a battle; only by keeping 2725
watch in prayer can one avoid falling into temptation.[74]

2613 Three principal *parables* on prayer are transmitted to us by St Luke: 546
– The first, 'the importunate friend',[75] invites us to urgent prayer: 'Knock, and
it will be opened to you.' To the one who prays like this, the heavenly Father
will 'give whatever he needs', and above all the Holy Spirit who contains all
gifts.
– The second, 'the importunate widow',[76] is centred on one of the qualities of
prayer: it is necessary to pray always without ceasing, and with the *patience* of
faith. 'And yet, when the Son of Man comes, will he find faith on earth?'
– The third parable, 'the Pharisee and the tax collector',[77] concerns the *humility* 2559
of the heart that prays. 'God, be merciful to me a sinner!' The Church continues
to make this prayer her own: *Kyrie eleison!*

2614 When Jesus openly entrusts to his disciples the mystery of
prayer to the Father he reveals to them what their prayer and ours
must be, once he has returned to the Father in his glorified humanity. What is new is to 'ask *in his name*'.[78] Faith in the Son introduces 434
the disciples into the knowledge of the Father, because Jesus is 'the
way, and the truth, and the life'.[79] Faith bears its fruit in love: it
means keeping the word and the commandments of Jesus, it means
abiding with him in the Father who, in him, so loves us that he
abides with us. In this new covenant the certitude that our petitions will be heard is founded on the prayer of Jesus.[80]

2615 Even more, what the Father gives us when our prayer is
united with that of Jesus is 'another Counsellor, to be with you for
ever, the Spirit of truth'.[81] This new dimension of prayer and of its 728
circumstances is displayed throughout the farewell discourse.[82] In
the Holy Spirit, Christian prayer is a communion of love with the
Father, not only through Christ but also *in him*: 'Hitherto you
have asked nothing in my name; ask, and you will receive, that
your joy may be full.'[83]

---

[72] Mk 1:15.
[73] Cf. Mk 13; Lk 21:34–36.
[74] Cf. Lk 22:40, 46.
[75] Cf. Lk 11:5–13.
[76] Cf. Lk 18:1–8.
[77] Cf. Lk 18:9–14.
[78] Jn 14:13.
[79] Jn 14:6.
[80] Cf. Jn 14:13–14.
[81] Jn 14:16–17.
[82] Cf. Jn 14:23–26; 15:7, 16; 16:13–15, 23–27.
[83] Jn 16:24.

Jesus hears our prayer

2616 Prayer *to Jesus* is answered by him already during his minis-
548 try, through signs that anticipate the power of his death and
Resurrection: Jesus hears the prayer of faith, expressed in words
(the leper, Jairus, the Canaanite woman, the good thief)[84] or in
silence (the bearers of the paralytic, the woman with a haemorrhage who touches his clothes, the tears and ointment of the sinful
woman).[85] The urgent request of the blind men, 'Have mercy on
us, Son of David' or 'Jesus, Son of David, have mercy on me!',[86]
has been renewed in the traditional prayer to Jesus known as the
2667 *Jesus Prayer*: 'Lord Jesus Christ, Son of God, have mercy on me, a
sinner!' Healing infirmities or forgiving sins, Jesus always responds
to a prayer offered in faith: 'Your faith has made you well; go in
peace.'

> St Augustine wonderfully summarizes the three dimensions of Jesus'
> prayer: 'He prays for us as our priest, prays in us as our Head, and is
> prayed to by us as our God. Therefore let us acknowledge our voice in
> him and his in us.'[87]

The prayer of the Virgin Mary

148 2617 Mary's prayer is revealed to us at the dawning of the fullness
of time. Before the incarnation of the Son of God, and before the
outpouring of the Holy Spirit, her prayer co-operates in a unique
494 way with the Father's plan of loving kindness: at the Annunciation, for Christ's conception; at Pentecost, for the formation of the
Church, his Body.[88] In the faith of his humble handmaid, the Gift
of God found the acceptance he had awaited from the beginning
490 of time. She whom the Almighty made 'full of grace' responds by
offering her whole being: 'Behold I am the handmaid of the Lord;
let it be [done] to me according to your word.' *Fiat*: this is Christian prayer: to be wholly God's, because he is wholly ours.

2674 2618 The Gospel reveals to us how Mary prays and intercedes in
faith. At Cana,[89] the mother of Jesus asks her son for the needs of a
wedding feast; this is the sign of another feast – that of the wedding
of the Lamb where he gives his body and blood at the request of
the Church, his Bride. It is at the hour of the New Covenant, at the
726 foot of the cross,[90] that Mary is heard as the Woman, the new Eve,
the true 'Mother of all the living'.

---

[84] Cf. *Mk* 1 40–41; 5:36; 7:29; *Lk* 23:39–43.
[85] Cf. *Mk* 2:5; 5:28; *Lk* 7:37–38.
[86] *Mt* 9:27; *Mk* 10:48.
[87] St Augustine, *En. in Ps.* 85, 1: PL 37,
1081; cf. *GILH* 7.
[88] Cf. *Lk* 1:38; *Acts* 1:14.
[89] Cf. *Jn* 2:1–12.
[90] Cf. *Jn* 19:25–27.

2619 That is why the Canticle of Mary,[91] the *Magnificat* (Latin) or *Megalynei* (Byzantine), is the song both of the Mother of God and of the Church; the song of the Daughter of Zion and of the new People of God; the song of thanksgiving for the fullness of graces poured out in the economy of salvation and the song of the 'poor' whose hope is met by the fulfilment of the promises made to our ancestors, 'to Abraham and to his posterity for ever' *724*

IN BRIEF

2620 Jesus' filial prayer is the perfect model of prayer in the New Testament. Often done in solitude and in secret, the prayer of Jesus involves a loving adherence to the will of the Father even to the Cross and an absolute confidence in being heard.

2621 In his teaching, Jesus teaches his disciples to pray with a purified heart, with lively and persevering faith, with filial boldness. He calls them to vigilance and invites them to present their petitions to God in his name. Jesus Christ himself answers prayers addressed to him.

2622 The prayers of the Virgin Mary, in her Fiat and Magnificat, are characterized by the generous offering of her whole being in faith.

Article 3
IN THE AGE OF THE CHURCH

2623 On the day of Pentecost, the Spirit of the Promise was *731* poured out on the disciples, gathered 'together in one place'.[92] While awaiting the Spirit, 'all these with one accord devoted themselves to prayer.'[93] The Spirit who teaches the Church and recalls for her everything that Jesus said[94] was also to form her in the life of prayer.

2624 In the first community of Jerusalem, believers 'devoted *1342* themselves to the apostles' teaching and fellowship, to the breaking of bread and the prayers.'[95] This sequence is characteristic of the Church's prayer: founded on the apostolic faith; authenticated by charity; nourished in the Eucharist.

2625 In the first place these are prayers that the faithful hear and read in the Scriptures, but also that they make their own – especially those of the Psalms, in view of their fulfilment in Christ.[96] The Holy Spirit, who thus keeps the memory of Christ alive in his *1092*

---

[91] Cf. *Lk* 1:46–55.
[92] *Acts* 2:1.
[93] *Acts* 1:14.
[94] Cf. *Jn* 14:26.
[95] *Acts* 2:42.
[96] Cf. *Lk* 24:27, 44.

Church at prayer, also leads her towards the fullness of truth and inspires new formulations expressing the unfathomable mystery of Christ at work in his Church's life, sacraments and mission.

1200 These formulations are developed in the great liturgical and spiritual traditions. The *forms of prayer* revealed in the apostolic and canonical Scriptures remain normative for Christian prayer.

I. Blessing and Adoration

1078 **2626** *Blessing* expresses the basic movement of Christian prayer: it is an encounter between God and man. In blessing, God's gift and man's acceptance of it are united in dialogue with each other. The prayer of blessing is man's response to God's gifts: because God blesses, the human heart can in return bless the One who is the source of every blessing.

1083 **2627** Two fundamental forms express this movement: our prayer *ascends* in the Holy Spirit through Christ to the Father – we bless him for having blessed us;[97] it implores the grace of the Holy Spirit that *descends* through Christ from the Father – he blesses us.[98]

2096–2097 **2628** *Adoration* is the first attitude of man acknowledging that he is a creature before his Creator. It exalts the greatness of the Lord who made us[99] and the almighty power of the Saviour who sets us free from evil. Adoration is homage of the spirit to the 'King of Glory',[100] respectful silence in the presence of the 'ever greater' God.[101] Adoration of the thrice-holy and sovereign God of love

2559 blends with humility and gives assurance to our supplications.

II. Prayer of Petition

2629 The vocabulary of supplication in the New Testament is rich in shades of meaning: ask, beseech, plead, invoke, entreat, cry out, even 'struggle in prayer'.[102] Its most usual form, because the most spontaneous, is petition: by prayer of petition we express awareness of our relationship with God. We are creatures who are not our own beginning, not the masters of adversity, not our own

396 last end. We are sinners who as Christians know that we have turned away from our Father. Our petition is already a turning back to him.

---

[97] Cf. *Eph* 1:3–14; 2 *Cor* 1:3–7; 1 *Pt* 1:3–9.
[98] Cf. 2 *Cor* 13:14; *Rom* 15:5–6, 13; *Eph* 6:23–24.
[99] Cf. *Ps* 95:1–6.

[100] *Ps* 24:9–10.
[101] Cf. St Augustine, *En. in Ps.* 62, 16: PL 36, 757–758.
[102] Cf. *Rom* 15:30; *Col* 4:12.

2630 The New Testament contains scarcely any prayers of lamentation, so frequent in the Old Testament. In the risen Christ the Church's petition is buoyed by hope, even if we still wait in a state of expectation and must be 2090 converted anew every day. Christian petition, what St Paul calls 'groaning', arises from another depth, that of creation 'in labour pains' and that of ourselves 'as we wait for the redemption of our bodies. For in this hope we were saved.'[103] In the end, however, the Holy Spirit 'helps us in our weakness; for we do not know how to pray as we ought, but the Spirit himself intercedes for us with sighs too deep for words.'[104]

2631 The first movement of the prayer of petition is *asking forgive-* 2838 *ness*, like the tax collector in the parable: 'God, be merciful to me a sinner!'[105] It is a prerequisite for righteous and pure prayer. A trusting humility brings us back into the light of communion between the Father and his Son Jesus Christ and with one another, so that 'we receive from him whatever we ask.'[106] Asking forgiveness is the prerequisite for both the Eucharistic liturgy and personal prayer.

2632 Christian petition is centred on the desire and *search for the Kingdom to come*, in keeping with the teaching of Christ.[107] There is 2816 a hierarchy in these petitions: we pray first for the Kingdom, then for what is necessary to welcome it and co-operate with its 1942 coming. This collaboration with the mission of Christ and the Holy Spirit, which is now that of the Church, is the object of the prayer of the apostolic community.[108] It is the prayer of Paul, the apostle *par excellence*, which reveals to us how the divine solicitude for all the Churches ought to inspire Christian prayer.[109] By prayer every baptized person works for the coming of the 2854 Kingdom.

2633 When we share in God's saving love, we understand that *every need* can become the object of petition. Christ, who assumed 2830 all things in order to redeem all things, is glorified by what we ask the Father in his name.[110] It is with this confidence that St James and St Paul exhort us to pray *at all times*.[111]

III. Prayer of Intercession

2634 Intercession is a prayer of petition which leads us to pray as Jesus did. He is the one intercessor with the Father on behalf of all 432 men, especially sinners.[112] He is 'able for all time to save those who

---

[103] Rom 8:22–24.
[104] Rom 8:26.
[105] Lk 18:13.
[106] 1 Jn 3:22; cf. 1:7 – 2:2.
[107] Cf. Mt 6:10, 33; Lk 11:2, 13.
[108] Cf. Acts 6:6; 13:3.

[109] Cf. Rom 10:1; Eph 1:16–23; Phil 1:9–11; Col 1:3–6; 4:3–4, 12.
[110] Cf. Jn 14:13.
[111] Cf. Jas 1:5–8; Eph 5:20; Phil 4:6–7; Col 3:16–17; 1 Th 5:17–18.
[112] Cf. Rom 8:34; 1 Jn 2:1; 1 Tim 2:5–8.

draw near to God through him, since he always lives to make intercession for them.'[113] The Holy Spirit 'himself intercedes for us... and intercedes for the saints according to the will of God.'[114]

2571 2635 Since Abraham, intercession – asking on behalf of another – has been characteristic of a heart attuned to God's mercy. In the age of the Church, Christian intercession participates in Christ's, as an expression of the communion of saints. In intercession, he who 2577 prays looks 'not only to his own interests, but also to the interests of others', even to the point of praying for those who do him harm.[115]

2636 The first Christian communities lived this form of fellowship intensely.[116] Thus the apostle Paul gives them a share in his ministry of preaching the Gospel[117] but also intercedes for them.[118] The intercession of Christians recognizes no boundaries: 1900 'for all men, for kings and all who are in high positions', for 1037 persecutors, for the salvation of those who reject the Gospel.[119]

IV. Prayer of Thanksgiving

224 2637 Thanksgiving characterizes the prayer of the Church which, 1328 in celebrating the Eucharist, reveals and becomes more fully what she is. Indeed, in the work of salvation, Christ sets creation free from sin and death to consecrate it anew and make it return to the 2603 Father, for his glory. The thanksgiving of the members of the Body participates in that of their Head.

2638 As in the prayer of petition, every event and need can become an offering of thanksgiving. The letters of St Paul often begin and end with thanksgiving, and the Lord Jesus is always present in it: 'Give thanks in all circumstances; for this is the will of God in Christ Jesus for you'; 'Continue steadfastly in prayer, being watchful in it with thanksgiving.'[120]

V. Prayer of Praise

2639 Praise is the form of prayer which recognizes most immediately that God is God. It lauds God for his own sake and gives 213 him glory, quite beyond what he does, but simply because HE Is. It shares in the blessed happiness of the pure of heart who love God in faith before seeing him in glory. By praise, the Spirit is joined to

---

[113] Heb 7:25.
[114] Rom 8:26–27.
[115] Phil 2:4; cf. Acts 7:60; Lk 23:28, 34.
[116] Cf. Acts 12:5; 20:36; 21:5; 2 Cor 9:14.

[117] Cf. Eph 6:18–20; Col 4:3–4; 1 Th 5:25.
[118] Cf. 2 Th 1:11; Col 1:3; Phil 1:3–4.
[119] 1 Tim 2:1; cf. Rom 12:14; 10:1.
[120] 1 Th 5:18; Col 4:2.

our spirits to bear witness that we are children of God,[121] testifying to the only Son in whom we are adopted and by whom we glorify the Father. Praise embraces the other forms of prayer and carries them toward him who is its source and goal: the 'one God, the Father, from whom are all things and for whom we exist'.[122]

2640 St Luke in his gospel often expresses wonder and praise at the marvels of Christ and in his *Acts of the Apostles* stresses them as actions of the Holy Spirit: the community of Jerusalem, the invalid healed by Peter and John, the crowd that gives glory to God for that, and the pagans of Pisidia who 'were glad and glorified the word of God'.[123]

2641 '[Address] one another in psalms and hymns and spiritual songs, singing and making melody to the Lord with all your heart.'[124] Like the inspired writers of the New Testament, the first Christian communities read the Book of Psalms *2587* in a new way, singing in it the mystery of Christ. In the newness of the Spirit, they also composed hymns and canticles in the light of the unheard-of event that God accomplished in his Son: his Incarnation, his death which conquered death, his Resurrection and Ascension to the right hand of the Father.[125] Doxology, the praise of God, arises from this 'marvellous work' of the whole economy of salvation.[126]

2642 The *Revelation* of 'what must soon take place', the *Apocalypse*, is borne along by the songs of the heavenly liturgy[127] but also by the intercession of the *1137* 'witnesses' (martyrs).[128] The prophets and the saints, all those who were slain on earth for their witness to Jesus, the vast throng of those who, having come through the great tribulation, have gone before us into the Kingdom, all sing the praise and glory of him who sits on the throne, and of the Lamb.[129] In communion with them, the Church on earth also sings these songs with faith in the midst of trial. By means of petition and intercession, faith hopes against all hope and gives thanks to the 'Father of lights', from whom 'every perfect gift' comes down.[130] Thus faith is pure praise.

2643 The Eucharist contains and expresses all forms of prayer: it is 'the pure offering' of the whole Body of Christ to the glory of God's name[131] and, according to the traditions of East and West, it is *the* 'sacrifice of praise'.

1330

---

[121] Cf. *Rom* 8:16.
[122] 1 *Cor* 8:6.
[123] *Acts* 2:47; 3:9; 4:21; 13:48.
[124] *Eph* 5:19; cf. *Col* 3:16.
[125] Cf. *Phil* 2:6–11; *Col* 1:15–20; *Eph* 5:14; 1 *Tim* 3:16; 6:15–16; 2 *Tim* 2:11–13.
[126] Cf. *Eph* 1:3–14; *Rom* 16:25–27; *Eph* 3:20–21; *Jude* 24–25.
[127] Cf. *Rev* 4:8–11; 5:9–14; 7:10–12.
[128] *Rev* 6:10.
[129] Cf. *Rev* 18:24; 19:1–8.
[130] *Jas* 1:17.
[131] Cf. *Mal* 1:11.

IN BRIEF

2644 *The Holy Spirit who teaches the Church and recalls to her all that Jesus said also instructs her in the life of prayer, inspiring new expressions of the same basic forms of prayer: blessing, petition, intercession, thanksgiving and praise.*

2645 *Because God blesses the human heart, it can in return bless him who is the source of every blessing.*

2646 *Forgiveness, the quest for the Kingdom, and every true need are objects of the prayer of petition.*

2647 *Prayer of intercession consists in asking on behalf of another. It knows no boundaries and extends to one's enemies.*

2648 *Every joy and suffering, every event and need can become the matter for thanksgiving which, sharing in that of Christ, should fill one's whole life: 'Give thanks in all circumstances' (1 Th 5:18).*

2649 *Prayer of praise is entirely disinterested and rises to God, lauds him and gives him glory for his own sake, quite beyond what he has done, but simply because HE IS.*

Chapter Two

THE TRADITION OF PRAYER

2650 Prayer cannot be reduced to the spontaneous outpouring of interior impulse: in order to pray, one must have the will to pray. Nor is it enough to know what the Scriptures reveal about prayer: one must also learn how to pray. Through a living transmission (Sacred Tradition) within 'the believing and praying Church',[1] the Holy Spirit teaches the children of God how to pray.

2651 The tradition of Christian prayer is one of the ways in which the tradition of faith takes shape and grows, especially through the contemplation and study of believers who treasure in their hearts the events and words of the economy of salvation, and through their profound grasp of the spiritual realities they experience.[2]

Article 1

AT THE WELLSPRINGS OF PRAYER

2652 The Holy Spirit is the *living water* 'welling up to eternal life'[3] in the heart that prays. It is he who teaches us to accept it at its

---

[1] *DV* 8.
[2] Cf. *DV* 8.

[3] *Jn* 4:14.

source: Christ. Indeed in the Christian life there are several well-springs where Christ awaits us to enable us to drink of the Holy Spirit.

The Word of God

2653 The Church 'forcefully and specially exhorts all the Christian faithful. . . to learn "the surpassing knowledge of Jesus Christus" *133* (*Phil* 3:8) by frequent reading of the divine Scriptures. . . Let them remember, however, that prayer should accompany the reading of sacred Scripture, so that a dialogue takes place between God and man. For "we speak to him when we pray; we listen to him when *1100* we read the divine oracles."'[4]

2654 The spiritual writers, paraphrasing *Matthew* 7:7, summarize in this way the dispositions of the heart nourished by the Word of God in prayer: 'Seek in reading and you will find in meditating; knock in mental prayer and it will be opened to you by contemplation.'[5]

The liturgy of the Church

2655 In the sacramental liturgy of the Church, the mission of *1073* Christ and of the Holy Spirit proclaims, makes present and communicates the mystery of salvation, which is continued in the heart that prays. The spiritual writers sometimes compare the heart to an altar. Prayer internalizes and assimilates the liturgy during and after its celebration. Even when it is lived out 'in secret',[6] prayer is always prayer *of the Church*; it is a communion with the Holy Trinity.[7]

The theological virtues

1812–1829

2656 One enters into prayer as one enters into the liturgy: by the *368* narrow gate of *faith*. Through the signs of his presence, it is the Face of the Lord that we seek and desire; it is his Word that we want to hear and keep.

2657 The Holy Spirit, who instructs us to celebrate the liturgy in expectation of Christ's return, teaches us to pray in *hope*. Conversely, the prayer of the Church and personal prayer nourish hope in us. The Psalms especially, with their concrete and varied language, teach us to fix our hope in God: 'I waited patiently for the LORD; he inclined to me and heard my cry.'[8] As St Paul prayed:

---

[4] *DV* 25; cf. St Ambrose, *De officiis ministrorum* 1, 20, 88: PL 16, 50.
[5] Guigo the Carthusian, *Scala claustralium*: PL 164, 476C.

[6] Cf. *Mt* 6:6.
[7] *GILH* 9.
[8] *Ps* 40:2.

'May the God of hope fill you with all joy and peace in believing, so that by the power of the Holy Spirit you may abound in hope.'[9]

2658 'Hope does not disappoint us, because God's *love* has been poured into our hearts by the Holy Spirit who has been given to us.'[10] Prayer, formed by the liturgical life, draws everything into the love by which we are loved in Christ and which enables us to respond to him by loving as he has loved us. Love is the source of prayer; whoever draws from it reaches the summit of prayer. In the words of the Curé of Ars:

> I love you, O my God, and my only desire is to love you until the last breath of my life. I love you, O my infinitely lovable God, and I would rather die loving you, than live without loving you. I love you, Lord, and the only grace I ask is to love you eternally... My God, if my tongue cannot say in every moment that I love you, I want my heart to repeat it to you as often as I draw breath.[11]

'Today'

2659 We learn to pray at certain moments by hearing the Word of the Lord and sharing in his Paschal mystery, but his Spirit is offered us at all times, in the events of *each day*, to make prayer spring up from us. Jesus' teaching about praying to our Father is in the same vein as his teaching about providence:[12] time is in the Father's hands; it is in the present that we encounter him, not yesterday nor tomorrow, but today: 'O that *today* you would hearken to his voice! Harden not your hearts.'[13]

2660 Prayer in the events of each day and each moment is one of the secrets of the Kingdom revealed to 'little children', to the servants of Christ, to the poor of the Beatitudes. It is right and good to pray so that the coming of the Kingdom of justice and peace may influence the march of history, but it is just as important to bring the help of prayer into humble, everyday situations; all forms of prayer can be the leaven to which the Lord compares the Kingdom.[14]

IN BRIEF

2661 By a living transmission – Tradition – the Holy Spirit in the Church teaches the children of God to pray.

2662 The Word of God, the liturgy of the Church, and the virtues of faith, hope and charity are sources of prayer.

---

[9] *Rom* 15:13.
[10] *Rom* 5:5.
[11] St John Vianney, *Prayer*.
[12] Cf. *Mt* 6:11, 34.
[13] *Ps* 95:7–8.
[14] Cf. *Lk* 13:20–21.

Article 2
THE WAY OF PRAYER

2663 In the living tradition of prayer, each Church proposes to *1201*
her faithful, according to her historic, social and cultural context, a
language for prayer: words, melodies, gestures, iconography. The
Magisterium of the Church[15] has the task of discerning the fidelity
of these ways of praying to the tradition of apostolic faith; it is for
pastors and catechists to explain their meaning, always in relation
to Jesus Christ.

Prayer to the Father

2664 There is no other way of Christian prayer than Christ.
Whether our prayer is communal or personal, vocal or interior, it
has access to the Father only if we pray 'in the name' of Jesus. The *2780*
sacred humanity of Jesus is therefore the way by which the Holy
Spirit teaches us to pray to God our Father.

Prayer to Jesus

2665 The prayer of the Church, nourished by the Word of God
and the celebration of the liturgy, teaches us to pray to the Lord *451*
Jesus. Even though her prayer is addressed above all to the Father,
it includes in all the liturgical traditions forms of prayer addressed
to Christ. Certain psalms, given their use in the Prayer of the
Church, and the New Testament place on our lips and engrave in
our hearts prayer to Christ in the form of invocations: Son of God,
Word of God, Lord, Saviour, Lamb of God, King, Beloved Son,
Son of the Virgin, Good Shepherd, our Life, our Light, our Hope,
our Resurrection, Friend of mankind...

2666 But the one name that contains everything is the one that the
Son of God received in his incarnation: JESUS. The divine name *432*
may not be spoken by human lips, but by assuming our humanity
the Word of God hands it over to us and we can invoke it: 'Jesus',
'YHWH saves'.[16] The name 'Jesus' contains all: God and man and *435*
the whole economy of creation and salvation. To pray 'Jesus' is to
invoke him and to call him within us. His name is the only one that
contains the presence it signifies. Jesus is the Risen One, and
whoever invokes the name of Jesus is welcoming the Son of God
who loved him and who gave himself up for him.[17]

---

[15] Cf. *DV* 10.
[16] Cf. *Ex* 3:14; 33:19–23; *Mt* 1:21.

[17] *Rom* 10:13; *Acts* 2:21; 3:15–16; *Gal* 2:20.

2616 **2667** This simple invocation of faith developed in the tradition of prayer under many forms in East and West. The most usual formulation, transmitted by the spiritual writers of the Sinai, Syria and Mt Athos, is the invocation, 'Lord Jesus Christ, Son of God, have mercy on us sinners.' It combines the Christological hymn of *Philippians* 2:6–11 with the cry of the publican and the blind men begging for light.[18] By it the heart is opened to human wretchedness and the Saviour's mercy.

435 **2668** The invocation of the holy name of Jesus is the simplest way of praying always. When the holy name is repeated often by a humbly attentive heart, the prayer is not lost by heaping up empty phrases,[19] but holds fast to the Word and 'brings forth fruit with patience.'[20] This prayer is possible 'at all times' because it is not one occupation among others but the only occupation: that of loving God, which animates and transfigures every action in Christ Jesus.

478 **2669** The prayer of the Church venerates and honours the *Heart of Jesus* just as it invokes his most holy name. It adores the incarnate Word and his Heart which, out of love for men, he allowed to be pierced by our sins. Christian prayer loves 1674 to follow *the way of the cross* in the Saviour's steps. The stations from the Praetorium to Golgotha and the tomb trace the way of Jesus, who by his holy Cross has redeemed the world.

'Come, Holy Spirit'

683 **2670** 'No one can say "Jesus is Lord", except by the Holy Spirit.'[21] Every time we begin to pray to Jesus it is the Holy Spirit who 2001 draws us on the way of prayer by his prevenient grace. Since he teaches us to pray by recalling Christ, how could we not pray to the Spirit too? That is why the Church invites us to call upon the 1310 Holy Spirit every day, especially at the beginning and the end of every important action.

> If the Spirit should not be worshipped, how can he divinize me through Baptism? If he should be worshipped, should he not be the object of adoration?[22]

2671 The traditional form of petition to the Holy Spirit is to invoke the Father through Christ our Lord to give us the Consoler Spirit.[23] Jesus insists on this petition to be made in his name at the very moment when he promises the gift of the Spirit of Truth.[24] But the simplest and most direct prayer is also traditional, 'Come, Holy Spirit', and every liturgical tradition has developed it in antiphons and hymns.

---

[18] Cf. *Mk* 10:46–52; *Lk* 18:13.
[19] Cf. *Mt* 6:7.
[20] Cf. *Lk* 8:15.
[21] 1 *Cor* 12:3.

[22] St Gregory of Nazianzus, *Oratio* 31, 28: PG 36, 165.
[23] Cf. *Lk* 11:13.
[24] Cf. *Jn* 14:17; 15:26; 16:13.

Come, Holy Spirit, fill the hearts of your faithful and enkindle in them the fire of your love.[25]

Heavenly King, Consoler Spirit, Spirit of Truth, present everywhere and filling all things, treasure of all good and source of all life, come dwell in us, cleanse and save us, you who are All-Good.[26]

2672 The Holy Spirit, whose anointing permeates our whole *695* being, is the interior Master of Christian prayer. He is the artisan of the living tradition of prayer. To be sure, there are as many paths of prayer as there are persons who pray, but it is the same Spirit acting in all and with all. It is in the communion of the Holy Spirit that Christian prayer is prayer in the Church.

In communion with the holy Mother of God

2673 In prayer the Holy Spirit unites us to the person of the only *689* Son, in his glorified humanity, through which and in which our filial prayer unites us in the Church with the Mother of Jesus.[27]

2674 Mary gave her consent in faith at the Annunciation and *494* maintained it without hesitation at the foot of the Cross. Ever since, her motherhood has extended to the brothers and sisters of her Son 'who still journey on earth surrounded by dangers and difficulties'.[28] Jesus, the only mediator, is the way of our prayer; Mary, his mother and ours, is wholly transparent to him: she 'shows the way' (*hodigitria*), and is herself 'the Sign' of the way, according to the traditional iconography of East and West.

2675 Beginning with Mary's unique co-operation with the *970* working of the Holy Spirit, the Churches developed their prayer to the holy Mother of God, centring it on the person of Christ manifested in his mysteries. In countless hymns and antiphons *512* expressing this prayer, two movements usually alternate with one another: the first 'magnifies' the Lord for the 'great things' he did *2619* for his lowly servant and through her for all human beings;[29] the second entrusts the supplications and praises of the children of God to the Mother of Jesus, because she now knows the humanity which, in her, the Son of God espoused.

2676 This twofold movement of prayer to Mary has found a privileged expression in the *Ave Maria*:

Hail Mary [or Rejoice, Mary]: The greeting of the angel Gabriel opens this *722* prayer. It is God himself who, through his angel as intermediary, greets Mary.

[25] *Roman Missal*, Pentecost, Sequence.
[26] Byzantine Liturgy, Pentecost Vespers, Troparion.
[27] Cf. *Acts* 1:14.
[28] *LG* 62.
[29] Cf. *Lk* 1:46–55.

Our prayer dares to take up this greeting to Mary with the regard God had for the lowliness of his humble servant and to exult in the joy he finds in her.[30]

490   *Full of grace, the Lord is with thee*: These two phrases of the angel's greeting shed light on one another. Mary is full of grace because the Lord is with her. The grace with which she is filled is the presence of him who is the source of all grace. 'Rejoice... O Daughter of Jerusalem... the LORD your God is in your midst.'[31] Mary, in whom the Lord himself has just made his dwelling, is the daughter of Zion in person, the ark of the covenant, the place where the glory of the Lord dwells. She is 'the dwelling of God... with men'.[32] Full of grace, Mary is wholly given over to him who has come to dwell in her and whom she is about to give to the world.

435   *Blessed art thou among women and blessed is the fruit of thy womb, Jesus*: After the angel's greeting, we make Elizabeth's greeting our own. 'Filled with the Holy Spirit', Elizabeth is the first in the long succession of generations who have called Mary 'blessed'.[33] 'Blessed is she who believed...'[34] Mary is 'blessed among women' because she believed in the fulfilment of the Lord's word.
146   Abraham, because of his faith, became a blessing for all the nations of the earth.[35] Mary, because of her faith, became the mother of believers, through whom all nations of the earth receive him who is God's own blessing: Jesus, the 'fruit of thy womb'.

495   2677   *Holy Mary, Mother of God*: With Elizabeth we marvel, 'And why is this granted me, that the mother of my Lord should come to me?'[36] Because she gives us Jesus, her son, Mary is Mother of God and our mother; we can entrust all our cares and petitions to her: she prays for us as she prayed for herself: 'Let it be to me according to your word.'[37] By entrusting ourselves to her prayer, we abandon ourselves to the will of God together with her: 'Thy will be done.'

        Pray for us sinners, now and at the hour of our death: By asking Mary to pray for us, we acknowledge ourselves to be poor sinners and we address ourselves to the 'Mother of Mercy', the All-Holy One. We give ourselves over to her now, in the Today of our lives. And our trust broadens further, already at the present
1020   moment, to surrender 'the hour of our death' wholly to her care. May she be there as she was at her son's death on the cross. May she welcome us as our mother at the hour of our passing[38] to lead us to her son, Jesus, in paradise.

971, 1674   2678   Medieval piety in the West developed the prayer of the rosary as a popular substitute for the Liturgy of the Hours. In the East, the litany called the *Akathistos* and the *Paraclesis* remained closer to the choral office in the Byzantine Churches, while the Armenian, Coptic and Syriac traditions preferred popular hymns and songs to the Mother of God. But in the *Ave Maria*, the *theotokia*, the hymns of St Ephrem or St Gregory of Narek, the tradition of prayer is basically the same.

967   2679   Mary is the perfect *Orans* [pray-er], a figure of the Church.

---

[30] Cf. Lk 1:48; Zeph 3:17b.   [35] Cf. Gen 12:3.
[31] Zeph 3:14, 17a.   [36] Lk 1:43.
[32] Rev 21:3.   [37] Lk 1:38.
[33] Lk 1:41, 48.   [38] Cf. Jn 19:27.
[34] Lk 1:45.

When we pray to her, we are adhering with her to the plan of the Father, who sends his Son to save all men. Like the beloved disciple we welcome Jesus' mother into our homes,[39] for she has become the mother of all the living. We can pray with and to her. The prayer of the Church is sustained by the prayer of Mary and united with it in hope.[40]

972

IN BRIEF

2680 *Prayer is primarily addressed to the Father; it can also be directed toward Jesus, particularly by the invocation of his holy name: 'Lord Jesus Christ, Son of God, have mercy on us sinners.'*

2681 *'No one can say "Jesus is Lord", except by the Holy Spirit' (1 Cor 12:3). The Church invites us to invoke the Holy Spirit as the interior Teacher of Christian prayer.*

2682 *Because of Mary's singular co-operation with the action of the Holy Spirit, the Church loves to pray in communion with the Virgin Mary, to magnify with her the great things the Lord has done for her and to entrust supplications and praises to her.*

Article 3
GUIDES FOR PRAYER

A cloud of witnesses

2683 The witnesses who have preceded us into the Kingdom,[41] especially those whom the Church recognizes as saints, share in the living tradition of prayer by the example of their lives, the transmission of their writings and their prayer today. They contemplate God, praise him and constantly care for those whom they have left on earth. When they entered into the joy of their Master, they were 'put in charge of many things'.[42] Their intercession is *956* their most exalted service to God's plan. We can and should ask them to intercede for us and for the whole world.

2684 In the communion of saints, many and varied *spiritualities* *917* have been developed throughout the history of the Churches. The personal charism of some witnesses to God's love for men has been handed on, like 'the spirit' of Elijah to Elisha and John the Baptist, so that their followers may have a share in this spirit.[43] A distinct *919*

---

[39] Cf. *Jn* 19:27.
[40] Cf. *LG* 68–69.
[41] Cf. *Heb* 12:1.

[42] Cf. *Mt* 25:21.
[43] Cf. 2 *Kings* 2:9; *Lk* 1:17; *PC* 2.

1202 spirituality can also arise at the point of convergence of liturgical and theological currents, bearing witness to the integration of the faith into a particular human environment and its history. The different schools of Christian spirituality share in the living tradition of prayer and are essential guides for the faithful. In their rich diversity they are refractions of the one pure light of the Holy Spirit.

> The Spirit is truly the dwelling of the saints and the saints are for the Spirit a place where he dwells as in his own home, since they offer themselves as a dwelling place for God and are called his temple.[44]

Servants of prayer

1657 2685 The *Christian family* is the first place of education in prayer. Based on the sacrament of marriage, the family is the 'domestic church' where God's children learn to pray 'as the Church', and to persevere in prayer. For young children in particular, daily family prayer is the first witness of the Church's living memory as awakened patiently by the Holy Spirit.

1547 2686 *Ordained ministers* are also responsible for the formation in prayer of their brothers and sisters in Christ. Servants of the Good Shepherd, they are ordained to lead the People of God to the living waters of prayer: the Word of God, the liturgy, the theologal life [the life of faith, hope and charity], and the Today of God in concrete situations.[45]

916 2687 Many *religious* have consecrated their whole lives to prayer. Hermits, monks and nuns since the time of the desert fathers have devoted their time to praising God and interceding for his people. The consecrated life cannot be sustained or spread without prayer; it is one of the living sources of contemplation and the spiritual life of the Church.

2688 The *catechesis* of children, young people and adults aims at teaching them to meditate on the Word of God in personal prayer, practising it in liturgical prayer and internalizing it at all times in order to bear fruit in a new life. Catechesis is also a time for the
1674 discernment and education of popular piety.[46] The memorization of basic prayers offers an essential support to the life of prayer, but it is important to help learners savour their meaning.

2689 *Prayer groups*, indeed 'schools of prayer', are today one of the signs and one of the driving forces of renewal of prayer in the

---

44 St Basil, *De Spiritu Sancto* 26, 62: PG 32, 184.

45 Cf. *PO* 4–6.
46 Cf. *CT* 54.

Church, provided they drink from authentic wellsprings of Christian prayer. Concern for ecclesial communion is a sign of true prayer in the Church.

2690 The Holy Spirit gives to certain of the faithful the gifts of wisdom, faith and discernment for the sake of this common good which is prayer (*spiritual direction*). Men and women so endowed are true servants of the living tradition of prayer.

> According to St John of the Cross, the person wishing to advance toward perfection should 'take care into whose hands he entrusts himself, for as the master is, so will the disciple be, and as the father is so will be the son.' And further: 'In addition to being learned and discreet a director should be experienced... If the spiritual director has no experience of the spiritual life, he will be incapable of leading into it the souls whom God is calling to it, and he will not even understand them.'[47]

Places favourable for prayer

2691 The church, the house of God, is the proper place for the liturgical prayer of the parish community. It is also the privileged place for adoration of the real presence of Christ in the Blessed Sacrament. The choice of a favourable place is not a matter of indifference for true prayer.   1181 2179 1379

– For personal prayer, this can be a 'prayer corner' with the sacred Scriptures and icons, in order to be there, in secret, before our Father.[48] In a Christian family, this kind of little oratory fosters prayer in common.

– In regions where monasteries exist, the vocation of these communities is to further the participation of the faithful in the Liturgy of the Hours and to provide necessary solitude for more intense personal prayer.[49]   1175

– Pilgrimages evoke our earthly journey toward heaven and are traditionally very special occasions for renewal in prayer. For pilgrims seeking living water, shrines are special places for living the forms of Christian prayer 'in Church'.   1674

IN BRIEF

2692 *In prayer, the pilgrim Church is associated with that of the saints, whose intercession she asks.*

2693 *The different schools of Christian spirituality share in the living tradition of prayer and are precious guides for the spiritual life.*

2694 *The Christian family is the first place for education in prayer.*

---

[47] St John of the Cross, *The Living Flame of Love*, stanza 3, 30 in *The Collected Works of St John of the Cross*, ed. K. Kavanaugh OCD and O. Rodriguez

OCD (Washington DC: Institute of Carmelite Studies, 1979), 621.
[48] Cf. *Mt* 6:6.
[49] Cf. *PC* 7.

2695 *Ordained ministers, the consecrated life, catechesis, prayer groups and 'spiritual direction' ensure assistance within the Church in the practice of prayer.*

2696 *The most appropriate places for prayer are personal or family oratories, monasteries, places of pilgrimage, and above all the church, which is the proper place for liturgical prayer for the parish community and the privileged place for Eucharistic adoration.*

Chapter Three
THE LIFE OF PRAYER

2697 Prayer is the life of the new heart. It ought to animate us at every moment. But we tend to forget him who is our life and our all. This is why the Fathers of the spiritual life in the Deuteronomic and prophetic traditions insist that prayer is a remembrance of God often awakened by the memory of the heart: 'We must 1099 remember God more often than we draw breath.'[1] But we cannot pray 'at all times' if we do not pray at specific times, consciously willing it. These are the special times of Christian prayer. in both intensity and duration.

2698 The Tradition of the Church proposes to the faithful certain 1168 rhythms of praying intended to nourish continual prayer. Some are daily, such as morning and evening prayer, grace before and 1174 after meals, the Liturgy of the Hours. Sundays, centred on the 2177 Eucharist, are kept holy primarily by prayer. The cycle of the liturgical year and its great feasts are also basic rhythms of the Christian's life of prayer.

2699 The Lord leads all persons by paths and in ways pleasing to him, and each believer responds according to his heart's resolve and the personal expressions of his prayer. However, Christian tradition has retained three major expressions of prayer: vocal, meditative and contemplative. They have one basic trait in 2563 common: composure of heart. This vigilance in keeping the Word and dwelling in the presence of God makes these three expressions intense times in the life of prayer.

---

[1] St Gregory of Nazianzus, *Oratio* 27, 4: PG 36, 16.

Article 1
EXPRESSIONS OF PRAYER

I. Vocal Prayer

2700 Through his Word, God speaks to man. By words, mental or vocal, our prayer takes flesh. Yet it is most important that the *1176* heart should be present to him to whom we are speaking in prayer: 'Whether or not our prayer is heard depends not on the number of words, but on the fervour of our souls.'[2]

2701 Vocal prayer is an essential element of the Christian life. To his disciples, drawn by their Master's silent prayer, Jesus teaches a vocal prayer, the *Our Father*. He not only prayed aloud the liturgi- *2603* cal prayers of the synagogue but, as the gospels show, he raised his voice to express his personal prayer, from exultant blessing of the Father to the agony of Gethsemani.[3] *612*

2702 The need to involve the senses in interior prayer corresponds to a requirement of our human nature. We are body and spirit, and *1146* we experience the need to translate our feelings externally. We must pray with our whole being to give all power possible to our supplication.

2703 This need also corresponds to a divine requirement. God seeks worshippers in Spirit and in Truth, and consequently living prayer that rises from the depths of the soul. He also wants the external expression that associates the body with interior prayer, for it renders him that perfect homage which is his due. *2097*

2704 Because it is external and so thoroughly human, vocal prayer is the form of prayer most readily accessible to groups. Even interior prayer, however, cannot neglect vocal prayer. Prayer is internalized to the extent that we become aware of him 'to whom we speak'.[4] Thus vocal prayer becomes an initial form of contemplative prayer.

II. Meditation

2705 Meditation is above all a quest. The mind seeks to under- *158* stand the why and how of the Christian life, in order to adhere and respond to what the Lord is asking. The required attentiveness is

---

[2] St John Chrysostom, *Ecloga de oratione* 2: PG 63, 583.
[3] Cf. *Mt* 11:25–26; *Mk* 14:36.
[4] St Teresa of Jesus, *The Way of Perfection* 26, 9 in *The Collected Works of St Teresa*

of Avila, tr. K. Kavanaugh OCD and O. Rodriguez OCD (Washington DC: Institute of Carmelite Studies, 1980), II, 136.

difficult to sustain. We are usually helped by books, and Christians
127 do not want for them: the Sacred Scriptures, particularly the Gospels, holy icons, liturgical texts of the day or season, writings of the
spiritual fathers, works of spirituality, the great book of creation,
and that of history – the page on which the 'today' of God is
written.

2706   To meditate on what we read helps us to make it our own by
confronting it with ourselves. Here, another book is opened: the
book of life. We pass from thoughts to reality. To the extent that
we are humble and faithful, we discover in meditation the movements that stir the heart and we are able to discern them. It is a
question of acting truthfully in order to come into the light: 'Lord,
what do you want me to do?'

2707   There are as many and varied methods of meditation as
2690 there are spiritual masters. Christians owe it to themselves to
develop the desire to meditate regularly, lest they come to
resemble the three first kinds of soil in the parable of the sower.[5]
But a method is only a guide; the important thing is to advance,
2664 with the Holy Spirit, along the one way of prayer: Christ Jesus.

2708   Meditation engages thought, imagination, emotion and
desire. This mobilization of faculties is necessary in order to
deepen our convictions of faith, prompt the conversion of our
heart and strengthen our will to follow Christ. Christian prayer
516 tries above all to meditate on the mysteries of Christ, as in *lectio*
2678 *divina* or the rosary. This form of prayerful reflection is of great
value, but Christian prayer should go further: to the knowledge of
the love of the Lord Jesus, to union with him.

III. Contemplative Prayer

2709   What is contemplative prayer? St Teresa answers: 'Contemplative prayer [*oración mental*] in my opinion is nothing else than a
close sharing between friends; it means taking time frequently to
2562–2564 be alone with him who we know loves us.'[6]

Contemplative prayer seeks him 'whom my soul loves'.[7] It is
Jesus, and in him, the Father. We seek him, because to desire him is
always the beginning of love, and we seek him in that pure faith
which causes us to be born of him and to live in him. In this inner

---

[5] Cf. *Mk* 4:4–7, 15–19.
[6] St Teresa of Jesus, *The Book of Her Life*
8, 5 in *The Collected Works of St Teresa
of Avila*, tr. K. Kavanaugh OCD and

O. Rodriguez OCD (Washington DC:
Institute of Carmelite Studies, 1976), I,
67.
[7] *Song* 1:7; cf. 3:1–4.

prayer we can still meditate, but our attention is fixed on the Lord himself.

2710 The choice of the *time and duration of the prayer* arises from a determined will, revealing the secrets of the heart. One does not undertake contemplative prayer only when one has the time: one makes time for the Lord, with the firm determination not to give 2726 up, no matter what trials and dryness one may encounter. One cannot always meditate, but one can always enter into inner prayer, independently of the conditions of health, work or emotional state. The heart is the place of this quest and encounter, in poverty and in faith.

2711 *Entering into contemplative prayer* is like entering into the Eucharistic liturgy: we 'gather up' the heart, recollect our whole 1348 being under the prompting of the Holy Spirit, abide in the dwelling place of the Lord which we are, awaken our faith in order to enter into the presence of him who awaits us. We let our masks fall and turn our hearts back to the Lord who loves us, so as to hand ourselves over to him as an offering to be purified and trans- 2100 formed.

2712 Contemplative prayer is the prayer of the child of God, of the forgiven sinner who agrees to welcome the love by which he is loved and who wants to respond to it by loving even more.[8] But he knows that the love he is returning is poured out by the Spirit in his heart, for everything is grace from God. Contemplative prayer is the poor and humble surrender to the loving will of the Father in 2822 ever deeper union with his beloved Son.

2713 Contemplative prayer is the simplest expression of the mystery of prayer. It is a *gift*, a grace; it can be accepted only in humil- 2559 ity and poverty. Contemplative prayer is a *covenant* relationship established by God within our hearts.[9] Contemplative prayer is a *communion* in which the Holy Trinity conforms man, the image of God, 'to his likeness'.

2714 Contemplative prayer is also the pre-eminently *intense time* of prayer. In it the Father strengthens our inner being with power through his Spirit 'that Christ may dwell in [our] hearts through faith' and we may be 'grounded in love'.[10]

2715 Contemplation is a *gaze* of faith, fixed on Jesus. 'I look at him and he looks at me': this is what a certain peasant of Ars in

---

[8] Cf. *Lk* 7:36–50; 19:1–10.   [10] *Eph* 3:16–17.
[9] Cf. *Jer* 31:33.

the time of his holy curé used to say while praying before the tabernacle. This focus on Jesus is a renunciation of self. His gaze purifies our heart; the light of the countenance of Jesus illumines the eyes of our heart and teaches us to see everything in the light of his truth and his compassion for all men. Contemplation also turns its gaze on the mysteries of the life of Christ. Thus it learns 521 the 'interior knowledge of our Lord', the more to love him and follow him.[11]

2716 Contemplative prayer is *hearing* the Word of God. Far from being passive, such attentiveness is the obedience of faith, the 494 unconditional acceptance of a servant and the loving commitment of a child. It participates in the 'Yes' of the Son become servant and the *Fiat* of God's lowly handmaid.

533 2717 Contemplative prayer is *silence*, the 'symbol of the world to come'[12] or 'silent love'.[13] Words in this kind of prayer are not speeches; they are like kindling that feeds the fire of love. In this silence, unbearable to the 'outer' man, the Father speaks to us his 498 incarnate Word, who suffered, died and rose; in this silence the Spirit of adoption enables us to share in the prayer of Jesus.

2718 Contemplative prayer is a union with the prayer of Christ insofar as it makes us participate in his mystery. The mystery of Christ is celebrated by the Church in the Eucharist, and the Holy Spirit makes it come alive in contemplative prayer so that our charity will manifest it in our acts.

2719 Contemplative prayer is a communion of love bearing Life for the multitude, to the extent that it consents to abide in the 165 night of faith. The Paschal night of the Resurrection passes through the night of the agony and the tomb – the three intense moments of the Hour of Jesus which his Spirit (and not 'the flesh [which] is weak') brings to life in prayer. We must be willing to 2730 'keep watch with [him] one hour'.[14]

IN BRIEF

2720 *The Church invites the faithful to regular prayer: daily prayers, the Liturgy of the Hours, Sunday Eucharist, the feasts of the liturgical year.*

---

[11] Cf. St Ignatius of Loyola, *Spiritual Exercises* 104.
[12] Cf. St Isaac of Nineveh, *Tract. myst.* 66.
[13] St John of the Cross, *Maxims and Counsels* 53 in *The Collected Works of*

St John of the Cross, tr. K. Kavanaugh OCD and O. Rodriguez OCD (Washington DC: Institute of Carmelite Studies, 1979), 678.
[14] Cf. *Mt* 26:40.

2721 *The Christian tradition comprises three major expressions of the life of prayer: vocal prayer, meditation and contemplative prayer. They have in common the recollection of the heart.*

2722 *Vocal prayer, founded on the union of body and soul in human nature, associates the body with the interior prayer of the heart, following Christ's example of praying to his Father and teaching the Our Father to his disciples.*

2723 *Meditation is a prayerful quest engaging thought, imagination, emotion and desire. Its goal is to make our own in faith the subject considered, by confronting it with the reality of our own life.*

2724 *Contemplative prayer is the simple expression of the mystery of prayer. It is a gaze of faith fixed on Jesus, an attentiveness to the Word of God, a silent love. It achieves real union with the prayer of Christ to the extent that it makes us share in his mystery.*

Article 2
THE BATTLE OF PRAYER

2725 Prayer is both a gift of grace and a determined response on our part. It always presupposes effort. The great figures of prayer of the Old Covenant before Christ, as well as the Mother of God, the saints, and he himself, all teach us this: prayer is a battle. 2612, 409 Against whom? Against ourselves and against the wiles of the Tempter who does all he can to turn man away from prayer, away from union with God. We pray as we live, because we live as we pray. If we do not want to act habitually according to the Spirit of Christ, neither can we pray habitually in his name. The 'spiritual 2015 battle' of the Christian's new life is inseparable from the battle of prayer.

I. Objections to Prayer

2726 In the battle of prayer, we must face in ourselves and around us *erroneous notions of prayer.* Some people view prayer as a simple psychological activity, others as an effort of concentration to reach a mental void. Still others reduce prayer to ritual words and postures. Many Christians unconsciously regard prayer as an occupation that is incompatible with all the other things they have to do: they 'don't have the time'. Those who seek God by prayer 2710 are quickly discouraged because they do not know that prayer comes also from the Holy Spirit and not from themselves alone.

2727 We must also face the fact that certain attitudes deriving from the *mentality* of 'this present world' can penetrate our lives if

we are not vigilant. For example, some would have it that only
37 that is true which can be verified by reason and science; yet prayer
is a mystery that overflows both our conscious and unconscious
lives. Others overly prize production and profit; thus prayer,
being unproductive, is useless. Still others exalt sensuality and
2500 comfort as the criteria of the true, the good and the beautiful;
whereas prayer, the 'love of beauty' (*philokalia*), is caught up in the
glory of the living and true God. Finally, some see prayer as a
flight from the world in reaction against activism; but in fact,
Christian prayer is neither an escape from reality nor a divorce
from life.

2728 Finally, our battle has to confront what we experience as
failure in prayer: discouragement during periods of dryness; sadness
that, because we have 'great possessions',[15] we have not given all
to the Lord; disappointment over not being heard according to
our own will; wounded pride, stiffened by the indignity that is
ours as sinners; and our resistance to the idea that prayer is a free and
unmerited gift; and so forth. The conclusion is always the same:
what good does it do to pray? To overcome these obstacles, we
must battle to gain humility, trust and perseverance.

II. Humble Vigilance of Heart

Facing difficulties in prayer

2729 The habitual difficulty in prayer is *distraction*. It can affect
words and their meaning in vocal prayer; it can concern, more
profoundly, him to whom we are praying, in vocal prayer (liturgical or personal), meditation and contemplative prayer. To set
about hunting down distractions would be to fall into their trap,
2711 when all that is necessary is to turn back to our heart: for a distraction reveals to us what we are attached to, and this humble
awareness before the Lord should awaken our preferential love for
him and lead us resolutely to offer him our heart to be purified.
Therein lies the battle, the choice of which master to serve.[16]

2730 In positive terms, the battle against the possessive and
dominating self requires *vigilance*, sobriety of heart. When Jesus
insists on vigilance, he always relates it to himself, to his coming on
2659 the last day and every day: *today*. The bridegroom comes in the
middle of the night; the light that must not be extinguished is that
of faith: ' "Come", my heart says, "seek his face!" '[17]

---

[15] Cf. *Mk* 10:22.   [17] *Ps* 27:8.
[16] Cf. *Mt* 6:21, 24.

2731 Another difficulty, especially for those who sincerely want to pray, is *dryness*. Dryness belongs to contemplative prayer when the heart is separated from God, with no taste for thoughts, memories and feelings, even spiritual ones. This is the moment of sheer faith clinging faithfully to Jesus in his agony and in his tomb. 'Unless a grain of wheat falls into the earth and dies, it remains alone; but if it dies, it bears much fruit.'[18] If dryness is due to the lack of roots, because the word has fallen on rocky soil, the battle requires conversion.[19]

1426

Facing temptations in prayer

2732 The most common yet most hidden temptation is our *lack of faith*. It expresses itself less by declared incredulity than by our *2609, 2089* actual preferences. When we begin to pray, a thousand labours or cares thought to be urgent vie for priority; once again, it is the moment of truth for the heart: what is its real love? Sometimes we turn to the Lord as a last resort, but do we really believe he is? Sometimes we enlist the Lord as an ally, but our heart remains presumptuous. In each case, our lack of faith reveals that we do not *2092* yet share in the disposition of a humble heart: 'Apart from me, you *2074* can do *nothing*.'[20]

2733 Another temptation, to which presumption opens the gate, is *acedia*. The spiritual writers understand by this a form of depres- *2094* sion due to lax ascetical practice, decreasing vigilance, carelessness of heart. 'The spirit indeed is willing, but the flesh is weak.'[21] The greater the height, the harder the fall. Painful as discouragement is, it is the reverse of presumption. The humble are not surprised by *2559* their distress; it leads them to trust more, to hold fast in constancy.

III. Filial Trust

2734 Filial trust is tested – it proves itself – in tribulation.[22] The principal difficulty concerns the *prayer of petition*, for oneself or for *2629* others in intercession. Some even stop praying because they think their petition is not heard. Here two questions should be asked: Why do we think our petition has not been heard? How is our prayer heard, how is it 'efficacious'?

Why do we complain of not being heard?

2735 In the first place, we ought to be astonished by this fact:

---

[18] *Jn* 12:24.
[19] Cf. *Lk* 8:6, 13.
[20] *Jn* 15:5.

[21] *Mt* 26:41.
[22] Cf. *Rom* 5:3–5.

when we praise God or give him thanks for his benefits in general, we are not particularly concerned whether or not our prayer is acceptable to him. On the other hand, we demand to see the results 2779 of our petitions. What is the image of God that motivates our prayer: an instrument to be used? or the Father of our Lord Jesus Christ?

2559 2736 Are we convinced that 'we do not know how to pray as we ought'?[23] Are we asking God for 'what is good for us'? Our Father knows what we need before we ask him,[24] but he awaits our 1730 petition because the dignity of his children lies in their freedom. We must pray, then, with his Spirit of freedom, to be able truly to know what he wants.[25]

2737 'You ask and do not receive, because you ask wrongly, to spend it on your passions.'[26] If we ask with a divided heart, we are 'adulterers';[27] God cannot answer us, for he desires our well-being, our life. 'Or do you suppose that it is in vain that the scripture says, "He yearns jealously over the spirit which he has made to dwell in us"?'[28] That our God is 'jealous' for us is the sign of how true his love is. If we enter into the desire of his Spirit we shall be heard.

> Do not be troubled if you do not immediately receive from God what you ask him; for he desires to do something even greater for you, while you cling to him in prayer.[29]

> God wills that our desire should be exercised in prayer, that we may be able to receive what he is prepared to give.[30]

How is our prayer efficacious?

2738 The revelation of prayer in the economy of salvation teaches 2568 us that faith rests on God's action in history. Our filial trust is enkindled by his supreme act: the Passion and Resurrection of his 307 Son. Christian prayer is co-operation with his providence, his plan of love for men.

2739 For St Paul, this trust is bold, founded on the prayer of the 2778 Spirit in us and on the faithful love of the Father who has given us his only Son.[31] Transformation of the praying heart is the first response to our petition.

2740 The prayer of Jesus makes Christian prayer an efficacious

---

[23] *Rom* 8:26.
[24] Cf. *Mt* 6:8.
[25] Cf. *Rom* 8:27.
[26] *Jas* 4:3; cf. the whole context: *Jas* 4:1–10; 1:5–8; 5:16.
[27] *Jas* 4:4.

[28] *Jas* 4:5.
[29] Evagrius Ponticus, *De oratione* 34: PG 79, 1173.
[30] St Augustine, *Ep.* 130, 8, 17: PL 33, 500.
[31] Cf. *Rom* 10:12–13; 8:26–39.

petition. He is its model, he prays in us and with us. Since the heart of the Son seeks only what pleases the Father, how could the prayer of the children of adoption be centred on the gifts rather than the Giver? *2604*

2741 Jesus also prays for us – in our place and on our behalf. All our petitions were gathered up, once for all, in his cry on the Cross and, in his Resurrection, heard by the Father. This is why he never ceases to intercede for us with the Father.[32] If our prayer is resolutely united with that of Jesus, in trust and boldness as children, we obtain all that we ask in his name, even more than any particular thing: the Holy Spirit himself, who contains all gifts. *2606* *2614*

IV. Persevering in Love

2742 'Pray constantly', 'always and for everything giving thanks in the name of our Lord Jesus Christ to God the Father.'[33] St Paul adds, 'Pray at all times in the Spirit, with all prayer and supplication. To that end keep alert with all perseverance making supplication for all the saints.'[34] For 'we have not been commanded to work, to keep watch and to fast constantly, but it has been laid down that we are to pray without ceasing.'[35] This tireless fervour can come only from love. Against our dullness and laziness, the battle of prayer is that of humble, trusting and persevering *love*. This love opens our hearts to three enlightening and life-giving facts of faith about prayer. *2098* *162*

2743 *It is always possible to pray*. The time of the Christian is that of the risen Christ who is with us always, no matter what tempests may arise.[36] Our time is in the hands of God:

> It is possible to offer fervent prayer even while walking in public or strolling alone, or seated in your shop... while buying or selling... or even while cooking.[37]

2744 *Prayer is a vital necessity*. Proof from the contrary is no less convincing: if we do not allow the Spirit to lead us, we fall back into the slavery of sin.[38] How can the Holy Spirit be our life if our heart is far from him?

Nothing is equal to prayer; for what is impossible it makes possible, what

---

[32] Cf. *Heb* 5:7; 7:25; 9:24.
[33] 1 *Th* 5:17; *Eph* 5:20.
[34] *Eph* 6:18.
[35] Evagrius Ponticus, *Pract.* 49: PG 40, 1245C.

[36] Cf. *Mt* 28:20; *Lk* 8:24.
[37] St John Chrysostom, *Ecloga de oratione* 2: PG 63, 585.
[38] Cf. *Gal* 5:16–25.

is difficult, easy... For it is impossible, utterly impossible, for the man who prays eagerly and invokes God ceaselessly ever to sin.[39]

Those who pray are certainly saved; those who do not pray are certainly damned.[40]

2745 Prayer and *Christian life* are *inseparable*, for they concern the same love and the same renunciation, proceeding from love; the same filial and loving conformity with the Father's plan of love; the same transforming union in the Holy Spirit who conforms us more and more to Christ Jesus; the same love for all men, the love with which Jesus has loved us. 'Whatever you ask the Father in my name, he [will] give it to you. This I command you, to love one another.'[41]

2660

He 'prays without ceasing' who unites prayer to works and good works to prayer. Only in this way can we consider as realizable the principle of praying without ceasing.[42]

Article 3
THE PRAYER OF THE HOUR OF JESUS

2746 When 'his hour' came, Jesus prayed to the Father.[43] His prayer, the longest transmitted by the Gospel, embraces the whole economy of creation and salvation, as well as his death and Resurrection. The prayer of the Hour of Jesus always remains his own, just as his Passover 'once for all' remains ever present in the liturgy of his Church.

1085

2747 Christian tradition rightly calls this prayer the 'priestly' prayer of Jesus. It is the prayer of our high priest, inseparable from his sacrifice, from his passing over (Passover) to the Father to whom he is wholly 'consecrated'.[44]

2748 In this Paschal and sacrificial prayer, everything is recapitulated in Christ:[45] God and the world; the Word and the flesh; eternal life and time; the love that hands itself over and the sin that betrays it; the disciples present and those who will believe in him by their word; humiliation and glory. It is the prayer of unity.

518

820

2749 Jesus fulfilled the work of the Father completely; his prayer, like his sacrifice, extends until the end of time. The prayer of this hour fills the end-times and carries them towards their consummation. Jesus, the Son to whom the Father has given all things, has

---

[39] St John Chrysostom, *De Anna* 4, 5: PG 54, 666.

[40] St Alphonsus Liguori, *Del gran mezzo della preghiera*.

[41] *Jn* 15:16–17.

[42] Origen, *De orat.* 12: PG 11, 452C.

[43] Cf. *Jn* 17.

[44] Cf. *Jn* 17:11, 13, 19.

[45] Cf. *Eph* 1:10.

given himself wholly back to the Father, yet expresses himself with a sovereign freedom[46] by virtue of the power the Father has given him over all flesh. The Son, who made himself Servant, is Lord, the *Pantocrator*. Our high priest who prays for us is also the one who prays in us and the God who hears our prayer.   2616

2750 By entering into the holy name of the Lord Jesus we can   2815 accept, from within, the prayer he teaches us: 'Our Father!' His priestly prayer fulfils, from within, the great petitions of the Lord's Prayer: concern for the Father's name;[47] passionate zeal for his Kingdom (glory);[48] the accomplishment of the will of the Father, of his plan of salvation;[49] and deliverance from evil.[50]

2751 Finally, in this prayer Jesus reveals and gives to us the 'know-   240 ledge', inseparably one, of the Father and of the Son,[51] which is the very mystery of the life of prayer.

IN BRIEF

2752 *Prayer presupposes an effort, a fight against ourselves and the wiles of the Tempter. The battle of prayer is inseparable from the necessary 'spiritual battle' to act habitually according to the Spirit of Christ: we pray as we live, because we live as we pray.*

2753 *In the battle of prayer we must confront erroneous conceptions of prayer, various currents of thought and our own experience of failure. We must respond with humility, trust and perseverance to these temptations which cast doubt on the usefulness or even the possibility of prayer.*

2754 *The principal difficulties in the practice of prayer are distraction and dryness. The remedy lies in faith, conversion, and vigilance of heart.*

2755 *Two frequent temptations threaten prayer: lack of faith, and acedia — a form of depression stemming from lax ascetical practice that leads to discouragement.*

2756 *Filial trust is put to the test when we feel that our prayer is not always heard. The Gospel invites us to ask ourselves about the conformity of our prayer to the desire of the Spirit.*

2757 *'Pray constantly' (1 Th 5:17). It is always possible to pray. It is even a vital necessity. Prayer and Christian life are inseparable.*

2758 *The prayer of the hour of Jesus, rightly called the 'priestly prayer' (cf. Jn 17), sums up the whole economy of creation and salvation. It fulfils the great petitions of the Our Father.*

---

[46] Cf. Jn 17:11, 13, 19, 24.
[47] Cf. Jn 17:6, 11, 12, 26.
[48] Cf. Jn 17:1, 5, 10, 22, 23–26.
[49] Cf. Jn 17:2, 4, 6, 9, 11, 12, 24.
[50] Cf. Jn 17:15.
[51] Cf. Jn 17:3, 6–10, 25.

Section Two

THE LORD'S PRAYER: 'OUR FATHER!'

2759 Jesus 'was praying at a certain place, and when he ceased, one of his disciples said to him, "Lord, teach us to pray, as John taught his disciples." '[1] In response to this request the Lord entrusts to his disciples and to his Church the fundamental Christian prayer. St Luke presents a brief text of five petitions,[2] while St Matthew gives a more developed version of seven petitions.[3] The liturgical tradition of the Church has retained St Matthew's text:

**Our Father who art in heaven,
hallowed be thy name.
Thy kingdom come.
Thy will be done on earth, as it is in heaven.
Give us this day our daily bread,
and forgive us our trespasses,
    as we forgive those who trespass against us,
and lead us not into temptation,
but deliver us from evil.**

2855 2760 Very early on, liturgical usage concluded the Lord's Prayer with a doxology. In the *Didache*, we find, 'For yours are the power and the glory for ever.'[4] The *Apostolic Constitutions* add to the beginning: 'the kingdom', and this is the formula retained to our day in ecumenical prayer.[5] The Byzantine tradition adds after 'the glory' the words 'Father, Son, and Holy Spirit'. The *Roman Missal* develops the last petition in the explicit perspective of 'awaiting our 2854 blessed hope' and of the Second Coming of our Lord Jesus Christ.[6] Then comes the assembly's acclamation, or the repetition of the doxology from the *Apostolic Constitutions*.

Article 1
'THE SUMMARY OF THE WHOLE GOSPEL'

2761 The Lord's Prayer 'is truly the summary of the whole gospel.'[7] 'Since the Lord... after handing over the practice of prayer, said elsewhere, "Ask and you will receive", and since everyone has petitions which are peculiar to his circumstances, the regular and

---

[1] *Lk* 11:1.
[2] Cf. *Lk* 11:2-4.
[3] Cf. *Mt* 6:9-13.
[4] *Didache* 8, 2: SCh 248, 174.

[5] *Const. App.* 7, 24, 1: PG 1, 1016.
[6] *Titus* 2:13; cf. *Roman Missal* 22,
   Embolism after the Lord's Prayer.
[7] Tertullian, *De orat.* 1: PL 1, 1255.

appropriate prayer [the Lord's Prayer] is said first, as the foundation of further desires.'[8]

I. At the Centre of the Scriptures

2762 After showing how the Psalms are the principal food of Christian prayer and flow together in the petitions of the *Our Father*, St Augustine concludes:

> Run through all the words of the holy prayers [in Scripture], and I do not think that you will find anything in them that is not contained and included in the Lord's Prayer.[9]

2763 All the Scriptures – the Law, the Prophets and the Psalms – *102* are fulfilled in Christ.[10] The Gospel is this 'Good News'. Its first proclamation is summarized by St Matthew in the Sermon on the Mount;[11] the prayer to our Father is at the centre of this proclamation. It is in this context that each petition bequeathed to us by the Lord is illuminated:

> The Lord's Prayer is the most perfect of prayers... In it we ask, not only for all the things we can rightly desire, but also in the sequence that they *2541* should be desired. This prayer teaches us not only to ask for things, but also in what order we should desire them.[12]

2764 The Sermon on the Mount is teaching for life, the *Our Father* *1965* is a prayer; but in both the one and the other the Spirit of the Lord gives new form to our desires, those inner movements that animate our lives. Jesus teaches us this new life by his words; he teaches us to ask for it by our prayer. The rightness of our life in *1969* him will depend on the rightness of our prayer.

II. 'The Lord's Prayer'

2765 The traditional expression 'the Lord's Prayer' – *oratio Dominica* – means that the prayer to our Father is taught and given *2701* to us by the Lord Jesus. The prayer that comes to us from Jesus is truly unique: it is 'of the Lord'. On the one hand, in the words of this prayer the only Son gives us the words the Father gave him:[13] he is the master of our prayer. On the other, as Word incarnate, he knows in his human heart the needs of his human brothers and sisters and reveals them to us: he is the model of our prayer.

---

[8] Tertullian, *De orat.* 10: PL 1, 1268–1269; cf. *Lk* 11:9.
[9] St Augustine, *Ep.* 130, 12, 22: PL 33, 503.
[10] Cf. *Lk* 24:44.
[11] Cf. *Mt* 5 – 7.
[12] St Thomas Aquinas, *STh* II-II, 83, 9.
[13] Cf. *Jn* 17:7.

2766 But Jesus does not give us a formula to repeat mechanically.[14] As in every vocal prayer, it is through the Word of God that the Holy Spirit teaches the children of God to pray to their Father. Jesus not only gives us the words of our filial prayer; at the same time he gives us the Spirit by whom these words become in us 'spirit and life'.[15] Even more, the proof and possibility of our filial prayer is that the Father 'sent the Spirit of his Son into our hearts, crying, "*Abba!* Father!"'[16] Since our prayer sets forth our desires before God, it is again the Father, 'he who searches the hearts of men', who 'knows what is the mind of the Spirit, because the Spirit intercedes for the saints according to the will of God.'[17]

690 The prayer to our Father is inserted into the mysterious mission of the Son and of the Spirit.

III. The Prayer of the Church

2767 This indivisible gift of the Lord's words and of the Holy Spirit who gives life to them in the hearts of believers has been received and lived by the Church from the beginning. The first communities prayed the Lord's Prayer three times a day,[18] in place of the 'Eighteen Benedictions' customary in Jewish piety.

2768 According to the apostolic tradition, the Lord's Prayer is essentially rooted in liturgical prayer:

> [The Lord] teaches us to make prayer in common for all our brethren. For he did not say 'my Father' who art in heaven, but 'our' Father, offering petitions for the common Body.[19]

In all the liturgical traditions, the Lord's Prayer is an integral part of the major hours of the Divine Office. In the three sacraments of Christian initiation its ecclesial character is especially in evidence:

2769 In *Baptism* and *Confirmation*, the handing on (*traditio*) of the
1243 Lord's Prayer signifies new birth into the divine life. Since Christian prayer is our speaking to God with the very word of God, those who are 'born anew...through the living and abiding word of God'[20] learn to invoke their Father by the one Word he always hears. They can henceforth do so, for the seal of the Holy Spirit's anointing is indelibly placed on their hearts, ears, lips, indeed their whole filial being. This is why most of the patristic commentaries on the *Our Father* are addressed to catechumens and neophytes.

---

[14] Cf. *Mt* 6:7; 1 *Kings* 18:26–29.
[15] *Jn* 6:63.
[16] *Gal* 4:6.
[17] *Rom* 8:27.
[18] Cf. *Didache* 8, 3: SCh 248, 174.
[19] St John Chrysostom, *Hom. in Mt.* 19, 4: PG 57, 278.
[20] 1 *Pt* 1:23.

When the Church prays the Lord's Prayer, it is always the people made up of the 'new-born' who pray and obtain mercy.[21]

2770 In the *Eucharistic liturgy* the Lord's Prayer appears as the prayer of the whole Church and there reveals its full meaning and efficacy. Placed between the *anaphora* (the Eucharistic prayer) and the communion, the Lord's Prayer sums up on the one hand all the petitions and intercessions expressed in the movement of the *epiclesis* and, on the other, knocks at the door of the Banquet of the Kingdom which sacramental communion anticipates. *1350*

2771 In the Eucharist, the Lord's Prayer also reveals the *eschatological* character of its petitions. It is the proper prayer of 'the end-time', the time of salvation that began with the outpouring of the Holy Spirit and will be fulfilled with the Lord's return. The petitions addressed to our Father, as distinct from the prayers of the Old Covenant, rely on the mystery of salvation already accomplished, once for all, in Christ crucified and risen. *1403*

2772 From this unshakeable faith springs forth the hope that sustains each of the seven petitions, which express the groanings of the present age, this time of patience and expectation during which 'it does not yet appear what we shall be.'[22] The Eucharist and the Lord's Prayer look eagerly for the Lord's return, 'until he comes'.[23] *1820*

IN BRIEF

2773 *In response to his disciples' request 'Lord, teach us to pray' (Lk 11:1), Jesus entrusts them with the fundamental Christian prayer, the* Our Father.

2774 *'The Lord's Prayer is truly the summary of the whole gospel',*[24] *the 'most perfect of prayers'.*[25] *It is at the centre of the Scriptures.*

2775 *It is called 'the Lord's Prayer' because it comes to us from the Lord Jesus, the master and model of our prayer.*

2776 *The Lord's Prayer is the quintessential prayer of the Church. It is an integral part of the major hours of the Divine Office and of the sacraments of Christian initiation: Baptism, Confirmation and Eucharist. Integrated into the Eucharist it reveals the eschatological character of its petitions, hoping for the Lord, 'until he comes' (1 Cor 11:26).*

---

[21] Cf. 1 *Pt* 2:1–10.
[22] 1 *Jn* 3:2 ; cf. *Col* 3:4.
[23] 1 *Cor* 11:26

[24] Tertullian, *De orat.* 1: PL 1, 1255.
[25] St Thomas Aquinas, *STh* II-II, 83, 9.

Article 2
'OUR FATHER WHO ART IN HEAVEN'

I. 'We Dare to Say'

2777 In the Roman liturgy, the Eucharistic assembly is invited to pray to our heavenly Father with filial boldness; the Eastern liturgies develop and use similar expressions: 'dare in all confidence', 'make us worthy of...' From the burning bush Moses heard a voice saying to him, 'Do not come near; put off your shoes from your feet, for the place on which you are standing is holy ground.'[26] Only Jesus could cross that threshold of the divine holiness, for 'when he had made purification for sins', he brought us into the Father's presence: 'Here am I, and the children God has given me.'[27]

> Our awareness of our status as slaves would make us sink into the ground and our earthly condition would dissolve into dust, if the authority of our Father himself and the Spirit of his Son had not impelled us to this cry... 'Abba, Father!'... When would a mortal dare call God 'Father', if man's innermost being were not animated by power from on high?[28]

270

2778 This power of the Spirit who introduces us to the Lord's Prayer is expressed in the liturgies of East and of West by the beautiful, characteristically Christian expression: *parrhēsia*, straightforward simplicity, filial trust, joyous assurance, humble boldness, the certainty of being loved.[29]

2828

II. 'Father!'

2779 Before we make our own this first exclamation of the Lord's Prayer, we must humbly cleanse our hearts of certain false images drawn 'from this world'. *Humility* makes us recognize that 'no one knows the Son except the Father, and no one knows the Father except the Son and anyone to whom the Son chooses to reveal him', that is, 'to little children'.[30] The *purification* of our hearts has to do with paternal or maternal images, stemming from our personal and cultural history, and influencing our relationship with God. God our Father transcends the categories of the created world. To impose our own ideas in this area 'upon him' would be to fabricate idols to adore or pull down. To pray to the Father is to enter into his mystery as he is and as the Son has revealed him to us.

239

---

[26] *Ex* 3:5.
[27] *Heb* 1:3, 2:13.
[28] St Peter Chrysologus, *Sermo* 71, 3: PL 52, 401C-D; cf. *Gal* 4:6.

[29] Cf. *Eph* 3:12; *Heb* 3:6; 4:16; 10:19; 1 *Jn* 2:28; 3:21; 5:14.
[30] *Mt* 11:25-27.

The expression God the Father had never been revealed to anyone. When Moses himself asked God who he was, he heard another name. The Father's name has been revealed to us in the Son, for the name 'Son' implies the new name 'Father'.[31]

2780 We can invoke God as 'Father' because *he is revealed to us* by his Son become man and because his Spirit makes him known to us. The personal relation of the Son to the Father is something that man cannot conceive of nor the angelic powers even dimly see: and yet, the Spirit of the Son grants a participation in that very relation to us who believe that Jesus is the Christ and that we are born of God.[32] *240*

2781 When we pray to the Father, we are *in communion with him* and with his Son, Jesus Christ.[33] Then we know and recognize him with an ever new sense of wonder. The first phrase of the *Our Father* is a blessing of adoration before it is a supplication. For it is the glory of God that we should recognize him as 'Father', the true God. We give him thanks for having revealed his name to us, for the gift of believing in it, and for the indwelling of his Presence in us. *2665*

2782 We can adore the Father because he has caused us to be reborn to his life by *adopting* us as his children in his only Son: by Baptism, he incorporates us into the Body of his Christ; through the anointing of his Spirit who flows from the Head to the members, he makes us other 'Christs'. *1267*

> God, indeed, who has predestined us to adoption as his sons, has conformed us to the glorious Body of Christ. So then you who have become sharers in Christ are appropriately called 'Christs'.[34]

> The new man, reborn and restored to his God by grace, says first of all, 'Father!' because he has now begun to be a son.[35]

2783 Thus the Lord's Prayer *reveals us to ourselves* at the same time that it reveals the Father to us.[36] *1701*

> O man, you did not dare to raise your face to heaven, you lowered your eyes to the earth, and suddenly you have received the grace of Christ: all your sins have been forgiven. From being a wicked servant you have become a good son... Then raise your eyes to the Father who has begotten you through Baptism, to the Father who has redeemed you through his Son, and say: 'Our Father...' But do not claim any privilege. He is the Father in a special way only of Christ, but he is the common Father of us all, because while he has begotten only Christ, he has created

---

[31] Tertullian, *De orat.* 3: PL 1, 1257A.
[32] Cf. *Jn* 1:1; 1 *Jn* 5:1.
[33] Cf. 1 *Jn* 1:3.
[34] St Cyril of Jerusalem, *Catech. myst.* 3,

1: PG 33, 1088A.
[35] St Cyprian, *De Dom. orat.* 9: PL 4, 541.
[36] Cf. *GS* 22 § 1.

us. Then also say by his grace, 'Our Father', so that you may merit being his son.[37]

2784 The free gift of adoption requires on our part continual
1428 conversion and *new life*. Praying to our Father should develop in us two fundamental dispositions:

First, *the desire to become like him*: though created in his image, we are restored to his likeness by grace; and we must respond to
1997 this grace.

> We must remember... and know that when we call God 'our Father' we ought to behave as sons of God.[38]

> You cannot call the God of all kindness your Father if you preserve a cruel and inhuman heart; for in this case you no longer have in you the marks of the heavenly Father's kindness.[39]

> We must contemplate the beauty of the Father without ceasing and adorn our own souls accordingly.[40]

2562 **2785** Second, *a humble and trusting heart* that enables us 'to turn and become like children':[41] for it is to 'little children' that the Father is revealed.[42]

> [The prayer is accomplished] by the contemplation of God alone, and by the warmth of love, through which the soul, moulded and directed to love him, speaks very familiarly to God as to its own Father with special devotion.[43]

> Our Father: at this name love is aroused in us... and the confidence of obtaining what we are about to ask... What would he not give to his children who ask, since he has already granted them the gift of being his children?[44]

III. 'Our' Father

443 **2786** 'Our' Father refers to God. The adjective, as used by us, does not express possession, but an entirely new relationship with God.

2787 When we say 'our' Father, we recognize first that all his promises of love announced by the prophets are fulfilled in the *new*
782 *and eternal covenant* in his Christ: we have become 'his' people and he is henceforth 'our' God. This new relationship is the purely gratuitous gift of belonging to each other: we are to respond to

---

[37] St Ambrose, *De sacr.* 5, 4, 19: PL 16, 470.

[38] St Cyprian, *De Dom. orat.* 11: PL 4, 543.

[39] St John Chrysostom, *De orat. Dom.* 3: PG 51, 44.

[40] St Gregory of Nyssa, *De orat. Dom.* 2: PG 44, 1148B.

[41] *Mt* 18:3.

[42] Cf. *Mt* 11:25.

[43] St John Cassian, *Coll.* 9, 18: PL 49, 788C.

[44] St Augustine, *De serm. Dom. in monte* 2, 4, 16: PL 34, 1276.

'grace and truth' given us in Jesus Christ with love and faithfulness.[45]

2788 Since the Lord's Prayer is that of his people in the 'end-time', this 'our' also expresses the certitude of our hope in God's ultimate promise: in the new Jerusalem he will say to the victor, 'I will be his God and he shall be my son.'[46]

2789 When we pray to 'our' Father, we personally address the Father of our Lord Jesus Christ. By doing so we do not divide the Godhead, since the Father is its 'source and origin', but rather confess that the Son is eternally begotten by him and the Holy Spirit proceeds from him. We are not confusing the persons, for we confess that our communion is with the Father and his Son, Jesus Christ, in their one Holy Spirit. The *Holy Trinity* is consubstantial and indivisible. When we pray to the Father, we adore and glorify him together with the Son and the Holy Spirit. [245] [253]

2790 Grammatically, 'our' qualifies a reality common to more than one person. There is only one God, and he is recognized as Father by those who, through faith in his only Son, are reborn of him by water and the Spirit.[47] The *Church* is this new communion of God and men. United with the only Son, who has become 'the firstborn among many brethren', she is in communion with one and the same Father in one and the same Holy Spirit.[48] In praying 'our' Father, each of the baptized is praying in this communion: 'The company of those who believed were of one heart and soul.'[49] [787]

2791 For this reason, in spite of the divisions among Christians, this prayer to 'our' Father remains our common patrimony and an urgent summons for all the baptized. In communion by faith in Christ and by Baptism, they ought to join in Jesus' prayer for the unity of his disciples.[50] [821]

2792 Finally, if we pray the *Our Father* sincerely, we leave individualism behind, because the love that we receive frees us from it. The 'our' at the beginning of the Lord's Prayer, like the 'us' of the last four petitions, excludes no one. If we are to say it truthfully, our divisions and oppositions have to be overcome.[51]

2793 The baptized cannot pray to 'our' Father without bringing before him all those for whom he gave his beloved Son. God's

[45] *Jn* 1:17; cf. *Hos* 2:21–22; 6:1–6.
[46] *Rev* 21:7.
[47] Cf. 1 *Jn* 5:1; *Jn* 3:5.
[48] *Rom* 8:29; cf. *Eph* 4:4–6.
[49] *Acts* 4:32.
[50] Cf. *UR* 8; 22.
[51] Cf. *Mt* 5:23–24; 6:14–15.

604 love has no bounds, neither should our prayer.[52] Praying 'our' Father opens to us the dimensions of his love revealed in Christ: praying with and for all who do not yet know him, so that Christ may 'gather into one the children of God'.[53] God's care for all men and for the whole of creation has inspired all the great practitioners of prayer; it should extend our prayer to the full breadth of love whenever we dare to say 'our' Father.

IV. 'Who Art in Heaven'

2794 This biblical expression does not mean a place ('space'), but a
326 way of being; it does not mean that God is distant, but majestic. Our Father is not 'elsewhere': he transcends everything we can conceive of his holiness. It is precisely because he is thrice-holy that he is so close to the humble and contrite heart.

> 'Our Father who art in heaven' is rightly understood to mean that God is in the hearts of the just, as in his holy temple. At the same time, it means that those who pray should desire the one they invoke to dwell in them.[54]

> 'Heaven' could also be those who bear the image of the heavenly world, and in whom God dwells and tarries.[55]

2795 The symbol of the heavens refers us back to the mystery of the covenant we are living when we pray to our Father. He is in heaven, his dwelling place; the Father's house is our homeland. Sin has exiled us from the land of the covenant,[56] but conversion of
1024 heart enables us to return to the Father, to heaven.[57] In Christ, then, heaven and earth are reconciled,[58] for the Son alone 'descended from heaven' and causes us to ascend there with him, by his Cross, Resurrection and Ascension.[59]

2796 When the Church prays 'our Father who art in heaven', she is professing that we are the People of God, already seated 'with
1003 him in the heavenly places in Christ Jesus' and 'hidden with Christ in God';[60] yet at the same time, 'here indeed we groan, and long to put on our heavenly dwelling.'[61]

> [Christians] are in the flesh, but do not live according to the flesh. They spend their lives on earth, but are citizens of heaven.[62]

---

[52] Cf. NA 5.
[53] Jn 11:52.
[54] St Augustine, De serm. Dom. in monte 2, 5, 18: PL 34, 1277.
[55] St Cyril of Jerusalem, Catech. myst. 5, 11: PG 33, 1117.
[56] Cf. Gen 3.
[57] Jer 3:19 – 4:1a; Lk 15:18, 21.
[58] Cf. Is 45:8; Ps 85:12.
[59] Jn 3:13; 12:32; 14:2–3; 16:28; 20:17; Eph 4:9–10; Heb 1:3; 2:13.
[60] Eph 2:6; Col 3:3.
[61] 2 Cor 5:2; cf. Phil 3:20; Heb 13:14.
[62] Ad Diognetum 5, 8: PG 2, 1173.

IN BRIEF

2797 *Simple and faithful trust, humble and joyous assurance are the proper dispositions for one who prays the Our Father.*

2798 *We can invoke God as 'Father' because the Son of God made man has revealed him to us. In this Son, through Baptism, we are incorporated and adopted as sons of God.*

2799 *The Lord's Prayer brings us into communion with the Father and with his Son, Jesus Christ. At the same time it reveals us to ourselves (cf. GS 22 § 1).*

2800 *Praying to our Father should develop in us the will to become like him, and foster in us a humble and trusting heart.*

2801 *When we say 'Our' Father, we are invoking the new covenant in Jesus Christ, communion with the Holy Trinity, and the divine love which spreads through the Church to encompass the world.*

2802 *'Who art in heaven' does not refer to a place but to God's majesty and his presence in the hearts of the just. Heaven, the Father's house, is the true homeland toward which we are heading and to which, already, we belong.*

Article 3
THE SEVEN PETITIONS

2803 After we have placed ourselves in the presence of God our Father to adore and to love and to bless him, the Spirit of adoption stirs up in our hearts seven petitions, seven blessings. The first three, more theologal, draw us toward the glory of the Father; the last four, as ways toward him, commend our wretchedness to his grace. 'Deep calls to deep.'[63]   2627

2804 The first series of petitions carries us toward him, for his own sake: *thy* name, *thy* kingdom, *thy* will! It is characteristic of love to think first of the one whom we love. In none of the three petitions do we mention ourselves; the burning desire, even anguish, of the beloved Son for his Father's glory seizes us:[64] 'hallowed be thy name, thy kingdom come, thy will be done. . .' These three supplications were already answered in the saving sacrifice of Christ, but they are henceforth directed in hope toward their final fulfilment, for God is not yet all in all.[65]

2805 The second series of petitions unfolds with the same movement as certain Eucharistic epicleses: as an offering up of our   1105

---

[63] Ps 42:7.
[64] Cf. Lk 22:44; 12:50.

[65] Cf. 1 Cor 15:28.

expectations that draws down upon itself the eyes of the Father of mercies. They go up from us and concern us from this very moment, in our present world: 'give *us*... forgive *us*... lead *us* not... deliver *us*...' The fourth and fifth petitions concern our life as such – to be fed and to be healed of sin; the last two concern our battle for the victory of life – that battle of prayer.

2656–2658 2806 By the three first petitions, we are strengthened in faith, filled with hope and set aflame by charity. Being creatures and still sinners, we have to petition for us, for that 'us' bound by the world and history, which we offer to the boundless love of God. For through the name of his Christ and the reign of his Holy Spirit our Father accomplishes his plan of salvation, for us and for the whole world.

2142–2159 I. 'Hallowed Be Thy Name'

2807 The term 'to hallow' is to be understood here not primarily in its causative sense (only God hallows, makes holy), but above all in an evaluative sense: to recognize as holy, to treat in a holy way. 2097 And so, in adoration, this invocation is sometimes understood as praise and thanksgiving.[66] But this petition is here taught to us by Jesus as an optative: a petition, a desire and an expectation in which God and man are involved. Beginning with this first petition to our Father, we are immersed in the innermost mystery of his Godhead and the drama of the salvation of our humanity. Asking the Father that his name be made holy draws us into his plan of loving kindness for the fullness of time, 'according to his purpose which he set forth in Christ', that we might 'be holy and blameless before him in love'.[67]

2808 In the decisive moments of his economy God reveals his 203, 432 name, but he does so by accomplishing his work. This work, then, is realized for us and in us only if his name is hallowed by us and in us.

2809 The holiness of God is the inaccessible centre of his eternal mystery. What is revealed of it in creation and history, Scripture 293 calls 'glory', the radiance of his majesty.[68] In making man in his image and likeness, God 'crowned him with glory and honour', but by sinning, man fell 'short of the glory of God'.[69] From that time on, God was to manifest his holiness by revealing and giving 705 his name, in order to restore man to the image of his Creator.[70]

[66] Cf. *Ps* 111:9; *Lk* 1:49.
[67] *Eph* 1:9, 4.
[68] Cf. *Ps* 8; *Is* 6:3.

[69] *Ps* 8:5; *Rom* 3:23; cf. *Gen* 1:26.
[70] *Col* 3:10.

2810 In the promise to Abraham, and the oath that accompanied it,[71] God commits himself but without disclosing his name. He begins to reveal it to Moses and makes it known clearly before the eyes of the whole people when he saves them from the Egyptians: 'he has triumphed gloriously.'[72] From the covenant of Sinai onwards, this people is 'his own' and it is to be a 'holy [or 'consecrated': the same word is used for both in Hebrew] nation',[73] *63* because the name of God dwells in it.

2811 In spite of the holy Law that again and again their Holy God gives them – 'You shall be holy, for I the LORD your God am holy' – and although the Lord shows patience for the sake of his name, the people turn away from the Holy One of Israel and profane his name among the nations.[74] For this reason the just ones of the Old *2143* Covenant, the poor survivors returned from exile, and the prophets burned with passion for the name.

2812 Finally, in Jesus the name of the Holy God is revealed and *434* given to us, in the flesh, as Saviour, revealed by what he is, by his word, and by his sacrifice.[75] This is the heart of his priestly prayer: 'Holy Father... for their sake I consecrate myself, that they also may be consecrated in truth.'[76] Because he 'sanctifies' his own name, Jesus reveals to us the name of the Father.[77] At the end of Christ's Passover, the Father gives him the name that is above all names: 'Jesus Christ is Lord, to the glory of God the Father.'[78]

2813 In the waters of Baptism, we have been 'washed... sanctified... justified in the name of the Lord Jesus Christ and in the Spirit of our God'.[79] Our Father calls us to holiness in the whole of *2013* our life, and since 'he is the source of [our] life in Christ Jesus, who became for us wisdom from God, and...sanctification',[80] both his glory and our life depend on the hallowing of his name in us and by us. Such is the urgency of our first petition.

> By whom is God hallowed, since he is the one who hallows? But since he said, 'You shall be holy to me; for I the LORD am holy', we seek and ask that we who were sanctified in Baptism may persevere in what we have begun to be. And we ask this daily, for we need sanctification daily, so that we who fail daily may cleanse away our sins by being sanctified continually... We pray that this sanctification may remain in us.[81]

---

[71] Cf. Heb 6:13.
[72] Ex 15:1; cf. 3:14.
[73] Cf. Ex 19:5–6.
[74] Ezek 20:9, 14, 22, 39; cf. Lev 19:2.
[75] Cf. Mt 1:21; Lk 1:31; Jn 8:28; 17:8, 17–19.
[76] Jn 17:11, 19.
[77] Cf. Ezek 20:39; 36:20–21; Jn 17:6.
[78] Phil 2:9–11.
[79] 1 Cor 6:11.
[80] 1 Cor 1:30; cf. 1 Th 4:7.
[81] St Cyprian, De Dom. orat. 12: PL 4, 543–544; Lev 20:26.

2814 The sanctification of his name among the nations depends
2045 inseparably on our *life* and our *prayer*:

> We ask God to hallow his name, which by its own holiness saves and makes holy all creation... It is this name that gives salvation to a lost world. But we ask that this name of God should be hallowed in us through our actions. For God's name is blessed when we live well, but is blasphemed when we live wickedly. As the Apostle says: 'The name of God is blasphemed among the Gentiles because of you.' We ask then that, just as the name of God is holy, so we may obtain his holiness in our souls.[82]

> When we say 'hallowed be thy name', we ask that it should be hallowed in us, who are in him; but also in others whom God's grace still awaits, that we may obey the precept that obliges us to pray for everyone, even our enemies. That is why we do not say expressly 'hallowed be thy name "in us"', for we ask that it be so in all men.[83]

2815 This petition embodies all the others. Like the six petitions
2750 that follow, it is fulfilled by *the prayer of Christ*. Prayer to our Father is our prayer, if it is prayed *in the name* of Jesus.[84] In his priestly prayer, Jesus asks: 'Holy Father, protect in your name those whom you have given me.'[85]

II. 'Thy Kingdom Come'

2816 In the New Testament, the word *basileia* can be translated by
541, 2632 'kingship' (abstract noun), 'kingdom' (concrete noun) or 'reign' (action noun). The Kingdom of God lies ahead of us. It is brought near in the Word incarnate, it is proclaimed throughout the whole Gospel, and it has come in Christ's death and Resurrection. The
560, 1107 Kingdom of God has been coming since the Last Supper and, in the Eucharist, it is in our midst. The Kingdom will come in glory when Christ hands it over to his Father:

> It may even be... that the Kingdom of God means Christ himself, whom we daily desire to come, and whose coming we wish to be manifested quickly to us. For as he is our resurrection, since in him we rise, so he can also be understood as the Kingdom of God, for in him we shall reign.[86]

451 2817 This petition is '*Marana tha*', the cry of the Spirit and the
2632, 671 Bride: 'Come, Lord Jesus.'

> Even if it had not been prescribed to pray for the coming of the kingdom, we would willingly have brought forth this speech, eager to embrace our hope. In indignation the souls of the martyrs under the altar cry out to the

---

[82] St Peter Chrysologus, *Sermo* 71, 4: PL 52, 402A; cf. *Rom* 2:24; *Ezek* 36:20–22.
[83] Tertullian, *De orat.* 3: PL 1, 1257A.
[84] Cf. *Jn* 14:13; 15:16; 16:24, 26.
[85] *Jn* 17:11.
[86] St Cyprian, *De Dom. orat.* 13: PL 4, 544–545.

Lord: 'O Sovereign Lord, holy and true, how long before you judge and avenge our blood on those who dwell upon the earth?' For their retribution is ordained for the end of the world. Indeed, as soon as possible, Lord, may your kingdom come![87]

2818 In the Lord's Prayer, 'thy kingdom come' refers primarily to the final coming of the reign of God through Christ's return.[88] *769* But, far from distracting the Church from her mission in this present world, this desire commits her to it all the more strongly. Since Pentecost, the coming of that Reign is the work of the Spirit of the Lord who 'complete[s] his work on earth and bring[s] us the fullness of grace.'[89]

2819 'The kingdom of God [is] righteousness and peace and joy in *2046* the Holy Spirit.'[90] The end-time in which we live is the age of the outpouring of the Spirit. Ever since Pentecost, a decisive battle has *2516* been joined between 'the flesh' and the Spirit.[91]

Only a pure soul can boldly say: 'Thy kingdom come.' One who has *2519* heard Paul say, 'Let not sin therefore reign in your mortal bodies', and has purified himself in action, thought and word will say to God: 'Thy kingdom come!'[92]

2820 By a discernment according to the Spirit, Christians have to distinguish between the growth of the Reign of God and the progress of the culture and society in which they are involved. This *1049* distinction is not a separation. Man's vocation to eternal life does not suppress, but actually reinforces, his duty to put into action in this world the energies and means received from the Creator to serve justice and peace.[93]

2821 This petition is taken up and granted in the prayer *of* Jesus *2746* which is present and effective in the Eucharist; it bears its fruit in new life in keeping with the Beatitudes.[94]

III. 'Thy Will Be Done on Earth, As It Is in Heaven'

2822 Our Father 'desires all men to be saved and to come to the *851* knowledge of the truth.'[95] He 'is forbearing toward you, not wishing that any should perish.'[96] His commandment is 'that you love one another; even as I have loved you, that you also love one *2196*

---

[87] Tertullian, *De orat.* 5: PL 1, 1261–1262; cf. *Heb* 4:11; *Rev* 6:9; 22:20.

[88] Cf. *Titus* 2:13.

[89] *Roman Missal*, Eucharistic Prayer IV, 118.

[90] *Rom* 14:17.

[91] Cf. *Gal* 5:16–25.

[92] St Cyril of Jerusalem, *Catech. myst.* 5, 13: PG 33, 1120A; cf. *Rom* 6:12.

[93] Cf. *GS* 22; 32; 39; 45; *EN* 31.

[94] Cf. *Jn* 17:17–20; *Mt* 5:13–16; 6:24; 7:12–13.

[95] 1 *Tim* 2:3–4.

[96] 2 *Pt* 3:9; cf. *Mt* 18:14.

another.'[97] This commandment summarizes all the others, and expresses his entire will.

59 2823 'He has made known to us the mystery of his will, according to his good pleasure that he set forth in Christ... to gather up all things in him, things in heaven and things on earth. In Christ we have also obtained an inheritance, having been destined according to the purpose of him who accomplishes all things according to his counsel and will.'[98] We ask insistently for this loving plan to be fully realized on earth as it is already in heaven.

475 2824 In Christ, and through his human will, the will of the Father has been perfectly fulfilled once for all. Jesus said on entering into this world: 'Lo, I have come to do your will, O God.'[99] Only Jesus can say: 'I always do what is pleasing to him.'[100] In the prayer of his 612 agony, he consents totally to this will: 'not my will, but yours, be done.'[101] For this reason Jesus 'gave himself for our sins to deliver us from the present evil age, according to the will of our God and Father.'[102] 'And by that will we have been sanctified through the offering of the body of Jesus Christ once for all.'[103]

2825 'Although he was a Son, [Jesus] learned obedience through what he suffered.'[104] How much more reason have we sinful crea- 615 tures to learn obedience – we who in him have become children of adoption! We ask our Father to unite our will to his Son's, in order to fulfil his will, his plan of salvation for the life of the world. We are radically incapable of this, but united with Jesus and with the power of his Holy Spirit, we can surrender our will to him and decide to choose what his Son has always chosen: to do what is pleasing to the Father.[105]

> In committing ourselves to [Christ], we can become one spirit with him, and thereby accomplish his will, in such wise that it will be perfect on earth as it is in heaven.[106]

> Consider how [Jesus Christ] teaches us to be humble, by making us see that our virtue does not depend on our work alone but on grace from on high. He commands each of the faithful who prays to do so universally, for the whole world. For he did not say 'thy will be done in me or in us', but 'on earth', the whole earth, so that error may be banished from it, truth take root in it, all vice be destroyed on it, virtue flourish on it, and earth no longer differ from heaven.[107]

---

[97] Jn 13:34; cf. 1 Jn 3; 4; Lk 10:25–37.
[98] Eph 1:9–11.
[99] Heb 10:7; Ps 40:7.
[100] Jn 8:29.
[101] Lk 22:42; cf. Jn 4:34; 5:30; 6:38.
[102] Gal 1:4.
[103] Heb 10:10.
[104] Heb 5:8.
[105] Cf. Jn 8:29.
[106] Origen, De orat. 26: PG 11, 501B.
[107] St John Chrysostom, Hom. in Mt. 19, 5: PG 57, 280.

2826 By prayer we can discern 'what is the will of God' and obtain the endurance to do it.[108] Jesus teaches us that one enters the kingdom of heaven not by speaking words, but by doing 'the will of my Father in heaven'.[109]

2827 'If any one is a worshipper of God and does his will, God listens to him.'[110] Such is the power of the Church's prayer in the name of her Lord, above all in the Eucharist. Her prayer is also a communion of intercession with the all-holy Mother of God[111] and all the saints who have been pleasing to the Lord because they willed his will alone: *2611*

> It would not be inconsistent with the truth to understand the words, 'Thy will be done on earth as it is in heaven', to mean: 'in the Church as in our Lord Jesus Christ himself'; or 'in the Bride who has been betrothed, just as in the Bridegroom who has accomplished the will of the Father'.[112]   *796*

IV. 'Give Us This Day Our Daily Bread'

2828 'Give us': the trust of children who look to their Father for everything is beautiful. 'He makes his sun rise on the evil and on the good, and sends rain on the just and on the unjust.'[113] He gives to all the living 'their food in due season'.[114] Jesus teaches us this petition, because it glorifies our Father by acknowledging how good he is, beyond all goodness.   *2778*

2829 'Give us' also expresses the covenant. We are his and he is ours, for our sake. But this 'us' also recognizes him as the Father of all men and we pray to him for them all, in solidarity with their needs and sufferings.   *1939*

2830 'Our bread': the Father who gives us life cannot but give us the nourishment life requires – all appropriate goods and blessings, both material and spiritual. In the Sermon on the Mount, Jesus insists on the filial trust that co-operates with our Father's providence.[115] He is not inviting us to idleness,[116] but wants to relieve us from nagging worry and preoccupation. Such is the filial surrender of the children of God: *2633*

> To those who seek the kingdom of God and his righteousness, he has promised to give all else besides. Since everything indeed belongs to

---

[108] *Rom* 12:2; cf. *Eph* 5:17; *Heb* 10:36.
[109] *Mt* 7:21.
[110] *Jn* 9:31; cf. 1 *Jn* 5:14.
[111] Cf. *Lk* 1:38, 49.
[112] St Augustine, *De serm. Dom.* 2, 6, 24:

PL 34, 1279.
[113] *Mt* 5:45.
[114] *Ps* 104:27.
[115] Cf. *Mt* 6:25–34.
[116] Cf. 2 *Th* 3:6–13.

227   God, he who possesses God wants for nothing, if he himself is not found
           wanting before God.[117]

2831 But the presence of those who hunger because they lack
bread opens up another profound meaning of this petition. The
drama of hunger in the world calls Christians who pray sincerely
to exercise responsibility toward their brethren, both in their personal behaviour and in their solidarity with the human family.
This petition of the Lord's Prayer cannot be isolated from the
1038 parables of the poor man Lazarus and of the Last Judgement.[118]

2832 As leaven in the dough, the newness of the Kingdom should
make the earth 'rise' by the Spirit of Christ.[119] This must be shown
1928 by the establishment of justice in personal and social, economic
and international relations, without ever forgetting that there are
no just structures without people who want to be just.

2790 2833 'Our' bread is the 'one' loaf for the 'many'. In the Beatitudes
2546 'poverty' is the virtue of sharing: it calls us to communicate and
share both material and spiritual goods, not by coercion but out of
love, so that the abundance of some may remedy the needs of
others.[120]

2834 'Pray and work.'[121] 'Pray as if everything depended on God
2428 and work as if everything depended on you.'[122] Even when we
have done our work, the food we receive is still a gift from our
Father; it is good to ask him for it and to thank him, as Christian
families do when saying grace at meals.

2835 This petition, with the responsibility it involves, also applies
to another hunger from which men are perishing: 'Man does not
live by bread alone, but... by every word that proceeds from the
mouth of God',[123] that is, by the Word he speaks and the Spirit he
breathes forth. Christians must make every effort 'to proclaim the
2443 good news to the poor'. There is a famine on earth, 'not a famine
of bread, nor a thirst for water, but of hearing the words of the
LORD'.[124] For this reason the specifically Christian sense of this
fourth petition concerns the Bread of Life: the Word of God
1384 accepted in faith, the Body of Christ received in the Eucharist.[125]

---

[117] St Cyprian, De Dom. orat. 21: PL 4,
551.
[118] Cf. Lk 16:19–31; Mt 25:31–46.
[119] Cf. AA 5.
[120] Cf. 2 Cor 8:1–15.
[121] Cf. St Benedict, Regula 20; 48.
[122] Attributed to St Ignatius of Loyola;

cf. Joseph de Guibert SJ, The Jesuits:
Their Spiritual Doctrine and Practice
(Chicago: Loyola University Press,
1964), 148, n. 55.
[123] Dt 8:3; Mt 4:4.
[124] Am 8:11.
[125] Cf. Jn 6:26–58.

2836 'This day' is also an expression of trust taught us by the 1165
Lord,[126] which we would never have presumed to invent. Since it
refers above all to his Word and to the Body of his Son, this 'today'
is not only that of our mortal time, but also the 'today' of God.

> If you receive the bread each day, each day is today for you. If Christ is
> yours today, he rises for you every day. How can this be? 'You are my
> Son, today I have begotten you.' Therefore, 'today' is when Christ
> rises.[127]

2837 'Daily' (epiousios) occurs nowhere else in the New Testa- 2659
ment. Taken in a temporal sense, this word is a pedagogical repetition of 'this day',[128] to confirm us in trust 'without reservation'.
Taken in the qualitative sense, it signifies what is necessary for life,
and more broadly every good thing sufficient for subsistence.[129] 2633
Taken literally (epi-ousios: 'super-essential'), it refers directly to the
Bread of Life, the Body of Christ, the 'medicine of immortality', 1405
without which we have no life within us.[130] Finally in this connection, its heavenly meaning is evident: 'this day' is the Day of the 1166
Lord, the day of the Feast of the Kingdom, anticipated in the
Eucharist that is already the foretaste of the Kingdom to come. For
this reason it is fitting for the Eucharistic liturgy to be celebrated 1389
each day.

> The Eucharist is our daily bread. The power belonging to this divine
> food makes it a bond of union. Its effect is then understood as unity, so
> that, gathered into his Body and made members of him, we may become
> what we receive... This also is our daily bread: the readings you hear
> each day in church and the hymns you hear and sing. All these are
> necessities for our pilgrimage.[131]

> The Father in heaven urges us, as children of heaven, to ask for the bread
> of heaven. [Christ] himself is the bread who, sown in the Virgin, raised
> up in the flesh, kneaded in the Passion, baked in the oven of the tomb,
> reserved in churches, brought to altars, furnishes the faithful each day
> with food from heaven.[132]

V. 'And Forgive Us Our Trespasses, As We Forgive Those Who Trespass Against Us'

2838 This petition is astonishing. If it consisted only of the first
phrase, 'And forgive us our trespasses', it might have been 1425
included, implicitly, in the first three petitions of the Lord's

---

[126] Cf. Mt 6:34; Ex 16:19.
[127] St Ambrose, De sacr. 5, 4, 26: PL 16, 472; cf. Ps 2:7.
[128] Cf. Ex 16:19–21.
[129] Cf. 1 Tim 6:8.

[130] St Ignatius of Antioch, Ad Eph. 20, 2: SCh 10, 76; Jn 6:53–56.
[131] St Augustine, Sermo 57, 7: PL 38, 389.
[132] St Peter Chrysologus, Sermo 67: PL 52, 392; cf. Jn 6:51.

Prayer, since Christ's sacrifice is 'that sins may be forgiven'. But, according to the second phrase, our petition will not be heard 1933 unless we have first met a strict requirement. Our petition looks to 2631 the future, but our response must come first, for the two parts are joined by the single word 'as'.

And forgive us our trespasses...

2839 With bold confidence, we began praying to our Father. In begging him that his name be hallowed, we were in fact asking him that we ourselves might be always made more holy. But though we are clothed with the baptismal garment, we do not 1425 cease to sin, to turn away from God. Now, in this new petition, we 1439 return to him like the prodigal son and, like the tax collector, recognize that we are sinners before him.[133] Our petition begins with a 'confession' of our wretchedness and his mercy. Our hope is firm because, in his Son, 'we have redemption, the forgiveness of sins.'[134] We find the efficacious and undoubted sign of his forgive-1422 ness in the sacraments of his Church.[135]

2840 Now – and this is daunting – this outpouring of mercy cannot penetrate our hearts as long as we have not forgiven those who have trespassed against us. Love, like the Body of Christ, is indivisible; we cannot love the God we cannot see if we do not love the brother or sister we do see.[136] In refusing to forgive our 1864 brothers and sisters, our hearts are closed and their hardness makes them impervious to the Father's merciful love; but in confessing our sins, our hearts are opened to his grace.

2841 This petition is so important that it is the only one to which the Lord returns and which he develops explicitly in the Sermon on the Mount.[137] This crucial requirement of the covenant mystery is impossible for man. But 'with God all things are possible.'[138]

... as we forgive those who trespass against us

2842 This 'as' is not unique in Jesus' teaching: 'You, therefore, must be perfect, *as* your heavenly Father is perfect'; 'Be merciful, even *as* your Father is merciful'; 'A new commandment I give to you, that you love one another; even *as* I have loved you, that you also love one another.'[139] It is impossible to keep the Lord's com-

---

[133] Cf. *Lk* 15:11–32; 18:13.
[134] *Col* 1:14; *Eph* 1:7.
[135] Cf. *Mt* 26:28; *Jn* 20:23.
[136] Cf. 1 *Jn* 4:20.

[137] Cf. *Mt* 6:14–15; 5:23–24; *Mk* 11:25.
[138] *Mt* 19:26.
[139] *Mt* 5:48; *Lk* 6:36; *Jn* 13:34.

mandment by imitating the divine model from outside; there has to be a vital participation, coming from the depths of the heart, in *521* the holiness and the mercy and the love of our God. Only the Spirit by whom we live can make 'ours' the same mind that was in Christ Jesus.[140] Then the unity of forgiveness becomes possible and we find ourselves 'forgiving one another, *as* God in Christ forgave' us.[141]

2843 Thus the Lord's words on forgiveness, the love that loves to the end,[142] become a living reality. The parable of the merciless servant, which crowns the Lord's teaching on ecclesial communion, ends with these words: 'So also my heavenly Father will do to every one of you, if you do not forgive your brother from your heart.'[143] It is there, in fact, 'in the depths of the *heart*', that every- *368* thing is bound and loosed. It is not in our power not to feel, or to forget, an offence; but the heart that offers itself to the Holy Spirit turns injury into compassion and purifies the memory in transforming the hurt into intercession.

2844 Christian prayer extends to the *forgiveness of enemies*,[144] *2262* transfiguring the disciple by configuring him to his Master. Forgiveness is a high-point of Christian prayer; only hearts attuned to God's compassion can receive the gift of prayer. Forgiveness also bears witness that, in our world, love is stronger than sin. The martyrs of yesterday and today bear this witness to Jesus. Forgiveness is the fundamental condition of the reconciliation of the children of God with their Father and of men with one another.[145]

2845 There is no limit or measure to this essentially divine for- *1441* giveness,[146] whether one speaks of 'sins' as in *Luke* (11:4), or 'debts' as in *Matthew* (6:12). We are always debtors: 'Owe no one anything, except to love one another.'[147] The communion of the Holy Trinity is the source and criterion of truth in every relationship. It is lived out in prayer, above all in the Eucharist.[148]

> God does not accept the sacrifice of a sower of disunion, but commands that he depart from the altar so that he may first be reconciled with his brother. For God can be appeased only by prayers that make peace. To God, the better offering is peace, brotherly concord and a people made one in the unity of the Father, Son and Holy Spirit.[149]

---

[140] Cf. *Gal* 5:25; *Phil* 2:1, 5.
[141] *Eph* 4:32.
[142] Cf. *Jn* 13:1.
[143] Cf. *Mt* 18:23–35.
[144] Cf. *Mt* 5:43–44.
[145] Cf. 2 *Cor* 5:18–21; John Paul II, *DM* 14.
[146] Cf. *Mt* 18:21–22; *Lk* 17:3–4.
[147] *Rom* 13:8.
[148] Cf. *Mt* 5:23–24; 1 *Jn* 3:19–24.
[149] St Cyprian, *De Dom. orat.* 23: PL 4, 553; cf. *Mt* 5:24.

VI. 'And Lead Us Not into Temptation'

2846 This petition goes to the root of the preceding one, for our sins result from our consenting to temptation; we therefore ask *164* our Father not to 'lead' us into temptation. It is difficult to translate the Greek verb used by a single English word: the Greek means both 'do not allow us to enter into temptation', and 'do not let us yield to temptation'.[150] 'God cannot be tempted by evil and he himself tempts no one';[151] on the contrary, he wants to set us free from evil. We ask him not to allow us to take the way that leads to *2516* sin. We are engaged in the battle 'between flesh and spirit'; this petition implores the Spirit of discernment and strength.

2847 The Holy Spirit makes us *discern* between trials, which are necessary for the growth of the inner man,[152] and temptation, which leads to sin and death.[153] We must also discern between *2284* being tempted, and consenting to temptation. Finally, discernment unmasks the lie of temptation, whose object appears to be good, a 'delight to the eyes' and desirable,[154] when in reality its fruit is death.

> God does not want to impose the good, but wants free beings... There is a certain usefulness to temptation. No one but God knows what our soul has received from him, not even we ourselves. But temptation reveals it in order to teach us to know ourselves, and in this way we discover our evil inclinations and are obliged to give thanks for the goods that temptation has revealed to us.[155]

2848 'Lead us not into temptation' implies a *decision of the heart*: 'For where your treasure is, there will your heart be also... No one can serve two masters.'[156] 'If we live by the Spirit, let us also walk by the Spirit.'[157] In this assent to the Holy Spirit the Father gives us *1808* strength. 'No testing has overtaken you that is not common to man. God is faithful, and he will not let you be tempted beyond your strength, but with the temptation will also provide the way of escape, so that you may be able to endure it.'[158]

540, 612 2849 Such a battle and such a victory become possible only through prayer. It is by his prayer that Jesus vanquishes the Tempter, both at the outset of his public mission and in the ultimate struggle of his agony.[159] In this petition to our heavenly Father,

---

[150] Cf. *Mt* 26:41.
[151] *Jas* 1:13.
[152] Cf. *Lk* 8:13–15; *Acts* 14:22; *Rom* 5:3–5; 2 *Tim* 3:12.
[153] Cf. *Jas* 1:14–15.
[154] Cf. *Gen* 3:6.
[155] Origen, *De orat.* 29: PG 11, 544C-D.
[156] *Mt* 6:21, 24.
[157] *Gal* 5:25.
[158] 1 *Cor* 10:13.
[159] Cf. *Mt* 4:1–11; 26:36–44.

Christ unites us to his battle and his agony. He urges us to *vigilance* of the heart in communion with his own. Vigilance is 'custody of *2612* the heart', and Jesus prayed for us to the Father: 'Keep them in your name.'[160] The Holy Spirit constantly seeks to awaken us to keep watch.[161] Finally, this petition takes on all its dramatic meaning in relation to the last temptation of our earthly battle; it asks for *final perseverance*. 'Lo, I am coming like a thief! Blessed is he *162* who is awake.'[162]

VII. 'But Deliver Us from Evil'

2850 The last petition to our Father is also included in Jesus' prayer: 'I am not asking you to take them out of the world, but I ask you to protect them from the evil one.'[163] It touches each of us personally, but it is always 'we' who pray, in communion with the whole Church, for the deliverance of the whole human family. The Lord's Prayer continually opens us to the range of God's economy of salvation. Our interdependence in the drama of sin *309* and death is turned into solidarity in the Body of Christ, the 'communion of saints'.[164]

2851 In this petition, evil is not an abstraction, but refers to a person, Satan, the Evil One, the angel who opposes God. The *391* devil (*dia-bolos*) is the one who 'throws himself across' God's plan and his work of salvation accomplished in Christ.

2852 'A murderer from the beginning. . . a liar and the father of lies', Satan is 'the deceiver of the whole world'.[165] Through him sin and death entered the world and by his definitive defeat all creation will be 'freed from the corruption of sin and death'.[166] Now 'we know that anyone born of God does not sin, but He who was born of God keeps him, and the evil one does not touch him. We know that we are of God, and the whole world is in the power of the evil one.'[167]

> The Lord who has taken away your sin and pardoned your faults also protects you and keeps you from the wiles of your adversary the devil, so that the enemy, who is accustomed to leading into sin, may not surprise you. One who entrusts himself to God does not dread the devil. 'If God is for us, who is against us?'[168]

[160] *Jn* 17:11; cf. *Mk* 13:9, 23, 33–37; 14:38; *Lk* 12:35–40.
[161] Cf. 1 *Cor* 16:13; *Col* 4:2; 1 *Th* 5:6; 1 *Pt* 5:8.
[162] *Rev* 16:15.
[163] *Jn* 17:15.
[164] Cf. *RP* 16.

[165] *Jn* 8:44; *Rev* 12:9.
[166] *Roman Missal*, Eucharistic Prayer IV, 125.
[167] 1 *Jn* 5:18–19.
[168] St Ambrose, *De sacr.* 5, 4, 30: PL 16, 472; cf. *Rom* 8:31.

2853 Victory over the 'prince of this world'[169] was won once for all at the Hour when Jesus freely gave himself up to death to give
677 us his life. This is the Judgement of this world, and the prince of this world is 'cast out'.[170] 'He pursued the woman'[171] but had no
490 hold on her: the new Eve, 'full of grace' of the Holy Spirit, is preserved from sin and the corruption of death (the Immaculate
972 Conception and the Assumption of the Most Holy Mother of God, Mary, ever virgin). 'Then the dragon was angry with the woman, and went off to make war on the rest of her offspring.'[172] Therefore the Spirit and the Church pray: 'Come, Lord Jesus',[173] since his coming will deliver us from the Evil One.

2854 When we ask to be delivered from the Evil One, we pray as well to be freed from all evils, present, past and future, of which he is the author or instigator. In this final petition, the Church brings before the Father all the distress of the world. Along with deliverance from the evils that overwhelm humanity, she implores the precious gift of peace and the grace of perseverance in expectation
2632 of Christ's return. By praying in this way, she anticipates in humility of faith the gathering together of everyone and everything in him who has 'the keys of Death and Hades', who 'is and who was and who is to come, the Almighty'.[174]

Deliver us, Lord, we beseech you, from every evil and grant us peace in our day, so that aided by your mercy we might be ever free from sin and
1041 protected from all anxiety, as we await the blessed hope and the coming of our Saviour, Jesus Christ.[175]

Article 4

THE FINAL DOXOLOGY

2760 2855 The final doxology, 'For the kingdom, the power and the glory are yours, now and for ever', takes up again, by inclusion, the first three petitions to our Father: the glorification of his name, the coming of his reign and the power of his saving will. But these prayers are now proclaimed as adoration and thanksgiving, as in the liturgy of heaven.[176] The ruler of this world has mendaciously attributed to himself the three titles of kingship, power and

---

[169] Jn 14:30.
[170] Jn 12:31; Rev 12:10.
[171] Rev 12:13–16.
[172] Rev 12:17.
[173] Rev 22:17, 20.
[174] Rev 1:8, 18; cf. 1:4; Eph 1:10.
[175] Missale Romanum, Embolism after the Lord's Prayer, 126: Libera nos,

quaesumus, Domine, ab omnibus malis, da propitius pacem in diebus nostris, ut, ope misericordiae tuae adiuti, et a peccato simus semper liberi, et ab omni perturbatione securi: expectantes beatam spem et adventum Salvatoris nostri Iesu Christi.
[176] Cf. Rev 1:6; 4:11; 5:13.

glory.[177] Christ, the Lord, restores them to his Father and our Father, until he hands over the Kingdom to him when the mystery of salvation will be brought to its completion and God will be all in all.[178]

2856 'Then, after the prayer is over you say "Amen", which 1061–1065 means "So be it", thus ratifying with our "Amen" what is contained in the prayer that God has taught us.'[179]

IN BRIEF

2857 In the Our Father, the object of the first three petitions is the glory of the Father: the sanctification of his name, the coming of the Kingdom and the fulfilment of his will. The four others present our wants to him: they ask that our lives be nourished, healed of sin and made victorious in the struggle of good over evil.

2858 By asking 'hallowed be thy name' we enter into God's plan, the sanctification of his name – revealed first to Moses and then in Jesus – by us and in us, in every nation and in each man.

2859 By the second petition, the Church looks first to Christ's return and the final coming of the Reign of God. She also prays for the growth of the Kingdom of God in the 'today' of our own lives.

2860 In the third petition, we ask our Father to unite our will to that of his Son, so as to fulfil his plan of salvation in the life of the world.

2861 In the fourth petition, by saying 'give us', we express in communion with our brethren our filial trust in our heavenly Father. 'Our daily bread' refers to the earthly nourishment necessary to everyone for subsistence, and also to the Bread of Life: the Word of God and the Body of Christ. It is received in God's 'today', as the indispensable, (super-)essential nourishment of the Feast of the coming Kingdom anticipated in the Eucharist.

2862 The fifth petition begs God's mercy for our offences, mercy which can penetrate our hearts only if we have learned to forgive our enemies, with the example and help of Christ.

2863 When we say 'lead us not into temptation' we are asking God not to allow us to take the path that leads to sin. This petition implores the Spirit of discernment and strength; it requests the grace of vigilance and final perseverance.

---

[177] Cf. Lk 4:5–6.
[178] 1 Cor 15:24–28.

[179] St Cyril of Jerusalem, Catech. myst. 5, 18: PG 33, 1124; cf. Lk 1:38.

2864 *In the last petition, 'but deliver us from evil', Christians pray to God with the Church to show forth the victory, already won by Christ, over the 'ruler of this world', Satan, the angel personally opposed to God and to his plan of salvation.*

2865 *By the final 'Amen', we express our* fiat *concerning the seven petitions: 'So be it.'*

INDEX OF CITATIONS

SACRED SCRIPTURE

PROFESSIONS OF FAITH
(Cited by DS numbers)

ECUMENICAL COUNCILS
(Cited by DS numbers, except for Vatican II)

PARTICULAR COUNCILS AND SYNODS
(Cited by DS numbers)

PONTIFICAL DOCUMENTS

ECCLESIASTICAL DOCUMENTS

CANON LAW

LITURGY

ECCLESIASTICAL WRITERS

SUBJECT INDEX

Prefatory Note to Index

The main entry words are printed in bold type. The sub-headings that follow main entries provide additional information about the same or closely related topics (for example **Abraham:** call of Abraham 59, 72, 762). Cross-references with 'see' or 'see also' supply information about relevant main entry words. The primary objective in constructing this index was to provide the most comprehensive survey possible of the contents, and repetitions have been avoided where possible. For most Biblical references please see the Index of citations.

desires all men to be saved 74
does not abandon man after the fall 410
God alone can satisfy man's desire for
	happiness 1718
God's work 1, 275
predestines no one to damnation 1037
reveals himself 35
reveals himself in history as liberator
	2084
wants glorification of man 2012
attributes
	characteristics of a father 370
	characteristics of a husband 370
	characteristics of a mother 370
	goodness 385
	love 218–21, 733
	neither man nor woman 370
	truth 214–17, 2465
existence of God 33, 231
God the Almighty
	God can reveal the future 2115
	God's omnipotence 268–74, 275–78
		and evil 277, 309–12, 314, 395,412
		in Holy Scripture 269
		is not despotism 271
	God's providence 302–14
	the mystery of God's apparent
		powerlessness 272–74
God the Creator
	as 'first cause' 300, 304, 308
	Creator of the world 295–300
	Creator from nothing 296–98
	dignity of creatures 308
	God is acting in creatures 308
	God transcends creation 300, 303
	in his image 355–61, 1701–09
	sustainer of the world 301
God the Creator of man 362, 371, 704
	allowed man to co-operate in his
		creation 307, 1884
	created man as rational, free person
		1730
	created man 1
		out of love 1604
		to know God 286
God the Holy One
	as mystery of his divinity 2807
	God's holiness and glory 2809
	in the life and prayer of the Christian
		2814
	in the revelation of the Old Testament
		2810–11
	in the revelation of Jesus 2812
name
	abuse of God's name forbidden 2146,
		2161–62

God's name in oaths 2150, 2164
God wants to be called personally 203
magical use of God's name
	forbidden 2149
names of God
	Adonai 209
	Kyrios 209
	YHWH 206, 250–51, 213–14
significance of the revelation of God's
	names 203–14, 2143
sin as offence against God 1850
speaking about God 39–43, 48
special salvific actions
	calls Israel 62–64, 218–19, 2060, 2085
	inspires the authors of Holy Scripture
		105–06
	New Covenant 64
	reveals himself to Moses 205
	saves Israel from sin 435
	sends his Son 422

God's plan

angels as messengers of 331
Christ and Church in economic activity
	7, 112, 751–80, 851, 2426
family in 2201–06
providence 302–14
Satan and 2851, 2864
Virgin Mary and 502–07, 723, 2617

Good

God as source of all 14, 1723, 2052
in judging an action 1755–56, 1865
tree of knowledge 396

Good News see Gospel

Goodness

as fruit of the Holy Spirit 736, 1832

Gospel

and the Law of the Old Covenant 1964
as Good News 571
as revelation of God's mercy 1846
command to proclaim 2
formation 126
instinct 1676, 1679
place and significance in the New
	Testament 125–27
record of Jesus' life 514–15, 534, 573
two ways of recording Jesus' message 76

Government 24, 36, 1884, 1899–901,
	1922–23

Grace

as God's gift
	as charism 2003
	as gift of the Holy Spirit 2003

memorial in the mystery of salvation 1099
participation in Christ's prayer 1073
response of faith 1083
source of prayer 2655
work of the Trinity 1077–109
Jewish and Christian 1096
liturgical seasons 1163–78
  liturgical year 1168–73,1194
  as unfolding of Paschal mystery 1171, 1217
  commemoration of Mary 1172
  commemoration of saints 1173, 1195
  liturgical interpretation from Easter on 1168
  liturgical meaning shapes the seasons 1095
Liturgy of the Hours
  and other forms of devotion 1178
  contents 1176–77
  participants 1175
  purpose 1174, 1196
Liturgy of the Word 1103, 1154, 1346, 1349, 2183
  and the Sunday obligation 2183
  as part of the Eucharistic celebration 1346, 1349
  function 1103
  popular religion and 1674–74
Sunday
  as Day of Lord 1166–67, 1193
  importance of Sunday Eucharistic celebration 2177–79
  occasion for the celebration of Sunday 1166
  purpose of Sunday 1167
  mystery of the liturgy 1075
  Word of God in the liturgy 1100–02, 1190

Lord's Day see Sunday

Lost property 2409

Love 1766
celibacy for love of God 1599
conjugal love 1604, 1643
interpretation and place
  and freedom 1828
  and the law of Christ 1824
  as 'soul of sanctification' 826
  as 'soul of the apostolate' 864
  as fundamental passion 1765
  as most important social commandment 1889
  as source of prayer 2658
  as virtue

love of enemies 1825
new commandment of love 1823
liturgy as 1083
love of God and love of neighbour
  Christ's love as source of all human merit before God 2011
  commandment to love one's neighbour 2196
  consecrated life as expression of God's love 914–30
  God created man out of love 1604
  relationship of love of God to love of men 2069
preferential 2729, 2732
sin as offence against love 1849. 1855
see also Charity

Lukewarmness 2094

Lust 1866, 2351, 2514, 2529, 2530, 2542

Luxury 1866, 2351

Lying 2482
discernment of truth and lies 1954, 2847
evils of 215, 2483–86
father of lies 392, 2482

Magic 2115–17, 2138

Magisterium see Church

Man
as creature
  as a good creation 374
  purpose 358
  recognition of limitations as creature 396
  with body and soul 327, 355, 362–65, 382, 1703, 1711
  with reason 1704
  with understanding and free will 311, 396
calling of man 1260
  to eternal life 1998
  to God 1878
  to love 1603–04
  to the Kingdom 543
  to union with Christ 521, 542
characteristics and actions
  action of man 16, 2085
  capacity for natural knowledge of God 32, 46
  common humanity and needs 361, 842, 1947–48
  desire for happiness 1718
  desire to do good 1706–07
  endowed with freedom 1705
  expresses himself in signs and symbols 1146

is a religious being 28, 44–45
constant struggle to decide in favour of
the good 409
needs social life 1879–80
obligation to follow his conscience
1706, 1713
striving of man for truth 2467
virtuous man 1803–04
Christ's right to judge men 679
Church proclaims full revelation about
man 2419
consequences of sin
according to Sacred Scripture 399–400
choice between eternal life and eternal
death 1470
deprived of resemblance to God 705
every man affected from birth on 403
freedom and original sin 396–401
harm through the activity of the devil
395
temptation of man 394
through sin, the devil has a certain
power over man 407
woundedness of human nature 405
consummation at the end of time 1045
duty to protect and help the sick or
handicapped 2276
end of 16, 356, 260
equality of all men and women 2393
according to nature, origin and goal
1934
human dignity as fundamental element
1935, 1945
unjust inequalities 1938
with differences in aptitudes 1936–37
God–man relationship 30, 101, 109, 285,
2566–67, 2826
profession of faith 199
question of God's existence 33, 41
human dignity, rights and duties
basis for and importance of human
dignity 1700
communion with God 27, 357, 1700
dignity of the creature's co-operation
with the Creator 306–08
harmed by sin 1487
human dignity 27
human dignity manifested in moral life
1706; in free choice 2339
origin of human rights in human
dignity 1930
rights 1738, 1930
human sexual identity
created as 'male and female' 355, 383
difference and complementarity of the
sexes 369–73, 1605, 2333

equal dignity of both sexes 369, 2334,
2393
vocation to love and communion
2331–32
in creation
everything created for him 358
goal of creation 358
hierarchy of creatures 342
importance of the order of creation 346
interdependence of creatures 340
original harmony 374–79, 384
respect for the order of creation 339,
346
responsibility for the world 373
unique place of man 343, 355, 1951
in humanity
brotherhood of all men 361, 1947–48
origin and goal of the whole human
race 842
unity of mankind 360
not abandoned by God after the fall 410
origin
created out of love by God 1, 315, 1604
promise to restore man's likeness to God
705
sin and the rejection of God 29, 398,
1739
sin as offence to human nature 1849,
1714
resemblance to God
before and after redemption by Christ
1701
created in the image of God 356–61,
380, 1702
whole of man willed by God 362
respect for personal dignity 1738
right to a good reputation 2479, 2507
right to act in accord with one's
conscience 1782
right to freedom of religion 2106
search for God
God calls man first 2567
knowledge of God
God speaks in human words 101, 109
through reason 50
through revelation 35, 50, 52, 208
ways 31
man always in search of God 30, 2566
sexuality
importance 2332, 2362
importance of conjugal union 2335
integration in the human person 2337
twofold purpose of Matrimony
2360–63
see also Matrimony
sin, consequences of 399–400

all implicated 402–03
common destiny 1046
death enters world 1008
harmony lost 400
loss of communication with God 1607
loss of likeness to God 705
nature violated 405
original sin 396–401, 403
subjection to error 1714
war of spirit and flesh 2516
weakness 208, 396, 1500, 2448
transmission of life 372
vocation 1878, 1710, 2133
divinization of man as Jesus' goal 460
to communion with God 27
to co-operation in God's creation 307, 378
to eternal beatitude 1703
to free submission to God 144, 396
to friendship with God 355, 396
to life in the Holy Spirit 1699
to manifest God 2085

Manna 1094, 1334

Manichaeism 285

Maranatha 451

Market economy
within the state's responsibility 2431

Marriage see Matrimony

Martyrdom
as bearing witness to the truth 2473, 2506
importance for the Church 2474

Martyrs 2473
acts of 2474
behaviour of 2113
cult of 957, 1173

Mary
and the Church
in Mary the Church is all-holy 829
Marian dimension of the Church 773, 973
Mary supports the beginning of the Church through her prayer 965
place of Mary in the mystery of the Church 963–72
place of Mary inseparable from Christ 964
Annunciation 484, 490
as example and model
Christian example of holiness 2030
example of obedience 144, 148–49

example of faith in God's omnipotence 273
assent of 148, 490, 494
Assumption into heaven 966, 974
beliefs about Mary based on beliefs about Christ 487
conceived and gave birth to the Son of God 485, 509, 723
devotion to Mary
in the liturgical year 1172–370, 2043, 2177
in the liturgy of the Church 971
not adoration 971
in God's plan of salvation
free from sin 411
'full of God's grace' 490
God's choice of Mary 488–93, 508
'Immaculate Conception' 490–93
preparation in the Old Covenant 489
interpretation
dwelling of the Son and of the Holy Spirit 721
'Mother of Grace' 968–70
as mediator, not source, of God's grace 969, 970
in restoration of supernatural life to souls 968
intercessor before God 969, 975
only through the mediation of Christ 970
predestined 488–89, 508
'Mother of the Church' 963
Panagia 493
personification of the Church 507
'Seat of Wisdom' 721
Theotokos 495
type' of the Church 967
obedience of faith of Mary 144, 494, 511
prayer of Mary 2617–19
prayer to 2675–79
prepared by the Holy Spirit 722
prophecy of Jesus' birth 484
sinless during her life 411
union with her Son 964
virginity of Mary 496–507, 510
as sign of her faith 506
in God's plan of salvation 502–06
in the faith of the Church 499
in the gospels 497–98, 500
in the Tradition of the Fathers 496
visitation to Elizabeth 717

Mass see Eucharistic celebration

Masturbation 2352

Materialism 285

as foundation of Christian moral
activity 1813, 1840
faith, hope, and charity as theological
virtues 1813, 1841
charity 1822–29, 1844
faith 1814–16, 1842
hope 1817–21, 1843
truthfulness 2468, 2505
in human relationships 2469
lies as offence against the virtue of
truthfulness 2486, 2508

Vocation
of Abraham 762
of our first parents 54
to follow Christ 1694
to sanctity 825
to the catholic unity of the People of
God 836
call of all by Jesus 3, 542–43
call of all by the Creator 1
society and vocation 1907, 2461
see also Evangelical counsels

Vows 2102
dispensation from 2103
of the evangelical counsels 915, 2103
see also Evangelical counsels; Promises

Voyeurism 2523, 2525

Wagers 2413

Wages
just wage as legitimate fruit of work 2434
unjust wages 2409

War
and the moral law 2312, 2328
arms race 2315, 2329
blind obedience 2313
disorders threatening peace 2317
duty to prevent war 2307–08, 2327
genocide 2313
'just war' 2309
obedience in war 2313
production and sale of arms 2316
treatment of the wounded and civilians
2313
weapons 2314

Way, ways
ways of mission 852
ways of Providence 314
ways of the Kingdom 1987

Way of the Cross 2669

Weakness
and prayers of saints 956, 1053

Holy Spirit and 741, 2630
human 268, 517, 540, 978, 1264, 1426,
1505, 1508, 1550, 2602
mystery of apparent weakness of God
272

Wealth
and the Kingdom 2544, 2556
happiness and wealth 1723
love of rich and poor 2445
passion for 2536

Wedding see Matrimony

Wedding Feast
at Cana 1613, 2618
in the Kingdom 1027, 1335
mystical 923
of the Lamb 1244, 1329, 1602, 1612,
1642, 2618

Widows, consecrated see Evangelical
counsels

Will
faith and will 143, 155
morality and the will 1755, 1853
passions and the will 1767–68
strengthening the will's mastery 1734,
1809
see also Man

Wisdom
as gift of the Holy Spirit 1831
man shares wisdom of God 1954
moral law as 1950

Witchcraft see Sorcery

Witness
Apostles and 857
as authentication 2044
Confirmation and 1285, 1303
duty of 1816, 2087, 2471
effect of 30
false 2464, 2476
in education 2226
intercession of 2683
laity as 904–05, 913, 942, 2242
martyrdom as 2473
matrimony and 1631
meaning of 995
of consecrated life and secular institutes
929, 932
of the saints 688
Resurrection, of 642

Women
as image of the Church 1368, 2853

calling of
created in image of God 355, 369–70, 2335
defence of 1610
dignity of 1645, 2334, 2393
in the salvation history of the Old Covenant 489
man 'created as male and female' 355, 383
ordination of 1577–78
original harmony of man and woman 376, 384
relations between men and women 409, 1606–07
religious life 918, 924
see also Mary; Man: human sexual identity

Word see Scripture, Catechesis

Work 1368
access to employment 2211, 2433, 2436
conflicts 2430
day of rest 1193, 2172, 2184–88
just wage as legitimate fruit 2434
meaning and value 2427–28, 2460
solidarity and 1940
strikes 2435.
unemployment 2436

World

Church and 782, 863, 2105
created by God 295, 325, 327, 337–49, 760
creation of the 'visible world' 325, 337
end of 681, 1001, 1243
Jesus as Lord and saviour of the world 450, 457–58, 608, 728, 1355
'sin of the world' 408, 2844
subjugation by man 373
'third world' 2440
transitoriness 677
'world of men' 326
world order and natural law 341
world renewed 655, 670, 916, 1042–50
see also Creation

Worship
as the first act of the virtue of religion 2096, 2135
meaning of worship 2097
in liturgical celebration 1070
see also Adoration

YHWH see God: names of God; Jesus Christ

Youth
education of 5, 1632, 2526, 2685, 2688
dangers to 2282, 2353, 2389

Zeal 579, 2442

A GUIDE TO THEMES IN THE *CATECHISM*

The *Catechism of the Catholic Church* was published in English in 1994. It proved an immediate success. However, no one could pretend that it was a particularly easy read. For many readers the waters were quite uncharted, and difficult to navigate.

Recently the definitive Latin version of the *Catechism* was published in Rome. This incorporated a considerable number of corrections and amendments – mostly fairly small – to the original text, as well as a much developed index. This present edition includes these changes to the original text. It also includes a guide for readers, prepared for the French edition, to help chart the waters and to make reading the full text both easier and more profitable for the reader.

The guide has been prepared, at least partly, through listening to what readers of the original text were saying. There are around two dozen themes drawn directly from the *Catechism*, which together show how the whole document, varied though its content is, is a true unity. In presenting each of these themes there is first a short section (in *italic*) in which some of the questions that people have asked about the given theme are put. These provide the context for a set of explanatory comments about the theme, which are eventually rounded off in a simple statement. The text of the *Catechism* itself is referred to throughout.

Readers are thus invited to follow a thematic journey through the *Catechism*, and by listening to questions put by searcher, critic, catechumen, or interested Christian, to try to make a deeper sense of their lives and of their faith in the Church.

DAVID KONSTANT
Bishop of Leeds

READER'S GUIDE TO THEMES IN THE CATECHISM

1. In Search of Meaning: Why a Catechism?

Our human understanding rightly seeks to dispel life's lack of meaning, to ask why things — and life — are as they are and to give a point to existence. In this quest, people today insist on thinking for themselves. They are aware of their freedom to believe or not. From among the diversity of available beliefs, they tend to choose those that best correspond to their hopes. From that point of view, what use to them is a Catechism presenting a compendium of doctrines, rites and obligations?

Far from ignoring these questions, the *Catechism of the Catholic Church* explores their roots. Our created nature and earthly condition explain our human quest for truth and happiness. This quest is our greatness; our powerlessness to satisfy it is our weakness. The Christian faith identifies our origin and our misfortune in this duality. On the one hand, we have come forth from our creator 'in his image and likeness'; on the other, we are subject to the burden of sin. From these two realities arises our difficulty in finding the truth and happiness that beckon us.

The *Catechism*'s only rationale is to help us enter into the knowledge of the mystery of God and the salvation he wants for us, by clearly and precisely setting forth the Catholic faith. But it cannot say all there is to say. And it cannot answer all the questions that may be asked about the faith concerning the Church. Intended primarily for believers and those enquiring about the Church's teaching, the *Catechism* presents the essence of what the Church believes, affirms and celebrates.

Human greatness and weakness

From its first pages, the *Catechism of the Catholic Church* presents the Christian vision of humanity. This vision is fundamentally positive: the human person is a being of greatness and nobility by virtue of 'his openness to truth and beauty' (33), aspiration for the infinite and hope for happiness (cf. 1718). 'Human freedom is a force for growth and maturity in truth and goodness' (1731). 'Moral conscience ... enjoins [the person] at the appropriate moment to do good and to avoid evil' (1777). Thus people seek what is absolute. Even if we are mistaken regarding our goal, it is still God whom we ultimately seek to encounter; our quest is universal (29).

The Christian faith, inspired by the Scriptures, bears witness to a human dignity which is based on the creation of man and woman 'in the image and likeness of God' (31, 225, 355ff.).

Human beings find within themselves and in others the experience of the 'drama of sin' (309). 'Sin weighs heavy on human life and history' (386). 'The human heart is heavy and hardened' (1432). 'This dramatic situation makes man's life a battle' (409). The reality of sin that weighs on every person cannot be avoided (385, 401). The 'most secret desires of the human heart' (2126) remain the mark of everyone's dignity and identity (1700).

Because faith considers our human nature to be of the essence, it draws the following conclusions concerning that nature: we are called to know the truth (150, 154, 2087), to follow our consciences (1706, 1776) and to fulfil our earthly destiny completely, in expectation of immortality (366). In responding to these calls, we realize our vocation and can grasp the meaning of our existence.

Nevertheless, faith is not limited to this assurance that life has meaning. Christian salvation, to which faith bears witness, is of another order. Beyond meaning that responds to a need for coherence and unity, there is grace.

We receive grace as a free gift from God (52, 54, 153), offered through the redemption of his Son (55) to those who believe in him (1996). Christians know that we are in God's hands (270, 305). And in the response we give to the grace that comes from God, we find fulfilment in the accomplishment of our lives (2002, 2005).

Before our eyes stands the model of perfect humanity, revealed to us in the person and message of Jesus Christ, the Son of God (520, 1701).

Why a Catechism of the Catholic Church?

The Pope and the bishops gathered in synod in 1985 decided to commission a *Catechism of the Catholic Church*, which was intended to be a compendium of all Catholic doctrine regarding both faith and morals (10).

Faith is not a mere feeling, but rather embraces the believer's whole life (154). Yet the believer also seeks to understand the convictions and loyalties that faith entails (15, 94).

Believers are not alone. Their faith places them in a relationship with other believers (166). The Church has a role and a mission to acquire and to transmit to the faithful the language of faith that permits communication and unity in thought and prayer (170–171).

The Church gathers the faithful, scattered through all the regions of the earth. The Church legitimately affirms her catholic or universal character, which guarantees to all believers the identity of the faith, in the truths she proclaims, the rites she celebrates and the moral demands to which she bears witness (182, 186–187).

It is further necessary to stipulate that the *Catechism of the Catholic Church* places its teaching outside all coercion (160). It affirms the right to religious liberty (2104–2106). Since this right is based on the very nature of the human person (1907), it implies that society must respect it as a civil right though its exercise is bound by legal principles in conformity with the moral order (2109).

If the question of meaning makes sense in the reflections of people of our time, and even somewhat painfully to young people who seek truth and certainty, the Church cannot dispense herself from taking it into account. But the message she transmits only addresses the question of meaning by transcending it through the faith she presents as a response to a call that itself comes from above and beyond human consciousness. *The Catechism of the Catholic Church* is not intended to be an instrument of proselytizing for the Church in the 'marketplace of religions'. The *Catechism* can help its readers the better to hear and understand that call. 'Take and read.'

2. The Mystery That Disturbs Our Idea of God

Belief in God is not evident to everyone. Nevertheless, the idea of God that reason can contrive has some truth to it. To be capable of apprehending the existence of an infinite and absolute being beyond the reality of things and people is the glory of the human mind. But according to the Christian faith, Revelation sees in God an altogether different mystery from that glimpsed by reason.

The Christian faith rests on a revelation of God who is beyond what reason acknowledges. Yet faith does not deny the capacity of reason to attain some knowledge of God. Faith gives credit to reason for establishing God's existence and transcendent being. But the conception of God that reason may acquire cannot be compared with what God has said about himself in Revelation. God is one, in three distinct persons: the Father, the Son and the Holy Spirit. By faith, Christians accept this mystery, which God has made known by his Word. The mystery of the Trinity is the basis of all the teaching contained in the *Catechism of the Catholic Church*.

The greatness and the limits of reason

From its first chapter, the *Catechism* confirms the Church's position, which recognizes that 'God can be known with certainty through his works, by the [natural] light of human reason' (31, 286).

Atheism's professed denial of God (2123–2126) and agnosticism's refusal to pronounce on this subject (2127–2128), even if they are explained by different motivations (29), nevertheless betray a real deficiency in the exercise of human intelligence.

There are several means of attaining knowledge of God (31–35). By exploring these means, the human mind can validly say something about God (40, 41, 43).

The Church does not disregard the historical conditions (culture, secularized society . . .) in which people find themselves; she acknowledges the difficulties in knowing God with certainty by reason alone (37).

Nevertheless, the Church's attitude towards human reason remains positive. The *Catechism* affirms that the mind's aptitude for knowing God prepares it to 'welcome [his] revelation in faith' (35). It also leads to 'seeing that faith is not opposed to human reason' (35, 159).

Welcoming Revelation

Christians hold by faith that God has made himself known to us. No matter how meritorious reason's efforts to approach God may be, it cannot attain the fullness of his mystery. To know God, it is not enough that we should seek to encounter him, but God himself must to come to meet us.

The knowledge of what God says about himself is of an entirely different order than that which reason can attain (50); it is based on the Word of God received in faith (142–143, 153ff.).

God expresses himself in the Revelation of his Word (68, 101), contained in the Scriptures gathered together in the Bible, the book of the Word of God (105, 107, 135), and transmitted by the Church in her Tradition (35, 84). Adherence to the Word of God makes one a believer (142ff).

The God of reason causes us to consider the distance that separates him, in the infinity of his greatness, power and eternity, from us (42). In his Word, God reveals himself in his closeness to his creatures (35, 206); the simple fact that he speaks (30, 51) indicates that he is not a mere mental construct, an 'anonymous force' (203), but a personal and living being (50, 52). God has a name (203, 213).

Above all, God reveals himself as the one whose love and loving-kindness for us extends even to compassion and forgiveness (210–211, 319). He is the faithful God (207, 215, 220).

In all he does to make himself known, both in the creation of the universe (282, 295, 315) and in his Revelation (50), God is seen to be the one who is totally other, whose 'mystery is beyond words' (230). He is the one who shows his greatness in his tenderness and compassion for us (231).

God reveals himself in his Son

The clearest sign of God's love is the Incarnation of his Son (65, 219). In his Son, come in our flesh, true God and true man, God fulfils his plan of salvation for the human race. In his Son, God has said everything; he has no other word to give us (65). In his Son, God has made known 'the mystery of his will', through which we 'should have access to the Father, through Christ, the Word made flesh, in the Holy Spirit' (51).

Since Jesus Christ came, we have known the mystery of the one God in its fullness; we have known him in three distinct persons: the Father, the Son, and the Holy Spirit (253). This is the mystery of the Holy Trinity (233).

This mystery makes us enter into God's 'inmost Being'; it is 'the central mystery of the faith and the Christian life' and is 'inaccessible to reason alone' (237). This mystery is penetrated by faith (144, 150ff.). Christians grow into this mystery through prayer, which brings about their union with the divine persons.

In the perfect equality of their divine nature (253), the three persons are equally present and active in the accomplishment of the work of salvation (258). But they are present and active, each in keeping with 'his unique personal property' (258); thus, the Son's Incarnation and the Spirit's coming are appropriated to the second and third persons of the Trinity.

....

As intellectual history attests, the human mind has always been preoccupied with knowing and saying something about God. The Christian faith, without scorning this preoccupation, welcomes the divine mystery that baffles reason and limits it to saying that God is never what it thinks he is. Yet faith does not set reason aside, but indeed requires the understanding of reason even within the adherence it gives to the revealed mystery. So it is that the ancient words remain contemporary: faith seeks understanding.

....

3. Human Language and God's Word

How can anyone accept the belief of the monotheistic religions that God speaks to humanity? Is it not an abuse of language to attribute language to God? Our idea of God must exclude every anthropomorphism, that is, every projection onto the supreme being of that capacity of expressing oneself in speech that is proper only to human beings.

It must be understood that the truths of faith are of an order different from human wisdom. The doctrine of Revelation, that is, the teaching that God expresses himself to us in order to divulge his mystery, is precisely what has been denied most radically by rationalist thought, in particular by the philosophers of the Enlightenment. Simply because they rejected this doctrine, they could no longer accept the faith. But the mystery of God does not lie in his silence. It lies, rather, in the creating and revealing Word about all that he has done for his people's salvation and happiness, a Word that is not only speech but deed. The Word reveals as much by the realities and events it decrees as by the words it causes to be heard. In the Holy Scripture contained in the Bible, the Word is conveyed through writing in human terms. Scripture is understood and interpreted by the Tradition of the Church, which has been sent to transmit and celebrate the Word.

God expresses himself in the Word

God encounters us in the Word. He reveals his name (203, 206) and his plan of salvation (50, 54) to us.

The Father reveals himself fully by sending his Son, the incarnate Word (50, 65, 238), and the Holy Spirit, who leads believers 'into all truth' (243, 50, 79, 729).

Thus there is a divine method (*pedagogy*) in God's patient revelation of his being and his saving action towards humanity (73, 708).

This revelation, which is progressive, 'culminates in the person and mission of the incarnate Word, Jesus Christ' (53).

Revelation is given 'simultaneously by deeds and words which are intrinsically bound up with each other and shed light on each other' (53). The Word is not only God's speech, but it also accomplishes what it proclaims, in the work of creation (115, 299), in the events of the history that prepared for Christ's coming (54ff.), and in the sacraments of the Church (1127), especially Baptism (1128), the Eucharist (1375), and Reconciliation (1441).

In the *Holy Scripture*, under the inspiration of the Holy Spirit, the Word of God is conveyed in writing (81, 105).

In order to reveal himself to us, God speaks in human language in the Scriptures (101).

God is the author of Scripture (105). He has chosen 'certain men' to be the 'human authors' (106) of the sacred books contained in the Bible (120).

The inspiration with which the sacred writers were privileged must be properly understood. As the Second Vatican Council said, and the *Catechism* repeats, the sacred writers 'made full use of their own faculties and powers so that, though [God] acted in them and by them, it was as true authors that they consigned to writing whatever he wanted written, and no more' (106). Thus 'all that the inspired authors or sacred writers affirm should be regarded as affirmed by the Holy Spirit' (107).

The Spirit at the heart of the Word

'Through all the words of Sacred Scripture, God speaks only one single Word, his one Utterance in whom he expresses himself completely' (102, 65). But because Jesus Christ is the Son, he reveals the Father in the fullness of his fatherhood at the heart of the Trinity (240, 443).

The same Trinitarian mystery causes the Holy Spirit to be seen as the Paraclete promised by the Son and sent by the Father to remind the disciples of 'all that the Son had taught them' (243, 687).

The Spirit is always at the heart of divine revelation. He inspired the sacred books of the Old and New Testaments (105) and guided the apostles so that they could transmit the Word (244). The Spirit always assists the Church in the knowledge of the Gospel (94) and assures the fidelity of her Tradition, the 'living memorial of God's Word,' in guarding the 'deposit of the faith' (84, 110–111). Equally, the Spirit allows Christians to understand the Scriptures and to be nourished by them in prayer, especially in the liturgical assembly (91, 1100, 2653).

The Spirit who inspires God's Word and makes it come alive speaks today to the Church, as he spoke to the Churches in the vision of the *Apocalypse of St John* (*Revelation* 2:7). The Table of the Word, in liturgical assemblies, is always united with the Eucharistic Table (103). The Spirit continues to act in the Christian community and in the heart of each of its members.

Although the book of the Scriptures is always present in its thought and prayer, Christianity must not be reduced to a religion of the book (108). The believer's vision does not stop at the written letter. The Spirit discloses, beyond the letter, the living Word that calls believers to live in keeping with the faith it reveals.

....

4. The Creation of the World

In the context of scientific attempts to explain the origins of the world, does the doctrine of a creating God stand any chance of being accepted? Is the believer who accepts it placed in opposition to or on the margins of every scientific effort to explain the origin of the world?

The *Catechism of the Catholic Church* does not disregard this objection. The problem of the origin of the cosmos draws a line of demarcation between scientific thought and 'believing' thought. The first kind asks about the how of origins; the scientific thought of some people concludes that the world could have made itself. On the contrary, believing thought, common to all the great religions, recognises a God who is the creator of the universe. The Christian faith respects scientific research for the explanation it tries to give of the process by which the cosmos appeared in time. But Christian faith goes farther: in the birth of the universe, faith sees and celebrates the work of the creating God who, in his absolute otherness, reveals his Trinitarian mystery.

God created the world

The *Catechism* interprets the doctrine of creation as faith's response to people's elementary questions: 'Where do we come from?' and 'Where are we going?' are two 'questions that are inseparable' (182). They have become the objective of a permanent 'quest', because human thought has always been intrigued by the question of origins and has given all kinds of answers to it (285).

In its attempt at explaining creation, science has made its contributions. Although science has 'enriched our knowledge' (283), the question of origins nevertheless goes beyond its 'proper domain' (284). 'It is not only a question of knowing when and how the universe arose physically, or when man appeared, but rather of discovering the meaning of such an origin' (284).

The Christian faith brings a clarification that permits us to place the question of origins in its proper context. To be sure, as most religions attest (28, 2566), human reason can grasp the existence of a creating God on the basis of his works (31–32, 36, 286). But in the light of Revelation, contained in the Scriptures

(289), believers embrace the truth of creation 'with firm certainty and with no admixture of error' (38).

It must be understood that creation bears witness to God's sovereign power and to his radical difference from his creatures (269); as the classic expression articulates it: God created the world from nothing. God 'needs no pre-existent thing or any help in order to create' (296–297, 338–339).

It must also be understood that God did not create for nothing. The created world 'proceeds from God's free will; he wanted to make his creatures share in his being, wisdom and goodness' (293, 295, 341).

Because the God in whom we believe is one God in three persons, the Father, the Son and the Holy Spirit (232–233), creation must be considered the common work of the Holy Trinity (292ff., 685–686).

Creation is the work of the Father. By creating the world, the Father reveals creation as 'the first step' towards his covenant with his people, 'the first and universal witness to God's all-powerful love' (288).

Creation is the work of the Son, the 'Word through whom all things were made' (*John* 1:1–13). 'All was created through him and for him' (*Colossians* 1:16–17) (291). 'The mystery of Christ casts conclusive light on the mystery of creation' (280).

Creation is the work of the Holy Spirit, 'the giver of life'. He is the 'Spirit creator'. The Word and the Spirit are the Father's 'hands' (292). 'The Word of God and his Breath are at the origin of the being and life of every creature' (703–704).

At the summit of creation

The human person is 'the only creature on earth that God has willed for its own sake' (356). God created the world 'as a gift addressed to man, an inheritance destined for and entrusted to man' (299). God has entrusted us with 'the responsibility of "subduing" the earth and having dominion over it' (307).

And so everyone is called to take on the responsibilities imposed by our 'intelligent and free' human nature, in order to 'complete the work of creation' (307). Moreover, our human nature grounds and legitimates the necessity for research and progress in knowledge and for mastering the universe through scientific research and technology (2293–2294). 'The glory of God is man fully alive', according to St Irenaeus (294).

Nevertheless the limits imposed by the order of creation must be respected in the fulfilment of this vocation. 'Each creature possesses its own particular goodness and perfection' (339). The 'integrity of creation' is what is meant here. The 'dominion ... granted by the Creator is not absolute; it is limited by concern for the quality of life of [our] neighbour, including generations to come' (2415).

The integrity of creation should motivate human conduct in questions concerning the union of man and woman in marriage and the love they give each other (1603), human life from conception to death (2258, 2270), the use of the world's resources (2415) and the universal destination of the earth's goods, and our relationship with the animals (2416–2418).

The natural law has been given to us precisely to enable us to harmonize our moral conduct with the order of creation (1951). 'The natural law is nothing other than the light of understanding placed in us by God; through it we know what we must do and what we must avoid. God has given us this light or law at the creation' (1955).

Praying to God the Creator

Faithful believers are not content to affirm the convictions of their faith in the creating God, but also strive to make him the object of their personal prayer (2692, 2699). They celebrate these convictions in the community gathered for liturgical prayer (2655).

'Prayer is lived in the first place beginning with the realities of creation' (2569). 'Adoration is the first attitude of man acknowledging that he is a creature before his Creator' (2628). 'To adore God is to acknowledge him as God, as the Creator and Saviour, the Lord and Master' (2096). 'To adore God is to acknowledge, in respect and absolute submission, the "nothingness of the creature" who would not exist but for God' (2097, 2779).

Finally, it is necessary to mention the place that the praise of God occupies in the Eucharistic liturgy, the 'sacrifice of praise in thanksgiving for the work of creation' (1359). 'We offer to the Father what he himself has given us: the gifts of his creation, bread and wine' 1357). In liturgical prayer, creation is always associated with God's other works: redemption and the grace of salvation (1352).

Thus, Christians cannot think of creation without understanding it as the first manifestation of God's plan for the world and humanity.

5. Is God Responsible for Evil?

Evil exists and scandalizes. Whether provoked by natural cataclysms or resulting from human deficiencies or vanity, evil always causes shock and indignation, especially when it strikes the innocent. A feeling of rebellion is added to a sense of fatalism. Why? Whose fault is it? Is God to be held responsible for the evil that occurs in our world?

The *Catechism of the Catholic Church* ignores neither the reality of evil that makes creation appear so violent and wretched nor the spontaneous reflex, born of a need to understand, that blames the Creator for evil, in the absence of any other explanation. Christians cannot cling to an attitude of judgement, but rather draw assurances from revelation to provide an answer to the scandal of evil. This answer must be sought in faith in the mystery of Christ, the Son of God and innocent victim on the cross of human sin.

The presence of evil

That evil exists is an evident fact. But where does it come from (385)? Its existence implies a 'question as pressing as it is unavoidable and as painful as it is mysterious' (309). Faith in God 'can be put to the test by the experience of evil and suffering. God can sometimes seem to be absent' (272).

There is no 'quick answer' to the question of evil. 'Only Christian faith as a whole constitutes the answer to this question … There is not a single aspect of the Christian message that is not in part an answer to the question of evil' (309).

Moral evil, related to sin and therefore 'more harmful', is to be distinguished from physical evil, associated with the 'becoming' of a creation in process towards its perfection (310, 302).

Sin has been 'present in human history' (386) from the beginning; it has 'invaded' and 'inundated' the world. Sin is 'universal' (401). Various explanations have been supplied for this universal presence of evil and sin in creation. One such explanation is based on the duality of two principles that have opposed each other since the beginning: Good and Evil, Light and Dark (285).

Such dualism is not compatible with faith in God, the Creator of the universe (286), and is not to be confused with what the Gospel teaches us about the one whom Jesus calls the 'father of lies' and a 'murderer from the beginning' (John 8:44; see 394). He is speaking here of the devil, the 'Evil One' (2851), whose influence and seductive power over individuals and society are undeniable, yet cannot be compared with the Creator's sovereign power (395).

An incomplete creation

Christian thought, nourished by the sacred writings, cannot identify God's almighty power with blind domination over his creatures' existence (271–272). It must be understood from the start that 'creation did not spring forth complete from the hands of the Creator' (302), who has entrusted us with the 'responsibility of "subduing" the earth and having dominion over it' (307, 373). We are God's 'stewards'. There is, then, a kind of 'human lordship over creation' which legitimates scientific research and technology (2293–2294).

Above all, it must be considered that 'God grants his creatures not only their existence but also the dignity of acting on their own' (306). They 'have to journey toward their ultimate destinies by their free choice' (311). The freedom given to us implies 'the possibility of choosing between good and evil' (1730–1732).

By becoming 'slaves to sin' (1733), we can frustrate God's plan. But God respects our freedom (387, 311). God is in no way 'directly or indirectly, the cause of moral evil' (311).

Christians, like all people, are subject to the experience of sin and evil. Only in faith can they give meaning to these realities (312). Is human suffering, which is born of physical affliction and slaughters even the innocent, more unjust than the passion and death of Christ, the innocent victim on the cross (601)? Christians also know that every instance of suffering gains redemptive value for our sins from the suffering of Christ (618, 1506).

Ultimately, it must not be denied that the mystery of evil is a stumbling block on the journey of faith, a mystery that can only be illuminated by Revelation, which presents in its entirety the plan of salvation willed by God and accomplished by Christ (616, 411–412).

Giving meaning to suffering

Any reflection on the problem of evil will be inadequate if not completed by two considerations: one on the place occupied by suffering in human life as a whole (1500–1501) and the other on our prayer 'not to be led into temptation and to be delivered from evil' (2846, 2850).

Suffering reveals itself in many guises. It gives us the experience of our powerlessness, limitations and finite nature (1500). Christians, no less than others, are not exempt from the trials that can 'lead to anguish, self-absorption, sometimes even despair and revolt against God' (1501). But to eyes purified by God, Christians are united in their pain with Christ, alone and abandoned, and offered as a victim on the cross. Invited by him to carry their own crosses, they know that they are associated with the mystery of his compassion and redemption (604, 618, 1506).

Finally, there is prayer. When the Lord taught the Our Father to his disciples, he formulated its last two petitions, which implore the grace of being freed and delivered from that reign of sin that continues to seduce and violate us. The Lord himself addressed this prayer to his Father: 'I am not asking you to take them out of this world, but I ask you to protect them from the Evil One' (*John* 17:15; see 2850).

> We conclude with this beautiful passage from the Catechism: 'In this final petition, the Church brings before the Father all the distress of the world. Along with deliverance from the evils that overwhelm humanity, she implores the precious gift of peace and the grace of perseverance in expectation of Christ's return' (2854).

6. Only One Life

What may survive after death remains for many a vexed, or even anguished, question. The idea of reincarnation is very seductive. Why does the Church reject it? What can we know about a life after life?

In fact, the *Catechism* does not simply justify the rejection of reincarnation (1013). Just as the Church acknowledges the logic of human reason (39) and legitimates the natural law (1954ff.), so too, concerning our human destiny, she confirms, clarifying it by faith, the common opinion as human wisdom and philosophical reflection have expressed it. All members of the human race are individual and personal beings, endowed with an immortal soul, and are free in the acts by which they forge their present and future destinies. To think that our earthly life is only a transitory stage within a succession of existences, lived out as reincarnations, would be to dissolve the identity of the individual self and to deny the value of our earthly lives.

The individuality of the person

In many passages, the *Catechism* recalls the individual reality and unique character and existence of every person, who is 'not something, but someone' (357). Endowed with personal dignity (1730, 1935), each person has been 'willed' for his or her 'own sake' (1703) and is loved by God (605). Everyone has a conscience (1781–1782).

The immortal soul (366) is united to the body to form 'a unique nature' (365). Thus the body shares in the dignity of God's image (364). This unity of soul and body is a major truth of the Christian faith, a truth that permits us to understand that 'every human life, from conception until death, is sacred' (2319, 2258).

Human beings are free and the 'masters' of their acts (1730–1734). They are therefore responsible for their conduct, for freedom implies 'the possibility of choosing between good and evil' (1732). All will be judged on the basis of their conduct and will receive 'eternal retribution' in their 'immortal soul at the very moment of death' (1022, 1036). It is therefore here below that we outline our eternity: 'The Last Judgement will reveal even to its furthest consequences the good each person has done or failed to do during his [or her] earthly life' (1039, 679).

The permanence of the person

How are we to accept the absolute nature of such affirmations in the perspective of reincarnation? The *Catechism* is precise: 'Death is the end of earthly life; ... as with all living things on earth, death seems the normal end of [human] life; ... remembering our mortality helps us to realize that we have only a limited time in which to bring our lives to fulfilment' (1007). 'Death is the end of man's earthly pilgrimage, of the time of grace and mercy which God offers him so as to work out his earthly life in keeping with the divine plan, and to decide his ultimate destiny ...' (1013). When our life on earth is ended, 'we shall not return to other earthly lives' (1013).

For Christians, the Paschal mystery of Christ's death and Resurrection (1681) gives death its meaning. Death inaugurates the fulfilment of our 'new birth begun at Baptism' (1682), whose fruit ripens all through life, by means of an interior purification that opens the way to the Kingdom (654).

Here the doctrine of purgatory (1030ff.) finds its meaning. Far from obliterating the personal identity of each person, this doctrine allows us to uphold the permanence of the individual self, something excluded by the very idea of reincarnation. The personal soul in purgatory, as distinct from the souls of those condemned to hell, experiences a purification that prepares it to know at last the beatific vision of heaven. Prayer for the dead loses all meaning if it is not destined for beings remembered for who they were and known for what they remain in the beyond (1032).

The greatest caution must be exercised towards all claims, from near or far, that pretend to be able to divine the mysteries of the beyond. The Church does not fail to warn believers against all aberrant practices of communicating with spirits or of magic (2116–2117).

Only in faith can we come to know the truth about the life to come in a beyond that remains mysterious because it surpasses 'all understanding and description' (1027). Scripture reveals the life to come by means of images (1027). But Christ's definite language about his own Resurrection (994) allows no equivocation about eternal life and the Resurrection of the body (655, 658), promised to all who believe in him (1020ff.).

Faith affirms many things about our earthly condition, the salvation revealed to us that has been accomplished in Jesus Christ, the hope of heaven in the life to come, and the moral demands derived from it. All these affirmations lead us to think that the entire structure of the truths of the faith contradicts and opposes reincarnation. The Christian creed loses all meaning if reincarnation lies at the end of our existence here below.

Nor can the deep agreement on this point between Christian doctrine and humanist thinking be disregarded. We are not worthy of ourselves except in our personal consciences and in the appeal they make to us to take our lives in hand and so to embrace our destiny. The myth of reincarnation can only discourage a sense of self-respect and the enterprise of being human.

7. Jesus Christ in our history

The natural idea of God balks at the Church's teaching that Christ is at the same time the Son of God and a man 'born of a woman' (Galatians 4:4). The Catechism regards Jesus as the foundation and heart of all that must be believed (151, 450, 463). But how can we accept the God-Man, his Birth, Miracles, Resurrection . . . ?

In its teaching about Christ, the *Catechism* firmly and resoundingly holds that the Church's faith is centred on the mystery of the Incarnation, that is, on the fact that Jesus Christ is both man and God. The son of Mary of Nazareth is the Son of God. He has taken flesh in order to accomplish the redemption and salvation of humanity. Although the *Catechism* insists on affirming Jesus' human identity and the historicity of his life, it regards as even more important to show all that the coming of God's Son in our human condition represents for the faith of the Church and the practice of believers.

The historical truth of Christ

Everything affirmed about the mystery of Christ would be deprived of foundation if its Gospel source (514–515) did not allow us to know with certainty of Jesus' historical existence.

With regard to historians, Jesus' existence is undeniable: witnesses in secular history (573), outside the Gospel, attest it.

In the Gospel accounts, there are undeniably many indications of a geographical or chronological order that allow us to situate Jesus' life in space and time (125–126).

The *Catechism of the Catholic Church* presents the authors of the four Gospels as credible witnesses: 'They transmit faithfully what Jesus, the Son of God, while he lived among men, really did and taught' (126). 'The fourfold Gospel holds a unique place in the Church' (127). The apostles' initial doubt after Christ's Resurrection confirms the historicity of that fact as reported by the evangelists (642–644).

Despite differences in their approaches, the four Gospels evoke in their accounts a portrait of Jesus whose human condition obeys the common law of existence, except for sin. Like common mortals, he is born (525), grows up (531), prays (2599), suffers (612) and dies (624). There is not a single account that does not testify to the reality of Jesus' human nature, in his daily conduct and behaviour as well as in his encounters with others.

All four Gospels give accounts that present elements commonly regarded as supernatural: he is born of a virgin (497, 502), performs miracles (547–548), and, above all, he rises on the third day (638ff.). These signs (*Acts* 2:22) intend to establish the precise point that Jesus is not an ordinary man. 'They bear witness that he is the Son of God; ... they are not intended to satisfy people's curiosity or desire for magic' (548). They reveal what must be called the supernatural and divine level to which they belong. 'His whole life is a mystery' (517). 'What was visible in his earthly life leads to the invisible mystery of his divine sonship and redemptive mission' (515).

Precisely because the events of Jesus' earthly life cannot be understood 'except in the light of the mysteries of Christmas and Easter' (512), any biography of Christ, in the usually understood sense, is regarded as an impossible challenge.

In fact the Gospels were written only to elicit or confirm the faith of the first communities of Christians who were converted to Christ by the preaching of the apostles, whom he sent to transmit the Good News (512). 'The Gospels were written by men who were among the first to have the faith and wanted to share it with others' (515). Their aim is to cause 'the meaning of Christ's actions and words and of the signs worked by him' (426) to be understood, and to make him known as 'the Holy One of God' (438).

The Gospels are concerned with 'proclaiming Jesus Christ in order to lead others to faith in him' (425). They cannot be understood outside of this perspective. The historical truth of Jesus is necessary but not at all sufficient to cause one to come to faith in his mystery.

The mystery of Christ

The Church's faith, especially in the first years following the death of the apostles, 'worked' on the Gospels and the 'deposit of faith' they contain (85). Statements of faith in the mystery of Christ dating from the time of the apostles are extant (449, 461).

Since Jesus Christ came, the mystery of God can no longer be confined within the limits of the one God as the religion of Israel could know and worship him. Christ, the Son of God, has revealed the God's inmost being, the mystery of the three persons (see the section on the Trinity).

Since Jesus Christ came, humanity is no longer handed over to the inevitability of evil and sin (385). A human being like every other, the Son of God mastered the forces of evil and sin by his death and Resurrection. He has restored us to our dignity by giving us the ability to live as sons and daughters of God (460), called to reach the perfection of the 'Father who is in heaven' (459, 2013).

Finally, since Jesus Christ came, all creation, especially humanity, having become a 'new creation', bears within it the sign of the Creator's presence, closeness, and love (518–519). The Word of God has become man: he shares his condition with us: he is everyone's brother. 'By his incarnation', the Second Vatican Council said, 'the Son of God is in some way united to every man' (521). And the face of Christ is encountered in even the lowliest of human beings (521, 1934). With regard to Christians, the actual demands of social life – solidarity and justice – are based on the conviction that everyone reflects the image of Christ (2407, 2419).

....

In conclusion, in order to safeguard the mystery of Jesus Christ, the God-Man, which stands at the heart of human and created realities, the Church of the first centuries, by means of long and

difficult debates, tried to clarify the doctrine of the Incarnation
(464–469). This is what is summarized in the formula of the Council of Nicaea: 'True God from true God, begotten, not made, of
one being with the Father.'

8. Christ's Death and Resurrection

*Faith in Christ, who died and rose, gives rise to scandal. This was already
true at the time of St Paul and remains true today: faith often encounters
scepticism and rejection. For some, Jesus' Resurrection seems to belong in
the realm of mythology. How can an event that challenges history and
especially a belief that defies the common experience of human destiny
be given any credit?*

Without disputing the fact that the very idea of resurrection
after death is unthinkable to many, the affirmation of Christ's
Resurrection nevertheless confers on the faith of Christians its
full dimension of truth and salvation. The Gospel is Good News
primarily because it proclaims, with Jesus Christ's Passion and
Resurrection, the victory of the Son of God over the powers of
death and forces of evil from which they arise. Many passages
of the *Catechism of the Catholic Church* (Part One, Section Two)
elaborate on Christ's Paschal mystery, which is presented in connection with the whole of Revelation to which this mystery provides the chief basis at the origin of the faith of the Christian
communities, as the apostolic preaching shows.

Understanding the death of Christ

The *Catechism* begins with this majestic witness: 'The Paschal
mystery of Christ's cross and Resurrection stands at the centre of
the Good News that the apostles, and the Church following them,
are to proclaim to the world' (571; see 422, 425, 638).

'God's saving plan was accomplished "once for all" by the
redemptive death of his Son Jesus Christ' (571).

'Everything in Jesus' life was a sign of his mystery' (515). The
Gospel accounts narrating the circumstances of his Passion and
death are particularly evocative of the sacrifice and sufferings
accepted by Christ 'for us men and for our salvation', as the Creed
says about the coming of God's Son in our flesh (456, 601).

Indeed, 'Jesus' violent death' must not be considered 'the result
of chance in an unfortunate coincidence of circumstances' (599).
On this subject, the *Catechism* takes pains to denounce the all-
too-persistent tradition that tries to impute the 'collective'
responsibility for Jesus' death to the Jews. Although certain Jews

were 'players' in his trial, all of them must not be included in a common reprobation (595–597).

Faith brings a different view: 'sinners were the authors and the ministers of all the sufferings that the divine Redeemer endured' (598). Christ died because of human sin. Many references to this teaching are found in the apostolic writings: 'He gave his life in ransom for the many' (*Matthew* 20:28). 'There is the Lamb of God who takes away the sins of the world' (*John* 1:29), the suffering servant prophesied by Isaiah (*Isaiah* 53:7). Thus St Paul could write: 'Christ has died for our sins in accordance with the Scriptures' (*I Corinthians* 15:3; 601; see 608, 602).

There is no greater test of love

There was nothing inevitable about Christ's death or the Passion that preceded it. Although he foresaw and foretold it to his disciples (554–557) as the hour to which 'he must come' (*John* 12: 27; see 607, 2605, 2746), he freely determined to go to Jerusalem, where his cross awaited him (557). He freely presented himself to his judges and to the violence of his executioners (609).

Christ made known the meaning of his death (609, 601): to 'give one's life' (*John* 15:15) is the supreme act of love. It is the absolute pledge of communion with the Father and of his submission to the Father's plan of salvation (606). Because he 'tasted death' (*Hebrews* 2:9), the Resurrection resulted from it (*Matthew* 16:21, *Luke* 24:26–27; see 554, 572, 624).

Thus Christ's death is 'both the Paschal sacrifice that accomplishes the definitive redemption of men ... and the sacrifice of the New Covenant, which restores man to communion with God' (613). 'In his suffering and death, his humanity became the free and perfect instrument of his divine love which desires the salvation of men' (609).

The central truth of the faith

The exceptional character of Christ's Passion and death acquires meaning only in connection with the event of the Resurrection. The same act of faith that accepts and understands that Christ 'died for our sins and was buried' also accepts and understands that he was raised 'on the third day' (*I Corinthians* 15:3–4). Without the assent of faith, Christ's Resurrection will also scandalize natural understanding. The *Catechism*, in its exposition of Christ's Resurrection, strives less to explain it than to show all that it represents for believers and for the Church.

The Resurrection is 'the crowning truth of our faith in Christ, believed and lived as the central truth by the first Christian community, handed on as fundamental by Tradition' (638).

The testimonies reported in the four Gospels and in the letters of the apostles mention the circumstances surrounding the Resurrection of Jesus Christ. The tomb found empty on Easter morning (640) and the appearances that marked the Lord's return (641) are the main facts that lend the Resurrection its historical credibility. Christ's Resurrection is 'a real event' (639, 1085) inscribed in history, but it also 'transcends and surpasses history' (647).

The apostles, the first witnesses to Christ's return, had to give evidence despite their doubt. They did not know how his passage from death to new life had occurred (647). Jesus' humanity, which they recognized, was the same, yet different: the same, because his body still bore traces of his Passion; different, because it was freed from the constraints of time and space (645). How could it not be clothed with the glory that shone forth on the day of his Transfiguration (555)?

At the heart of the Gospel proclamation

The overwhelming importance of Christ's Resurrection in the first proclamation of the Gospel message is well known. It is the nucleus of the apostles' preaching (642). The assurance of St Paul's observation is also well known: 'If Christ has not been raised, then our preaching is in vain and your faith is in vain' (*I Corinthians* 15:14) (651).

The Resurrection gives to Christ's mystery its definitive and decisive character. With the Lord's Ascension, which follows it, the Resurrection completes his saving mission to humanity and confirms 'all Christ's works and teachings' (651). He died for our sins and has been raised so that 'we might walk in newness of life' (*Romans* 6:4). This gift of divine grace, which St Paul calls our justification, is the fruit of the Paschal event (654, 1992, 1694–1695).

With the mystery of Christ, the mystery of the Holy Trinity is also revealed by the Resurrection. The Father's power is shown forth in his deliverance of Christ from the 'pains of death' (*Acts* 2:24). The working of the Holy Spirit 'gave life to Jesus' dead humanity and called it to the glorious state of Lordship' (648).

By his Ascension to the right hand of the Father, the risen Christ enters into the Father's glory with his humanity, which has become the source of grace and salvation for all (659, 1084). Jesus Christ is Lord: by his glorious humanity, he 'recapitulates' human history and all creation (668).

Finally, Christ's Resurrection affords to Christians no little assurance: their bodies, too, will be raised from the dead at the end of time (655, 989ff.).

A certainty for the Christian faith

Such is the importance of the Paschal mystery that it is not limited to providing a solid foundation for the certainties of faith: it motivates the Christian life, both in what it animates (654) and in what it celebrates (1067).

Baptism, which makes of each a 'member of the Body of Christ' (1267), gives the grace of belonging to 'him who died and rose for us' (1269). Faith is both lived out and witnessed to by those who possess an inner fidelity to the Spirit, who makes us share 'in Christ's Passion by dying to sin, and in his Resurrection by being born to a new life' (1988; see 729, 737, 1691, 1992).

Especially by celebrating the 'sacred *Triduum*' that ushers in the feast of Easter, the Church commemorates the mystery of Christ's death and Resurrection (624)

The Eucharist is the pre-eminent 'memorial' of 'the Lord's Passion and Resurrection' (1330; see 610, 611, 2643). Sunday, 'the Lord's Day' (2174), retains its significance as the day for the assembly of the faithful to celebrate this memorial (1166–1167).

If Christ's Resurrection is a stumbling block on the path leading to faith, it becomes for those who believe a certainty that clarifies and enlightens all that Revelation can express about the Christian mystery. In the doubting heart it elicits a trust in the invincible love of the Lord of hosts (Isaiah 9:7) that will grow in the inner self.

---

9. Speaking about the Holy Spirit

The Holy Spirit has no face. Is this the reason why he remains, too often, absent from Christian imagery? Despite the real renewal of interest in the Spirit stemming from spiritual movements in today's Church, catechesis and preaching still find it difficult to make the Holy Spirit a vital presence in the common faith of Christians. Is there a difficulty in speaking about the Spirit? Is his mystery so remote or abstract that it defies all language?

In order to forestall these difficulties, the Catechism devotes a number of passages to defining the Holy Spirit, his divine identity within the Trinity, his role in the history of salvation and his presence in the Church and in hearts of believers. This teaching, imbued with the Scripture and the best thought of the Fathers, leads us to conclude that the mystery of the Spirit gives Christianity its definitive uniqueness. Without this mystery, God's Revelation, our knowledge of Christ and the Church, the moral life and prayer of the baptized, and, indeed, the whole Creed itself is emptied of meaning.

The *Catechism*'s approach, as set forth here, relies on Christ's words to his apostles: 'When the Spirit of truth comes, he will lead you into all truth' (*John* 14:17) (243). It is first of all a matter of discerning the role of the Holy Spirit in understanding the four bases of the faith: the Trinitarian mystery, the Son's Incarnation, the Church's mission, and the interior experience of the believer.

The Revelation of the Trinity

'No one comprehends what is truly God's except the Spirit of God' (*I Corinthians* 2:11). This quotation from the Apostle Paul introduces the catechesis on the Holy Spirit (683, 687). He is the Paraclete foretold and promised by Christ to lead us 'into all truth'. The truth of God lies far beyond what human reason can describe, in the truth of the three persons of the Holy Trinity. And the Spirit must reveal this truth (684).

'The Spirit will not speak on his own' (*John* 16:13). The Spirit does not speak directly of himself; we do not hear him directly. 'We know him only in the movement by which he reveals the Word to us and disposes us to welcome him in faith' (687).

Thus the Spirit reveals himself in his work (688). He himself is the one who reveals the Word that tells forth the mystery of God (111). He is the author of the sacred books he inspired (105, 1100). He gives us to understand the Word (111, 1101). The Spirit disposes the believer to welcome the Word in faith (91, 92, 108) and to grow in it (94, 158).

Above all, the Holy Spirit is the Spirit of love who reveals the very being of God – love – that is the 'inmost secret' of the Trinity (221), in the exchange that unites the three persons (255). The Spirit makes known to us the whole truth about the mystery of God (152). The Spirit 'searches everything, even the depths of God' (*I Corinthians* 2:10).

....

If the Holy Spirit were removed from the field of faith, that would not only cut out one of the Creed's essential articles, but even remove the Trinity from the Christian view.

....

The mystery of Christ

'No one can call Jesus 'Lord' except in the Holy Spirit' (*I Corinthians* 12:3). 'It is the Holy Spirit who reveals to men who Jesus is' (152). Believing in Christ, the Son of God, is the work of the Spirit (153). Recognizing Christ as the Redeemer is also the work of the Spirit.

The Spirit was present at the saving event that was accomplished in Christ's life. He was 'sent to sanctify the womb of the Virgin Mary and divinely fecundate it, causing her to conceive the eternal Son of the Father' (485, 504–505, 690). Thus the Spirit conferred on Jesus the anointing that made him the Christ, sent to proclaim the Good News (486). The Spirit was present at Jesus' baptism (535); he led Christ into the desert (538) and onto the mountain to pray at his Transfiguration (555). Christ's Resurrection is the work of the Spirit (648).

If the Spirit were to be removed from Christ's life, the mystery of the Son of God would go with him. Christ would become a simple human figure of moral greatness and sacrifice.

The Body of Christ, which is the Church

The Church's title 'universal sacrament of salvation' (776) is justified because, the Holy Spirit is present and active in her, most especially in the sacraments she is sent to confer (1091–1092).

The Church has received from the Spirit the gifts that make her the Body of Christ (798). He assures her unity (813) and obtains for each of her members the spiritual gifts (767, 799, 951, 1830) that contribute to making the Church the Temple of the Holy Spirit (797).

And the Church has received from the Spirit, 'sent by the Father', the 'four characteristics' (811), the marks that define her: she is one (813), holy (828), catholic (830) and apostolic (861, 864).

The Holy Spirit, 'the Church's living memory' (1099), acts essentially in her through the liturgical action (1108) and the sacraments, in order to 'bring us into communion with Christ and so to form his Body' (1108). In the sacraments a presence and action is revealed that make the Church known 'in all truth' (1117). The forgiveness of sins and birth to a new life called to greatness by faith (1123) come from the Spirit. The seven sacraments, through the sacramental grace proper to each (1129), are the 'places' where the Spirit works in the hearts of believers in order to sanctify them, 'by uniting them in a living union with the only Son, the Saviour' (1129).

The gifts of the Spirit, 'many elements of sanctification and of truth, are found outside the visible confines of the Catholic Church' (819). At the crossroads where the separated Churches meet, scarred as they are by the wounds to unity, the Spirit is present and calls them to open the way to a return to unity (820).

If the Spirit were to be removed from the faith-giving vision of the Church, she would be no more than a social institution at the service of a religious system like any other, with her beliefs and rites emptied of every inner, significant dimension of the Body of Christ. The ecumenical enterprise would then lose all meaning.

'Live by the Spirit' (*Galatians* 5:16)

'By the power of the Spirit, God's children can bear much fruit' (736). Since they have become the 'Temple of the Holy Spirit', Christians are called to bear 'the fruit of the Spirit' (*Galatians* 5: 22). 'He enlightens and strengthens us to live as "children of light" (*Ephesians* 5:8)' (1695).

The Holy Spirit is 'the interior Master of life according to Christ', who 'inspires, guides, corrects and strengthens this life' (1697). 'The moral life of Christians is sustained by the gifts of the Holy Spirit' (1830). Each Christian, aware of his or her weakness, must follow the Spirit's 'calls to love what is good and shun evil' (1811).

The grace of the Holy Spirit has 'the power to justify us, that is, to cleanse us from our sins and to communicate to us "the righteousness of God"' (1987). Justification is the chief grace received in Baptism (1992).

'Infused by God', the theological virtues 'are the pledge of the presence and action of the Holy Spirit in the faculties of the human being' (1813). Faith is the first fruit of the Spirit (153–158). The hope that makes us await and desire the 'heritage of eternal life' (*Titus* 3:7) is the fruit of the desire inscribed in us by the Spirit (1817, 2541). Charity, or love, which is the new commandment, is the Holy Spirit's pre-eminent gift.

The Holy Spirit acts in us so as to harmonize our lives to the way taught and followed by Christ (1696). The Spirit maintains in our hearts a desire for moral perfection and a taste for virtue (2543). Thus the Spirit lies at the origin of the acts performed by disciples of the Gospel, who want to keep the commandments and to follow Christ (1724). The Spirit of God leads the Christian into the whole truth of the moral life.

The Master Within

Along with the gift that 'justifies and sanctifies us', together with the sacramental graces, the Spirit gives special graces, called charisms. They are 'at the service of charity which builds up the Church' (2003).

'The inner man' (*Ephesians* 3:16) is conceived in us by the interior Master (1995, 2672). But, like everything of the supernatural order, the action of the Spirit 'escapes our experience and cannot be known except by faith' (2005). We must use discernment in the evaluation of spiritual gifts, especially charisms. The Holy Spirit contributes to discernment by the gifts of wisdom and counsel (1831).

Discernment is equally necessary when the moral choice of the individual's conscience is confronted by delicate situations in which 'judgements are less assured and decision difficult' (1787). It is necessary in such cases to make use of 'the virtue of prudence, ... the advice of competent people and ... the help of the Holy Spirit' (1788).

Sometimes tempted to confuse the growth of the Kingdom of God with the progress of society, Christians need a process of discernment to help them understand that 'the Kingdom of God is justice, peace and joy in the Spirit' (*Romans* 14:17, see 2819–2820).

Discernment is the work of the Holy Spirit within us and is important on the spiritual level so that we do not confuse trial with temptation, and temptation itself with the consent given to it (2847). For this reason, spiritual direction, or companionship on one's journey, is justified (2690).

Finally, the 'Master within' (2672) is the one who inspires in us the filial confidence and love that impel us to cry out, 'Abba, Father!' (2766). How can Christian prayer not be the work of the Spirit, for it imitates Christ's prayer (2600), in all its forms (2625) and expressions (2658)? Moreover, we must pray to the Spirit in order to be helped and conformed to the desire he elicits (2670).

If the Holy Spirit were removed from the prayer and moral life of Christians, these would be no more than conformity and legalistic observance of external precepts. The moral life would become a moralism without enthusiasm and prayer a soulless ritual.

10. Does Faith Need the Church?

To live as a Christian without the Church, to believe in God without distraction, and especially without the distraction of the institution and rituals that all religion imposes – this idea is in the air today. If so, to be a believer would be to give oneself the freedom to be open to the Gospel without being constrained to follow the rules of a Church or to become a member of a community.

The teaching of the Church presented by the *Catechism* aims at justifying to Christians their membership in a social body: the community of his disciples willed by Christ. This membership, because it has its own logic, cannot be reconciled with a syncretism that, by abolishing the boundaries of all religions, tends to pour them all into the same mould. To do so would be to depart from fidelity to the Catholic faith as the biblical and ecclesial Tradition have presented it.

The *Catechism* testifies to the Church's social and communal aspect. It articulates its teaching around its two poles: communion, which assures the unity of the faith, and mission, which summons the Church to spread the Gospel. In order to guarantee the permanence of these two poles, the Church is hierarchically structured and claims for each of her members an active part in her own life and in her apostolic service in the world.

The sacrament of salvation

Although faith is 'a personal act', it is not an 'isolated act' (166, 781). Before being appropriated by a baptized person as his or her personal faith, it is already the faith professed by the Church (168). She is our Mother in the faith (169).

Revelation testifies that God's plan of salvation is intended for all humanity (50, 56, 776). But individuals are only included in this plan (781) by their membership in the People God has chosen: this is the reason for God's call to Abraham (60, 761–762).

The Church is the fulfilment of God's covenant with the People of Israel (763). The Church is the 'People of God', instituted by Christ (764–765) and clearly distinguished from 'all other religious, ethnic, political or cultural groups found in history' (782). The Church's identity is made clear in the marks or notes professed in the Creed: she is one, holy, catholic and apostolic (811).

Indeed, the Church, because she is the People of God of the New Covenant, possesses the three 'characters' that Christ, the Son of God, received in his anointing as Messiah. Because Christ is priest, prophet and king (783), the Church has a priestly voca-

tion to offer spiritual sacrifice (784), a prophetic duty to speak
the Word of God and bear witness to it (785), and a royal office
to assure the service of the Gospel in the world (786). The Church
exercises these three functions by the power of the Spirit who
lives and acts in her.

But all that the Church says and does, she says and does only in
the name of Jesus Christ, the one mediator (711). The Church
does not take Christ's place; she is only his 'instrument' (776, 738).

Thus, as the Second Vatican Council specified, the Church is
the 'sacrament – a sign and instrument, that is, of communion
with God and of unity' among all people (775).

The Church is communion

Not only is the Church 'gathered around' Christ, but she is also
'united in him' (789). Two expressions of St Paul help us understand this fact: the Church is Christ's 'Body' (791–795) and his
'Bride' (796).

The unity of the Body of which Christ is the Head establishes
a requirement of unity among the members of the Church, a
unity called communion and based first of all on the union of the
baptized with Christ (197, 787, 813–814, 2655).

Communion in the Church is accomplished by the presence
and action of the Holy Spirit (798, 1108), so much so that the
Fathers spoke of the Church as the place 'where the Spirit flourishes' (749). The Church is the Temple of the Spirit (797).

The bonds of unity that assure this communion are the following: one faith, one and the same sacramental liturgy, and the same
fidelity to apostolic succession (815, 830). Prayer is the privileged
expression of this communion (2565).

Here the question arises of the Catholic Church's relationship
with the other Christian confessions. The *Catechism* deals tactfully
with the 'wounds' to Christian unity (817) and acknowledges
'elements of sanctification and truth' in the other confessions. It
speaks of these elements as the work of the Spirit in them (819).
It also affirms that the 'call of the Spirit' impels us to work for
the reconciliation of the Churches and for their unity (820–822).

The Church is mission

The *Catechism*, in its first pages, points out the Word of God is
addressed to all people (74; see 759). From the beginning, the
task of proclaiming the Gospel has fallen to the Church (767, 776)
as her essential mission (851, 863).

Established in succession to the apostles, who were the first to preach the Gospel (857–860), the Church is catholic because she knows that 'she has been sent out by Christ on a mission to the whole of the human race' (831).

The Holy Spirit, by means of his gifts, assures the apostolic vitality of the Church and guides her 'on her missionary paths' (852).

The Church has a 'sacred right' to be missionary and to transmit the Gospel (848). The frequently misunderstood adage: 'Outside the Church there is no salvation' must be interpreted in this sense. Far from pronouncing exclusion (847), it signifies nothing more than a missionary dynamism at the service of the Gospel of salvation (845, 846, 851).

Moreover, in the wake of the Second Vatican Council, the *Catechism* takes pains to discern whatever 'goodness and truth' is to be found in non-Christian religions (839ff.) as 'a preparation for the Gospel' (843) that can lead to knowing the truth (851).

To build up the Church

In her constitution, the Church rests on the apostolic succession (857, 861–862), signified by the sacrament of Orders (1087, 1536). This sacrament confers on bishops the anointing of the Spirit that gives them the authority to exercise the three offices of sanctifying, teaching and ruling (1558), in union with 'the Pope, Bishop of Rome and Peter's successor' (882). Thus the bishops represent the 'hierarchy', in which priests (1536, 1554, 1562ff.) and deacons (1569–1570) also have a share at their respective levels.

But this ministry does not exclude the right of baptized lay people to exercise their own responsibility at the service of communion and mission in the Church (897). In the diversity of vocations and gifts (873), all participate in the Church's life and in her witness in society (872, 898, 900, 909, 912).

This responsibility of lay people is firmly established in the grace of baptism that allows them to share in the priestly dignity of the People of God (782, 901). Thus, there is a 'common priesthood of the faithful' (1268, 1547) that permits lay people to take part in catechesis (904), the liturgical celebration (901) and apostolic witness (905), in harmony with the initial experience of the community of Jerusalem (84, 949), as described in the *Acts of the Apostles* (*Acts* 2:42).

The laity exercise these responsibilities in the midst of local communities; it must be recognized that 'it is in these [communities] and formed out of them that the one and unique Catholic Church exists' (833).

It follows that every baptized person has the right and duty to be not only a partner in the faith, but also and especially a living and active member, enlivening the Church. We are born as Christians by Baptism, but we become Christians by our commitment in the midst of the People of God, which is the Church. It is a contradiction in terms to profess oneself to be a 'Christian' and yet to refuse to do what would justify this title.

11. The Question of Infallibility

Is infallibility a qualification, a privilege or an assurance? In the opinion of many, infallibility is surely one of the most misunderstood and confusing notions. What does the fact that the Pope is acknowledged by the faithful to be infallible add to his dignity and moral authority?

In a clear and calm style, the *Catechism* offers certain explanations in order to present a correct idea of papal infallibility. First of all, it recalls our human weakness in seeking and possessing the truth. It then shows how infallibility belongs first to God, to his Son Jesus Christ who came to bear witness to the truth (*John* 18: 37), and to the Spirit who leads us into all truth (*John* 16:13). It affirms that Christ willed to share his infallibility with his Church in all things concerning the truths contained in God's Word, which she is sent to transmit. Finally, it observes that the Church's infallibility precedes papal infallibility. For the service of the Word, the Pope, assisted by the Holy Spirit, has been declared infallible. The exercise of his teaching authority and its infallible expression are bound by certain conditions, which the *Catechism* clarifies.

God is the source of truth

People searching for truth, despite their desire for it and their openness to it (33), often remain powerless and weak in the use of their intelligence alone to know what surpasses human understanding (37).

Thus, we need a revelation in order to attain what Vatican I calls 'those religious and moral truths which of themselves are not beyond the grasp of human reason, so that even in the present condition of the human race, they can be known by all men with ease, with firm certainty and with no admixture of error' (38).

The infinite perfection of the mystery of God (41) cannot be understood apart from the attribute of truth that is its very being (215, 2465). Because God is truthful (2465), he can neither be deceived nor deceive us; therefore, believers can put faith in his Word (156). And so the source of all infallibility must be considered to reside in God.

This divine infallibility is reflected in the Son (217, 241), who 'came into the world to bear witness to the truth' (*John* 18:37). The Son's teaching is not his own, but belongs to him who sent him (*John* 7:16; see 427, 2471).

The Holy Spirit is the spirit of truth (*John* 14:17), sent to lead Christ's disciples into 'all truth' (*John* 16:13; see 91, 2466). The Spirit is present in the Church, most especially to assist her pastors in their ministry of transmitting and teaching the Word (857, 862).

The Church is endowed with infallibility

The Body of Christ, of which he is the Head, is infallible, because Christ willed to share with his Church (889) his own infallibility, less as a privilege than as an assurance that she cannot fail in transmitting the faith (890).

The Holy Spirit assists the Church in all her members so that, faithful in guarding the 'deposit of faith' (84), she may 'bear witness to God who is the truth and who wills the truth' (2464). The Spirit assists the pastors, the 'teachers of the faith' (1558), in the exercise of their prophetic office, identified with the mission of the *Magisterium* (94, 875). He likewise assists the faithful in maintaining the integrity of the faith they have received by giving their assent to the Word transmitted to them (91, 889).

Because faith is first of all knowledge of the truth of the revealed mystery, it needs to be expressed in words that translate it (40, 89). This is the reason for dogmas defined by the *Magisterium* of the bishops united with the Pope (77, 88). Dogmas are formulas of the faith deriving from the Church's Tradition (78), the 'living memory' of divine revelation (78). Dogmas are pledges of the Holy Spirit's assistance and guarantees of the Church's infallibility.

The personal infallibility of the Pope

On account of the primacy he exercises in the Church (881–882), the Bishop of Rome, successor of Peter, personally possesses infallibility in the exercise of his teaching office (891).

This papal infallibility must not be understood as the privilege of being assured of freedom from temptation and sin, or as a pledge of a superhuman superiority, or still less as the right to say and decide anything at all.

The Pope exercises his infallibility under certain precise conditions. Its object is limited to the field of faith and morals (891,

2035). It must also respect the prescribed forms: infallibility concerns solemn and public declarations, addressed to the whole Church (2035), as is designated by the expression *ex cathedra*, 'from the [papal] chair'. It must be said that the exercise of papal infallibility has been very rare. Since the definition of papal infallibility by the First Vatican Council, the Pope has only once made use of it, to define the Assumption of the Blessed Virgin Mary (966).

The Pope is not the only one who can proclaim a dogmatic definition. The bishops assembled in an ecumenical council, that is, gathered as representatives of the universal Church, also have infallible authority to define a truth of the faith (891). But they can only do so in union with the Pope and with his consent. This was the case at the First Vatican Council, which proclaimed the personal infallibility of the Bishop of Rome.

The ordinary *Magisterium*

The solemn or 'extraordinary' *Magisterium* described above must be distinguished from the 'ordinary' papal or episcopal *Magisterium*, so-called because it is exercised under the more ordinary forms of declarations or exhortation addressed, in particular circumstances, to the People of God. It belongs to the pastors of the Church to exercise the responsibility of teaching the faithful in order to affirm and educate their faith (892).

This ordinary *Magisterium* is exercised especially in terms of morality and the conduct of life in harmony with the Gospel (2032–2034).

On the concrete level of natural law (2036), the problems of justice (2246, 2420) and familial and sexual morality, critical opinion is often tempted to dispute the *Magisterium*. The Church refers Christians back to their consciences, assisted by the Holy Spirit, to accept and to give their filial assent (2040) to a teaching that aims only at conveying the challenges and moral obligations that flow from Baptism (2039).

....

Far from considering the charism of infallibility to be a sort of favour attached to the offices of Pope and bishop, it must be seen as a precaution given by the Lord to those whom he has called to serve his Church. The beautiful Byzantine prayer of priestly ordination, cited by the *Catechism* (1587), bears witness to this: 'Lord, fill with the gift of the Holy Spirit him whom you have deigned to raise to the rank of the priesthood, that he may be worthy to stand without reproach before your altar, to proclaim the Gospel of your kingdom, to fulfil the ministry of your word of truth.'

....

12. Power or Service in the Church

A persistent prejudice tends to consider the ordained ministers of the Catholic Church as possessing a hierarchical power too absolute not to seem domineering. Whether they are deacons or, especially, priests or bishops, their authority risks paralysing or applying the brakes on the presence and action of lay people who share in the life and mission of the Church.

The *Catechism* avoids all polemics. It holds resolutely to the apostolic succession and the sacrament of Orders, whose three degrees make up the Church's ministry. The power that flows from the sacrament has the sole purpose of serving the People of God. This consideration of the People of God is primary: it gathers all the baptized who share in the common priesthood of all the faithful in order to bear witness to their communion both in faith and in their mission to proclaim the Gospel. For a more exclusive service of the People of God, the Church sends those whom she has called and consecrated by the laying-on of hands. Their ministry is not so much a pledge of dignity or superiority as the fulfilment of a service.

The Church, the People of God

Let us recall briefly the essential elements of the section based on the *Catechism*'s teaching on Church, the People of God.[1] In Christ, who is the Father's 'yes' to his covenant promises to Israel (2 Corinthians 1:20), the Church is the People of the New Covenant (762).

The Church is called to carry out the three offices of Christ, who received his Messianic anointing from the Father (783). Christ is priest, prophet and king; his Church is invested with priestly, prophetic and royal offices (784ff.)

All members of the Church participate in these three functions (871, 1140, 1144). This vocational dignity is based on the grace and character of baptism (872, 900) and is shared by all members of the Church (872). It produces its fruits in the order of communion and mission by the action of the Holy Spirit who is present to the Church and acts in her (798).

Although all members of the Church take part in her communion and mission, they nevertheless exercise differentiated services (873). Christ chose the apostles to be the founders of communities (857, 860) and willed that they should designate their successors (861–862) by the laying-on of hands (1536, 1538).

[1] See above, 'Does faith need the Church?'

The lay faithful, although sharing their baptismal vocation, have different gifts and charisms at their disposal, each in his or her situation, in order to carry out their responsibilities in the Church (873).

Hierarchical order in the Church

By calling the Twelve, Christ himself instituted the apostolic college to which the college of bishops has succeeded (877). In doing so, he established the hierarchical order of his Church (874).

By the sacrament of Orders (875), the Church confers on those she calls to ministerial service (1585) the power to exercise the functions pertaining to the competence of the diaconate, the presbyterate or the episcopate. These are the three degrees of the sacrament (1536, 1554).

The highest degree is that of bishop (1555), who possesses what is called 'the fullness of the priesthood'. By right of this fullness, the bishop exercises a privileged role in transmitting the faith (888), administering the sacraments (893), and governing the People of God (894). 'Taking the place of Christ', the bishop is teacher, high priest and shepherd (1558, 1561).

The bishop has a direct and personal responsibility for the local (particular) church, whose shepherd he is (886, 1560). But as successor of the apostles, the bishop, in communion with the Bishop of Rome and the other bishops, has a responsibility, which is called 'collegial', towards the universal Church (1560).

The presbyterate or 'priesthood' is the second degree of the ministerial priesthood (1562). From ordination conferred by the bishop, priests receive a power that enables them to participate in the bishop's power. Like the bishop, whose 'support and instrument' they are (1567), the priests are entrusted with the tasks of teaching the Gospel, dispensing the sacraments and governing the People of God (1564) gathered in the territory of the local community (1567) committed to them. They are 'servants of forgiveness' through the sacrament of Reconciliation (1466) and the Anointing of the Sick (1516), and they preside at the Eucharist (1142).

Like the bishop, priests act in the name of Christ (*in persona Christi*); they share in 'the authority by which Christ builds up and sanctifies and rules his Body' (1563). Together they make up the diocesan *presbyterium*, united with the bishop by bonds of 'love and obedience' (1567).

'At the lower end of the hierarchy are to be found deacons, who receive the imposition of hands not unto the priesthood but unto the ministry' (1569). It is well known that the Second Vatican Council re-established the permanent diaconate, which may be conferred on married men (1571). The deacons carry out specific duties in the service of the People of God (875).

A vocation to service

Although the *Catechism* vigorously affirms the hierarchical structure of the Church and the power of those who have received the sacrament of Orders, it clearly identifies this power as a service of the People of God. This idea of service is present throughout the *Catechism*. Service is intrinsically connected with the ministry (876).

Thus, the ordained or ministerial priesthood is at the service of the baptismal priesthood (1120), that is, of the common priesthood of the faithful (1547). The power transmitted to ordained ministers is the power of Christ (1548), whose living image (1549) and icon (1142) they are, especially the bishops and priests.

Because they represent Christ, when ordained ministers celebrate, they also represent the Church, his Body (1553). It is therefore, first of all and fundamentally, a participation in the priesthood of Christ that is an entirely different thing from delegation from the community (1553, 1538).

It follows that ordained ministers must conform themselves to the model of the shepherd, which Christ revealed in the Gospel. This requirement is imposed first of all on the bishop (896), all of whose authority must be exercised in a 'spirit of service' (894); it is also imposed on priests (893) and deacons so that their ministry may be assimilated into Christ, the Servant of all (1570).

Because priests must exercise their ministry for the integral service (1579) of the People of God, they are chosen in the Latin Church from among believers who have a vocation to celibacy.[2] The Liturgy of the Hours, the divine office they pray each day, signifies both their union with Christ who prays in them and their care for the Church they are sent to serve (1175).

The presence and mission of lay people

Far from absolving lay people from all responsibility in the ecclesial community, the *Catechism* offers repeated references that should

---

[2] Because it operates at the magisterial level, which involves the Church's doctrinal teaching, the *Catechism* does not deal with the questions, so controversial today, of the ordination of married men or that of women. It only seeks to bear witness to the discipline of the sacrament of Order, inherited from the secular tradition of the Western Church, itself based on biblical revelation as it has always been interpreted.

motivate the presence and apostolic commitment of lay people (900, 913) through the common priesthood of the faithful (1120, 1547, 1545, 871–872, 904, 909).

As related above, the unity of the Body of Christ is accomplished in the harmony of gifts and charisms that differentiate its members (799, 800, 814, 897ff.). Thus the Church presents in this regard the appearance of an organism, even as St Paul describes it (790, 797).

The cohesion of the Body of Christ can be perfected only if the different functions that must be carried out in it (910–912) are respected. While the *Catechism* does not deal with the possible conflicts that may arise in Christian communities, it refuses to regard them as a mere rivalry between clerics and lay people for 'power'. Yet it is important to recall that everyone responds to his or her vocation (739) in personal union with Christ (893, 901) and with an inner docility to the Holy Spirit.

> In principle and in whatever forms its exercise by men of flesh and blood may take, ministerial service cannot oppose the vocation of the lay faithful to participate in the life and mission of their Church. But the idea must be excluded that, in order to foster the presence of responsible lay people, the Catholic Church should come to renounce her hierarchical constitution. She will never be a democracy in the sense that the exercise of power in the Church would be the result of delegation by means of voting, as it is in civil society. Although the procedure for designating people for certain responsibilities in the Church is sometimes by election, it is usually at a subordinate level and within the framework of hierarchical authority.

13. Mary in God's plan

Rather paradoxically, devotion to the Blessed Virgin Mary has caused division, not only among the Christian confessions, but also among Catholics themselves. Some think that one cannot do or say too much where Mary is concerned. Others have a tendency to maintain a certain reserve, indeed to justify in the name of faith the distance they keep from certain Marian devotions they suspect of nourishing a piety that is more sentimental than reflective.

Relying on the Scripture and the most ancient Tradition of the Church, Eastern as well as Western, the *Catechism of the Catholic Church* formulates the teachings that support Marian devotion. After mentioning the different forms this devotion has taken in the Church, the Catechism places them on the foundation of the Virgin's role in the whole plan of salvation, as Revelation has made it known. It cannot be denied that Mary occupies a privileged place in the fulfilment of Redemption and in the communion of saints.

Marian devotion in the Church

The Church's devotion to the Blessed Virgin is an intrinsic part of Christian worship (971). The *Catechism* quotes the declaration of Pope Paul VI that justifies the Marian feasts of the liturgical cycle (1172), the 'countless hymns and antiphons' dedicated to her (2675), and the privileged devotion of the *Rosary* (2676), which is 'an epitome of the whole Gospel' (971).

The *Catechism* offers two clarifications. On the one hand, although it is 'very special', Marian devotion 'differs essentially from the adoration which is given to the incarnate Word and equally to the Father and the Holy Spirit' (971). On the other hand, prayer to the Blessed Mother of God always remains centred 'on the person of Christ manifested in his mysteries' (2675). All that we believe about Mary is based on our faith in Christ (487).

The Virgin, perfect model of faith and holiness

The Second Vatican Council presented the Virgin's life as a 'pilgrimage of faith' (165). Following the Council's teaching, the *Catechism* begins its Marian teaching with the fact that gives Mary of Nazareth her privileged place among all creatures: 'her complete adherence to the Father's will, to his Son's redemptive work, and to every prompting of the Holy Spirit' (967). Thus, for the Church, Mary is the model of faith and love; she is the 'exemplary realization', the very type of the Church (967).

There are many references to Mary's life that make her absolute faith in the Word of God evident. Mary is 'she who believed' (*Luke* 1:45) in the word of the angel at the Incarnation (148, 273, 484, 494, 506). She is the one who remains a virgin in faith and accepts the promise of motherhood (506). Mary is the one whose faith, 'until her last ordeal, never wavered' (149).

Mary's prayer is entirely inspired by her faith. She gives voice to praise in the *Magnificat* (722, 2097, 2619). She asks for and obtains from Jesus his first miracle at Cana (2628). She is present with the apostles in the Upper Room: the Spirit is in her, as will be made clear at Pentecost (723, 726, 965, 2097).

Mary's absolute fidelity to the Word caused St Augustine to

say that 'Mary is more blessed because she embraces faith in Christ than because she conceives the flesh of Christ' (506).

'Full of grace', Mary is holy, endowed with a holiness that preserved her from sin (411) and grew in her throughout her life through her obedience to the Holy Spirit (722f.). She deserves the beautiful title *Panhagia*, the 'All-Holy', granted by the unchanging tradition of the Eastern Churches (493).

Thus Mary is the perfect model of what all the baptized are called to become (829, 2030). The beauty of holiness that the Church should radiate until the end of time is perfected in Mary (773, 972). The *Catechism*, following the Council, calls Mary 'the eschatological icon of the Church' (972).

The Mystery of Mary

By considering God's plan of redemption in all its fullness, faith allows us to comprehend the Virgin's singular destiny (487).

The early Church recognized Mary as the New Eve, preserved from the inherited stain of original sin and set apart by divine grace from all sin (411, 488, 493, 494). This privilege is articulated by the dogma of the Immaculate Conception.

But this privilege does not place the Virgin outside the universal sphere of redemption. Mary has received all that she is from Christ. She is the first to be redeemed by the blood of the cross (492).

In view of her divine motherhood, the Virgin was endowed, from her own conception, with the grace that sets her apart (488, 494). Because the one conceived in her flesh is 'the Father's eternal Son, the second person of the Holy Trinity, ... the Church confesses that Mary is truly "Mother of God", "*Theotokos*", according to the expression of the Eastern Churches' (495, 466).

After she had conceived Jesus by the power of the Holy Spirit, Mary remained a virgin. The *Catechism*, in several passages, tries to show how Mary's virginal conception of Jesus can only be understood in the light of the mystery of the Incarnation of God's Son. The virginal conception is 'the sign that it truly was the Son of God who came in a humanity like our own' (496). The vision of faith has allowed the Church to probe more deeply into the meaning of the Scriptures concerning the promise (497–498) and to grasp 'the mysterious reasons why God in his saving plan wanted his Son to be born of a virgin' (502).

In the same vision of faith that leads us to establish ties and connections among the truths of revelation, unifying the Christian mystery, the awareness of believers has grown since the beginning in the knowledge of the mystery of Mary. Among her Assumption, her virginal conception of Jesus, and her Immaculate Conception, there is a sort of common harmony: in her body and soul, the Virgin is free from sin. How could her earthly destiny not receive its perfect fulfilment in her Assumption (967)?

Anticipating the final Resurrection, the Virgin Mary, present in heaven and sharing the glory of the Father with the Son and the Spirit, is both the perfect image of the Church and her Mother, just as she is the mother of all in the order of grace (967). She is the mediatrix of our salvation, sharing in the unique mediation of the Redeemer from her place as a redeemed creature (970).

> The Marian doctrine professed by the Catholic Church does not result from an unwarranted intuition or an excessively exaggerated devotion to the Virgin. Rather, this doctrine attests to a real development of the faith that, since the early Church, has sought to understand what has been entrusted to the prayer and thought of believers by the Word that reveals the divine mystery, both in its unity and in its manifold relationships. The attentive and dispassionate study of this development should further ecumenical progress.

14. Being Born a Christian and Becoming One

Do the three sacraments of initiation, Baptism, Confirmation and Eucharist, conferred by the Church at the beginning of the Christian life, still make sense in our strongly secularized society? Although it is still customary to receive them, especially Baptism, a gap seems to be growing between the offer and the demand, that is, between the Church's offer of the sacrament and the understanding of those who request it. On the other hand, is it wise to confer Baptism on infants?

The *Catechism* does not aim to present specific rules and directives that derive for the most part from canon law and, in their application, from the pastoral judgement of those responsible for the Christian community. Therefore, it does not offer an immediate answer to questions such as those posed above. On this point, as on many others, the Catechism essentially restricts itself to making clear what the sacramental rites represent in the Church's tradition and discipline. It limits itself to presenting the doctrinal notes that contribute to pastoral discernment. There is today perhaps too great a tendency to consider the three sacraments of initiation only in relation to children. There is a risk in doing so of forgetting that the adult catechumenate lies at the origin of the Church's sacramental practice.

The sacraments of Christian initiation

The first three sacraments form part of the group of the seven sacraments (1113, 1210). The *Catechism* recalls that all the sacraments were willed by Christ (1114, 1127) to be instruments of his grace for nurturing and cultivating the Christian life at each of the stages or events experienced in the course of a human life (1210).

The sacraments of Christian initiation stand at the beginning of an existence lived out, from then on, under the sign of faith. They lay the foundations for such a life (1212). They are sacraments of beginning, whether they concern adults recently converted to the Gospel or children born of Christian parents (1229).

The sacraments of initiation, like the others, are not mere rites (1084, 1127–1128). Rather, they bear within themselves the most powerful symbolism of the Christian mystery (1086) that demands to be understood and received at the end of a period of catechesis, either of catechumens (1230, 1248, 1309) or of parents (2221) who request baptism for their child.

In reality, each of the three sacraments of initiation consists of a natural symbol appropriated to the spiritual reality it represents and signifies: water for Baptism (1213), chrism (perfumed oil) for Confirmation (1293), and bread and wine for the Eucharist (1333). Each of these signs speaks for itself and 'God speaks to us' through them (1147).

Sacraments are not only of a symbolic order, but they also accomplish what they signify. By the spoken word, a spiritual gift is conferred on those who receive the sacrament. This word, by the action of the Holy Spirit (1155), brings the specific sacramental form to the rite celebrated (1153). The Word makes the sacrament.

New birth

The Biblical symbolism of water is various (1217ff.). In its transparency, water is a sign of purity; in its violence, it is a sign of death; in its liveliness, it is a sign of renewal and life. All this symbolism is attached to the water of Baptism. By the words, '*I baptize you in the name of the Father and of the Son and of the Holy Spirit*', the baptized are purified and justified, transformed and renewed from within (1227).

The salvation of Jesus Christ operates in the soul. The stain of original sin, inherited from our first parents, is washed away (1263–1264). With the outpouring of the Spirit and the gifts of grace a new birth is brought about for a new life (1265–1266). Finally, the baptized are incorporated into the Church.

This entire inner change is a sign of the Lord's Passover, and also its fruit. Baptism makes us share in the mystery of Christ, who died for our sins and rose to new life (1227, 1262). The rite of immersing the baptized in the blessed water clearly illustrates this wholly spiritual passage from death to life (1214, 1239).

The importance of Baptism is understood precisely in terms of its meaning (1213, 1257). Baptism truly determines the Christian life, opens the way to evangelical faithfulness, qualifies the baptized to be active members of the Church (1270), sharing in the common priesthood of the faithful (1268) by reason of the indelible character that configures them to Christ (1272).

The necessity of Baptism is so fundamental that, in cases of absolute emergency, in the absence of an ordained minister, anyone can baptize, provided it is done with the intention of the Church and according to her rite (1256). Although Baptism is necessary for salvation, both the desire to be baptized ('Baptism of desire') and dying for the faith ('Baptism of blood) can be substituted for Baptism in water (1258ff.).

Here arises the problem of infant Baptism. For what reasons does the Church keep its tradition of baptizing the very young, who are not yet aware of or responsible for their decisions? These reasons are related to the confidence placed by the Church in the decision of the parents themselves (2220). It must be remembered that in apostolic times, new converts who chose to follow the 'way' were baptized together with their entire households (1251–1252).

The Baptism of little children is motivated only by the act of faith of parents who want to set their child on the way of salvation and grace from birth (1250, 2222, 2228). The child's whole developing existence is invested from the beginning with the presence of the Spirit. There is nothing magical about it. It demonstrates the realism of faith. The family is a 'domestic church': everything experienced within it is marked by faith (2204). 'The sheer gratuitousness of the grace of salvation is particularly manifest in infant Baptism' (1250).

Under the sign of the Spirit

Confirmation, the second sacrament of Christian initiation, although distinct from Baptism, is not separate from it. Confirmation prolongs Baptism and, as its name indicates, confirms it (1289).

Confirmation presents two peculiarities in the way it is conferred. First, it bears witness to the proper ministry of the bishop, because, on or before Holy Thursday, he consecrates the sacred chrism (1297), the instrument of the sacrament, and, in the Latin rite, is the ordinary minister of the sacrament (1313).[3] On the other hand, Confirmation illustrates the initiative Christ has left to his Church in the control of the administration of the sacraments. This is so because the rite of Confirmation has varied since the beginning (1288–1289) and two traditions, the Eastern and the Latin, have been established for the administration of the sacrament (1290ff.).

The essential rite is anointing with sacred chrism (1289, 1300), which follows the laying-on of hands (1288–1289). Chrism is a perfumed oil that symbolizes 'abundance and joy' as well as 'healing' and 'strength' (1293).

The words spoken by the minister are very simple: 'Be sealed with the Gift of the Holy Spirit' (1300).

Therefore the seal of the Holy Spirit, in a sense, is given to the soul of the confirmed by this sacrament (1295–1296). Confirmation bestows this gift in a definitive way; it cannot be repeated. The character imparted by Confirmation, like that of Baptism, is indelible (1304).

The fruits of the Spirit flow from Confirmation (1303): firmness in the faith, spiritual maturity (1308), fidelity and commitment to the Church, powerfully signified by the ministry of the bishop who confers the sacrament (1313).

The required age for Confirmation has varied in the Churches of the West (1307). In many countries, for pastoral reasons connected with religious development, it has seemed preferable to delay the sacrament until adolescence. It then becomes, for baptized young people, a choice they personally have to make. Beyond the rite itself, Confirmation is recognized as the sacrament of commitment.

Eucharistic Communion

The *Catechism* presents communion within the global framework of the Eucharistic liturgy, which is the subject of a separate section (see no. 16).

....

The sacraments of initiation 'equip' Christians to live in faith and to share their ecclesial commitment with others. 'It is more difficult to become a Christian when one already is, than to become a

---

[3] Second Vatican Council, Dogmatic Constitution on the Church, *Lumen Gentium*, 26: *originarius*.

Christian when one is not'. To be born into the faith is not all there is; it is only a beginning. A whole life is not enough to bear witness to our fidelity. The help of the Holy Spirit is necessary, for with the seal imparted in Baptism and Confirmation, the Spirit provides indispensable gifts for maintaining 'the obedience of faith' (*Romans* 16:26) throughout the course of our days.

15. Why the Sacraments?

Do we come to God by way of a personal journey, concerning only ourselves? Then why does the Church intervene in this encounter? She places herself between God and us by means of rites called sacraments. Don't the sacraments render faith something external and formalistic? What do they bring to the believer's journey?

The *Catechism* raises these questions and answers them even as it transcends them. First of all, it makes it clear that every religious journey relies on rituals. Moreover, it recalls that Christ himself gave the sacraments to the Church. Finally, it attests that Christ fulfils the promise of God's covenant with us through the sacraments. He continues to act in the Church by signifying through the sacraments the gifts of grace deriving from his Paschal mystery.

The sacraments of Christ

Although our religious journey is personal (27, 1779), it remains no less true that 'as a being at once body and spirit, man expresses and perceives spiritual realities through physical signs and symbols' (1146). 'We are body and spirit, and we experience the need to translate our feelings externally' (2702). 'The great religions of mankind witness' to this need (1149).

Man is also a 'social being; man needs signs and symbols to communicate with others ... The same holds true for his relationship with God' (1149). The Church's sacraments have a communal function, for they bind all the faithful to one another in common worship (1140–1141).

Christ willed the sacraments he established (1114, 1117, 1210) to be 'accessible to our human nature' (1084). Each sacrament is made up of a tangible reality, an element of the material world or of a gesture of social life (1145, 1148). Thus, the 'divine pedagogy' (1145) intended for what is visible to represent and to signify the invisible reality of the salvation of Jesus Christ (1148). 'The sacraments of the Church do not abolish but purify and integrate all the richness of the signs and symbols of the cosmos and of social life' (1210).

The seven sacraments in some way touch the whole of human existence. They were established by Christ (1113, 1114, 1117) so that we might benefit from them at all the stages and in all the different conditions of our lives (1210).

Some of the sacraments exist to establish the foundations of the Christian life (Baptism, Confirmation, and Eucharist); these are called sacraments of initiation. Others are for *healing* (Reconciliation and the Anointing of the Sick). Still others are for the 'service of communion and the mission of the faithful' (Orders and Marriage) (1210, 1212, 1421, 1534).

The sacraments of the Church

We can only understand the Church's sacraments by entering into the heart of the mystery of the covenant on which they are founded and which they themselves signify. This is the Paschal mystery, the mystery of Christ who, having accomplished our salvation by his death and Resurrection, remains present and living in the Church in order to act in her and to sanctify her members (1085, 1116, 1118).

The Church's liturgical action, which is carried out through the sacraments, is the work of the Holy Spirit whom the risen Christ gave to the apostles when he imparted to them his 'power of sanctifying' (1087). Thus the Spirit is the artisan of the sacraments (1091). 'The Spirit and the Church co-operate to manifest Christ and his work of salvation in the liturgy' (1099). As a result, the sacraments, especially the Eucharist, the 'source and summit of the Christian life' (1324), are the 'memorial of the mystery of salvation' (1099).

Faith does not consider the sacraments to be mere signs of the Paschal mystery they represent. It regards them also as pledges of the Lord's covenant and the efficacious instruments of his grace (1084). 'In them, Christ himself is at work' (1127). The Church is convinced that when she baptizes, Christ himself baptizes. Christ 'acts in his sacraments in order to communicate the grace that each sacrament signifies' (1127). The sacraments make Christ's grace present to believers 'independently of the personal holiness of the minister' (1128, 1584).

It must again be made clear that three of the sacraments not only transmit the Lord's grace but also confer a very particular anointing, what the Church calls an 'indelible character', because it marks out the Christian for ever (1121). These three sacraments are Baptism (1272–1273), Confirmation (1304–1305) and Orders (1581–1583).

In giving the sacraments a full development, the *Catechism* aims only at uncovering what must be considered the Church's sacramental universe. Because the sacraments are acts of Christ who acts in her, it can be affirmed in all truth that they make the Church (1118). Far from nourishing religious formalism, the sacraments are sacred rites at the service of the believer's most personal and innermost faith (1123). They make it grow and enter into the very heart of the paschal mystery of Jesus Christ. What would the Christian faith be if it were not first of all a way into that mystery?

16. Liturgy: More than Ritual

The celebrations and services of the Church unfold in such a universe of rite and word that the uninitiated may be tempted to regard them as mere ritual.

It must be acknowledged that the *Catechism* does not discuss liturgy under its simplest aspect. Far from reducing liturgy to a protocol of gestures and symbols, which would risk provoking a feeling of alienation in those who do not know their meaning, the *Catechism* broadens the believer's vision to include the horizon of the infinite in the liturgical action. The mystery of God himself is captured by the celebration. This mystery is revealed in the Lord's Passover. The liturgy contemplates it, meditates on it, sings it – in a word, celebrates this mystery. 'Through the liturgy Christ ... continues the work of our redemption in, with and through his Church' (1069–1070).

The *Catechism* seeks to make it clear that the liturgy places the Church in a state of vigilance. She concentrates on faith and prayer; she lets herself be guided by the Spirit to bear witness to the Father, in an attitude of adoration and praise, and to give thanks for the redemption and salvation accomplished by the Son. She thus unites herself to the praise of the glory of the heavenly Jerusalem and desires to wait in joyful hope for 'the new heavens and the new earth' (Revelation 21:1).

Heavenly liturgy and celebration

The Church's liturgy, in heaven or on earth, is entirely the celebration of the salvation accomplished by Christ in the mystery of his death and Resurrection (1076, 1082, 1085, 1104, 2655).

The sacrifice of the Son accomplishes this work of redemption and salvation, in obedience to the Father's will, and is followed by the sending of the Spirit (1092).

One cannot fail to be struck by the *Catechism*'s many references to the heavenly liturgy (1107, 1186, 1130, 1325, 1329, 1344, 1370, 1402, 1409). The angels and saints in heaven sing the hymn of praise and thanksgiving to the three persons of the Trinity. The earthly liturgy of the Church must be viewed in relation to the liturgy of the 'holy city of Jerusalem' (1090).

The liturgy celebrated by the faithful is a 'foretaste' of the liturgy of heaven (1090). This fact gives our celebrations their spirit and meaning.

Indeed, the spirit and meaning of our liturgies, sacramental or Eucharistic, must be sought in praise (2639) and thanksgiving (2637) for the blessings received from the Father who 'has blessed us in his Son, in order to give us the Spirit of filial adoption' (1110; see 1077–1081). Christian worship is first of all a movement of adoration (2626), which turns our hearts towards the Father for his infinite greatness and goodness shown forth through all his benefits, and above all for the grace of the salvation won for us by his Son's Passover (1082, 1088).

The movement of homage we make through the 'offering of his own gifts' is joined to this movement of adoration of the Father. By means of this offering, we ask the Father to send the Holy Spirit, so that he may produce the fruits of a life devoted 'to the praise and glory of his grace' (*Ephesians* 1:6), in communion with Christ the High Priest.

The liturgical celebration

Every celebration takes place in the time of the Church, that 'new era' ushered in by the 'gift of the Spirit' for the 'dispensation of the mystery' (1076). Christ lives and acts in the Church through the sacraments, in the 'sacramental economy' that aims only at dispensing the fruits of the Paschal mystery (1076).

The whole community, the Body of Christ united with its Head, celebrates the liturgy (1140, 1144). By virtue of their common priesthood, all the baptized take part in the celebration (1141). But they do not all have the same function, Some of them are ordained so that they can act in the person of Christ for the service of all (1142); thus, the liturgical life is structured (1087).

In every celebration are encountered signs and symbols that express 'the divine pedagogy of salvation' (1145). Signs in the human world (1146), natural symbols connected with the cosmos (1147) or with the realities of social life (1148), signs of the covenant and of the events of Biblical history (1150), and, above all,

Gospel signs recognized in the life of Christ (1151), all enter into the vast concert of liturgical and sacramental symbolism (1152).

If the liturgy is gesture deployed by visible physical rites, it is also word, in as much as the Word of God is present to accompany the rites and to elicit the response of faith (1154). In the sacraments, the importance of the word that effects and accomplishes the spiritual fruit signified by the symbol (1155) is made known.

The liturgical action, because it takes place in the time of the Church (1163ff.), which is also the time of humanity, unfolds in keeping with the rhythm of seasons and days that make up the liturgical year (1168), culminating with the Easter Triduum (1168–1169). Sunday, 'the Lord's Day', stands out as especially significant (1166, 1343, 2177).

The liturgical action needs a place of worship (1180). A church is a house of prayer and a house of the Father's children, because it is the house of God (1181, 1186, 2179).

The celebration is structured around the Liturgy of the Word and the Liturgy of the Eucharist (1346–1347). Each follows a ritual whose course belongs to the most ancient tradition and whose 'substance' cannot be modified (1356, 1205). Together, Word and Eucharist constitute 'one single act of worship' (1346).

It must be deduced from this that the Eucharistic celebration, our Mass, is not something to be invented anew. It is received from the Church. If there can be different styles of celebration, the structure of the Mass must remain the same, in harmony with the norms established by a long tradition.

Another fact is that before being shared, Christian liturgy is praise and thanksgiving. The movement of acknowledgement of the gifts of God precedes the movement of encountering God and 'exchanging gifts' with him.

The memorial and the sacrifice

The Eucharist, which completes Christian initiation, is, as the Second Vatican Council attests, 'the source and summit of the Christian life'. In the Eucharist 'is contained the whole spiritual treasure of the Church, namely Christ himself, our Pasch' (1322–1324, 2771–2772).

This fullness of meaning attached to the Eucharist is revealed in the richness of vocabulary designating it. Each designation opens a new perspective on the 'mystery of faith' (1328–1332).

Bread and wine are the signs of the sacrament (1333) instituted by Christ at the Last Supper, at the time of the Passover, in memory of his death and Resurrection (1337–1339) and of his intercession for 'his own' in the presence of the Father (1341).

Thus, Christ gave his own definitive meaning to the Jewish Passover, inaugurated the new Passover, and proclaimed the Church's final Passover (1341, 1343). The whole Paschal mystery is present in the Eucharistic memorial.

The Eucharist is not only a memorial; it is also a sacrifice. Or rather, because it is a memorial, it is a sacrifice (1365). 'When the Church celebrates the Eucharist, she commemorates Christ's Passover, and it is made present: the sacrifice Christ offered once for all on the cross remains ever present' (1364, 1366).

It must be understood that the sacrifice of Christ and the sacrifice of the Eucharist are one and the same sacrifice. Only the manner of offering is different: bloody on the cross, unbloody on the altar (1367). And the Eucharist is no less the sacrifice of the Church, because she is united with Christ in his self-offering to the Father. The Eucharist makes present again today the sacrifice of the cross (1368–1369).

The sacrament of the presence

The 'real' presence of Christ under the 'species' of bread and wine consecrated on the altar by the priest is assuredly one of the greatest difficulties of the faith. The purest faith says 'yes' to it, with the sole assurance that it is hearing and welcoming the Lord's words (1381). Indeed, the resistance and dispute among the disciples of Jesus at the first announcement of the 'bread of life' is well known (1332).

We must therefore return to the words of the Lord that fulfil the promise: 'This is my body which will be given up for you' (1374). 'It is by the conversion of the bread and wine into Christ's body and blood that Christ becomes present in this sacrament' (1375). This 'realism' of Christ's substantial presence in the Eucharist guarantees the word that brings about the change designated by the rather technical term 'transubstantiation' (1376).

This change is accomplished today in the Eucharistic celebration by the action of the Holy Spirit, present to the Church, as he is for all the sacraments (1375). The prayer of *epiclesis*, before the consecration of the bread and wine, has the specific purpose of asking the Father to send the Spirit to effect the change (1353).

By reason of Christ's substantial presence, the Eucharist is the greatest of the sacraments (1374). It is received by the faithful in communion, whose spiritual fruits are listed by the *Catechism* (1391–1398).

Among all these effects, the unity of the Body of Christ (1396) and commitment to the poor (1397) must be recalled in particular. The realism of faith appeals to the realism of charity. In all truth, we celebrate the Eucharist in order to 'make' the Church (1396).

> So great is the importance of the Eucharistic inheritance Christ has bequeathed to his Church that, paraphrasing St John in concluding his Gospel, we may say, 'There are, in this sacrament, many other aspects that are not written here. But these are written so that you may come to believe that Jesus is the Messiah, the Son of God and that through believing you may have life in his name' (*John* 20:30).

17. The Divided Self

Who has not experienced being torn between desiring to do what is good and being tempted to do what is evil? The drama of the human conscience lies in living out this contradiction, of which St Paul writes in Romans 7:19. The nobility of our consciences lies in their judgement of our free choices. Why does the Church classify as sin what is evil in the eyes of conscience? How does the faith she proposes explain this presence of evil in the human heart?

The *Catechism* often returns to the dignity and greatness of the human person, 'created in the image and likeness of God', the Creator (1700). It also recalls that the freedom with which each person is endowed (1705, 1730) conveys to everyone the power to be, so to speak, 'the father of his acts' (1749), for better or worse (1732, 1776ff.).

The *Catechism* recalls, too, that a moral conscience exists in every person, as the 'voice of God' (1706) that judges the conduct of each, in order to make known what is good and what is evil.

The *Catechism* also clarifies that what the human conscience judges to be sin, the Christian faith recognizes as sin, that is, an 'offence against God' (1850).

Finally, faced with a picture of humanity that, at all times and everywhere in the world, reveals the universality of sin, the *Catechism* affirms the Christian vision that recognizes in every actual sin the consequence of a sin at the very origin of our creation (1707, 1739).

The reality of sin

Because we are endowed with freedom (1731), and are 'fathers' of our acts, we enter into the realm of morality: we are 'moral subjects' (1749). We are responsible for our conduct (1734). In order to determine if an act is right or wrong, we must take into account its nature, our intention and the circumstances surrounding it (1750ff.)

When we do so, it is proper for us to exclude acts that, by their very nature, are morally unworthy of us and reprehensible in and of themselves (1756).

What conscience considers a fault that 'wounds' human nature (1849), faith considers a sin. For sin is 'an offence against God, ... disobedience, a revolt against God' (1440, 1850). Thus it is not enough for Christians to admit guilt, but they must also acknowledge that they are sinners before God. In this way the call to conversion is discovered, 'which requires convincing of sin' and 'includes the interior judgement of conscience' (1848).

There exists a great diversity of sins (1852). The Tradition of the Church has established the distinction between mortal and venial sin. Mortal sin turns us radically away from God and 'destroys charity in the heart' (1855). Venial sin 'does not break the covenant with God' but does display 'a disordered affection for created goods' (1863).

Because certain vices are contrary to the evangelical virtues and can give rise to many moral faults, they are called 'capital sins' (1866).

It is appropriate to note here that the *Catechism of the Catholic Church* never mentions sin without referring at the same time to forgiveness and mercy (1846, 1851). Only God forgives sins (1440). 'Slow to anger and abounding in steadfast love', God always offers his forgiveness (1846, 1851). The call to conversion (1428, 1430) disposes us to receive the 'sacrament of forgiveness' that Christ instituted for the reconciliation of sinners (1444). By giving his apostles the 'power of the keys' (982), Jesus entrusted this ministry to his Church. Therefore, 'reconciliation with the Church is inseparable from reconciliation with God' (1445).

Finally, the role of prayer in purifying the heart and seeking pardon from God must not be forgotten. This is the purpose of the fifth petition of the 'Our Father' (2631, 2838–2839).

The origin of sin

The experience of sin is so universal (386, 401, 408) in the history of humanity as a whole and of each person in particular that an explanation common to the human species must be presumed. From the revelation transmitted by the Church, believers possess a certain knowledge of human origins that must be properly understood: the doctrine of original sin (385–412).

The *Catechism* is not lacking in realism when, in several places, it refers to the 'drama of sin' (309). It observes that 'the human heart is heavy and hardened' (1432). It bears witness that 'angels and men, as intelligent and free creatures . . . can go astray. Indeed, they have sinned' (311). 'The world is virtually inundated by sin' (401).

Above all, the *Catechism* tries to establish the conviction that the origin of sin cannot be understood outside of Revelation (387). Universal salvation in Christ has made clear the universal presence of sin; 'we cannot tamper with the revelation of original sin without undermining the mystery of Christ' (389).

The *Catechism* makes a number of references to the 'figurative language' of the Bible in the book of *Genesis* (390). It clarifies the meaning of this kind of language by showing first of all that sin, from the origin, has been a test of freedom (396).

After discussing the 'fall of the angels' and the power of death, which is attributed to Satan (394–395), the *Catechism* shows us of what, essentially, the first human sin consisted: 'man preferred himself to God; he chose himself over and against God' (398).

'Adam and Eve committed a personal sin, but this sin affected the human nature that they would then transmit in a fallen state' (404). Original sin would henceforth be a sin 'contracted' and not 'committed'. It is 'a state and not an act' (404).

It must be understood that 'original sin does not have the character of a personal fault in any of Adam's descendants.' It is 'a deprivation', but 'human nature has not been totally corrupted' (405). In spite of sin, every human being remains beloved by God, 'who desires everyone to be saved' (*I Timothy* 2:4).

The first effect of Baptism, a new birth, is to remove what must be called the stain of original sin (981, 1263). Yet Baptism does not suppress the need for Christians, with the help of divine grace, to master their passions, the marks in us of our 'wounded nature' (409, 1264, 2515). This is the whole meaning of the phrase 'spiritual struggle' (2516).

....

Ultimately, the problem of original sin in its totality cannot be clarified except in the light of Revelation as a whole. 'There is not a single aspect of the Christian message that is not in part an answer to the question of evil' (309).

....

18. Christian Morality, Human Morality

On what basis and by what right does the Catholic Church, when she articulates the moral law, presume to include all humanity under this law? Isn't the morality she proclaims intended only for the faithful and not for all people in general? Isn't a universal ethic of human rights sufficient for our secular society?

If the Church arrogated to herself a monopoly on morality, coercing consciences to follow her, such presumption would indeed be unbearable. But the Church possesses, from divine revelation, a very high conception of human dignity. From Christ, who knew 'what was in everyone' (*John* 2:25), the Church also knows that there exists in every human being a call to the good that is continually fragmented and thwarted by the attraction of evil. In order to help each person in the conduct of his or her life, the Church, teaching the faithful the principles and obligations of the moral life, cannot help but challenge humanity's conscience. In the *Catechism*, there are more references to human dignity than to anything else. The *Catechism* affirms the basis for that dignity and defines its characteristics and the rights derived from it. It derives from it the moral obligations for the conduct of individuals, society and those who govern it.

The basis of human dignity

Human dignity comes primarily from the nature of the person, who is a rational being, made up of a body and a soul (365, 1703).

Endowed with freedom (1705), people are responsible (1731), the 'fathers' of their acts (1734). Our free will gives us autonomy: we are 'somebodies' (357).

Our freedom gives us an aptitude for choosing good or evil (1732). It makes us moral subjects (1749). The practice of the moral life testifies to the dignity of the human person (1706).

Conscience is the 'most secret core' in everyone (1776). Conscience expresses the judgement of reason, which recognizes the moral quality of personal acts (1778).

This vision of humanity, recalled many times by the *Catechism*, expresses the wisdom of Christian humanism (1676). It confidently accepts the wisdom of all the political and cultural thought valued by the modern world of human rights. Long before the philosophy of the Enlightenment, which saw the emergence of such rights, the Church had always proclaimed the eminent dignity of the human person. The Church bases this dignity on the Word of God, which reveals human origins: we are 'created in the image and likeness of God' (27, 355).

Our immortal souls, created immediately by God (366), are open to the desire for God. 'Only in God' will we 'find the truth and happiness' for which we never stop searching (27). The most sublime aspect of our dignity lies in our knowing that we are 'religious beings' (28).

The human body shares in the dignity of God's image (364). Thanks to the spiritual soul, the material body is a human and living body: the union of body and soul forms a single human nature (365).

The Second Vatican Council expressed the most significant Christian thought about the human person, 'the only creature on earth that God willed for its own sake' (356).

Claims and rights

Human dignity is universal (1934). It has no frontiers. It belongs to all people (1676), because God's image is in everyone (1702). 'Equal natural dignity implies a universal common good' (1911). 'The human race forms a unity' (360), with the result that 'all men are truly brethren' (361) and this demands solidarity, since 'the goods of creation are destined for the whole human race' (2402).

More particularly, man and woman possess equal dignity: on the one hand, they share a 'perfect equality as human persons, on the other, in their respective beings as man and woman' (369, 1645, 2203, 2334–2335, 2387).

One's own dignity implies fundamental rights for all people, indispensable for their personal existence (1935, 1956) and for their social life (1906). The equality of all people also rests on these fundamental rights (1906).

Because the human person is 'the principle, the subject and the end of all social institutions' (1881, 1929), his or her rights are prior to society and are indispensable to it (1940, 2426). The moral legitimacy of authority is based on them (1930).

In particular, the right to exercise freedom, especially in moral and religious matters, is 'inseparable' from human dignity (1738, see 2106–2108).

Moral obligations and rules

The body of moral obligations and rules, set out in the third part of the *Catechism*, is entirely derived from its consideration of the human person and of his or her dignity and vocation (2070).

This body of moral teaching is contained in the Ten Commandments of God (the Decalogue), which articulate the Lord's demands on the People of Israel to be faithful to the Word of the Covenant (2056)

Expressed most often in the form of prohibitions, the commandments indicate the limits of the path we must follow so as not to deviate from the order of creation (2057). In this sense, we may speak of a natural law (2070) as the reflection of the divine law (1955).

The honour and dignity of the human person are always the purpose of the precepts contained in the Decalogue. They appeal to the conscience of everyone who has the choice between what is good and what is evil (1777), what accords with human dignity and what does not (1956, 1959).

Thus the obligations and duties of whoever wants to live up to human greatness must be understood. These include respect for human life (2261–2267), the demands of social justice (1929, 2426ff.), sexual moderation and fidelity in love (2334ff.), integrity in relation to the well-being of others (2407ff.), the use of the goods of creation and the duty to do and speak the truth (2467ff.)

One of the major precepts underlying the others is the one that commands us to avoid doing to others what we would not want done to ourselves. This is the ancients' Golden Rule, recalled four times by the *Catechism* (1931, 1789, 1970, 2407).

Solidarity also has an international dimension: rich countries have a duty towards those who have not yet emerged from a state of underdevelopment (1911, 2437ff.).

All civil authorities have responsibilities incumbent upon them. They must guarantee the common good, in particular by respecting the rights of persons (1907, 1959, 2237), especially the rights to freedom of conscience and religious liberty.

People's moral endeavour carried out in the midst of life's realities signifies the accomplishment of their destiny at the very level of their personal dignity (1955). This is the logic of the ethic of human rights.

In terms of faith, this dynamic of the moral life challenges our human nature fragmented by sin. The moral life can only be upheld and can only await what it hopes for, if the Gospel is heard and recourse is had to divine grace and the help of the Holy Spirit (1960). Here is the specific contribution of Christian morality.

....

It does not follow from the fact that the Church has received her own vision of humanity from the Word of God that her moral teaching departs radically from the ethic of human rights. For both, there is the same consideration of human dignity, the same

requirement of respect for the most fundamental rights (2246).
But the Church prescribes a morality that comes from on high
and goes farther than human wisdom. In bearing witness to it,
the Church does not coerce consciences, nor does she oppose the
humanistic rules of our secular societies. She proclaims a Gospel
that regards love as the 'perfection of the law' (2196). Thus, while
the Church respects the ethic of human rights, she transcends its
demands. She strengthens it by exercising a 'prophetic function'
(2036) in affirming that only that which surpasses humanity really
corresponds to it.[4]

19. Can the Virtuous Save Themselves?

*In many areas of existence, the individualism of today inclines us to solve
our own problems by ourselves. On the moral and religious planes, we
also think that we are sufficient unto ourselves. We all have consciences
and presume that our own intentions are pure. What need do we have
for the help that the Church says is supernatural and calls 'grace'?*

Voluntarism in religious and moral matters has always been a
factor. This temptation is called 'Pelagianism' after the fourth-
century monk who affirmed the human power to attain perfection
and to achieve salvation without any help other than the firmness
of our characters and the bending of our wills to virtuous effort.
The Church has always reacted against this claim, which excludes
divine grace from the field of the moral and spiritual lives of
Christians. She has held fast to the Lord's words: 'Without me
you can do nothing' (*John* 15:5). The *Catechism of the Catholic
Church* develops three teachings: the limitations of our human
nature for doing good, the help of grace won for us by Christ's
redemption, and God's presence in the faithful hearts of believers,
in solidarity with their brothers and sisters in the Church.

Wounded and vulnerable humanity

As recalled above in the section 'The divided self,' faith has a
realistic vision of humanity and its earthly condition. This vision
recognizes both our greatness (355ff.) and our vocation (1730,
1719). It also testifies to our fragility and our limitations (1739),
neither overvaluing our dignity nor showing any tendency to
grovel in the face of our human weaknesses.

[4] Cf. German Bishop's Conference: *The Church's Confession of Faith: A Catholic Catechism for Adults* (San Francisco: Ignatius Press, 1987) p.39

Humanity's experience of sin is universal (386, 1860). Conscience always struggles with the choice between good and evil (1732). It is sometimes exposed to difficult choices; virtue and a sense of moral obligation stumble over conflicts of duties (1787–1788).

The Word of God reveals that we live with sin, and makes clear its malice and perversity. The Gospel denounces the Pharisaic attitude that shuns the truth about ourselves, which the judgement of our consciences has disclosed.

Faith calls us to a conversion of the heart (1427–1428). In struggling against evil instincts (1723), believers are renewed within by a 'new heart' (1433). This 'endeavour of conversion is not just a human work' (1428).

Interior change is the fruit of that divine help called 'grace' and of our human freedom (1742); grace makes virtue grow within us (1810) by the assistance it brings.

Welcoming God's gift

'Salvation comes from God alone' (169). Because 'God is love' (1 John 4:8; see 221, 753), he, 'from the fullness of his love, addresses men as his friends ... in order to invite and receive them into his own company' (142).

Salvation is the work of the whole Trinity (258). 'The Father did not send his Son into the world to condemn the world, but so that the world might be saved through him' (John 3:16). By his glorious cross, the Son has won for us the fruits of the grace of redemption (605, 654). The Holy Spirit is present in the believer's soul and works through the gifts of the Spirit (734–736).

God's first gift to humanity is his creation (295, 299).

God also bestows the gift of his Word on the human race. The Word reveals God's plan of love on our behalf and makes us hear the call of our vocation (1701, 1719). Speaking to our hearts by the inner voice of conscience (1776), the Word of God helps us to know him in truth (387) and to ponder the weight of the earthly goods that hinder us on the way marked out by the Beatitudes (1723).

God's gift is the living water of grace revealed to the Samaritan woman (John 4:10; see 2559). Welcomed in faith and received in the sacraments, this grace produces the work of justification (1987–1996). This rather technical word is intended to signify a very simple reality: the conformity of our being and behaviour with God's justice, that is, his holiness (1991).

This grace of justification was won for us by the Passover of

Jesus Christ (1741), the Saviour of the world (601, 654). It makes the Holy Spirit present within us to fulfil, by his gifts (1830), our vocation as the Father's sons and daughters in the wake of Christ, the first-born Son (736).

'The grace of Christ is not in the slightest way a rival of our freedom' (1742). There is a kind of interplay, or synergy, between human freedom and divine grace. Freedom tests itself in order to attain what is good; grace liberates and purifies it, elevates and sanctifies it. The 'interior Master', the Spirit, is at work within us (1995).

The practice of the human virtues enters into this interior dynamic movement led by the Holy Spirit (1810). 'Moral balance', so difficult to achieve and maintain, gains confidence in the gift of the Spirit (1811).

Yet the *Catechism* warns against the idea that we can be saved by wisdom apart from faith ('illuminism'). Because grace is of a supernatural order, it 'escapes our experience and cannot be known except by faith' (2005). It is enough for Christians to remember Christ's words, 'By their fruit you shall know them' (*Matthew* 7:20), to consider that grace is present in themselves and in the lives of all the faithful, especially the saints (2005).

Nothing is virtuous in or by itself

The teachings collected in the *Catechism* have shown sufficiently that our efforts to lead a moral life need the interior co-operation of divine grace in order for us to remain faithful to the Gospel and to grow in wisdom and virtue.

Faith itself is a free gift of the Lord (162). It needs to be affirmed by prayer and hearing the Word.

Continuity in faith has a price, the spiritual battle that frees us from the weight of sin (409) and the obstacles encountered in prayer (2725). An inner openness to the Holy Spirit makes present within us an 'ever more intimate union with Christ' (2014).

Personal prayer acquires all its importance here (2697), since through it, each person is responsive and obedient to the Father's will as his son or daughter (2610).

If Christians cannot feel personal self-satisfaction in the accomplishment of their salvation, they also cannot separate themselves from all that the community of believers gathered in the Church brings to them (2655).

Everyone needs others (1936). This need, which is part of human nature, is equally true for Christ's disciples (781).

'Faith is a personal act' (166), since we are baptized individually and are individually responsible for our conduct and actions, for which we will be judged individually (2158, 1022). Nevertheless, we receive the Word of God, which stands at the origin of our faith, from and by the Church (875, 2). We receive the sacraments, which convey Christ's grace and the life of the Spirit (1118, 2030), from and by the Church. In the Church, we celebrate the Eucharist, which signifies the unity of the People of God (1141) on pilgrimage towards the heavenly Jerusalem, where the saints and angels gather together (757, 1138, 2788).

Because of this solidarity of grace and vocation, Christ taught his disciples to pray 'Our Father, who art in heaven' (2792). These words express that sharing in spiritual goods that the Church calls 'the communion of saints' (949).

From beginning to end, the Christian's spiritual experience rests on the conviction that God himself is its beginning, its cause and its end. We must pray as if everything depended on him and act as if everything depended on us (2834). St Augustine replied to the monk Pelagius with this prayer: 'Lord, command me what you will, but give me what you command.' For it is true that, in the Christian life, all is grace.

20. Seeing My Brother and Sister in Everyone

What does the Gospel message of love for others have to say to a contradictory society such as ours, which excludes people even as it asserts human rights?

We must recall certain powerful affirmations, often repeated in the *Catechism* concerning human dignity and the vulnerability that stems from sin, the natural equality of all and the violence that divides us, our fundamental and universal rights and the disparities that produce injustice.[5] The *Catechism* presents the most specific and most essential elements of the Gospel's demand for Christians to love one another. It emphasizes the connection between the command to love and the duty of justice. It develops the consequences of this connection for human relations and its implications for the amendment of morals and the conduct of each person.

The 'sacrament' of brotherhood

In many passages in which the *Catechism* discusses the love of

[5] See in particular the sections above: 'The divided self', 'Christian morality, human morality' and 'Can the virtuous save themselves?'

neighbour, it associates it with the demand for justice (2401, 2479, 2820, 2487). The two virtues are connected with each other (1889).

The virtue of justice (1807) governs obligations founded on the equality of all (360, 1878, 1934), the universal destination of the goods of creation (2402ff.), and the personal integrity (357, 1930) that belongs to everyone.[6] 'All men are truly brethren' (361).

Charity, the greatest virtue (1822, 1827), creates the obligation to love one's neighbour. Each Christian must become 'a neighbour to others' (1932). The commandment to love one's neighbour is parallel to the commandment to love God (1878, 2196). Love accomplishes (2196) the 'perfection of the law' (*Romans* 13:10).

The seven final commandments of the Decalogue summarize our obligations as regards to our love of others (2055).

Fraternal charity excludes no one. Following the example of the Lord, we must 'love as he does, even our enemies, and ... love children and the poor as Christ himself' loves them (1825).

The duty of solidarity or 'social charity' bears witness to this human and Christian brotherhood. This duty is based on 'the equality in rational nature of all men, whatever nation they belong to' (1939; see 2407). Charity is the greatest social commandment (1889). From this perspective, it is understood that the 'hinge' of the moral life is the 'sense that the other is one's equal' together with 'the desire for God and submission to him' (1955).

The new commandment

Christ revealed the most profound dimension of charity for others in the new commandment (1823), the new law (1965, 1972) that he entrusted to his disciples. What is new is not the precept to love others, but to love them 'as I have loved you' (*John* 15:12). He loved all people; indeed, he loved them unto death (605, 601, 1741). He called everyone to the Kingdom he proclaimed and promised (543). He identified himself with those who are sorely tried (544).

Do we fully understand what Christ meant when he ended the parable of the Last Judgement with these words: 'Every time you did it to one of the least of my brethren, you did it to me' (*Matthew* 25:40)? Christ reveals his face in those who are in need (678,

---

[6] For the social dimension of the duty of justice, see the section below, 'The challenge of the Church's social teaching'.

1932). Our neighbours, and most particularly those who are most defenceless, are signs, 'sacraments' of Christ's presence (2449).

In the Eucharistic liturgy, the reception of the Body of Christ in communion cannot be separated from a commitment to the poor (1397).

Thus, if Christians want to be faithful to the Gospel, they are called to recognize the face of Christ in all who await a sign of love and affection, especially those who have been 'wounded by life'. This recognition is a very real and effective pledge of the solidarity that contributes to building up, in our human relationships, the harmony and peace indispensable to the social compact (1889, 1931) and to the lessening of human suffering (2448).

Those whom we must love

Because charity towards others is never exclusive, the Golden Rule (1970) must apply to all: 'In everything do to others as you would have them do to you' (*Matthew* 7:12).

After affirming the principle of charity for all, the *Catechism* turns to certain human situations in which love for others is usually exercised: in the heart of the family (2204, 2212), in the filial devotion of children (2215) and in the affection of parents (2228).

Above all, Christians must follow Christ's example of being attentive to the needs of all who live with some distress in their bodies or souls, and of being helpful to them (544, 1503, 1509). Christians are called to practise in their regard the gestures and acts of charity called 'the works of mercy' (2447).

The Church cherishes a particular compassion for the poor (716) to whom she accords a 'preferential love' (2448). She wants to be faithful to the Gospel's example and the Beatitudes (2444).

The demands of charity inspire respect for believers of other Christian confessions (818) and other religions (2104): the Jewish people, Muslims and other non-Christians (841–842). The spirit of dialogue (856) is based on the common origin and destiny of the human race (842).

Again, this consideration of the unity of the human race, in the diversity of peoples and races, creates the duty of solidarity among nations (1939), with all the moral obligations of justice and charity that flow from it (2439).

Forgiveness of enemies is one of the most difficult demands of the virtue of charity, but it is nonetheless essential to living in accordance with the logic of the Gospel. 'The teaching of Christ goes so far as to require the forgiveness of offences. He extends the commandment of love ... to all enemies' (1933, 2262, 2303).

The fifth petition of the 'Our Father' teaches us to ask for the spiritual strength to forgive (2840, 2814). It is significant (2841) that forgiveness is the only disposition to which Christ returns and which he develops in the Sermon on the Mount (*Matthew* 5: 23–24; 6:14–15).

Conversion of the heart

Detachment from self, required by love for others, will remain an impossible challenge without a conversion of the heart, that is, the interior transformation that elicits 'the desire and resolution to change one's life' (1431). The 'poverty of spirit' of the Gospel's first beatitude (2544–2545) calls us to shun disordered covetousness (2535), and therefore to banish envy (2538), which is a refusal to love (2540).

The respect of justice and charity for others creates the duty to avoid everything that could damage anyone's personal reputation, such as detraction and calumny (2479) and false witness (2476).

Lying (2486–2487) and invasion of privacy (2492) are likewise to be avoided. In the same vein, one must refuse to allow oneself to be guided by egoism and animosity.

Giving scandal (2284–2285) also offends seriously against charity.

A truly Christian life, according to the Gospel, is discerned by the evidence of its charity, for which we must pray. One must have a childlike attitude (2734) to ask the Father for 'a humble and trusting heart' (2785), a spirit of vigilance to remain in communion with Christ (2860), and, above all, a willingness to forgive (2864).

Because we pray to the Father to forgive us (1631), we ourselves can grant others our forgiveness, the fruit of the 'high-point of Christian prayer' (2844).

....

In conclusion, both for individual relationships as for the sake of society, we can only make this adage, which sums up the whole Christian ideal, our own: 'At the evening of life, only love remains.'

....

21. The Challenge of the Church's Social Teaching

Why should the Catholic Church intervene in the social and economic sphere? It is not her domain. She runs the risk of seeming to be in collusion with certain political ideologies and the regimes and powers that represent them.

On account of the numerous problems raised by the social question in the sphere of justice, the defence of rights, and the demands of solidarity, that question cannot be a matter of indifference to the Church, her pastors or her faithful. The Church would fail in her mission if she did not recall, in the name of the Gospel, what is at stake in the social life and economic activity. She addresses those responsible for that life and activity so that they may assure the conditions of justice and equity so indispensable to the harmony and equilibrium of societies and peoples.

A certain vision of humanity

In two long chapters, one devoted to life in society (1877–1942) and the other to social justice (2401–2442), the *Catechism* develops the principles governing human relations within every social community.

First of all, the Church makes her voice heard because, in the field of social and economic life, our human condition and destiny are at stake. The Church intervenes to bear witness to her vision of humanity (2244), a vision she has received from the Gospel (2419).[7]

Moreover, the Church does not disregard the injustices and disorders that too frequently afflict our social and economic life. She sees in them a further incentive to make herself heard. In several passages, the *Catechism* mentions the 'structures that are the fruits' of human sin (408) that exist in social institutions and the economy. She denounces 'social sin' (1869), the inversion of means and ends (1887), inequalities (1938), and human bondage (2414), and she recalls the obligation to respect fundamental human rights (1907, 1930).

The Church does not intervene out of an ambition to dominate minds and morals, still less to exercise direct political power (2442, 2245). 'In the moral order, her mission is distinct from that of political authorities' (2420).

A message of social truth

The Church recalls several elementary truths about the need for social life (1879, 1836), the nature of society (1980) and the presence of a guiding authority (1897), and the service of the human

---

[7] See the other sections of this guide that refer to human dignity: 'The divided self', 'Christian morality, human morality', 'Seeing my brother and sister in everyone'.

person, who is 'the principle, the subject and the end of all social institutions' (1881).

She does not disregard, in the majority of societies, 'a certain pre-eminence of man over things' (2244). But she feels obliged to affirm 'the transcendent character of the human person' (2245). She owes it to herself to proclaim the principles of morality, even in what concerns the social order (2030).

In terms of the history and evolution of societies (2421), the Church has articulated a body of social teaching (2422) that 'proposes principles for reflection, . . . provides criteria for judgement, . . . [and] gives guidelines for action' (2423).

Moreover, by speaking in the name of the Gospel, the Church brings the Gospel spirit of solidarity to the social life. This spirit transcends human laws (1932, 1940) and must remain present in human relations, excluding violence from them; it goes so far as to demand the forgiveness of enemies (1933). There is a 'mutual good will' that 'is not limited to guaranteeing rights' (2213). Throughout her history, the Church has borne witness to the requirement of solidarity in society and has been able to open up new paths for the development of temporal goods (1942).

It pertains to the Church's mission 'to pass moral judgements even in matters related to politics, whenever the fundamental rights of man or the salvation of souls requires it' (2246, 2420).

The bishops have the duty, in the exercise of their teaching office, to transmit the message of truth (890) in moral matters (2036–2037). When they proclaim this message, their word is prophetic.

The lay faithful are also the Church (897). They must also share in the Church's mission. Their initiative is particularly necessary in the area of social, political and economic realities, in order to imbue them with the spirit of the Gospel (899, 905, 909, 2442).

The lay faithful must nevertheless be careful not to confuse 'the rights and duties which they have as belonging to the Church and those which fall to them as members of the human society' (912, 2820).

Obligations and duties of the social life

The authority of those responsible for public life must be exercised 'as a service' (2234, 1902).

This authority must respect the hierarchy of values (1886, 2234) in order to promote the common good of society, which requires respect for the person and for his or her rights, social wellbeing and development, security and peace (1906–1911).

In order to respond to this first requirement, those responsible must satisfy several major obligations. These obligations include fostering voluntary associations and the participation of all (1882), promoting subsidiarity in the exercise of responsibilities (1883–1185), assuring respect and support for the family (2209–2211), guaranteeing the defence of life (2273) and health care (2288), encouraging respect for political rights and, above all, respect for the 'right to exercise freedom, especially in religious and moral matters' (1738; 1740).

Other duties are joined to the preceding ones: guaranteeing the right of citizens to freedom of information (2498) and, when the situation requires it, affirming respect for professional secrecy (2491).

The duties of citizens correspond to the obligations incumbent on the authorities. These duties include paying taxes, exercising the right to vote, defending the country (2240), and obeying legitimate authority (1900). This last does not exclude resisting the directives of those in power when these violate 'the demands of the moral order', the 'fundamental rights of persons or the teachings of the Gospel' (2242–2243).

The demands of social justice

As for social justice, the state cannot do everything. It has the duty 'of overseeing and directing the exercise of human rights in the economic sector' (2431).

It is up to social partners and those responsible for business enterprises (2432) to assure access to work (2433, 2427, 2436) and just wages (2434). The conflicts of interest that cause social groups to oppose one another must be handled first by negotiation (2429). Recourse to strikes is 'morally legitimate' (2435) when, in certain situations, they cannot be prevented.

The *Catechism* highlights the need for international solidarity and the responsibility of the nations to bring it about. The social question has acquired a 'world-wide dimension' (2438): rich nations have a duty of solidarity and sometimes of justice towards poor nations (2439). There is a universal common good (1911) that cannot dispense them from being attentive to the development of countries suffering from the violence of hunger or exploitation (2440). The acceptance of immigrants is also a form of assistance and solidarity (1911, 2433).

The social ethic proposed by the Church to those responsible for civil life and economic action opens out to an interior and moral dimension that invites consciences to come forward to act in truth. The virtue of prudence (1806) permits preliminary judgements and moral decisions (1780). In order to resist the temptations created by power, inner conversion is required (1916). 'Social changes' must not be achieved without taking proper account of the laws and customs of the society that one seeks to serve (1888).

> The teaching of the Church in social and economic matters involves no programme of rights to be defended and duties to be fulfilled. It certainly involves no ideological system that could be compared with others (2425). It is as much a spirit to be promoted as a conviction to be shared. This spirit is one of solidarity coming from the Gospel. The conviction clarified is related to the strict sense of human greatness that must be safeguarded by protecting it from threats. In this sense, the Church's social message always poses a challenge.

22. Talking about Sexuality

Sexuality always seems to have frightened the Church. This is probably because sexuality is lived out in the 'flesh' and the Church always speaks of the flesh with a certain reserve! Consequently, isn't her moral discourse disqualified in the face of a public opinion that is more and more aware of the presence of sex in the culture and the media?

Although in the past some religious literature could nourish prejudices about the Church's thought, she must present the truth of her teaching on human sexuality that she seeks to offer in the name of the Gospel. No, sex is not taboo. The Church has no bias against it and does not seek to inflict guilt on consciences. We shall see here how the *Catechism* presents sexuality in the light of creation and how the morality the Church proposes is also the morality of a humanism that strives to balance, by the help of divine grace, our carnal impulses with our desire for true inner freedom.

Creation and sexuality

Let us recall how the *Catechism* presents the origin of the human being as created to be male and female, in a perfect personal equality (355, 369).

Made up of body and soul, the human being is endowed with a sexuality that differentiates man and woman (2333), but which also renders them complementary to each other (372, 2332).

Because 'sexuality affects all aspects of the human person' (2332), 'everyone, man and woman, should acknowledge and accept' his or her own sexual identity (2333).

By reason of the duality of body and soul (362), a tension exists in our tendencies and impulses, some of which arise from the 'spirit', while others arise from 'the flesh', according to St Paul (2525–2526).

The 'human heart' (368, 2563, 2527) is the place where this tension arising from our 'passions' is expressed (1767). It is also the place where they can find their balance (2517).

Complementary and different, man and woman are made for each other (371–372). The vocation to marriage is 'written in the very nature of man and woman' (1603, 1605).

Love is 'the fundamental and innate vocation of every human being' (1604). The love that unites man and woman is 'an image of the absolute and unfailing love with which God loves' them (1604).

The sexual condition is not a misfortune. Although that condition is scarred by 'the heritage of sin' (2516), Christians cannot forget that Christ came to restore humanity and creation (2536). They recognize that the body is called to become 'the temple of the Holy Spirit' (2519). They know that the body is destined for resurrection (298, 988).

Far from devaluing the human body, the Church declares that it shares with all creation the quality of being the reflection of its creator (2335). The body therefore has a natural goodness and enters into the order and wisdom that presided over creation (299, 307, 341). From this goodness is derived the duty to respect the laws that maintain the body's integrity.

It is precisely this limit that the human genius of scientific and technological research must impose on itself in carrying out the task given to humanity to 'subdue' creation (307, 373). In the light of this principle, the norms of bioethics in the area of sexuality and the relations between man and woman must be understood (2293–2294, 2376–2377).

Towards a discipline of sexuality

In prescribing the rules of sexual morality, the Church is merely recalling the precepts of the natural law (1954, 1959) contained in the sixth (2331ff.) and ninth (2514f.) of the Ten Commandments.

The key word that encompasses the norms of sexuality is 'self-mastery': 'the alternative is clear: either man governs his passions and finds peace, or he lets himself be dominated by them and becomes unhappy' (2339).

This self-mastery is identified with the virtue of chastity (2337, 2345). It assures 'the successful integration of sexuality within the person' and 'the inner unity of man' (2337).

Connected with the cardinal virtue of temperance (2341), chastity is not acquired once and for all (2342). It requires a true apprenticeship (2339), especially in the years of childhood and adolescence (2342). Its growth is always threatened and it requires a constant effort at all stages of life (2342).

The practice of chastity varies according to one's state of life: celibacy and the consecrated life require continence; the bonds of marriage are lived out in conjugal chastity (2349).

Through the self-mastery it demands, chastity is ordered to the gift of self (2346), to a relationship with others that can blossom into friendship (2347–2348).

Sexuality and married life

In the relationship of spouses, chastity permits the integral gift of one to the other (2362). Because sexuality is not of a 'purely biological' order and involves 'the innermost being' of man and woman, it attains its true dimension only in a love that is the total gift of self to the other (2361). The 'source of joy and pleasure' for the spouses (2362) is found in this gift.

Among the baptized, the Lord has raised the marriage covenant establishing a community of life between a man and a woman to the dignity of a sacrament (1601).

By the very nature of the union of spouses, the gift they give each other is irrevocable. Fidelity expresses the constancy of the commitment of marriage, which is one and indissoluble (1614–1615, 2364–2365).

'Conjugal love naturally tends to be fruitful'; a child 'springs from the very heart of that mutual giving' (2366). In this love an absolute link exists between the union of the spouses and procreation (2366, 2363, 2369). In affirming this link, the Church expresses a truth about human beings that comes from creation itself. She sees in this truth the vocation of spouses to 'share in the creative power and fatherhood of God' (2367).

Here the very controversial problem of the regulation of births arises (2368–2371). It is fitting, in recalling the moral norms clarified by the Church, to consider the importance of what they represent. Do sexual relations exist only for their own sake or must they, by respecting these norms, be open and go beyond a carnal egoism that, by illicit means, refuses to conceive a child and bring it to birth?

It is also appropriate to uphold the conviction that a child is not something owed but a gift (2378). Is there not a real contradiction in demanding both a 'right to a child' and unconstrained freedom with regard to conception?

Sexuality astray

Like most human realities, sexuality is not sheltered from deviations and even perversions. In a realistic page, the *Catechism* presents offences against chastity (2351–2356).

While taking a firm stance on homosexuality, the *Catechism* nevertheless recognizes that it is a trial for many who are marked with it and demands that they should be 'accepted with respect, compassion and sensitivity' (2358–2359).

Without illusions about the 'march of sex', the *Catechism* denounces moral permissiveness, which rests on a false idea of freedom (2526). It also has no tolerance for anything that encourages 'voyeurism' in publicity and the media (2523).

The challenge of chastity

Chastity seems to public opinion to be an impossible challenge. If chastity is a moral virtue, it is also a gift of God, a grace that we must know how to request (2345).

For the baptized, there is an imperative command to take means to remain chaste (2340). This is the indispensable struggle for purity (2526, 2530).

The *Catechism* pays special attention to careful and modest comportment (2521). Modesty protects the mystery of persons and their love. It maintains silence or reserve in the face of unhealthy curiosity (2522) or exhibitionistic tendencies.

Marriage does not shelter Christian spouses from the 'wounds of sin' (1607–1608). 'Nothing is impossible with God.' By power of the Holy Spirit, Christian marriage can renew the human heart (298) and purify it (2520). This is the whole meaning of a conjugal spirituality.

....

At a time when a current of thought is being articulated, that seeks to relativize the institution of marriage and risks shaking the very foundations of society, is it really of no importance to recognize in the Church's moral thinking the surest guarantee for maintaining the values indispensable to the whole social life?

....

23. Is Prayer an Obligation or a Grace?

Is it necessary to be a believer in order to pray? The Church asks us to 'make our prayer'. But isn't prayer something other than a rite to be observed? Prayer should express the depths of the heart, what each person feels when encountering his or her own self. More than an obligation, prayer is first of all a grace for those who want to breathe deeply within themselves in God's presence. Why then has the Church codified the times and formulas of prayer by her prescriptions?

First of all, it must be stated that the *Catechism* devotes its entire Part Four to prayer (2558–2865), thereby expressing the importance it attaches to prayer for Christians. After making clear the place occupied by prayer in the actual experience of faith, the *Catechism* stresses that the Spirit's presence must lie at the heart of the journey of prayer. It justifies the educational role of the Church, which discloses to the faithful the different paths of prayer, whether personal or communal.

The believer's prayer

Whatever form it may take, prayer expresses faith, for it is 'the raising of one's mind and heart to God' (2559). Prayer allows us to establish a relationship with God (2562).

Prayer is born in the heart, 'our hidden centre, beyond the grasp of our reason and of others' (2563).

Prayer is universal because the 'search for God' is present everywhere. 'All religions bear witness to' it (2566). Prayer is also present throughout human history: it is 'the relationship with God in historical events' (2568).

Christian prayer is the response to a call that comes from within. The Holy Spirit, the 'Master Within' (741), makes prayer 'spring forth' in us and directs it to the Father (2564, 2652, 2670, 2672). Christ thirsts within us, as he did at the well in Samaria (2560).

Prayer is a battle (2725). 'Prayer cannot be reduced to the spontaneous outpouring of interior impulse: in order to pray, one must have the will to pray' (2650). Prayer must face many obstacles, in particular, all the prejudices deriving from contemporary mentalities and currents of opinion (2726). Moreover, one cannot disregard the difficulties proper to the actual practice of prayer (2729).

Prayer is first of all a question of love (2742). The disposition of the heart purifies the petitions expressed in prayer and accepts the fact that God hears and answers our prayer only for our benefit (2735–2737). It is not enough for us to say, 'Lord, Lord' (*Matthew* 7:21), but we must dispose our 'heart to do the will of the Father' (2611).